Health, Illness, and the Social Body

A Critical Sociology

Second Edition

Peter E. S. Freund

Montclair State University

Meredith B. McGuire

Trinity University

Prentice Hall
Englewood Cliffs, New Jersey 07632

Library of Congress Cataloging-in-Publication Data

FREUND, PETER E. S.
    Health, illness, and the social body : a critical sociology /
Peter E. S. Freund, Meredith B. McGuire. — 2nd ed.

        p.   cm.
    Includes bibliographical references and index.
    ISBN 0-13-155491-3
        1. Social medicine.   2. Sick—Psychology.   3. Medical care.
    I. McGuire, Meredith B.   II. Title.
    RA418.F753   1995
    306.4′61—dc20   94-20753
                                                            CIP

Acquisitions editor/editor in chief: *Nancy Roberts*
Associate editor: *Sharon Chambliss*
Editorial/production supervision: *Kim Gueterman*
Cover design: *Bruce Kenselaar*
Buyer: *Mary Ann Gloriande*

1995, 1991 by Prentice-Hall, Inc.
A Simon & Schuster Company
Englewood Cliffs, New Jersey 07632

Printed in the United States of America

10   9   8   7   6   5   4   3   2   1

ISBN 0-13-155491-3

Prentice-Hall International (UK) Limited, *London*
Prentice-Hall of Australia Pty. Limited, *Sydney*
Prentice-Hall Canada Inc, *Toronto*
Prentice-Hall Hispanoamericana, S.A., *Mexico*
Prentice-Hall of India Private Limited, *New Delhi*
Prentice-Hall of Japan, Inc., *Tokyo*
Simon & Schuster Asia Pte. Ltd., *Singapore*
Editora Prentice-Hall do Brasil, Ltda, *Rio de Janeiro*

Contents

7   THE ILLNESS EXPERIENCE   143

8   SEEKING HEALTH AND HELP   169

Preface

Society has profound influence on human bodies, as well as on our ideas and perceptions about those bodies. For this text we have selected key themes in the sociology of health and illness that highlight the complex interrelationship of body, mind and society. Although we describe various interpretive approaches and review much conventional literature in several related disciplines, rather than writing a standard medical sociology, we present a critical, holistic interpretation of health, illness and human bodies that emphasizes *power* as a key social-structural factor in health and in societal responses to illness.

Writing this second edition has made us even more aware of the importance of power issues in health and healing. Some of the most interesting recent health-related research explores precisely those areas of social life where power differences are evident: gender, race and ethnicity, poverty and wealth, work and professions, abuse and violence, the physical and social environment, health care financing and delivery, among others. The politics of the debate over U.S. health care "reform" also illustrates the importance of power and wealth—especially of corporate actors—in setting the very terms of discourse, not merely affecting the policy outcomes.

This text does not attempt to cover every relevant topic, but is organized as a set of core essays around which to build a course. Thus, for example, the topics of women's health issues, ethnic factors in health and illness, and AIDS are discussed in several different sections, rather than all under one heading. Students using the Index will find a wealth of information and references for further research on these and other important issues. Using this text as a core reading, instructors can assign related articles, monographs or readings to complement their own emphases.

Chapter One is an introduction that outlines relevant problems and key concepts in the field, and especially shows how this text links materialist and social-constructionist theories of health and illness through the unifying theme of power. Chapter Two introduces students to social epidemiology, and outlines broad patterns of morbidity and mortality. Chapters Three through Five describe the social production of unhealthy bodies and develop interpretations of the nature of connections among mind, body, and society. Chapters Six through Nine discuss the social context of ideas and experiences of health and illness. Chapters Ten through Twelve examine social and cultural factors in the medical system's treatment of sick persons and the political economy of health care in the United States.

While presented in an orderly arrangement, the book's chapters may be used in a different sequence. Each chapter introduces relevant key concepts and a limited number of sociological theorists or researchers. For reasons of practical flexibility, we have reiterated explanations of a few key terms in more than one chapter. Authors mentioned by name in the text have been generally selected for the importance of their theoretical contributions. Others are cited in the recommended readings and references, which have been included both to acknowledge our intellectual debts and to provide students with extensive useful references for further research.

Each chapter ends with an annotated list of some recent recommended readings: Two appendices suggest further useful materials. Appendix A outlines major resources for a search of the literature in the field. Students preparing term papers or theses will find these resources essential. The book's extensive bibliography should also be invaluable for researchers. Appendix B is an annotated list of film and video resources. We have found good visual presentations to be invaluable aids in concretizing and illustrating points that are often far from students' personal experiences, as well as for stimulating discussion.

In writing this second edition, we have received additional help from several persons, whose assistance we gratefully acknowledge: John Donahue, Miriam Fisher, George Martin, Jim Spickard, and Sheryl Tynes. Also very welcome were the advice and encouragement of our editors, Nancy Roberts and Sharon Chambliss, and reviewers Deborah A. Sullivan and Kathy Charmaz. We appreciate the assistance of Linda Baird, Pat Cummins, Rachel McGuire, Kieran McGuire, and Janaki Spickard-Keeler in manuscript preparation. Finally, we want to thank our families, Miriam Fisher, Kieran and Rachel McGuire, and Jim, Janaki, and Dmitri Spickard, for putting up with us during the writing of this book and for illustrating by their very lives why sociologists should care about health.

CHAPTER ONE

A Sociological Perspective on Health, Illness, and the Body

When we think of health and illness, we usually think of eating properly and other healthy habits, of institutions such as hospitals, and of health professionals such as doctors and nurses. While we may be dimly aware that health has its social dimensions, we may not think of health as a topic for social scientists.

Sociological analysis emphasizes that the occurrence of illness is not random. Eckholm (1977: 18–19) notes:

> Individuals who enjoy good health rightly think of themselves as fortunate: But luck has little to do with the broad patterns of disease and mortality that prevail in each society. The striking variations in health conditions among countries and cultural groups reflect differences in social and physical environments. And increasingly the forces that shape health patterns are set in motion by human activities and decisions. Indeed, *in creating its way of life, each society creates its way of death* [emphasis added].

The sociology of health and illness studies such issues as how social and cultural factors influence health and people's perceptions of health and healing, and how healing is done in different societies. Social structures and cultural practices have concrete consequences for people's lives.

We like to think that a newborn infant is as yet untouched by these abstract forces and has possibilities for health limited only by the child's genetic makeup. Even at birth, however, these abstract forces have begun to inscribe themselves on the baby's body. The very life chances of this infant, including the probabilities that she will live, be well, acquire the skills for success in her culture, and achieve and maintain that success, are powerfully influenced by all of the social circumstances and forces she will encounter throughout her life. In short, the baby's life chances, including possibilities for health and long life or sickness and death, are shaped or constructed by society itself.

The baby's birth weight, for example, is influenced by her mother's diet, which in turn is partly a product of her society, her culture, and her social class. Other features of the mother's social context have direct consequences for the newborn's health, including the mother's smoking or drug habits, the housing and sanitary conditions in which the infant is born, and the like. Later, whether the baby is a victim of cholera, bubonic plague, schistosomiasis, or lead poisoning depends upon public health measures taken in her environment. What other factors in the baby's home life and environment will shape her sense of self and self-esteem, and her ability to cope with stress and manage her environment? As she matures, how will her gender, race, ethnicity, and social class influence her life chances?

Later in life, her experiences as a worker will place her in various physical environments and social relationships that will affect her health. Her culture will shape what she likes to eat, how she experiences stress, whether she drinks alcohol, and how she feels about her body. How she experiences the process of giving birth will be shaped by her culture's meanings of childbirth as well as by the social context of birth, such as whether it takes place in a hospital under the supervision of an obstetrician trained in Western notions of pregnancy as a medical problem.

The infant is born into a social structure and culture that also powerfully influence what will be considered illness and how that illness will be treated. When this person gets sick, social forces play an important role in determining her chances of becoming well. How does she decide when she is sick and needs help? If she is sick, for example with a bad cold, how will others respond? If she develops multiple sclerosis, how will the attitudes and responses of others, and the quality of her social and physical environment affect her very life chances? What will happen if she develops a stigmatizing illness, such as leprosy or AIDS?

What resources are available to her in dealing with her needs when ill? If she approaches the medical system for help, how does she pay for it? How do her social class, age, race, and ability to pay influence the quality of her medical care? How does the institutional context of her medical care (for example, a public versus a for-profit private hospital, or a nursing home compared to a hospice or home care) help determine its quality? In addition to the quality of life, even the quality of death is linked with such social contexts.

Medical systems involve concrete organizations that reflect the economic interests of such groups as doctors and other professionals, insurance companies, pharmaceutical industries, manufacturers of medical equipment, hospitals, research organizations, government agencies, and medical schools. They all compete for resources, influence policy, and try to set health care and research agendas. Health care systems differ greatly from society to society in how they define and meet the needs of individual citizens. The baby's life chances are, therefore, intimately intertwined with these seemingly remote, social organizations.

The fates of individual bodies are thus linked to the workings of the social body. A person's life chances are not some deterministic fate nor a purely accidental, random result. Rather, a person's chances for illness and successful recovery are very much the result of specifiable social arrangements, which are in turn products of human volition and indeed deliberate policy choices made by identifiable groups and individuals. In large part, illness, death, health, and well-being are socially produced.

THE SOCIAL CONSTRUCTION OF THE BODY

To construct is to make or build something. Clearly, societies do not literally make or produce bodies, but they can influence, shape, and misshape them. Just as an artist can mold clay to construct an object (which is constrained by the physical properties of the clay), social groups and the cultures they share can shape members' bodies. Obvious examples of the deliberate cultural shaping of the human body include the foot binding practiced in traditional Chinese society, the cradle boards used to shape infants' heads among the Kwakiutl Indians, the stays and corsets worn by nineteenth-century middle-class European and American women, and the high heels and pierced earrings favored today. Similarly, having to live in a polluted environment or to sit at a desk, to work on an assembly line, or to bend over all day in a mine shaft are examples of social conditions that can indirectly shape the body and in turn the body's health.

Those things that happen to human bodies are closely related to the working and anatomy of the social body. Illness is not merely a physical experience but also a social experience. The sick body is not simply a closed container, encased in skin, that has been invaded by germs or traumatic blows; rather, it is open and connected to the world that surrounds it. Thus the human body is open to the social body. Similarly, our material (or physical) environment, such as the urban landscape, the work place, or our foods, are influenced by our culture, social structure, and relationships. And these in turn influence our bodies.

THE SOCIAL CONSTRUCTION OF IDEAS ABOUT THE BODY

Ideas too are constructions. Every society has many levels of shared ideas about bodies: What is defined as healthy and beautiful in one society might be considered unhealthily fat and ugly in another; what is seen as thin and lean in one group might be defined as sickly in another. Aging may also be defined as something to be either conquered, feared, accepted, or revered. Likewise, some societies picture the body as working like a machine, whereas others see it as a spiritual vessel.

Health Beliefs and Practices

Because they are social constructions, one's ideas of the body and its health and illness are influenced by both one's culture and one's social position, such as class or gender. Both cultural and social structural factors are important in understanding people's behavior and health. People act as they do not only because of their beliefs about health (the cultural aspects) but also because of structural aspects, such as how power is distributed and relationships are organized. Thus, although we conceptually distinguish cultural and social structural aspects, in actuality they overlap.

Culture is the beliefs, values, actions, and material objects shared by a people. Culture includes such elements as language, beliefs about the universe and the nature of good and evil, ideals such as justice or freedom, and more mundane considerations such as what constitutes appropriate food, dress, and manners. Culture also encompasses objects that a people produce and share. Cooking utensils, films, cemeteries, blueprints, crucifixes, musical scores, and flags are among the items that represent cultural values and notions.

How do our cultural conceptions of a person's physical abilities affect those abilities? In our society, we used to believe that women were unable to carry heavy objects. While biology contributes somewhat to women's physical abilities, so do cultural ideas. In a patriarchal society, women's expectations that they will be weak, together with the experience of being treated as weak because of their social status, have a self-fulfilling result: Women do not become strong. Culture can affect health by shaping behaviors, such as diet, or by influencing how people change their environments, which in turn affects their health (Brown and Inhorn, 1990).

Social structure (or social organization) is the relatively stable, ongoing pattern of social interaction. In a particular society, there are recognizable patterns of interaction that are appropriate to different social positions and relationships, such as parent-child, supervisor-employee, teacher-student, and friend-friend. Behavior in these relationships is regulated through a number of mechanisms, including social control and shared cultural values. Various persons in social relationships occupy different social statuses. These relationships are often part of larger social organizational contexts; for example, the supervisor and employee positions may be part of a business corporation.

Social status is an individual's position in any system of social ranking. People can be stratified or ranked according to such dimensions as class, ethnicity, age, and gender. Social class (often measured by income or occupation or both) is one important indicator of social location; it influences how much power individuals have to manage their bodies and their external environment.

Class is not the only determinant of power. The particular position of power we occupy in our family (e.g., child or parent) and our gender, race, and ethnicity are also all important factors. Even health status (being chronically ill, for instance) will determine the stressors to which we are exposed and the coping resources that are available to us. Our position in institutional arrangements, such as being a hospital patient, can also affect our health (Volicer, 1977, 1978).

In understanding health and illness, cultural aspects to be considered might include people's eating and hygienic habits, and their ideas about health, illness, and healing. By contrast, structural elements might include a person's position and relationships in the work place, family, and medical settings as well as such social status indicators as gender, race, age, and class.

Both scientific and nonscientific ideas about health, illness, and the body are the result of social construction, as are the facts that we assemble as evidence for our ideas about the world. *All* descriptions, including medical descriptions, are constructions in that they include some information and exclude other information. Similarly, definitions of health are social constructions. For example, the *International Dictionary of Medicine and Biology* defines *health* as "a state of well-being of an organism or part of one, characterized by normal function and unattended by disease" (Becker, 1986: v. 2, 1276). This definition delineates well-being only in terms of bodily functioning and the absence of disease. But are we necessarily healthy if we simply lack disease? And are all diseases necessarily unhealthy? Is it healthy to function under all (however miserable) conditions? Why should functioning be such an important criterion? Is it because our society places so much cultural emphasis upon certain forms of functioning?

The Medical Model

Our culture derives many of its ideas about the body from the Western biomedical model. A sociological perspective on health and illness, however, does not take this model as "truth." Rather, medical ideas of the body and its diseases are also seen as socially constructed realities that are subject to social biases and limitations. Biomedical ideas are based upon a number of historical assumptions about the body and ways of knowing about the body; the following are some of these historically created assumptions that have become embedded in the Western medical model. Chapter Nine develops these concepts in more detail.

 One biomedical assumption is *mind-body dualism*. The medical model assumes a clear dichotomy between the mind and the body; physical diseases are presumed to be located solely within the body. As a result, biomedicine tries to understand and treat the body in isolation from other aspects of the person inhabiting it. The history of Western medical science suggests several of the sources of this image of the body as separate from mind or spirit (some are described in Chapter 9).

 Not only does the medical model dichotomize body and mind, but also it assumes that illness can be reduced to disordered bodily (biochemical or neurophysiological) functions. This *physical reductionism* excludes social, psychological, and behavioral dimensions of illness. One result is that medicine "sees" disease as localized in the *individual* body. Such conceptions prevent the medical model from conceiving of the *social* body or how aspects of the individual's social or emotional life might affect physical health. Thus, medicine generally ignores social conditions contributing to illness or promoting healing.

A related assumption of the biomedical model is what Dubos (1959) called the *doctrine of specific etiology*. This belief holds that each disease is caused by a specific, potentially identifiable agent. The history of Western medicine shows both the fruitfulness and the limitations of this assumption. Dubos noted that while the doctrine of specific etiology has led to important theoretical and practical achievements, it has rarely provided a complete account of the causation of disease. An adequate understanding of illness etiology must include broader factors, such as nutrition, stress, and metabolic states, which affect the individual's susceptibility to infection. As noted in Chapter 2, the search for specific illness-producing agents worked relatively well in dealing with infectious diseases but is too simplistic to explain the causes of complex chronic illnesses. Also, as Dubos observed, this approach often results in a quest for the "magic bullet" to "shoot and kill" the disease, producing an overreliance on pharmaceuticals in the "armamentarium" (stock of "weapons") of the modern physician.

The machine metaphor is another implicit assumption in the medical model. Accordingly, the body is a complex biochemical machine, and disease is the malfunctioning of some constituent mechanism (e.g., a "breakdown" of the heart). Other cultures use other metaphors; for example, ancient Egyptian societies used the image of a river, and Chinese tradition refers to the balance of elemental forces (yin and yang) of the earth (Osherson and AmaraSingham, 1981). In combination with the assumption of mind-body dualism, the machine metaphor further encouraged an instrumentalist approach to the body; the physician could "repair" one part in isolation from the rest (Berliner, 1975).

Partly as a product of the machine metaphor and the quest for mastery, the Western medical model also conceptualizes the body as the proper *object of regimen and control*, again emphasizing the responsibility of the individual to exercise this control in order to maintain or restore health. This assumption meshes with other values, resulting in the medical and social emphases upon such standardized body disciplines as diets, exercise programs, routines of hygiene, and even sexual activity (Turner, 1984: 157–203).

THE CENTRALITY OF POWER IN THE SOCIOLOGY OF HEALTH AND ILLNESS

One of the unifying themes of this text is the social construction of both ideas about the body and the body itself. In this process power and control play an important role. In the most general sense, **power** is the ability to get what one wants and to get things done.

Power is a ubiquitous factor in our daily lives. It both enables us to accomplish tasks (such as to get enough food) and constrains the number and types of possibilities open to us. This text emphasizes the relationship between health and power, such as the power of workers over their work pace; the power of people to control the quality of their physical environments; the power of various groups or societies to shape health policy or to deliver what they consider healing; the power of people of different statuses to control, receive, and understand information vital to their well-being; and the power of the mass media to shape ideas about food and fitness. In addition to these objective manifestations of power, we also subjectively experience power. A person's sense of empowerment—a feeling that one can handle stressful situations, for instance—is important to health and well-being, and is strongly related to one's ability to manage one's environment and to feel safe and secure in it. The power of individuals is not simply personal but also usually has a social basis.

The concept of social power in particular implies that the will of one individual or group can prevail over that of others. One's statuses (e.g., age and social class) in society determine the resources available for the exercise of power. For example, if I own a business and control its resources, I can decide how they will be used; generally, I have power in my work place and have more resources to enforce my will than do the workers in my business.

Often our experiences deal not with overt power or control but relative, implicit power. For example, if I feel in control of my family life, I thus feel able to resist others' attempts to wrest control, whether by direct confrontation or by subtle manipulation. For this reason, power is typically enhanced when its exercise is accepted as legitimate. Likewise, when people do not recognize that power is being exercised, they may submit to control unwillingly and unknowingly. Thus concepts like "social status" and "social control" are significant in understanding the relationship between power and the body. **Control** refers to the exercise of power in a particular situation. Like a sense of empowerment, control is related to one's ability to manage one's environment and to feel safe and secure in it.

Social control may be defined as those ways in which a society assures itself of its members' proper and respectable behavior, appearances, productivity, and contributions. Social control assures the relatively smooth functioning of the social order and the maintenance of hierarchical relationships such as class.

This control may rely on violence, force, persuasion, and/or manipulation. Internalized forms of control, such as individual conscience, are far more subtle and effective means of assuring uniformity. The standards by which persons learn to measure themselves are another way in which society uses the social self as a means of control. Social organizations also use their control of information to maintain power. For example, the regulation that workers have to punch a time clock is a device for assuring work attendance. Social control measures also affect those who are in power, as when they become their own "slave drivers."

THE PERSPECTIVE OF THIS TEXT

While our focus is sociological, we have drawn from many other disciplines and subdisciplines, such as medical sociology, medical anthropology, socio- and psychophysiology, medical economics, sociology of health and illness, social psychology, history, philosophy of the body, and ethics. Each has its separate focus, and persons contributing to one discipline are often unaware of related work in other fields. We emphasize synthesizing work from several disciplines to achieve a more holistic appreciation of health and illness that views healing and prevention in the broadest sense: The body is not treated as a self-enclosed machine, and health and illness are understood in their social, cultural, and historical contexts.

A holistic perspective is necessary but difficult, because it requires us to go beyond the rigid separations of concepts about the body, mind, and society. As Scheper-Hughes and Lock (1986: 137) wrote:

> We are without a language with which to address mind-body-society interactions, and so are left hanging in mid-air, suspended in hyphens that testify to the radical disconnectedness of our thoughts. We resort to such fragmented concepts as the biosocial, the psychosomatic, the psychosocial, the somatosocial, as feeble ways of expressing the complex and myriad ways that our minds speak to us through our bodies, and the ways in which society is inscribed on the expectant canvas of our flesh and bones, blood and guts.

We stress the interactions of mind, body, and society, and the importance of symbols and subjective experience in understanding health and illness. The narrow focus and unifactorial models of disease characterizing much of modern medicine and some of the sociology of health and illness deflect attention from the social issues implied by persisting inequalities in health status within most modern societies (Comaroff, 1982: 61), as well as the yet greater gaps of inequality between so-called "developed" and less-developed nations.

SUMMARY

This text on the sociology of health and illness deals with the social construction of bodies, with an emphasis on how power shapes this construction. How cultural and social structural factors and central power relationships influence us physically and how we perceive, care for, maintain, and "repair" our bodies constitute the major questions to be addressed. The perspective of this book is a holistic one, emphasizing the interpenetration of mind, body, and society.

The first part, Chapters 2 through 5, deals primarily with the ways in which society and culture affect physical functioning, and the material environments in which people exist. The second part, Chapters 6 through 9, emphasizes people's experience of their own and others' bodies, especially social aspects of the illness experience. The last part, Chapters 10 through 12, examines social and cultural factors in the medical systems' treatment of sick persons, and the political economy of health care in the United States.

CHAPTER TWO

Who Becomes Sick, Injured, or Dies?

Sickness does not just "happen." Rather, there are discernible patterns in the distribution and frequency of sickness, injury, and death in human populations. **Social epidemiology** is the study of these patterns and the *social* factors that shape them (Mausner and Bahn, 1985).

Noticing relationships between specific illnesses and people's social situation is hardly a new phenomenon: Early Greek and Egyptian writers made such connections (Sigerist, 1960). Popular lore also includes awareness of the linkage between, for example, an occupation and a sickness. *Alice in Wonderland's* Mad Hatter was a plausible "madman" because people had recognized a connection between the occupation of hat-making and bizarre behavior long before the relationship was traced to the effects of the mercury with which hat-makers regularly worked (Stellman and Daum, 1971: 255). Similarly, long before medicine identified the problem, villagers living by the Niger River in Africa recognized that their proximity to the river was related to the prevalence of a horrible sickness characterized by intense itching and eventual blindness. Often they would move away, abandoning valuable farmlands, when the sickness had affected too large a proportion of the community (Eckholm, 1989).

During the late eighteenth and early nineteenth centuries, the historical process of industrialization set the stage for the development of the disciplines of both sociology and epidemiology (Spruit and Kromhout, 1987). The changes that accompanied industrial capitalism created radically different conditions for health and illness:

> The rates of smallpox, typhus, typhoid fever, diphtheria and scarlet fever all increased: two cholera epidemics had swept through the warrens of the Great Towns, a third was on its way. . . . The reordering of the circumstances of everyday life . . . ensued. Industrial capitalism gave rise to novel physical arrangements for work and dwelling (the factory, the company town), created new patterns of economic exploitation (mass displacements from land, urban migration in unprecedented numbers, wage labor). . . . Hazardous and fatiguing work, damp cold and stifling living quarters, cheap gin and adulterated foods, demoralization—the legacy of disease bequeathed by early capitalism stems from such an environment (Susser et al., 1985: 4).

Epidemiology, as a discipline, evolved from early studies of epidemics among people living in such environments. Like sleuths tracing the path of a suspected criminal, epidemiologists examined clues to the path of a suspected source of infection. For example, in 1854 a cholera epidemic broke out in London. Sir John Snow pinpointed known cases of the disease on city maps, thus narrowing the search to certain neighborhoods. He then interviewed survivors and neighbors of cholera victims about everyday behavior, such as what the victims had eaten, where they had played, and so on. Snow discovered that all of the victims had obtained their water from the same pump. He concluded that there was a relationship between this source of water and cholera infection, and he had the pump shut down, thereby ending the epidemic (Snow, 1855).

While modern epidemiologists have far more sophisticated tools such as computers and complex bacteriology laboratories, their underlying method remains much the same as Snow's: They search for patterns linking the types and incidence of sickness of a people with their way of life. Thus epidemiological studies often highlight the political and social contexts of health and illness. (See Box 2.1.) The famous nineteenth-century epidemiologist Rudolf Virchow declared, " 'Medicine is a social science, and politics is nothing but medicine on a grand scale' " (quoted in Susser et al., 1985: 6). Political and social factors are readily evident in studies showing certain diseases to be characteristic mainly of the rich, while others occur almost exclusively among the poor. Political implications also follow, for instance, from epidemiological studies demonstrating certain occupations to be the causes or major contributing factors in certain illnesses and death. Epidemiology is only one of many approaches to understanding the connections between social arrangements and sickness or death, but epidemiological data receive special attention from policymakers because they describe large-scale differences that are applicable to entire industries or nations.

COMPLEX WEBS OF CAUSAL FACTORS

Epidemiology examines the interaction of complex disease-producing factors: a "web of causation" (MacMahon and Pugh, 1970: Chapter 2). This web is composed of three main, intertwining aspects: agent, host, and environment. The *agent* is the source of a disease, such as a virus in an infection or asbestos fibers in asbestosis. The agent is a necessary but not sufficient cause of disease; disease does not occur without an agent, but the agent alone is not sufficient to produce the disease (Mausner and Bahn, 1985).

BOX 2.1 *FUR FASHIONS AND PLAGUE*

The outbreak of Manchurian plague at the turn of this century constitutes a well-documented example of the role of living patterns in disease causation. The plague bacillus is widely distributed among the wild rodents of Asia. Manchurian marmots normally harbor this microbe, but they do not suffer from the infection under usual circumstances. Around 1910, a change in women's fashions in Europe suddenly created a large demand for the fur of the Manchurian marmot, and a number of inexperienced Chinese hunters began to hunt this wild rodent. Until then it had been hunted only by Manchurians who had a taboo forbidding them to hunt sick animals. In contrast, the inexperienced Chinese trapped every animal within reach, especially the sickest who were slower and easier to catch. As it turned out, the sick marmots were suffering from plague, and many Chinese hunters contracted the infection from them. When the hunters met in the crowded and ill-ventilated Manchurian inns, those who had caught the microbe spread it to their neighbors, thereby initiating a widespread epidemic of pneumonic plague. A change in women's fashions in Europe thus indirectly caused an epidemic of pneumonic plague in Manchuria.

Source: René Dubos, *Man, Medicine and Environment.* Baltimore: Penguin, 1968: 113.

The site within which an agent creates a disease is called the host. The host and agent interact within a biosocial environment, which includes the external conditions linking the agent to the host (such as unsanitary living conditions); the vector, or the means through which the agent is carried (such as diseased marmots or contaminated drinking water); and the condition of the internal environment of the host (such as relative immunity). To cause disease effectively, an agent must be able to survive in the environment and find a susceptible, fertile host (Johnson and Sargent, 1990). For example, a human body (host) may harbor tubercular bacilli (agent), but if the body's resistance (environment) is high, this disease agent cannot produce infection. Thus disease is not the outcome of just one factor; rather, many factors contribute to the complex "web of causation." Epidemiology is a generally more holistic approach to health and illness.

As the name implies, epidemiology arose from the study of widespread infectious diseases, or epidemics. The maturing field has more recently begun to include study of the distribution, spread, and cause of noninfectious diseases, such as heart disease or cancer. The epidemiology of these sicknesses is, however, more difficult, because they develop more slowly, often over decades. The causal factors are thus obscured by time. A 60-year-old victim of a heart attack is not likely to be able to recall accurately relevant information about his life as much as 40 or 50 years earlier.

Noninfectious diseases also often involve multiple contributing factors rather than a single infectious agent. Thus it is difficult to identify all possible factors and determine their relative weight. For example, the hormones in birth control pills have been implicated in the development, many years after their use, of breast cancer. It is difficult, however, to determine just how significant a factor they may be for several reasons. The disease does not develop in clinically observable forms immediately upon use of "the pill." Other factors (such as the age of the onset of menstruation) are also involved and, in combination, greatly increase probability of developing the disease. It is extremely difficult to determine the relative importance of these various other factors (such as the woman's leanness, her age at the birth of her first baby, and whether she breastfed her babies) or even whether some possible factors are not being considered. It is difficult to determine, many years after the fact, exactly how much or which type of hormones women received; formulations for early contraceptive pills contained much higher dosages of hormones and in different combinations than more recent formulations. If a woman is now 48, she may have taken several different formulations for many periods of varying length since the age of 18 (cf. Kolata, 1989).

Early epidemiological studies examined relatively crude social factors, such as occupation or social class. Increasingly, social epidemiology is trying to tease out more refined categories of social influences on morbidity and mortality. For example, rather than look only at broad categories of occupation, research might examine the health impact of characteristic patterns of work-place time pressures or supervisor-worker relationships. Subsequent chapters describe some of these studies.

METHODOLOGICAL ISSUES

Epidemiology proceeds by observing statistical correlations between two or more variables pertaining to health, sickness, or death. The data for these statistical procedures are often drawn from records that are kept for other institutional purposes; researchers must therefore contend with discrepancies or errors created by the original records.

Statistical Associations

The existence of a statistical correlation between two variables is not sufficient evidence of a causal link between them. Many statistical relationships are spurious. For example, a nineteenth-century observer noted that the incidence of cholera was inversely correlated with the altitude of a community; low-lying places had higher rates of the disease than did those at higher altitudes. This correlation confirmed a prevalent notion that stagnant air (miasma) caused cholera; accordingly, because their air was "fresher," communities at higher altitudes had less miasma and thus less cholera. Later epidemiological discoveries showed that impure water was actually the vector (means of spreading the agent) for cholera. Because low-lying places were more likely to have both stagnant air and impure water, investigators were led to a spurious correlation between the disease and miasma (Mausner and Bahn, 1985).

It is often difficult to determine whether a statistical correlation is the product of an indirect relationship actually explained by intervening variables. For example, epidemiological data from the rural southern regions of the United States may show a statistical correlation between low birth weight and childhood deaths from diarrhea. Does that mean that low birth weight causes subsequent death from diarrheal dehydration? This is a plausible interpretation, since birth weight may affect the child's susceptibility to illness, but birth weight may be only a by-product of some other causal factors. One clue to these other factors is to ask a somewhat oversimplified question: What kind of children are likely to experience both low birth weight and diarrhea? The profile of children with these conditions suggests several related features: They are likely to be from poor families in which the mother was young and received little or no prenatal care (Stevens, 1988). To establish a direct causal link between low birth weight and death due to diarrhea, it would be necessary to identify and hold constant all other factors. Any causal analysis must take into account multiple factors that may operate at several levels in the web of causality.

Data Bases

Many records upon which epidemiological studies are based are seriously flawed. Some statistics come from the records of schools, industries, insurance companies, hospitals, and public health departments. Since these data are kept for various other institutional reasons, they are often of limited accuracy for epidemiological purposes. For example, industrial accident statistics can be distorted by an industry's attempt to give the impression of a low accident rate.

Likewise, death certificates are very inaccurate and unreliable sources of information about the causes of death (Hill and Anderson, 1988; 1991). A Connecticut study found that 29 percent of death certificates inaccurately stated the cause of death, based upon autopsy reports and patients' medical records (Kircher et al., 1985). In a further 26 percent of the cases, the autopsy and death certificate gave the same general disease category but attributed death to different specific diseases. Thus more than half of the certificates provided seriously flawed data about the cause of death. Similar conclusions about the inaccuracy of death certificates were found in a Scottish study of postmortems (Cameron and McGoogan, 1981). Interviewing doctors in a Scottish city, Bloor (1991) found wide variations in how deaths were certified.

The usefulness of data from both medical records and death certificates may also be diminished by judgments made by the medical personnel who keep the records. Deliberate misrepresentations often occur when the cause of death is a stigmatizing sickness, such as alcoholism or AIDS. Such reporting problems make it difficult to assess the scope and actual impact of these important health problems. Not only the concern over stigma but also political, economic, and ideological considerations often figure into the deliberate underreporting of the incidence of AIDS. Data have been flawed, for example, by racist attitudes, fears of hurting tourism, and the assumption that AIDS affects only stigmatized minorities (Bolton, 1989: 93–94).

Death certificates also often state only a final cause of death, rather than the initial or contributing causes. For example, a person who dies of a gunshot wound may be listed as having died of internal bleeding. Although the bleeding is a fact in the case, the gunshot wound does not appear in the mortality statistics. Certain causes of death, such as adverse reactions to prescribed medications, are also systematically underreported (Altman, 1988b).

The *International Statistical Classification of Diseases, Injuries and Causes of Death*, revised about every ten years by the National Center for Health Statistics of the United States, specifies standards to be used by attending doctors, coroners, and others in an attempt to produce internationally comparable data. Changes in these guidelines for classification, however, yield different rates of morbidity and mortality. One revision of the manual required coders to disregard medically induced (iatrogenic) causes of death, such as postsurgical bleeding or drug reaction, and instead to record the medical condition that first necessitated the treatment (Bloor et al., 1987). The proposed new form of death certificates in the United States asks for the immediate cause of death and a sequential listing of *all* underlying causes. It is likely that these new data will result in the "discovery" of comparatively high rates of medically induced conditions leading to death.

Despite recent efforts to change the format of U.S. death certificates to allow for more complex and thorough reporting, the data entered upon them remain problematic. Most death certificates are based upon doctors' clinical judgments about the cause or causes of death; autopsies are expensive and performed for a decreasing proportion of cases. Whereas in the 1950s, autopsies were performed on about half of all patients who died in a hospital, current rates are only about 12 percent, performed disproportionately for forensic (i.e., legal) evidence and, thus, hardly a representative sample (Hill and Anderson, 1991). Even when an autopsy subsequently contradicts the certificate or adds significant new information, physicians often do not amend it (Altman, 1988b).

Even if autopsy findings are included on death certificates, these data may be slanted by the criteria used to select cases for autopsy. Women are less likely to be autopsied than men. In some states, nonwhite deaths are less likely to be investigated than those of whites (Bloor et al., 1987). Social status and/or the perceived social worth of the victim may also influence the thoroughness with which a death is investigated (cf. Sudnow, 1967). Thus the cases autopsied are not a representative sample of all deaths.

"Errors" or variations in diagnosis are not random; they are often socially produced. For example, medical personnel's judgments may vary according to the perceived social class of the dead person. In earlier medical reporting, the cause of a professional person's death from heart disease was likely to be labeled as "angina," whereas the cause of death of a working-class person with the same condition was usually classified as something else (Marmot et al., 1987). Similarly, diagnoses (and thus morbidity statistics) are influenced by doctors' attitudes toward patients' social characteristics, such as gender, social class, or occupation, as discussed further in Chapters 9 and 10. For example, earlier data indicated that the rate of deaths due to alcoholism in Scotland were about twice those in England and Wales; these data are now in question, because studies show that doctors in England and Wales are much less likely than those in Scotland to attribute death to alcohol-related diseases such as cirrhosis (see Altman, 1988b).

Cultural differences in medical practice, even among Western industrial nations and among doctors trained in modern biomedicine, account for some variations in diagnoses. For example, blood pressure readings considered hypertensive in the United States would be considered normal in England (Payer, 1988). Doctor characteristics may also affect the diagnosis or reported cause of death. Because of differences in their training, younger British doctors were less likely than older ones to report stomach cancer as a diagnosis (Bloor et al., 1987). Thus a falling rate of mortality due to stomach cancer may be at least in part an artifact of differences in doctors' education.

These examples show that many health statistics may be *artifactual*, or produced by the social arrangements by which the statistics themselves are gathered and processed. Such artifactual evidence is misleading and often altogether incorrect. With these limitations in mind, let us examine some results of epidemiological investigation. The cautious use of epidemiological information can give us a broad "picture of health."

CHANGES IN LIFE EXPECTANCY IN THE TWENTIETH CENTURY

American males born in 1900 could expect to live 46.3 years and females, 48.3 years. By 1989 the life expectancy for both sexes had increased, but so had the gap between male and female rates. Males born in 1989 can expect to live 71.8 years, while females born that same year could live on the average to the age of 78.6 years. Figure 2.1 shows the dramatic increase in life span in the United States from 1900 to 1990 (U.S. Dept. of Health and Human Services, 1992). There was a general decline of infant mortality and the increasing difference in life expectancy between men and women that began to emerge around 1920. In 1990, the infant mortality rate for the United States was 9.1 deaths per 1,000 (Hilts, 1991). Figure 2.2 shows U.S. patterns of infant mortality between 1920 and 1990. There are also dramatic differences between blacks and whites in both general life expectancy and infant mortality.

Along with life expectancy changes, there have also been changes in the causes of death in Western industrial societies. Despite the recent development of some infectious diseases such as AIDS, there has been a general decline in death rates due to infectious diseases and an increase in death rates due to chronic degenerative diseases (McKinlay et al., 1989). Figure 2.3 illustrates this important change.

Table 2.1 shows the changing causes of death in order of their frequency. In 1900 acute infectious diseases (pneumonia, influenza, and tuberculosis) were the foremost causes of death in the United States. Chronic diseases (heart disease and cancer) were the major killers in 1985. Since the 1950s, the death rate from coronary heart disease in the United States has been decreasing. This is perhaps due to changes in diet, exercise patterns, and smoking habits (Sytkowski, et al., 1990). Rates of death from cancer have increased during the same time (Pear, 1984).

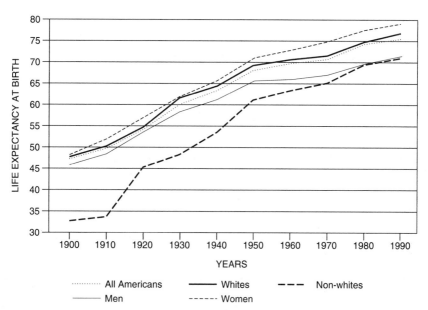

FIGURE 2.1   Changes in U.S. Life Expectancy, 1900–1990. (Sources: U.S. Bureau of the Census, Statistical Abstract of the United States, 1992. Washington, DC, 1992; U.S. Bureau of the Census, Historical Statistics of the United States, Colonial Times to 1970. Bicentennial edition, part 2. Washington, DC, 1975.)

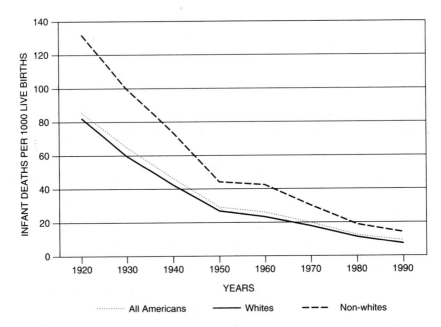

FIGURE 2.2 Changes in U.S. Infant Mortality, 1920–1990. (Sources: U.S. Bureau of the Census, Statistical Abstract of the United States, 1992. Washington, DC, 1992; U.S. Bureau of the Census, Historical Statistics of the United States, Colonial Times to 1970. Bicentennial edition, part 2. Washington, DC, 1975.)

TABLE 2.1   Causes of Death in the United States, 1900 and 1990

	1900		1990
Causes of Death	Death Rate (per 100,000)	Causes of Death	Death Rate (per 100,000)
All causes	1,719.0	All causes	861.9
Pneumonia and influenza	202.2	Diseases of the heart	289.0
Tuberculosis	194.4	Malignancies	195.1
Diarrhea, enteritis, and ulceration	142.7	Cerebrovascular disease	57.9
Diseases of the heart	137.4	Chronic obstructive pulmonary disease	35.5
Senility, ill-defined or unknown	117.5	Influenza and pneumonia	31.3
Intracranial lesions of vascular origin	106.9	Suicide and homicide	22.5
Nephritis	88.6	Diabetes mellitus	19.5
All accidents	72.3	Cirrhosis of the liver	10.2
Cancer and other malignant tumors	64.0	Arteriosclerosis	6.6

Sources: U.S. Department of Health and Human Services, National Center for Health Statistics, "Births, marriages, divorces, and deaths for 1985," *Monthly Vital Statistics Report* 34(12), 1986: 5; U.S. Department of Health and Human Services, *Health: United States, 1991.* Hyattsville, MD: National Center for Health Statistics, 1992.

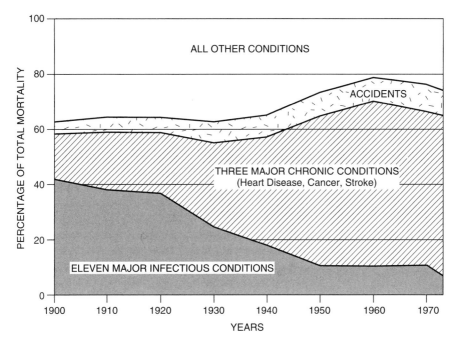

FIGURE 2.3   *Proportion of Chronic and Infectious Disease Contributing to U.S. Mortality, 1900–1973. (Source: John B. McKinlay and Sonja M. McKinlay, "The questionable effect of medical measures on the decline of mortality in the United States in the twentieth century," Milbank Memorial Fund Quarterly 55, 1977: 416. Reprinted by permission.)*

The increased incidence of chronic degenerative diseases cannot be attributed simply to the fact that people are living longer. It is true that the longer people live, the more likely they are to develop a chronic disease; however, increased longevity does not account for the fact that, beginning in the 1950s, even *younger* age groups have shown an increased incidence of these afflictions (Angier, 1991; Eyer and Sterling, 1977). This premature development of degenerative sickness may be the result of contemporary dietary, environmental, and social factors. Evidence that the social, biochemical, and physical environment of industrialized societies create new health problems, such as increased rates of cancer, comes from a comparison with preindustrial societies, which have lower incidence of these problems. Aspects of the way of life in industrialized societies are implicated because the rates of chronic degenerative diseases increase among groups that migrate from agricultural to industrial communities (Janes, 1986).

THE MYTH OF MEDICAL PROGRESS

Many people believe that "miracles" of medical progress have been responsible for the improved health and longevity in Western industrial countries since the turn of the century. Media imagery often contributes to the notion, but much evidence suggests the contribution of medical intervention to increased life expectancy has been rather limited. McKeown (1979) argues that improved nutrition and population control, the control of predators, and improvements in urban dwelling conditions and hygiene have played a much greater role in extending life expectancy than did medical technology. The impact of these various factors on health can be documented through epidemiological studies.

A study of mortality rates in the United States shows that medical intervention (such as inoculations) accounts for only a small percentage of the decline in mortality from infectious diseases during the early part of the twentieth century. Figure 2.4 shows that, of nine common infectious diseases, only poliomyelitis began to decline significantly *after* the introduction of the vaccine. All the other major infectious diseases had declined dramatically *prior* to the introduction of a vaccine or antibiotic (McKinlay and McKinlay, 1977). The decline of tuberculosis likewise preceded the introduction of chemical therapies (Friedman, 1987). Nonmedical factors, such as improved nutrition, clean water, garbage and sewage disposal, and other public health measures, may account for the primary decline in mortality due to many infectious diseases.

The precise contribution of medicine to increased life expectancy, to the reduction of morbidity, and to the quality of life is difficult—if not impossible—to assess. Some have argued that the iatrogenic (i.e., medically induced) health risks of modern medicine and its institutions outweigh its benefits (Illich, 1975). This position probably overstates the harmful effects of modern medicine. Nevertheless, any evaluation of the contribution of medical intervention must take into account its iatrogenic consequences, such as unneeded surgery, over- and misprescription of drugs, the negative side effects of medication, and infections transmitted in medical settings.

There is no doubt that medicine has made significant contributions to human health. It is effective in treating many acute diseases. Emergency medicine has saved many lives, and technological innovations in medicine since World War I have made it possible for many to survive previously mortal health crises. Medicine has also played a major role in the virtual eradication of some infectious diseases, such as smallpox and polio. The ability of medicine to treat or prevent chronic, degenerative diseases is, however, more limited. Furthermore, the benefits from medical progress must be distinguished from social-environmental changes and public health measures that have played a major part in improving people's health. The contributions of public health measures are often devalued by modern medicine, resulting in social policies that allocate the vast majority of health care expenditures to medical research and treatments rather than to preventive programs such as maternal nutrition or workplace safety.

MORBIDITY AND MORTALITY
IN THIRD WORLD COUNTRIES

The pattern of high rates of mortality due to infectious diseases seen in industrialized societies at the turn of the century still characterizes the health situation of many Third World societies. The average person born in Japan in 1990 can expect to live to about

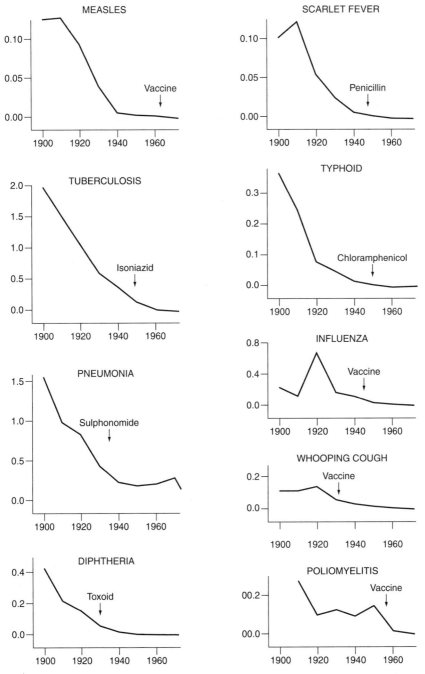

FIGURE 2.4 The Fall in the Standardized Death Rate (per 1,000 Population) for Nine Common Infectious Diseases in Relation to Specific Medical Measures in the United States, 1900–1973. (Source: John B. McKinlay and Sonja M. McKinlay, "The questionable effect of medical measures on the decline of mortality in the United States in the twentieth century," Milbank Memorial Fund Quarterly 55, 1977: 422–423.)

78.6 years; in Sweden and Canada, that person would live 77 or more years, and in the United States, 75.9 years. By contrast, the life expectancy of those born in 1990 in India is 59.1; in Somalia, 46.1; in Afghanistan, 42.5; and in Sierra Leone, 41 (United Nations Development Programme, 1993). Average life expectancies are somewhat misleading, however, because they do not reflect the variations between subgroups (e.g., class, gender, and rural-urban differences) within each society. In Third World countries, as in nineteenth-century Europe and America, such factors as inadequate diet and unsanitary conditions contribute greatly to the high mortality rate and prevalence of infectious diseases. Childhood diseases such as measles are much more likely to result in death where nutrition and sanitation are poor.

Many Westerners consider Third World countries to be inherently disease-ridden, eagerly awaiting the benefits of modern civilization. In the nineteenth century, Africa was viewed as a "white man's grave," a disease-filled "dark continent." Many diseases, however, such as smallpox, syphilis, measles, influenza, cholera, and tuberculosis, were introduced to Africa from Europe and Asia, devastating native populations, which had no immunity to diseases to which they had never been exposed. At the same time, sailors, explorers, colonists, and merchants were exposed to diseases, such as malaria, that were new to them. Since they had no immunity, they too were hard hit.

The colonization of Africa and the slave trade created massive sociocultural dislocations and altered patterns of land use. Migration to the cities and the attendant overcrowding, as well the ecological disruption of the land, generated conditions that bred and spread certain infectious diseases. In epidemiological terms, alterations in the environment made for a changed relationship among host, agent, and environment. For instance, in western Africa the development of logging, commercial agriculture, roads, railways, and other changes in the landscape created sites (infection reservoirs) for breeding mosquitoes and thus for spreading malaria (Epstein and Packard, 1987).

In countries such as South Africa, radically different pictures of health exist side by side in the same society. As a whole, South Africa has a highly developed economy. Nevertheless, the policy of apartheid produced the social and economic domination of a white minority over a nonwhite majority by radical segregation of housing, education, occupations, and legal status. This social arrangement resulted in very different living conditions for whites and nonwhites, and hence in different patterns of morbidity and mortality. The infant mortality for blacks in South Africa is approximately six times higher than that of whites. One-quarter of black children under fourteen years of age are chronically malnourished or undernourished. By contrast, there is hardly any malnutrition or undernutrition among whites, and whites generally die of "diseases of affluence," which are linked with affluent lifestyles such as high-calorie diets and sedentary occupations. Blacks, on the other hand, are more likely to die of infectious diseases, such as typhoid, cholera, tuberculosis, and measles (a disease that is rarely fatal in affluent societies). Thus, in one nation, two very different ways of life produce different health profiles. These differences are a dramatic illustration of how social-structural arrangements (i.e., apartheid) can produce different patterns of health, illness, and death (Frankel, 1986; Susser et al., 1985).

Not only are diseases themselves spatially and socially segregated, but various forms of segregation also reduce people's ability to know and understand others' way of life. Probably most members of the white minority in South Africa do not fully perceive the physical consequences of apartheid. The ability of the affluent to see the world of the hungry and poor is blocked by their spatial and social segregation from each other. Similarly, a reporter in Ethiopia noted that many members of the urban middle and upper classes did not have any knowledge of the famine in their *own* country until foreign correspondents wrote about it (May, 1985). A censored press, as in Ethiopia and South Africa, can thus mute social conscience. In many cities in the United States, economically comfortable middle-class persons may likewise live only blocks from squalor and never be truly aware of it.

THE EPIDEMIOLOGY OF AIDS

In the last quarter of 1991, 160 countries reported 500,000 AIDS cases. The United States has about 40 percent of the world's reported cases. As of July, 1992, there were over 200,000 cases of AIDS in the United States (Stine, 1993: 191). The U.S. Centers for Disease Control (C.D.C.) and the World Health Organization (W.H.O.) estimate that approximately 1 million Americans are now infected with H.I.V., the virus that is the agent of AIDS. W.H.O. estimates that worldwide some 10 million people are infected; 6.5 million of those infected are African (W.H.O., 1992, cited in Eckholm, 1992).

The transmission of the AIDS virus depends on the geosocial context in which it is spread. In North and South America, Western Europe, Australia, and New Zealand, AIDS affects mainly males. The mode of transmission often involves anal intercourse, whereas the rate from transmission by vaginal intercourse appears to be relatively low. In these countries, AIDS is concentrated primarily among homosexual men, contributing to the myth that it is essentially a "gay plague." Intravenous drug users are the second largest risk group; transmission occurs by sharing unsterile needles.

The epidemiological profile of AIDS in countries like the United States, however, may be changing. As of 1989, women were increasingly likely to become infected (Corea, 1992). More people in racial and ethnic minorities—men, women, and increasingly children—are becoming AIDS victims. In New York City, more than one-half of AIDS cases are among blacks and Hispanics (Shulman and Mantell, 1988). Among Hispanics, the rates are highest among Puerto Ricans, whereas the rates among Mexican-Americans are similar to those of non-Hispanic whites (Selik et al., 1989; U.S. Department of Health and Human Services, 1992). The use of broad categories such as "Hispanic" to designate high-risk groups, however, can be highly problematic since it obscures the wide range of differences *within* these groups (for instance, some Hispanic peoples have relatively low rates of intravenous drug use). Similarly, some epidemiological research "lumps" gays and bisexuals into one category (Schiller, 1992; Becerra et al., 1991). Prostitutes are often identified as a high-risk group but in the United States, for instance, there is no evidence of higher H.I.V. rates of infection among prostitutes than among other groups (Corea, 1992: 83).

The rate of new cases in the gay community may be leveling off because of dramatic changes in sexual practices (Fauci, 1988). Some of this change is due to social organizing by the gay community which, through education and condom distribution, has had an impact on sexual practices (Friedman, 1993; Nelkin et al., 1991). AIDS is also becoming more geographically widespread in the United States, with one-half of new cases occurring outside of major urban centers. This development may be even more dramatic than it appears because AIDS may be particularly underreported in regions like the Midwest and among persons of higher socioeconomic standing (Laumann et al., 1989).

In central Africa, the patterns of transmission to hosts and course of infection are quite different. One-third to one-half of all those with AIDS are women, with a large concentration of cases among prostitutes. This suggests that in Africa heterosexual intercourse is a more common means of transmitting AIDS than homosexual contact and intravenous drug use. In parts of Africa, prostitution is encouraged by practices of migratory labor (a heritage from the colonial past) and poverty. Millions of couples are separated for months at a time while men go to cities or plantations for work. Women, on the other hand, often have few alternate means of survival and may provide sex in exchange for economic survival (Eckholm, 1990). Their lack of social power renders them more vulnerable to AIDS. Men who resist the use of condoms and have multiple partners, transmit the virus from place to place during their travels for work (Corea, 1992; Turshen, 1989).

Scientists have speculated about the origins of the H.I.V. virus. At first, some argued that the virus originated in the African green monkey, but there is little evidence to support that hypothesis (Stine, 1993), and the attempt to locate the origins of the virus in Africa may reflect Western attitudes toward that continent as a source of disease. It is possible that the virus originated in the United States and was transported to Africa (Turshen, 1989: 221). In any event, the epidemiology of the AIDS virus may be affected by social policy and laws (e.g., regarding needle distribution), religious factors (e.g., the attitude of religious groups toward sexuality), as well as many other economic and cultural factors (Friedman, 1993).

VARIATIONS IN MORTALITY AND MORBIDITY

The wide range of mortality and morbidity within societies is distributed along basic sociological variables such as region, age, gender, ethnicity, and class. Variations in health and death are linked to people's different locations in social space and structure. The following discussion examines major variables in mortality and morbidity for the United States.

Age

As expected, death rates increase with age. In the United States, until the age of 40, death rates increase gradually. After 40, they virtually double for each decade of age (Mausner and Bahn, 1985: 120). Figure 2.5 shows population pyramids for the United States, which indicate, for a given year, the relative numbers of males and females in each age bracket. The data for 1910 take the shape of a conventional pyramid because the birth rates are balanced by death rates, for both sexes, in a somewhat even pattern. The 1991 pyramid, however, is less conventionally shaped because of decreased birth rates and lower death rates, a pattern that characterizes industrialized nations. This trend, in which fewer people are born and more live past the age of 50, has been called the "graying" of society because ever larger proportions of the population survive into old age. Demographic projections show that people aged 85 years or more are likely to be the fastest growing part of the population in the next few decades (Rice, 1990).

Although chronic degenerative diseases have been increasing in all age groups, their rates increase most dramatically for older people (Verbrugge, 1990). In 1965, one out of five Americans under 50 had chronic diseases; among those over 65, four out of five had such disorders, with heart disease most frequent (Susser et al., 1985). Only rates for death due to homicide, accidents, and suicide decline with age; rates of death due to chronic illnesses and disabling conditions increase. The increased number of people in our society with chronic illness and disabilities has raised a number of sociopolitical issues, discussed further in Chapter 8. Many chronic conditions are not a "natural" result of aging. For example, the rate of hypertension (high blood pressure) increases with age in American society but not in hunting and gathering societies. The nomadic !Kung bushmen of the Kalahari Desert in Africa consume large quantities of dietary salt, a factor that some have linked to hypertension, yet they do not show increased blood pressure with age (Schnall and Kern, 1981).

While aging seems to involve inevitably increased morbidity, some researchers suggest the possibility of "compressing" morbidity. They argue that while the life span is biologically limited, it may become possible to limit the period when an aging person is infirm (Fries, 1990). Others point out that while the compression of morbidity is a desirable goal, it is not occurring now and there is little evidence that it will in the near future (Guralnik and Schneider, 1990). On the other hand, although compression of morbidity may be possible, it pertains mostly to higher socioeconomic groups. Widespread compressed morbidity would require greatly increased social equality (House et al., 1990).

Gender

In the nineteenth century, women typically died younger than men. One explanation of the difference is that frequent pregnancies and childbirth involved considerable health risks. Also, under conditions of general material scarcity, women often got what food was left after men and children ate their share. Poor nutrition

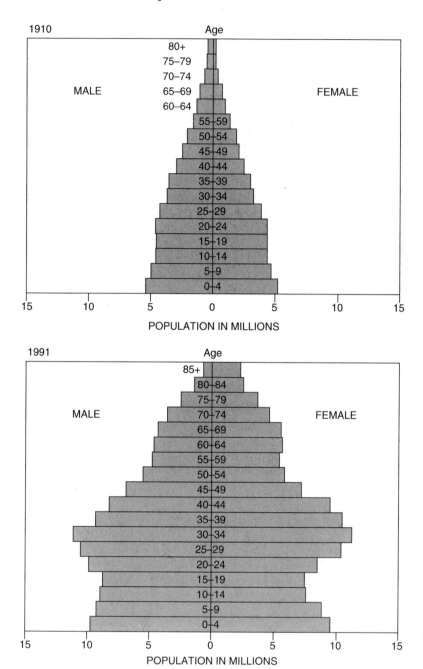

FIGURE 2.5   Age Composition of the U.S. Population, 1910 and 1991. (Sources: Population Reference Bureau, Population Bulletin 37 (2), 1982; U.S. Bureau of the Census, Statistical Abstract of the United States, 1992. Washington, DC, 1992.)

then compounded women's health difficulties (Shorter, 1982). By the 1920s, the gender patterns in mortality rates had changed, and women generally were living longer than men. By 1989 the life expectancy at birth for U.S. males was 71.8 years; for females, 78.6 (U.S. Dept. of Health and Human Services, 1992). At all ages, males have higher rates of mortality than females (Verbrugge, 1992). Similar differences between men and women exist in most Western industrialized countries (Waldron, 1994; Sagan, 1987); however, in some Third World countries, male life expectancy is greater than that for women (Waldron, 1994).

Biological factors may partially account for the higher mortality rates of males. Higher fetal mortality rates have been reported for males (Harrison et al., 1992). Because the male-female mortality rate difference occurs cross-culturally, it cannot readily be explained by social factors. There is evidence that female life expectancy is also higher among many other animal species (Sagan, 1987). This biological advantage for women may come from hormonal differences, although such differences may also produce in women higher rates of some sicknesses, such as gallstones (Friedman, 1987).

Men die earlier and have more life-threatening illnesses, but in general women become ill more frequently (Cleary, 1987: 55). Chronic illnesses are more prevalent among women than men, but they are less severe and life threatening than those of men (Cleary, 1987: 55; Verbrugge and Wingard, 1987; Verbrugge, 1992). Women also report more episodes of illness and more contact with physicians (Susser et al., 1985: 71). Women's higher rates of sickness and doctor visits can be partly explained by gynecological or reproductive problems, which men would not have, but the incidence of these problems is not great enough to account for the difference in morbidity rates between men and women. Perhaps women are more willing than men to admit they are sick and/or to visit physicians. If this is true, then lower morbidity rates for men are deceptive, since they are a function of the underreporting of sickness rather than differences in rates of actual disease (see Waldron, 1976). It has been suggested that women learn more effective coping skills and ways of caring for themselves (such as seeking care and calling in sick), but there is no firm evidence for this hypothesis (Verbrugge, 1985; 1992).

Men are more likely than women to engage in high-risk behavior, such as smoking or driving fast, and risks associated with work roles may be higher for men (Verbrugge, 1985; Waldron, 1991). Furthermore, there may be some differences in personal styles. Women are perhaps less likely to exhibit Type A ("coronary-prone") behavior, described in Chapter 5. The mortality gap between men and women may be narrowing in recent years. As women adopt more high-risk behaviors (e.g., smoking) and enter into work places with job stressors and other risks, and as men, by contrast, improve their health behaviors, the gap may narrow further (Cleary, 1987; Verbrugge and Wingard, 1987). While biological factors such as hormonal differences play some role, sociocultural factors linked with differences between men's and women's roles probably account for much of the sex-linked variations in mortality and morbidity rates.

Race and Ethnicity

Patterns of morbidity and mortality also vary among ethnic and racial groups in a society. Some differences may be explained by hereditary factors that are disproportionately characteristic of certain groups. Genetically transmitted sicknesses include sickle cell anemia (among blacks and some other groups) and Tay-Sachs syndrome (among persons of Eastern European Jewish descent).

Hereditary factors also combine with sociocultural factors to produce ethnic differences in morbidity and mortality. For example, Mexican-Americans are more likely to have inherent lactose intolerance than Anglo-Americans; lactose intolerance combined with social factors (e.g., higher rates of poverty) produces serious nutritional deficiencies (Schreiber and Homiak, 1981: 283). Similarly, genetic tendencies may be a component factor that, together with stressful living and working arrangements, leads to disproportionately high rates of diabetes among Mexican-American migrant workers (Angel, 1989; Scheder, 1988).

Patterns of variation are linked indirectly to ethnicity through other factors: nutrition, housing and sanitary living conditions, employment and types of occupation, family patterns, and lifestyle. Epidemiological data reflect these variables, but cannot always separate them neatly to show just how much variance is explained by any one variable. Other connections are more obvious. For example, a study of the incidence of childhood lead poisoning showing a large number of the victims to be inner-city black preschoolers could determine rather easily whether the causal connection was in fact that disproportionate numbers of urban blacks live in substandard, older housing where the crumbling lead paint may be ingested by young children. The following discussion gives some of the highlights of U.S. data about racial and ethnic variation in morbidity and mortality.

Black Americans constitute by far the largest racial/ethnic minority in the United States. Epidemiological data referring to "nonwhites" are thus mainly describing blacks. The pattern of health of black people is very different from that of whites. In 1989 black life expectancy was 69.6 years compared to 75.9 years for whites (U.S. Dept. of Health and Human Services, 1992). These rates represent a dramatic improvement since 1920, when life expectancy was 45.3 years for blacks and 54.9 years for whites.

One major factor in the lower life expectancy for blacks is their high rate of infant mortality. Figure 2.2 shows differences in infant mortality between white and nonwhite Americans between 1920 and 1990. Even though infant mortality has been steadily declining for both groups, the nonwhite rate has generally been about twice that of whites (LaVeist, 1992). Infant mortality is especially high among newborns with low birth weight or very young mothers or both. The rate of live births of babies with low birth weight (less than 2,500 grams) was 12 percent for blacks compared with 6 percent for whites; 38 percent of black mothers did not receive prenatal care until after the first trimester of pregnancy, compared to 20 percent of white mothers (Anderson et al., 1987). These factors are clearly linked with socioeconomic factors (LaVeist, 1992). Low birth weight is often the direct result of poor maternal nutrition and inadequate prenatal care. Compared to other industrialized countries, the U.S. infant mortality rate is frighteningly high, largely due to this country's failure to address the problems of poverty, especially nutrition and health care. Indeed, since 1980 cutbacks in federal spending resulted in reduced or inadequate prenatal care for poor mothers (cf. Physicians' Task Force on Hunger in America, 1985).

Since the mid-1980s, there has been a slight decrease in black life expectancy (while whites experienced a *slight* increase); changes in life expectancy of black males account for most of the decrease (Najman, 1993; U.S. Dept. of Health and Human Services, 1992). This decrease may be partly due to the rise of infectious diseases such as AIDS and increased conditions of poverty experienced disproportionately by blacks (Muwakkil, 1991).

The proportionately higher rates of hypertension and hypertensive heart disease among blacks compared with whites illustrate the complexities of causal factors with which epidemiological studies must contend. Factors accounting for these differences include genetic factors in susceptibility, greater stress due to racism, lower socioeconomic status, less access to good medical care, and a higher rate of obesity among blacks (Friedman, 1987). The genetic susceptibility explanation seems doubtful because cross-cultural studies found no such patterns among genetically comparable peoples of Africa. Whereas American blacks show a rapid increase in blood pressure after the age of about 24, African blacks living in tribal communities do not have increased blood pressure as they age. Migration to industrialized, urban settings, however, does promote increased blood pressure (Janes, 1986). The lower socioeconomic status of many blacks probably accounts for much of the differences in hypertension and other problems (Navarro, 1991). Even after one takes social class into consideration, however, some small yet significant differences remain (Navarro, 1989). Such factors as stress produced by racism and residential segregation, which influence even the more affluent blacks, may explain some of these remaining "racial" differences (La Veist, 1993; Mutchler and Burr, 1991; Reed, 1990).

Hispanics (e.g., Mexican-Americans, Puerto Ricans, Cuban-Americans) are a fast growing minority in the United States. Some are at increased risk for diabetes, hypertension, tuberculosis, AIDS, alcoholism, cirrhosis, specific cancers, and violent deaths. Among subgroups of Hispanics, Puerto Ricans have the poorest health. Many of these health disadvantages are due to low socioeconomic status (Council on Scientific Affairs, 1991). Such categories as "Hispanic" are, in fact, extremely heterogenous, so generalizations about ethnic differences in health must be treated with caution.

Some American ethnic groups comprise individuals whose families came to the United States in different waves of immigration. Thus comparative studies have the potential of identifying which factors in sickness and death are due to the particular living situation and lifestyle of a group in the United States compared with the country of origin. For example, while the rate of tuberculosis among Chinese-Americans is higher than among the general population, it is nevertheless lower than in the "old country." Similarly, both first- and second-generation Chinese-Americans have more coronary heart disease than Asian Chinese; diet and stress are both implicated (Gould-Martin and Ngin, 1981).

Patterns of morbidity and mortality among Native Americans reveal another set of factors. American Indians are among the most disadvantaged ethnic groups in the United States; their death rate is about 30 percent higher than that of the general U.S population (Weeks, 1986). Like many peoples of developing nations, Native Americans are experiencing a demographic and epidemiological transition over a relatively short period of time.

Demographic transition refers to the changes populations undergo (usually in the course of so-called modernization) as they move from a situation of high mortality and fertility to a stage in which mortality has declined but fertility is still high. The third phase is characterized by low fertility and mortality (Omran, 1971). Native American groups have experienced more decline in mortality than in fertility, and the decline in mortality is largely due to the reduction of epidemic infectious diseases. The resulting rates of morbidity and mortality, at this stage of transition, reflect a shift in causes of death. For example, among Navahos overall mortality has declined, especially mortality due to influenza, pneumonia, gastritis, and certain diseases of early infancy; at the same time, there is increased mortality due to accidents and alcohol-related diseases (Kunitz and Levy, 1981).

There thus appears to be considerable racial and ethnic diversity in the United States in rates of mortality and morbidity, but precise figures are not available since national epidemiological data do not differentiate among white ethnic groups or nonwhite ethnic groups (for critical summaries of various studies on urban black Americans, Chinese-Americans, Haitian-Americans, Italian-Americans, Mexican-Americans, Navajos, and mainland Puerto Ricans, see Harwood, 1981a; see also Polednak, 1989). Most differences, however, appear to be largely due to social-structural factors, especially class. Purely materialist explanations (i.e., those that focus on the impact of different material conditions on health differences) may not always completely explain ethnic differences in such health indicators as infant mortality (Andrews and Jewson, 1993). Cultural factors also influence diet, health-related behavior (e.g., smoking and drinking), reproduction, and the like.

Social Class

Social class is probably one of the most useful shorthand indicators of a person's power. Class is usually measured by income, education, occupation, or a combination of these factors. Generally, there is a consistently significant relationship between class and health (Dutton, 1986). The lower the social class, the higher the rates of morbidity and mortality. This relationship is not surprising, considering the important part that social class plays in the quality of our everyday lives (Mausner and Bahn, 1985). Infant mortality and social class are also clearly linked. While infant mortality has declined for the population as a whole in the past century, class differences are still quite large and have remained constant over the years (Wilkinson, 1986a).

Indeed, in the United States, class differences in health may have increased (Najman, 1993; Navarro, 1991). One study found that differences in mortality between socioeconomic groups (as measured by income and education) increased in the United States between 1960 and 1986. In recent decades, there have been similar increases in mortality-rate disparity between socioeconomic groups in other countries (Pappas et al., 1993).

The relationship between social class and rates of mortality has been documented for England, Wales, Denmark, Finland, France, Japan, New Zealand, and the United States (Marmot et al., 1987). Table 2.2 shows some relationships between social class (measured by occupational classifications) and morbidity, mortality, and health behavior in England and Wales. Lower-class persons had consistently higher rates of perinatal (infant) mortality, maternal mortality (the mother's death from pregnancy- or birth-related problems), and mortality from all causes. Studies in the United States and Australia also show a relationship between social class and infant mortality (Najman, 1993). Class differences are also linked to rates of coronary heart disease and diseases of the respiratory system. Morbidity rates (measured by respondents' reports of longstanding illness and the number of restricted activity days per year) show a regular correlation with social class. Class differences are particularly pronounced between the highest class (professionals) and lowest class (unskilled manual workers) (Rice, 1991).

In Scandinavia, longstanding illness is reported more frequently among blue-collar than white-collar groups (Rahkonen et al., 1993). There is a relationship between people's self-assessment of health and their income levels. The higher the income level, the more likely self-assessed health is excellent; the lower a person's income, the more likely health will be self-rated as poor (U.S. Department of Health and Human Services, 1992; Navarro, 1991; Blaxter, 1990).

These data illustrate that differences that at first appear to be individual are often actually social variations. While smoking is an individual behavior, for example, those in the lowest socioeconomic positions are almost three times as likely to smoke as those in the highest positions (Marmot et al., 1987), which may partially explain the higher rates of respiratory diseases among the lower classes. Similarly, alcohol consumption is highest among the lower classes, as is the incidence of obesity (Dutton, 1986). Deaths due to accidents also increase as socioeconomic status decreases (Quick, 1991).

The Black report, a famous British study on the relationship between class and health, concluded that lack of personal control over one's life was an important factor linking low social status with poor health (Black, 1980; see also Gray, 1982). A 1987 update of the Black report not only documented persisting class differences in morbidity and mortality, but also showed a widening gap in health between the upper and lowest classes (Townsend, 1990).

Syme and Berkman (1976) have argued that this lack of control and other adverse features of lower-class life create a "generalized susceptibility" to disease (see also Blaxter, 1990). The issues of generalized susceptibility, control, and health will be discussed further in the next three chapters.

The conditions of lower-class life include living and working in more polluted and crowded environments, exposure to higher noise levels and risks of accidents,

TABLE 2.2 Birth Weight and Mortality in England and Wales by Social Class.[a] Morbidity and Health Behavior in Great Britain by Socioeconomic Group.[b]

		SOCIAL CLASS[a]					
		I	II	IIIN	IIIM	IV	V
Birthweight ≤ 2500 g, 1980 (%)		5.3	5.3	5.8	6.6	7.3	8.1
Mortality							
Perinatal mortality/1,000, 1978–1979		11.2	12.0	13.3	14.7	16.9	19.4
Mortality 1–14, 1970–1972	M	74	79	95	98	112	162
	F	89	84	93	93	120	156
Maternal mortality, 1970–1972							
(standardized maternal mortality rate)		79	63	86	99	147	144
All cause mortality 15–64, 1970–1972							
(SMR)	Men	77	81	99	106	114	137
	Married women	82	87	92	115	119	135
	Single women	(110)	79	92	108	114	138
Coronary heart disease, men 15–64,							
1970–1972 (SMR)		88	91	114	107	108	111
Disease of respiratory system,							
men 65–74 (PMR)		60	74	82	105	108	123

		SOCIOECONOMIC GROUP[b]					
		1	2	3	4	5	6
Morbidity (age 45–64)							
% Reporting longstanding illness	M	35	31	41	42	47	52
	F	32	36	40	41	49	46
Average number of restricted activity	M	4	14	30	31	27	38
days per person per year	F	22	23	28	27	33	39
Health behavior							
Prevalence of cigarette smoking, 1984	M	17	29	30	40	45	49
	F	15	29	28	37	37	36
Participation in active outdoor	M	42		34	23	17	15
sports (%), 1977	F	30		27	17	14	11

[a]Registrar-General's Social Class: I, Professional etc; II, Intermediate; IIIN, Skilled occupations (non-manual); IIIM, Skilled occupations (manual); IV, Partly skilled; V, Unskilled.

[b]Socioeconomic group: 1, Professional; 2, Employers and managers; 3, Intermediate and junior nonmanual; 4, Skilled manual and own account nonprofessional; 5, Semiskilled manual and personal service; 6, Unskilled manual.

Source: M. G. Marmot, M. Kogevinas, and M. A. Elston, "Social/economic status and disease," *Annual Review of Public Health* 8, 1987: 113. Reproduced with permission from the *Annual Review of Public Health*, 8, © 1987 by Annual Reviews, Inc.

and inadequate housing and transportation. Medical care for the poor is less accessible and of lower quality than that for higher social classes. Furthermore, health problems of the poor are typically more serious, complex, and difficult to treat (Dutton, 1986).

As the Black report shows, for England, improved access to medical care does not by itself significantly reduce social class differences in health. Scandinavian countries, which provide citizens with excellent access to high-quality health care, nonetheless exhibit some class differences in health. A study of the Scandinavian situation concluded that "health care without social welfare and economic policy will be ineffective in reducing social inequalities in health" (Rahkonon et al., 1993: 77). To seriously reduce the effects of social class on health requires far more basic economic and social reforms (Hurowitz, 1993).

Measuring social class variables is difficult. Occupation is one frequently used indicator of social class, but occupational categories are often broad and not neatly tied with a single social stratum. For example, the category "teacher" might include a nursery school teacher and a professor at a prestigious university. How would the classification scheme distinguish between a farmer who owns 50 acres and cultivates them for family subsistence, and a "farmer" who owns 4,000 acres and hires numerous workers to cultivate them (Susser et al., 1985)?

Despite such definitional problems, studies of many societies document a consistent relationship between social class and health. Rates of mortality and social class are clearly linked, but the relationship between class and specific causes of death is not so consistent, and may change over time. Rates of coronary heart disease in England and Wales, for example, first began to increase in the 1930s among men of the upper classes. By 1950 the disease was more common among the lower classes. A similar downward shift in the incidence of coronary heart disease took place in the United States (Susser et al., 1985). A possible explanation of the variation is that the upper classes were initially more susceptible to coronary heart disease as a "disease of affluence" (for example, they may have eaten much more meat and enjoyed more sedentary leisure time). As lifestyles changed, however, concern with dieting and exercise became values for many middle- and upper-class persons, and coronary heart disease declined. The lower classes did not adopt such lifestyle changes, and thus their rates of coronary heart disease remained high (Marmot et al., 1987; Susser et al., 1985).

The epidemiology of poliomyelitis also illustrates how the relationship between class and mortality from specific diseases may change over time. In lower-class areas, characterized by overcrowding and poor sanitation, children often developed antibodies and hence immunity to polio after being exposed to the virus early in life. Thus the poor had lower risk of paralysis and death than the more "sheltered" middle and upper classes. When the polio vaccine was introduced in the mid-1950s, however, this relationship between class and vulnerability to the disease changed. Those upper- and middle-class children who were first vaccinated were the first to benefit. An education campaign eventually resulted in the widespread acceptance of immunization, but pockets of underimmunized persons still exist in the United States, particularly among lower-class minority groups (Susser et al., 1985: 229–231).

These examples show that the relationship between specific kinds of morbidity or causes of mortality may not follow the usual relationship with social class and may shift over time. At present, however, there are no major causes of mortality for which death rates are not higher among lower-class than upper-class persons. On the whole, the lower classes bear higher burdens of mortality and morbidity. The general incidence of morbidity and mortality decreases as one moves up the social ladder (Blaxter, 1990).

Even when data show a strong correlation between two variables, such as social class and health status, the direction of causality is sometimes difficult to determine. Does variable *A* produce variable *B;* does variable *B* produce *A;* or are they related in even more complex ways, mutually influencing each other or indirectly influencing each other through some third (intervening) variable? For example, do lower social status and the poor living conditions that accompany it produce poor health, or does poor health lead to downward mobility and lower income, or do both situations interact (Dutton, 1986)? The explanation that poor health results in downward mobility has been called the *drift hypothesis*, which suggests that those who acquire disabling diseases "drift" down the social ladder in the course of their lives (Lawrence, 1958).

Some evidence hints that serious illness in childhood is related to downward mobility in later life. Boys who were seriously ill are more likely than those who were healthy to gravitate to a social position below that of their fathers (Wilkinson, 1986b). Downward drift may be linked only to specific "diseases" such as schizophrenia (Marmot et al., 1987), so the drift hypothesis does not satisfactorily explain the entire relationship between social morbidity and mortality. The hypothesis does appear to hold more for chronic illness than for acute illness. The two explanatory models may, however, be complementary: Chronic illness may lead to lower socioeconomic status, the conditions of which may increase the likelihood the person will suffer acute diseases, thus producing a vicious downward circle for the disadvantaged (Wolinksy and Wolinsky, 1981).

Some of the relationship between social inequality and specific kinds of morbidity and mortality may be more artifactual—a product of the way the variables are measured—than real. An extensive critique of the Black report argues that the correlation between social class and mortality due to chronic degenerative diseases is essentially artifactual (Bloor et al., 1987). For example, the perceived social class of the deceased person influences whether the cause of death was classified as heart disease. The significance of such artifacts in the correlations between social class and health is not clear. Other reviews (compare Marmot et al., 1987) consider artifacts to be relatively unimportant in explaining the social class differences in health. They observe that a large number and variety of studies, done in several societies, indicate a strong relationship among class, health, and death.

SUMMARY

There are observable patterns to the frequency and incidence of human sickness and death. As opposed to the clinical-medical model, which focuses on individual bodies and a limited number of causal factors in disease, the epidemiological approach looks at social patterns of morbidity and mortality and the complex "web of causation." Epidemiological studies show that many patterns of morbidity and mortality are connected with social variables, such as the kind of society, race, ethnicity, age, social class, and gender. These epidemiological variables are also rough indicators of the social distribution of power and of the different power relationships people experience. With its broad generalizations, social epidemiology sets the stage for a more refined analysis of the ways a society produces, defines, experiences, and treats sickness and death.

RECOMMENDED READINGS

Article

John McKinlay and Sonja McKinlay, "The questionable contribution of medical measures to the decline of mortality in the United States in the twentieth century," *Milbank Memorial Fund Quarterly* 55, 1977: 405–428.

Books

Gary D. Friedman, *Primer of Epidemiology*, 3rd ed. New York: McGraw-Hill, 1987. A clearly written introduction to epidemiological concepts.

Sol Levine and Abraham Lilienfeld, eds., *Epidemiology and Health Policy*. New York: Tavistock, 1987. An excellent collection of articles dealing with problems such as nutrition, coronary heart disease, cancer, injuries, and occupational health.

Mervyn Susser, William Watson, and Kim Hopper, *Sociology in Medicine*. New York: Oxford University Press, 1985. An interesting interpretation of the sociology of health and illness from an epidemiological perspective.

Meredith Turshen, *The Politics of Public Health*. New Brunswick, NJ: Rutgers University Press, 1989. Lively, critical analysis of public health and epidemiological issues in a global context.

CHAPTER THREE

The Material Foundations of Health and Illness

Certain social practices contribute to the production of a healthy body; others lead to its destruction. The very condition of our bodies—whether we are healthy or sick, whether we live or die—depends not on luck but on social circumstances.

In Chapter 2 we discussed some of the patterns of distribution of sickness and death according to social variables like socioeconomic status, ethnicity, race, and gender. In this chapter we shall examine certain social environments and practices that produce physical conditions contributing to these differences in health and illness. Basic health requirements—a satisfactory diet and a safe, clean physical environment—are very much influenced by many cultural and social-structural arrangements.

Much in our social activities endangers our health. How we organize production, and what and how we produce and consume are central to creating our way of life as well as to producing health or illness. This discussion begins by examining material (i.e., physical) sources of health and illness, and how they are shaped by social factors, especially the power of different groups to control physical resources such as food and the quality of the physical environment.

FOOD

World Hunger

Every few years the news media alert the public in economically "developed" nations to widespread starvation in parts of the world such as Ethiopia or Bangladesh. The public conscience is mobilized, and money and food are collected. The furor then dies down, and for a while the public forgets the routine starvation that plagues much of the world. In 1991, more than half a billion adults (out of a world population of about 5 billion) experienced continuous hunger. About 1 billion people (20 percent of the world's population) lack the calories needed for an active work life (Cohen and Hoehn, 1991).

More common than outright malnutrition is undernutrition, or a diet that lacks certain basic nutrients (i.e., enough protein or vitamins). Over a billion people have nutritional deficiencies; for example, several million people have vitamin A deficiency, which can cause blindness and vision problems (Cohen and Hoehn, 1991). There are 350 million people (mostly women between the ages of 18 and 45) who suffer from iron-deficiency anemia (Latham, 1987: 330), which results in symptoms of constant fatigue. Thus, vitamin-deficiency diseases, such as scurvy, beriberi, rickets, keratomalacia (lack of vitamin A), pellagra, and mineral-deficiency diseases (e.g., anemia) are still widespread in the Third World (Brown and Inhorn, 1990). Mortality rates from measles are much higher in Third World countries such as Mexico and Ecuador. Differences in vulnerability to an infectious disease such as measles (which kills few people in the United States), tuberculosis, and even diarrhea[1] are partly due

---

[1]Diarrhea is a major killer of children in the Third World; an estimated 4.5 million children die from it each year. In the United States, about 200,000 children under the age of five are hospitalized each year because of diarrhea, and several hundred a year die from it. While vaccines against the virus that is the disease's primary agent are not yet available, the treatment of oral rehydration therapy is simple, safe,

TABLE 3.1   Per Capita Calorie Consumption by Region (1969–1971, 1988–1990)

Region	1969–71	1988–90
	. . . . . . kcal per caput/day	
World	2,430	2,700
Developed regions	3,190	3,400
North America	3,230	3,600
Europe	3,240	3,450
Oceania	3,290	3,330
Former USSR	3,320	3,380
Developing regions	2,120	2,470
Africa	2,140	2,200
Far East	2,040	2,450
Latin America	2,500	2,690
Near East	2,420	2,920

Source: United Nations, Food and Agriculture Organization (FAO), *The State of Food and Agriculture, 1992.* Rome, 1992: 21.

to nutritional factors (Eckholm, 1977: 48). One-third of all children under the age of five in "developing" countries are undernourished to the point of permanent developmental impairment (Cohen and Hoehn, 1991). While not starving, many people in the world suffer from stunted physical development, a greater vulnerability to disease, and a lowered quality of life brought on by undernutrition.

An adequate diet is characterized partly by the quality of food consumed and by a certain amount of various vitamins, protein, fiber, and other components. An adequate diet also requires the consumption of a sufficient number of calories to support the body's activity. (A calorie is a measure of how much energy is generated by food eaten.) Table 3.1 shows variations in per capita calorie consumption in selected regions of the world. We can see from this table that the figure for some regions, such as Africa in 1988–1990, was a little more than half that of countries such as the United States. Per capita figures, however, do not show how these calories are distributed within the population. Thus in Africa some are well fed, whereas others consume far *less* than their minimum daily caloric requirement.

There is a certain irony to the fact that although undernutrition and malnutrition are more common in Third World countries, they are also features of well-to-do countries such as the United States, where an entire industry is devoted to producing foods that taste like the "real" thing but lack caloric substance, and where some use jogging and other exercises to cope with the tendency to overconsume and overeat. In the 1960s, however, studies such as *Hunger U.S.A.* (1968) showed the extent of undernutrition in America. The introduction of food stamps, increased health care and welfare benefits, school lunches, and other "poverty" programs since that time

---

and inexpensive. The epidemiology of diarrhea shows that in America these preventable deaths occur disproportionately among poor black children in the rural South; social policies addressed to alleviating poverty, improving sanitation, and increasing access to health care and health care education could thus eliminate an entire category of infant mortality (Stevens, 1988).

has helped to decrease the incidence of hunger. Some evidence suggests that cutbacks in these programs under the Reagan administration in the 1980s led to increased incidence of hunger. The 1985 report of the Physicians' Task Force on Hunger in America estimated that approximately 20 million Americans are hungry and that about 500,000 children are undernourished. Approximately one child in eight under the age of 12 is vulnerable to hunger. The problem of hunger in the United States appears to be growing; indeed, in the 1990s, the U.S. food aid program helped a record number of eligible food stamp recipients (Cohen and Hoehn, 1991). Economic crises in the farming sector during the 1980s ironically increased hunger among the families of the nation's food producers (Schneider, 1987).

Overpopulation and Scarcity.   One common theory explains world hunger as a matter of overpopulation combined with lack of natural resources, such as arable land and favorable climate. Accordingly, poor people exceed their ability to feed themselves by reproducing too fast. This is often called a Malthusian explanation, after Thomas Malthus, a nineteenth-century British economist whose theories of population growth still have influence (Hess, 1987). Malthus ([1798] 1965) argued that the growth of the world's food supply would not be able to keep pace with the growing population unless it were reduced by "natural" forces such as war or famine, or by poor people's abstinence from sex. Innovations in agricultural productivity, which were already apparent in Malthus's time, cast doubt on his theory. His interpretations nonetheless influenced many social scientists and policymakers, particularly the nineteenth-century social Darwinists, who argued that social life and survival could be explained using the principles of evolution and that evolution favored the "survival of the fittest." Malthus's predictions were correctly characterized as "dismal" and led some (including the social Darwinists) to believe that while food aid and improved sanitary measures might help the poor in the short run, they would simply encourage them to breed more, thus creating more long-term suffering (Hess, 1987).

The Malthusian notion of an absolute scarcity of food and thus the need for poorer nations to control population growth still prevails. While there is some truth to this position, advocates often refuse to consider policy measures, such as land reform, that would more equitably redistribute the resources needed to grow food (Moore-Lappé and Collins, 1986).

Malthus, of course, could not fully grasp the potential of modern technology to stimulate the food supply. It is estimated that, with existing levels of technology, it is possible to feed a much greater number of people than the world's current population (Barraclough, 1991; Moore-Lappé and Collins, 1986; George, 1982). However, in many countries hunger seems to have increased just as the world food surplus has grown. In fact, many poor countries in which undernutrition and malnutrition prevail are *exporting* large quantities of food. During a 1984 drought, for example, Zimbabwe was exporting a record harvest of tobacco, soybeans, and cotton, and Kenya was exporting asparagus and strawberries (Bennett and George, 1987). During a famine in Mali, there were likewise increased exports of cotton and peanut cake, which is fed to European cattle (Moore-Lappé and Collins, 1986).

After the communist revolution, life expectancy in China increased dramatically, from the age of 24 in 1929–31 to 65 in 1982; infant mortality also sharply declined. Except for periods of famine in some areas caused by natural disasters, China has been able to feed its people not simply by increasing food production but also by more equitably distributing food (Barraclough, 1991; Warnock, 1987; Lardy, 1983; George, 1982).

The improved standard of living brought population growth to China. Agricultural practices and land use for urban areas and industry have subsequently decreased the available arable land, which, relative to other countries, was already minimal (Warnock, 1987). To increase its living standards and diversify people's diet further, China may have to import food. If the nation continues to increase its use of energy-intensive agricultural methods to increase crop yields, it will become dependent on oil imports.

Nevertheless, China—an extreme example of the Malthusian problem of many people and few resources—managed to bring about dramatic decreases in hunger through political changes (Barraclough, 1991). Population growth will be a significant factor in the long-term standard of living, but population is not the only factor, nor can the mechanisms that affect population growth be considered independently of sociopolitical and economic factors.

Emphasis on population control as the primary solution to hunger problems often places the burden of solutions on poor people whose attitudes toward birth control appear irrational to outsiders. High birth rates in developing countries may, however, be very rational to the people themselves, who believe they need more babies (in the face of high infant mortality) to care for them in old age and to provide a family labor force. Population growth is thus not simply the *cause* of poverty. Large families are a way of coping with impoverished conditions, and hence a *result* of poverty (George, 1982).

The scarcity argument also holds that many countries lack sufficient natural resources such as arable land. Only about 44 percent of the world's cultivable land is being used to grow food. Much lies unused for investment purposes (i.e., the owners are waiting for its value to increase). How land is used and who determines this use are thus important considerations. Colombia, for example, uses arable land for such export crops as carnations, which bring the large landowners more profit than subsistence crops. In Brazil, land that had once been used to grow food beans for local consumption is now cultivated in soybeans for export. Due to a diversion of land use for export crop production, bean prices tripled. At the same time Brazil's GNP (gross national product) increased, as did its supply of foreign currency. Brazil industrialized and its rich prospered, while hunger grew among the poor (Brooke, 1993; George, 1982). Moore-Lappé and Collins (1986) have argued that every country has enough land to feed itself, and that hunger is often the result of patterns of land use and ownership that are shaped by the social distribution of power in these societies.

While overpopulation and geography contribute to world hunger, more important reasons involve sociopolitical and economic factors as well as technology and knowledge.

Technology and Knowledge.   There is no doubt that modern technologies, such as farm machinery, allow people to work the land more effectively and often to increase food production. Indeed, some improvements in health in the Western world were the consequence of advances in agricultural production. Yet use of these technologies must be viewed in its sociopolitical and economic contexts.

Toxic substances are often a part of modern agricultural technologies, but developing countries do not have effective regulatory controls (Norris, 1982). Many of the world's countries have no effective legislation to control toxic chemicals. Many pesticides such as DDT and DBCP, which have been banned in the United States, continue to be sold and used in the Third World. Beyond their widespread and deadly effects on farmers who often do not know of their risks, these toxic chemicals often come back to our dining room as residues on vegetables and fruits, thus completing a "circle of poison" (Thrupp, 1991; Weir and Shapiro, 1981). Industrialized nations export substances that are banned in their own countries but that subsequently are imported back into their own food supply.

The high yield these agricultural technologies produce has other negative consequences. They are typically energy intensive, requiring considerable quantities of oil to build and fuel machinery, and to make pesticides and fertilizers. Thus a great deal of nonrenewable resources, like oil, is required to produce relatively little food energy. The need to import such resources for energy and for agricultural technology increases the foreign debts of many Third World countries, which means that more land must be devoted to producing export crops to pay those debts. Should the market price of a major export crop drop, the problem becomes more acute. When coffee prices dropped in 1981, for example, El Salvador had to spend 70 percent of its coffee earnings on oil imports (Everett, 1984).

Energy-intensive technology is a mixed blessing for many people. Small farmers cannot afford it, and its uncontrolled use may deplete the land and cause extensive pollution. Technological solutions alone are thus of little use to many developing nations. Many farmers would benefit from less energy-intensive ways of growing food, but such possible options are not likely to be developed by the companies that profit from existing technologies. In short, technologies do not develop in sociopolitical and economic vacuums.

Some critics attack many of the agricultural practices and consumption patterns of the Third World poor as irrational factors contributing to their hunger. On the surface, nothing appears more irrational than starving Hindus in India who will not eat their cattle. Harris (1985), however, has argued that many of these seemingly "irrational" practices make ecological sense, given local conditions. Cows can be used to plow land and produce milk, their blood (which can be drained without killing them) is a source of protein; and their manure provides fuel and fertilizers. In the context of Indian culture, large-scale meat production may actually be "ecologically impractical," since it takes about 20 pounds of grain to produce one pound of beef (George, 1982). In fact much of the world's grain is used for animal feed. The major barriers to subsistence are thus not the lack of technology, overpopulation, or a scarcity of land but rather economic, political, and social considerations that relate to land use, distribution, and control.

Land as a Resource: Use and Distribution. In South America, 90 percent of the land is controlled by 17 percent of the landowners (George, 1982). In Honduras, one of the poorest countries in Central America, 4 percent of the people control 65 percent of the arable land (Wijkman and Timberlake, 1988). In El Salvador, another extremely poor Central American country, 81 percent of the arable land is used to grow coffee and is owned by 3 percent of the population (Kotzsch, 1985). In the 1980s, 3 percent of landowners controlled two-thirds of the land in Guatemala, while almost 90 percent of the peasants (mostly indigenous peoples) were landless (Barraclough, 1991). This pattern of land ownership and use is typical of many Third World countries.

Bangladesh is an example of how patterns of land control are significant in explaining world hunger. In that country, the per capita calorie consumption is considerably less than the necessary nutritional minimum, yet Bangladesh actually produces enough food to be able to feed its hungry. In fact it exports large amounts of food. Between 1960 and 1984, the number of landless households (i.e., those with less than 0.2 hectares of land) tripled (Barraclough, 1991). Those who own less than 0.2 hectares of land or who own *no* land consume an average of 1,924 calories per day. People owning 1.2 hectares or more consume 2,375 calories per day, and consume 28 percent more protein than those with less land (Brown et al., 1987: 31). In short, farmers' access to land and their ability to grow what their family needs are prerequisites to subsistence. Land reform that would make this subsistence possible is very difficult to institute, however, since the parliament is dominated by landowners (Crittenden, 1981).

In southwestern India, the state of Kerala managed to improve its life expectancy and infant mortality rates, despite the fact that it has one of India's lowest per capita income rates. (In 1986, life expectancy in Kerala was 68 years, compared with the national rate of 57 years; its infant mortality rate was 27 per 1,000 live births, compared to 86 per 1,000 for India as a whole). The lower infant mortality rate and increased life expectancy were due to improved food intake. In 1969, a new state government instituted land reform, government control of food prices, large-scale public health actions, accessible medical care, and literacy training. Kerala was able to improve its health and nutritional status through political and social change rather than increased economic development and production (Franke and Chasin, 1992).

Hungry Bodies Are Socially Produced. A basic requirement for health is a good diet. At first glance, it would seem that the problem of hunger in many parts of the world revolves around issues of scarce resources, a lack of technology, and overpopulation. These undoubtedly *are* factors, but technology depends on who controls it, whether it is available to all, and whether it is geographically and culturally appropriate. Most countries have the resources to feed even very large populations, but the key factors in determining whether they do so appear to be political considerations as well as corporate control of technologies and often, of large amounts of land used to grow export crops.

Many have criticized food aid on the grounds that it is used as a political tool: Countries may withhold needed food aid from governments with policies of which they disapprove (Barraclough, 1991; Kinley et al., 1981). A more serious problem, however, is that much aid never reaches those who need it because of local power arrangements. A World Bank study of Bangladesh discovered that about one-third of the food aid went to police, military personnel, and civil servants; that about one-third went to the urban middle class; and that only one-third reached the rural poor, who constitute the vast majority of the hungry. A similar pattern prevails in other countries (Kinley et. al., 1981; Parker, 1981).

Hunger in poor countries is affected by their relationship with rich nations. Many Third World countries must contend with the impact of colonialism on their society, physical environment, and system of food production. Furthermore, rich nations' models of industrial food production may be inappropriate for less developed countries, and their pressure to adopt "advanced" food production methods often hinders the development of culturally and ecologically viable alternatives. Many Third World countries also serve rich nations as a source of markets, raw materials, and export crops. Fluctuations in global food prices are furthermore affected by the capitalist world market in which rich nations are a dominant force (Warnock, 1987).

The basic requirement of health, a good diet, therefore is linked to the distribution of power. It is easier to blame nature, scarcity, a lack of technology, or individual reproductive practices than it is to indict social systems. Yet it is the social systems and the way that power is distributed within them that shape the material world in which we live and hence the condition of our bodies.

The Sociocultural Dimensions of Eating Habits: "You Are What You Eat"

A society's habits of food consumption also play a role in nutritional problems. These eating habits are in turn influenced by sociocultural factors and issues of power. So-called affluent societies, with their diets high in animal fat, salt, and sugar, are often characterized by poor eating habits. At the end of the eighteenth century, sugar consumption in Europe (13 pounds per person per year) was already relatively high compared to previous times. With time sugar found even more and more uses as a flavor enhancer and preservative. By the middle of the twentieth century, sugar consumption in the United States was over 120 pounds per person per year (Mintz, 1979). In some respects our diets have become healthier (e.g., increased consumption of protein); however, in other ways (e.g., significantly increased consumption of food additives, sugar, animal fat, and salt), they have become unhealthier. We tend to view eating habits as a matter of individual free choice. While this is partly true, they also reflect sociocultural preferences, and the way we eat is shaped by sociopolitical and economic factors. In this section, the interrelationships among society, power, and food will be examined from that perspective.

We do not eat merely to survive or because food provides us with sensuous pleasure. For humans, food takes on symbolic meanings, and activities related to the consumption of food have social functions and dimensions. Sharing food reflects social bonds. A family dinner is an occasion to communicate, affirm social ties, and remind members of their respective social statuses. There are food taboos in virtually every society. For instance, Moslems and Jews prohibit the consumption of pork. A breach of a food taboo can affect one physiologically. A person who knowingly eats a proscribed food may get sick or even die. For example, when the Ponape, a people of the South Pacific, ate a forbidden fish, they would break out in hives (Farb and Armelagos, 1980).

Culturally rooted aversions to particular foods are not restricted to religious groups or preliterate societies. A priest in San Francisco once suggested that since Asian refugees in the area liked to eat dogs and cats, the humane society could supply them with stray animals (which unless adopted, would be killed anyway) to use as food; his proposal was met with a great deal of opposition. Many Americans would get physically ill if they discovered that they had just eaten "puppy parmigiana," yet in some parts of the world dogs are a normal source of meat protein and are even considered a delicacy. Americans enjoy cheese, but most Chinese people find it disgusting. Cultural factors thus shape our food preferences, our reactions to food, and our very appetites (i.e., when we feel hungry).

The diets of specific cultures are often well suited to the physical environments and biological constitution of the people who inhabit them. A genetic intolerance of lactose, a prime component of milk, is not uncommon among *most* peoples of the world (Harris, 1985; Overfield, 1985). Such physical intolerance, common among the Chinese, may partially explain their aversion to cheese, for example. Biological variations are not the only reason some foods are defined as unpleasant or preferred. Cultures also adopt certain food habits for practical benefits, as exemplified by the Hindu prohibition against eating cows (Harris, 1985). Some foods may be too costly in their demand on land, human, and fuel resources. The Chinese custom, for example, of rapidly cooking food in a wok over high flame developed because of fuel scarcity (Farb and Armelagos, 1980).

Sociocultural Change, Eating Habits, and Multinational Corporations. When external forces alter the eating habits or way of life of a culture, new nutritional problems can ensue. In many societies, dental cavities were rare until Western influences introduced large amounts of refined sugar into the diet (McElroy and Townsend, 1985). Several decades ago the Zuni Indians of the American Southwest had a very low incidence of diabetes. As farmers and hunters, their bodies had developed a capacity to store fat efficiently to survive periods of food shortage. Their cultural values defined being fat as healthy. As they "modernized," their lifestyle became more sedentary, and they replaced their traditional diet with the low-income food culture of fast food that was high in salt and sugar. Their biological capacity to store fat then became a liability, as they burned less energy and consumed more food. The incidence of diabetes subsequently increased (Peterson, 1986).

In recent years, multinational corporations have found new markets for their food products in the Third World. Often these products are promoted and introduced into sociocultural environments in which their widespread use may be inappropriate and unhealthy. Soft drinks and white bread, for example, have been aggressively promoted in countries like Malaysia and Mexico (Kaur, 1990; Barnet and Mueller, 1974). Advertising campaigns and the fact that these products are seen as coming from a "high-status" culture make them prestigious, and they may come to symbolize modernity and social status. Given the limited cash income of Mexican peasants, however, such products consume disproportionate amounts of the family budget and provide little nutritional return. In Malaysia, many farmers spend up to one-third of family incomes on cigarettes and alcoholic drinks (Kaur, 1990). In a marginally nourished population, this exchange is a poor trade.

In the 1960s and 1970s, several companies such as Nestlé promoted commercial baby formula in Third World countries. Their advertising presented bottle feeding as modern and healthy for babies. Bottle feeding, however, required much of the family cash income (from 15 to 85 percent, depending on the country), and many mothers diluted the milk to stretch supplies, thus unintentionally starving their babies. The lack of the clean water, fuel, and sanitary conditions needed for formula preparation and storage also prevented the product's safe use (Kaur, 1990). Even a marginally nourished mother can usually produce breast milk, which also transmits to the infant her natural antibodies that fight infection. As bottle-feeding practices were adopted in such places as Kenya, infant malnutrition increased. Doctors gave this form of commercially encouraged malnutrition a medical label: "bottle-baby syndrome." In recent years, because of an international boycott and other pressures, the transnational companies were persuaded to stop many of their practices promoting this inappropriate product in Third World countries (Norris, 1982).

The world's eating habits are increasingly influenced by global corporate interests, which not only control much food production but also influence the information disseminated through advertising. One author concluded, "Backed by such powerful advertising, the standardization of food values at a global level at the expense of the local specificities has divorced people's eating habits from their history and culture" (Mansour, 1987: 16). Large corporations have not only more and more control over the growing and processing of food, but also access to powerful means of disseminating information about their products (e.g., advertising). These factors increasingly shape the food habits of the world.

Nutritional and Commercial Practices in Industrialized Countries. Commercial messages that promote foods are often directed at such vulnerable targets as children. A considerable portion of Saturday morning television commercials, for example, promote sugar-laden cereals and snack food. With the exception of a few token public service nutrition ads, most commercials imply that such food is consumed by the viewer's heroes, and that eating it will result in personal pleasure and status among one's peers (Barnouw, 1978: 91–92; Gussow, 1978: 229). One study indicated that children influenced by these commercials may exert significant control over their mothers' shopping habits (Barnouw, 1978: 92–93).

Not only do individual advertising messages affect eating habits, but their cumulative tone also suggests a cultural attitude toward food. The more implicit messages often have a greater effect. Bottled drinks, such as beer and soft drinks, are heavily advertised. The implicit message is less a matter of which product one drinks, but rather that one should want a commercial drink instead of water or a home-produced beverage to satisfy thirst. Advertising has thus sold a behavior, not just a product (Gussow, 1978: 222). Some ads suggest that when people are hungry and do not have time to eat, they should deaden hunger pangs by consuming a candy bar, which produces a sugar "high." Other ads urge the audience to eat or drink more, even after the hunger or thirst is satisfied; expanded appetites are thus created. To sell products, commercials often urge people to override their bodies' signals by either deadening them or overconsuming. Their messages are often contradictory: "Be thin," "control your eating," "eat, drink, and be merry," and "gorge, gorge, gorge."

Affluent societies often consume overly rich diets with too much sugar, fat, and salt, and too little fiber. Absence of fiber in a diet has been linked to the high incidence of colon cancer (Burkitt, 1973). Food processing enables modern societies to preserve, store, and transport a wide variety of foods, increasing their availability throughout the year in regions far from their origins. Processing also increases the convenience of preparation of many foods. By its very nature, however, processing causes the loss of many nutrients (Farb and Armelagos, 1980: 211). It also frequently takes away some of the natural flavors; to compensate for lost flavor, manufacturers then add sugar, salt, or artificial flavoring (Silverstein, 1984).

The diet of our modern society is more varied, interesting, and in many ways more nutritious than that of our medieval ancestors, who, prior to the fifteenth or sixteenth centuries, subsisted on a plain fare mainly consisting of grains and vegetables with few spices (Braudel, 1973). Increased trade, the availability of new foods and seasonings, and advances in agricultural technology and food processing have made an improved diet possible. The growth of capitalism helped to stimulate trade and technology to the benefit of many. Food processing, however, is also used to increase profit. Technologies have been developed to store foods longer, to increase yield of products (e.g., hormones make chickens grow faster and fatter), to enhance flavor in place of using expensive ingredients, and to disguise products with artificial colors, scents, and shapes (Center for Study of Responsive Law, 1982). Yet rather than reducing food prices, processing often increases costs (Silverstein, 1984). Corporate control over food production and distribution also affects the choices available. Relatively few people have access to and can afford to buy unprocessed foods, which are now sold as part of a growing health food industry. In many places, supermarket fare is the only option.

Dieting and Fitness.   An estimated 10 to 20 percent of all children and 35 to 50 percent of middle-aged people in the United States are overweight (Eckholm, 1977). The excessive consumption of salt, sugar, and animal fats has been linked to many "diseases of affluence," such as hypertension, diabetes, and coronary heart disease (*Economist*, August 31, 1985). Since the mid-1970s, there has been a slight decrease in the number of deaths from heart disease in the United States. Some of this decrease has been linked to changes in habits of smoking, eating, and exercise (Sytkowski et al., 1990). Stress, other psychosocial factors, and environmental factors like pollution have also played a role.

The motivation and opportunity to consume a healthy diet and to exercise are socially distributed (Goldstein, 1992; Townsend, 1990). Several studies show a relationship between social status and obesity (Sagan, 1987). One study indicated that women from lower-class backgrounds are six times more likely to be obese than upper-class women. Eating disorders, such as anorexia, are more common in upper-class women (Yates, 1991). Some of this variation is explained by differences in availability of adequate nutrition (i.e., starchy food satisfies hunger and is cheaper). Another factor is that people overeat to manage stress; also, different classes assign different social meanings to obesity. Obesity is not as heavily stigmatized in the lower class. Dieting and fitness rituals are primarily a middle- and upper-class phenomenon (Goldstein, 1992), not motivated simply by a concern for better health. In some cultures fat is a sign of prosperity; in middle-class American culture, however, fat symbolizes loss of self-control. Such differences lead some anthropologists to consider obesity to be a culture-bound syndrome, or a condition that "makes sense" as an illness only in certain cultural contexts (Ritenbaugh, 1982). In recent years, there has been an increasing concern with thinness. The pressures to be thin are greater for women than for men.

What constitutes being overweight, and how much excess weight is unhealthy? Questions of overweight and overnutrition are difficult to calculate with precision. While "objective" scientific facts bear upon the definition of "normal" weight, the facts change, and various groups challenge particular standards of evaluation. Between 1960 and 1983, for instance, the standards for normal weight as established by actuarial tables (statistical calculations, especially of factors related to life expectancy) were revised upward. Groups like Weight Watchers, the American Cancer Society, and American Heart Association do not accept these changed standards as valid. In short, there is no tidy, universal standard for how much one should weigh (Attie and Brooks-Gunn, 1987; Schwartz, 1986).

Our cultural obsession with dieting and fitness reflects a concern not merely with health but also with self-control and physical appearances. In our society, looking good and feeling well tend to be confused. In all societies, health is judged to some degree on the basis of appearances, but in our society, a person's image is especially important, partly due to mass-media influence.

Concern about weight and fat is one expression of a generalized societal anxiety about physical appearances. Since the 1880s, societal tolerance for high weight may have narrowed, and the criteria for acceptable weight have become more demanding (Schwartz, 1986). Eating disorders are on the increase (Yates, 1991; Attie and Brooks-Gunn, 1987; Sagan, 1987: 55), while cultural standards for women's bodies have shifted from fat to thin. In recent decades, the number of articles and books about diets have increased (Hatfield and Sprecher, 1986). In 1986, 25 million people (mostly women) attended Weight Watchers meetings; 700,000 attended regularly, and $10 billion were spent on weight-reduction drugs alone (Kleinfield, 1986). Women's and increasingly men's anxiety about weight and fat constitutes a major source of profit. A 1985 survey found that in comparison to 1972 data, respondents (both male and female) showed more dissatisfaction with their body image. While the proportion of women expressing such dissatisfaction was still higher than in 1985, the differences in the level of dissatisfaction between the sexes had narrowed. Weight was the one physical feature that evoked the most anxiety among these males (Cash et al., 1986). A small 1981 survey found that 40 percent of the respondents considered "getting fat" to be a major personal fear (Schwartz, 1986: 246).

Such fears are not totally without foundation. Obesity is strongly stigmatized in our culture, particularly among the middle and upper classes (Attie and Brooks-Gunn, 1987). Negative attitudes toward obese people tend to be learned at an early age (Yates, 1991). One study showed ten- and eleven-year-olds pictures of a "normal" child, one with an amputated limb, one with facial disfigurement, one in a wheelchair, one with crutches and a wheelchair, and an obese child. When the children were asked to rank the pictures in terms of their preference for a friend, the majority made the obese child their *last* choice (Richardson et al., 1963).

Obesity *does* contribute to physical problems such as high blood pressure. While obesity functions to raise blood pressure because of the physical strain it puts on the body, other factors may also be involved. Perhaps the social meanings of obesity affect the body as well (Attie and Brooks-Gunn, 1987). Since obesity is perceived as a negative attribute, it may affect an individual's self-esteem. Anxieties about one's body may also contribute to increased blood pressure (Lynch, 1985).

Society's stigmatization of those who are overweight is related to the social norm of control, but there is a question of whether obesity is a metabolic disorder beyond some people's control (Brody, 1983). If this is the case, to focus on the individual's responsibility is cruel and futile. The regulation of appetites is not merely biological, however; there are important social factors too. To regulate our appetites, we need to know whether we are hungry. It is possible that obese people are more vulnerable to social forces that short-circuit hunger signals from their bodies. One study found that "normals" were more oriented to internal cues as signals as to when to eat, while obese people relied on external cues such as the appearance, taste, and smell of food and the time of day. In one variation of the experiment, a wall clock had been moved forward a few hours, displaying the wrong time. Subjects of normal weight did not eat the available food, even though the clock falsely signaled meal time, whereas the obese subjects ate (Schachter, 1968).

Some have observed that this culture encourages people to rely on external signals for eating. Snack ads urge us to deaden hunger signals; meal schedules encourage us to look to the clock for signs of hunger. In a culture that encourages high levels of consumption, physiological hunger and nutritional considerations may be eclipsed by advertising messages designed to create demand (Silverstein, 1984). If there are "natural" limits to human appetites (and this is debatable), the economic system's impetus to sell must overcome them. This factor does not explain individual differences in responding to social pressures, but it does suggest that cultural pressures may affect the way people perceive their bodies, and hence how they control their eating.

All societies value some degree of self-control, but in modern societies such a concern is pervasive. Turner (1984: 112) observes:

> We jog, slim and sleep not for their intrinsic enjoyment, but to improve our chances at sex, work and longevity. The new asceticism of competitive social relations exists to create desire—desire which is subordinated to the rationalization of the body as the final triumph of capitalist development. Obesity has become irrational.

The contemporary emphasis on fitness, especially among the middle class, is not simply a matter of health but of conformity to the norms of an eternally youthful, lean body. Moreover, fitness activities may be a way of displaying control over one's body and hence over one's self in a culture in which control is valued and yet powerlessness seems to be a pervasive experience (Glassner, 1989). The "ideal" body is not only slender, but also firm—tightly self-managed, self-constrained; this changed ideal may reflect society's increased emphasis on self-control and management, rather than externally imposed control and coercion (Bordo, 1990).

A study of workers in California's "Silicon Valley" suggests that their almost compulsive tendency to exercise and diet (along with compulsive shopping and extensive drug abuse) represents a way of coping with the powerlessness, alienation, stress, and loneliness of much of their lives (Hayes, 1989). As with dieting, a vast industry has arisen to meet fitness "needs," producing endless streams of commodities and specialized technologies, from electronic rowing machines to digital pulse meters. Commercialized diet and fitness thus transform simple needs into marketable commodities (Glassner, 1989).

In modern society, appearances are very important in achieving success in work, play, and sexual relationships. A competitive society makes such successes important to the individual's sense of self. To achieve them, a rational mastery over the body and appearances becomes a central concern in life. By these norms, then, obesity reflects an irrational inability to control oneself, and fitness activities (beyond their contribution to health) promote a sense of self-mastery.

Gender, Power, and Eating Disorders.   Much concern about weight is a concern about appearances. The standards for physical appearances or somatic (body) norms vary from time to time and place to place. The importance of conforming to such standards also varies. Our society tends to evaluate women by their appearances and men by their performance (such as occupational, athletic, and sexual). Despite some shift in attitudes, men are generally more anxious about functioning and women about appearances (Melamed, 1983; Lakoff and Scherr, 1984). Furthermore, the responsibility for whether one is successful in one's area of competence rests with the individual:

> Ours is a culture of personal responsibility; we are told to captain our own souls and "take responsibility" for our successes and failures. Traditionally, men have been able to demonstrate success through their achievements in work, but it has mainly been

> through what a woman does with her appearance that she has been able to exhibit her mastery and achievement to others and to herself (Millman, 1980: 155).

While this double standard is changing somewhat, it still prevails. A heavy man can be seen as solid and powerful. Think of media heroes like "Cannon" and "Ironsides." Heavy women television stars, however, are unlikely to have heroic roles (Silverstein, 1984: 107); they are typically portrayed as sloppy, weak willed, or comic.

Women are more likely than men to believe that they are overweight when in fact they are not, if judged by "objective" standards (which themselves are not so objective). A 1980 survey of college women found that 70 percent believed they were overweight, while only 30 percent actually fit insurance chart definitions of being overweight. Women's anxieties about weight are thus out of proportion to the facts. Fears about one's body and appearances are fueled by the mass media, which reminds audiences how inadequate their bodies are. One woman observes:

> The mass media tells us all day and all evening that we are inadequate, mindless, ugly, disgusting in ourselves. We must try to resemble perfect plastic objects, so that no one will notice what we really are. In ourselves we smell bad, shed dandruff, our breath has an odor, our hair stands up or falls out, we sag or stick out where we shouldn't. We can only rook people into liking us by using magic products that make us products too (quoted in Hatfield and Sprecher, 1986: 291).

Concerns about weight are a source of chronic stress for many women (Attie and Brooks-Gunn, 1987). Pressures on women to look thin may contribute to eating disorders like anorexia and bulimia (Fallon and Rozin, 1985), which are much more common among women than men. Anorexics lose the desire to eat and starve themselves. Bulimics binge, consuming vast amounts of food, and then purge themselves by vomiting or using laxatives.

Our culture gives members seriously conflicting messages about eating. On the one hand, people are urged to control their appetites and to diet in order to be sexy and desirable. At the same time, there is a conflicting message to enjoy life, to consume, to indulge ourselves and our appetites. The cultural contradiction of our times lies in the conflict between one set of messages, which emphasizes the importance of discipline as producers (i.e., the work ethic), and another, which stresses our role as pleasure-seeking consumers (Turner, 1984: 200). We are thus asked to be both ascetic (disciplined and in control of our flesh) *and* hedonistic (pleasure seeking and indulgent) at the same time. This dual expectation compounds problems for women, whose traditional role as nurturers and food providers places them in frequent contact with food (Charles and Kerr, 1986).

Anorexia can be interpreted as a woman's body discipline carried to an extreme. Families of anorexics often stress perfection and success (Yates, 1991). The anorexic woman takes the mandate to use diet to control appearance a step further than most would. The bulimic person perhaps responds to the contradictory messages of the culture by "both having her cake and eating it." The purge-and-binge cycle characterizing bulimics enables them to overindulge their appetites yet remain thin.

Eating disorders are extreme, self-destructive ways of responding to cultural conflicts that affect most women to some degree.

Advertising for a variety of products may promote the bulimic solution in a seemingly benign way. One "lite beer" commercial promises, "Oh, you can have it all!," trumpeting both a message of the good life and the promise of a beer that tastes like it has substance but in fact has little actual substance. A vast array of diet foods offers a "banquet without food," which promises all the pleasures of eating without its unwanted consequences (Schwartz, 1986).

Eating disorders are not really problems of appetite for food but rather self-destructive responses to cultural constraints and contradictions. Somatic norms of femininity limit female appetites (not only for food but also for public power, independence, and sexual gratification). Gender role norms expect women to feed and nurture others, and not the self. And the culture subtly promotes the expectation that women be circumscribed in their access to and amount of public space (Bordo, 1989).

Similarly, overeating is sometimes a means of asserting control. Millman (1980) found that some of the obese women she interviewed experienced eating as the one area of a controlled life where they felt able to "let go," while others used eating as a way of protecting themselves against parental domination. One respondent reported that she ate and gorged herself as a defiant response to her mother, who was always harassing her about her appearance. Millman (ibid., p. 73) observed:

> This woman (like several others I interviewed) has throughout her life used food and weight to assert and feel control in her relationships and her place in the world. And when these assertions run against the wishes of parents or husbands, eating and weight become associated with a refusal to bow to social control.

Others have argued that fat may represent a form of "armor" by which some women can protect themselves from unwanted sexual advances. Eating may also help to alleviate the anxieties about identity and devalued sense of self that our society engenders in women (Chernin, 1981). The double standards of physical appearances, together with the strong link that our culture encourages between women's looks and their sense of self, have led some writers to declare that "fat is a feminist issue" (Ohrbach, 1981). This approach suggests that eating disorders are not simply a loss of control but may reflect an attempt to *assert* control (albeit in ultimately self-destructive ways). It is simplistic to view eating disorders as a sign of personal weakness or as a purely individual matter, independent of social factors.

THE PHYSICAL ENVIRONMENT AND HEALTH

The physical environment is another crucial factor in health and illness that is profoundly shaped by sociocultural forces. The notion that clean air and healthy spaces are essential ingredients for well-being is by no means new. In the fifth century B.C. the Greek physician Hippocrates wrote about the importance of such factors. As described in Chapter 2, infectious diseases are more likely to develop and spread among poorly nourished, weakened "hosts." Even the earliest epidemiologists knew that environmental conditions, such as unclean water supply or poor sewage disposal, spread infectious diseases.

Development and Environment

Famine in parts of Africa has been blamed on unfavorable geography and climate. Some research suggests that colonialism disrupted traditional African farming practices that were adapted to the local environment. The best land was appropriated to grow export crops like peanuts. Brush and trees were cleared, thus hastening erosion and desertification (Warnock, 1987; Danaher, 1985a; Franke and Chasin, 1981). In the West African Sahel,

> while French science developed improved varieties of peanuts and the French vegetable oil business prospered, African farmers were being coerced through taxation and physical brutality into peanut mono-cropping that depleted the soil, overuse of fallow areas, seasonal labor migrations that interfered with millet production and a breakdown of mutually beneficial grain milk exchanges with pastoralists from the Sahara desert fringe, whose animals had also manured the farmer's fields (Franke, 1987: 462).

In Central America, Nicaragua's landscape has been damaged by the stripping away of its rain forest, pesticide pollution, and industrial contaminants. Deforestation and pollution were a legacy left by the dictator Anastasio Somoza, the small local landholding elite that supported him, and U.S.-based corporations that invested there. Expansion of cotton plantations and cattle ranches forced poor farmers away from the fertile lands into the forests that they cleared. U.S. lumber companies also deforested vast regions. Cotton growers used large quantities of toxic pesticides, which polluted the soil and poisoned local people in epidemic proportions (Karliner and Faber, 1988).

The Sandinista regime came into power in Nicaragua in 1979 and tried to rehabilitate the land, impose environmental regulation, reforest, and find less toxic ways of controlling pests. Their ongoing war with the "Contras," however, hampered these efforts by diverting government funds for environmental protection into the war effort. "Contra" targets also included environmental workers and reforestation projects. Similar ecological destruction as the result of political and social conditions similar to those that prevailed in Nicaragua under Somoza can be found in other Central American countries like Honduras and Guatemala (Karliner and Faber, 1988). In many developing countries, the poorer inhabitants face the hazards of unregulated development but share in few of its benefits.

The transformation of the land through unregulated development may result in unforeseen epidemiological consequences. Massive deforestation in South India, for example, facilitated the spread of Kyasanur forest disease, an influenzalike viral infection spread by ticks. With deforestation, formerly tree-dwelling monkeys began to spend more time on the ground, thereby coming into contact with ticks. Cattle grazed on the cleared forest edge and were also exposed to the ticks. Human contact with monkeys and cattle that carried the ticks created an epidemic of this disease among people. Agricultural workers, who had the most contact with the cleared land between forest and pasture, were the most vulnerable (Nichter, 1987).

As we manage to control and pacify various external threats, ironically it is many of our own activities that cause many modern health problems. Even so-called natural disasters, such as floods, famine, and drought, are themselves affected by human activity. Human practices exacerbate the effects of flooding (Wijkman and Timberlake, 1988). For example, deforestation destroys natural barriers against flooding and fosters mudslides. Some agricultural practices that destroy the soil's ability to absorb water may also aggravate flooding. Deforestation often speeds up erosion and the growth of deserts. In short, even "natural" disasters often have social and political dimensions.

The Social Organization of Space and Motion

Our fitness, health, and physical comfort depend in part upon the quality of the physical space we inhabit and our options for movement within it, which in turn depend greatly on the social organization of space and on the opportunities or constraints that social forces place on our movement. The social organization of space and motion is affected by the distribution of power in any given society. Some people have more influence in shaping their physical surroundings than others; some have more freedom of movement. The following examples of the work place and transportation illustrate how powerfully various social forces shape our physical space and motion with significant implications for our well-being.

Space, Motion, and Occupational Health.   The design of physical environments reflects social status. One indicator of social status is the amount and quality of an individual's space. Large private offices with windows, for example, are reserved for executives (Lindheim, 1985). Certain physical arrangements of the work place would appear to be essential for health, yet many low-status workers do not have access even to toilets or facilities to wash their hands. A 1984 study (Weinstein, 1985) showed that over one-third of U.S. farm workers did not have access to toilets and that one-fifth did not have access to drinking water. OSHA (Occupational Safety and Health Administration) has only recently passed regulations requiring employers to provide such necessities, the lack of which can spread infection. Because many farm workers work with toxic substances such as pesticides, the absence of washrooms is not just an inconvenience but also a health hazard.

Uncomfortable work environments are also problematic for the large proportion of employees who work in offices. The vast majority of jobs in the expanding information service sector are low-level positions in which workers have little control over their environment, which is designed to maximize cost effectiveness and worker control. The following arrangement is characteristic of white-collar offices:

> Of the people surveyed in one large modern office building by our Columbia University research team, 34 percent could not decorate or personalize their work areas in any way.

They couldn't even hang a picture or keep a plant. Ninety percent could not control the number of people passing by their desk area, and 69 percent had no say over whether others could come directly up to their desk at any time without permission. Eighty-four percent of the office workers reported that they were always in the view of someone else and had no way to avoid this contact; 80 percent also reported that they had no control over whether their work or conversations were overheard. The overwhelming majority of office workers could not alter the ventilation (88 percent), open the windows (96 percent), adjust the lighting (83 percent), rearrange the furniture or equipment (75 percent), or change the temperature (75 percent) (Stellman and Henifin, 1983: 112).

How the work place regulates our movements may literally shape or misshape our bodies. Friedrich Engels ([1845] 1973: 282–283), writing over 145 years ago, describes the crippling effects of their work on the bodies of women and children coal carriers:

> The first result of such over-exertion is the diversion of vitality to the one-sided development of the muscles, so that those especially of the arms, legs, and the back, of the shoulders and chest, which are commonly called into activity in pushing and pulling, attain an uncommonly vigorous development, while all the rest of the body suffers and is atrophied from want of nourishment. More than all else the stature suffers, being stunted and retarded.

Repetitive strain or trauma injuries in the United States are on the increase since 1983 (Wegman and Fine, 1990). It is estimated that about one-half of all U.S. workers have jobs with the potential for such injuries (National Safe Workplace Institute, 1990). People whose occupations require the use of their arm, wrists, or fingers in quick, repetitive motions, such as cashiers, meat packers, mail sorters, and typists, may suffer from inflamation of their tendons (tendonitis) or from compression of their nerves (carpal tunnel syndrome or tenosynovitis). Work pace is associated with higher rates of such repetitive strain injuries (Goldoftas, 1991; Wegman and Fine, 1990). Possible reasons for the recent increase in such injuries in the United States include the intensification of work pace and the alteration of work processes such that the range of motion is decreased (Goldoftas, 1991). Certain work movements may cause disproportionate wear and tear on certain parts of the body. While some of these problems are inherent to some degree in the type of activity involved in an occupation, they can be reduced by frequent breaks, job rotation, and opportunities to stretch as well as by the proper ergonomic design of equipment and work space. "Telegraphist's cramp," "cotton-twister's hand," "stitcher's wrist," and "bricklayer's shoulder" are some workers' expressions for such injuries (Goldoftas, 1991).

Ergonomics is the study of the relationship between the workers, their movements, and the physical features of their work environment. For example, is the chair designed to minimize backaches after long hours of sitting? Is the control panel easily readable and within comfortable reach? Ergonomic studies have tended to emphasize designing machines and work places that will enhance productivity; however, less attention has been directed toward worker health or comfort (Goldsmith and Kerr,

1982). Furthermore, ergonomists design work places with the "average" person in mind, with little provision for those whose bodies are not average.

In many work places, even basic ergonomic considerations are often ignored to enhance productivity and profits. Workers may be forced to work in cramped, uncomfortable positions. For instance, one welder comments:

> I got moved to a new job spot-welding where I had to stand on my toes with my head all the way against my back and my arms stretched out all day long. I told my boss that we had to disassemble the piece in order for me to do the job without injuring myself, and he insisted that I could do it the way it was. Well, I did it until finally I hurt my back so bad that I was out for 5 months (quoted in Back, 1981: 24–25).

Until a few decades ago, farm laborers were forced to use short-handled hoes, which raised productivity by increasing traction but also caused serious back pains. It was only after pressure from unions and workers that the farm owners finally allowed workers to use long-handled hoes. Healthy movements are thus related not just to the nature of the activity, but also to the design of the tools and environment.

Varying the position of the body frequently during the workday is important for orthopedic health and psychological well-being. Some workers come to experience themselves and their bodies as "spirit" or disoriented when their work involves uncomfortable, uninterrupted, repetitive motions:

> I sit in one place all day facing a wall. My fingers are moving all the time, my eyes are staring into a machine that is placed so I have to hold my neck stiff to see the words clearly. Everyone is typing or using machines so there is a lot of noise. It's impossible to talk or even to turn around and look at someone else. My job is basically to copy numbers and letters all day, but most of the time I'm not even aware of them. *It's like my hands and my eyes are alive and my mind and my body are dead* (quoted in Back, 1981: 41–42 [emphasis added]).

People can adapt to unhealthy environments, but often at a cost. A significant portion of time in our everyday lives is spent on such unnoticed forms of body activities as walking up and down, pacing, stretching our limbs, tapping our feet, drumming our fingers, smoothing our hair, and hugging our body. These kinds of activities are integral to our self-image and contribute to stress reduction and to fitness (Csikszentmihalyi, 1990). They may also foster a sense of self-control and physical-emotional satisfaction. The social arrangements of many work places affect workers' ability to engage in these natural activities.

The work place illustrates the relationship between the organization of space and the regulation of motion, and workers' psychophysical well-being. Disempowering spaces force people's bodies into standard forms or the motions of a machine. Workers need to vary their movements and to distribute more evenly the stressors that cause bodily wear and tear. The ability to control movements and to adapt work spaces to one's own well-being in turn depends on various political and economic factors.

Space, Motion, and Transportation. Another arena in which space and motion affect health is the automobile. In many parts of the United States, someone with no automobile transportation has severely curtailed access to medical care, shopping, leisure activities, friends, and work. It has been estimated that more than 38 percent of U.S. households with incomes under the poverty level do not possess a car. About 24 percent of households of elderly persons lack a car (Freund and Martin, 1993). Similarly, most youths and persons with disabilities are unable to transport themselves (Hillman et al., 1990b; Rosenbloom, 1988). In American society access to transportation is thus unequally distributed, based on race, income, age, and class (Yago, 1985). The system of transportation dominated by the individual passenger car was created not merely by individual consumer choices but also by political and corporate interests. The major portion of public funds spent on transportation in the United States goes for highways as opposed to mass transit (Freund and Martin, 1993; Snell, 1982).

Reliance on automobile transportation is related to various problems of physical fitness. Difficulties in commuting can increase stress; for example, the heart rate of a train passenger is lower than that of a passenger in a private car (Lundberg, 1976). Driving causes increased levels of stress hormones, blood sugar, and cholesterol (Robinson, 1988), and can create problems like "motorist's spine" and "driver's thigh" (Homola, 1968). Persons who drive a car for 20 miles or more a day are at special risk for lumbar disk herniation (lower back injury). Truck drivers suffer a high rate of back injuries (National Institute on Disability, 1987).

The shape of modern transportation networks is the result not merely of society's love affair with the automobile but also of concrete economic and political decisions that affect the location of corporation offices, shopping malls, industrial parks, and restaurants. These decisions thrust individuals into reliance on private automobiles, whether they love or hate them. Advertising campaigns of automobile companies, furthermore, have imbued the car with symbolic meanings of masculinity, freedom, and social status; reliance on cars is thus not simply a matter of preference. Through their various interventions in the marketplace, manufacturers have shaped social space to the needs of automobile transportation. According to Snell (1982), from the 1930s to the 1950s the automobile industry (specifically General Motors) promoted the homogenization of the urban landscape by dismantling alternate transportation networks (e.g., trains and trolleys) and replacing them with inefficient, polluting trucks, buses, and automobiles. Once other modes of transportation had declined, the automobile became a virtual necessity rather than a luxury (Freund and Martin, 1993).

Accidents: An Individual or Social Problem?

Following heart disease, cancer, and stroke, accidents are among the foremost causes of death in American society. Automobile accidents constitute a large percentage of total accidents; work-related injuries are another important component (U.S. Department of Health and Human Services, 1992). Accidents result from the interplay among an unsafe environment, unsafe equipment and tools, and the behavior of the individuals involved. Accidents are usually treated as the results of individual fault, but often social and environmental problems also play a significant causal role. Accidents are not random, unpredictable events but follow patterns (Smothers, 1991). The very definition of events as "accidents"—as opposed to socially produced, preventable incidents—has political and social policy implications (Freund and Martin, 1993).

Auto Accidents.   While the death rate due to auto accidents in the United States is by no means the highest among industrialized countries, some 43,000 to 53,000 Americans die each year in such accidents, producing a death rate of over 26 deaths per 100,000 population (National Safety Council, 1986). Worldwide, some 200,000 people died in traffic accidents in 1985 (Renner, 1988). There are approximately 4 to 5 million injuries related to motor vehicles each year in the United States. Of these, 500,000 people require hospitalization (averaging a stay of nine days). More deaths occur from automobile accidents than from any other injury-producing event. Motor vehicle accidents are the largest single trauma-induced cause of paraplegia and quadriplegia, and a major cause of epilepsy and head injuries (Claybrook et al., 1984); each year about 20,000 Americans develop epilepsy as a result of auto accidents (Schneider and Conrad, 1983). Auto accidents are a leading cause of death for young males aged 15 to 19. Per passenger mile, cars are more dangerous than trains, buses, or planes. Just as auto accident fatalities are socially distributed along lines of gender and age, they also vary by social class. In Britain, lower-class persons have the greatest risk of auto accident fatality; since fewer lower-class persons drive, not surprisingly, their pedestrian death rate is also high (Quick, 1991).

Why the automobile exacts such a high health risk is a complex question. Much public attention focuses on drunk driving. In 1990, 39.7 percent of U.S. road fatalities involved drivers with blood alcohol levels of 0.1 percent or more (a level defining intoxication). This figure represents a decline from 1982 when it was 46.3 percent (Smothers, 1991). These figures are somewhat misleading, however, since they include all traffic deaths in which any of the parties involved consumed alcohol, even if the person who was drinking was not at fault. Other estimates place the figure of alcohol-related deaths at 25 percent (Ross and Hughes, 1986). Many alcohol-related traffic fatalities, furthermore, involve cofactors such as fatigue, inexperience, poorly designed or inadequately lit roads, and unsafe cars (Gusfield, 1991). Such devices as air bags have been shown to significantly reduce fatalities, yet the automobile industry lobby has regularly worked to prevent the implementation of regulations to require air bags in cars (Baker et al., 1987).

Although individual drivers have a responsibility to drive safely, focusing merely on individual behavior neglects the social, cultural, and environmental dimensions of auto accidents. Some roads are designed without barriers between oncoming cars; cars lack protective devices like air bags, and drivers use vehicles capable of killing speed (Schrank, 1977: 77). When New Jersey residents were given the option of free and readily available public transportation on New Year's Eve, the accident rate declined. In many parts of this country, the automobile is the only available means of transportation, pressuring drunken drivers and other impaired persons (e.g., those with vision problems) into driving (Syme and Guralnik, 1987). Such factors in traffic fatalities are the result of social policies.

Policy responses to traffic accidents emphasize raising the *drinking* age, but few legislators would consider raising the *driving* age because in many parts of the country to be without a car is to be helpless, especially given an atrophied public transportation system. Social factors also explain why males are at particularly high risk. Many young males are socialized into taking lots of risks and into feeling or appearing invulnerable; media messages glorify speed and risk taking; many car-chase scenes convey a relatively carnage-free image of fast or reckless driving; advertisements glamorize cars as images of masculinity, speed, power, and excitement; and young men often view the use of seat belts as not "macho" (Quick, 1991; Horton, 1985).

Economic pressures may also contribute to vehicular accidents by promoting reckless behavior on the road. Truck drivers have a high rate of drug consumption (especially stimulants). Economic considerations lead them to drive longer hours with unsafe equipment and larger payloads. Thus, social-structural forces contribute to trucking accidents (Rothe, 1991).

Public policy has not given much attention to the health costs of a transportation system centered upon the auto. Accidents, of course, are only one of the costs, which also include health consequences from auto emissions (see Table 3.2), noise pollution, and so on. Diet, smoking, exercise, and alcohol are in the limelight as health-lifestyle issues, but because we take cars for granted as the primary means of transport and because of the political power of auto interests, there has been inadequate analysis of the health implications of pervasive auto use (Hunt, 1989).

In addressing the problem of automobile accidents, most policy focuses on changing individual behavior through education or various sanctions (Gusfield, 1981). However, individuals are hard to reach, influence, and control; traffic penalties are not consistently and rapidly imposed on violators; and to monitor and educate all drivers is difficult and not very cost-effective. By contrast, an **ecological approach** to the problem emphasizes changing the social and physical environment (e.g., building safer highways), producing safer cars, and making many alternative ways of traveling available to drivers (Syme and Guralnik, 1987). These kinds of preventive measures have, however, been consistently constrained by the marketplace. The political and economic power of the automobile industry, in consideration of the cost of designing safer vehicles and highways, seriously limits the government's power or willingness to choose and implement solutions to prevent auto accidents (MacLennan, 1988).

Work-Place Accidents: Unsafe Behavior, Unsafe Conditions?   Work-place *accidents* (some prefer the term *injury*, since an accident implies a random occurrence) differ from occupational *diseases* in that in the former the exposure to the source is sudden, and the damage as well as its cause is readily apparent (Baker et al., 1987: 177). By contrast, the cause of work-related diseases is not always apparent, and the effect may be gradual. Accidents are thus discrete, clearly identifiable events that happen suddenly.

Each year work-place accidents cause 1.7 million disabling injuries and 10,000 to 12,000 deaths (Moeller, 1992: 37). In 1989, the private sector reported 2,955,500 injuries with lost workdays (U.S. Department of Health and Human Services, 1992: 216). Like other health problems, their incidence and severity tend to be socially distributed. Lower-status jobs generally involve more accidents (Dutton, 1986). Because black males tend to work in high-risk occupations (e.g., coke-oven stokers) with little control over their work environment, they have 37 percent greater likelihood than whites of suffering occupational injuries or illnesses (Goldsmith and Kerr, 1982). The rate of injuries, particularly fatal ones, have generally declined somewhat in the past 50 years (Baker et al., 1987). The legislation of safety regulations, such as the 1969 Federal Mine Safety and Health Act, seems to have helped reduce injuries.

Data on work-place safety are highly problematic. Job injury rates are sometimes calculated in terms of the number of workdays lost per week, month, or year due to injury. However, employers often keep injured workers on the job or temporarily move them to easier jobs to keep injury rates down (Goldsmith and Kerr, 1982). Some companies simply do not report all injuries. In 1986 the Chrysler Corporation was fined a substantial sum for failing to report 182 injuries at one work site alone (Noble, 1986). Since official government data are based on company self-reports, these figures also tend to underestimate injuries. In 1985 the U.S. Bureau of Statistics reported that 3,750 workers died on the job, whereas the National Safety Council (an independent agency) reported 11,600 worker deaths (Noble, 1986). Part of this discrepancy is due to the fact that the government does not count injuries in private businesses employing fewer than 11 people. Because the current administration of OSHA uses injury rates to decide whether to inspect a work place, this undercounting of injuries has serious policy and regulatory implications.

Until recent decades, much research focused on work-place accidents rather than diseases, partly because the source of the damage is easier to identify. It is also easier to emphasize the individual's role in an accident. For example, textbooks on occupational health argue that changing the work environment reduces occupational diseases, but treat occupational accidents as essentially a problem of individual attitude and safety awareness (Baker et al., 1987: 197).

The concept of *accident proneness*, first coined in 1926, became the focus for whole generations of industrial psychologists who searched for specifiable characteristics causing some individuals to be especially likely to have accidents. In a chapter on industrial and occupational psychiatry, the 1966 *American Handbook of Psychiatry* described the "accident syndrome" as involving an "impulsive character" and "reaction of anxiety." The handbook does not suggest, however, that the psychiatrist should take into account the characteristics of the work place in which the "accident-prone" behavior occurs (Berman, 1978: 23–24). Empirical research has been unable to isolate any personality traits, independent of specific situations, that could be categorized as "accident proneness" (Members of the Working Party, 1975).

Environmental factors also contribute to accidents. Work-place accidents involve "accident prone" tools and environments, as well as social pressures that encourage risky behavior. As for automobile accidents, the ecological model appears more useful than the individual behavior model for understanding work-place accidents. At one steel plant, for example, the higher the rate of production grew, the higher the monthly injury rate rose (Hills, 1987). Similarly, in the past decade or so the meat-packing industry has been under increased competitive pressure. Wages have decreased, but productivity pressures in this shrinking industry have grown, simultaneously increasing the rate of on-the-job injuries (Glaberson, 1987; Noveck et al., 1990). Especially when linked with other factors such as increased job alienation, situational pressures enhance the likelihood of accidents (Back, 1981).

Design of equipment itself is sometimes the source of accidents. Although machines can be built in an ergonomically sound fashion to reduce accidents, more often they are designed mainly to enhance productivity (Goldsmith and Kerr, 1982). The burden of accident prevention in these environments is thus on the individual worker. An assembly-line worker commented:

> When there are accidents they always blamed us for not using safety equipment. Six of us had to work with an acid solution and we were all given plastic goggles. But no one could wear them because they didn't fit and you couldn't see very well with them on. This was a piece work job and there was no way we were going to make our bonus if we wore our glasses. I always felt caught between being worried about my health and being worried about not making production. You know it could've been fairly easy to put a shield over the whole operation so we wouldn't have to worry about it (quoted in Back, 1981: 15).

Engineering controls that alter the environment, such as putting a protective "shield over the whole operation," are typically more expensive than giving workers individual safety equipment, such as respirators to prevent breathing dust. So-called passive safety approaches, which rely on safe equipment and environment more than on behavior, are more effective but also more expensive (Baker et al., 1987). While respirators are cheaper for corporations, they create problems for workers. Respirators are physically uncomfortable, especially if worn the whole day under conditions of high temperature and noise. They may also be ineffective or create such side effects as breathing difficulty or heart strain. Work-place physical stressors, such as high noise levels and toxins, may also affect workers' perception, alertness, and reflexes, thereby producing "accident proneness."

Some social scientists consider accidents to be related to the social structure of the work place. In many work situations, there is a split between those who plan and organize work and those who execute it. As described in Chapter 6, this division may influence the perception and treatment of occupational health problems (Navarro, 1981). Experts who study accidents and occupational health problems are often far removed from the day-to-day routine of the work places they analyze. Furthermore, management concerns with productivity and cost-effectiveness are not always compatible with workers' needs for safe work places. Human error (e.g., due to drug use) and carelessness *are* important factors in work-place injuries. It is also important,

---

BOX 3.1   *SWEDISH ROAD TO BETTER CONDITIONS*

The Swedish approach to health and safety has four main features.

First, Swedish workers have won real power at the local level to prevent hazards. Sweden's OSHA—the National Board of Occupational Safety and Health—sets standards and inspects work places, but unions view its role as secondary to their own efforts.

Second, Swedish workers have the information and training to enable them to use that power.

Third, unions have a major voice in safety and health research and research is often geared to finding practical solutions to hazards.

Fourth, Swedish unions are concerned about the total work environment, not just safety and health as narrowly defined in the U.S. They consider physical safety hazards, chemical and noise exposures, heat, and cold, speed-up, boredom, and stress as related problems. The Swedish unions are concerned not only about injuries and illnesses but also discomfort, an unpleasant work place and lack of job satisfaction.

They believe that workers are entitled to a humane work environment and control over their jobs.

Source: In These Times, January 18–21, 1986: 17. Reprinted by permission.

---

however, to focus on how such variables as styles of managerial control also contribute to work-place health problems (Members of the Working Party, 1975: 74–75). One basic issue in occupational injuries is the conflict between, on the one hand, managerial pressures to enhance productivity, control, and profit margins, and, on the other hand, the needs of workers to work in the safest technologically feasible working environment. Box 3.1 illustrates some structural ways of reducing work-place injuries.

ENVIRONMENTAL POLLUTION

The concept of pollution usually carries the connotation of the fouling of the environment by humans, but volcanoes pollute the air and various nonhuman species pollute the environments with their excreta. In fact, most atmospheric pollution is not of human origin. Only 9 percent of the carbon monoxide in the air comes from human sources, such as automobile use. Of all particulates (i.e., bits of metal and the like) emitted into the air, only 11 percent comes from human activity (e.g., cars and industrial pollution). Various industrial processes account for 16 percent of the hydrocarbons in the atmosphere. About 45 percent of the sulfur dioxide in the atmosphere comes from human activity (Botkin and Keller, 1982: 172–173).

Table 3.2 shows the quantities and sources of major pollutants emitted in the United States. Government estimates suggest that up to 50,000 premature deaths occur from air pollution (National Safe Workplace Institute, 1990: 16). There was a sig-

TABLE 3.2   Air Pollution in the United States in 1989 (Calculated Emissions Estimates)

Type of Pollutant	All Sources	Transpor- tation	Stationary Fuel Combustion	Industrial Processes	Solid Waste	Other
Particulate matter[a]	7.2	1.5	1.8	2.7	1.1	1.1
Sulfur oxides[a]	21.1	1.0	16.8	13.3	(1)	(1)
Nitrogen oxides[a]	19.9	7.9	11.1	0.6	0.1	0.2
Carbon monoxide[a]	60.9	40.0	7.8	4.6	1.7	6.8
Lead[b]	7.2	2.2	6.4	2.3	2.3	(2)

[a]Emissions in 10^6 metric tons per year.

[b]Emissions in 10^3 metric tons per year.

(1) Emissions of less than 50,000 metric tons per year.

(2) No emissions calculated.

Source: U.S. Department of Health and Human Services, *Health, United States, 1991*, Hyattsville, MD: National Center for Health Statistics, 1992: 215.

nificant decrease of lead emissions between 1975 and 1980, coinciding with an approximately 50 percent decline in the use of leaded gasoline. Motor vehicles are a major source of carbon monoxide, a gas that interferes with the blood's ability to carry oxygen. Sulfur dioxides and nitrous oxides come from fuel combustion used to heat dwellings, generate electricity, and power motor vehicles (Renner, 1988). These emissions are important components of acid rain, which has a destructive impact on forests and the life in lakes and rivers, contributes to the erosion of building surfaces, and may contribute to human respiratory problems. Because acid rain often falls in regions distant from where the pollution originates, the economic activity in one region damages the environment in another, causing political strains between regions and nations, such as the United States and Canada.

While humans are not the only sources of global pollution, their activities have increasingly produced ecological changes in climate, atmosphere, and the very shape of the earth's surface. Our social institutions may not be able to effectively regulate the impact (Shabecoff, 1987b: A6). This impact of humans on the "spaceship earth" is not merely the result of technology or "progress" but is also linked to the failure of political, economic, and social policy to regulate the use of technology or to create "healthier" technologies.

Sometimes it is community-based groups that call attention to polluting activities of corporations and their health consequences for the people who live in those communities. Poorer communities are more likely to be victims of corporate pollution (Cushman, 1993). In one Massachusetts community, ordinary citizens collected information to understand the sources and effects of pollution in their area. Their efforts led to lawsuits against two corporations that had been dumping toxic wastes (Brown and Mikkelsen, 1990).

Discussions of pollution often pronounce that "we" (referring to humans in general) pollute. This expression, however, masks the sociopolitical dimension of environmental health by equating the individual "litterbug" with the corporate polluter whose impact on the environment is more far-reaching and potentially dangerous than that of the individual (Bookchin, 1962). Not all of "us" pollute equally, nor are we all equally affected by pollution.

"Don't Let the Smoke Get in Your Lungs": The Individual as Polluter

While tobacco smokers do not contribute significantly to atmospheric pollution, their habits do have a significant impact on health. They obviously pollute their own air, and are at increased risk of coronary heart disease, emphysema, bronchitis, and lung, bladder, and esophagal cancer (U.S. Department of Health and Human Services, 1987: 50). According to World Health Organization estimates, approximately 2.5 million people worldwide die each year from tobacco-related sickness. More than 1.5 million of these deaths occur in "developing" countries and about 400,000 deaths per year occur in the United States (Nichter and Cartwright, 1991). Some experts argue that smoking is as serious an addiction as heroin and, in the long run, perhaps even more damaging to the body (Weil and Rosen, 1993). Some research suggests that there may be a synergistic (i.e., mutually enhancing) relationship between smoking and air pollution from other sources. For example, smokers in urban areas of high air pollution are at a greater risk of lung cancer than their rural counterparts who smoke (Epstein, 1978).

In the United States, smoking has declined at about 2 percent a year since 1974; however, some of this reduction has been offset by the number of teenagers (especially females) who have taken up smoking. In 1989, approximately 32 percent of males and 27 percent of females smoked (Nichter and Cartwright, 1991; see also Chesney, 1991). By 1991, daily cigarette consumption rates per man, woman, and child were 5.6 in the United States and 4.6 in Britain (Macalister, 1992). In the United States, smoking is considerably more common among blue-collar than white-collar workers. Blacks are more likely to smoke than other racial and ethnic groups. Cigarette industry advertising has increasingly targeted these vulnerable groups (Stebbins, 1991).

Individuals who smoke also affect the quality of air shared by others in the enclosed spaces of offices, homes, and restaurants. Passive smoking (the inhaling of someone else's cigarette smoke) has been linked to a variety of health risks. Parents' smoking has an impact on the respiratory health of their children, and a smoker's spouse may have increased risk of lung cancer (Fielding and Phenow, 1988; Sandler et al., 1988). The effect of the smokers' habit on nonsmokers raises fundamental issues regarding individual rights as opposed to collective rights:

> Air pollution makes us take seriously the fact that we exist, not as isolated entities secure behind our fences, but as fellow creatures in a shared and threatened environment. While in some settings—when looking at second-hand smoke or workplace hazards—we can insist that individual consent remains fundamental, in others we may have to look beyond consent to autonomy and beyond the individual to a deeper sense of com-

munity. If anything is our birthright, it is the air that we breathe (Center for Philosophy and Public Policy, 1985: 5).

The passive smoking issue has helped to define "personal" habits as a social problem (Chapman et al., 1990). Might other "habits" such as the "excessive" use of automobiles also be viewed as social problems because of their pollution of "community" air (Freund and Martin, 1993)?

Increased awareness of the hazards of passive smoking has contributed to wider smoking restrictions and affected smokers' cigarette consumption. The passive smoking issue, thus, poses another threat to the tobacco industry (Chapman et al., 1990). Movements to restrict smoking in public places are becoming widespread in the United States (Cummings, 1984). One company told workers that they would either quit smoking or lose their jobs (*The New York Times*, January 25, 1986b). The courts subsequently overturned the company's efforts to control its workers' private lives (i.e., smoking outside of work). This company manufactures accoustical tiles and insulation containing various fibers that may contribute to respiratory problems and lung cancer. Union officials saw the company's emphasis on smoking as an attempt to evade the more costly issue of clearing the work-place air of these dangerous fibers. Smoking is often a way of dealing with the stress induced by the work place. To reduce employee smoking, employers might offer alternative ways for employees to cope with negative moods and work-related stress (Chesney, 1991). Are the employers who wish their workers to stop smoking willing to give them more breaks, alternative means of stress reduction, more relaxing work conditions, and a slower pace of work? The tendency to focus only on smoking may distract from issues of other sources of environmental pollution that are often heavily concentrated in work places (Fettner, 1987).

The tobacco producers form a major industry in the United States. On one hand, pronouncements and public service messages from the Surgeon General and Department of Health and Human Services condemn smoking; on the other hand, the Department of Agriculture continues to subsidize tobacco growers heavily. Taxes on tobacco sales are also a source of revenue for the government, so there may be some conflict of interest on the issue. The tobacco industry has compensated for its loss of revenues in the United States by increasing its exports, particularly to the Third World (Nichter and Cartwright, 1991; Stebbins, 1991) and eastern Europe (Macalister, 1992). The U.S. government has exerted pressure on such countries as Thailand and South Korea to allow American cigarette sales and advertising or to face trade sanctions (Nichter and Cartwright, 1991; Stebbins, 1991). Rather than deal with such massive economic and political issues, however, policymakers find it easier to focus on changing individuals' habits (Milio, 1985). While smoking is an individual behavior and only the individual can decide to stop, the practice of smoking is firmly rooted in a sociocultural context (Townsend, 1990). Advertising has glamorized smoking, associating it with vigor, sexiness, and sophistication. Other social factors supporting the habit include peer pressure among teenagers, and the use of smoking for sociability and for stress reduction. Smoke cessation programs, some argue, have little impact, because their focus is on changing individual behavior rather than addressing its sociocultural sources (Syme and Guralnik, 1987). As with accidents, an ecological method that considers individuals *and* their relationships to their social and cultural environment is a fruitful approach to supposedly "personal" addictions like smoking.

Pollution in the Work Place

Between 70,000 and 100,000 Americans die each year from occupational diseases—*not* including occupational injuries (National Safe Workplace Institute, 1990; Elling, 1986). About 390,000 new cases of disabling occupational diseases are diagnosed each year (Moeller, 1992). These estimates vary according to criteria for the category of "occupational diseases." Many respiratory problems experienced by coal miners, for example, were not immediately classified as black lung. They were so designated only after years of political conflict between mine owners, workers, unions, and various health professionals (Smith, 1981). The same symptoms were previously diagnosed as bronchitis, emphysema, or health problems resulting from workers' personal habits. In fact, occupational diseases are often hard to distinguish from "ordinary," nonwork-related problems (Elling, 1986: 18). To a physician untrained in diagnosing occupational diseases, lung cancer caused by asbestos looks like cancer due to smoking. Many cases of brown lung (a disease caused by inhaling cotton fibers) among textile workers go unrecorded, since the symptoms may be misinterpreted as emphysema (Guarasci, 1987). Stress-related diseases (discussed in Chapter 5) are also not included in occupational disease statistics.

Obtaining sound statistics on occupational disease is a complicated process because they vary depending upon who decides which health problems are job related. Company doctors, for example, are less likely to view symptoms as work related than union-affiliated doctors. One doctor working for the textile industry claimed that brown lung is:

> best described as a "symptom complex" rather than a disease in the usual sense. We feel that this term may be preferable, first in order not to unduly alarm workers, as we attempt to protect their health and secondly, to help avoid unfair designations of cotton as an unduly hazardous material for use in the textile industry, raising the fear that the engineering control of it may be costly, and that it may be better, therefore, to switch to some less costly material (quoted in Berman, 1978: 93).

Industry has focused on individuals, their lifestyle, and their "susceptibility" to occupational diseases (Epstein, 1990a). For years, instead of cleaning the air of cotton dust, the textile industry tried to identify hypersusceptible workers or "reactors" (Green, 1983). Employers' concern with workers' health is often inextricably tied to economic interests that influence what is or is not perceived and treated as occupational disease. As with accident prevention, management favors individual devices rather than "passive" engineering controls for the prevention of occupational disease. The issue of having the worker adapt to the work place rather than adapting the work place to the worker is thus not merely an economic one. Nelkin and Brown (1984: 70) observe that:

> the dispute over precautions extends beyond the question of immediate cost. Personal protective equipment places responsibility for protecting health on the workers themselves. Ill health can then be blamed on their failure to comply. Conversely, engineering controls place responsibility on management, shifting both the burden and the blame. To insist on personal precautions is to reinforce the belief that individuals are responsible for their own health and safety. To accept engineering controls is to accept the notion of corporate responsibility.

Because the people who study or make policy decisions about occupational health are often remote from the work place, workers' reports of symptoms are often ignored or invalidated, despite the fact that workers are often the first to recognize occupational health hazards. A Labor Department study found workers' self-reporting of health hazards to be highly reliable, except that workers tended to underestimate the effects of chronic diseases caused by occupational exposure (Nelkin and Brown, 1984: 31). Coal miners have, for generations, known of "miner's asthma" and black lung; their awareness is documented in song and popular writings. Such knowledge was, however, dismissed as unscientific or as excuses for malingering. While workers' reports are not based on scientific observation, ignoring their observations delays effective responses to occupational health hazards.

Workers do not always report work-related health problems, however; some may not complain out of fear of repercussions. Many others do not make the connection between low-level, long-term exposure to hazards and diseases that developed slowly or gradually. For example, the symptoms of asbestosis appear 20 to 40 years after asbestos exposure. Most private physicians have little training in occupational medicine and may not recognize patients' symptoms. One study of worker deaths from asbestos exposure showed that only 48 percent were correctly diagnosed on the death certificates. Only about half of U.S. medical school programs require course work in occupational health; among those that require the topic, the median time spent on occupational health topics is four hours (National Safe Workplace Institute, 1990: 18). Many doctors do not record a patient's occupational and work history, and often they fail to connect symptoms to work conditions.

Tens of thousands of different chemicals are used in commercial production processes, and the list grows at the rate of about a thousand a year. Of the 2 million known chemicals, only a few thousand have been tested for their dangerous properties, and only a few hundred of these have been thoroughly tested. Production processes often use several chemicals in conjunction with each other, but very little is known about health hazards created when these chemicals (which individually may be harmless) interact with each other (Nelkin and Brown, 1984). Regulatory standards are typically set only after a problem has been identified among workers. In this sense, workers often function as human guinea pigs.

As Epstein (1990b: 455) notes:

> The regulatory system is potentially only as valid as the information generated is reliable. When the ingredients are not identified, when the proper studies are not conducted, when the results of studies are not published for review, and when the results of studies state conclusions contrary to the actual data, effective regulation becomes virtually impossible. . . . An overwhelming record confirms the premise that scientific information generated and interpreted by institutions and individuals with direct or indirect economic interests in its outcome must be regarded as suspect until proven otherwise by independent validation.

Institutional interests do not necessarily intentionally alter data. Sometimes, however, industries such as asbestos mining and manufacturing have collected occupational health data and then systematically suppressed it (Lilienfeld, 1991).

Regulatory agencies such as the Environmental Protection Agency (EPA) or OSHA must rely heavily on company data about various chemicals. However, the very companies with an economic interest in producing the chemicals are often the ones that test them. Cutbacks in funding to regulatory agencies, such as those in the 1980s, further limit effective research to determine regulatory standards. In many cases, OSHA has not set standards even for those chemicals known to be carcinogenic (i.e., cancer causing).

Many dusts and particles inhaled by workers produce serious health problems. It is estimated that about 10 percent of active miners have black lung disease (pneumoconiosis). The inhalation of various fibers (such as cotton dust) affects about 85,000 U.S. textile workers, 35,000 of whom are disabled by brown lung (byssinosis) and other respiratory problems (Hills, 1987). Tunnel workers' asthma (silicosis) comes from inhaling particles of sand. Table 3.3 shows the number of male deaths due to exposure to some of these substances. Exposure to chemicals used in many manufacturing processes has also been linked to cancer and various other serious diseases.

Pollution in the work place is not confined to blue-collar or industrial jobs. For example, the computer industry, which seems "high tech" and clean, exposes workers to solvents, chemicals, and gases that may be toxic. Adequate health and safety standards have not been established for this relatively new industry (Hayes, 1989; Howard, 1985). Supposedly "clean" office work sometimes involves inhaling ozone,

TABLE 3.3 Death from Selected Occupational Diseases for U. S. Males, 1970–89

Cause of Death	1970	1975	1980	1984	1989
Malignant neoplasm of peritoneum and pleura	602	591	552	584	565
Pneumoconiosis	1,155	973	977	923	725
Asbestosis	25	43	96	131	261
Silicosis	351	243	202	160	130

Source: U.S. Department of Health and Human Services, *Health, United States 1991*, Hyattsville, MD: National Center for Health Statistics, 1992: 180.

a gas that can aggravate respiratory problems, from photocopiers or chemical copier fluids (Stellman and Henifin, 1983). Several studies document "office sickness" due to the high pollutant content of modern office buildings that are often airtight and rely on centralized air sources (Sterling et al., 1983). Persons who do housework may also be exposed to a variety of chemicals and air pollutants, such as fungal spores and bacteria (Chavkin, 1984).

The World Health Organization estimates that 30 percent of new and remodeled buildings, with efficient but "closed" ventilation systems, have indoor air quality problems (cited in National Safe Workplace Institute, 1990). Ironically, some workers in the EPA building itself wore respirators shortly after it was built because of indoor air pollution.

Work-place pollution spreads beyond the confines of the work place affecting workers' families. Factory pollution also tends to spread into the immediate vicinity. A high percentage of urban dwellers have some asbestos fibers in their lungs, even though they have not worked with asbestos. Atmospheric pollution from asbestos plants, construction sites, and even from auto brake linings spreads asbestos fibers into public spaces. An estimated 10 to 15 percent of lung cancer deaths is due to asbestos (Moss, 1980: 237).

Just as the fruits of production are not equally distributed, so too are the costs of production, such as pollution, unequally shared. The average age at death of blue-collar workers is more than a decade earlier than that of white-collar workers (National Safe Workplace Institute, 1990: 11). People living in urban poverty areas are exposed to larger quantities of chemical and air pollution than their middle-class suburban counterparts (Dutton, 1986). Likewise, developing countries experience increasing pollution and industrial hazards, even while already industrialized countries are achieving greater environmental and work-place health and safety regulation. Many developing countries want to attract industry, but they lack technical information to evaluate processes, resources for testing products, effective power to set and enforce standards, and worker organizations to voice concerns (Navarro and Berman, 1981).

In the United States, the Occupational Safety and Health Act of 1970 was passed to "assure as far as possible every working man and woman in the United States, safe and healthy working conditions." This assurance has not been realized, however, in large part due to political abuses and to underfunding of the vast task of researching and enforcing standards (see Elling, 1986; Howard, 1985; Simon, 1983; Szasz, 1983; Berman, 1978). The United States spent $0.63 per worker on job health in 1986, whereas Finland spent $12.29 in 1986 and Sweden $12.33 in 1988 (National Safe Workplace Institute, 1990). Compared to Sweden, Finland, East Germany, West Germany, and the United Kingdom, the United States ranked last, or tied for last place, on five out of six criteria for effective occupational safety and health: a strong national policy mandate for occupational health and safety; the provision and organization of services related to occupational health; workers' ability to control their work environment; the level of financing for occupational health activities; worker education; and the information about the work place available to workers and experts. Sweden and East Germany ranked highest on all six criteria (Elling, 1986).

Comparative data on actual levels of occupational health and safety in each of these countries are scant and difficult to evaluate because countries use different methods of collecting and categorizing information. Elling (1986) argues that those countries with the most protection have the lowest rates of occupational disease and injury. Calculating admittedly crude work-related death rates, he finds that the United States has the highest rate, with 50 such deaths per 100,000 workers; the United Kingdom has 2.5 per 100,000, and Sweden has 3.6 per 100,000. Comparing rates of occupational disease and injury, Sweden and East Germany have the lowest; Finland and the United Kingdom fall in the middle; West Germany is next, and the United States has the worst (Elling, 1986: 22). The other countries appear to have stronger regulations and generally safer working conditions than the United States (Goldsmith and Kerr, 1982). For instance, Swedish workers have the right to veto plans for new machines, work processes, or construction on health and safety grounds. They are also trained in health and safety (including ergonomics) at the employers' expense. In one SAAB automobile plant, the accident rate decreased 33 to 50 percent after some of these policies were implemented (Engler, 1986). Since a significant proportion of disease and disability in the United States is work related, issues of regulation and the politics of regulation become important health considerations (National Safe Workplace Institute, 1990).

SUMMARY

Sociopolitical factors and culture "construct" our physical environments and hence our bodies. Cultural meanings, shaped by social status as well as corporate and other political interests, influence physicial activities: working, eating, and fitness. Social factors determine people's opportunities for a healthy material environment and lifestyle. Thus, human activity produces important factors in bodily health and life, or illness and death.

RECOMMENDED READINGS

Articles

NICKE CHARLES and MARION KERR, "Food for feminist thought," *The Sociological Review* 34(3), 1987: 537–572.

CAROL A. MACLENNAN, "From accident to crash: The auto industry and the politics of injury," *Medical Anthropology Quarterly* 2(3), 1988: 233–250.

DAVID MICHAELS, "Waiting for the body count: Corporate decision-making and bladder cancer in the U.S. dye industry," *Medical Anthropology Quarterly* 2(3), 1988: 215–232.

MARK NICHTER, "Kyasanur forest disease: An ethnography of a disease of development," *Medical Anthropology Quarterly* 1(4), 1987: 406–423.

BARBARA ELLEN SMITH, "Black lung: The social production of disease," *International Journal of Health Services* 11(3), 1981: 343–359.

Books

MARK NATHAN COHEN, *Health and the Rise of Civilization*. New Haven, CT: Yale University Press, 1989. Comparing the health of those living in "civilized" societies with those in "primitive" hunting/gathering ones, Cohen concludes that the material circumstances of civilizations create health costs, not merely benefits.

PETER FREUND and GEORGE MARTIN, *The Ecology of the Automobile*. Montreal: Black Rose Books, 1993. An analysis of the ecological, social, and health effects of automobile-dominated transportation systems.

MARCIA MILLMAN, *Such a Pretty Face: Being Fat in America*. New York: W. W. Norton, 1980. An excellent, highly readable empirical study of dieting, "fat camps," the social meanings of obesity, and the relationship of such issues to gender.

JEANNE STELLMAN and MARY SUE HENIFIN, *Office Work Can Be Dangerous to Your Health*. New York: Random House, 1983. A well-written handbook for workers about the hazards of office work.

JOHN W. WARNOCK, *The Politics of Hunger: The Global Food System*. Toronto: Methuen, 1987. A comprehensive discussion of world food problems, with an emphasis upon both political and ecological aspects of the situation.

CHAPTER FOUR

Mind, Body, and Society

We have briefly reviewed some of the ways in which social and political factors affect the quality of and our use of our material environment. In previous chapters, we looked at physical determinants of health and at their social contexts. Here we shall examine other ways in which our bodies are affected less visibly, but perhaps more directly, by social relationships and structures. In this chapter and the next, we focus on the issue of sociopsychological stress and health. Stress and related concepts provide the basis for a holistic perspective in which individual minds and bodies are integrally interrelated with social environments.

"STICKS AND STONES MAY BREAK MY BONES, AND NAMES CAN ALSO HURT ME"

In everyday life, we are sometimes aware that sociopsychological factors affect our health. We might say, "I always get a cold after a tough exam."[1] Conversations contain various psychosomatic references such as, "You're a pain in the neck!" "She'll be the death of me yet!" "Grandma died of a broken heart!" These references show a commonsense awareness of the connections among the mind, body, and society. Particularly among middle-class persons, there appears to be a recent increase in self-consciousness about bodies and stress.

Despite this recent interest in mind-body relationships, psychological and social factors are not perceived to be truly important in determining health because they are not "real," that is, countable and tangible. Viruses, radiation, chemicals, and smoking are physical factors whose effects on the body can be measured and observed. Because medical science has viewed mind and body as separate entities to be studied and treated separately, doctors often do not assign these factors much reality or tangibility. Thus, while we may intuit the reality of psychosomatic connections, we also believe that "sticks and stones may break my bones, but words will never hurt me" (at least not physically!). Yet is this adage really true?

Some evidence suggests that a conversation with another person (even a non-threatening one) will automatically raise our blood pressure; a conversation with our boss, even more so (Lynch and Rosch, 1990; Lynch, 1985). What are we to make of accounts of "voodoo death," when a chieftain utters a death curse at a woman who violates a tribal taboo, and the woman, who believes her death to be inevitable, soon dies of no clear physical causes (Cannon, 1942)?[2] Modern equivalents of voodoo death occur in such cases as sudden death after retirement or widowhood. Engel (1971) argued that such phenomena are due to intense emotional arousal, which in-

---

[1]In fact, studies do show that immunity to disease among medical students is lower than usual during finals (Kielcolt-Glaser and Glaser, 1991).

[2]There may well be other mechanisms involved in voodoo death besides being scared to death. For example, other people, such as relatives, friends, and neighbors, withdraw their emotional support from the victim. Funeral rites may be carried out while the person is still alive, thus symbolically defining the individual as dead. (This has been called social death.) However, there may also be a withdrawal of material support, such as refusing the victim water. The literature on voodoo death differs on how the process works. Some argue that dehydration (loss of body fluids) is a vital factor. Relatives may withhold water,

terrupts the regular rhythm of the heart; in other words, it causes a cardiac arrhythmia that can be deadly. We do not wish to overstate the case that words can kill, but do want to make the point, developed further later, that human physiology is responsive to its social environment and that symbolic meanings can physically affect us.

Placebos: A Case of Mind or Body?

Research on placebos provides some suggestive linkages between mind and body. A placebo is a chemically inert or inactive substance (e.g., a sugar pill) that looks like real medication. It is a sham treatment that is supposed to have no actual physical effects. The Latin word *placebo* means "I will please." Doctors sometimes give placebos to patients who want and expect treatment yet seem to have no physical, organic basis to their complaints. Placebos are also used in tests of drugs and treatments to determine how much of a drug's effectiveness is due to its specific physical properties and how much is due to subjective or psychological factors. The placebo is used as a standard (or a control) against which a drug being tested can be compared.

While chemically inert, placebo "pain medication" can actually reduce pain in as much as 35 percent of patients (Beecher, 1959). In the late 1950s, there was even a controversial experiment with placebo surgery. (Recent tighter rules for experiments with human subjects prohibit such experiments.) It was found that an early version of coronary by-pass surgery (called mammary artery ligating surgery) was no more effective than sham surgery, in which patients were put to sleep and had an incision made, although no actual surgery was performed on the heart arteries (Cobb et al., 1959). Some observers have suggested that current coronary by-pass surgery may likewise derive part of its success from a placebo effect. Many by-pass patients experience considerable relief, even though their surgery produced *no* functioning, patent grafts (i.e., it did not improve ventricular function). The operation's symbolic and metaphorical effects may thus account for much of the patients' relief from angina pain (Moerman, 1983). Since patients usually hope that treatment will work, almost all treatments involve an element of the placebo effect. Medical settings—with their impressive equipment, diplomas and certificates on doctors' office walls, white uniforms, clipboards and stethoscopes—contribute to this "faith" or expectancy.

Some researchers view the placebo effect as being all in the mind and having no physical basis. Others suggest that placebos actually induce internal physical changes in the body (Eisenberg et al., 1993; Horwitz et al., 1990; Cousins, 1989; Weil, 1988; Bakal, 1979). For instance, placebos may stimulate the body's production of natural opiates, called endorphins (Davis, 1984; Levine et al., 1978). If this is

---

and the victim believing he is doomed, loses the desire to drink or obtain water (Eastwell, 1982). Thus according to some, voodoo death has mainly physical causes (e.g., dehydration), with psychological causes being secondary. Others argue that while physical causes are important, psychologically giving up on life produces lethal physical consequences (such as cardiac arrhythmia). There is some laboratory evidence that animals who give up die because their physiological systems have been depressed to a point of death (McElroy and Townsend, 1985).

true, it may be an oversimplification to consider the pain-relieving properties of a placebo merely psychological. Doctors' "bedside manner" or communication may likewise have concrete physical effects, such as reducing pain or speeding recovery. As one physician notes,

> But what if it is demonstrated in the future that reassurance provided by a health professional is capable of releasing endogenous morphine-like substances within a patient's brain? Without doubt, the phrase "laying on of hands" will acquire a new meaning (Bakal, 1979: 251).

The Western assumption of a division between mind and body is not shared by all cultures. In many cultures being sick or being healed is neither all biological nor all psychological but a psychophysiological process (Grossinger, 1990; Weil, 1988; Kleinman, 1978). We shall examine this issue in later chapters. For our present purpose, research on placebos illustrates that they may have a psychophysiological effect and that biomedicine's assumption of a mind-body split may not be supportable. A growing body of evidence suggests that the assumption of such a mind-body dualism limits medicine's ability to understand health and illness.[3] Furthermore, mind and body exist in a social environment with which they also interact. Thus social meanings, pressures, and relationships have at least *some* impact on us. The following sections sketch some of the possible pathways through which social pressures (or stressors) can become the source of psychophysical troubles.

The value of placebos is sometimes misconstrued as a simplistic mind-over-matter argument, which leads to the trap of another form of mind-body dualism: the mind ruling the body. Mind and body must be seen as interacting and not as separate elements. Diseases clearly have biological components, but they also have a psychosocial dimension. Psychosocial factors, however, do not magically transform bodies. Psychosocial pressures generally take years to exact their toll; for instance, social stress does not generate coronary heart disease or hypertension overnight. Some health problems experienced in adulthood may have begun much earlier in the person's life, even early childhood, when the organism is not yet fixed in its patterns of physical responses. Physical damages brought on by long-term stress, for example, may not be easily reversible. The fact that a health problem is affected by social factors, however, does not make it any less real.

[3]There is not always definite evidence, and much of the research is controversial, yet it is very suggestive. The research comes from a host of disciplines with a bewildering array of names, including psychological medicine (Bakal, 1979), psychosomatic medicine, psychophysiology (Suter, 1986), health psychology (Millon et al., 1982), sociophysiology (Barchas and Mendoza, 1984a, 1984b; Waid, 1984) and recently psychoneuroimmunology, (Ader et al., 1991; Pelletier and Herzing, 1988; Locke et al., 1985). These names become less intimidating if we break them down into smaller units of meaning. In the case of psychoneuroimmunology, *psycho* refers to the mind, *neuro* to the nervous system, and *immuno* to immunity. The ending *-ology* generally means *study of*. Thus psychoneuroimmunology is the study of the interactions among the mind, the nervous system, and the immune system. A central theory that underlies much research in this area is that the immune system may be the connecting point between psychosocial experiences and diseases (Solomon, 1985). For instance, such factors as social stress may have an impact on immunity, which in turn lowers a person's resistance to disease.

The Open Quality of Human Bodies:
Dogs Don't Brood

All creatures interact intimately with their environments; they have an impact on their environmental conditions and in turn are affected by them. When studying organisms and their surroundings, we have a tendency to make a sharp distinction between the environment and the creatures inhabiting it (Levins and Lewontin, 1985), but this distinction is misleading. We speak of animals adapting to their environments, but creatures also transform the world they live in, often modifying it to their needs and in turn being shaped by the world they have shaped. Humans, more than other creatures, can transform their social and physical environments, but they are also more liable to being affected mentally and physically by the world they create.

Creatures are shaped not only by physical surroundings but also by their social relationships and expectations. Social relationships affect physical responses. The social position of animals, for instance, affects their behavioral responses to amphetamines. Given amphetamines, both dominant and submissive monkeys increased dominant and submissive behaviors "appropriate" to their status. When a monkey changed its social position, so did its response to the drug. Thus, under amphetamines a monkey with increased status changed its behavior from being submissive to being more threatening and making more dominant displays (Haber and Barchas, 1984).

In a similar experiment with humans, four subjects were told that they would be given a sleeping pill, but one of the four was actually given a stimulant. All *four* subjects became drowsy and quiet (including the one who had unknowingly been given the stimulant). This study shows the importance of social expectations, the influence of the experimenter, and the behavior of one's peers (in this case the other three subjects) for one's physical response. Psychosocial factors were thus as important as the drug's biochemical properties in influencing people's behavior (Bakal, 1979: 180). Becker (1967) argued that culture and social learning affect how the individual experiences the effects of drugs. The ability of the hallucinogen LSD, for example, to produce a psychotic episode does not depend merely upon the chemistry of the drug but also on the sociocultural setting in which it is experienced.

Human physical functioning is more responsive than that of other animals to its environment (Berger and Luckmann, 1967: 47–50). This is true for a number of reasons:

1. Human beings leave the womb more unfinished than other creatures and exist in an extrauterine social womb of dependence on others. Social learning begins before we are biologically complete (e.g., our central nervous system is not fully developed) for an extended period after birth. Since human young are more open and malleable, early social learning has a deeper impact on them both physically and mentally. Although rats are far more "closed" than humans, studies show that activity and social stimulation can modify the brain of infant (and even adult) rats (Diamond, 1988). The role of early stimulation in constructing human physiology is much greater. Because human interconnectedness and dependence on others are thus partly a result of biology, human physiological functioning is more deeply affected by social surroundings (Birke, 1986: 85).

2.   Humans communicate through the use of symbols, which allows them—unlike other creatures—to reflect on themselves and their bodies, and to attach meanings to events (Berger and Luckmann, 1967). Symbols allow humans to remember experiences in a way that other creatures cannot. Humans reflect on their past and anticipate their future, but dogs cannot brood about old grudges. This is not to say dogs do not remember past pain or wait in anticipation, but relative to humans, they tend to be more grounded in the here and now. Such a capacity to reflect on the meaning of events may generate a chronic, low level of stress, since our brooding can contribute to a constant degree of psychophysical arousal. The capacity to symbolize widens the range of events to which humans respond as psychologically and physically stressful. A human can respond to the fear of being humiliated in the same way that an animal responds to physical threat. Unlike animals, however, humans do not generally respond to threats motorially (i.e., by running or fighting) but by mulling them over in our minds. This response has an impact on our health, because the wider range of anxiety and guilt about our past, present, and future that may result can affect us physically.

3.   Research shows ways in which seemingly involuntary physical processes, such as blood pressure, digestion, and the functioning of the immune system, can be changed in "lower" animals by conditioning (i.e., reward and punishment) and in humans by learning (such as learning through biofeedback). People are capable of a great deal of voluntary self-regulation and, as yogic practitioners demonstrate, can initiate the regulation of even "involuntary" aspects of physical functioning (Pelletier, 1992). While one can *condition* an animal to lower its blood pressure, humans can *place themselves* into states of mind that will alter their blood pressure. This means that the regulation of blood pressure and other supposedly involuntary physical functions are not closed systems that simply operate automatically, but rather that they are responsive to the psychosocial environments of which the person is a part. Human sexual responses are modulated by "higher" cognitive functions. Fantasies may amplify or diminish excitement (Cohen and Taylor, 1976). All organisms are capable of *self*-organizing their physical functioning; in humans this capacity seems greater. This capacity may be affected by moods, emotions, and feelings about ourselves that are in turn connected to our social existence (Buytendijk, 1974).

In sum, one might loosely characterize human physiology, relative to that of other creatures, as more responsive to its environment and more capable of self-regulation. Humans have more open and more controllable bodies; hence, we are more "makeable." Our bodies have greater access to the outer physical and social world because humans are free from fixed instinctual patterns and have greater capacity for self-regulation. One human aspect of our bodily nature is this particular openness to the world. "Our body in its relative independence has an opening to a formed outer world" (Buytendijk, 1974: 19).

Through these mind-body "thoroughfares," our movements are shaped by the physical constraints of our world, and our internal environment fluctuates to some extent with our experiences in the social and physical world. The way in which conversation can raise blood pressure serves as an example. Our way of life in a society and how we experience this way of life are linked to the functioning of our bodies through muscular, neurohormonal, cardiovascular, respiratory, and other systems. Due to our developed self-consciousness and capacity to reflect, the self can dampen or incite the physical systems and in turn be affected by them.

The ability to communicate symbolically (which is intrinsically tied with this open quality) makes us susceptible to a wider range of stressors than other forms of life experience. Humans respond physically to both physical and socially symbolic threats. Most psychosomatic illnesses are therefore peculiarly human. Humans also possess a greater ability to modify stressors' impact by the way we interpret them.

Body and society can intersect in many ways. We have reviewed some obvious connections, such as the impact that cultural and social factors have on our diet and hence on our physical condition. Other interrelationships between body and society are more subtle, such as ways our biochemistry may be influenced by the temporal rhythms of social environments or relationships. Some body-society influences involve surface modifications of our muscular-skeletal structure, including our posture, movements, and the shape of our bodies. Others may penetrate our body by changing blood pressure or the responsiveness of our nervous system. While showing relative internal stability, our bodily systems are "never completely withdrawn from a relationship to a way of existence" that is constantly changing and affecting these bodily systems (Buytendijk, 1974: 29).

Respiratory functioning, which is both voluntary and involuntary, exemplifies such body-society connections. We breathe automatically, yet can hold our breath (Suter, 1986: 56). How we breathe may be affected by our mood. Anxious people breathe more shallowly. Anxiety in turn may be produced by social settings. What we have here is a kind of society-mind-body bridge. Similarly, blood pressure, blood sugar, and immunity are affected by patterns of neuroendocrinological arousal (Gruchow, 1979), which are themselves linked to the way we live and respond to our life experiences. The early empirical and theoretical foundations for such linkages can be found in the pioneering works of W. B. Cannon (1929) and his student who became the father of contemporary stress research, Hans Selye (1956).

The Neurohormonal Connection: Stressor and Stress Response

Of all the bridges that connect the body to the mind and to the "outside" world, the best known and explored is the neurohormonal connection. A **stressor**, or a stress situation (Suter, 1986), refers to stimuli, or environmental conditions or events, that elicit stress. We include here those stimuli that come from our minds, such as recalling a frightening event. The threat of a dog's bite is a stressor, and our body's response to that stressor is called the **stress response** or **fight-or-flight response**. The stress response is the body's way of getting ready to deal with the stressor by mobilizing itself to either fight or to flee. This "fight-or-flight reflex," as Cannon (1929) called it, involves neurohormonal changes in the body (Suter, 1986: 73), which elicit a particular pattern of arousal or excitation in the nervous system and the release of certain hormones. One function of these hormones is to "stimulate and coordinate distant organs" (Selye, 1975: 148).

Hormones are released by the endocrine glands directly into the body, and they stimulate or depress various physical functions. These hormones act as the body's chemical messengers, telling it to step up or to slow down its activities. Adrenaline (also known as epinephrine) and noradrenalin (norepinephrine) are examples of a class of stress hormones known as catecholamines. The stress response involves changes in the central nervous system (CNS; the brain and nerves in the spinal cord) and the release of some of these hormonal substances.

Other examples of stress hormones are the corticosteroids (e.g., cortisol). Research since Selye, however, has suggested that many other hormonal substances, including peptide hormones (e.g., endorphins) play a role in the stress response. Thus, to speak of specific stress hormones may be misleading (Weiner, 1992; Pelletier and Herzing, 1988). We could think of hormones as "information substances" (Hill, 1989). One function of hormones is to stimulate and coordinate distant organs (Selye, 1975). Another may be to provide communication links between different physiological systems. Thus, peptide hormones, for example, influence communication between the brain and immune system (Pelletier and Herzing, 1988). Both the organism and its relationship with its environment can be conceptualized in informational terms, with neuroendocrinological functions acting as information networks within the organism (Weiner, 1992).

The fight-or-flight response, according to Selye, is a general physiological response that involves a number of systems throughout the body and can be evoked by any number of nonspecific stimuli (stressors) in the environment. Selye noted that his medical training encouraged a blind spot for the idea of nonspecific factors. In the course of his medical education, specific diseases and their causes "assumed an ever increasing importance and pushed the syndrome of just being sick, the question 'what is disease in general?' out of my consciousness into that hazy category of the purely abstract arguments that are not worth bothering about" (Selye, 1956: 17). In contrast to Selye, other researchers (Weiner, 1992) argue that stressors evoke physiological responses specifically attuned to those specific stressors. Furthermore, prior rhythms of the organism, genetic predispositions, social contexts, and other factors influence physiological responses to stressors. We examine some sources of variability in physiological responses to stressors further in this chapter.

The stress response, in the form of this neurohormonal activity, creates a number of nonspecific changes in the body[4] that adapt the organism for fight or flight (Sapolsky, 1990):

---

[4]The stress response can never be measured directly. In a sense, a stress researcher is like an investigator who tries to deduce what is happening inside a factory on the basis of noises he or she hears while standing on the outside (Suter, 1986). Some measures of stress include the calculation of the amount

1. Blood pressure is increased. Blood flows to the muscles and heart, and much is diverted from the peripheral (outer) parts of the body; this is why cold feet and hands are often a symptom of stress. Blood is also diverted away from functions, like digestion, not needed for fleeing or fighting.
2. Sugars and fats (including cholesterol) are released to give the body energy.
3. Immunity is temporarily depressed to allow the body to tolerate possible invasions, such as wounds.

These changes suggest how prolonged, uninterrupted stress might create physical problems. For example, does the continued release of fats and sugars into the blood help to explain the connection between stress and coronary heart disease? Can prolonged stress affect the mechanisms that regulate blood pressure? These are some of the issues investigated by stress research.

Weiner (1992) suggests that research focus on disturbances—what he calls "perturbations" of neuroendocrinological rhythms and ways in which stressful experiences relate to those disturbances. He advocates looking at both organic (disease) and functional (ill health) problems from this holistic model.

Some researchers believe that stress-induced neuroendocrinological changes generally only contribute to causing disease (as a cofactor along with others, such as prior structural damage and genetic factors). Furthermore, they argue stress-induced changes contribute more to ill health than to the onset of disease. Bodies manifest ill health in a wide range of symptoms such as sleeplessness, fatigue, hyperventilation, chronic pain, and so on. These symptoms often do not have a clear-cut organic basis (Weiner, 1992). Even though such forms of distress are common medical complaints, medicine has neglected them since they lack clear organic sources. Given the tendency for medicine to see mind and body as separate, often doctors do not take such problems seriously.

The events in modern life that elicit the stress response in humans are not usually physical but more typically social and symbolic in nature (e.g., the threat of being humiliated). Furthermore, modern conditions do not always make the adaptive response of fleeing or fighting a practical one. We may be provoked by a boss to fight or run, but we have learned that neither response would be appropriate. Thus the body may be continuously geared up for action but not allowed by the rules of "civilized" behavior to act.

Any demanding situation, such as climbing a dangerous trail for enjoyment or mining coal in a dangerous mineshaft for a living, can be stressful. Not all stressors are negative, however; some can energize and challenge. Stress itself is not inherently unhealthy. It is a part of life, and a totally stressless environment would be both impossible and boring.

---

of electrical activity in the nervous system and the biochemical analysis of blood and urine, but all of these methods have problems. For instance, while the quantity of catecholamines in a person's urine reflects different levels of stress, it may also be a function of that person's unique way of metabolizing (processing) such substances, since some people will excrete such hormones more rapidly than others.

Negative and positive stressors are not necessarily equal in their impact on us. Are there qualitative differences in how people respond to negative or positive stressors? Research (Glass, 1977; Dohrenwend and Pearlin, 1982) suggests that it is not just change or environmental demands that are stressful. The uncontrollability of the stressor-event seems to increase its destructive consequences for the body. Stressors are likely to have a negative effect when the individual feels helpless in the face of them.

The Relationship Between Physical and Sociopsychological Stressors

A physical stressor may have an impact on psychological states as mood (Bullinger, 1990). For example, noise levels may not only have physical consequences, such as damage to hearing, but may also influence mood and act as a psychological stressor. Furthermore, there is evidence that physical and sociopsychological stressors interact with each other. By lowering immunity, stress can aggravate an individual's vulnerability to infectious microorganisms. Being physically run-down may also make it harder to cope with social stresses. Often different kinds of stressors interact with each other and may in fact *increase* one another's impact on the body. Such a mutually enhancing interaction is called a synergistic relationship. Each factor may "feed" into the other, amplifying effects that either one alone might have had.

The relationship between diet and stress exemplifies synergism. In our fragmented ways of looking at health and illness, we often focus on one factor (such as diet) as *the* determinant of health. Some think that eating properly will save them from heart disease and other woes, yet diet cannot be considered in isolation from other factors. A high cholesterol diet *combined* with high levels of social stress can increase the likelihood of atherosclerosis (hardening of the arteries), over and above the effect of diet by itself (Kaplan et al., 1983; Eyer, 1984). Smoking and stress combined may interact synergistically to raise blood pressure and heart rate (Ratliff-Crain and Baum, 1990; Karasek and Theorell, 1990).

House and his colleagues (1979) studied workers who were exposed to chemicals known to cause respiratory problems. They found that the workers suffered even higher levels of these disorders if, simultaneously to being exposed to the noxious chemicals, they were also exposed to "noxious" supervisory pressures. Social stress increased the effect of physical (chemical) stressors on the body. Supervisory pressure and noxious chemicals thus interacted in a synergistic fashion. Although Dew et al. (1989) did not find significant synergistic effects between occupational exposure of blue-collar women to organic solvents, such as glues, and levels of perceived occupational stress, they argue that the synergy hypothesis is nonetheless compelling and worth further investigation (see also Karasek and Theorell, 1990: 141–142).

A QUESTION OF SUSCEPTIBILITY

Why do two people react very differently to the same stressors? Some of us face stress with confidence; others with fear, despair, and a sense of hopelessness. While some people seem to weather life's crises without much damage, others break easily.

Clearly, it is not only the stressor itself that determines the reaction, but also how the individual experiences and deals with the stressor. Furthermore, research suggests that even physiological reactions to stress vary from person to person. Some people's bodies react very strongly to a stressor; others' less so. What factors account for such variations in individual susceptibility?

Although there are important individual variations in reactions to stress, we should avoid individualistic interpretations that ignore the social circumstances contributing to these variations. Such approaches tend to blame the victim of stress rather than to examine the social situations that might account for variations in individual susceptibility. Three interrelated kinds of individual variations in stressor reaction exemplify this problem; the mere presence of a stressor does not account for a person's physical reaction to it. First, there are differences in the way people's bodies respond to stressors (**physiological reactivity**). Second, there are variations in how people perceive stressors and assess what is happening to them (**cognitive-emotional appraisal**). Third, there are differences in the way people manage stressors (**coping**).

Physiological Reactivity

While the basic pattern of the stress response remains essentially the same from person to person, researchers have found recurring *individual* patterns in the way people's bodies respond to stress. Some individualized physical responses are more fixed or rigid than others. Two people faced with the same stressor will show differences in the level to which their blood pressure rises. The pressure of persons who have hypertension tends to fluctuate more dramatically than that of those whose blood pressure at rest is "normal" (Suter, 1986; Buytendijk, 1974).

Individuals also differ in their patterns of neurological excitation. In some people the ergotrophic response, in which sympathetic arousal is high, is more easily elicited. Other people respond more quickly with a tropotrophic response, in which parasympathetic excitation predominates (Suter, 1986). Individuals may also differ in how readily their bodies shift between these two responses, physically changing from being in a state of fight or flight to being in a state of relaxation (Gellhorn, 1969).

Individuals have varying hormonal reactions (Bieliauskas, 1982: 5). In some laboratory studies, men produced more epinephrine in response to stressors than did women. A study of women in nontraditional "male" occupational roles, however, showed that women meet demands with almost no sharp increase in epinephrine like the men's (Frankenhaeuser, 1991). It is nonetheless possible that this difference has genetic and natural bases. Perhaps men overreact to stress, thus producing an inefficient excess of stress hormones (Frankenhaeuser, 1991; Polefrone and Manuck, 1987; Overfield, 1985). Some physiological variations may reflect differences in biological make-up. Perhaps men and women *do* differ biologically to some extent in hormonal reactions. Perhaps some individuals are genetically predisposed to hypertension or coronary heart disease. Such issues are by no means resolved, and the research results are mixed.

Variations in physiological reactivity, such as differences in catecholamine reactivity, may also be the result of social factors, at least to some extent. Men and women are socialized to deal with stress in different ways. It may well be that these learned patterns also affect their way of responding physically (Birke, 1986; Lowe and Hubbard, 1983). The fight-or-flight response tends to elevate blood pressure. A long-term exposure to stressors and a learned typical way of responding to them might eventually lead to a regular pattern of reacting physically, as some animal studies suggest (McCarty et al., 1988). One study suggests that chronic occupational stress in blue-collar workers may, over an extended period, modify the way the heart and blood pressure respond to stressors (Siegrist and Klein, 1990).

Moss (1973) has argued that given a certain cognitive-emotional orientation to stressors, over time the nervous system might become "tuned" into a particular pattern of arousal. Thus the sympathetic nervous system's reaction to situations might become amplified and fixed in that amplified pattern. The parasympathetic nervous system would not, therefore, be as readily activated. The person could be easily excited and would find it hard to "unwind." Individual physiological patterns in responding to stress might be partly the result of learning and other social experiences (Suter, 1986: 84). The distinction between physiological factors (e.g., individual differences in hormonal output) and social factors (social situations which promote physical changes) in health is thus not always clear-cut.

Cognitive-Emotional Appraisal

Cognitive-emotional appraisal is the physiological impact of a person's interpretation and emotional reaction to a stressful event. In one study of this phenomenon, Lazarus (1966) and his associates showed male students different versions of a film that depicted ritual operations on the genitals: circumcision (cutting around the penis to remove the foreskin) and subincision (cutting the penis lengthwise). One version of the film had no sound and showed only the operations. Another version had a soundtrack that emphasized the harmlessness of the procedures and the fact that the participants in the rites saw them as an honor. A third version contained the narration of an anthropologist who, in an intellectual tone, constantly commented on events as the interesting and "exotic" customs of other societies. The researchers measured the level of physiological stress response of each member of the audiences. Those exposed to the second or the third version of this film showed lower physiological levels of stress. Lazarus concluded that one's physical reaction to a stressor is affected by how one interprets it. In this case, the soundtracks helped the audiences interpret the stressor as less threatening. Although watching a stressful event on a film is not the same as seeing it in person or having it done to oneself, such experiments illustrate that our interpretations of events have a significant effect on how we react to them.

Several theories emphasize the importance of an individual's cognitive-emotional appraisal of situations in linking stress to illness (see Totman, 1979; Moss, 1973). Antonovsky (1987: 13) proposes that people with a high "sense of coherence" are healthier, because they have

> a global orientation that expresses the extent to which one has a pervasive, enduring though dynamic feeling that 1) the stimuli deriving from one's internal and external en-

vironments in the course of living are structured, predictable and explicable; 2) the resources are available to one to meet the demands posed by these stimuli; and 3) these demands are challenges worthy of investment and employment.

Antonovsky (1990) conceptualizes this sense of coherence as "dispositional orientation" (rather than personal "trait") toward experiencing stressors as comprehensible, manageable, and meaningful.

Cultural factors and an individual's position in a social structure can affect this sense of coherence. Antonovsky does not, however, thoroughly examine the ways environments disempower people, nor does he systematically consider how conditions that attack a person's sense of coherence are built into the social organization of institutions such as the work place and the family. He also does not explore in sufficient depth the impact of social and economic systems such as capitalism on individuals' sense of coherence.

These theories emphasize the importance to health of feeling a sense of empowerment or control.[5] What they clearly do not distinguish is how a person feels or perceives the world, as opposed to conditions that lead a person to emotionally and mentally appraise the world a certain way. The emphasis on cognitive appraisal in the stress literature often implies that how one perceives an event is the result of a psychological attribute or quality inherent in the person, independent of the event itself. This approach treats *how* we perceive things as almost unrelated to *what* we are perceiving. Such a focus may downplay common, objective environmental stressors such as poverty (Moos and Swindle, 1990). Furthermore, people may react physiologically to a stressor but not be consciously aware of it (Krohne, 1990).

While individuals do vary in the way they appraise stressors at any given time, these differences are often the result of former social experiences with past stressors. Feeling helpless may come from some set of previous objective experiences. If, for instance, people were once overwhelmed and made to feel powerless by social class, economic, or familial events, later in life they may find it harder to believe that a stressor now confronting them is a manageable one (even if it is!).

Seligman (1992) observed that animals placed in laboratory conditions of help-

---

[5]Antonovsky (1979: 127–128) claimed that it is important to differentiate a sense of control from one of coherence, because a sense of control implies that "I am in control," which reflects a cultural bias that equates a *sense* of control with *self*-control. However, people do not have to be in control to have a sense of coherence, but simply be participants in shaping their fate and believe that who or whatever is in control (e.g., their god or leader) is controlling events in the people's interest and is a legitimate authority. Indeed one can feel that the world is relatively safe and in control and yet not *be* in control.

But two issues must be raised: First, self-control *is* important in Western industrialized societies. Second, however much events can be "in the hands of the Lord," so to speak, individuals still must feel the world is manageable and not working against them. It is inconceivable that persons could tolerate feeling that they were puppets or that their actions were not their own. To be unable to connect one's actions with more or less predictable outcomes would be most disturbing. While control need not be totally in individuals' hands, they, as Antonovsky admitted, must feel themselves to be participants in their actions and that the world is being managed in their interest. It is in this way that we argue that theories such as Antonovsky's emphasize a *sense* of control, which we would agree is not synonymous with *self*-control.

lessness for a long enough period were unable to cope with subsequent stress or possible activity. He has linked such "learned helplessness" to depression, poor health, and a generally heightened susceptibility to stressors. The experience of powerlessness in everyday situations at work or home may produce a similar learned helplessness in humans (Lennerlof, 1988). Other authors have introduced similar concepts, for example, the "giving-up complex" (Schmale, 1972) and the "paralysis of will" (Bakal, 1979). Likewise, the notion of "surplus powerlessness" (Lerner, 1992) suggests that if individuals were once made to feel powerless, the expectation that they will again be powerless builds up and keeps them from acting when confronted with stressors (even when they are able). People's present reactions to stressors are thus linked to their past experiences with empowering or disempowering situations. A lifetime of social exploitation or domination will certainly have an impact on whether a person feels empowered.

Coping

Coping refers to all of the ways of managing the tension a stressor produces (Mechanic, 1978: 51). As Syme and Berkman (1976: 6) observed:

> Generalized susceptibility to disease may be influenced not only by the impact of various forms of life change and life stress, but also by differences in the way people cope with such stress. Coping, in this sense, refers not to specific types of psychological responses but to the more generalized ways in which people deal with problems in their everyday life. It is evident that such coping styles are likely to be products of environmental situations and not independent of such factors.

One's cognitive-emotional appraisal of a situation is in itself a way of coping or managing stress. Some people "overact" emotionally; seeing the glass as half-empty, they give up. Others see a glass that is half-full and keep striving. Coping is not merely a matter of attitude, perception, or emotional response, however; it also involves action—that is, doing something about the stressor.

The focus of much stress literature on individual coping leads to two blind spots. First, these studies fail to consider how power affects people's ability to do something about stress. How does social class, ethnicity, gender, or work situation influence resources for effective coping? Second, much research tends to separate coping and stressor, thereby missing the fact that the conditions creating stress often also limit both the possibility of and options for coping. One's social position (such as one's status as a woman) often limits options for coping. In some areas of life, such as in friendships, certain personal styles of coping strategies are possible, but in much of everyday life people's options for managing stress are very limited. The world of work, for example, allows most people only limited coping strategies (Pearlin and Schooler, 1978).

The early literature on stress gives the impression that stress is a problem primarily for high-powered, white-collar workers. Yet research indicates that while these groups do face a great deal of stress, they also have access to resources that allow them to cope with it more effectively than those who lack resources. Even among animals the "top dog" generally has more resources to handle stressors than the "bottom dog." One study of baboons found that, in response to stress, high-ranking males showed faster increases in cortisol, a stress hormone, than subordinate baboons; however, their basal level (i.e., the ordinary amount when not exposed to stress) of the hormone was lower than that of the subordinates. Furthermore, when the stressful event ended, the amounts of cortisol in high-ranking baboons returned more rapidly to the basal levels than did those of their subordinates. The more effective coping of these "top bananas" was attributed to such advantages as better choice of food, mates, and living conditions (Sapolsky, 1982, 1989, 1990). Another researcher found that rats that can control the source of stress or predict when stress will occur also cope more effectively and show fewer pathological effects of stress than do rats that cannot control or predict stressors (Pelletier and Herzing, 1988: 32; Weiss, 1972). The blood pressure and cardiovascular reactivity of rats in response to stressors have been shown to be linked to their position in the social hierarchy (Bohus et al., 1991). A wide range of physiological patterns is associated with subordinate rank in animals; these patterns vary as the social status of the animal changes. They are, thus, a function of the animal's social status (Weiner, 1992: 176). Although animal studies cannot be used uncritically to generalize about human situations and behavior, executives and other "top bananas," whose job conditions allow for control and provide resources for coping (such as more control over the use of one's time), can probably cope with stress more effectively than those who do not experience such advantages.

One might argue that nonexecutive stress is a more serious health hazard than executive stress. A study of 5,100 Swedish and American men found the highest risk of coronary heart disease among workers with both heavy job demands (i.e., numerous stressors) and a "low ability to influence how their tasks are done" (Karasek and Theorell, 1990; Nelson, 1983). Thus one's social position (such as on the job) may influence both the amount of stress one faces and the resources one has for coping. The most stressful occupations are those that combine high levels of stress with little control over those stressful conditions. Being a telephone operator or a waitress may therefore be more stressful than being a bank officer, sales manager, or physician. For example, a National Institute of Occupational Safety and Health study found that clerical women who had low control over their work with VDTs (video display terminals) showed higher levels of job stress than the highly pressured air traffic controllers, who also work with such terminals (Howard, 1985: 73). Thus the social circumstances in which people find themselves influence not only the demands to which they are exposed but also their ability to handle those demands.

In recent years, corporate health programs have proliferated in the United States. Sponsored mainly by larger corporations, they emphasize exercise, meditation, diet control, and smoke cessation (Conrad, 1988; Pelletier, 1985). While programs for blue-collar and lower-echelon white-collar workers exist, many are directed toward executives, who present potentially more expensive health-related losses for the corporation. These programs seem to have developed in an economic environment of escalating medical costs to corporations and governments (Alexander, 1988). However, there is no definitive evidence yet that, in the long run, they do prevent illness (Conrad, 1988). Indeed, they may be attempts to impose new forms of social control on the workers through a new corporate health ethic, by shaping values and attitudes of workers toward their lifestyles and also toward work. Such an ethic stresses the *individual* worker's fitness, strength, diet, and health habits, while avoiding scrutiny of social contexts that affect health (Conrad and Walsh, 1992).

While their overt function is to use prevention to reduce health care costs and loss of workdays, corporate health programs may also direct attention away from political and environmental issues in the work place. They do not generally encourage workers to examine critically the social conditions under which they work, such as work pace, vacations, breaks, or participation in decisions affecting their work. The implicit message to employees is that their health (and the costs they incur by being sick) are their individual responsibility (Glassner, 1989). Such programs may even be used to justify cutting back on medical benefits. The corporate image also benefits by such programs, and other parts of the business sector profit by selling the equipment and services for these programs (Alexander, 1988).

Stress and Power

Young (1980: 133) observes that both scientific and lay discussions of stress tend to "subvert sociological reasoning" by removing people from their social contexts and from class and group conflicts. They tend to emphasize subjective factors and the way individuals *perceive* events, or in other words, psychological as opposed to sociological factors.[6] The way people see things gets confused with the way that things are (Young, 1980: 145). Instead of beginning analyses of stress and health by looking at coping responses, cognitive-emotional appraisal, or individual forms of coping, why not begin by examining social conditions of inequality or structural arrangements, such as those that force a person to work under pressure or do not allow time to relax?

Scheder's (1988) analysis of diabetes among Mexican-American migrant farm workers illustrates the relationship among psychosocial stress, limited options for managing stress, and social inequality. Much research on diabetes has focused on factors of nutrition, obesity, and health behavior. While these variables are important influences, exclusive emphasis on them obscures the role of such factors as social inequality. Diabetes is more common among low-status and low-income people (Scheder, 1988). The exact role that psychosocial stress plays in the disease is not clear; however, some evidence suggests stress may influence its onset and course (Scheder, 1988; Jacobson and Leibovich, 1984). Stress can also affect health behavior, such as excessive eating and drinking. The neuroendocrinological arousal generated by high levels of chronic stress may also affect blood sugar metabolism (Jacobson and Leibovich, 1984). Scheder found that rates of adult-onset diabetes (Type II diabetes mellitus) were much higher among those who had spent a long time

---

[6]We therefore do not agree with Mechanic (1978:71), who after reviewing literature on helplessness and health, concluded that whether we in fact control our external environment is a "philosophical issue." What is significant, he said, is our subjective response to conditions, or our sense of helplessness.

as migrant farm workers and had frequent experiences of stressful life events. Obesity did not distinguish those who got diabetes from those who did not. Scheder concluded that the high levels of stress experienced by these migrant workers as a result of their low social position, disrupted social networks, social marginality (i.e., being outsiders in American culture), discrimination, heavy workloads, job insecurity, poverty, and feelings of hopelessness and helplessness, contributed to catecholamine-produced impairments in glucose levels. This study suggests the kinds of questions we need to ask about the effects on health of power, psychosocial stress, and a personal sense of control.

SUMMARY

Material environments and our interactions with them affect our bodies. Symbolic and social factors, however, may also influence bodies through neurohormonal and other physical changes, which in turn may even mediate the interaction between our bodies and the physical environments they inhabit.

Stress is not merely in the eyes of the beholder, nor are the ways in which people handle stressors merely a matter of our individual resourcefulness. The economic organization of a society, the various social pressures to which its members are subjected, and their membership in sociological categories such as class, race, ethnicity, gender, and age are very important considerations. In the next chapter, we shall look at qualities of social environments that both empower and disempower to emphasize the effects of social-structural factors, such as stratification and social control, upon people's bodies and health.

RECOMMENDED READINGS

Articles

HOWARD BECKER, "History, culture and subjective experience: An exploration of the social bases of drug-induced experience," *Journal of Health and Social Behavior* 8, 1967: 163–176.
GEORGE L. ENGEL, "Sudden and rapid death during psychological stress: Folklore or folk wisdom?" *Annals of Internal Medicine* 74, 1971: 771–782.
LENNART LENNERLOF, "Learned helplessness at work," *International Journal of Health Services* 18(2), 1988: 207–222.
K. W. PETTINGALE, "Towards a psychobiological model of cancer: Biological considerations," *Social Science and Medicine* 20(8), 1985: 779–787.

Books

AARON ANTONOVSKY, *Unraveling the Mystery of Health: How People Manage Stress and Stay Well.* San Francisco: Jossey Bass, 1987. An elaboration and application of Antonovsky's "sense of coherence" perspective.

ROSALIND BARNETT, LOIS BIENER, and GRACE K. BARUCH, eds., *Gender and Stress*. New York: The Free Press, 1987. A good collection of articles dealing with gender differences in experiencing and responding to stress.

ROBERT KARASEK and TÖRES THEORELL, *Health Work: Stress Productivity and the Reconstruction of Working Life*. New York: Basic Books, 1990. Excellent analysis of the conditions of work that are sickeningly stressful.

MARTIN SELIGMAN, *Helplessness: On Depression, Development and Death*. San Francisco: W. H. Freeman, 1992. An introduction to the concept of learned helplessness that presents evidence for its various applications.

STEVE SUTER, *Health Psychophysiology: Mind-Body Interactions in Wellness and Illness*. Hillsdale, NJ: Laurence Erlbaum, 1986. An introduction to the psychophysiology of stress, basic relevant anatomy, and applications of the psychophysiological perspective to several illnesses.

ANDREW WEIL, *Health and Healing*. Boston: Houghton Mifflin (revised edition), 1988. A very readable critique of biomedicine and presentation of a holistic perspective.

CHAPTER FIVE

Social Organization, Health, and Illness

In the previous chapter we described how a sense of manageability and control over our circumstances can affect our health. What kinds of conditions empower or disempower us? As we suggested in Chapter 4, the amount of stress a person experiences in the work place, for example, partly depends upon certain social conditions. Social status and the social organization and regulation of activities are crucial in structuring these social conditions.

ORGANIZATIONAL SETTINGS AND EMPOWERMENT: SOCIAL STATUS AND CONTROL

A number of factors can either contribute to our feeling of empowerment or erode our sense of coherence, and thus affect the stressfulness of life events and the effectiveness of our responses to those events. These factors include: (1) the ways activities are scheduled and the individual's attitudes toward time; (2) how social relationships and circumstances either affirm or assault a person's sense of self; (3) whether social environments provide sufficient information important to individual well-being and security; and (4) the quality of social support systems.

Social stratification and control are closely linked with both empowering and disempowering situations in the social production of health and illness (Freund, 1982). They shape whether we experience time as stressful; how we feel about ourselves, our abilities, our competence, and our ability to predict the outcomes of our behavior; and the quality of social relationships that support us.

Our examples of social stratification and control are generally drawn from Western capitalist societies, with an emphasis on the illness-producing organizational properties of capitalism as a socioeconomic system. These properties are, however, by no means confined to such societies. The former USSR, for instance, had experienced a significant deterioration in life expectancy and infant mortality since the mid-1960s (Feshbach, 1984; but see also Cooper, 1987). Lifestyle factors, such as a high rate of alcohol consumption and smoking, and a poorly functioning health care system contribute to these problems (Feshbach, 1984). Some observers have speculated, however, that Soviet health problems are caused by social organizational properties similar to those found in capitalist societies. Large social status differences, for example, affect health and access to health care (Cooper and Schatzkin, 1982). As in monopolistic capitalist societies, the thrust toward "the efficient accumulation of capital" (Eyer, 1977: 38), productivity, and control over workers takes precedence over workers' health. Soviet industry has eagerly appropriated capitalist techniques of increasing labor productivity, such as the assembly line (Braverman, 1974). Social inequality and oppressive forms of control are thus not exclusive to capitalism.

KILLING TIME AND BRIDLING MOTION

Control over time—our own or other people's—is a form of power. Powerful persons have the ability to regulate other people's time and labor. The ability to manage our own schedules is limited by our position in society. Wealthy persons have more resources for managing the stress of demanding schedules. A teacher can keep a student waiting, but students should not be late for their appointments with a teacher, since a teacher's time is assumed to be more valuable. *Time is socially organized, and the ability to schedule time and to manage it is socially distributed.* Those with more power have more control over time.

From the moment we enter the world as babies, we are subject to a social calendar that is not of our own making, and we are taught to respect the constraints of time. The fragmentation and structuring of time and space in adult terms begins early. In some societies, however, adults and children do not experience such sharp time distinctions between work and play (Cherfas and Lewin, 1980).

In our society, the emphasis is on productivity. The social organization of our economic life is the basis of much of our social scheduling of time. This organization demands intense productivity and encourages us to internalize certain attitudes toward time. **Internalization** is the process by which people take on and make their own the attitudes, beliefs, and ways of looking at and acting on the world held by others. The work ethic, one such internalized complex of attitudes toward time, affects us not only at work but even at leisure.

The social organization of time and learned attitudes toward time can have a profound effect on our health. The rhythms of time and motion demanded of people and the way people respond to these demands are very important sources of stress; they also shape our ability to cope with these stressors. Personal ways of responding to environmental demands are socially learned. The family, for instance, can teach its members to become obsessed with time. Controls over time can be both externally and internally imposed. The time clock at the factory, the doctor's appointment, the classroom bell, and the income tax deadline exemplify externally imposed controls over time. The so-called Type A way of responding to time is an example of a self-imposed, or internalized, form of control over time. Type A behavior is the result of socialization during which some individuals learn to respond to time in a socially approved way.

How members of a society collectively use time and the different degrees of control over their own or other people's time are central sociopsychological factors in health. They determine the frequency and intensity of stressors as well as the effectiveness of means of dealing with those stressors. For example, work time can be stressful for many people; factors such as social or occupational status influence how well they can cope with work time.

Time and Work

In the beginning of the twentieth century, the intense control by employers over work time, which had characterized the growing capitalist society of the nineteenth century, was further extended. Workers became more and more paced by the rhythms of the machine. With the emergence of the assembly line and "scientific management" of work activity, new, more systematic, "scientific" or rationalized forms of control predominated in the work place. For instance, standards for workers were increasingly set by time-and-motion studies.

The work of Frederick Taylor epitomizes the attempt to impose rationalized, scientific controls over time and motion. In *The Principles of Scientific Management* ([1911] 1947), Taylor argued for a sharp division between those who *plan* work and those who *do* it. The planning was to be carried out exclusively by managers trained in scientific management. Jobs were to be divided and subdivided into the smallest, easiest-to-learn unit of activity. Time-and-motion studies would determine the most efficient way to move and the optimum unit of time each subdivided task should take. These studies would then set standards for precisely how and how fast all the workers would move. Taylor argued that such a system of management should take precedence over the idiosyncratic rhythms and needs of individual workers (Karasek and Theorell, 1990). While his system is no longer widely applied in most work places, the attitudes and assumptions of Taylorism still prevail among many managers.

Work in industrial manufacturing in particular was highly regulated by machines and specific, limiting instructions. Tasks were broken down into short, simple, repetitious units of activity (Braverman, 1974). The result of this form of control, used in the pursuit of productivity, was to place workers increasingly into environments that moved too fast, were deadeningly boring, and controlled the motions of the body in an unnatural and uncomfortable way.

The quest for increased productivity has been most intense in industrial manufacturing. This drive has put greater pressure on industrial workers in the form of ever-increasing demands on pace and the effective use of working time, and decreasing options for variety, relaxation, and social interaction at work. Various studies show that poor mental health, psychosomatic disorders, and sick leaves are most common in low-status industrial manufacturing jobs (Frankenhaeuser and Gardell, 1976).

The pace and motion of factory work has been extended to white-collar office work. The movements of some typists, keypunch operators, and other office machine operators have taken on "automaton-like characteristics" (Stellman, 1977: 55). The growth of computer technologies since the 1950s has opened up new work possibilities, but it has also led to more highly repetitive, boring, machine-paced work in the office. Computer technology provides for increased control over individual workers. A terminal on a supervisor's desk can monitor the number of strokes made by each individual keypunch operator (National Safe Workplace Institute, 1990; Garson, 1988).

Bell Telephone computers print 15-minute summaries of how many operators were on duty, how many calls each operator handled, the average speed of an operator's answer, and how long they spent talking to each customer (Howard, 1985: 63). Citicorp Bank uses Management Information System (MIS) software, which provides management with data about work places hundreds of miles away. Each clerk's printout shows the amount of time spent processing records, talking on the phone, and the like. The records are then evaluated according to standards set by Citicorp's time-and-motion specialist (Howard, 1985: 30–31). A National Association of Working Women's survey found that 35 percent of its members, in jobs as diverse as bank teller, data entry clerk, waitress, and truck driver, were monitored by computer (Howard, 1985: 62). Even middle-level managers and executives are subject to closely monitored time controls; some must submit accounts of work done every half-hour (Garson, 1988). Thus the tendency in office and professional work, as in factory work, is toward greater standardization of work and control over time (Garson, 1988). There is a growing de-emphasis on skill and on individual control over the work process (Glenn and Feldberg, 1977).

Load Balance.   Some environments demand too much, too fast, while others demand some degree of involvement but make too few demands and are boring. The different rhythms of working (and of living in general) may be conceived of in terms of load balance: Do they demand too much or too little? How much pressure (or how much of a load) is imposed on a person? A load imbalance may involve either overload or underload, or both, as temporal rhythms. A chronic load imbalance may adversely affect one's health. While our examples of time rhythms are drawn from the work place, the problem of load balancing may apply equally to the lives of the unemployed, the elderly, and persons with disabilities (Frankenhaeuser, 1981).

Underload and **overload** are products of the degree of control one has over the rhythm of one's work. Temporal demands are not as stressful when self-generated. However, they are stressful when they are imposed and combined with little control over how one's work is done (Karasek and Theorell, 1990). Such jobs are likely to be held by low-status workers. Overload may involve piecework, such as being paid by the number of letters typed each hour. Overload usually results from a work environment that moves too fast for comfort. Underload often involves machine-paced work, such as an assembly line. Workers' movements are standardized but also demand their attention. Underload tends to be boring and tiring work. Clearly some boring work need not be stressful. A night watchman can read, walk, and chat; this work may thus not be as stressful as boring work that requires sustained alertness and attention, such as watching a machine.

Work often involves both underload and overload (Frankenhaeuser and Gardell, 1976). A dramatic example is the labor process at a Canadian meat packing plant:

> Two lines run during the day, one on the night shift. The pace is maintained by the skinning machine operators who place the hams with skins removed on the conveyer. . . . Workers holding razor sharp knives are forced to match the pace of machine operators. If a worker cannot keep up, the others down the line must work faster just to maintain the pace. Arguments occur among workers, accusations of going too fast or too slow. Stress on the job is high due to the surrender of control to the machine-paced line combined with the need to maintain a constantly high level of attention. A momentary loss of attention can lead to error or injury. Indeed, the sense of stress is heightened by congestion as workers are sandwiched between the moving table and large vats for waste and trim located two feet away. From management's perspective, however, the changes are viewed positively, because workers put pressure on each other to keep up production speeds (Novek et al., 1990: 49, 292–293).

One can imagine the multiplicity of health risks that characterize this job, such as the danger of injury from knives and sharp machines, as well as repetitive strain injury.

There is also the psychosocial stress produced by the pressure of time and the boredom coupled with the demand for constant alertness. Many jobs involve such a combination of extremes of hectic and boring work, together with strict control over time and movements that is physically and psychologically uncomfortable.

Overload and underload have been linked to increased excretions of catecholamine, a stress hormone (Spillane, 1984; Frankenhaeuser, 1981; Kahn, 1981). A study of sawmill workers found that those whose jobs were characterized by a lack of control over their situation (as a consequence of overload and underload) were most likely to have increased catecholamine excretions in their urine. These workers also reported feeling tired, tense, anxious, and ill more frequently than other workers (Frankenhaeuser and Gardell, 1976). Low control coupled with fast pace increases cortisol and adrenaline excretions (Karasek and Theorell, 1990). Some research has linked chronic work overload among blue-collar workers to myocardial infarction (Weiner, 1992: 88). Higher hospitalization rates for myocardial infarction (heart attacks) were related in another study to hectic monotonous work, lengthy and irregular work hours, and low degree of influence over timing holidays (Haynes, 1991: 159).

At times the pace and lack of control over motion may even produce a "stress epidemic" that is manifested through mass symptoms of dizziness, nausea, headaches, and hallucinationlike phenomena (Chase, 1980). This is most common where the work is routine, repetitive, and boring (Alexander and Fedoruk, 1986). Similar group outbreaks have also occurred in schools (Small and Borus, 1983). Some observers have noted that women are more susceptible to stress epidemics. However, this is not really due to gender but to the fact that women are more likely to end up with the lowest-status industrial manufacturing jobs (Chase, 1980). While such outbreaks have been attributed to purely psychological factors, exposure to solvents (even in levels below government standards for risk) might have, in fact, played a part in such outbreaks (Dew et al., 1989: 341).

The machine-paced nature of much work means that, in a sense, the human body must function like a machine. Since machines can tolerate what humans cannot, the gearing of the body to the rhythm and movements of a machine may have destructive physical effects. A sociologist who worked in a Hungarian tractor factory described how the time pressure of machine-paced work affected the way workers paid attention to physical signs that they are tired or uncomfortable:

> The best way I can put it is like this: *I* cease to exist. When the huge side doors of the workshop are opened and the transporters rattle in loaded with material, I *know*—without having a thought as such, I simply *know*—that I am in a freezing draught, but I do not *feel* that I am cold. My back aches, there is a cramp in my fingers, the piece rate is ridiculous: I don't feel or think any of this (Haraszti, 1978: 112).

One's working conditions can thus put one out of touch with one's own body.

Social class may be related to the individual's degree of sensitivity to illness (Koos, 1954). The fact that lower-class persons show decreased sensitivity to such symptoms as backaches, headaches, chronic tiredness, and coughing may be due to social conditions that deaden awareness of the body's messages. Tight and complex schedules, long hours, and shift work are the results of attempts to control workers' time in the interests of productivity. They often do so at the expense of workers' control over the quality of their lives.

To argue that our contemporary work hours are long may seem absurd in comparison to the nineteenth-century workweek of around 70 hours (Friedmann, 1961: 105). That period, however, was not typical. Industrial capitalism was then becoming a dominant force in Western society, and productivity was being enhanced mainly by lengthening the workday. By contrast, in agricultural societies the workweek was shorter (around 30 hours a week) and more in gear with seasonal rhythms, and workers frequently labored only about 15 weeks a year (Johnson, 1978; Eyer and Sterling, 1977).

In the United States, the number of hours per year that people work has increased since the late 1960s. From 1969 to 1987, the increase for men was nearly 100 work hours per year and for women, about 300 more hours a year. In Europe in recent decades, work hours have decreased, perhaps because of stronger unions. Paid vacation time required by law in Europe ranges from four to five weeks a year (Schor, 1992); the United States has no requirements for paid vacations and the standard paid vacation in the United States is less than half as long as in Europe.

Shift Work.   Working on shifts is another kind of temporal rhythm that is utterly unknown in many societies. As capitalism became the predominant form of economic and social organization in Western society, shift work became more common. By 1980, 11 percent of full-time U.S. workers were on late shifts (U.S. Department of Labor, 1981). Roughly 20 to 25 percent of U.S. workers are on some form of shift work (Blyton, 1985). In Europe the proportion of workers on shifts has increased overall since World War II, with the greatest increases among women and nonmanual (white-collar) workers (Blyton, 1985). Shift work became more common as the investment in machinery became greater and as it became profitable to sustain production around the clock. Some shift work is needed for technical reasons, such as a specific manufacturing process that cannot be interrupted. Certain service jobs (like those in hospitals) also require round-the-clock coverage. Most shift work, however, is instituted because it increases profits by maximizing the use of the equipment and space in which capital has been invested.

There are many different systems for arranging shifts. The most common is to have an early morning, late afternoon, and night shift (e.g., 5 A.M. to 1 P.M., 1 P.M. to 9 P.M., and 9 P.M. to 5 A.M.). The number of days worked on the same shift is called the rotation period. The most common rotation period is one week (Baker, 1981: 109).

Shift work often goes against the rhythms governing many bodily functions. Heart rate, body temperature, the production of various hormones, and metabolic rates all vary with the time of day, and seem to follow a 25-hour cycle called a circadian rhythm (Åkerstedt, 1990). One researcher suggests that shift work often violates workers' physiological rhythms by not giving them enough time to adjust from one cycle to another (Levi, 1981, 1978). One study exposed 100 volunteers to rotation periods that shifted between three days and three nights of continuous work. It was found that the circadian rhythms, geared to being awake during the day, persisted. The author concluded that although the endocrine system will eventually adapt to the shift, *long* rotation periods are necessary to adapt (Levi, 1978). However, most shift arrangements do not allow for this.[1] Studies show higher rates of sleep and digestive disorders among shift workers (Åkerstedt, 1990). While some argue that shift work has not demonstrated long-term serious effects on health (Poole et al., 1992), one study found a connection between cardiovascular disease and the amount of shift work done. Higher levels of serum cholesterol also were found among shift workers (Knutsson et al., 1986).

The time of the day a person must work affects sensory-motor performance (e.g., quickness of reflexes). It also has an impact on the metabolism (i.e., the body processing) of various chemicals and toxins to which individuals are exposed in the course of their work. How quickly the body absorbs a medication depends on what time of day it is taken. Similarly, how chemicals and other physical stressors affect the body may depend on the time of day of exposure, an issue that has not received much attention in research on time, work, and health (Baker, 1981: 117). Social factors often interact with physical stressors in complex ways.

Shift work, like overtime, may be formally voluntary in the terms of a union contract, but often financial pressures or fear of denying a superior's request may make what is formally voluntary in practice almost compulsory (Pfeffer, 1979: 87–88). Working overtime or on different shifts, furthermore, has social consequences for workers and their families. Shift work often intrudes into the worker's personal life, affecting leisure and social networks such as family and friendships. These changes in turn influence eating habits and sleep patterns, and may produce such adverse health consequences as digestive disorders. For these reasons, some countries, such as Sweden and Belgium, have laws that strongly limit the prevalence of shift work.

Some experiments allowing employees to have some control over their own time (e.g., flextime), by choosing to work longer days and shorter weeks or other alternatives to nine-to-five daytime hours, have been tried in the United States and Europe. In West Germany and Switzerland about 40 to 45 percent of the work force is on flextime; it is mainly a white-collar prerogative, but more blue-collar workers are on flextime in those countries than in the United States. About 8 percent of the U.S. work force has flextime, and those workers are concentrated in the service sector and among nonmanual workers in large-scale business enterprises (Blyton, 1985). Unfortunately, flextime experiments are often limited by overriding fears of declining productivity and managerial control.

---

[1]Some individuals adjust better than others; some prefer certain time cycles, and there are sometimes ways of arranging shifts so that workers have an opportunity to adjust. However, most workers, as opposed to owners or managers, do not have sufficient control over these matters and cannot set up temporal structures compatible with their individual needs.

Internalized Time Pressure

In addition to the workers' *externally* imposed time pressures, which are related to health problems, individuals also *internally* impose such pressures on themselves. Certain social structures, especially the hierarchical division of labor in modern societies, encourage and reinforce individual motivation to overwork. These hierarchical and manipulated job settings reflect larger societal stratification and cultural values (Garfield, 1980). Self-motivated workers, however, have internalized these values, becoming their own "slave drivers." The "workaholic," sometimes described as having a Type A personality, displays a behavior pattern produced by cultural values and social pressures experienced in the contexts of school, family, work, and other settings (Ivancevich and Matteson, 1988).

One of the dimensions of Type A behavior is a "time sickness"—an obsession with time and a constant time urgency. The physicians Friedman and Rosenman (1974) first became aware of this distinct pattern of behavior when they noticed that in the waiting room for their heart patients the front of the seats were all worn down: Their patients were literally sitting on the edge of their seats. Other dimensions of Type A include a competitive attitude, hostility, repressed anger, and a compulsion to be perfect.

Some studies have linked Type A behavior with health problems, especially coronary heart disease (Suls and Sanders, 1988; Haynes et al., 1980; Rosenman et al., 1975). Other research found that in response to high demands and loss of control Type A persons show more elevated heart rate, stress hormones, and blood pressure than Type B persons (Ivancevich and Matteson, 1988). Although research on the connection between Type A behavior and health problems has produced conflicting results (see Suls and Sanders, 1988; MacDougall et al., 1985; Shekelle et al., 1985), the concept is suggestive of some ways that cultural values and social pressures encourage the internalization of "sickening" attitudes.

People's socialization to these attitudes leads them to become their own source of time pressure. Type A is a personal style that motivates people to overload themselves constantly. Such personality patterns are encouraged by the norms and patterns of socialization characteristic of the future orientation, restlessness, and driven quality of modern capitalist-industrial societies. Middle-class socialization in the United States encourages a certain style of aggression and strongly emphasizes performing and achieving (Houben, 1991). In our society, with its work ethic and emphasis on constantly producing, getting ahead, and being competitive, many people incorporate such traits into their personality and practice them in extremes (Drummond, 1980).

Type A behavior is not simply a personality trait belonging to certain types of *individuals*; rather, it is produced in certain *social situations*. Many researchers see it as "in the nature of Type A people to produce Type A behavior" (Young, 1980: 139); however, this approach treats the style as an attribute, existing independently of the person's social situation. Nobody's behavior is totally independent of the situation that they are facing at a given moment. Even a Type B person will be more anxious if supervisory pressure is high. Some studies suggest that coronary-prone behavior patterns can be elicited by work settings (McQueen and Siegrist, 1982), especially those that are time pressured and competitive, and threaten personal control (Karasek and Theorell, 1990; Ivancevich and Matteson, 1988). Type A behavior may not be a *significant* risk factor in coronary heart disease unless combined with such stressful situations. The distinction that is often made between personality and social forces is a misleading one, however, since much of our personality is shaped in the course of our social experience.

Work Time, "Free" Time

A time urgency characterizes behavior not only in work time but also in *free* time. In fact, the character of leisure time is affected by work time. The two-week vacations that are common in the United States (compared to the average of four to six weeks in many other industrial countries) are directly affected by the other 50 weeks of work. Temporal rhythms of underload and overload affect life experiences other than work (Antonovsky, 1979: 187). A college professor who worked in a factory on his year of academic leave observed:

> Except for shopping at supermarkets that are open all kinds of hours, I could hardly run errands, go see a doctor, or do anything in the community. . . . I found myself torn between spending those few precious hours of waking leisure with my son, with my wife or by myself. I found myself, in short and with some important differences no doubt, trying to live with drastically curtailed and compressed free time as millions of American workers have learned to live, snatching moments of personal satisfaction largely from time not sold to others (Pfeffer, 1974: 41).

People who work in dull and restricting jobs tend to be less likely than those with interesting jobs to engage in "leisure activities requiring planning, participation and effort" (Frankenhaeuser, 1981: 492). Workers do not typically compensate for dull jobs with exciting, challenging leisure-time activities.

Not only may the rhythms of work time seep into the lunch hour, weekends, and holidays, but the *physiological* responses to work stress may also continue long after the workday is done. The physiological effects of work overload may spread to leisure hours, thus delaying their full impact (Frankenhaeuser, 1991). Many of us have experienced a form of work time carrying over into our free time when we are unable to adjust our sleep patterns during vacations and continue to wake up to an inner "alarm clock" geared to the memories of work time. The inability to unwind is accompanied by the hormonal system's inability to slow down, even in the absence of environmental demands. Thus workers who have been working overtime show elevations of catecholamines not only at work but through the next evening as well. The process of unwinding may be accompanied by an increase in psychosomatic problems (Levi, 1981: 53).

The inability to relax during free time is also the consequence of media and peer pressures to consume frenetically. While some people may shop as a way of relaxing or even as a means of affirming themselves ("I shop, therefore I am," is one mock motto), often free time ends up as rigidly scheduled as work time. The activity of consuming requires that commodities be bought, kept, and maintained. More time must be scheduled and compartmentalized to allow for shopping, getting to sales on time, and having goods repaired, waxed, shampooed, trimmed, and polished. Because time spent consuming must to some extent be scheduled, leisure time is therefore regimented. Sports and amusements may also mirror the rhythm and movement of the work world. One observer commented:

> Even days ostensibly outside daily routine, holidays, are occupied with "organized" sports and amusements which, far from being liberating forms of leisure facilitating participation in subjective atemporality, are ritualistic reaffirmations of the daily grind, veritable sermons or morality plays on the value of efficient use of "on" time and the rewards of synchronized cooperation. Indeed, unprogrammed, "idle," or "non-productive," time, eagerly sought and jealously safeguarded in more subjective cultures, is experienced as malaise in machine culture (Dye, 1981: 58–59).

A disciplined worker and a disciplined consumer go together hand-in-hand in our society.

So-called leisure time is often consumed by unpaid labor in the form of housework and the care of dependent children and elderly. In our society, this burden falls disproportionately on women. Parenting and housework are work, even though they are not socially recognized as paid, "productive" labor. These forms of work are characterized by recurring, boring, repetitive tasks; long hours; social isolation in the home; and many features, such as underload and overload, that characterize factory work (Chavkin, 1984; Stellman, 1977). Working mothers thus carry a double burden from both paid work and housework (Schor, 1992; Hochschild, 1989). Furthermore, those household tasks for which women are responsible tend to be those that must be done daily at a fixed time, whereas men's household tasks (e.g., fixing the car) allow for more flexibility in scheduling (Frankenhaeuser, 1991).

In one study, male managers "wound down" physiologically more rapidly after leaving work than did female managers, indicating the continued work pressures of a "second shift" that women face. Similar results have been found for women physicians (Theorell, 1991). Another study concluded that if men's and women's roles were more equal and they spent their time in the same way, "women would experience better health than men, more consistent with their greater longevity" (Bird and Fremont, 1991: 126).

The standardization of work time (such as the practice of working for eight hours from nine to five) also means that many people are excluded from paid work, including mothers who cannot afford child care, elderly people who must rest more often, and disabled people who may not function as effectively on a nine-to-five schedule. Since the industrial "revolution," there has been a trend to separate spheres of activity. Paid work is increasingly done *outside* the home, while in earlier days it was often done *at* home. This segregation of activities of work and home, together with the standardized workday, makes it difficult or impossible for mothers and others who cannot function on "normal" time to participate in the paid labor force.

It would be simplistic to assume that the unemployed poor merely have "time on their hands," without examining the quality of this time. The poor, both unemployed and employed, are unable to enjoy the privileges of time use that go with higher social class levels. For example, they spend a great deal of time waiting for various services in places such as emergency rooms, clinics, welfare offices, and courts. Such waiting can cost precious wages, especially since many services are not available after working hours. Middle-class people can take time off, and upper-status people can have the service brought to them (Henley, 1977). One's social position also influences the degree of access to other people's time and control over one's own use of time (Henley, 1977; Schwartz, 1973).

Elderly or disabled persons sometimes find themselves in surroundings that overwhelm them because they are unable to function at the speed demanded. In the right context, however, they might still be able to function well. Older people's disorientation and inability to function are sometimes interpreted as signs of senility; others' inability to function at "full speed" may be seen as a sign of mental or social disturbance. Thus, instead of seeing these problems as responses to environments that move uncomfortably fast or slow, we tend to treat them as personal, *internal* states of mind. When the environment of college students was experimentally sped up so that they could not maintain the pace, they also began to show irritability and the inability to function (Kastenbaum, 1971). Retirement and institutionalization lead people to experience "standard" time as irrelevant, thus atrophying time-related coping skills and contributing to behavior that may be incorrectly interpreted as evidence of senility.

There is an important relationship between time and health. The standard ways of socially scheduling activity often conflict with one's personal pace or biorhythms. A sharp discrepancy between the two will have an impact on one's health. Such a split between social time and our ability to keep up is prevalent in time-pressured, production-oriented Western societies. In a society as productive as ours, a shorter workweek with longer breaks, more flexible hours, and less time-pressured work should not be impossible. Despite two-day weekends and labor-saving devices, we seem to live in a world that is more time pressured than past societies and many present ones.

HEALTH AND SELF: BEING HELPLESS, FEELING WORTHLESS AND HOPELESS

What is the relationship between our sense of self and our health? Our sense of self is our experience of ourselves as unique and distinct persons. Our self-concept refers to our thoughts and feelings, both positive and negative, about ourselves as individuals. Much of our sense of self is developed during our socialization in response to other people's attitudes and treatment of us. How we feel about ourselves depends very much on both the extent to which various social interactions validate or affirm our sense of self and our social position (e.g., class, gender, and age). How competent and capable we feel to manage various stressors also contributes to our sense of self and health (Ben-Sira, 1985). Similarly, our self-image is related to ways we display ourself to others, or our presentation of self (Goffman, 1959). Some social settings force us to present ourselves in ways that are incompatible with our fundamental sense of who we are and what we are feeling; they may affect our sense of self and health. For example, salespersons who must smile in the face of insults and tirades from rude customers may experience this as an assault on their feelings about themselves and possibly also their health.

Our health is affected by our sense of self or self-presentation. An empowered self, one experiencing a sense of coherence (Antonovsky, 1987, 1979), can produce health. By contrast, "giving up" on life can be a significant catalyst for disease (Seligman, 1992; Levy and Heiden, 1990; Pelletier and Herzing, 1988; Engel, 1976; Schmale, 1972). A "dispirited" self (Jourard, 1964), characterized by a poor sense of self, a lack of a sense of control, and a feeling of being overwhelmed by events, has been linked to depression and anxiety (Johnson and Sarason, 1978). People with a poor conception of themselves take longer to recover from mononucleosis (Anderson, 1978). A study of West Point cadets found those who were unable to live up to their expectations of themselves were at higher risk for infectious mononucleosis (Kielcolt-Glaser and Glaser, 1991). Other studies found a sense of failure and self-devaluation to be characteristic in heart patients, patients with respiratory problems, and those suffering from ulcerative colitis (Totman, 1979). These and related studies suggest that intense and prolonged social invalidation, particularly when it is incorporated into a person's self-concept, may contribute to weakened bodily defenses, make it harder to cope with stressors, or heighten the sensation of such symptoms as pain (Feuerstein and Skjei, 1979).

Structural Sources of Self-Invalidation

Attacks on one's identity can be stressful (Cockerham, 1978) because the self is regarded as a sacred object in modern Western cultures. While being degraded or treated as incompetent has always been painful, the importance attached to the self has varied historically. Only in recent times has the self been conceived as an object, much less as a sacred object. How we feel about ourselves and who we are has become significant only in the last few centuries; the idea of a self-concept in psychology emerged in the twentieth century (Burns, 1979). The significance that people attach to the self, how they think about it, the importance they attach to various aspects of the self (such as self-control), and above all the social standards by which they judge themselves all depend on social and historical circumstances. As psychologist Fromm (1965: 311) observed,

> Thus modern man, instead of having to be forced to work as hard as he does, is driven by the inner compulsion to work which we have attempted to analyze in its psychological significance. Or instead of obeying overt authorities, he has built up an inner authority—conscience and duty—which operate more effectively in controlling him than any external authority would ever do.

The inability to live up to the demands of this "inner authority" leads to a sense of personal failure, even when the causes of failure are beyond an individual's control. This is particularly true given our society's emphasis on each individual's responsibility for one's fate. While modern Western society puts a value on the self and self-expression, it also systematically produces assaults on the self and limits self-expression. To some extent, the invalidation of people is built into the characteristic structure of economic and social inequality.

The effects of social inequality are aggravated in America by the myth that everyone can succeed and that if they fail, it is their own fault. In the nineteenth century, when this myth had somewhat greater basis in reality, American economic structure was more fluid and open, but now success may be harder to attain. Only a few achieve any measure of success in this system, while many are left behind. Sennett and Cobb (1972: 58) observe that "the creation of badges of ability requires the mass to be invisible men." The success ladder is endless, without a top rung, and plastic images of greater and greater success are flashed before people as constant reminders of their inadequacies. The media create superstars and celebrities of the moment. Even those who do achieve moderate success pay psychic costs in terms of their own guilt and the resentment of others. Sennett and Cobb argue that such guilt and resentment are built into the competitive social relationships that characterize our society. Because society pressures people to keep striving to escape a damaged sense of self, and because defeated people are more likely to blame themselves rather than the existing social arrangements, "American society benefits when it makes people feel anxious, defeated and self-reproachful for an imperfect ability to command the respect of others" (Sennett and Cobb, 1972: 153). These assaults on the self are attributed to personal deficiencies rather than to the *condition* of individual powerlessness. Many situations in our society make people feel powerless. One of the major sources of identity is work, yet significant assaults on people's sense of self take place in the work place.

Work, Self, and Health.   A sociopsychological approach to work is based on the assumption "that challenge and pride in work are fundamental ego needs and that any serious threat to these needs will endanger the individual's total well being" (Frankenhaeuser and Gardell, 1976: 39). Much work undermines workers' sense of self-esteem and job satisfaction. The absence of these two interrelated psychological factors, however, is a more important predictor of the risk of coronary heart disease than the presence of other relevant factors, such as poor diet, a lack of exercise, and smoking (House, 1974).

Pride and challenge in work are increasingly absent in many work places. Some surveys indicate that in the 1970s and early 1980s, workers have been more dissatisfied and discontented with their work than in previous decades (Pelletier, 1985). The reasons for increased dissatisfaction are not clear, but may include changes in the kind of people in the work force, lowered motivation, or greater willingness to voice criticism. Some of the increased dissatisfaction, however, may be due to changes in the work place itself.

Worker autonomy is being destroyed under bureaucratic and scientific management. Since World War II, more jobs have been "deskilled" (i.e., they require fewer skills, and are less complex, less challenging, and more boring). Machine-paced work, in addition to being stressful, may also have symbolic meanings—for instance, symbolizing a low-status job or that one is, oneself, a machine (Houben, 1991: 319). The rhythms and motions of the assembly line have come to characterize even white-collar work and help to erode self-esteem and job satisfaction (Howard, 1985; Glenn and Feldberg, 1977; Braverman, 1974).

Workers may perceive the stressfulness of machine-paced work conditions but see their inability to cope as a sign of their own lack of competence. Insofar as they take the situation as natural and accept company production norms as demands that *should* be manageable, their inability to manage stressors erodes their sense of self. The impersonal nature of controls in places like the computerized work place, described earlier, makes it harder to locate the actual agent responsible for imposing stress. The problem is "in the system," and since it is hard to get angry at a system, workers often fault themselves (Howard, 1985: 89–90). One author observed that "to the degree that workers internalize the values of corporate culture, they tend to blame themselves for its contradictions" (Howard, 1985: 137).

Supervisors may constantly remind many workers of their childlike status. They address workers in terms appropriate for children, such as calling women "girls." Some workers have to ask their supervisor for permission to go to the bathroom and are reprimanded for overly lengthy bowel evacuations (Howard, 1985; Pfeffer, 1979; Garson, 1977). *Reader's Digest* gave its employees report cards, perpetuating a child-like treatment typical of school settings (Garson, 1977). One phone company manager, referring to women working in his department, stated: "These girls are just an interface between the customer and computer" (quoted in Howard, 1985: 56). Thus workers may be treated not only as children ("these girls"), but even worse, as a *thing* ("an interface").

Negative sanctions that stigmatize the individual for deviations from, for instance, norms of productivity, are among the means organizations use for social control. They label workers who deviate as "shirkers," "disloyal" employees, "malingerers," and so on. These labels assault the person's sense of self and may be a source of chronic stress in work organizations. Similarly, workers may feel "underappreciated" and not respected as individuals. Sanctions used as a means of social control in work settings may thus act as chronic stressors by affecting a worker's sense of self (Houben, 1991).

Unemployment and Health.   If work can be a health hazard, so too can unemployment (Catalano, 1991). In our society work is an important source of many people's sense of self. The loss of one's job involves more than a loss of financial resources; it may also result in loss of part of one's work-related social network. The stress of unemployment can place a strain on one's relationships with family and friends (Atkinson et al., 1986). Nonemployment, as well as loss of employment, may adversely affect health. Some studies show that women who are employed outside the homes (even if they also do housework) tend to have better health than those who are not employed (Hibbard and Pope, 1993; Vågero, 1992; Loscocco and Spitze,

1990; Cleary, 1987). Underemployment may also affect self-esteem because people who need to work settle for jobs that do not utilize their abilities or pay adequate wages and fringe benefits. People with disabilities and women with children are especially likely to be underemployed, since the work place seldom accommodates their special needs (see Serrin, 1989).

Massive unemployment, such as a factory closing, can rip apart the social fabric of a community, affecting not only those who are laid off but also neighborhoods where workers owned homes and local businesses patronized by workers. Unemployment statistics do not adequately capture the concrete psychophysiological effects of unemployment on health. As one author observed,

> Unemployment, with its associated alienation and loss of self-esteem, takes a heavy toll on the lives of Western psychotics. The negative symptoms of schizophrenia—apathy, withdrawal, restricted emotions and lack of interest in the world around—may be to a degree the common psychological effects of long-term unemployment. Every time the economy goes into a decline, mental-hospital admissions for psychosis in working-age people increase. Economic stress and unemployment, by triggering the onset of new cases or worsening already apparent illness, may well account for this phenomenon (Warner, 1986: 51—52).

Brenner (1976) has estimated that between 1970 and 1975, a 1.4 percent increase in unemployment was related to an additional 1,500 suicides, 26,000 deaths from cardiovascular and kidney diseases, 870 deaths from cirrhosis of the liver, and 5,500 mental hospital admissions. A relatively small increase in unemployment thus produced extensive human mental and physical costs. Because he found that there is a consistent relationship, over a number of decades, between an increase in unemployment and higher mental hospital admissions and stress-related diseases, Brenner (1979) argued that economic instability and insecurity increase the likelihood of unhealthy habits and that the stress of unemployment disrupts social networks. In addition to having a direct physiological impact on people's bodies, the stress of unemployment may increase the tendency to adopt destructive coping habits (e.g., smoking and drinking) and may strain social relationships. Brenner's research has been questioned, however, because it is not clear whether the factors he implicated were actually the cause or the result. Perhaps poor health itself tends to produce unemployment, rather than the reverse. Although his findings need to be supplemented by more small-scale and detailed qualitative studies, on the whole, such studies seem to confirm the general relationship between unemployment and illness (Buss and Redburn, 1983; Liem, 1981).

Case studies of particular communities have documented the link between unemployment and some mental problems such as suicide, schizophrenia, and depression (Buss and Redburn, 1983; Jahoda et al., 1971). Detailed analyses of small samples also confirm the connection between unemployment and health. Cobb and Kasl (1977) applied sophisticated psychological and physiological measures to study a small group of people before and after a plant closing. They found that job loss increased the likelihood of suicide. The workers' levels of cholesterol, norepinephrine, and epinephrine (i.e., stress hormones) were also higher after the layoffs, which suggests that unemployment may increase the likelihood of such physiological problems as coronary heart disease and hypertension.

Another study found that the economic recession in the early 1980s had significant health-damaging effects (Kessler et al., 1987). One advantage of this study was that the researchers controlled for the possibility that during periods of layoffs, workers' psychological and physical health might affect how quickly they would be laid off, a selection bias that would obscure the relationship between unemployment and health. Unemployment itself should not be treated as a stressor utterly independent of a host of other factors affecting the stressfulness of the unemployment experience. High levels of social support may buffer a person against the stressful effects of being out of a job, although unemployment may also put a strain on social support resources.

Some researchers have suggested that health is adversely affected not only by unemployment and downward swings in the business cycle but also by periods of relative prosperity when unemployment is *low*. Eyer (1977) argued that in these "boom" times, mobility and the attendant social dislocation, as well as job stress and pressures to succeed, are especially high; all of these factors increase health risks. Eyer noted that death rates are lower during periods of high unemployment and higher in times of rapidly expanding employment (Eyer, 1977; Eyer and Sterling, 1977). Is this difference due to greater exposure to job-related physical risks or increased psychosocial stress? Relationships between the fluctuation of business cycles and changes in health status are difficult to assess, in part because there are often time lags between the experience of a stressor and its health consequences. Such studies, while raising intriguing questions, are done on such a broad and general scale that they can yield only crude results that must be interpreted cautiously. Numerous studies, however, confirm at least some connection between unemployment and illness.

Other Contexts of Self-Invalidation. Social conditions encountered later in life can reinforce a lack of self-esteem that often builds upon an already injured sense of self that developed as a part of the individual's early family experience. Pearlin (1983: 6) concluded that:

> the family does have a dimension to its place in the stress process that sets it apart from occupations, however. It is, of course, a major reservoir of problems and tribulations. Multiple facets of marital relations, parent-child encounters, and the transitional points along the family life cycle have been viewed as fertile ground out of which stress can grow. It is likely, too, to be an arena in which problems generated elsewhere are transplanted. But the family domain, unlike occupation, is also the place where the wounds that people incur outside are most likely to be healed. The family is truly many things to its members: it is commonly an active and rich source of pain, and it is just as commonly where people turn to find relief from pain. In the stress process, it stands in a uniquely pivotal position.

Several studies suggest that those whose families make them feel powerless, force them to surrender their autonomy, or inhibit their displays of anger in response to arbitrary authority will experience subsequent health problems (Seligman, 1992; Doherty and Campbell, 1988; Sagan, 1987; Pratt, 1976; Schneider, 1975; Laing and Esterson, 1965).

Those who display physical or mental "brokenness" are particularly likely to experience attacks on their sense of self. Our society, with its strong values on the ability to work, has little use for those who are not productive by these standards. Thus it devalues physically or mentally handicapped, aged, and disabled persons. One of the primary goals of self-help movements, such as the Gray Panthers, an activist organization for the young and old, and the Center for Independent Living in Berkeley, California, has been to escape the trap of being treated as invisible, socially dead, and nonexistent.

Some invalidating consequences of the social structure are amplified by total institutions (such as hospitals) and social service organizations. An ethnographic study of a nursing home provides an excellent example of such structurally produced invalidation (Gubrium, 1975). In this institution, as in others, top staff, floor staff, and patient-residents inhabited very different social worlds; the communication that passed between them was distorted by hierarchical arrangements. In making room assignments and other decisions, the top staff worked from simplified, one-dimensional pictures of patient-residents that were constructed with input from the floor staff, but very little input from the patients themselves. Some evidence suggests that individuals' freedom of choice in entering a nursing home is an important predictor of their longevity (Seligman, 1992). A sense of control over one's life affairs—a sense of being empowered—may be crucial in dealing with institutional stressors, such as those found in hospitals (Volicer, 1978, 1977).

In the course of people's experiences in the family, work situations, and other institutional settings, they may be "persuaded" that they are incompetent or worthless as they simultaneously learn to value competence and control, and to regard the self as a sort of sacred object. Invalidation of our selves can be stressful, even when it is not internalized and made part of our self-conception.

Dramaturgical Stress.   One author suggested that "stress could be induced when an individual perceives his chosen face or performance in a given situation to be inconsistent with the concept of self he tries to maintain for himself and others in that situation" (Cockerham, 1978: 49). **Dramaturgical stress** is generated by role playing, managing the impression one makes on others, and particularly by being forced to keep up social appearances that are inconsistent with one's real feelings and concept of self. Some research suggests that there are physiological consequences to situations of great discrepancy between the way one must present oneself to others and the emotional-psychological reaction to others that the situation elicits. In one experiment, some subjects responded to provocative situations by expressing overt hostility ("anger out"). Persons displaying "anger in" responses were more likely to blame themselves and not express overt hostility. "Anger in" respondents exhibited more extended physical stress reactions than the "anger out" group (Funkenstein et al., 1957).

Some researchers have identified a complex of coping patterns, which they call "Type C" and describe as "being 'nice', stoic or self-sacrificing, cooperative and appeasing, unassertive, patient, compliant with external authorities, and unexpressive of negative emotions, particularly anger" (Temoshok, 1990: 209). One component of this coping style, the suppression of emotions such as anger, has been linked tentatively to cancer progression (Temoshok, 1990: 209). Links between emotional states or personal styles and development of cancer are *very* tenuous, and we should be cautious not to isolate personal tendencies from ongoing social contexts, viewing responses as characteristics of individuals. Nonetheless, these findings suggest that some people are socialized to respond habitually to social circumstances in ways that may heighten adverse health consequences.

In a laboratory experiment, anger was induced experimentally by having a colleague arbitrarily harass and insult subjects while they were trying to solve a problem. The subjects' anger resulted in increases in their blood pressure. Those who could express their hostility toward the experimenter's colleague by giving him what they believed was a mild electric shock (actually a fake one) had their blood pressure return to normal more rapidly. Those who were not allowed to display anger in this fashion continued to show signs of elevated blood pressure long after the harassment had stopped (Hokanson and Burgess, 1962). Similarly, when a person's overt physical movements (such as jumping up) in response to a stressor (such as hearing a gunshot) are repressed, it takes longer for that person's physical functions to return to a prestress response state (Gellhorn, 1969). Such laboratory experiments only suggest how everyday life situations that continuously require certain people, such as powerless social minorities, to repress their anger in the face of the arbitrary exercise of power, might lead to permanently elevated blood pressure.

Minority Status.   Fanon, the Algerian psychiatrist, has dealt with the connections between racial and colonial domination and psychological and physical well-being. In the following passage, he linked muscular tension and illness in Algerians to their powerlessness in the face of French colonial authority:

> This particular form of pathology (a generalized muscular contraction) had already called forth attention before the revolution began. But the doctors described it by portraying it as a congenital stigma of the native, an "original" part of his nervous system where it was stated, it was possible to find the proof of a predominance of the extra-pyramidal system in the native. The contracture is in fact simply the postural accompaniment to the native's reticence and the expression in muscular form of his rigidity and his refusal with regard to colonial authority (Fanon, 1963: 293).

Since it was not possible for the colonized Algerians to express anger openly toward colonial authority, it was held in but manifested itself in the form of muscular tension. Note also that the effects of a social problem (colonial rule) were viewed by the colonial doctors as an inherited, individual problem.

Encounters with authority, particularly when it is experienced as arbitrary or oppressive, can be stressful, even when the invalidation stemming from such situations is not internalized. Some researchers suggest that the high rates of hypertension among black males cannot be explained by diet, genetic, and other factors alone. They speculate that since black males may be exposed to more anger-provoking encounters with arbitrary authority (e.g., in regard to housing, employment, and the law) than other groups but cannot express their anger, the invalidation of their emotional responses might well contribute to their greater incidence of hypertension (Harburg et al., 1973). Suppressed anger has been implicated in the development of hypertension (Pickering et al., 1991). Socialization to suppress hostility may be especially high among the "respectable poor" of the upwardly mobile, upper-lower class, who emphasize the importance of politeness, or those who respect and emulate upper-status people (Harburg et al., 1973). The demand that one always be polite and civil—no matter how rude someone else may be—represents a form of social control. The strict control over anger is a norm in our society (Stearns and Stearns, 1986; Elias, 1982, 1978).

Other relatively powerless minorities also experience much dramaturgical stress. Those who must cope with a social stigma by concealing their identity under a cloak of "normal" appearances face special stresses. For example, in our society the widespread fear of homosexuality (homo-phobia) pressures homosexuals to hide their true selves in order to survive psychological and social expectations, yet trying to "pass" as heterosexuals may place them under considerable dramaturgical stress. In addition to the self-hatred that comes from internalizing antigay values and the repressed anger that results from discrimination, they may suffer from the constant fear of disclosure:

> Visible lesbians are treated as outcasts or queers. They are ignored, fantasized about, and played with. Lesbians are subject to verbal and physical harassment. Closeted lesbians live in fear of being found out. A lesbian's family may be a source of stress for her as coming out to one's family can often mean risking anger, pain or exile. Drifting apart from one's family may be the result of not coming out (O'Donnel, 1978: 14).

"Closets" are the refuge of the powerless, but the use of this refuge has its price. "Closets are a health hazard" was a slogan first used by the physicians marching in the 1981 Gay Freedom Day Parade in San Francisco.

Dramaturgical Stress and Work

As more and more people work in corporate and bureaucratic settings, a great deal of control over the presentation of self becomes an important part of their work skills. To get along, manners and politeness become tools for the efficient and effective accomplishment of work (Mumford, 1963: 139). Many skills of self-presentation require what Hochschild (1983) calls "**emotion work**," or the activity through which we control how we show our feelings. Emotion work involves both repressing "undesirable" emotions, such as displays of anger, and forcing oneself to appear happy and enthusiastic, even when one does not feel that way.

The proportion of jobs providing services has increased in our economy. Those that involve some form of selling (e.g., salesclerk or stockbroker) or provide emotional services such as friendliness or reassurance (e.g., social worker or flight attendant) have especially increased (Hochschild, 1983). These service jobs demand elaborate skills in self-presentation and in managing one's emotions (both of which entail emotion work). As Fromm (1965: 268) observed,

> If you do not smile you are judged lacking in a "pleasing personality" and you need to have a pleasing personality if you want to sell your services whether as a waitress, a salesman or a physician. Only those at the bottom of the social pyramid, who sell nothing but their physical labor, and those at the very top do not need to be particularly pleasant.

In his description of the white-collar stratum that has replaced more entrepreneurally oriented middle class, Mills (1956: xvii) noted that the management of one's personality has increasingly become an essential work skill "of commercial relevance and required for the more efficient and profitable distribution of goods and services." This demand for "pleasing personalities," particularly in the face of job conditions that are anything but pleasing, can be highly stressful and often require workers to deny their emotional responses to those stressors.

A study of bank employees found that when the emotional and physical appearances demanded of workers conflicted with their own sense of self, they began to experience self-artificiality. Bureaucratized structures, particularly those with commercial goals, are most likely to produce this tension between the public face and private self (Karasek and Theorell, 1990: 33; Jackall, 1977). The rude customer who "is always right," the demand for geniality in the face of social isolation within the office, the interpersonal competitiveness, and the hierarchical pressures all produce dramaturgical stress in the work place (Freund, 1982).

Emotion work entails more than merely assuming a smiling mask, because that would come across as insincere. Rather one must convince oneself, to some extent, that one's angry reaction is not valid. Hochschild (1983) describes how flight attendants are taught to see the nasty customer as a victim and one's own angry response as unnecessary. In other words, they are expected to convince themselves that they feel something other than what they are feeling. Such invalidation of one's emotions may have long-term health consequences, especially as the split between what one feels and what one shows may become automatic, not merely a temporary mask that one assumes voluntarily.

Furthermore, one may lose touch with one's visceral ("gut") reactions because of the constant work requirement to "sell" a certain kind of personality and feelings.[2] Emotion work may short-circuit the experience of signals about people and places that feelings provide (Hochschild, 1983), and put people out of touch with their own bodily reactions. (See Box 5.1.)

---

[2]Those prone to high blood pressure may respond to stress neuroendocrinologically in more dramatic fashion. They are "high reactors" who in their demeanor show a "cool" exterior, are more controlled emotionally, and do not experience sudden and large fluctuations in their blood pressure; for instance, they usually do not blush (Lynch, 1985). It would be worth investigating how these psychosomatic splits are encouraged by such work conditions as the ones just described.

BOX 5.1   *DRAMATURGICAL STRESS AND BLOOD PRESSURE: THE CASE OF A
HOSPITAL ADMINISTRATIVE AIDE*

Researchers placed blood pressure and pulse monitors on participants in one study and
correlated the changes in these stress indicators with activities and social pressures
throughout the day. The case of one hospital aide exemplifies workplace stress.

Her peak reading at the office—a diastolic pressure of 77—came in the morning
when she was mediating a dispute between two secretaries . . . . She hit this level again
just before lunch when she was in that perennial secretarial bind: politely taking orders
from someone who annoys you.

In this case, it was a patient, a tense, well-dressed suburban matron convinced that
something was wrong with her despite repeated tests showing she was healthy. . . . At
that moment, there were two real emergencies going on—doctors were rushing in and
out of the office to consult about a women near death on an operating table, and a cardiac patient from another hospital needed to be transferred by helicopter to the medical
center. In the midst of all this, Collins spent 15 minutes negotiating appointments for
the matron; her voice remaining pleasant, but her diastolic pressure peaking and her
pulse hitting 90.

Source: John Tierney, "Wired for Stress," *The New York Times Magazine*, May 15, 1988: 81.

INFORMATIONAL TROUBLES AND
INSTITUTIONAL CONTEXTS

Appropriate and adequate information about our environment can significantly help
us manage our lives and their stressors and strains by providing a sense of security
as well as feelings of efficacy and competence. **Informational troubles** occur when
people do not get enough feedback about their actions or about potential threats in
their environment, and can seriously affect our health. Workers, patients, students,
inmates, and other relatively powerless groups often may not understand the rationale behind actions such as firings, hirings, reprimands, parole denials, and tenure
denials. Chronic discrepancies between an institution's logic and individuals' understanding of reality is a source of informational troubles.

The following story of institutional life illustrates the impact of short-circuited
information on a resident's sense of personal efficacy and health:

A female patient who had remained in a mute state for nearly 10 years was shifted to a
different floor of her building along with her floor mates, while her unit was being re-
decorated. The third floor of this psychiatric unit where the patient in question had been
living was known among the patients as the chronic, hopeless floor. In contrast, the first
floor was most commonly occupied by patients who held privileges, including the freedom to come and go on the hospital grounds and to the surrounding streets. In short, the

first floor was an exit ward from which patients could anticipate discharge fairly rapidly. All patients were given medical examinations prior to the move, and the patient in question was judged to be in excellent medical health though still mute and withdrawn.

Shortly after moving to the first floor, this chronic psychiatric patient surprised the ward staff by becoming socially responsive such that within a two week period she ceased being mute and was actually becoming gregarious. As fate would have it, the redecoration of the third-floor unit was soon completed and all previous residents were returned to it. Within a week after she had been returned to the "hopeless" unit, this patient, who like the legendary Snow White had been aroused from a living torpor, collapsed and died. The subsequent autopsy revealed no pathology of note, and it was whimsically suggested at the time that the patient had died of despair (Lefcourt, 1973: 422).

This woman may have given up on life because of the way she *perceived* her return to the chronic ward. Her previously learned helplessness may have aggravated her despair. Another important element, however, is how the social structure of the hospital contributed to her death. The institution was unaware of her perceptions, the implications of her changed behavior, and the consequences of returning her to a "helpless" chronic ward. Her inability to make her needs known to the staff and the staff's inability to perceive her needs were linked to two factors that were to some extent built into the hospital: her social status as a resident and her powerlessness in the face of how the institution regulated behavior and made decisions about her life. Her "giving up," while an extreme reaction, was thus not simply a feature of her personality or state of mind but also her response to institutional conditions that were neither created nor readily changeable by her.

Informational Troubles and Illness

Uncertainty about information important to one's security has physiological consequences that in the long run may adversely affect one's health. Research on rats found that lack of predictability is linked to greater pathological responses to a stressor (Weiss, 1972) and to changes in the immune system (Mormede et al., 1988). Other studies connect uncertainty with neurohormonal changes (Levine and Wiener, 1989).

Studies suggest that social environments may be damaging when they leave a person uncertain in the face of a threat (Kiritz and Moos, 1974). Similarly, situations in which individuals receive inadequate or inaccurate feedback from their environment are especially stressful, because people literally cannot know what to expect and hence how to act (Levin and Idler, 1981). Ambiguities about one's appropriate role and one's effectiveness in that role may also be unhealthful (Garfield, 1980). Unsatisfactory connections between expectations and actual experience have been linked to stress and eventually to lowered immunity (Moss, 1973). While some informational troubles are due to disturbances in the individual's own perceptions, many organizational settings generate or amplify informational uncertainty. Similarly, structural factors (such as social class and age) contribute to informational troubles by creating chronic discrepancies between expectations[3] and experience, and between actions and their consequences:

> An individual's appraisal of his own performance, his self-esteem and sense of identity are partly dependent on his value system and the information feedback he received from his social milieu. When the promulgated values are discrepant and conflicting, the individual will have greater difficulty in choice and decision-making as well as in attaining a sense of competence, which enhances self-esteem and satisfaction (Lipowski, 1973: 523).

In short, the lack of information and adequate feedback from one's environment has an impact on one's self-esteem and sense of competence.

Informational Troubles in the Work Place

Informational troubles are generated by features inherent in various bureaucratic and corporate structures of everyday modern life. In work settings, much production is characterized by a marked organizational split between those who manage work and those who execute various tasks. On an informational level, the split is between knowledge about the planning and control of production and about its execution.

One of the "social functions of ignorance" is the maintenance of control over clients or workers (Moore and Tumin, 1949). As a college teacher who worked in a factory during his sabbatical observed:

> As indicated, the factory worker's subordinate and related vulnerability is affected in part by the company's keeping from the workers sufficient advance information about the factors of production and intentions of the company so likely to affect their lives. . . . Keeping workers ignorant also helps management control them. Ignorance particularly in the face of economic instability, makes workers insecure, hanging on for information in company handouts that consistently come too late for a meaningful response. Management treats information as a part of its private property and uses information to protect its own authoritarian rule (Pfeffer, 1979: 103–104).

Workers, for example, are seldom told the rationale for establishing production goals (Haraszti, 1978: 61), even though they structure and affect the quality of working life.

Management also controls information about dangers in the work environment. Many companies do not tell their workers, or the workers' doctors, the generic names of the chemicals to which workers are exposed. Because these substances as well as dangerous production processes are often protected as "trade" secrets, only the trade name, a code number, or a general description of its use is provided (Howard, 1985).

Workers who experience symptoms such as nausea, rashes, or headaches may

---

[3]Although Moss (1973), Antonovsky (1987, 1979), and Totman (1979) have suggested that informational troubles can affect health, they do not adequately demonstrate how the degree of power that accompanies one's social status and the way behavior is regulated in various social settings create informational troubles. Further research needs to establish more clearly the connections among social structure, controls specific to that structure, various kinds of informational troubles, and the stress they produce.

suspect that the cause is the substances they work with, but they cannot get definitive information from management (Howard, 1985; Nelkin and Brown, 1984; Berman, 1978; Scott, 1974). Their only knowledge about the effects of these chemicals may come from rumors or indirect indicators, such as the fact that those working in high-risk areas are asked to "spit in the can" (i.e., give specimens for sputum cytologies) or give urine samples (Kingsport Study Group, 1978: 61). A local doctor in a Tennessee Eastman (a part of Eastman Kodak) "company town" reports seeing telltale symptoms of work-related health problems in many of his worker-patients or hearing accounts of illness their coworkers are experiencing. He concluded, "But you never read about this in the paper. The only way you get it is through the grapevine. Some of the grapevine is probably inaccurate, but I have a feeling as a physician that I'm seeing the tip of the iceberg" (quoted in Kingsport Study Group, 1978: 60). One worker in the microchip electronics industry, where the work often involves solvents and acids remarked,

> People don't know what they are working with because they're never *told* what they're working with. I was never informed of the hazards. Oh, I was told that I was working with acid and that it could burn me, yes. But I was never told about the possible carcinogens or the effects of the solvent inhalation (quoted in Howard, 1985: 158).

Like the doctor-patient and professional-client relationships, the manager-worker relationship is characterized by unequal access to important information. Management's monopoly over knowledge is a resource that keeps management's options open, and protects against lawsuits, strikes, and other critical actions. Such managerial control over information, however, also affects client or worker security, autonomy, and often health.

Imagine feeling some symptoms, having an uneasiness about the substances you work with, or hearing rumors, and yet being uncertain of how those substances might affect you.[4] Such uncertainty aggravates an individual's sense of powerlessness and insecurity. These informational troubles often result in an inability to predict and plan or know the sources of one's distress. To remedy some of this uncertainty, Norway has legislation requiring that workers be informed about systems used in planning and controlling of production, that they be given training to understand such systems, and that they be able to influence their design. In Sweden, the law requires that workers on all levels be given comprehensive information about working conditions and their hazards (Levi, 1981: 119–120).

SOCIAL SUPPORT

As discussed in Chapter 4, humans' biological makeup makes them open to influences from the social environment, including relationships with other people. The loss of a spouse or intimate friend can be a stressor of such magnitude that it precip-

---

[4]Recall the study by House et al. (1979) cited in Chapter 4. How might informational stress interact with the respiratory effects of the chemical (i.e., the chemical stressor)?

itates something like voodoo death (Engel, 1971). Bereavement can increase the risk of coronary problems (Pilisuk and Parks, 1986: 33) and lower immunity (Bartrop et al., 1977). Mourning and separation from loved ones can affect levels of stress hormones (Pilisuk and Parks, 1986: 45). Yet although the withdrawal of social support or a diminished quality of social relationships can have a sickening impact on us, social bonds also have the potential to heal us.

Social support is one source of the individual's sense of empowerment. It may seem strange and perhaps a bit clinical to think of our relationships with lovers, family, friends, and fellow workers or students in terms of power, yet social ties can serve as nets that hold us up or keep us from falling when we are threatened. They function as sources of information and financial or other kinds of aid, and as mirrors that help to reflect back to us messages of self-affirmation. Just as a fetus needs a womb to receive nourishment, shelter, warmth, and life support, human beings cannot function effectively as isolated individuals.

Social support is a general term for the many different resources that aid persons in times of crisis and help them cope with life. Social relationships empower individuals by making them feel that they are part of a larger social order. They are also a source of self-validation and a sense of personal security (Pilisuk and Parks, 1986). As symbols of those relationships, physical contact and intimacy can be empowering. Other people can remind us that we are alive and have someone to lean on and depend on when necessary, and generally enhance our sense of security and self-confidence. Emotional support is one of the most important ways social support empowers individuals (House, 1981).

This support may involve touch. Since many measures of social support use paper-and-pencil methods such as questionnaires, human touch has not been adequately investigated as a medium of emotional support. Giving social support may involve subtle cues like body language and tone of voice, which often go unnoticed by the researcher-observer (Pilisuk and Parks, 1986: 39). While the effects of social contact may not be mentally perceived, they still may have an impact on our bodies. Lynch (1979) cited some clinical observations that a nurse's touch can affect the blood pressure of even a comatose patient. Under the stress of electric shocks, dogs who were petted responded to these stressors with fewer pathological consequences than animals who were not touched. Another study found that rabbits on a high-fat diet that were not touched were more likely to develop heart disease than those that were cuddled and petted (House et al., 1988). While animal experiments should be used cautiously when generalizing to humans, these studies suggest that nonverbal aspects of social relationships may have health consequences.

Pearlin (1983) emphasizes that social support reduces strain by preventing the loss of self-esteem and aiding a sense of mastery that overwhelming stressors can erode. Social support empowers by giving individuals a sense that they are valued, esteemed, cared for, and belong to a network of mutual obligation. These are primarily *emotional* functions of social support, which also serves an *instrumental* purpose. Social support can provide useful information and material resources (such as financial aid) as well as other help (Levin and Idler, 1981). Support can also encourage recovery from an illness, for example, by encouraging a family member to do therapeutic exercises. Other social networks also promote such health habits as regular exercise, good eating habits, and adequate sleep.

Social Support and Health

In the classic study *Suicide*, Durkheim ([1897] 1951) found a relationship between rates of suicide and the degree to which individuals were integrated into their group, which he measured with indicators such as divorce rates. Thus a group with high rates of divorce should show a high rate of suicide. Conversely, a more integrated group should have a lower rate.[5] Durkheim was the first social scientist to demonstrate that suicide was not simply an *individual* psychological issue but also to some extent a social and cultural phenomenon influenced by such factors as the strength of social bonds. Much of the literature on social support and health follows in this tradition by making similar associations between social isolation and poor health. We must also consider the possibility of a reverse causal relationship, that is, that poor health may lead to social isolation (House et al., 1988).

Social isolation itself can be stressful. Some research indicates that low integration into social networks contributes to poor health, even when significant stressors are absent (Gore, 1978: 158). A comprehensive study showing the link between social factors and health was conducted by Berkman and Syme (1979) on a large population in Alameda County, California. They used measures of four types of social contact: (1) marriage partners, (2) close friends and relatives, (3) members of a church, and (4) informal or formal associations. Those who had contacts with any of these groups evidenced lower mortality rates than those who did not. The authors of this study recognized the problem of *causal direction:* Does illness cause a person to withdraw and others to withdraw from that person, or does social isolation generate sickness? Therefore, they analyzed groups with every kind of health status and found that even among those who were sick, persons with higher levels of social contact had lower mortality rates. Persons with extensive social connections were likely to smoke and drink less, and to eat and sleep more regularly than those with few social connections. This finding suggests that social relationships also protect health by encouraging good health habits (Wallston et al., 1983).

Another study, analyzing pregnancy complications, found that neither high stress nor the lack of support, in and of themselves, increased such problems. When major stressors were combined with a low degree of social support, however, there were significantly higher numbers of complications. Women who had high stress and high levels of social support experienced fewer difficulties than those who had a lot of stressful events but not much support. When the levels of stress were low, the absence of social support did not have a notable impact on complications (Nuckolls et al., 1972). This evidence suggests that social support helped to buffer women against

---

[5]Durkheim also recognized that groups fostering *too much* integration could encourage what he called "altruistic suicide," such as the deaths of Japanese Kamikaze pilots who crashed their planes into Allied warships during World War II.

the effects of high stress. Most research finds social support to be either a primary *causal* factor (i.e., a *main* effect) in determining health or a *mediating* factor, which may protect the person from the full impact of the stressor.

Lynch (1979) argues that social isolation can both contribute to coronary heart disease and adversely affect a person's recovery from a heart attack. Although much of his evidence is indirect and the quality of his data uneven, as a whole it provides compelling evidence that social isolation can influence us physiologically and hence affect our health. Lynch emphasized that social contact (or what he calls "dialogue") is of chief importance for health.

Mortality rates are considerably lower among those who are married than among those who are single or formerly married. Some studies also show differences between those who are married and those who are not in death rates from cirrhosis of the liver, tuberculosis, and pneumonia (Levin and Idler, 1981; Lynch, 1979). While such evidence is in line with our cultural assumptions about the importance of family life, it must be interpreted cautiously. Marital status tells us nothing about the quality of social contact. Many people are formally married but psychologically live alone and feel isolated from each other, whereas divorced and other single people may participate in rich social lives. Unhappy marital relationships can cause greater health risk than can the absence of a partner (Kielcolt-Glaser and Glaser, 1991: 860–861).

Social support is also a potential mediator of negative effects of unemployment on health by offering a sense of empowerment. A longitudinal study of men who were laid off from work found that those with higher degrees of social support reported fewer symptoms of illness and showed lower levels of cholesterol. Conversely, those with lower levels of support had higher levels of cholesterol and reported more illness symptoms (Gore, 1978).

Social support is also important in the work place, where it buffers work-related stress (Hibbard and Pope, 1993; Waxler-Morrison et al., 1991; House, 1981; LaRocco and House, 1980). A study of NASA workers found that good work relationships protected them from the effects of such stress (Caplan, 1972). Further investigation is needed on how particular organizational forms encourage or discourage social support. For example, how do cultural factors, such as an emphasis upon competitiveness and individualism, affect the possibility for supportive relationships in the work place? As two authors observed, "social currents of careerism, autonomy, mobility, privacy and achievement that disrupt our traditional roots and ties also make difficult the continuity of new bonds" (Pilisuk and Parks, 1986: 59). Do stressors in the work place, such as high noise levels, also inhibit social interaction? While social support may be empowering, it is also important to examine how control over work conditions makes social support possible.

Limitations of Social Support Research

Much of the social support literature makes several assumptions that are problematic. First, social support should not be treated as a stable, constant factor; levels of social support do not necessarily remain the same over time. Second, stressful events (stressors) and social support are not independent factors, but rather interact with each other (Atkinson et al., 1986). Just as social support may protect a person against a stressor (such as unemployment), so too may a stressor (such as unemployment) affect levels of social support. For example, a spouse's unemployment may put a strain on the entire family relationship and in turn reduce the support given by family members. Some evidence further suggests that economic stressors *and* the amount of support available are socially distributed by class: "It's as simple as that. If you are poor, you have more stress and less supportive resources" (Pilisuk and Parks, 1986: 58).

The research tends to focus only on the *beneficial* aspects of social support. Although it is popularly believed that it is always good to have family and friends around in times of trouble, social support is not necessarily helpful and at times can be counterproductive. For example, persons experiencing a health crisis can be overprotected, which slows recovery. Family members may also try to communicate supportive messages ("You can do it!") that may be interpreted by the ill person as a form of pressure to get well (Horton, 1985a). Social support may undermine sick people's sense of personal competence by making them feel that they cannot do anything on their own or that they cannot possibly reciprocate the help they have been given (Pilisuk and Parks, 1986: 39). One study indicates that *perceived* support may be more important than *received* support in coping with stressful events.[6] It concluded that it is possible that "the perception of one's network being ready to act can be as important—if not more important—than actual supportive behavior" (Wethington and Kessler, 1986: 84).

Perhaps the most significant blind spot in this area of research is the failure to consider the larger contexts of the power in which social support takes place. For example, people in economic need may have difficulties with their social networks. Their social and economic powerlessness in turn places a strain on their social networks, and may also limit their access to supportive social relationships. Working-class people on the whole have less developed social networks and group affiliations than middle-class people (Fischer, 1983). One study showed how poverty limits social involvement because of a lack of funds for transportation, recreation, or association dues (Pilisuk and Parks, 1986: 60). Income and education seem to have an impact on the influence of social support on minimizing stress (Ratliff-Crain and Baum, 1990).

The notion of social support is very much in fashion in stress research (McQueen and Siegrist, 1982), partly because of its appeal to common sense: We would all agree that "we get by with a little help from our friends." The thrust of many studies is that people who have—or perceive themselves to have—access to emotional, material, and other kinds of support are healthier and are at an advantage when dealing with life's crises, including sickness. One group of researchers reported, "We found that individuals showed a greater level of depressive symptoms if they experienced a most

---

[6]A problem in this study is that measures of both perceived and received support were based on the recall of subjects; they are therefore subjective and may have been perceptually modified by the respondents.

important and undesirable event. This effect was reduced if help came from strong rather than weak ties" (Lin et al., 1985: 259). This interpretation seems to represent a scientific way of saying something that we all know, yet the evidence does not always support this conclusion (McQueen and Siegrist, 1982: 359). One researcher observed that "it appears that lack of support in combination with deficiencies in self-esteem or mastery may account for differential vulnerability to life difficulties" (Thoits, 1983: 90). Thus an important factor in determining individuals' ability to cope with stress is how empowered they feel themselves to be.

The current emphasis on social support seems to be in tune with some of the other ideological biases we have discussed. Social support puts the emphasis on the individual and institutions such as the family in which individuals have some power. One consequence of the focus on the importance of social support may be to force people to fall back on their own *private* resources (Fischer, 1983), for it is in the private sphere of family life and friendship in which people have some control (Pearlin, 1983). In such public settings as the work place or school, social support may not be available, and individual coping mechanisms may not be effective. Thus coping difficulties and limits to social support derived from societal structures outside the private sphere are seldom addressed.

Studies on the availability of social support make little mention of class and power. For example, how does capitalism, as a social system, help to generate competitiveness, individualism, and social mobility that make social support difficult? How do controls in the work place affect social support as well as self-esteem and self-mastery? How does the distribution of power in existing social networks such as families affect social support? Social support can be a means of empowering the individual, but it is also a part of the social and cultural environments that determine its quality and availability. The research emphasis on social support should not blind us to the many other ways in which these social environments empower or disempower individuals, making it more difficult for them to control their own bodies.

SUMMARY

In this chapter we have examined social-organizational conditions of disempowerment, and how these conditions create psychosocial stress and affect the individual's responses to stress. Social stresses that attack one's sense of self and self-concept are particularly problematic in modern society, given the extreme importance attached to both concepts. Social class and work situations affect our self-concept. Dramaturgical stress also affects health, especially because contemporary society puts a great deal of emphasis on the importance of self-presentation as part of social and work skills. When people must "grin and bear it" under the most uncivil conditions, health problems may ensue.

Appropriate and adequate information is a significant source of security and help in coping with environmental demands. Institutional settings (such as the work place or a hospital) can generate informational troubles, which are related to illness and the inability to cope adequately. Social support is a means of being and feeling empowered. The absence of such support can itself give rise to stress and deprive individuals of a resource for coping with stress. The sociopsychological conditions of modern life reviewed here are related to chronic degenerative diseases—the "diseases of civilization."

RECOMMENDED READINGS

Articles

JOSEPH EYER and PETER STERLING, "Stress-related mortality and social organization," *Review of Radical Political Economics* 9(1), 1977: 1–44.

MARIANNE FRANKENHAEUSER, "Coping with stress at work," *International Journal of Health Services* 11(4), 1981: 491–510.

GERARD J. HOUBEN, "Production control and chronic stress in work organizations," *International Journal of Health Services* 21(2), 1991: 309–327.

JAMES S. HOUSE, KARL R. LANDIS, and DEBRA UMBERSON, "Social relationships and health," *Science* 214, July 1988: 540–545.

Books

PETER E. S. FREUND, *The Civilized Body: Social Domination, Control and Health*. Philadelphia: Temple University Press, 1982. An elaboration of the perspective of this chapter.

ARLIE HOCHSCHILD, *The Managed Heart: Commercialization of Human Feeling*. Berkeley: University of California Press, 1983. Introducing the concepts of emotion work and emotional labor, this study of flight attendants discusses the increase of emotion work in the service sector.

ROBERT HOWARD, *Brave New Workplace*. New York: Penguin, 1985. An examination of social control, alienation, and health hazards in computerized work places and in the computer industry.

RICHARD M. PFEFFER, *Working for Capitalism*. New York: Columbia University Press, 1979. The account of a college professor's experiences working in a factory.

JULIET B. SCHOR, *The Overworked American*. New York: Basic Books, 1992. As the title suggests, an analysis of the causes and consequences of increased time pressure experienced by U.S. workers.

CHAPTER SIX

The Social Meanings of Sickness

What does it mean to be sick? In some ways a tree's disease is similar to a human's disease: Trees can recover or they can die of disease; branches become lifeless, leaves wither, and roots and trunks function poorly. Unlike trees, however, humans must also grapple with the experiential aspects of sickness. Humans are capable of reflecting upon themselves, their bodily conditions, and their self-perceptions. This reflexiveness means that humans typically suffer not merely from disease but also from their experience of illness and the meanings that they and others attach to it.

Sickness is upsetting to the social group too. Because it is a breech of the ideals or norms of the society, it is disruptive. Illness represents a threat to the order and meanings by which people make sense of their lives and organize the routines of their everyday existence. Sickness also raises moral questions, such as, "Who (or what) is responsible for this misfortune?"

ILLNESS AS DEVIANCE

The very notion of health is a social ideal that varies widely from culture to culture or from one historical period to another. For example, in the nineteenth century the ideal upper-class woman was pale, frail, and delicate. A woman with robust health was considered to be lacking refinement (Ehrenreich and English, 1978). In other periods, cultures, or subcultures, however, the ideal of health might be identified with traits such as strength, fertility, spirituality, righteousness, the absence of pain, the presence of certain pain, fatness, thinness, or youthfulness. The ideal of health thus embodies a particular culture's notions of well-being and desired human qualities. Standards of health in any culture reflect that culture's core values. Through ritual action and symbols (especially language), the social group continually reproduces these central, shared meanings (Durkheim, [1915] 1965).

Durkheim ([1895] 1938: 68–69) observed that deviance serves to remind the entire social group of the importance of certain collective values. Like crime, sickness is a form of **deviance**, or departure from group-established norms. Society typically imputes different kinds of responsibility for crime than for sickness. Durkheim asserted that the very existence of social norms—however defined—means that there will be deviance in all societies. The way a society reacts to sickness and crime reaffirms its core values. Furthermore, the practices for sanctioning deviance (such as punishing the criminal or treating the sick person) reaffirm and revitalize the collective sentiments and maintain social solidarity. Durkheim ([1893] 1964: 108) argued that societal reaction against deviance "is above all designed to act upon upright [nondeviant] people. . . ." This function suggests that the treatment of the sick in all healing systems serves to reaffirm cultural norms and ideals for the sick and the well alike.

Thus, deviance is more a description of the social group that defines it than a quality of the individual considered deviant. Labeling of an attribute or behavior as deviant is, in fact, a social product (Waxler, 1980; Becker, 1963). Cultures vary widely as to whether they consider deviant such bodily conditions as facial scars, obesity, shortness, and paleness. One cultural standard, for example, considers a certain amount of hair on a man's chest to be desirable, representing fortitude, robustness, and manliness. Much less hair on the chest is treated as too effeminate; much more is considered coarse and animallike. Other cultures (and subcultures), however, have different definitions of desirable body hair and different connotations of deviance from those norms.

As Chapter 9 illustrates, defining deviance is a social process involving factors such as power and stratification. Power in a society includes having significant influence in setting social norms and labeling deviance. It also involves having control over the social mechanisms by which these norms are taught and enforced. Indeed, one function of social control is to perpetuate the dominance of those in power in establishing the norms. Socially established norms are *imposed* on people, regardless of their own beliefs. Power is a factor in both the creation of a deviance label and its application to some individual persons.

The Sick Role

Society must deal with individuals who differ significantly from its norms. As indicated in Chapter 1, the concept of social control refers to all mechanisms a society uses to try to contain its members' behavior within various norms, including deterrents, incentives, rewards, and punishments. How society responds to an instance of perceived deviance depends largely upon its determination of the individual's responsibility for the deviant behavior.

Like all social roles, the **sick role** is primarily a description of social expectations (including those of the sick person). While these expectations strongly influence behavior, the sick role does not describe how sick persons actually behave (cf. Twaddle, 1981b: 56–58).

According to Parsons (1951: 428–447), the sick role entails certain responsibilities as well as certain privileges:

1. The individual's incapacity is a form of deviance from social norms, but since it is not deliberate, the individual is not held responsible;
2. The sickness is legitimate grounds for being exempted from normal obligations, such as work or school attendance;
3. The legitimacy of this exemption is, however, predicated upon the sick person's intent to get well;
4. The attempt to get well implies also seeking and cooperating with competent help to treat the illness.

The sick role of someone with pneumonia exemplifies Parsons's use of this concept. A person with serious pneumonia would not be expected to report to work, to do housework, or to keep an appointment. Failure to perform such basic social obligations is a form of deviance that is typically sanctioned, for example, by firing an employee. Having pneumonia, however, is usually considered an acceptable, but temporary, excuse for not meeting these obligations. The employer does not hold the sick person immediately responsible. This part of the sick role concept is thus connected with Parsons's larger concern with how societies maintain their equilibrium in the face of deviance and disruptions such as sickness.

Although having pneumonia is a legitimate excuse for not reporting to work, the sick person is expected to "act sick" and try to get well. The employer would be less than happy to see the "sick" employee at a baseball game later that day, for example. According to Parsons, part of trying to get well involves seeking competent health care from a trained physician. The social expectations for a person with pneumonia thus include going to a doctor, obtaining and taking the doctor's prescription, and otherwise conforming to whatever regimen the doctor ordered. Thus, he tied the sick role inevitably with the role of medical professionals. (Parsons was especially interested in the development of professionalism as a feature of modern society.) In his usage, the sick role directly implies the patient role; by contrast, we explore the patient role as a separate role, which sick persons may or may not enter, depending upon whether their sickness is brought to the attention of medical professionals (see Chapter 10).

Parsons's concept of the sick role is valuable in that it highlights the social control functions of how society treats sickness. It also emphasizes the extent to which social definitions of sickness reflect larger cultural values of modern Western societies (Parsons, 1972: 124). Some of the cultural narrowness of Parsons's sick role concept is due to his explicit focus on American values, such as the emphasis upon individual achievement and responsibility. His conception of the sick role was thus primarily a description of American modes of dealing with the problems of deviance and motivation in the face of the potential disruptions when individual members feel unable to meet normal obligations. The sick role, however, is not as clear-cut as Parsons's model suggests. Four problems with his approach are discussed next.

The Sick Role Is Not Necessarily Temporary.   Parsons's conception of the sick role is based upon only one, relatively narrow class of health problems. The obligations and exemptions described in his model appear to fit serious, acute illnesses reasonably well. **Acute illnesses** characteristically occur suddenly, peak rapidly, and run their course (i.e., result in death or recovery) in relatively short time. Examples include influenza, measles, and scarlet fever.

Chronic illnesses, by contrast, are of long duration—typically as long as the sufferer lives. They often result in the steady deterioration of bodily functioning. Examples include emphysema, diabetes, multiple sclerosis, epilepsy, and heart disease. Furthermore, some acute illnesses are considered chronic when they become a continuing pattern in an individual's life; examples include chronic bronchitis, asthma, and ulcers. Additionally, a number of chronic, disabling conditions (e.g., paraplegia from a car accident) do not involve any ongoing disease, but may result in an ambiguous, lifelong sick role.

While many acute conditions can be cured (or are self-limiting), most chronic conditions are permanent. Treatment of chronic illness is aimed at best at controlling the deterioration caused by the disease and at *managing* the illness. Many of the most dangerous acute (usually infectious) diseases of earlier generations have been brought under control in developed countries through improved sanitation, nutrition, housing, and the like. Inoculations, antibiotics, and other medical treatments have also had some effect in curing infectious diseases (although, as Chapter 2 shows, their role has been somewhat overstated). By contrast, the proportion of persons suffering chronic illnesses has greatly increased, and modern medical intervention does not appear so potent in the face of such conditions.

The nature of chronic illness does not fit Parsons's sick role pattern. Obviously, his assumption of the necessity of an "intent to get well" is irrelevant if the illness is, by definition, permanent. His sick role conception presumed that the benefits were conditional, but chronic illnesses make most of the conditions meaningless (Alexander, 1982). Unlike infectious disease, chronic ailments are more likely to be considered partly the fault or the responsibility of the sufferer. Whereas few people consider a case of chicken pox, for example, to be the sick person's fault, lay and medical conceptions of many chronic conditions, such as lung cancer, high blood pressure, and cirrhosis of the liver, are believed to be brought on—at least partially—by the sufferer's own lifestyle.

Feelings about whether a chronic illness is sufficient grounds for exemption from normal responsibilities are also ambiguous. Since the condition is not temporary, the exemptions are all the more problematic for both the sufferer and those who would grant the exemptions. Just how disabling is the condition? Is a partial exemption feasible? Often persons suffering chronic illnesses do not want total exemption from normal responsibilities, but the illness prevents them from fulfilling some usual duties. For example, a person with emphysema may be able to work but at a much slower pace, and a person with chronic back pain may need more frequent breaks. Societal values enforced by the sick role suggest why persons with chronic illness have considerable difficulty negotiating such concessions.

As a means for maintaining stability and social control, the sick role allows temporary exemptions from normal role requirements without changing those requirements. Routine deviance from the requirements is, however, far more disruptive if judged by criteria of maximizing productive efficiency. If, for example, an employer expects all clerk-typists to put in eight-hour days, it would be highly disruptive to adjust work expectations to accommodate several workers' various chronic illnesses (e.g., by allowing one worker to work only six hours with frequent breaks, another to type at a very slow pace, and yet another to work only those days when the chronic condition was not flaring up). Thus, the legitimate exemptions of the sick role are not readily granted to many chronically sick persons.

Similarly, many other "deviant" health conditions do not fit the sick role model of acute diseases and thereby lead to ambiguities about expectations. Should a person born with a physical handicap be treated as sick? What about accident victims or the mentally ill? In a process known as the medicalization of deviance, more and more problems that do not fit the sick role model are being defined as sicknesses (cf. McKinlay, 1972). Medicalization produces a proliferation of sicknesses, few of which can be medically cured. Like chronic illness, these conditions are typically only medically controlled or managed. The individual may be identified as sick, but the benefits and responsibilities of the sick role simply do not apply. Thus, there is considerable ambiguity over the role expectations of those deemed to be "sick" with such conditions as pregnancy, menopause, hyperkinesia, alcoholism, pyromania, and PMS (premenstrual syndrome).

The Sick Role Is Not Always Voluntary.   Parsons's model holds that the sick person, in exchange for the advantages of the sick role, is motivated to assume that role and voluntarily cooperate with the agents of social control in the appropriate therapy for the deviant condition. In the preceding case of the worker with pneumonia, for example, the person's discomfort and fear of complications would presumably motivate the individual to see a doctor, have blood tests and X-rays, get bed rest at home or in a hospital, and take medications. Parsons thus assumed that, in contrast to the criminal deviant, the sick person voluntarily enters the socially prescribed role.

Not all persons, however, want to enter the sick role, even when they feel ill. Many people resist the expected childlike dependency the role often entails; many others have strong aversion to medical treatments, especially in the hospital. A Scottish study of lower-class women found considerable negative moral evaluation of persons who give in, or "lie down," to illness (Blaxter and Paterson, 1982). Some people, furthermore, simply cannot afford to withdraw from normal obligations; the sick role is a threat to their subsistence (Kasl and Cobb, 1966).

Some sicknesses carry a negative connotation or stigma. While the sick person would obtain some benefits (such as exemption from work or other duties) from the sick role, these negative attitudes toward that illness could be worse than the condition itself. For example, a person suffering epilepsy may actively avoid being socially identified as having the disease because of the repulsion and often outright discrimination associated with the illness (Schneider and Conrad, 1980).

Many persons are placed into the sick role by others, regardless of their own wishes. Children and the dependent aged are generally not considered competent to decide for themselves whether to assume the role; instead their caretakers make the decision for them. Likewise, some conditions force an involuntary entrance into the sick roles. The most straightforward example is a loss of consciousness. Other ambiguous situations arise when someone's family (or unrelated caretakers, such as doctors, social workers, or police) decide that an individual is too "sick" to have good judgment and then place the person into the sick role. Because many people thus do not enter the sick role voluntarily, their cooperation with the medical regimen cannot be assumed. In many such cases, the social control functions of the sick role are more coercive and less benign than portrayed by the model.

By contrast, some persons seek to enter the sick role and are denied access. A process of subtle social negotiation occurs when an individual claims the sick role. This claim must then be accepted as legitimate by others, especially authoritative others. Often medical personnel such as the school nurse and the company doctor are the critical gatekeepers who have the power to determine who will be admitted to the sick role in their institutional setting. Informal negotiation also typically takes place as the person claiming the sick role attempts to convince family and others of the legitimacy of the claim, and the others judge—and sometimes test—that legitimacy. Entry into the sick role is thus essentially a social and political process.

Variability in Sick Role Legitimacy. Parsons's conception of the sick role also presumes that a single, stable value system is operative for all persons in a society. Historically, however, the legitimate exemption of sick persons from various obligations is highly variable. The criteria for such an exemption may also differ according to gender, social class, and subcultural expectations.

Legitimate exemptions from work obligations, for example, vary enormously, typically according to social class. Unskilled workers, for example, may not have any paid sick days, whereas white-collar workers may have a given allowance of such days proportionate to their rank or seniority. Indeed, the idea that absence due to sickness should not be a basis for dismissal is relatively recent; even today sickness is not a legitimate exemption for many workers, and they have no legal protection of their jobs.

The meaning of the sick role itself varies considerably according to social class. The same sickness has different connotations according to the class or gender of the sufferer. For example, in the nineteenth century consumption (tuberculosis) was a romanticized illness among the middle and upper classes. This sick role implied a "consuming" passion as expressed in artistic sensitivity and creativity. Some of the physical effects of tuberculosis were considered beautiful: slenderness, fever-bright eyes, pallor, and a transparent complexion accompanied by pink cheeks. One young woman with consumption wrote in her diary:

> Since yesterday I am white and fresh and amazingly pretty. My eyes are spirited and shining, and even the contours of my face seem prettier and more delicate. It's too bad that this is happening at a time when I am not seeing anyone. It's foolish to tell, but I spent a half-hour looking at myself in the mirror with pleasure; this had not happened to me for some time (Marie Bashkirtseff's Journal of 1883, quoted in Herzlich and Pierret, 1987: 81).

The well-to-do sufferer was " 'apart,' threatened but all the more precious for it" (Herzlich and Pierret, 1987: 25). While the disease was more prevalent and devastating among the lower classes, no such privileged or positive sick role was available to them.

The sick role was considered especially appropriate for women of that era because it was thought to reflect ladies' refinement and delicacy. It was expected and even stylish for well-to-do women to faint frequently and to retire to bed for "nerves," "sick headaches," "female troubles," and "neurasthenia." Lower-class women, by contrast, were considered to be more robust, as evidence of their coarseness and less civilized nature (Ehrenreich and English, 1978).

Upper-class Victorians could obtain exemption from normal obligations by claiming the sick roles of neurasthenia or hysteria, illnesses of the "nerves" believed to afflict particularly intellectual or sensitive persons. The label of neurasthenia appears to have been especially useful for men, whose normal role expectations of fortitude and active participation in the world outside of the home made it difficult for them to exhibit dependency or weakness. The vague symptoms identified as neurasthenia, however, were a legitimate basis for men to assume the sick role (Sicherman, 1978; see also Drinka, 1984).

Cultural expectations of the sick role also vary, perhaps widely. There is some evidence that cultures differ in the degree of legitimacy they accord various illnesses and their resulting claims to exemption from responsibilities. For example, neurasthenia is a legitimate basis of the sick role among contemporary Taiwanese, whereas in the United States it is a far less common diagnosis or culturally recognized reason for assuming the sick role (cf. Kleinman, 1980). Similarly, persons of Hispanic background would be more likely than those of Anglo-Saxon heritage to consider a certain "fright" (*susto*), such as being startled by an animal or a possible assailant, to be a legitimate basis for the sick role (Rubel et al., 1984). Since cultures vary in how they understand various illnesses, they also have different expectations for the behavior of persons occupying the sick role, such as the amount of pain and disability they may experience (cf. Angel and Thoits, 1987). These examples illustrate that the expectations identified as a sick role change; problems that were identified in the past as a legitimate basis for claiming the role are no longer appropriate, while other problems—formerly unrecognized or discounted—are now accepted as legitimate.

Responsibility for Sickness. Parsons's model of the sick role held that, unlike crime, sickness was not the responsibility of the deviant person. Furthermore, he considered the professional diagnosis and treatment of medical deviance to be purely technical, neutral, and unbiased. As Chapter 9 illustrates, however, the very definition of illness is socially constructed, and social groups often impute responsibility for illness to the sick person.

Freidson (1970) observed that certain conditions are typically viewed as the responsibility of the sick individual and thus are treated relatively punitively, like crimes. Examples include various sexually transmitted diseases as well as substance abuse and conditions derived from such abuse. Freidson noted that the attitudes of both the society and the medical profession, while greatly expanding the range of conditions considered to be properly "medical" problems, do not necessarily abolish the negative moral connotations attached to these conditions. He also described another category of sicknesses that, while not technically considered the fault of the sick person, are nonetheless stigmatized (Freidson 1970: 234–237). **Stigma** is a powerful discrediting and tainting social label that radically changes the way an individual is viewed as a person (Goffman, 1963: 2–5). For example, being an illegitimate child was (historically more than currently) an enormous barrier to presenting oneself as a "normal," upright citizen.

Many sicknesses carry a stigma. Leprosy, epilepsy, and AIDS, for example, all carry connotations of disreputability and even evil. The sick role for someone with a stigmatized illness is clearly different than that for a person with a "neutral" sickness. Stigmas can result in various forms of discrimination: Persons with epilepsy, for instance, have experienced job discrimination, difficulty in obtaining a driver's license, prohibitions against marrying, and difficulties in obtaining insurance (Schneider and Conrad, 1980). Even after someone has been treated and pronounced "cured" of such a condition, the stigma often remains on that person. Furthermore, the stigma frequently spreads to the family and close friends of the sick person in what Goffman (1963: 30–31) calls a "courtesy stigma." For example, families and friends of persons with epilepsy, cancer, or AIDS sometimes find themselves being shunned or harassed (Conrad, 1986).

The source of stigma is not the disease itself but rather the social imputation of a negative connotation. Leprosy is highly stigmatized in India, but far less so in neighboring Sri Lanka. Lepers in India are treated as outcasts, whereas many lepers in Nigeria remain in the village and carry on normal social lives (Waxler, 1981). Because cultures vary in the stigma imputed to different sicknesses, the sick role for those illnesses vary accordingly.

The degree of stigma and responsibility attached to a sickness may also change over time, often as notions about an illness change. In the nineteenth century, when tuberculosis was considered to be a somewhat romantic sickness resulting from an inherent disposition of passion and creativity, the illness had relatively little stigma. Later, however, when tuberculosis was considered infectious, those with the disease were seen as carriers to be avoided, isolated, and feared (Herzlich and Pierret, 1987).

Specific social and historical conditions lead to the stigmatizing of a sickness. Before the middle of the nineteenth century, leprosy in Hawaii was of minor importance and not stigmatized. As international trade and colonialism began to change the islands' social and economic situation, however, many outsiders came to the islands. Large numbers of Chinese immigrants arrived to work on the plantations, and the Hawaiians believed that they had brought leprosy. Although the Chinese immigrants were hard working and frugal, they were viewed as an inferior ethnic-racial group that threatened the jobs of other working-class persons. In 1880 Hawaii enacted laws to exclude the Chinese, partly on the basis of a belief that they carried disease. Health data suggest that the Chinese were not, however, an important source of leprosy, which more likely came to the islands through the ethnically mixed crews of ships from countries where the disease was prevalent. The Chinese were stigmatized in part because they were thought to be the source of leprosy, which at the same time became stigmatized because it was identified with the Chinese. Thus, a relatively unknown and unimportant disease was transformed into a morally threatening sickness (Waxler, 1981).

The stigma attached to AIDS in recent years is a parallel situation. AIDS can and does affect all kinds of people, including many newborns. However, since most people identify the disease with homosexuals and drug users, it carries a considerable stigma. The widespread imputation of responsibility and stigma to sick persons suggests that Parsons's sick role model understates the moral judgment and social control aspects of sickness.

The Medicalization of Deviance

Religious, legal, and medical institutions have all contributed to the definition of deviance in society. For example, "Thou shalt not steal" is a religious norm: Stealing is a sin. Legal systems define similar norms of behavior, and violation of the norms is a crime. In a process called the **medicalization of deviance**, medical systems increasingly also define what is normal or desirable behavior: Badness becomes sickness.

The relative influence of religious, legal, and medical institutions in defining deviance has shifted in Western societies. As the Middle Ages waned and these three institutions became increasingly differentiated from each other, the religious organizations still had the greatest weight in defining deviance. This preeminence continued into the eighteenth century, but in America and France (and later in other European countries), the legal mode of defining deviance gained ascendancy (see Freidson, 1970: 247–252). In America, the increasing preeminence of the legal definitions was promoted by religious pluralism and by the increasingly rational organization of the nation-state (cf. Hammond, 1974).

The significance of legal definitions of deviance has diminished somewhat in the twentieth century, and medical definitions have gained in importance. This shifting balance is clearly reflected in the 1954 precedent-setting case *Durham* v. *United States* (214 F.2d 863), in which the court ruled that "an accused is not criminally responsible if his unlawful act was the product of a mental disease or mental defect." The shift in balance favoring medical definitions of deviance corresponds chronologically with a period of the rapid professionalization of medicine, when medical discoveries and technology proceeded quickly, and public faith in science and medicine was increasing.

Part of the reason for the declining importance of religious definitions is that they appear too nonrational and, in a religiously pluralistic country, lack societywide acceptance. Legal definitions, while more rational, seem to hinge too greatly upon human decisions, such as the judgment of twelve ordinary citizens on a jury. Medical definitions, by contrast, appear to be more rational and scientific, and based upon technical expertise rather than human judgment.

The concept of sickness, however, far from being a neutral scientific concept, is ultimately a *moral* one, establishing an evaluation of normality or desirability (Freidson, 1970: 208). The medical profession (especially its psychiatric branch) has defined a wide range of disapproved behavior as "sick": alcoholism, homosexuality, promiscuity, drug addiction, arson, suicide, child abuse, and civil disobedience (Conrad and Schneider, 1992). Social stigma adheres to many sicknesses, such as leprosy, AIDS, pelvic inflammatory disease, and cirrhosis of the liver. Moral judgment is also applied in the evaluation of "good" patient behavior, defined as acknowledging the necessity of medical care and following "doctors' orders" for various conditions, which may include receiving prenatal care, accepting blood transfusions, obtaining inoculations for one's children, and following prescribed drug and dietary regimens. Issues of moral judgment and responsibility are at stake.

When sicknesses thus labeled are defined as "bad," the doctors who join or organize efforts to eradicate or control them function as "**moral entrepreneurs**" (Becker, 1963: 147–163), or those who make an enterprise out of moral concerns.

The "discovery" of an illness category called hyperkinesis (or minimal brain dysfunction) involved such entrepreneurial action in a recent example of the medicalization of deviance. Virtually all of the persons labeled with this syndrome have been children; most are boys. The characteristic behaviors identified with hyperkinesis include excess of motor activity, short attention span, restlessness, impulsivity, and inability to sit still in school and comply with rules. These behaviors, however, have been frequently observed among schoolchildren, probably since the invention of the institution of the school. While no organic basis for "minimal brain dysfunction" has been identified, the "discovery" of hyperkinesis is explained in part by social factors such as the development and vigorous promotion of psychoactive drugs (specifically, Ritalin [methylphenidate]) for controlling hyperkinetic behavior, and the crusading efforts of moral entrepreneurs, including doctors, educators, and parents. Although hyperkinesis has been a medical category for only a brief time, it rapidly became an attractive diagnosis, and the drug Ritalin accounted for significant proportions of the pharmaceutical industry's profits (Conrad and Schneider, 1992: 156–158).

Moral entrepreneurs engage in considerable political efforts to get their definitions of sickness accepted and implemented. Professional colleagues must be convinced; related professionals who could make referrals must be informed; and relevant regulatory agencies must be persuaded. The attempt to define participation in religious cults as a medical problem illustrates how the illness label is a product of such political efforts (Robbins and Anthony, 1982). The 1980 and 1987 editions of the American Psychiatric Association's *Diagnostic and Statistical Manual of Mental Disorders* (DSM-III and DSM-III-R) contained several changes from previous editions in order to characterize participation in new religious movements or in non-Western religions in the United States as characteristic of mental disorder (Post, 1992). For example, in the definition of paranoid personality disorder, the revised manual stated that "individuals with this disorder are over-represented among leaders of mystical or esoteric religions and/or pseudoscientific and quasipolitical groups" (American Psychiatric Association, 1987: 308). Thus an evaluation of someone's mental health includes a judgment as to whether the individual's religious, scientific, or political persuasion is deviant. Interestingly, the efforts to define participation in new religious movements as "sick" were primarily those of a relatively small number of therapists who made their living "deprogramming" former members or testifying as expert witnesses in court cases involving such religious or other social movements. These moral entrepreneurs were establishing a specialized professional territory for themselves by creating illness labels (Richardson, 1993; Maloney, 1987).

While the boundaries of what is called mental illness are generally more malleable than those of physical illnesses, similar political processes are often involved in the classification of physical ailments. Ideas about the etiology of an illness (and, by extension, responsibility for it) are often politically debated. For example, a syndrome called miners' nystagmus has been the subject of continual political negotiation as a medical category. In the nineteenth century, this syndrome, characterized by oscillation of the eyes and spasms of eyelids, frequently accompanied by other complaints such as tremors of muscles of the neck, dizziness, headaches, sensitivity to light, and troubled sleep, was a recognized diagnostic category. Later, however, it had become an expensive item of compensation, so the British mining industry engaged in continual medical-legal debates as to whether it was a legitimate illness. The incidence of nystagmus complaints was often related directly to changes in conditions of work (e.g., production schedules) in the mines. As the result of complex social interactions involving doctors, management, labor, and government agencies, this illness was eventually psychologized, and thereby both recognized as a problem yet invalidated as a compensable illness (Figlio, 1982).

Zola (1983: 261) argued that "if anything can be shown in some way to affect the workings of the body and to a lesser extent the mind, then it can be labelled an 'illness' itself or jurisdictionally 'a medical problem.' " Thus, even normal and healthy physical conditions or processes, such as menstruation, pregnancy and childbirth, body and facial shape and size, and aging, have been brought under medicine's jurisdiction (Dull and West, 1991).

One recent example of this tendency has caused considerable ethical controversy: In 1993, the National Institute of Health (NIH) resumed recruiting healthy children for an experiment on the effects on stature from a course of injections with a genetically engineered human growth hormone. Bioethicists, however, were disturbed by the project's definition of natural physical traits as "diseases" that can/should be "cured" with expensive surgery or drugs (a year's treatment with human growth hormone costs about $20,000). They argued that an inherited characteristic deemed socially undesirable (such as height, skin color, or gender) should not be defined as a "medical problem" needing medical treatment (Hotz, 1993). Modern societies must face many such moral judgments about whether or how to use genetic engineering; however, by trying to define the issues as "mere" medical problems with technical responses, researchers and their commercial sponsors are evading profound social and moral issues.

The Medicalization of Moral Authority

The same historical processes that brought about the preeminence of medical definitions of deviance also led to a much stronger role for medical authority in moral issues, such as what is right or wrong?, what is good or bad?, and whose good should prevail? Sometimes court events involve a clash of several sources of authority.[1]

In one representative court case, claims were made from legal, medical, parental, and religious bases of authority. A young person had been comatose for months, and was "as good as dead" in the common-sense view. Her body was being kept alive by technological intervention, and eventually her parents sought legal permission to terminate these "extraordinary" measures. Because no single authority held uncontested legitimacy, the case was complicated. Medical experts gave their opinions on the medical definitions of death. Legal experts raised issues of the legal rights and guardianship of comatose patients. Theological experts offered briefs on the borderlines of life and death, and the girl's father made a thoughtful personal statement about his request. The relevant issue is not merely the uncertainty of the outcome but also that it was the court in which medical, legal, religious, and parental figures vied to have their statements taken seriously (Willen, 1983; Fenn, 1982).

---

[1]This section is adapted with permission of the publisher from *Religion: The Social Context*, Third Edition, by Meredith B. McGuire, © 1992, by Wadsworth, Inc.

The situation of difficult childbirth illustrates the growing role of physicians as arbiters in several such moral issues. For example, sometimes the infant's head is too large for the pelvic opening, making vaginal delivery difficult or impossible, and jeopardizing the lives of both the mother and the infant. In the late nineteenth and early twentieth centuries, several medical technologies were developed to deal with this crisis: high forceps (instruments to reach and reposition or pull the fetus), symphysiotomy (surgical severing of cartilage to separate the pubic bones), pubiotomy (cutting of the pubic bones), Caesarian section (surgical opening of the abdominal wall), and craniotomy (surgery on the fetal head to enable it to fit through the pelvic opening). Because none of these procedures was without risk to the woman or the fetus or both, each operation involved some moral concern for whose good was paramount.

Particular moral problems developed, however, in dire cases in which an emergency craniotomy was the last resort to save the mother's life. Initially, these moral decisions involved the doctor, the woman and her family, and sometimes the family's religious advisers as well. Gradually, however, the medical experts successfully asserted their autonomy and authority by their exclusive control of the relevant technical knowledge and by removing childbirth from home to hospital (and therefore out of the arenas of influence of family or clergy). Physicians tried to justify their own authority in this moral decision on the grounds of technical expertise and presumed rationality, but analysis of their rhetoric shows that their decisions were often based on social attitudes about women's childbearing role as much as were the previous decisions of other moral authorities (Leavitt, 1987).

The growing legitimacy of medical authority, relative to other sources of judgment, is further illustrated by contemporary court decisions upholding medical judgments to perform Caesarian sections. Caesarian sections are increasingly common, now accounting for about one in four births in the United States. They involve major abdominal surgery, with its concomitant risks and complications. An investigation of court cases between 1979 and 1986 showed that courts often accept physicians' decisions to operate over the objections of patients, their families, or religious persuasion, even though subsequent medical developments suggest that many of these operations were not necessary (Irwin and Jordan, 1987).

Medical dominance has effectively reduced the legitimacy of actions of other "encroaching" institutional areas such as religion and the family. Several courts have overruled religious or moral objections to various medical procedures. Jehovah's Witnesses, for example, believe that blood transfusions are forbidden by scripture, but the courts have generally upheld the medical authorization of such treatments, even for unwilling recipients (*United States* v. *George*, 239 F. Supp. 752, 1964). Medical authority was also ruled to supersede parental authority in decisions presumed to determine life or death (precedent cases in 1952, 1962, and 1964 are cited in Burkholder, 1974: 41). Even in instances in which the medical ability to prevent death is doubtful, greater legitimacy is given to medical rather than parental authority. In 1977, for example, a Massachusetts court ordered that parents of a child dying of leukemia submit the child to medically prescribed chemotherapy, rather than to a less unpleasant (but also less respectable) nonmedical alternative therapy.

Social Control and Power

The labeling of deviance is an issue of legitimacy on another level as well, for the power to define sickness and to label someone as sick is also the power to discredit that person (Zola, 1983: 276–278). If a person's mental health is called into question, the rest of society does not have to take that person seriously. The individual then becomes the locus of the "problem." During the Vietnam War, a physician refused to train medical personnel for the army, claiming that his religious conscience compelled him to refuse this service. The army insisted that his compulsions were psychological rather than religious (Fenn, 1978: 57). By thus raising doubt about his psychological health, the army was able to evade his religious dissent as well as his legal claim to protection under the First Amendment of the Constitution.

Medical control in defining deviance also produces medical power in certifying deviance, which is another aspect of social control. The societal acceptance of medical definitions of deviance gives the medical profession unique power to certify individuals as sick or well. If a back disorder is a legitimate basis for taking the sick role (and thus to be excused from work or to claim insurance), a physician is considered to be the appropriate agency for certifying a valid claim. One study found that sick persons typically use "feeling" terms to describe internal states that they experience as illness; they say, for example, "I don't feel good" or "I feel too dizzy to stand." Thus, especially when the bodily condition of sickness is not obvious to their audiences, they need doctors' substantiation to legitimate their claims to being sick (Telles and Pollack, 1981). One of the functions of physicians, then, becomes the role of gatekeeper (Stone, 1979a, 1979b).

Physicians became the chief arbiters of claims for worker compensation for "repetitive strain" injuries; not surprisingly, company doctors selected by manufacturers or insurers typically were less likely to certify the injury or provide sympathetic care than were personal physicians (Reid et al., 1991). Similarly, from 1952 to 1979, when homosexuality was a legitimate basis for denying a person U.S. citizenship, psychiatrists were given the power to certify that a homosexual should be thus denied (see Szasz, 1970).

When a person is certified as deviant, the agency of social control must then deal with this offender. Religious responses to deviance include counseling, moral indignation, confession, repentance, penance, and forgiveness. Legal responses include parallel actions, such as legal allegations, confession, punishments, rehabilitation, and release with or without the stigma of a record. In the medical model, the responses entail other parallels: diagnosis and therapy.

The process of reintegrating the deviant individual into the social group is therapy, which for even relatively minor deviance involves a form of social control (such as getting a young mother "back on her feet" so she can resume her family responsibilities). The social control functions of therapy are clearly evident in their grossest forms, such as the kidnapping and forcible "deprogramming" of persons with deviant religious or political views (Robbins and Anthony, 1982), and the mental hospitalization of political dissidents in Russia (Medvedev and Medvedev, 1971); similar use of medical definitions for political purposes in the United States is exemplified by the treatment of Ezra Pound and General James Walker (Freidson, 1970: 246; see also Turner, 1977).

The use of psychoactive drugs for social control is one area of particular concern. The above example of drug prescription for difficult-to-manage children shows how matters of social control are medically managed. Similarly, several United States and Canadian studies have documented the very large proportion of the elderly receiving drugs that affect the central nervous system, such as tranquilizers, analgesics, antidepressants, sedatives, hypnotics, and anticonvulsants. One function, deliberate or not, of the use of these drugs is the management of elderly persons. For example, older persons need shorter but more frequent periods of sleep than younger adults, but sedatives are often prescribed in many institutions to try to keep the elderly in an eight-hour sleeping pattern, so the staff can better supervise them at night (Harding, 1981; see also Harding, 1986).

Social control is also involved in the use of drugs to make it possible for persons to accommodate themselves to an unsatisfactory social role. When workers experience severe stress in the work place, treating their stress-related health conditions with drugs keeps them performing their roles without challenging the work conditions or the appropriateness of those roles.

In 1987, a pharmaceutical company was investigated by the U.S. Food and Drug Administration for sending doctors an advertising brochure depicting on the cover a very tense air traffic controller at the computer monitor in a hectic control tower. The caption reads, "He needs anxiolytic [tranquilizer] therapy . . . but alertness is part of his job." Inside the folder, the worker is portrayed as cheery and smiling, and the text reads, in part, "BuSpar. . . . For a different kind of calm." While the ad was criticized as misleading in its downplaying of negative side effects of the drug, the more serious sociological issue is the notion that a tranquilizer is the solution to work-place stress brought on by specific policy decisions. According to a U.S. Government Accounting Office study, air controllers suffered very low morale, extreme overwork, and other pressures due to chronic and serious understaffing—a major problem since President Reagan had fired 11,000 striking air traffic controllers in 1981 (*Health Letter*, 1987; Hinds, 1987).

Research in the United States, Canada, Germany, and Italy showed that women were the overwhelming majority of recipients of prescriptions for tranquilizers and sedatives (Harding, 1986). Pharmaceutical company advertising to doctors specifically recommended such psychoactive drugs to deal with women's dissatisfaction with their social roles. An advertisement for Valium (diazepam) showed a troubled young woman sitting at a table in a school gymnasium; the photo was labeled,

Symbols in a life of psychic tension: M.A. (Fine Arts), PTA (President-elect), GYN repeated examinations normal (persistent complaints). . . .

Rx: Valium . . . M.A. (Fine Arts) . . . PTA (President-elect) . . . representations of a life currently centered around home and children, with too little time to pursue a vocation for which she has spent many years in training . . . a situation that may bespeak continuous frustration and stress: a perfect framework for her to translate the functional symptoms of psychic tension into major problems. For this kind of patient—with no demonstrable pathology yet with repeated complaints—consider the distinctive properties of Valium (diazepam). Valium possesses a pronounced calming action that usually relieves psychic tension promptly, helping to attenuate the related somatic signs and symptoms.

Like the air traffic controller, this young woman is identified as suffering from the stress and frustration of her social role. The solution of prescribing tranquilizers serves the social control function of keeping people in their roles without questioning the role demands themselves (for a review of the literature on prescription of psychotropic drugs for women, see Ettorre and Riska, 1993).

Social control may seem more pleasant or humane when the deviance is treated as sickness rather than as crime or sin, but the potency of the control agencies is just as great. Certain medically defined deviance can permanently spoil the individual's identity (cf. Goffman, 1963). Even when the condition is considered medically "cured" or under control, stigma still adheres to such "illnesses" as alcoholism, drug abuse, mental disorders, syphilis, and cancer. This problem of stigma is especially evident in the case of epilepsy and other conditions involving deviance from one very important cultural norm: self-control. Chapter 7 further examines the problems of stigma and control in chronic illness and handicaps.

Sickness and Social Dissent

The social control functions of the sick role and of some medical interventions demonstrate that society's constraints on individual behavior are real, even when individuals do not agree with the norms for behavior. Although social control measures may be objectively powerful in a society, their effect is never total. Society's members are never fully socialized and compliant. Thus, deviance such as sickness can also be a form of social dissent—usually unorganized, but sometimes organized—against existing social arrangements.

Sickness is, as the sick role concept shows, an act of refusal that is potentially threatening to the established order. In effect, the sick person is saying, "I will not any longer." By claiming the sick role, the individual may refuse to go to school or work, to be responsible for dependents, to serve in the armed forces, and to participate in everyday social obligations. Indeed, in its extreme form sickness is a refusal to cope, to struggle, and to endure. As such, claiming the sick role resembles the activist strategy of passive resistance (Scheper-Hughes and Lock, 1991; Lock and Scheper-Hughes, 1990; see also Herzlich and Pierret, 1987: 183–184; Kleinman, 1992). Taking the sick role is thus often a way of expressing dissent from other social roles. Many social historians consider the epidemic of hysteria among Victorian women to be an expression of their dissent against the constraints of their social roles

(Ehrenreich and English, 1978; Sicherman, 1978). Similarly, workers' job dissatisfaction is often expressed by high rates of absenteeism for sickness.

Sickness is, however, not necessarily an effective form of dissent. Waitzkin (1971) suggested that the sick role has latent (i.e., not recognized or intended) functions that maintain the status quo in society and reduce conflict and change. For example, if disgruntled workers take sick leave to relieve the tensions of their job satisfaction, the sick role reduces the likelihood that those tensions would be addressed politically, such as in a confrontation with management. The sick role instead provides a temporary safety valve to reduce pressure in various institutional settings, such as the family, prisons, and the military.

While the sickness may not be able to change social arrangements, such as social class or gender hierarchies, it may be effective in obtaining actual advantages or relief for the sick person. Some secondary gains of sickness, such as receiving extra attention in the family, may be such a result. For example, in many African societies there are special healing cults for women, such as the *zar* cult of the predominantly Moslem peoples in Ethiopia, Egypt, Sudan, and Somalia. Some anthropologists have interpreted the *zar* affliction, in which the sick person is believed to be possessed by spirits, as women's assertion of dissatisfaction with their lack of social and economic power (Lewis, 1971). Taking the sick role can be a relatively successful (albeit manipulative) assertion of power of the subordinate members of the society. It poignantly expresses women's dissent, but does not fundamentally alter the social arrangements.

Similarly, sickness is sometimes the attempt to cope (although not always constructively) with an intolerable social situation, as discussed in Chapter 4. Sickness expresses frustration, dissatisfaction, and anger turned against oneself. Alcoholism and other substance abuse, depression, and suicide exemplify this potentially self-defeating attempt. To interpret, for example, the alcoholism of a middle-aged, unemployed, impoverished Native American on a reservation as a purely individual sickness is thus to miss the likelihood that it is the expression of his frustration and hostility in the face of his utterly marginalized social condition (Scheper-Hughes and Lock, 1991). Likewise, to interpret an immigrant woman's severe case of "nerves" as a quaint relic of old-country, folk beliefs misses the meaning of nerves (or "nervios," or "nevra," and so on) as a physical expression of real distress (Finkler, 1989; see also Guarnaccia et al., 1989). Her distress, expressed in the physical symptoms of "nerves," may be produced by the perceived disorder of daily life in a society where she experiences exploitation as a worker and discrimination as a member of an ethnic minority, and in a culture which lacks the values by which she would have been honored in her native culture (Lock, 1990).

Scheper-Hughes and Lock (1991) argued that modern medicine has so thoroughly individualized its image of sickness that it has lost sight of the extent to which sickness may be the expression of social dissent about frustrated and unmet human needs. They stated:

> In summary, we wish to stress that while illness symptoms are biological entities they are also coded metaphors that speak to the contradictory aspects of social life, expressing sentiments, feelings, and ideas that must otherwise be kept hidden. As patients—all

of us—we can be open and responsive to the hidden language of pain and protest, rage and resistance, or we can silence it, cut it off by relegating our complaints to the ever expanding domains of medicine ("It" is in the body) or psychiatry ("It" is in the mind). Once safely medicalized, however, the social issues are short-circuited and the message in the bottle—the desperate plea for help and the scream of protest—is forever lost (Scheper-Hughes and Lock, 1991: 422–423).

Some of these metaphorical aspects of the body and sicknesses are described in more detail next.

PROBLEMS OF MEANING AND ORDER

Illness is upsetting because it is experienced as a threat to the order and meanings by which people make sense of their lives. Suffering and death create problems of meaning not simply because they are unpleasant, but also because they threaten the fundamental assumptions of order underlying society itself (cf. Berger, 1967: 24). For the individual, illness and affliction can likewise be experienced as assaults on the identity, and on the ability to predict and control central aspects of one's own and one's loved ones' lives. Healing, in all cultures, represents an attempt to restore order and to reassert meaning.

Illness disrupts the order of everyday life. It threatens our ability to plan for the immediate or distant future, to control, and to organize. Even a relatively minor malady, such as a head cold, can disturb the order of daily life; how much more so can serious, potentially fatal, or debilitating illnesses, such as cancer or polio, throw our lives into disorder! A study of the impact of childhood leukemia found two characteristic experiences of sufferers and their families: uncertainty and the search for meaning (Comaroff and Maguire, 1981).

There are a number of ways by which medical systems in all cultures restore order in the face of illness. Diagnostic action, whether accomplished by divination or CT (computer tomography) scan, divine revelation or physical examination, is a means of naming the problem and giving it a culturally recognizable form. Naming the illness imposes order on a previously chaotic set of experiences, thereby giving the sick person a set of expectations and some basis for acting. Etiologies likewise contribute to restoring a sense of order, because they reflect important values of the social group, especially by identifying a causal relationship between sickness and socially prescribed normal or ideal social relationships. In applying particular etiologies to a given illness episode, the medical process ritually reaffirms these values (Young, 1976).

In many cultures, the healing process addresses not only individual disruption but also disordered *social* relations. The healing role of the African Ndembu diviner is to identify (in symbolic guise) the agents of affliction. Sickness is understood as an eruption of social conflict and divisiveness in one symbolic place. For example, the Ndembu attribute menstrual disorders to *chisaku* (misfortune due to displeasure of ancestral shades or breach of taboo). The healing ritual propitiates the ancestors and exorcizes the evil influences of both living and dead. Significantly, it involves the woman's matrilineal kin, with whom there may be a problem for the woman and her husband. The larger aims of the healing ritual include restoration of problematic kinship ties, reconstruction of the woman's relationship with her husband, and enhanced procreation, thereby benefiting both the marriage and the lineage. Because the disordered body is the expression of disordered social relations, healing consists of reunifying and reordering the entire group, of which the sick person is only an individual expression (Turner, 1969, 1968).

Similarly, faith healing in many Christian groups restores order through healing the metaphorical body (McGuire, 1982). For example, some Christian groups believe that healing a troubled marriage should involve bringing the "body" (wife and children) into proper relationship (i.e., submission) with the "head" (husband and father). The importance of the body as a natural symbol suggests that, even in Western cultures, illness and healing may be ways of symbolizing order and meaning on several levels.

The Body as a Symbol

The human body is a natural symbol. The meanings of the symbol are not intrinsic in it, but are socially constructed and attached to it. Douglas (1970: 93) stated that:

> The social body constrains the way the physical body is perceived. The physical experience of the body, always modified by the social categories through which it is known, sustains a particular view of society. There is a continual exchange of meanings between the two kinds of bodily experience so that each reinforces the categories of the other. As a result of this interaction the body itself is a highly restricted medium of expression.

Thus, she argued that bodily control is social control and that attitudes toward the body reflect the social concerns of the group (Douglas, 1970: 11–18; see also Douglas, 1966).

Body symbolism works on several levels; often the body and its parts are used as metaphors. For example, when we say a person is upright, we are referring to both a moral evaluation and a physical posture. Similar body metaphors are applied when we evaluate people as spineless, underhanded, open-eyed, heartless, cold-blooded, brown-nosed, blue-blooded, sinister, thickskinned, or gutless. Social relations are likewise reflected in body metaphors, such as, "He is a pain in the ass," or "They are thicker than blood."

Consider all the symbolic meanings we give to various body parts and body products, including hands, heart, womb, hair, eyes, milk, blood, spit, feces, and sweat. These meanings are not inherent in the physical properties but are applied by a social group. In socialization, we learn our society's meanings. A baby is not born with an aversion to the sight of blood. A young child must learn to be disgusted by the feel of feces (usually only after having played with them and receiving several reprimands).

Through the meanings attached to the body, social structure shapes individual bodily expression. At the same time, bodily expression reflects the social structure. There have been numerous studies of various cultures, including Western industrialized societies, showing how core values are revealed in body-related beliefs and practices, such as eating (Banks, 1992; Turner, 1982), beauty and adornment (Kunzle, 1981; Turner, 1980), birth and death (Davis-Floyd, 1992; Comaroff, 1984), sex (Turner, 1984; Foucault, 1978), pollution and cleanliness (Elias, 1978; Douglas, 1966), fitness (Bordo, 1990), and health and healing (McGuire, 1988; Comaroff, 1985; Crawford, 1984; Westley, 1983).

The Meaning of Affliction

Illness is also upsetting because it raises the questions of meaning: Why is this happening to me? Why now? Who's responsible? How could God allow this to happen? Why do the good suffer and the evil prosper? In many cultures, the medical system and the religious system are inextricably interwoven. Religious meaning is thereby connected with illness explanations.

In his analysis of religious systems, Weber noted the importance of **theodicies**, or religious explanations of meaning-threatening experiences, for sickness, suffering, and death ([1922] 1963: 138–150). Theodicies tell the individual or group that the experience is not meaningless but is rather part of a larger system of order, a religious cosmology (see also Berger, 1967: 24). Some successful theodicies are in fact nothing but assertions of order. A woman discussing her personal meaning crisis after her husband's premature death said, "I finally came to understand that it didn't matter whether *I* understood why he died when he did, but that God had a reason for it, and that was all that mattered." For this believer, knowing that an order exists behind events was more important than knowing what that order was. Theodicies do not necessarily make the believer happy or even promise future happiness; they simply answer the question, Why do I suffer?

At the same time that Western societies are experiencing the increasing medicalization of authority, Western medicine is having difficulty dealing with sufferers' problems of meaning. Anthropologists remind us that however well Western medicine deals with the symptoms the sick person suffers, it fails to address the problem of "who sent the louse" (Comaroff, 1978). Illness etiologies in Western medicine typically deal with proximate causes (e.g., germs, viruses, or genetic defects), but these notions are not adequate explanations for many people, since questions of meaning frequently beg for ultimate causes.

A foremost characteristic of the institution of medicine in modern Western societies is its differentiation from other institutions that provide meaning and belonging. **Institutional differentiation** is the process by which the various institutional spheres in society become separated from each other (see Parsons, 1966). For example, religious functions are focused in special religious institutions, which are separate from other institutions, such as the educational, political, and economic. The medical institution has limited itself to the cure of disease, as a biophysical entity, and to the physical tending of the diseased individual. The functions of healing that provide meaning and belonging are treated as relatively unimportant, and are relegated to the private-sphere institutions of family and religion. These private-sphere institutions are allowed, even encouraged, to handle the meaning problems of the sick, but only so long as their beliefs and actions do not interfere with the medical management of the disease (McGuire, 1985).

Just as the physical body is a potent symbol of one's selfhood, so too are experiences of suffering linked with one's identity, as discussed in Chapter 7. Practically, being unwell implies being disabled, in the sense of being made unable to do what one wants or needs to do; it implies reduced agency. It means losing some control (an especially important quality in this society), and it involves losing one's routines—the very patterns by which daily existence is ordered (Cassell, 1982; see also Comaroff, 1982).

Suffering is not connected with disease or pain in any precise causal or proportionate way. The pain of childbirth, for example, may be more severe than the pain of angina, but it generally causes less suffering because it is perceived as temporary and is associated with a desired outcome. A disease may be incurable yet cause little suffering if it does little damage to the person's sense of self and ability to engage in everyday life. For example, a chronic fungal infection of the big toe may cause less suffering than a temporary but disfiguring episode of Bell's palsy. Many people may seek help and healing less for disease itself than for suffering and affliction.

Cassell (1982: 639) has suggested that suffering poses difficulty for the biomedical system, because it is "experienced by persons, not merely by bodies, and has its sources in challenges that threaten the intactness of the person as a complex social and psychological entity." He observed that medical personnel can unknowingly cause suffering when they do not validate the patient's affliction, and when they fail to acknowledge or deal with the personal meanings the patient attaches to the illness. Cassell (1982: 642) noted that "people suffer from what they have lost of themselves in relation to the world of objects, events and relationships." One woman still suffered greatly from a hysterectomy she had undergone six years earlier. As she explained, "It meant losing a huge part of my future." Unmarried, childless, and only 29 years old, she lost hopes and dreams for the future. She expressed enormous anger at the insensitivity of physicians and hospital staff who had treated her "like an ungrateful child, crying over spilt milk" (quoted in McGuire, 1988). The medical personnel, even if thoroughly well intentioned, probably felt their sole duty was the correct treatment of her specific uterine problem; the woman's suffering was not their problem nor relevant to their tasks.

Whether brought on by a physical problem or not, affliction often results from a threat to the *coherence* of a person's world. As noted in Chapter 4, a sense of coherence itself is related to health and healing. People suffer from a loss of connectedness—links with loved ones, valued social roles, and groups that are important to them. As Chapter 7 shows, the illness experience often involves such losses. In the face of affliction, people seek meaning and order to address this essential coherence (Cassell, 1982; see also Antonovsky, 1984).

SUMMARY

Sickness is not merely the condition of an individual, but is also related to the larger social order. It is connected with moral issues and the imputation of responsibility for deviance from social norms. Society deals with such deviance through social control mechanisms, including the sick role. Sick role expectations, however, vary historically and cross-culturally. The discrepancies between the ideal image of the sick role, which is based upon certain forms of acute illness, and chronic and other nonacute conditions result in ambiguous expectations for those whom society defines as sick. The medicalization of deviance and the social stigma of illness highlight the social control functions of medicine, which are yet another connection between power and health. The medical profession has successfully asserted primacy in the defining deviance and the corollary function of certifying deviance, thereby becoming a primary moral authority in modern societies.

A related issue is the problem of meaning created by illness, suffering, and death. Because of the importance of the human body as a natural symbol, bodily control and healing practices reflect social relationships and concerns. The problems of meaning brought on by illness are particularly difficult in modern Western medical settings, due to the differentiation of medical institutions from meaning-providing institutions such as religion and family. The biomedical model, with its nearly exclusive focus on physical conditions, does not adequately deal with suffering and the subjective experience of affliction.

RECOMMENDED READINGS

Articles

SUSAN BORDO, "Reading the slender body," pp. 83–112 in M. Jacobus, E. F. Keller, and S. Shuttleworth, eds., *Body/Politics: Women and the Discourses of Science*. New York: Routledge, 1990.

JEAN COMAROFF, "Medicine: Symbol and ideology," pp. 49–68 in P. Wright and A. Treacher, eds., *The Problem of Medical Knowledge: Examining the Social Construction of Medicine*. Edinburgh: Edinburgh University Press, 1982.

ROBERT CRAWFORD, "A cultural account of 'health': Control, release, and the social body," pp. 60–103 in J. B. McKinlay, ed., *Issues in the Political Economy of Health Care*. New York: Tavistock, 1984.

MARGARET LOCK and NANCY SCHEPER-HUGHES, "A critical-interpretive approach in medical anthropology: Rituals and routines of discipline and dissent," pp. 47–72 in T. M. Johnson and C. F. Sargent, eds., *Medical Anthropology: A Handbook of Theory and Method*. New York: Greenwood Press, 1990.

NANCY E. WAXLER, "Learning to be a leper: A case study in the social construction of illness," pp. 169–194 in Elliot G. Mishler, Lorna R. AmaraSingham, Stuart T. Hauser, Ramsay Liem, Samuel D. Osherson, and Nancy E. Waxler, *Social Contexts of Health, Illness, and Patient Care*. Cambridge: Cambridge University Press, 1981.

Books

PETER CONRAD and JOSEPH W. SCHNEIDER, *Deviance and Medicalization: From Badness to Sickness*. Philadelphia: Temple University Press, 1992. This highly readable volume explains the medicalization process, illustrating it with detailed examinations of the medicalization of mental illness, alcoholism, opiate addiction, hyperkinesis, child abuse, homosexuality, and criminality.

CHAPTER SEVEN

The Illness Experience

Illness is a profoundly human experience that calls into question normal expectations about our bodies and capacities. When illness is not part of our life, we take the relationship between our bodies and our selves for granted. Indeed, we are not likely to think about our bodies or be particularly conscious of many bodily sensations. In health, we expect our bodies to be able to function and to sustain a presentation of our selves as normal, reliable participants in social interaction (Dingwall, 1976: 98). What we call illness is a disturbance in body processes or experience that has become problematic for the individual.

ILLNESS AND SELF

The experience of illness, even if only temporary, reminds us of our limitations, of our dependencies—present and potential, and of our ultimate mortality. When ill, our bodies inform us that they cannot always be counted on to be able for what we want them to do. Because our very sense of who we are and our important social relationships are intimately connected with our bodies and their routine functioning, being ill is disruptive and disordering. We identify our selves with our bodies, as evidenced by one physician's introspective account of his own accident and gradual recovery. He exclaimed, "What seemed, at first, to be no more than a local peripheral breakage and breakdown now showed itself in a different, and quite terrible, light—as a breakdown of memory, of thinking, of will—*not just a lesion in my muscle, but a lesion in me*" (Sacks, 1984: 67).

Thus, the illness experience is much more than a biophysical event; it has far-reaching social, emotional, moral, and spiritual implications. Kleinman's (1988, 1978) distinction between disease and illness is useful. According to his definitions, **disease** refers to the biophysical condition—the problem as seen from the biomedical practitioner's perspective. The physician transforms the patient's and the family's expressions of illness into terms that fit the theoretical models of disease. By contrast, **illness** refers to "how the sick person and the members of the family or wider social network perceive, live with, and respond to symptoms and disability" (Kleinman, 1988: 3–6). Because doctors of Western medicine have been trained to focus almost exclusively on disease, they have difficulty in dealing with the illness experience (Kleinman, 1978).

This chapter focuses on the experiences of illness and pain, especially as shaped by social structure and culture. While even the most minor illness can be problematic for the sufferer, we shall emphasize those illnesses most likely to have a damaging effect on the person's identity and sense of self (see Oleson et al., 1990). Most everyday illnesses are not profoundly disruptive, although they too remind the sufferer of personal limits and dependencies. If I have a bout of the flu, I may be very miserable, fall far behind in my work, and be temporarily dependent on family and friends, unable to reciprocate their care; however, such illness does not significantly challenge my relationships and my identity. Likewise, many accidents wounding the body and many acute illnesses, while temporarily very discomforting or even seriously threatening, do not damage the ill person's sense of self. If I suffer acute pneumonia, the condition may be life-threatening and require dramatic medical intervention—hospitalization, antibiotics, and intense nursing care—but I emerge to retain my essential relationships and identity. Other illnesses, however, are deeply disruptive, threatening the ill person's important relationships and very sense of self (Bury, 1991).

Loss is one factor that can make an illness experience profoundly disruptive. People actively grieve because the loss of body parts (e.g., amputation of an arm) or functions (e.g., partial blindness) represent loss of integrity—the wholeness of the person (Cassell, 1982). People suffer not only from the loss of present capacities and roles, but also from being robbed of their future: the teenager who is a paraplegic after a car accident, the childless young woman who has a hysterectomy, the middle-aged lawyer who loses her eyesight, the elderly musician whose arthritis makes playing a beloved instrument impossible.

Chronic illness and pain in particular force the sufferer to come to new terms with the experience of time. Sometimes a life-threatening acute illness or a serious accident has such impact, but an acute condition is—by definition—temporary. Chronic illness, by contrast, often leads to a radical reassessment, in light of changed and yet-changing capacities, of one's self in relationship to one's past and future. The experience of chronic illness thus involves both a sense of loss and a heightened self-consciousness (Charmaz, 1991; 1987). Chronic illness often demands complex strategies for managing symptoms. Adhering to drug regimens must be balanced against the side effects of drugs; symptoms may be concealed from other people; life must be scheduled around symptom flare-ups or to avoid flare-ups (Bury, 1991; Pinder, 1988). These strategies break up taken-for-granted rhythms and activities of daily life and heighten self-consciousness.

Illness is especially damaging to the self when it is experienced as overwhelming, unpredictable, and uncontrollable because it paralyzes the person's ability to manage life, to plan, and to act. Enormous attention must be given not merely to actual crisis periods in the illness but also to minute, mundane worries such as: Can I visit my friend's apartment without having an asthma attack? Can I make it to the bathroom quickly enough? If I attempt sexual intercourse, will my back pain flare up? Do I risk a heart attack if I take on this interesting project at work? Can I negotiate the path from my car to the store? (cf. Kleinman, 1988: 44). Unpredictability and uncontrollability result in a disjunction between the person and the body; the functioning that was once taken for granted is gone, and the person in effect feels, "I cannot count on my body. *It* fails *me*." The body becomes an "other"—at best an unpredictable ally.

Illness that results in ongoing social marginality is also particularly damaging to the self. Much of our web of social relationships is predicated upon the assumptions that members will be able to reciprocate, that one member will not be utterly dependent upon others, and that all give and receive. Some illnesses undermine the assumption of reciprocity and thus make social relationships precarious. Losing independence is threatening to one's sense of self not just because of pride in self-sufficiency (a related value in our culture), but more because it impairs one's ability to

participate as an equal in important social relationships. Valued friendships and social roles become strained or lost altogether. Often the individual lives in a deliberately collapsed world because the larger world becomes unmanageable or threatening.
One woman commented:

> What is really so awful is that illness, I believe, really makes you very lonely. . . . One
> is really out of the world. *When there is illness one is, and one stays, alone.* It's very
> hard to get help. . . . It destroys what one would like to do, it isolates you. . . . If I got
> into very poor health, I could no longer take care of them as I do. . . . I would be cut off
> from my family, life would have to be organized without me, I would not play the role
> that I play now. I believe that one who is sick is outside of normal life (quoted in Herzlich
> and Pierret, 1987: 178).

Pain and treatment often become a focus for the chronically ill, forcing them
to withdraw into themselves. Lack of access to everyday activities also fosters isolation. Others, unable to deal with chronic problems, socially withdraw, and thus a
spiral of increasing isolation is set into motion: The less one can or wants to do, the
less one socializes; but the less one socializes, the more others withdraw, and in turn
the more the person with a chronic illness withdraws. One man with severe rheuma-
toid arthritis said:

> Now the only place I go now is down to the local club. Everybody knows me sort of
> thing. They might say it's a shame for him, but nobody bothers me, they accept me as
> I am. But if I go anywhere else . . . people are embarrassed. People say 'bloody hell, is
> that . . . ? Dear me, what's the matter with him?' And they try not to catch your eye, if
> you will. People tend to stay away from you. I don't know, they just don't want to be
> involved. You tend to do the same then (quoted in Bury, 1982: 176).

All the more marginalizing are illness experiences involving stigma, which by
definition has the potential to discredit the self that the individual is trying to present
to others. For example, one young woman had undergone a colostomy in which a
large part of her colon was surgically removed, necessitating the perpetual wearing
and cleaning of a device that collected and held the contents of her bowels. She exclaimed:

> I feel so embarrassed by this—this thing. It seems so unnatural, so dirty. I can't get used
> to the smell to it. I'm scared of soiling myself. Then I'd be so ashamed I couldn't look
> at anyone else. . . . Who would want a wife like this? How can I go out and not feel un-
> able to look people in the eyes and tell them the truth? Once I do, who would want to
> develop a friendship, I mean a close one? How can I even consider showing my body
> to someone else, having sex? (quoted in Kleinman, 1988: 163).

Since control is so strongly valued in our culture, loss of control is especially
problematic. People experience an assault on their sense of self when their illnesses
involve losses of control, such as incontinence, loss of bowel control, flatulence,

seizures, stumbling and falling, tics and tremors, and drooling. We rely on relative control of our bodies to present ourselves in socially valued ways (Schneider and Conrad, 1983; Goffman, 1963), but chronic illness and disability disrupt that control. Furthermore, in a culture in which productivity, vigor, beauty, and youth are very important values, disability and aging are especially threatening. Disability and chronic illness may remind people of their vulnerability (Livneh, 1991; Murphy, 1987). Thus, certain chronic illnesses and disabilities are especially likely to threaten the individual's sense of self and connectedness with others.

Even with nonfatal chronic illnesses, such as arthritis, the illness experience requires individuals, families, and personal networks to continually confront problems of uncertainty, dependency, and understanding. It also necessitates the negotiation of new role relationships with others. Sometimes a chronic illness may result in outright conflict or rejection (Bury, 1988; see also Schott and Badura, 1988). A retired lawyer described the effects on himself and his family of his wife's ten years of decline with Alzheimer's disease:

> Our children come and they cry. And I cry. We reminisce about old times. We try to recall what Anna was like before this happened. But I can see it wears them out just being here for a day or two. They've got their own troubles. I can't ask them to help out any more than they do already. Me? It's made a different person out of me. I expect you wouldn't have recognized me if you had met me ten years ago. I feel at least ten years older than I am. I'm afraid what will happen if I go first. I haven't had a half hour free of worry and hurt for ten years. This illness didn't just destroy Anna's mind, it has killed something in me, in the family, too. If anyone asks about Alzheimer's, tell them it is a disease of the whole family (quoted in Kleinman, 1988: 183).

Illness is not experienced merely by the individual in whose body the symptoms are located; often the family and other close members of the sufferer's social network also feel the disruptiveness of illness. For example, the husband of a woman with cancer said:

> I keep saying we felt, like I guess I feel like this is my disease, too. That's because it's so drastic. It's a fight that she has to undertake, so it's partly mine, too. It's a psychological thing, the helplessness for the husband. This is not just her disease, it is my disease, too (quoted in Wilson, 1991).

The human response to illness is to give it meaning, to interpret it, to reorder the disordering experience. To make sense of what is happening to us, we draw upon socially available categories from a large cultural repertoire and from personal and family stories and meanings absorbed from our particular ethnic and religious backgrounds. In the case of minor illnesses, the interpretations might include our underlying definitions of health and illness, and our notions about why we got sick and how to get well. Seriously disruptive illnesses are likely to evoke further interpretations about the meaning of life, moral responsibility, suffering, relationships, and death.

LAY CONCEPTIONS OF HEALTH

How do you know you are sick? How do you know if your condition is potentially serious enough to warrant "doing something" about the illness? Long before any outside help (medical or otherwise) is sought, individuals interpret their own condition. Underlying all such evaluations is a set of ideas about health and illness. The concepts and logic of these ideas are not those of science or medicine, although they may be borrowed, accurately or inaccurately, from those formal systems of knowledge. Rather they are the concepts and logic of ordinary people whose experiences, socialization, cultural background, and immediate social network shape and continually develop their notions of health and illness.

Many people think of health as being simply the absence of illness. For example, a Scottish study of older persons found that key dimensions of health mentioned were an absence of illness, a reserve of strength, and a feeling of being generally fit or capable of accomplishing daily tasks (Williams, 1983). Corroborating evidence came from a study of middle-aged French subjects, who described health in terms of an absence of illness, an equilibrium in daily life, and a capacity to work (Herzlich and Pierret, 1987; Herzlich, 1973).

Other research found that while both working-class and middle-class persons shared the notion that health meant the absence of illness, working-class people tended to emphasize what was essential for their everyday lives: the ability to carry out their tasks, especially job and family duties (Blaxter and Paterson, 1982). Middle-class persons were more likely to mention broader, positive conceptions of health that included such factors as energy, positive attitudes, and the ability to cope well and to be in control of one's life (Saltonstall, 1993; Calnan, 1987; Herzlich, 1973). These views are illustrated by the following comments of a middle-class woman:

> I think that [truly healthy persons] . . . are very spontaneous and flexible, and I think they have more options that they experience. . . . They are feeling connected to a larger purpose and connected with other people. . . . I would also say that being in power, feeling powerful in your life, feeling responsible for your life is a very important part of it (quoted in McGuire, 1988).

The sense of being in control may be particularly important to the middle class, for it meshes with their experiences of making decisions and having a degree of control in their work and daily life. By contrast, because working-class persons have control over far fewer areas of their lives, this value may be remote or inconceivable to them. Crawford (1984: 78) argued that middle-class values have expanded the notion of health to something that must be actively achieved and proven, since "to be healthy [in this culture, means] to demonstrate to self and others appropriate concern for the virtues of self-control, self-discipline, self-denial, and will power."

There are important differences in lay conceptions of health and illness within various subcultures as well. Persons raised in different ethnic subcultures—Chicano, Irish, Appalachian, or Polish, for example—typically learn their group's ideas about health and illness, including: What is health? What can cause illness? What does a given illness mean? How can I protect myself and loved ones from illness? How can I counteract illness when it occurs? What can I expect to experience with different illnesses? What resources can I turn to for help in the face of illness?

Religious subcultures likewise influence not only their members' responses to illness but also their very definitions of health and illness. One member of a Christian healing group stated, "Health, wholeness—all these words to me are Scripture and salvation. It all goes together. A healthy person to me would be one that was whole in spirit, soul, mind, and body" (quoted in McGuire, 1988: 39). A study of middle-class spiritual healing groups found that, as persons became more actively involved, they expanded their notions of what needed healing in their lives. Because health was an ideal encompassing all their religious ideals, healing was a continual part of the process of striving for those goals (McGuire and Kantor, 1988, 1987).

Although there are few studies about other kinds of subcultural groups, it is probable that they too influence members' conceptions of health, illness, and healing. For example, to what extent is an adolescent subculture (and not just chronological age) a factor in the health notions of teenagers? Are there health belief systems communicated by other subcultures, such as homosexuals or the military? We have only begun to explore the diversity of lay conceptions of health and illness. The sketches we have thus far, however, illustrate the importance of lay conceptions for understanding people's behavior in the face of illness.

LAY UNDERSTANDINGS OF ILLNESS

Just as laypersons' notions of health are shaped by their social and cultural background, so too are the ways people understand their illnesses. People seek to comprehend what is wrong with them: What is the nature of this illness? Where did it come from? Why me? Why now? What can be done about this illness? What can be done to protect myself from other illness? Individual belief systems about illness are typically drawn from, but not necessarily rigidly determined by, larger cultural belief systems, which give shape to the illness experience, help the individual to interpret what is happening, and offer a number of choices about how to respond.

Lay images of various diseases reveal why certain responses "make sense." A study of middle-class New Yorkers found that people regularly refer to disease and diseased body parts as "its"—as objects separate from the person. This image allows ill persons to distance themselves from their problems. The concept of disease as an "it" also meshed with notions that the problem had its source in some external agent that invaded the body (Cassell, 1976). Because lay images of illness reflect people's diverse experiences, they vary by such factors as social class, gender, ethnicity, and religion.

A study of Scottish women showed the predominance of the image of disease as a thing that one "has," "gets," or "catches." Accordingly, "it" attacks, strikes, or sets in. One respondent said, "My family wis never bothered wi' their chest . . . it wis always their throats. It always went for their throat, not their chest" (quoted in Blaxter, 1983: 61). The regional idiom of "taking" a disease distinguishes temporary (typically infectious) illnesses from chronic illnesses or a clear physical abnormality. One might "take" pneumonia, measles, bronchitis, or scarlet fever, but not a tumor, cyst, arthritis, or cancer (Blaxter, 1983).

People employ their lay conceptions to explain the nature and causes of specific maladies. In one English community, respondents tended to think of their illnesses in terms of hot or cold and wet or dry; for example, a chest cold fit the wet-cold image, whereas a fever was depicted as hot-dry. By extension, then, certain maladies were linked especially with damp, cold weather or house environment. People held explicit images of the germs and viruses to which they attributed some illnesses. They often depicted these agents as clouds of tiny particles or as minute, invisible insects. Medical professionals sometimes participated in the use of these images, for example by explaining a problem as "a tummy bug" (Helman, 1978).

The causal categories used by laypersons may not be correct in bioscientific terms but are generally rational and based upon the kinds of empirical evidence available to laypersons. One Scottish study showed the most commonly invoked lay causal categories were, in rank order: (1) infection; (2) heredity or familial tendencies; (3) agents in the environment, such as "poisons," working conditions, and climate; (4) secondary products of other diseases; and (5) stress, strain, and worry (Blaxter, 1983; similar categories were found by Locker, 1981: 67).

The interpretation of illness is an ongoing process. People reinterpret their situation at various stages of their illness. They look back at earlier experiences and actions, and reinterpret them to make sense of subsequent events and new beliefs. Interaction with physicians is only one source, among many, of people's reinterpretations (Hunt et al., 1989). Interaction with important others is another source of new interpretations. One purpose for this ongoing reconstruction is to make sense of a whole sequence of events, rather than viewing each part as an episode that just "happened." Thus, for example, cardiac patients retrospectively noticed the symptoms which had built up to their heart attack. Their reconstruction of the meaning of the sequence of events made the heart attack seem less threatening and more understandable (Cowie, 1976).

Cross-cultural research suggests that several explanatory logics are used by laypersons, including those in "modern" Western cultural settings. One category of logic is that of invasion, in which an outside agent is believed to come into the body to cause the illness. Examples include notions of possession, germ theory, or object intrusions. Another logic involves degeneration, in which the illness is explained as due to the breakdown of the body or its parts from such causes as exhaustion or the accumulation of toxic substances. Mechanical models provide another logic, explaining illness as the result of misalignment of body structures, or blockages of digestive or nervous channels, for example. A fourth logic commonly used is the notion of equilibrium, which attributes illness to the failure to maintain harmony (individual or social), balance, and order (Chrisman, 1977). While these categories can be used to analyze the logics of other cultures, they are all used extensively by laypersons in modern Western societies.

Lay understandings of illness typically address the broader issues of meaning, such as those discussed in Chapter 6: Why must I suffer? Why me and not someone else? Why now? Have I done something bad to bring this upon myself? Indeed, in much lay thinking cause and meaning are not separate interpretive categories. Serious illnesses in particular evoke broader causal interpretations that are often used in combination with medical interpretations. For example, one young woman accepted the medical etiology of her vision problems, but simultaneously employed a broader causal meaning to her illness: " 'With my eye problem, there was something that I didn't want to see. I couldn't get well until I opened my eyes to that something' " (quoted in McGuire, 1988).

NOTICING ILLNESS

How do people know they are ill? In addition to these underlying ideas about health and illness, a number of other social factors influence whether an individual will perceive a particular disturbance and come to define it as distressing enough to warrant further attention. People react to the meaning of a symptom, not merely the symptom itself. The significance of symptoms is not self-evident; the person must actively give attention and interpretation to them. Sometimes a bodily disturbance is sufficiently acute and obvious to merit certain treatment. A person with a gaping and painful wound that is bleeding profusely is not likely to ignore the bodily disturbance. Other disturbances, however, are more open to varying interpretations, including those that make the person less likely even to notice them. Mechanic (1976) suggested that the ordinary response to such disturbances involves testing hypotheses by observing the situation over time. Part of this process involves assuming a wait-and-see stance to test such hypotheses as: This is something minor, the body will heal itself, and further symptoms may develop to give a better idea of what this could be.

Typically, people try to normalize their symptoms. They interpret disturbances as within the range of "okay," or at least understandable. A man who was hospitalized for a heart attack stated:

> I just felt rotten and I had a pain in my chest and I thought it was indigestion. I'd been rushing in the lunch hour and lifted a heavy box and all this sort of thing, and it was, oh three quarters of an hour after the actual rush that I felt the pain (quoted in Cowie, 1976).

Normalizing a disturbance, however, does not necessarily make it unimportant or less real. For example, a person might normalize an excruciating abdominal pain by interpreting it as a bout of recurring gall bladder problems. For this reason, the response to acute illnesses is typically different from the response to chronic illnesses. One U.S. study found that for acute problems, people focus on the symptoms. The amount of effort the individual puts into some form of treatment often depends upon the severity of the symptoms themselves. For chronic problems, by contrast, people develop strategies of management over a long term. When problems flare up, the response is routinized and not necessarily directly related to the severity of symptoms of that single episode (Verbrugge and Ascione, 1987).

PAIN AND ITS PSYCHOSOCIAL DIMENSIONS

The sociocultural and psychological dimensions of pain demonstrate how profoundly greater the illness experience is compared to its mere biophysical aspect. Because the medical model does not adequately encompass these dimensions, it often fails to meet the needs of pain sufferers. Pain is a form of biofeedback essential to our survival. Occasionally someone is born without the capacity to feel pain. In one such case, the person was deformed by the age of 25 because he had severely burned his hand and suffered other injuries without feeling them. Further, the ulceration and wearing down of bodily extremities characteristic of leprosy were once thought to be symptoms of the disease, until it was discovered that they were produced by its deadening of the victim's ability to feel pain (Neal, 1978: 47–50). Although pain is an essential warning system for the body, it can also be a scourge and a terrible existential reality, a source of fear and anxiety that in some cases becomes all-consuming and overwhelming.

Pain is the symptom that people report most frequently when they see a doctor. Musculoskeletal problems (e.g., lower back pain, joint pain, or arthritis) are the leading causes of disability among people in their working years; back pain is second only to respiratory problems as a reason for missing work (Osterweis et al., 1987). Approximately 7 million Americans have serious back problems (Bogin, 1982). A nationwide sample of 1,254 adults revealed that about 75 percent of Americans suffer from occasional headaches and more than 50 percent from back and muscular pain. People who reported high levels of stress also reported high levels of all kinds of pain (Schmeck, 1985). Pain seems to be a very individual and personal matter. As a physical sensation, it does not seem to be subject to sociocultural influences, yet there are many ways in which the private world of pain interacts with the sociocultural world.

The clinical reality of pain is, however, complex, and involves three components: a person's actual sensation of pain; a person's tolerance *threshold* for pain; and a person's expression of pain. Pain is unique as a medical phenomenon, since its measurement relies on individuals' accounts of what they are feeling as well as the doctors' observations of pain-related behavior. The doctor can observe a person's gait or flex limbs to see if pain is inhibiting movement, but all indicators are based on what the patient says or does. In other words, pain measurement depends on patients' intended or unintended expressions of the pain they are feeling. Although of limited reliability, several laboratory techniques (e.g., thermography and positron emission tomography scans) attempt to measure organic signs of pain without relying on patients' reports, but these are only indirect measures of the manifestations of pain, such as the degree of sympathetic nervous system activity (Osterweis et al., 1987: 141–142). Thus, clinicians must rely heavily upon the individual sufferers to describe or show what they feel.

Pain as a Biosocial Phenomenon

Pain is obviously a sensation; a cut finger produces a "simple" physical sensation. Pain generally involves more than simply a physical sensation, however, because it is imbued with meaning. For some ballet students or athletes, the pain that comes with a workout is "good pain," or a normal, acceptable consequence of well-done exercise, whereas a sharp, sudden new pain of unknown origin would signal that something fundamental has gone wrong. One doctor observed that the wounded soldiers he was treating during World War II complained of less pain and requested less pain medication than civilians who had suffered equally serious wounds. The soldiers, for whom the wounds meant leaving the battlefield and further danger of death, apparently experienced and tolerated pain differently (Beecher, 1956).

While pain obviously involves physical sensations, it is often more than just sensations. As something that accompanies disease or a serious injury, pain takes on meaning as a form of suffering. "People in pain report suffering from pain when they feel out of control—when the pain is overwhelming, when the source of pain is unknown, when the meaning of the pain is dire or when the pain is chronic" (Cassell, 1982: 641). In short, when pain threatens one's integrity as a person and one's physical existence, it becomes suffering (Cassell, 1982). These negative meanings of pain may in turn amplify the physical sensations the person experiences (Kleinman, 1988).

In Chapter 4, we argued that the mind and the body should be seen as an interrelated whole. Placebos, for example, do not merely relieve pain "in the mind" but can also generate physical changes by stimulating the release of pain-relieving endorphins. The spinal-gate control theory of pain suggests another mind-body-society thoroughfare by proposing that activity in the nervous system affects the opening and closing of "gates" in the spinal cord that modulates the flow of pain messages. Most theories of pain hold that a specific pain stimulus produces an input in the form of a pain message that travels upward along the spinal cord to a pain center in the brain, where an "alarm" is set off. In contrast, the spinal-gate control theory argues that pain messages from the frontal cortex (a higher brain center), from the limbic system (a midbrain area that controls emotions), and from other parts of the body can affect the opening and closing of these spinal gates, and thus modify incoming pain messages (Melzack and Wall, 1983). The experience of pain is, however, more than an incoming sensation, since it is affected by emotional states and higher-order cognitive mental functions (Bendelow, 1993; Osterweis et al., 1987). Indeed, pain does have important biopsychosocial and cultural dimensions (Bates, 1987; Freund, 1982).

There may be ethnic variations in the experience of pain as well (Bates, 1987). Some studies suggest that men and women may differ in pain tolerance, with the male threshold allegedly being higher. Racial differences have also been indicated; whites appear to have the highest tolerance for pain, and blacks and orientals, less (Woodrow et al., 1972). Of course major individual variations within groups exist, and all of these measures of tolerance are based on pain expressions and the way they are interpreted. The research is by no means conclusive, but it strongly suggests that such variations exist. But are they biological, cultural, or biocultural (Bates, 1987; Overfield, 1985)?

Sociocultural Variations in Pain Expression

Pain expression refers to how a person shows and behaviorally responds to pain. Pain expression is clearly influenced by sociocultural factors. Cultures in which emotional control is valued encourage stoicism about pain. "Big boys don't cry!" reveals a cultural expectation that adult males should repress the expression of pain. The ability to control the social presentation of pain even under conditions that inflict a great deal of pain may be a sign of one's moral status (i.e., one's "manhood," moral uprightness, or reliability). An elder of the Kuranko society of Sierra Leone in Africa, for example, describes the circumcision of an adolescent going through a puberty rite:

> Even when they are cutting the foreskin you must not flinch. You have to stand stone still. You must not make a sound from the mouth. Better to die than to wince or blink or cry out (quoted in Jackson, 1983).

In the Kuranko society, control over pain expression symbolizes the ability to assume an adult male role. Painful procedures such as tatooing and scarification are endured by adolescents partly because the expression of pain is negatively sanctioned, and perhaps because the meaning and honor of the procedure affects the experience of pain itself. Many athletes endure pain that most other people would not. On the whole, however, our culture teaches that pain can and should be avoided, and we tend to medicate it extensively (Kleinman, 1988; Bogin, 1982).

Under some situations, persons suffer excruciating pain, yet must quickly learn to manage their expression in order not to threaten a group's morale or its ability to function. Medical settings are an excellent example of this. Were one to scream hysterically in a dentist's chair, what influence would this have on waiting patients, especially small children? In hospitals the treatment for severe burns, which includes scrubbing the wounds, scraping away dead tissue, and applying new dressings and medication, inflicts a lot of pain in addition to the extreme pain of the burns themselves. However, burn victims are socialized into enduring the pain by the "coaching" of staff as well as of other patients who have been through similar experiences (Fagerhaugh and Strauss, 1977).

People from varying cultural backgrounds present their symptoms, including pain, in different ways (Good and Good, 1981). Zborowski's (1969, 1952) study of hospitalized male patients suffering from back pain and spinal lesions found that Jewish and Italian men were particularly vocal and disturbed about their pain. While Italians were concerned with immediate pain relief, however, the Jews worried about the pain's implications for their future. Anglo-American patients wanted the pain taken care of but were not as vocal in their pain expression. Irish patients were the most stoic and likely to deny pain. Zborowski's work has been criticized for its limited sample, broad and overly stereotypic generalizations about ethnic groups, and the fact that subjects were studied only in a medical setting. Yet Zborowski's study pointed the way to understanding cultural variations in the expression and possibly also the experience of pain. Zola (1983, 1966), for example, also found ethnic differences in how people showed and talked about their symptoms. Italians, for instance, described their symptoms more expansively and emotionally. Another study found ethnic differences in responses to pain from Asians, Afro-West Indians, and Anglo-Saxons (Thomas and Rose, 1991).

Generalizations about different groups' responses to pain must be used cautiously and not become the basis of stereotyping. While we may have typical ways of expressing ourselves, social situational factors can affect how we will express ourselves. Expressing pain must not be confused with *feeling* pain; for instance, acting stoic does not mean that one feels no pain. Even if people from various social categories (e.g., social classes, gender, or cultures) do present their pain differently, social and cultural factors also influence how observers interpret their pain expressions.

Responses to other people's pain expressions are influenced by cultural assumptions about what those expressions mean. An African woman's response to stomach pain due to infection may seem exaggerated to a Western-trained male doctor, but the woman's response is reasonable given her fears about infertility, a source of shame in her culture. The same woman, however, may handle the pain of childbirth without complaints (Susser et al., 1985: 136). One study of burn patients found Samoans (in contrast to, for instance, American burn patients) were calmer, more "stoic," accepting of the situation, and less complaining (Ablon, 1986). Zborowski (1969, 1952) and Zola (1983, 1966) found that because Italians expressed their pain so dramatically, non-Italian doctors tended to question the credibility of their Italian patients, interpreting their problems as "psychiatric." Such differences in the social and cultural backgrounds of doctor and patient can thus lead to very different interpretations of pain. One study found that

> the pain of women was treated later and less directly than the pain of men. Women suffered longer before being referred to the Pain Unit. They were less often treated with procedures specifically intended to cure the pain. The men in a shorter period since pain onset were operated upon twice as often as the women. Paradoxically, women reported twice as many surgical procedures unrelated to pain (Lack, 1982: 62).

Women were also given more minor tranquilizers, antidepressants, and analgesics, and fewer narcotics than men. This difference implies that the doctors took women's pain less seriously, interpreting it as of psychological origin; however, they accepted men's pain as "real" and prescribed painkillers. Was this difference due to variation in how men and women showed pain, or because of how male doctors interpreted women's presentations of pain? Other studies (e.g., Bendelow, 1993) suggest that health workers were more likely to believe that women's pain was more likely to be psychogenic.

The visibility of the source of pain is another significant factor in determining how seriously people take another's pain symptoms. It is often hard to see the cause of pain. Patients with chronic back pain may, for example, learn to conceal signs of pain, such as masking a limp caused by sciatic nerve pain. Because they look healthy, their pain may not always be taken seriously (Fagerhaugh and Strauss, 1977). By contrast, a bloody gash—even on a part of the body with relatively little nerve sensitivity—is taken seriously as a source of pain.

Chronic Pain

By definition, chronic pain is recurring or ongoing. It is not simply continuous but is experienced qualitatively differently from acute pain episodes. Because it is ongoing, chronic pain often has profound implications for a sufferer's life and very identity. People with chronic pain face continuing problems in symptom management (Strauss, 1975). How does one deal with pain and live life as normally as possible? People in chronic pain may not be able to tolerate regular employment, to follow schedules, or even to meet the demands of home life. Chronic pain is not always constant, but is often intermittent and unpredictable, flaring up unexpectedly (Bogin, 1982). Each day sufferers must manage a host of problems associated with activities that are taken for granted by others: They must pace their activities in order to tolerate or not aggravate the pain, and they must balance the undesired side effects of medication against the benefits of pain reduction.

Chronic pain also poses basic problems for the sufferer's sense of self. One person explained:

> Our personalities have been shaken to the core, and what we most counted on—our close relationships, our marriages, our jobs—may well have fallen by the wayside. Our whole sense of life has radically changed since pain became a part of it, yet no one seems to understand our listlessness, our loss of hope, our lack of optimism. Other people can't *see* our pain, so how can they imagine what it's done to us? Only someone who has lived with chronic pain knows how insidious the process is (Bogin, 1982: 4).

Acute pain goes away and does not become an ongoing, major focus of everyday existence. Chronic pain, by contrast, is a "somatic reminder that things are not right and may never be right. This reminder, phenomenally situated in one's own body, is inescapable" (Hilbert, 1984: 370). The body as subjectively experienced is transformed into an object with pain. One "moment one is one's body, the next one has a body" (Bergsma, 1982: 111). Chronic pain demands constant attention and can become all-consuming.

People in chronic pain often face invalidating responses from others, particularly if their pain is not believable or if an organic basis of pain is not apparent. One sufferer stated that she had considered unneeded surgery so that she would have a scar to show (Hilbert, 1984: 373). Another believed his several surgical treatments had worsened the pain but at least gave him scars that symbolized, to himself and others, the physical reality of the pain (Kleinman, 1988: 68). Core values in American culture may contribute to the invalidation experienced by chronic pain sufferers. Some anthropologists (Good et al., 1992: 205), writing on chronic pain, observed:

A number of our subjects complained of something akin to a North American *tyranny of health*. The dominant images in the popular culture extol physical vitality and deny anything short of robust health. Blemishes, illnesses that cannot be rapidly cured, and especially grave infirmities that suggest disability or death are banished from everyday life. A strong will, we are told, can influence the body, so infirmity is often associated with a lack of individual strength. The chronically ill feel great discomfit in this ethos. They are discredited as burdensome, anomalous, and, in some unspoken but definite way, responsible for their condition. Suffering is accorded no positive value. To bear distress and pain is not the same thing in the post-Reagan era as it was in Colonial, Jacksonian or Victorian America. It now carries no moral virtue. Quite the contrary, in the society of instant crises and quick remedies, of risk management for the unexpected, the very idea of *chronicity*, of predictable, serious long-term trouble, is unacceptable. Thus, the chronically ill—especially those with conditions that are at the borderline of respectability—feel that they are culturally illegitimate, unaccepted in the wider society.

Invalidating responses often come from doctors (Hilbert, 1984: 368), particularly when they are frustrated by their inability to treat effectively or find an organic cause for the pain (Kleinman, 1988; Bogin, 1982). Chronic pain challenges doctors' sense of competence and control. More significantly, chronic pain raises issues about mind-body relationships that threaten sharp distinctions between "real" versus "imagined," "psychological" versus "physical" pain (Good et al., 1992). "Physical" experiences of pain may be influenced by "perturbed" neuroendocrinological rhythms (Weiner, 1992). Physicians are unlikely to look for those factors and, given their assumptions about the nature of pain, would not "notice" them.

Invalidation of the reality of the experience of pain is particularly disconcerting because sufferers are being told that what their bodies are telling them is not real. Since our bodies and physical sensations are primary sources of our sense of reality, this invalidation is especially devastating (Kleinman, 1992; Ware, 1992; see also Ewan et al., 1991; Hilbert, 1984; Kotarba, 1977). Chronic pain sufferers find themselves in a bind. On the one hand, concealing signs of their pain reduces the likelihood that their claims to being in pain will be taken seriously. On the other hand, persons who regularly display and dramatize their pain risk wearing down other people's sympathy, placing a strain on their social support networks.

Somatization

In all cultures, the body serves as a means of expressing and communicating cultural, as well as personal, messages. Pain is a legitimate reason to assume the sick role (described in Chapter 6), thereby perhaps avoiding some undesired activity. Pain is one way people communicate social distress or a sense of social powerlessness. Sometimes, being in pain may be a way of avoiding difficult decisions. For example, a young adult's parents may be stifling her autonomy, but to leave home means to alienate them and to face an uncertain, perhaps hostile, existence away from home. Pain may be both a way of delaying the difficult decision and a means of communicating something about the conflicts she is experiencing (Kleinman, 1988).

Somatization is "the communication of personal and interpersonal problems in a physical idiom of distress and a pattern of behavior that emphasizes seeking of medical help" (Kleinman, 1988: 57). Somatization does not mean that the pain is inauthentic, except in cases of outright malingering. Pain may be physical in origin but sustained and amplified by sociopsychological factors. Social distress may create the physiological changes that amplify existing pain or create an experience of pain (Kleinman, 1988). In her study of Mexican women's sickness and pain, Finkler (1994) refers to the damaging effects of women's distresses, social situation (especially gender roles), and cultural beliefs as "life's lesions."

The particular idiom of distress used is drawn from a cultural repertoire. For example, in Iran "heart distress" is a meaningful expression linking an entire set of social concerns: infertility, attractiveness, sexual intercourse, pollution, and old age. Thus, when an Iranian complains of a "pressed heart," that complaint must be understood in terms of its cultural meanings (Good, 1977; cf. Guarnaccia and Farias, 1988). Even when it has sociopsychological sources, however, pain is not simply "in the mind" but also is a bodily phenomenon.[1] Labeling an illness *psychosomatic* or *psychogenic* delegitimates people's real suffering. Because their pain is expressed in body idioms, it is too easily medicalized and, thereby, distorted or trivialized. For example, to label the suffering of a Salvadoran refugee as posttraumatic stress disorder is to isolate and euphemize the consequences of pervasive political violence (Kleinman, 1992; Kleinman and Kleinman, 1991).

CHRONIC ILLNESS AND DISABILITY: THE POLITICS OF IMPAIRMENT

Because chronic illness and disability more seriously disturb the person's essential relationships and very sense of self, they result in a very different illness experience than acute illness. An **impairment** is the loss of some physiological or anatomical function, whereas a **disability** is the consequence of such an impairment, such as the inability to walk, climb stairs, or travel (Scheer and Croce, 1988: 23). Many people with disabilities object to the term *handicap* because of its negative connotations, especially when it implies that the whole person is handicapped. We shall, therefore, speak of persons with disabilities (Zola, 1993).

Although some people with chronic illnesses are impaired and disabled, chronic illness does not inevitably lead to disability. For example, diabetes may interfere only

[1]While pain always involves sociopsychological aspects, this should not detract from the reality of the physical aspects. A doctor who cannot discern organic sources of pain should not assume that there are none; biomechanical causes, for example, that were not detectible by earlier technologies (e.g., X-rays or myelograms) may appear through newer technologies (e.g., CT scans and magnetic resonance imaging). Is it possible that painful social experiences at one point in one's life (e.g., sexual abuse in childhood) may alter a person's physiological reactivity to pain later in life? Can socially distressing life circumstances increase pain sensitivity or amplify the painful effects of physical trauma? Perspectives such as Kleinman's (1988), that stress the biopsychosocial aspects of pain recognize the relationship between social life and pain, including the subjective reality of somatized pain.

minimally with some people's functioning. Some people with an impairment and a disability (for example, from an automobile accident) are not sick and may object to being defined as such. The sick role (described in Chapter 6) temporarily exempts people from normal activities; however, people with disabilities who are treated as though they were sick may find themselves prevented from participating in normal social activities and placed in a state of perpetual dependence. Nonetheless, many people with chronic illness have impairment and share problems with those who have experienced a loss of functioning at birth or due to a trauma (e.g., an accident).

Impairment is relatively verifiable in "objective" medical terms.[2] Disability, however, is not as easily defined separate from the social and cultural context of impairment. In a small Egyptian village, for example, trachoma (an infection that affects the eyelids) is widespread, but the "Western" standards of blindness do not apply to those who are afflicted. Instead, the social and cultural arrangements make it possible for many villagers with severely impaired vision to function without disability:

> Most visually impaired adults are illiterate, so they do not need signs to read. There are no street signs or house numbers to read in the hamlet. The structure of the village changes very slowly. If a new house is built every five years the visually impaired can learn to find their way around it. . . . Plowing, sowing seed and harvesting ripe produce do not require much vision. If there is some small task they are unable to do, their extended family does it for them. Thus, they do not perceive themselves as disabled (quoted in Cockburn, 1988: 13).

Until the 1940s, a significant proportion of the inhabitants of Martha's Vineyard in Massachusetts was deaf. The whole community knew sign language, and hearing people used it even among themselves. Sign language became a natural and ordinary form of communication. People with impaired hearing worked, married, and were not thought of as separate, significantly different, or as "special." They were, in short, not considered handicapped (Sacks, 1990).

Thus, whether an "objective" impairment becomes a disability depends on the environment, the expected daily activities, and the attitudes of others. A disability is not just the result of the limitations of a person's sensory, motor, cognitive, or other capabilities, but a "function of the interaction between the individual's condition and the environment, both physical and attitudinal—in which they live" (Gartner and Joe, 1987: 1). Impairment is universal, found among people in all societies; however, social and cultural responses and the "design" of social environments vary (Scheer and Croce, 1988). The sociological focus, therefore, is not on disabled people but on disabling attitudes and environments.

One definition used in the United States considers disability to be "an inability to engage in gainful employment"; more broadly, it refers to a reduction of activity, a "restricted activity day" (Mausner and Bahn, 1985: 113). Estimates of the number of Americans with disabilities range from about 35 to 43 million people, depending on who is counting and how (National Institute on Disability and

---

[2]Even in this respect, there is still the question of what is a "normal" body.

Rehabilitation Research, 1993; Shapiro, 1993: 6–7). Most common is difficulty in walking and lifting (*The New York Times*, 1986a). Nonwhite disabled people outnumber white disabled people by a ratio of about two to one (National Institute on Disability, 1986). These figures suggest that disabilities are not as uncommon as many believe. Our perceptions are based partly on the fact that Western society, especially the United States, tends to deny and to segregate disability, old age, and death. Furthermore, the likelihood of having a disability is socially distributed, as are individual resources for coping with disability.

Categorizing people as disabled has implications for social policy, as Zola (1982: 242) pointed out:

> By trying to find strict measures of disability or focusing on "severe," "visible" handicaps we draw dividing lines and make distinctions where matters are very blurry and constantly changing. By agreeing that there are 20 million disabled or 36 million, or even that half the population are in some way affected by disability, we delude ourselves into thinking there is some finite, no matter how large, number of people. . . . Any person reading the words on this page is at best momentarily able-bodied. But nearly everyone reading them will, at some point, suffer from one or more chronic diseases and be disabled, temporarily or permanently, for a significant part of their lives.

Being disabled is a "normal" condition of humanity, and categorizing people by disability status can create misleading distinctions. Such definitions are social and political constructions, as illustrated by the fact that the boundaries are historically shifting and cross-culturally variable (Fine and Asch, 1988; Osterweis et al., 1987).

Chronic illness is, by definition, ongoing, recurrent, and often degenerative. Conrad (1987) suggested that there are different types of chronic illnesses, each with its own social implications: "lived-with" illness, such as asthma and diabetes; "mortal" illness, such as some cancers; and "at risk" illnesses, which include inherited, "environmental," or "personal" behavior risks. People with disabilities or chronic illnesses in our society face a number of common problems regarding the social organization of their environments, the attitudes of others, and their sense of self.

Disability, Chronic Illness, and the Social Organization of Space and Time

The organization of the spaces in which people move and the time arrangements of their activities are related to the quality of life and health. Building codes, government ordinances, financial considerations, and many other factors structure the qualities of the buildings in which we work, live, and play (Hahn, 1988). Social and political considerations influence the quality and accessibility of transportation. Zola (1982: 208) described the inhospitable nature of many environments for a person wearing a leg brace:

> Chairs without arms to push myself up from; unpadded seats which all too quickly produce sores; showers and toilets without handrails to maintain my balance; surfaces too slippery to walk on; staircases without bannisters to help me hoist myself; buildings

without ramps, making ascent exhausting if not dangerous; every curbstone a precipice; car, plane, and theatre seats too cramped for my braced leg; and trousers too narrow for my leg brace to pass through. With such trivia is my life plagued. Even though I am relatively well off, mobility is a daily challenge.

Imagine trying to walk about in a physical space designed only for those in wheelchairs. The doors would be too low, the floors would be too slippery for walking, and no chairs would be provided for sitting. People with physical impairments simply have more specialized or individual physical needs than those without impairments. The failure of social environments to account for individual rhythms and patterns for comfortable movement contributes to problems in health and the quality of life for all people, but to a greater degree for people with impairments.

While technological advances have made it possible for many people with disabilities to survive and potentially to function, such advances have not generally been applied to the design of public, work, and living environments. We live increasingly in humanmade, artificial spaces that are not currently adapted to a wide spectrum of bodies but could be so modified. In recent years, however, there has been a slight shift toward creating more environments of "universal" or "transgenerational" design, geared to the needs of persons with some physical impairment (Shapiro, 1993). While no environment can accommodate everyone's needs, "universally" designed spaces are intended for use by the widest possible range of bodies. One example is a park recently built for access both by able-bodied and disabled people; its tennis, pool, and special swings are designed for use by people in wheelchairs (Brown, 1988).

Much research on chronic illness and impairment focuses on malingering and whether government financial benefits motivate people not to work; instead, however, research should examine how work conditions themselves discourage the chronically ill from maintaining their jobs. The nature of the job, such as the pace of work and the physical design of the work place, is an important determinant of work disability (Osterweis et al., 1987; Yelin, 1986). During World War II people with disabilities assumed many of the jobs vacated by those who went to war. For all workers during that time, there were lower rates of absenteeism, work-related accidents, and turnover, and higher rates of production. After the war, workers with disabilities were replaced by returning "able-bodied" veterans (Struck, 1981: 26). The nature of the job, such as the pace of work and the physical design of the work place, is an important determinant of work disability (Osterweis et al., 1987; Yelin, 1986). Shorter, more flexible work schedules, opportunities for breaks, and general social-temporal arrangements that accommodate slower or differently paced rhythms would allow individuals with impairments to function more effectively.

People with chronic impairments do not usually challenge disabling time limitations and pressures. They do not generally question the arrangements of work and living spaces in which they must function; rather, they typically assume such arrangements to be natural and given (Charmaz, 1983). People come to believe that their inability to squeeze their bodies and rhythms of movement into inadequate social-spatial arrangements are signs of their *personal* inadequacy. Disabling environments and attitudes thus contribute to a loss of sense of self and to suffering among those who have chronic physical impairments (Charmaz, 1991).

Disabling Attitudes and Sense of Self

Our society often places people who violate somatic norms into institutions or segregates them behind the scenes of everyday life (Baird, 1992). One woman with multiple sclerosis commented:

> I once asked a local advertiser why he didn't include disabled people in his spots. His response seemed direct enough. "We don't want to give people the idea that our product is just for the handicapped," he said. . . . If you saw my blind niece ordering a Coke, would you switch to Pepsi lest you be struck sightless? No, I think the advertiser's excuse masked a deeper and more anxious rationale: to depict disabled people in the ordinary activities of daily life is to admit that there is something ordinary about disability itself, that it might enter anybody's life. If it is effaced completely or at least isolated as a separate "problem," so that it remains at a safe distance from other human issues, then the viewer won't feel threatened by her or his own physical vulnerability (Mairs, 1987: C2).

The suffering created by such discrediting attitudes is not just a matter of the personal attitudes themselves but also the social conditions that engender them (Charmaz, 1983).

The stigmatizing opinions of others have a strong impact on one's sense of self. A stigma is a deeply discrediting attribute that, when visible, can brand a person as less than human, as pitiable, horrible, and publicly discreditable. The degree to which an attribute is stigmatizing depends on its sociohistorical context and the status of the person who possesses such an attribute:

> Conjure in your mind a military man with an eye patch. Is there not something romantic and heroic about the injury? Doesn't it suggest a dark and complex past, a will of uncommon strength, perhaps a capability for just enough brutality to add a trace of virile unpredictability to the man? Now replace the image of the mysterious man who wears an eye patch with the image of a 7-year-old girl who wears one. For most people, something strange happens. The romance and mystery disappear; what we see is a handicapped child. There is something sad and even pitiful about her; we fear for her future and worry about her present. We think: this poor kid is going to have a hard time growing up and making it in this world (Gliedman and Roth, 1980: 29).

In all societies, certain deviations from somatic norms are considered stigmatizing, but there are no inherently stigmatizing attributes. Rather, stigma is a social construction that depends on person and context.

In our society, those with "severe" impairments are sometimes viewed as

> visually repulsive; helpless; pathetic; dependent; too independent; plucky, brave and courageous; bitter with chips on our shoulders; evil (the "twisted mind in a twisted body"); mentally retarded; endowed with mystical powers and much else (Sutherland, 1981: 58).

Some of these attitudes are changing. The mass media, however, perpetuate stereo-types that associate disability with evil and criminality (e.g., characters like Frankenstein's hunchbacked assistant), a loss of self-control, an attempt to compensate for their impairment, and a tendency to either be asexual or "perversely" preoccupied with sex (Longmore, 1987).

Media images project some heroic role models: the blind skier, the one-legged pitcher who made it to the major leagues, and Helen Keller and her many achievements.[3] These examples show people's ability to transcend the most limiting of conditions, and in that respect they are inspiring. They may, however, imply another message: "that if a Franklin Delano Roosevelt and a Wilma Rudolph could *overcome* their handicap, so could and should all the disabled. And if we fail, it is our problem, our personality, our weakness" (Zola, 1982: 204–205). Many media "success" stories similarly communicate a message in the tune with the American ethos of rugged individualism and responsibility for oneself. This imagery, however, deflects from an understanding of the mundane problems faced by those with impairments and the many barriers that most humans simply cannot overcome.

Sexual expression is an important source of pleasure, tension release, and sense of self. Until recently, however, the prevalent attitude, even among many professionals working with people with disabilities, was to deny or avoid recognition of their sexuality. The deviation of persons with disabilities from somatic norms often arouses an aesthetic anxiety in others, particularly in Western societies, which put a high premium on "supernormal standards of bodily perfection" (Baird, 1992; Hahn, 1988: 42). Our sexual fantasies are saturated with images from advertising and the entertainment world. Media-driven standards of sexual attractiveness, particularly for women, result in even greater disadvantages for people whose bodies deviate from the ideal (Sutherland, 1987: 27). Zola (1982) described a Swedish experiment in which counselors acted as sex surrogates with their clients who had disabilities; the experiment was stopped, however, because the counselors began to enjoy their contacts. The fear that "deviant" bodies may be "deviant" only in the eyes of the beholder made this experiment a threat. Some societies have begun to accept sexual pleasure as a *right* for the disabled. In 1992, a government agency in the Netherlands ruled that a municipality must pay a person with a disability a monthly stipend to cover the services of a sex surrogate (Stalk, 1992).

People with disabilities also face special problems in the management of such emotions as anger. First, the impairment itself may inhibit anger expression. Being physically weak or on crutches may make the direct, motoric, dramatic expression of emotions difficult. Furthermore, disabling attitudes and environments force people into a state of dependency beyond the biological consequences of their impairments.

People with disabilities are also socialized out of their anger. They are expected to be grateful for what help they receive and cannot "afford" the luxury of overt anger

---

[3]Very few people know that Helen Keller was displayed for a while as an exhibit, like the Elephant Man, in a vaudeville show!

expression for fear of risking the alienation of the people on whom they depend (Zola, 1982). Like fat people, people with disabilities are expected to tolerate their situation quietly and to be cheerful and jolly (Charmaz, 1991: 201). When people regularly and vocally respond to frustrating or disempowering conditions, they further risk having their anger treated as a by-product of their impairment rather than as an appropriate response to their social environment or living conditions. The docudrama "Captives of Care" depicted a resident of an institution who was angry with the staff for the arbitrary limits imposed by institutional life. In one encounter, he lashed out at a nurse for invading his privacy. The nurse did not understand his reaction, and a colleague explained to her that "that's the way he is because he is twisted." Because his physical impairment was thus seen as explaining his behavior, his protest over institutional conditions was invalidated.

The constant emotional work involved in managing anger often results in repressing the anger, and turning it inward and against oneself. Zola (1982: 222) argued that depression among those with disabilities is partly due to constraints against getting angry. This depression is often viewed as the individual's problem rather than a normal response to social pressures. Thus turning socially provoked anger inward is socially functional, but individually repressive.

One strategy for avoiding the potential stigma of some disabilities is *passing*, or concealing a discrediting social status or stigmatizing attributes. In some cases, disclosure or "selective telling" can act as a means of forestalling a negative reaction from another person. Schneider and Conrad (1983) described how people with epilepsy weigh the stigma potential of their condition against positive consequences (e.g., having someone to help in case of seizure) of revealing the fact. Concealing one's condition is sometimes a way of avoiding stigmatizing attitudes. Because people with impaired vision may consider a cane to be a stigma symbol or an overt sign of disability, they may prefer a less obtrusive folding cane, even though it may not be as effective an instrument. Charmaz (1991: 151) observes: "An appliance that simplifies logistical problems and arduous tasks can confound self-image and social identity. Hence some ill people prefer to stay at home or risk heart failure, a fall or exhaustion rather than use a walker, wheelchair or a handicapped parking space." The refusal to use highly visible prosthetic devices, however, is not necessarily irrational, but may be based on well-founded fears of being viewed as a "cripple."

In Chapter 4, we suggested that assaults on one's sense of self may have physical consequences, including an impact on the immune system. Certain chronic illnesses, such as herpes, leprosy, epilepsy, and AIDS, carry a load of powerful negative meanings that define afflicted persons and our perception of them. In addition to the fear of death, disfiguring treatments, and the usual threats to one's self-concept that accompany any debilitating disease, sufferers of AIDS are also faced with highly stigmatizing responses from others. It has evoked irrational fears of contagion, not unlike leprosy did in the past. Because of its association with homosexuality, it has also evoked intense homophobic reactions. People with AIDS have been dismissed from their jobs, evicted from their homes, rejected, and isolated by friends and relatives. Even the family, friends, or colleagues of victims may become stigmatized by association, a pattern that Goffman calls "courtesy stigma" (Goffman, 1963). AIDS victims may also be ostracized by medical personnel whose fears override their knowledge about contagion. Studies indicate that the risk of spreading infection from AIDS patients to health care workers is minute (Heyward and Curran, 1988), yet one patient with AIDS commented,

> The nurses are scared of me; the doctors wear masks and sometimes gloves. Even the priest doesn't seem too anxious to shake my hand. What the hell is this? I'm not a leper. Do they want to lock me up and shoot me? I've got no family, no friends. Where do I go? What do I do? God, this is horrible! Is He punishing me? The only thing I got going for me is that I'm not dying—at least, not yet (quoted in Kleinman, 1988: 163).

Such attitudes contribute to distress and unneeded suffering; they may also have biophysical consequences. Further research is needed on the impact of the social stress produced by the stigma of AIDS in further assaulting a person's immune system (Kaplan et al., 1987).

Disability as a Minority Status

People with disabilities constitute a minority group because of their relative powerlessness and their identifiability, both of which promote discrimination and stigmatization. Unlike other minority groups, however, the disabled do not usually share a subculture, a geographical location, or history. Their cultural status is ambiguous: They are "betwixt and between," neither healthy nor sick. Murphy (1987) argues that because such ambiguity is threatening to normals, the isolation and discrimination faced by those with disabilities may come from their anomalous and ambiguous status in our system of cultural classification. Nevertheless, like other minority groups, such as women, blacks, Hispanics, and gays, they do experience similar problems of being powerless objects of stereotypes and discrimination.

A Harris poll in 1984 showed that 74 percent of persons with disabilities do identify with one another, and that 45 percent consider themselves a minority in the same sense as blacks or Hispanics (Fine and Asch, 1988). Some people who are deaf, for instance, are resistant to "technical fixes," such as cochlear implants (in which the inner ear is wired to a receiver), precisely because the technology denies people who are deaf their identity in a deaf culture, such as participating in the use of sign language (Barringer, 1993). Some studies suggest that physically "normal" people view those with impairments, such as blindness, as inferior to members of ethnic minority groups (Susser et al., 1985). One study found a hierarchy of attitudes toward persons with disabilities, with those who were blind ranked below those with cerebral palsy, total paralysis, or epilepsy. Other studies show that blacks as a group were ranked close to the blind in terms of social preference. Such biases develop as early as the age of six (Gliedman, 1979).

Perhaps the most important feature that people with disabilities share with racial and ethnic minorities is the tendency for others to attribute their perceived inferiority and "differentness" to biological factors alone, rather than to social conditions. Disabling attitudes and environments create a self-fulfilling prophecy that legitimates individualistic and biologistic assumptions about the disabled. Because such environments and attitudes exclude people with disabilities from the community and from work places, the nondisabled conclude that this exclusion is evidence that the disabled cannot function in such settings. "Like racists, able-bodied people often confuse the results of social oppression with the effects of biology" (Gliedman and Roth, 1980: 28).

Disability Civil Rights Movements: Recapturing Self and Access

Stimulated by the 1960s civil rights movement, people with disabilities became politically active, working from the assumption that they constituted a minority group deprived of their civil rights. Shifting their focus from individual problems to attacking unfair social structures, they began demanding equal access to housing, jobs, transportation, and health care. The activism of the 1960s had widened the definition of political issues to include the personal, everyday problems faced by various groups. Various forms of **identity politics** (Anspach, 1977) attempted to forge a new identity and sense of self (e.g., "Gay is proud," and "Black is beautiful"). Often these politics revolved around particular stigmatizing definitions. For example, women's groups resisted the medical definition of menopause as a disease (McCrea, 1983) (see Chapter 9). Similarly, disability rights activists realized that definitions of disability were sociopolitical (Scotch, 1988).

After World War II, environmental barriers kept people with disabilities from participating fully in society, despite technological developments that made such a life increasingly possible. Those who had *acquired* an impairment (e.g., from polio or war wounds) were not used to being dependent and had higher expectations than those who were *born* with an impairment. The struggle for civil rights represented an attempt by people with raised expectations to remove barriers by ending employment discrimination, increasing architectural access, opening admission to universities and other institutions, and pursuing other policy goals (Scotch, 1988). Groups like the Center for Independent Living in California and Disabled in Action on the East Coast, which are staffed largely by people with disabilities, sought to define issues such as access not as charity or welfare but as basic civil rights. Many workers in human services, however, still view people with disabilities as clients with problems to be treated. By contrast, the disability rights movement emphasizes the involvement of citizens with disabilities in shaping their own fate (Shapiro, 1993).

In the United States, the disability rights movement contributed to the passage of the Americans with Disabilities Act of 1990, the first comprehensive civil rights legislation for people with disabilities (Shapiro, 1993). This law prohibits employers from discriminating against people with disabilities; it requires businesses to provide reasonable accommodations to workers and customers with disabilities, and it orders accessible public transportation and other reasonable public accommodations for persons with disabilities. One of the main contributions of the movement has been to heighten public awareness of discrimination and chronic illness as sociopolitical issues, not merely medical problems.

SUMMARY

Illness is the complex set of ways in which the sick person (and family and friends) perceive, manage, and respond to symptoms and disability. The experience of illness reminds us of our limitations, dependencies, and ultimate mortality. While ordinary, even minor illnesses disrupt one's life, certain illness experiences are likely to have a damaging effect on the sick person's identity and sense of self. Certain disabling conditions and chronic pain and illnesses are especially problematic, because they involve a sense of loss; they are overwhelming, unpredictable, and uncontrollable; and they produce social marginality for the sufferer. The chronic illness experience is not limited to the sick person but often involves family and friends as well. People interpret their illness, giving it meaning, form, and order. These meanings in turn shape their perception of their symptoms and pain.

Disability and pain are important features of the illness experience, especially chronic illness. Social and political factors are involved in both the definition and management of disability. Disabling social and physical environments and attitudes are responsible for many of the problems suffered by persons with chronic illness or impairments. Similarly, both the experience and expression of pain are linked with sociocultural factors. Suffering is often increased, however, when others invalidate the reality of the pain. Since the majority of serious illnesses today are chronic, in contrast to the acute illnesses predominant in the recent past, we need to appreciate their powerful impact upon the sufferer's daily life, social relationships, and very self.

RECOMMENDED READINGS

Articles

LINDA ALEXANDER, "Illness maintenance and the new American sick role," pp. 351–367 in N. J. Chrisman and T. W. Maretzki, eds., *Clinically Applied Anthropology.* Dordrecht, Netherlands: D. Reidel, 1982.

KATHY CHARMAZ, "Loss of self: A fundamental form of suffering of the chronically ill," *Sociology of Health and Illness* 4, 1983: 167–182.

SHARON R. KAUFMAN, "Toward a phenomenology of boundaries in medicine: Chronic illness experience in the case of stroke," *Medical Anthropology Quarterly* 2 (4), 1988: 338–354.

JESSICA SCHEER and NORA CROCE, "Impairment as a human constant: Cross-cultural and historical perspectives on variation," *Journal of Social Issues* 44(1), 1988: 23–37.

Books

SHIZUKO FAGERHAUGH and ANSELM STRAUSS, *Politics of Pain Management: Staff-Patient Interaction.* Reading, MA: Addison-Wesley, 1977. A study of the social organizational contexts—especially power relations—for the perception of pain and pain management.

ARTHUR KLEINMAN, *The Illness Narratives: Suffering, Healing, and the Human Condition.* New York: Basic, 1988. A sensitive witness to narratives of illness experiences, especially those that are chronic and disabling or disfiguring.

ROBERT F. MURPHY, *The Body Silent.* New York: Henry Holt, 1987. An anthropologist's account of his increasing paralysis due to a spinal tumor and his personal perspective on the sociocultural aspects of disability.

JOSEPH W. SCHNEIDER and PETER CONRAD, *Having Epilepsy: The Experience and Control of Illness*. Philadelphia: Temple University Press, 1983. A sociological look at epilepsy, and the management of its symptoms and stigma.

JOSEPH P. SHAPIRO, *No Pity: People with Disabilities Forging a New Civil Rights Movement*. New York: Random House, 1993. A very readable account of the disability rights movement in the United States.

IRVING K. ZOLA, *Missing Pieces: A Chronicle of Living with a Disability*. Philadelphia: Temple University Press, 1982. An excellent combination of sociological insights and Zola's personal experiences with disability, as well as his participant-observations as a guest in a Dutch village adapted to the needs of people with disabilities.

CHAPTER EIGHT

Seeking Health and Help

How do people conclude that they are ill, and what actions do they choose to take in response? There are a number of implicit and often utterly incorrect assumptions about how people seek health and respond to health problems. Probably each one of us can think of instances in our own experiences when these assumptions did not hold:

> People know for sure when they are ill.
>
> As soon as they realize they are ill, they seek competent help, specifically a medical doctor (or dentist, psychiatrist, or other appropriate professional).
>
> When they consult the professional, they give an explanation of the problem that is as medically correct as possible.
>
> The doctor understands what they are saying about their problem.
>
> The doctor's explanation of the problem makes sense to them.
>
> When the doctor prescribes therapeutic action, they follow that advice carefully until it takes effect or until the doctor changes the instructions.
>
> People know for sure when they are well, and are satisfied when this state of health is restored.

The fact that these assumptions are rarely accurate is a source of considerable tension and outright dissatisfaction on the part of both medical professionals and patients. One key reason for this tension is the enormous, and generally unrecognized, chasm between the medical models of illness and the conceptions used by laypersons in understanding and making decisions about their own health and illnesses. This gap is built into the structure of professionalized medicine, where—by definition—the layperson does not share the specialized body of knowledge used by the professional (Freidson, 1970: 278–279).

Most modern societies tend to treat professional interpretations as vastly superior to lay understandings. Medical professionals tend to demean lay conceptions, often labeling them as superstition, ignorance, foolishness, or instances of persons being unwilling to take proper care of themselves. From this perspective, the doctor is viewed as the expert whose rational pronouncements are the result of legitimate authority, whereas the patient should be passive and obedient, deferring all judgment to the expert.

By contrast, West (1979: 162) argues that attention should be directed to "the person as a conscious, reflective actor engaged in the process of making sense of various kinds of body changes within the framework of his own 'lay' knowledge." Studies of decision making in health matters show that most laypersons *do* make conscious choices that are rational, within the framework of their understanding of the illness (Locker, 1981). We will examine the vast range of interpretations and decisions the ordinary person makes in seeking health.

Contrary to the common misconception, health seeking is largely *not* a process of getting professional medical care. Most health-enhancing or preventive measures are nonmedical, and only a very small portion of ailments are ever brought to a physician's attention. As Zola (1983: 111) commented,

> Virtually every day of our lives we are subject to a vast array of bodily discomforts. Only an infinitesimal amount of these get to a physician. Neither the mere presence nor

the obviousness of symptoms seems to differentiate those episodes which do and do not get professional treatment.

This observation is corroborated by recent studies documenting the "iceberg of morbidity"—the vast majority of physical problems that are never brought to medical (or formal health statistics) attention (Verbrugge, 1986). The Health in Detroit Study found, on the basis of health diaries, that persons over 18 experienced an average of 23 health problems in 16 days within a six-week period (Verbrugge and Ascione, 1987). This means that people experienced discomfort sufficient to be considered a health problem more than one-third of the days of the study (which itself was scheduled to avoid the height of hay fever and winter colds seasons, so this figure is probably conservative). The *least* commonly mentioned action in response to these problems was medical care; on only 5 percent of days on which they experienced problematic symptoms did respondents have medical contact of any kind (office visit, appointment scheduling, medical advice by telephone, or hospital visit). The study found that people typically responded promptly to symptoms, but that "for most symptoms of daily life, people opt to do something on their own without medical help" (Verbrugge and Ascione, 1987: 549).

This society generally and medical professionals in particular hold an ambiguous norm: Responsible persons *should* get professional medical care for all serious, medically treatable ailments and, at the same time, *should not* bother doctors or use medical facilities for unimportant or nontreatable ailments. This norm furthermore assumes that people share the professional definition of which ailments are serious or treatable and are able to assess their own situations adequately to determine into which category they fit. While physicians strongly urge professional attention for health problems, they simultaneously dislike being bothered with trivial problems or problems that they do not know how to treat effectively (Klein et al., 1982).

A British study found that 25 percent of general practitioners surveyed complained that patients consulted doctors for unimportant reasons. At the same time, 56 percent complained that patients did not have enough humility in accepting the medical expert's judgments (Cartwright, 1967). The contradictory or ambiguous norm is that laypersons should be actively expert in judging correctly which ailments to refer to the professional, and then assume a humbly passive role when under the care of the professional.

SELF-TREATMENT AND THE DECISION TO GET HELP

The vast majority of actions people take to prevent illness or to treat everyday health problems are done without expert help, either medical or nonmedical. A British study found that women respondents most frequently listed the following ways of keeping healthy: good diet, exercise and fitness, no smoking, sufficient sleep and rest, and fresh air. Very few respondents (less than 10 percent) mentioned medical checkups or screening (Calnan, 1987: 101–130).

Likewise, the individual or family typically responds directly, without lay or professional help, to ordinary health problems. The Health in Detroit Study found that self-dosing with prescription or nonprescription drugs was the most common response, used during 58 percent of the days on which people experienced symptoms. Self-imposed restriction of activities (such as cutting down on errands and chores) was also common, used on nearly 24 percent of the days on which symptoms were noticed (Verbrugge and Ascione, 1987).

British researchers found that although 91 percent of adults studied reported symptoms during the two weeks prior to interview, only 16 percent had consulted a physician. Indeed, only 28 percent had consulted their doctor at all during the previous 12-month period, even though, under the British National Health Service, the cost of consulting a doctor is not a deterrent, as it is for many in the United States. A far more frequent action in response to symptoms was taking medicine. In the 24 hours before the interview, 55 percent of adults had used some medicine; in the two weeks before the interview, they had taken an average of 2.2 different items of medication. Some were taken for preventive purposes, but most were taken in response to specific symptoms: a temperature, headaches, indigestion, and sore throats. Self-medication also includes the decision to take medicines prescribed and often kept for long periods, to be taken "as needed." Prescription drugs for the central nervous system (such as tranquilizers and sedatives) were frequently self-dosed. In a sample of households in England, Wales, and Scotland, 99 percent of homes kept one or more medicines; the average number was 7.3 nonprescribed and 3.0 prescribed. A fifth of the households kept sedatives, tranquilizers, or sleeping pills, and two-fifths kept some medication that the respondent could not identify (Dunnell and Cartwright, 1972).

Some responses to illness are not merely physical. If the person's belief system attributes illness to nonphysical causes, such as emotions or spiritual factors, then it is logical for a sick person to choose nonphysical approaches to treating the illness. If, for example, a person believes that she is especially vulnerable to infections when she is lonely or "blue," she might choose to treat an ailment by doing things that cheer her up or by visiting a close friend. Similarly, if someone believes that God will intervene to heal his illness, then prayer for healing constitutes a therapeutic action.

Such nonphysical responses are rarely done to the complete exclusion of physical treatments, and often they are meshed in interesting combinations. For example, when a person chooses to treat a bad case of the flu by consuming a bowl of steaming chicken soup or a concoction of milk toast, is the treatment merely the ingestion of a therapeutic substance or the soothing emotional connotations of the food, or both? Likewise, when a sick person says a blessing prayer over a bottle of prescription pills, is the treatment purely a physical response to illness?

The Health in Detroit Study found that about half the time people responded to their health problems by talking with family or friends (Verbrugge and Ascione, 1987). This response is both therapeutic in itself and also a way of consulting with other laypersons about what to do. Laypeople rely upon their own networks of contact for advice, including suggestions about where to seek further help. Family, friends, neighbors, and colleagues at work, school, a religious group, or a social club all constitute potential sources of advice. The sick individual, however, must decide whose advice is sought and whose advice is heeded. For example, your grandmother might be a valued source of home remedies, and her burn ointment may be more effective than any commercial salve you have tried, but you might not want her advice on what might be a sexually transmitted disease, since the advice is likely to come with a lecture on sin. Individuals are typically selective in their choices of lay advice.

There is some evidence that these lay advice networks rely especially upon women as knowledgeable sources of referrals and as the seekers of health advice both for themselves and for members of their families (Graham, 1985). The division of labor in many households allocates to women more than to men such duties as caring for sick family members or selecting and arranging for appointments with medical and/or nonmedical practitioners.

Not all lay advice comes from existing networks, however. Sometimes people seek out new sources of advice or create a new network of lay advisers. A person with Parkinson's disease, for example, may look for a group of fellow sufferers, whose advice on some matters may be more valued than that of longtime friends or even doctors who have not experienced the disease themselves.

One specific form of advice is the lay referral to a source of help (Freidson, 1970: 290). Through lay referrals, the individual learns of many treatment options (which are usually linked with their lay advisers' evaluation of what might be the problem), including a favorite (or least favorite) doctor; the type of specialist to try; less orthodox practitioners, such as an herbalist or acupuncturist; self-help health groups; and alternative healing groups, such as a psychic healing circle, prayer group, or meditation center.

A study of Puerto Ricans in a small northeastern city, for example, found that sick persons with effective networks of kin and fictive kin (*compadrazgo*) received much concrete assistance in selecting and negotiating entry to both institutional health resources (e.g., prenatal care programs) and noninstitutional help (e.g., *espiritistos—* spiritual healers). The study concluded that such kin networks should be viewed as health educators because of their role in teaching members where to seek help, how to select among available help resources, and how to deal with bureaucratic and other roadblocks to getting help (Schensul and Schensul, 1982).

Social interaction with family, friends, and acquaintances often plays an important part in the decision to seek help. One study of the decision to take a health problem to a clinic found that the individual rarely sought help at the physically sickest point. Rather, the nature of symptoms themselves appeared to be less significant than social interaction in prompting the decision to see a doctor:

> For our patients the symptoms were "really" there, but their perception differed considerably. There *is* a sense in which they sought help because they could not stand it any longer. But what they could not stand was more likely to be a situation or a perceived implication of a symptom rather than any worsening of the symptom *per se* (Zola, 1983: 118).

For example, a person might be motivated to seek help after a friend's description of some serious disease that could possibly be related to her symptoms; symptoms that were formerly not worrisome then become significant, even though she had experienced no change in the symptoms themselves. Similar factors are probably involved in the decision to seek nonmedical forms of help. Thus, the motivation to do something about a health problem often results from social interaction that heightens the significance imputed to the symptoms.

People do not always seek help mainly to *cure* a health problem. For example, a person might go to a *shiatsu* (Japanese acupressure) therapist for pain relief but not accept the diagnostic interpretations the therapist gives. Some people consult medical doctors for diagnoses more to rule out feared serious outcomes than actually to treat the symptoms. Similarly, some people want the medical diagnosis but distrust the medical treatment (especially certain drugs or surgery). One middle-class American woman said, "I still think they give you too much medication, which I accept gratefully and then don't take" (quoted in McGuire, 1988). We have too little data on what patients actually hope to accomplish by consulting medical and nonmedical health experts, but probably much of what professionals call noncompliance (discussed further in this chapter) is due to the fact that the doctors' orders are not necessarily what laypeople want when they seek professional help.

THE HIDDEN HEALTH CARE SYSTEM

Far too often, when people speak of the health care system, they refer only to the professionalized, institution-oriented *illness care* system of doctors and other professional health workers, hospitals, clinics, insurance companies, pharmaceutical companies, and government agencies. This form of care is important, because it is complex and powerful. It also has extensive economic significance, as discussed in Chapter 12. There is, however, another highly important system of health care.

Home and Family Care

The **hidden health care system** refers to all the laypersons who are often the real *primary* health care providers (Levin and Idler, 1981).[1] The vast majority of efforts to maintain health take place in the home and other private spheres of action, including diet, rest, recreational exercise and relaxation, hygiene, adequate shelter, avoidance of dangerous substances, and prevention of accidents and injuries (Pratt, 1976).

Likewise, most health care takes place in the home, and is either self-administered or given by members of the family. Virtually all care of minor illnesses occurs outside the formal health care system. Imagine how many people in any given day may be taking care of themselves or someone else who is miserable with such illnesses as chicken pox, a bad head cold, or stomach flu! Even for health problems that

---

[1]This usage differs from the common one in the literature, where "primary providers" refers to general practitioners, pediatricians, and other medical doctors or nurse practitioners who, in contrast to specialists, are supposed to be the first to evaluate patients' needs.

have been treated in the formal system, most of the actual care is done at home: giving medications, tending a person restricted to bed, changing dressings, and monitoring symptoms. Furthermore, throughout the society enormous amounts of energy and time are also required to care for persons with chronic illnesses, disabilities, and mental retardation, and those who are dying. A 1979 survey (Feller, 1983) found an estimated 4.9 million adults with chronic health problems who lived in the community rather than in institutions such as nursing homes or hospitals, but required help for everyday activities such as walking, bathing, dressing, preparing meals, and eating. In addition to these nonmedical forms of health care, an estimated 1.3 million people received some form of medical or nursing treatments (e.g., injections or physical therapy) at home. Older adults accounted for the vast majority of persons needing home care, and the rates of persons needing assistance increased dramatically for those over age 85. The "graying" of modern societies, described in Chapter 2, results in a larger proportion of members surviving to an age at which they need long-term care for chronic health problems.

Even in nations with large government expenditures for health care, the formal health care system is predicated upon the expectation that most care will be given at home. Indeed, the transfer of even part of these services (for example, complete care of all victims of Alzheimer's disease or AIDS) to the public sphere would probably swamp the system. Informal health care, which provides care at little or no cost to the government or insurers, has thus remained a part of the domestic economy.

There are several health-related benefits to self-treatment and home treatment, especially compared with treatment of the same problems in a formal, usually institutional, setting. Those who participate in the care of their own illness are more likely to experience a sense of independence, mastery, self-confidence, and control than those who are the passive recipients of care. A number of studies show the benefits of self-care, especially in treatment of chronic illnesses such as diabetes, hemophilia, and kidney disease (see Levin and Idler, 1981: 79–80).

Home care of illness and injury is typically more personal than formal or institutional care, although personal ties can be problematic, since care givers can have negative as well as positive feelings for the sick person. Home care is also likely to involve more nurturance than perfunctory tending, although the actual care too varies from home to home. Another advantage of home care is greater continuity; the patient will not have to face an unfamiliar shift of nurses or a new specialist. Finally, home care is usually not as isolating as institutional care. Persons whose chronic illnesses are cared for at home may participate, perhaps in a limited way, in the "normal" worlds of the household, school, community, and even work.

For most of us, the idea of home care raises cozy images of our comfortable room, surrounded by our favorite home entertainments, with Mom bringing us whatever we want for comfort: home-cooked special foods, a hot-water bottle, or a soothing drink. This image is, however, not the reality for many sick persons. For instance, what is the reality of home care for the widowed elderly person living alone in a bare furnished room, or the single mother who is seriously ill?

Nor are all families loving sources of nurturing care. Many families offer their members—especially children and elderly dependents—daily lives of negligence or outright abuse (Steinmetz, 1988; Straus et al., 1980). Indeed, the very health-related problems for which they need care may exacerbate these victims' abuse by other family members. Constant demand for help negotiating stairs or bathrooms, for example, might drive a tired care giver "over the edge" to abuse or neglect. Some long-term or arduous care tasks can also strain the emotional and physical resources of even a well-intentioned family.

Just as persons with disabilities need special enabling environments, so too is the optimum setting for recuperation or the management of chronic illness one that is enabling. Much home care, like many institutional settings, is disabling. For example, a person with a debilitating chronic illness may require assistance with treatments (e.g., dialysis or injections), the management of routine activities (e.g., bathing or fixing meals), and transportation (e.g., climbing stairs or riding to a friend's apartment). Like institutional care, home care given by families, volunteers, or paid workers sometimes subordinates the sick person's needs to other household goals, such as keeping to a certain schedule. Home care sometimes increases sick people's dependency rather than enabling them to manage on their own as much as possible.

U.S. health care policies have barely begun to explore (much less fund) a vast range of physical and social arrangements that would support such enabling environments as noninstitutional collective living situations, copatienting, adequate services to sick persons living independently, barrier-free physical settings for chronically ill persons, and well-trained and well-paid institutional and home health workers. Satisfactory funding for home care of the disabled, the chronically ill, or people recuperating from accidents or acute illnesses needs to include the full range of help needed. Most existing programs are oriented to the treatment of acute conditions and fund only skilled nurses and certified therapists; however, some people might need homemaker help with grocery shopping, child care, or personal care, services not covered by most insurance unless the person is institutionalized (Soldo, 1985). Even in communities where home health support services are available, there is enormous variation in the degree to which individuals are eligible for the help they need at costs they can afford.

Women's Roles

When people speak of home care, they typically mean care by a *woman* (e.g., wife, mother or daughter), an assumption that becomes particularly problematic in light of women's changing roles within the larger society. It is estimated that three quarters of care giving in the home is provided by unpaid relatives, of whom 70 percent are women (Shapiro, 1993: 252). The assumption that it is the wife-mother who should care for the family's sick results in real restrictions upon women's opportunities in the public sphere, especially the world of work. Mothers, far more often than fathers, nurse sick children. Employed mothers reported three times as many hours of work lost due to family (primarily children's) illnesses compared to employed fathers (Carpenter, 1980). Missing work to care for a child who has a sore throat is not a mere inconvenience; it may also seriously reduce a woman's job opportunities. The world of work assumes key participants will not be taking off time to care for dependents; anyone (female or male) who takes home responsibilities more seriously than work risks losing promotion opportunities or even the job itself.

Furthermore, the care-giving role requires many women to forgo paid jobs to care for a chronically disabled relative. Although there may also be some rewards for such duties, caring for some homebound sick persons can be a 24-hour-a-day responsibility, leaving little time for personal needs. One study found that 40 percent of the women in households that included older parents requiring care spent the equivalent time of a full-time job providing that care (Newman, 1976). A report issued by the Older Women's League noted that women spend an average of 17 years caring for children and 18 years assisting aged parents. Some 35 percent of the persons giving care to the elderly are themselves older than 65 (cited in *The New York Times*, May 13, 1989; see also Abel, 1991; Brody, 1990; Lewin, 1989).

Few families can afford many of the time- or labor-saving arrangements that might relieve care givers' burdens; domestic help, day care, or elevators, and hydraulic lifts, for example, are expensive. Where they exist, some community nursing and social service agencies and volunteer groups do help families with certain of these needed resources. For example, in the United States the hospice movement provides support services for some families of persons who choose to die at home rather than in the hospital. Other support available in some areas include adult day care centers, hot meal delivery services, and visiting physical therapists. Especially in the United States, however, very few of the costs of home health care are provided under the terms of health insurance or government medical programs, and many Americans lack adequate insurance coverage to pay even for available services (see, for example, an analysis of policies and resources for family care of elderly and disabled persons by Moroney, 1980).

The assumption that the health and illness care role belongs to the wife-mother is so pervasive that media and health education programs assume that women will rearrange their lives to provide for the health of their families. One British health education project published a pamphlet urging measures women should take to prevent their husbands from having heart attacks. It recommended, for example, that:

> The sensible wife will first decide whether her husband should lose weight, and then plan his menu accordingly. Pressure and pace at work, family responsibilities and general worries can be controlled to some extent by the man himself. . . . But perhaps more important is the tolerance and understanding of his wife. Let your husband talk about his worries, and whenever possible take the work from him—draft letters, pay bills, arrange for the plumber to come yourself (quoted in Graham, 1985).

In efforts to contain rising medical costs, insurers (including Medicare) have emphasized outpatient treatment and home health provision (discussed further in Chapter 12). Earlier discharge from hospitals, for example, means that recuperating patients return home needing more extensive lay nursing care for longer periods. New technologies make possible the home administration of some fairly sophisticated therapies, such as kidney dialysis and intravenous feeding and medicating. The cost savings of performing these procedures at home is considerable. For example, in 1988 kidney dialysis in a hospital or clinic cost about $2,000 per month, compared with $1,200 per month for home dialysis; feeding by the tube cost about $23,800 a month in a hospital, but only $6,000 a month at home (Findlay, 1988). These procedures are not usually done by the sick person without help, however. In addition to requiring visits from skilled nurses who teach the procedures, supervise home treatment, and monitor the sick person's condition, much home care involves the extensive commitment of family members. Their unpaid labor increasingly includes providing complex nursing medical care previously done only by physicians, registered nurses, or therapeutic specialists (Glazer, 1990). In recent years, both government and corporate (i.e., insurance companies' and hospitals') policy changes have resulted in considerable "work transfer" for women providing health care, paid and unpaid. Economists and public policy analysts typically conceptualize domestic production (i.e., work done in the home) as separate from the larger (public) economy, but the ability of these public-sphere institutions to extract cost savings or profits by transferring labor "costs" to unpaid women workers in the home shows how inaccurate such an idea is. Indeed, it suggests that public-sphere institutions use the notion of duty to one's family as an ideological legitimation for extracting unpaid labor (Glazer, 1993).

This policy shift toward home care is developing precisely at a time when women are beginning to achieve somewhat greater equity in educational and occupational opportunities. Not only are women workers less eager to take on such additional care burdens, but the larger proportion of women in the work force also results in fewer (women) volunteers available for neighborhood assistance to those who need help at home. The policy shift also comes as nurses and other health care workers are struggling to achieve greater recognition (and pay) for the work they do (Brown, 1983).

Although moving more care of the sick to the home superficially appears to be demedicalization, note that it is not the *doctors'* tasks or fees that are being reduced by earlier release from the hospital, but rather the more "menial" tasks of care, which are being transferred to the family or family-paid workers. Whereas previously these tasks would have been done in the hospital by low-paid nurses' aides and practical nurses (LPNs), they are now transferred to unpaid relatives, who are sometimes assisted by very low-paid home health workers; all are women typically (see Fine, 1988). On the other hand, it is nurses—not doctors—who usually make the home visits and monitor acute episodes of the home-bound sick. Cost-cutting measures during the 1980s, however, severely restricted the amount of actual nursing care given by visiting nurses and greatly increased their caseloads at the same time that patients were increasingly released from hospitals while seriously ill (Glazer, 1990). The nature of professional home nursing does appear to be a move away from a highly medicalized model, partly because it emphasizes teaching the sick person and family to care for themselves.[2] One community health nurse noted that her work was unlike that of doctors or hospital nurses because she works with the patient in the physical and social context of the family and home life, emphasizing the personal caring aspect of nursing. She added, "In a holistic sense, community health nurses are healers."

The policy move to community-based health care has *not* usually reduced physician control and potential income, however. The home birth movement, for example, has been vigorously suppressed. In the United States, although some physicians have supported the practice of out-of-hospital births, professional organizations such as the American College of Obstetricians and Gynecologists have vigorously opposed it. Certification for trained midwives is available only to registered nurses who have taken extra training, but even these certified nurse-midwives have been severely restricted in their attempts to practice independent of physician control and have had great difficulty obtaining malpractice insurance. The virtual monopoly of obstetricians and hospitals has thus been preserved (Levin and Idler, 1981: 83–103; Romalis, 1985).

Mutual Aid

Self-help and mutual aid groups are another form of hidden health care. These voluntary associations offer *reciprocal* help, usually among persons with similar health needs. The mutual quality of this aid is the key feature distinguishing these groups from professional health care. Members exchange roles as provider and receiver of health and illness care (see Levin and Idler, 1981; Katz and Levin, 1980; Katz, 1979; Caplan and Killilea, 1976; Katz and Bender, 1976; Levin et al., 1976). Examples include support groups such as those for persons with certain diseases (e.g., epilepsy and Parkinson's disease) or disabling conditions (e.g., chronic pain), or who have undergone certain operations (e.g., mastectomies or colostomies) or other traumatic experiences (e.g., the suicide of loved one or rape). Some communities also have volunteer health help that is more one-sided, such as volunteer ambulance and emergency squads.

Self-help groups typically offer their members much mutual social support, concrete suggestions about how to manage the many day-to-day problems, information about their condition and various therapeutic possibilities, and advice about dealing with family, friends, and medical professionals (cf. Droge et al., 1986; Morgan et al., 1984). One aim is to break the isolation of those whose regular networks may

---

[2]The work of community health nurses (including many nurse-practitioners and nurse-midwives) is comparable to that of their predecessors, public health nurses, who since the 1920s enjoyed greater professional autonomy and respect in their work than did hospital- or office-based nurses (see Melosh, 1982: 113–157). Physicians, however, have perceived them as professional competitors and have often fought to prevent laws that would permit these nurses to work independently. Since nurse-practitioners can provide primary care, comparable to physicians', for about 80 percent of the patients in ambulatory clinics, there are many possibilities for status and role conflicts between the two gender-stratified occupations (Little, 1982; see also Lurie, 1981).

not include anyone in a similar situation. As one member explained, " 'In the beginning one is truly cut off, one feels completely different from everyone else. . . . The healthy cannot understand the sick, one really belongs to a world apart' " (quoted in Herzlich and Pierret, 1987: 220).

Mutual help groups appear to be feature of lay health care especially in the United States, where they mesh with cultural values and historical experience of mutual and self-reliance (see Risse et al., 1977). The movement is also widespread in northern Europe and growing rapidly throughout Europe (World Health Organization, 1981). While not specifically organized as self-help groups, similar functions are also performed by healing cults in many traditional societies. For example, in rural Turkey a traditional form of reciprocity is *dertleşmek*, in which neighbors express and share their joys, sorrows, and problems. The therapeutic value of *dertleşmek* has been demonstrated among Turkish immigrant women in Belgium (Devisch and Gailly, 1985).

There is considerable diversity in the social organization of these groups, with many of the long-term groups imitating professional, bureaucratic health care organizations, yet many others remaining adamantly loosely organized lay groups. Some are formed at lay initiative; others have been created by helping professions for their clients. Thus there is a difference in the degree of independence of power experienced, for example, by a group of chronically ill persons who organize to do something for themselves and each other, as compared with a therapy group organized by the outreach staff of a hospital.

Mutual help groups also vary greatly in the degree to which they have assumed any political agenda or recognized any of the political issues implicit in self-care or mutual aid. The Independent Living Movement for persons with disabilities and chronic illnesses and the Women's Health Movement have taken a politically activist stance (see Tudiver, 1986; Crewe and Zola, 1983; Doyal, 1983; Ruzek, 1979). Out of one such women's support group emerged the now-famous "handbook" for women's health: *Our Bodies, Our Selves* (Boston Women's Health Collective, new edition, 1992).

Assuming self-care and mutual responsibility in the face of illness, however, also have *implicit* political consequences because the sick persons take an active and often knowledgeable role in the treatment of their own sickness. They often consider their proficiency in treating their particular illness to be superior to that of the professionals (cf. Herzlich and Pierret, 1987: 217–218). For example, diabetics who must give themselves frequent injections and persons with renal (kidney) failure who may perform their dialysis at home often distrust having those services performed in hospital. People who have had long experience managing their chronic illness or disability often gain considerable expertise about their condition, and are more likely to expect doctors and other medical personnel to share power with them.

Our recognition of this hidden health care system helps us to understand better the full range of activities people engage in to keep well or to treat illnesses. Not all outside help is professional medical care. Beyond the lay help of home, neighborhood, and mutual aid groups, there are a number of nonmedical healing alternatives that people may seek.

ALTERNATIVE HEALING SYSTEMS

People's belief systems inform their decisions as to when they need help and which kinds of help are appropriate. Even in modern Western societies, where biomedicine is the dominant medical paradigm, people may use several healing systems simultaneously with biomedicine. A study (McGuire, 1988) of middle-class Americans who used various alternative, spiritual healing approaches (e.g., Christian faith healing, psychic healing, and Eastern or occult healing) found that virtually all adherents used both biomedical *and* alternative systems. Furthermore, their beliefs shaped how they combined these various approaches. For example, one man had his broken arm X-rayed and set in a cast by medical professionals at the hospital, but followed this treatment with frequent prayers at home and in his religious group. He believed that the prayers resulted in faster and more effective healing. Adherents of the various alternative healing approaches felt that medical doctors were not necessarily the best source of help for such problems as chronic pain and illness, because they treat the symptoms, not the cause. These adherents believed that the "real" causes of such illnesses were spiritual (or the socioemotional by-products of spiritual problems). Thus, by definition, modern medicine alone was not a sufficient source of help (McGuire, 1988).

Even people who are not consciously using alternative belief systems seek different sources of healing help, depending upon how they understand or express their problems. Someone with back pain, for example, might consult a pharmacist, massage therapist, orthopedist, physiatrist, or chiropractor, depending upon how the person interpreted the pain, its seriousness, and its possible causes. For many people, seeking help for health or illness includes several options in addition to orthodox medical care.

Nonallopathic Practitioners

One longstanding alternative source of health-related help is a professional practitioner from a formal healing system other than allopathy. Although allopathy is only one approach to doctoring, as described in Chapter 10, it has attained a virtual monopoly of medical education, licensing, and practice in the United States and Canada. It is also the dominant form of medicine practiced in most of Europe, although some non-allopathic approaches have greater legitimacy and freedom there than in North America. Medical systems that dissent from the dominant one have often been called sects, being seen as analogous to religious sects that dissent from the established church (see Jones, 1985). These medical systems are based upon completely different, competing paradigms of illness causation and cure.

Probably the best-known alternatives in the United States are two nineteenth-century challenges to allopathy: chiropractic and osteopathy, therapeutic systems based on the idea that malalignments of the musculo-skeletal system also produce problems in the neuro-endocrine system. Osteopathy has become largely subordinated within regular (allopathic) medical practice and licensing. Until the 1980s, chiropractic was actively suppressed by the AMA and licensing legislation. Although it has since gained greater legitimacy and recognition (e.g., chiropractic treatment is now covered by much health insurance), chiropractic is still viewed by many (or most) medical practitioners as an unacceptable alternative to diagnosis and treatment by a medical doctor (Baer, 1987, 1984; see also Coburn and Biggs, 1986; Wardwell, 1982; Albrecht and Levy, 1982)

There are few studies on how patients combine the use of both chiropractic and medical doctors. Apparently some persons use the chiropractor as their main physician, turning to medical doctors occasionally if referred by the chiropractor or if they believe they need medication (which chiropractors cannot prescribe). Others use medical doctors as their primary physician, seeking chiropractors when the malady is something medical doctors do not treat effectively. Relatively few medical doctors reciprocate in referring patients to chiropractors. Indeed, until 1979 the AMA forbade its members to make such referrals (*The New York Times*, 1979).

Homeopathy, a holistic form of pharmacological therapeutics developed in the early nineteenth century (Kaufman, 1971), is now more common in Europe and Latin America than in the United States. In England, for example, homeopathic physicians are licensed to practice and are reimbursed under the National Health Service. The homeopathic movement also encourages laypersons to self-treat certain illnesses and to learn to use some of the homeopathic medicines (Coulter, 1984).

Like homeopathy, naturopathy utilizes presumably milder medicines, primarily herbs. One form of naturopathy, Thompsonism, was influential in the United States in the eighteenth and nineteenth centuries because it was linked with the rising tide of political populism and the needs for lay modes of healing in frontier and other rural communities (Cassedy, 1977; Numbers, 1977). The various natural health movements were generally suppressed in the United States, but in some European countries, such as Germany, these practices were more acceptable as a complement to biomedicine (Maretzki and Seidler, 1985; Roth, 1976). Contemporary versions of naturopathy as well as homeopathy appear to be increasingly used in the United States and Britain, perhaps as a result of dissatisfaction with the dominant, allopathic medical system (Sharma, 1992; Taylor, 1984).

Another extant nineteenth-century alternative to allopathy is hydrotherapy, which utilizes water (e.g., baths, mineral water, and mud) for treatments. There are few sociological studies of the extent of use of these alternative therapeutic systems, but evidence suggests that they are used in conjunction with biomedicine, although without the knowledge of the patients' medical doctors (Eisenberg et al., 1993b; McGuire, 1988). One German study found that an estimated 30 to 40 percent of patients of medical doctors also consulted such nonallopathic practitioners as homeopaths, naturopaths, and hydrotherapists (Haehn, 1980).

Some traditional Oriental medical practices have recently been introduced into Western societies.[3] The paradigms of illness and healing of such therapies as acupressure, acupuncture, and Oriental herbal medicine are very different from those of

---

[3]Professionalized practice is also a feature of other Asian medical traditions, such as Ayurvedic and Yunani medicine, but these have not been extensively "borrowed" by Westerners (see Kleinman et al., 1978; Leslie, 1976).

Western biomedicine. Acupressure, or *shiatsu*, is generally administered like a massage, so it is not in direct competition with licensed medicine, but neither is it typically covered by medical insurance. Acupuncture, which involves the insertion of needles, is under tighter legal control. In most of the United States nonphysician acupuncturists are required to work under the supervision of licensed doctors, although some states have made allowances for licensing nonphysician acupuncturists (who, ironically, are often better trained as acupuncturists than physicians who took relatively brief training in the method). Patients who utilize acupuncture alongside regular medical treatment often do not tell their own physicians for fear of alienating them (Kotarba, 1975; see also Wolpe, 1985).

Because these alternative medical systems are in direct competition with allopathic medicine, political and legal maneuvers regarding their practice have concrete economic effects. Like allopathic medicine, these alternatives are organized as professional practices, with their own body of knowledge, training and certification standards, code of ethics, and organizations (see the review of literature in Cassidy et al., 1985; see also Saks, 1992; Sharma, 1992; Cant and Calnan, 1991). Like bio-medicine, they rely largely upon learned diagnostic and therapeutic techniques, which do not require the patient to understand or agree with the underlying paradigm in order to be effectively treated.

Indigenous Healers and Healing Groups

The acceptance of an underlying belief system is more likely to be a feature of **indigenous healing**, or native, folk, or popular practices for health and healing. Anthropologists have documented a vast array of such systems around the globe. The early literature, however, generally assumed that as societies became modernized and Westernized, they would shed these "primitive" beliefs and practices and substitute the biomedical system, but this expectation has not been borne out (Kleinman, 1984).

Furthermore, indigenous healing has remained widespread in modern industrialized societies. Social scientists once interpreted these beliefs and practices as remnants of peasant, old-country traditions or as characteristic of uneducated, lower-class persons who could not afford modern medical treatment. Although there appear to be different healing systems operating in the various subcultures of modern societies, indigenous healing beliefs and practices are in fact relatively widespread among educated, fully acculturated, and economically secure persons (McGuire, 1988). A 1990 survey estimated that 34 percent of Americans had used some kind of alternative therapy that year; 72 percent of those using nonmedical therapies did not tell their doctors that they were using other approaches in their treatment (Eisenberg et al., 1993b).

The sheer diversity of indigenous health and healing beliefs and practices makes it very difficult to generalize about these alternative options. Some indigenous practices are conducted by healers—lay specialists who have particular knowledge and/or spiritual or natural "gifts" for healing. Other indigenous healing is done by the sick person or nonspecialists in the group. In the United States, for example, indigenous healing approaches include those of spiritual healers, mediums, shamans, herbalists, lay midwives, fire doctors (for burn pain), bone setters, leg lengtheners, astrologists and spiritual advisers, and occult healers. Indigenous healing also includes a wide variety of meditation approaches, prayer, spiritual exercises, massage and other "body work," exercise disciplines, and martial arts.

Although most indigenous healing occurs outside orthodox medical practice and is generally denigrated by the medical establishment, a number of medical doctors have incorporated some of these alternative practices into their treatment of patients. One study of these physicians found that their personal web of experiences, including religion and spirituality or their own illness or pain experiences, led them to integrate alternative approaches with mainstream medical practices. It concluded that dissention among physicians may be greater than the professional organizations would like to acknowledge, and that many so-called mainstream physicians hold views about health and healing and behave in ways that deviate from mainstream medical norms (Goldstein et al., 1987).

One small fringe of both indigenous *and* orthodox medical practice includes what has been called "quackery," or fraudulent healing, usually for financial gain. Much labeling of quackery has been the effort of the medical profession to suppress any competition to its professional dominance. For example, the AMA funds a Bureau of Investigation to trace "quacks" and aid in their legal control and prosecution (Young, 1967). This effort also polices the AMA's ranks, since many "quacks" are medical doctors who deviate from acceptable professional standards (Roebuck and Hunter, 1975; Young, 1967).

Because indigenous healing, by contrast, is loosely organized, there are no clear-cut boundaries for acceptable practice. To the extent that indigenous healers are members of an established community in which they work, however, ordinary social control is operative. Someone who is believed to be pretending to heal and exploiting neighbors' needs in time of trouble would almost certainly be punished. When indigenous healing occurs more anonymously (e.g., by a traveling healer or advertised nostrums), there is greater potential for deliberately fake healing. Most indigenous healing, however, is comparatively sincere; it is practiced by people—healers and patients alike—who, to some degree, share a belief system in which that approach to healing is plausible and indeed advisable. (See Box 8.1.)

Some of these alternative approaches are systematized by recognized movements; others are developed by independent healers, often drawing eclectically from a wide range of Western and non-Western traditions. The various spiritual healing approaches are generally based upon a larger religious belief system. For example, healing done in pentecostal prayer groups is not an isolated activity of the group but an expression of the groups' larger belief that God acts directly in believers' everyday lives in response to their prayer and faith.

Spiritual healing is rather widespread, even in modern Western societies. Obvious examples include Christian faith healing, Christian Science and other New Thought healing, psychic healing, and healing approaches imported from various Eastern spiritual traditions such as Zen and Tibetan Buddhism and Jainism (English-Lueck, 1990; McGuire, 1988, 1982; Johnson et al., 1986; Poloma, 1985; Wagner,

BOX 8.1   *ONE AMERICAN HEALER*[4]

Marge is a 48-year-old pediatric nurse employed full-time in a large hospital in a suburban community. She is successful in her career, with the appropriate advanced degrees and experience for high level positions, although she has not chosen to leave active nursing for administration. Her husband is a senior partner in a law firm in a nearby city. The couple has four grown children. . . .

Marge is involved . . . in several groups using alternative healing. She personally utilizes some Eastern methods . . . but she does not teach these methods nor is she affiliated with a group in which Eastern spirituality is a focus. As a nurse, she has used Therapeutic Touch for about three years. She uses her psychic healing methods to "get in touch with" the pain and suffering of the children in her ward; patients do not need to know that she is "sending" them healing energies. Privately, she has been practicing psychic healing for about six years; her methods are eclectic and she tries new "modalities" as she learns about them, discarding some approaches, keeping others. Her main support group is a psychic healing circle that meets each week in members' homes. . . . When she seeks healing for herself, she usually turns to the members of this group. In addition, she attends the monthly or weekly meetings of three regional holistic health and metaphysical societies. These meetings are important sources of new ideas and techniques. She has also taken numerous workshops and short courses on various alternative methods: foot reflexology, rebirthing, and crystal and color healing.

Marge does healing almost any time, any place and with anyone—including many people who do not know she is "sending" them healing energy. Marge described working on healing herself and others even while doing the dishes or in the elevator at work. Sometimes she engaged in it deliberately; other times, she felt, it was simply a part of her being. She stated: "I believe that in every moment of my life I release energy to those around me. I think everybody needs it every moment. . . . I feel that whoever makes connection with me or I make connection with them, I'm using my energy to heal."

She is also a good example of the general lack of clear financial motivation on the part of many "expert" alternative healers. She charges private clients only a nominal fee (from $15 to $30, depending upon ability to pay) for a thirty-to-ninety-minute session, and she earns about $100 to $150 (depending upon the number of registrants) for teaching a day-long workshop. These services are, however, occasional and minor sources of income for Marge. Her professional salary, combined with that of her husband, supports a high standard of living; Marge views her paid work as healer as a sideline, done mainly as a service.

Source: From *Ritual Healing in Suburban America* by Meredith B. McGuire with the assistance of Debra Kantor. Copyright © 1988, by Rutgers, The State University. Reprinted with permission of Rutgers University Press.

1983; Westley, 1983; Tipton, 1982; Csordas and Cross, 1976; Moody, 1974; Skultans, 1974).

Ethnic and other subcultural belief systems inform the indigenous healing practices of most ethnic groups in the United States (and elsewhere). The healing actions of such persons as the Mexican-American *curanderos*, Navaho singers, Puerto Rican

[4]This is a composite portrait to protect the identity of the actual healers studied.

espiritistos, Hawaiian *kahunas*, Eskimo shamans, or Haitian voodoo healers are based upon complex systems of ideas about illness and power (Roeder, 1988; Snyder, 1983; Gill, 1981; Trotter and Chavira, 1981; Garrison, 1977; Harwood, 1977; Scott, 1974; Snow, 1974; Hill, 1973; Vogel, 1970; Kiev, 1968).

The Effectiveness of Indigenous Healing

The foremost reason why people use indigenous healing is that it *makes sense* to them. Indigenous healing beliefs are plausible, especially to people who grew up in a culture or subculture in which they were common. Indigenous healing "works" partly by fitting into people's understandings of their world and how it operates. Young (1976: 8) pointed out that therapies are considered efficacious not merely when they are a means of curing sickness, but "equally important, [when] they are a means by which specific, named kinds of sickness are defined and given culturally recognizable forms."

Indigenous healing forms and transforms the illness experience. It utilizes symbols and ritual action, meaningful to believers or members of that culture, that can produce change on several levels: social, bodily, and emotional.[5] A number of studies of symbolic healing suggest that just as mind, body, and society are linked in illness causation, so too are they (potentially at least) part of the healing process (Lyon, 1990; Devisch, 1987; Dow, 1986; Csordas, 1983; McGuire, 1983; Moerman, 1979).

The therapeutic practices themselves also make sense to members of the subcultural group. To an outsider, the Vermont folk remedy of a honey-vinegar mixture may seem nonsensical and repulsive. To persons raised in that rural New England subculture, however, it may be a plausible and appealing way of conceptualizing problems of health and illness; the remedy invokes images of benign nature, living "near to the soil," and being in harmony with the laws of nature by which health is maintained and produced (Atkinson, 1978).

In summarizing several outcome studies, which generally evaluate the results of healing efforts in terms of Western medical as well as indigenous standards, Kleinman (1984: 150) observed, "These studies document three things: that folk healers are frequently effective, that there are limits to their efficacy, and that, while toxicities of folk healing are infrequent, they do occur."[6]

This summary, along with Kleinman's caution that each form of healing has to be viewed in its own social context, probably also applies not only to folk healers but to the full range of alternative healing practices in modern Western societies.

---

[5]Biomedicine also uses symbols of power to enhance its effectiveness. For example, a pill may symbolize medical power to cure inside the body (Pellegrino, 1976). Surgery, lab tests, and diet regimens may likewise be used as ritual symbols (cf. Posner, 1977). Medical costumes and settings (e.g., stethoscopes and white uniforms) symbolize professional expertise. Such symbols increase trust and expectancy and, indirectly, may increase healing effectiveness (Frank, 1973). Much of what is called the placebo effect may in fact be related to symbolic healing (Moerman, 1983).

[6]We need to keep in mind that the *exact* same generalizations could be made about healing by medical doctors: They are frequently effective, their efficacy is limited, and some treatments are dangerous or iatrogenic. This evaluation does not mean, however, that one should not consult a doctor, but it does imply

ADHERENCE TO THERAPEUTIC RECOMMENDATIONS

Part of the health-seeking process is whether and how the sick person follows the recommended therapeutic procedures. For example, is a recommended diet followed? Are prescriptions filled and medicines taken? A medical doctor's recommendations may not be the only course of action to which a sick person would adhere; the advice of a lay consultant, an herbalist, a massage therapist, or spiritual healer might also be considered. Some sick persons deliberately seek several opinions—medical or otherwise—and therefore obtain several therapeutic recommendations. Adherence thus implies actively choosing which advice to follow.

Some formulations of the sick role have included following the doctor's orders as a role expectation (see Chapter 6). Many doctors, likewise, consider it a patient's duty to comply with their therapeutic regimen. The very notion of patient compliance implies a power relationship: The doctor is treated as authoritative and powerful, the patient as powerless and appropriately obedient (Chrisman, 1977; Stimson, 1974). The idea that the patient should comply may, thus, have ideological functions for the physician (Trostle, 1988).

A number of studies show that health care professionals greatly underestimate the amount of patients' nonadherence to medical regimens (see the review of literature in DiMatteo and Friedman, 1982: 35–57; Kasl, 1975; Stimson, 1974). One estimate suggests that some 20 percent of prescriptions are never filled; 30 to 50 percent of medications prescribed are taken incorrectly (National Council on Patient Information and Education, as cited in Brody, 1992). When doctors' "orders" involve major lifestyle changes (such as changing eating or exercise patterns), compliance is even less common. Doctors often experience patient nonadherence to their recommendations as an affront to their authority; they blame patients as irresponsible.

Often, however, there are many other reasons why patients do not adhere to recommended therapies. Since patients do not want to alienate their doctors, they often hide their nonadherence to the doctors' recommendations and the extent of their search for other opinions. Many patients, especially those dealing with chronic illnesses, develop their own strategies for managing their illness. Such strategies include the selective use of biomedical approaches, but often also involve other therapeutic approaches, advice from more than one doctor, and/or their tailoring of the doctor's advice. From the patients' point of view, such noncompliant health-seeking behavior is rational, and it preserves for them some element of control (Herzlich and Pierret, 1987; see also Alexander, 1982).

Rather than conceptualizing the sick person's role in terms of degree of com-

---

we should be cautious about naive assumptions that medical treatment is necessarily beneficial or safe. Likewise, we should avoid romantic notions that folk healing is necessarily beneficial or safe. The effort to evaluate or compare the effectiveness of folk healing with medical healing is greatly complicated by the fact that because they typically operate with totally different paradigms, their notions of what constitutes a "successful" healing are very different. While there is much overlap in what problems they consider to need healing, folk and medical healing usually have very different goals. Thus efforts to compare them or to evaluate one by the terms of the other are greatly confounded.

pliance with doctors' orders, it is useful to understand the meaning of medications and other therapies from the perspective of the sick person. One study found that many people with epilepsy modify and self-regulate their use of prescribed medications in an attempt to assert a degree of control over their condition (Conrad, 1985; see also Donovan and Blake, 1992; Trostle et al., 1983). In a similar assertion of control, hemodialysis patients from a wide range of educational and ethnic backgrounds utilized nonprescribed treatments (e.g., special diets and exercises, religious and folk healing, herbal treatments, massage, and acupuncture) without the knowledge of their medical doctors (Snyder, 1983).

Noting the extent of nonadherence to doctor's recommendations, Zola (1983: 217) argued that

> to "take one's medicine" is in no sense the "natural thing" for patients to do. If anything, a safer working assumption is that most patients regard much of their medical treatment as unwanted, intrusive, disruptive, and the manner in which it is given presumptuous.

The patient is engaged in an ongoing process of evaluation of recommended therapies; whether the recommendation is medically correct is only one, sometimes minor criterion in this evaluation. Other criteria include such matters as: Does the doctor appear to understand my illness correctly? Do the doctor's methods of diagnosis, interpersonal style, and treatment meet my expectations of competent? Is there a safer, more pleasant, or less drastic alternative (especially to surgery and powerful medications)? Does it feel like this therapy is working? When dissatisfied, patients may try to modify the treatment either by negotiating with their doctor or by modifying the plan by themselves (i.e., noncompliance). Both approaches represent patients' attempt to assert some control (Donovan and Blake, 1992).

Much patient nonadherence can be traced to difficulties of understanding and communication in the doctor-patient interaction (Svarstad, 1976), as described further in Chapter 10. Part of the "problem," however, is due to important differences in the perspectives and goals of doctors and their patients. The doctor's focus is typically upon curing or managing the specific disease presented by the patient. Laypersons, by contrast, are more likely to have a broader notion of health and illness and to be concerned with all aspects of their life, not merely one health problem, no matter how serious. For example, a patient may feel that the depression experienced as a side effect of blood pressure medicine is so debilitating that continuing the medication is not worth the price (cf. Twaddle, 1981b).

Often the decision not to follow the doctor's recommended course of action (or not to seek professional help in the first place) is due to a discrepancy between the layperson's and the professional's understandings of the sickness. For example, in rural Appalachian culture there is a common belief that the purpose of medical treatment is to cure sickness. There is a profound suspicion of medical practitioners, especially in their treatment of chronic illnesses (such as coal miners' black lung disease), because they charge fees and require repeated visits but cannot actually cure the disease. Lay conceptions of black lung in particular hold the progressive deterioration to be an inevitable, irreversible consequence of working in the mines. Thus, health care programs designed to ameliorate some effects of the disease have not had much success in attracting participants or generating adherence to regimens of exercise and diet (Friedl, 1982).

Similarly, a Louisiana study of black women with hypertension (high blood pressure) found that their cultural beliefs and folk-illness models affected their adherence to the medical regimen prescribed. For example, many of these women conceptualized their sickness as "high blood," a folk-illness condition in which the blood is too rich, thick, and hot, and total blood volume is too great; this conceptualization is not what doctors mean by high blood pressure. When health professionals failed to understand that medical diagnostic terms invoked a whole different set of cultural meanings for these patients, they inadvertently contributed to patient noncompliance (Heurtin-Roberts and Reisin, 1990).

A Massachusetts study of sufferers of specific chronic illnesses found that primary care physicians and nurse practitioners showed very limited knowledge of their patients' conceptions of these illnesses. While professionals were more likely to know the beliefs of college-educated patients than those of less educated patients, overall they understood the lay explanatory models used by less than half of the patients in the study (Helman, 1985). This lack of shared understanding of the nature of the illness is likely to lead to considerable nonadherence to doctors' orders and to dissatisfaction on the part of both medical professionals and their patients.

Adherence to any therapeutic regimen is likely to require some effort. The sheer logistics of putting all recommendations into effect are enormous, especially for chronic illness, for which the therapeutic regimen must last a lifetime and is likely to become more demanding as the condition deteriorates. Health seeking is an active process throughout, but the active participation of the sick person is especially evident when it comes to choosing and putting some or all therapeutic advice into effect.

SUMMARY

The process by which people seek health is an active one. Both preventive care and the treatment of problems involve numerous decisions about the body and its needs. Self-treatment is far more common than treatment by professionals, medical or nonmedical. In addition to professional medical care, there is a vast hidden health care system providing advice, preventive and therapeutic care, emotional and practical support, and guidance in the search for professional care.

Orthodox Western biomedicine is only one of several healing systems available in most societies. Other options include nonallopathic practitioners, and various indigenous healers and healing groups. The individual, then, has a range of health-seeking options. Even after consulting outside help, the individual also chooses which advice or therapeutic regimens to accept and put into practice.

RECOMMENDED READINGS

Articles

NOEL J. CHRISMAN, "The health-seeking process: An approach to the natural history of illness," *Culture, Medicine, and Psychiatry* 1, 1977: 351–377.

HILARY GRAHAM, "Providers, negotiators, and mediators: Women as the hidden carers," pp. 25–52 in E. Lewin and V. Olesen, eds., *Women, Health, and Healing: Toward a New Perspective.* New York: Tavistock, 1985.

Books

ALAN HARWOOD, *Rx: Spiritist as Needed: A Study of a Puerto Rican Community Mental Health Resource.* New York: Wiley, 1977. This highly readable ethnography describes the beliefs and practices underlying the use of Puerto Rican spiritual healers in a U.S. urban environment.

LILY M. HOFFMAN, *The Politics of Knowledge: Activist Movements in Medicine and Planning.* Ithaca: State University of New York Press, 1989. The author presents case studies of activist movements that challenged the occupational self-interest of professions, especially the medical profession.

LOWELL S. LEVIN and ELLEN L. IDLER, *The Hidden Health Care System: Mediating Structures and Medicine.* Cambridge, MA: Ballinger, 1981. A highly readable synthesis of the literature on the role of families, self-care, religious groups, community groups, and mutual aid in the larger system of health care.

MEREDITH B. MCGUIRE, with the assistance of Debra Kantor, *Ritual Healing in Suburban America.* New Brunswick, NJ: Rutgers University Press, 1988. This study describes the beliefs and practices of middle-class, educated, suburbanites who use various nonmedical healing alternatives (such as faith healing, meditation, psychic healing, acupressure, and massage) in addition to medical treatment.

CHAPTER NINE

The Social Construction of Medical Knowledge

Our culture and social structure shape the way we understand and interpret our bodies, illness, and disease as well as whether or how we perceive illness. This chapter examines how what we know about illnesses is socially constructed, used, and changed.

A sociological approach to knowledge about illness differs from the biomedical approach in that it does not assume the objective existence of what medicine categorizes as disease.[1] The sociologist does not take for granted that disease entities exist in nature and await "discovery." This perspective does not mean that people's health conditions have no objective foundation. People do experience real pain, sickness, and death. This approach does, however, mean that laypersons' and professionals' *ideas* about illness are **social constructions**, or the result of human activity. Therefore, no matter how empirically precise these ideas are, they are always open to the influence of social factors in their production, transmission, and development. The very fact that medical ideas are bound by assumptions implicit in a language and a culture's rules for producing knowledge means they are always delimited in their representation of the real world (see Young, 1978).

MEDICAL IDEAS AND SOCIAL FORCES

These ideas about body, health, and disease are nonetheless very powerful in shaping a society's medical reality. The knowledge held by any given culture or group is the product of its social history. Western medicine's knowledge of its disease categories is a social product, as is the knowledge of diseases in other medical systems, such as Ayurvedic medicine in Asia and *curanderismo* in Latin America.

In Chapter 8 we described lay conceptions of health, illness, and the body. By contrast, formal medical knowledge in Western societies is typically highly specialized and based upon bioscientific theories and categories of thought. The contemporary medical paradigm represents a major historical change in how the body is viewed. Scientific **paradigms** are frameworks of formal knowledge that members of a given scientific community share, mainly due to having undergone similar educations and professional initiations; to sharing a common professional language, rules of evidence, and conceptual schemes; and to relying on the same professional literature and communication of the same scientific community (Kuhn, 1970: 176). These paradigms are rather like lenses; the world viewed through one paradigm looks very different from the world viewed through another. We shall examine briefly the recent history of current medical paradigms and how they have come to have such powerful impact upon the practice of medicine and the development of the medical profession.

Although Western medical practice is based upon scientific knowledge, the practitioners themselves are not typically scientists. The scientist's objective is to gather empirical data, and to analyze, interpret, and generalize from these findings.

---

[1]Any social constructionist approach to knowledge must recognize how sociological ideas are in turn influenced by social processes and historical developments.

Scientists are not necessarily concerned with the practical application of scientific knowledge. By contrast, the practitioner's goal is more pragmatic: to deal with the specific conditions of individual patients or clients. What the practitioner needs to know is likewise more practical. The only portion of medical knowledge relevant to doctors is that which relates to conditions they are most likely to encounter in clinical practice. Much medical knowledge is thus often "recipe knowledge," or "knowledge limited to pragmatic competence in routine performances" (Berger and Luckmann, 1967: 42). For example, pediatricians' use of immunizations does not require their detailed understanding of the latest scientific theories about the operations of the body's immune system (although their medical education typically introduced this subject). Rather, they rely upon "recipe knowledge" of which immunizations are recommended for children, at which ages, and with what common side effects and contraindications. They also rely upon knowledge of where to turn when a situation is no longer routine.

A person's access to or possession of a valued form of knowledge can be an important factor in determining one's power and prestige in any society. For example, if the knowledge of how to make a valued ritual potion is held only by the women of a particular family, then their knowledge is the basis of some power or honor. Knowledge is unevenly distributed in a society, often along lines of gender, social class, age, ethnicity, and the division of labor (Berger and Luckmann, 1967: 76–81). Access to and possession of specialized, formal knowledge, such as medical knowledge, is particularly uneven. Because very few people in modern societies possess advanced medical knowledge or technical skills, being able to control such knowledge is the basis of rewards (e.g., high fees), power, and privilege. People who control specialized knowledge are thus in a position to limit the access of others to that knowledge (e.g., by controlling professional school admissions and discouraging laypersons from gaining knowledge). The social distribution of knowledge both reflects and shapes social distinctions of power and prestige.

"Discovering" Disease: A Historical Example

Many diseases that were diagnosed frequently in the past either are not commonly found today or are no longer recognized as diseases. Similarly, some conditions diagnosed as disease nowadays may very well cease to fit any disease category in the future. The forces shaping the "discovery" of disease categories are not purely objective, scientific factors; rather, value judgments, economic considerations, and other social concerns frequently enter the process. For instance, a famous physician during the American Revolution identified a disease he called "revolutiona," which was characterized by presumably irrational opposition to the "natural rule" of the English monarch (Conrad and Schneider, 1992: 49). In the 1850s, the classification of "diseases of the Negro race" included "drapetomania," which caused slaves to run away from their masters, and "dysaesthesia aethiopis," which accounted for laggard work habits among slaves (see Cartwright, 1851). Disease categories thus have political uses, and those on whom they are imposed may suffer serious consequences.

A prime example of changing medical definitions is a disease, prevalent in the latter half of the nineteenth century and the first part of the twentieth century, that had the following characteristics:

It retards the growth, impairs the mental faculties and reduces the victim to a lamentable state. The person afflicted seeks solitude, and does not wish to enjoy the society of his friends; he is troubled with headache, wakefulness and restlessness at night, pain in various parts of the body, indolence, melancholy, loss of memory, weakness in the back and generative organs, variable appetite, cowardice, inability to look a person in the face, lack of confidence in his own abilities.

When the evil has been pursued for several years, there will be an irritable condition of the system; sudden flushes of heat over the face; the countenance becomes pale and clammy; the eyes have a dull, sheepish look; the hair becomes dry and split at the ends; sometimes there is a pain over the region of the heart; shortness of breath; palpitation of the heart . . . ; the sleep is disturbed; there is constipation; cough; irritation of the throat; finally, the whole man becomes a wreck, physically, morally and mentally.

Some of the consequences of [this disease] are epilepsy, apoplexy, paralysis, premature old age, involuntary discharge of seminal fluid, which generally occurs during sleep, or after urinating, or when evacuating the bowels. Among females, besides these other consequences, we have hysteria, menstrual derangement, catalepsy and strange nervous symptoms (Stout, 1885: 333–334).

This serious disease was onanism, better known as masturbation. The fact that the doctor writing this description of symptoms slips easily into referring to it as an "evil" alerts us to the strong moral connotations that this disease label carried. This supposedly scientific medical category thus clearly reflected the moral and social judgments of the doctors who applied it (cf. Engelhardt, 1978).

What functions did the identification of masturbation as a disease serve? For the distraught parents of a moody teenager, the label explained a wide range of behaviors. It is less likely that the young person experienced much relief at having this diagnosis applied to symptoms such as poor appetite, headaches, or split ends. Another important function was to establish this "disease" as within the proper jurisdiction of the medical profession. The author of the preceding description concluded emphatically that "the treatment of this disease should be undertaken only by a skillful physician" (Stout, 1885: 334).

Applying the category of disease to masturbation implied etiological explanations. The **etiology** of an illness is a set of ideas about its causality in general or about the origins of a particular illness episode. Like all ideas, they are human constructions that change over time. Early etiological theories of masturbation implicated the loss of seminal fluid, whereas later theories emphasized the overstimulation of the nerves, which led to general debility. Several authorities held that all sexual activity was potentially debilitating, but that masturbation was especially injurious because it was "unnatural" and thus more likely to disturb the nerve tone (Engelhardt, 1978: 15–17). The diagnosis of masturbation as a disease syndrome is no longer common; indeed, in many medical and lay conceptions it is now considered to be quite normal and healthy.

Identifying a person's problems as the disease of masturbation subsequently implied a particular course of therapy in accordance with etiological ideas about the disease. Therapies were supposed to, first, eliminate the practice and, second, calm the nerves and rebuild the person's sapped strength. Some of the more tolerant therapies included hard work, a simple diet, tonics, cold baths, sedatives and narcotics such as opium, and alternative sexual outlets such as prostitutes or mistresses (Engelhardt, 1978: 19). If these therapies were not successful, more drastic measures were often recommended, such as restraining devices, acid burns and rings inserted in the foreskin to make masturbation painful, circumcision (of males and females), clitoridectomy (surgical removal of the clitoris), vasectomy, acupuncture of the prostate or testicles, and even castration (Engelhardt, 1978; Barker-Benfield, 1975). Such a seriously debilitating disease required serious measures, including drastic surgery.

Those symptoms once clustered and classified as signs of the insidious disease of masturbation may still exist (e.g., some teenagers still have variable appetites, split ends, and dull, sheepish looks), but the characteristics are no longer classified as a disease. Conversely, new classifications, such as premenstrual syndrome, have been defined into existence as a disease. The diagnostic category of PMS (premenstrual syndrome) is a social construction which, like the diagnosis of onanism, embodies a set of cultural ideas and values. The considerable controversy within the American Psychiatric Association over whether to include the diagnosis (called "Late Luteal Phase Dysphoric Disorder") in the revised Diagnostic and Statistical Manual (DSM-III-R, 1987) illustrates the social value considerations implicit in the definition and diagnosis of PMS, or LLPDD. The attempts by medical doctors to define PMS are similarly problematic; some definitions are so broad that they classify as PMS the normal variance during as much as 17 days of the 28-day cycle in virtually all women with menstrual cycles. Accordingly, they define almost all adult women as having a medical problem (and presumably needing medical treatment). Despite lack of strong empirical evidence, doctors, lawyers, psychologists, journalists, and laypersons have used the notion of PMS and other hormonal cycle variance to "explain" women's violent crimes, automobile driving patterns, accident proneness, suicidal impulses, and quarrelsomeness. Thus, like the nineteenth-century diagnosis of hysteria, a "modern" medical diagnosis—seemingly factual and empirically based—comes to embody old cultural assumptions that women's reproductive systems cause irrationality and "sick" behavior (Rodin, 1992).

Such new categories both justify medical control and legitimate the expense of medical care for that disease. For example, in the United States socially constructed disease categories are the only basis for most insurance reimbursement. Socially constructed disease categories, accepted as legitimate by the medical establishment, become the basis for funding research, treating patients, and institutionally establishing treatment programs. By putting these ideas into practice, medicine gives the disease categories a reality of their own. The process by which symptoms are selectively clustered and defined as disease is a social process and reflects cultural assumptions and power relationships (see Johnson, 1987).

Science as a Social Product

With its emphasis upon a scientific model, biomedicine has developed increasingly complex **nosologies** or typologies of diseases. The medical model held that each particular disease could be characterized by a specific pathological configuration and attributed to a definite, unique cause. Thus medicine has emphasized the classification and description of all diseases. The movement toward ever more precise differentiations of medical nosologies and etiologies is based upon the assumption of **disease specificity**—the medical belief that each disease or syndrome has characteristic qualities and causes that are specific to that category of disease. This assumption has led to a focus on the individual rather than the social and contextual locus of sickness (Cassell, 1986; see also Dingwall, 1976: 50).

Medical ideas are the product of social processes and are continually changing. All scientific work involves the social construction of facts and interpretive schemes (Latour and Woolgar, 1979: 243; Berger and Luckmann, 1967: 60–72). Modern medical science strives to be as empirically neutral as possible, for example, by conducting blind experiments in which neither administrator nor subject knows whether a substance being given is the experimental substance or an inert control substance. Nevertheless, much medical research cannot be readily conducted neutrally, because—among other reasons—live human bodies are not readily detached from the persons who inhabit them. Thus, neither the scientific observers nor the objects of scientific observation can have their influential social characteristics and attitudes eradicated.

Social, economic, and political factors greatly influence the scientific discovery of new diagnostic categories. Funding for research is largely dependent upon what is socially defined as a serious problem at the moment. For example, a disease syndrome known as GRID (Gay-Related Immune Deficiency) received relatively little medical attention or research funding, but when the same syndrome was later considered to be a national threat to the heterosexual population and redefined as AIDS (Acquired Immune Deficiency Syndrome), enormous increases in research funding enabled scientists to identify several variants of the syndrome and to describe some of the complex ways it can damage the body (see Shilts, 1987). Funding for research on what is now recognized as a serious international health problem was thus significantly delayed due to the politics surrounding a stigmatized illness. Similarly, research on women's health risks and responses to therapies has been funded at a much lower rate than men's. Only 13 percent of the National Institute of Health's budget is used to research women's health problems, such as heart disease (Weider, 1991). Thus, diagnoses and therapies for women have been based primarily on research done on men, despite considerable clinical evidence that diseases in women's bodies and women's responses to usual therapeutic approaches are different from those of men.

Often the development of new disease categories is connected with the assertion of a new occupational specialization. Considerable professional prestige is attached to "discovering" and describing a "new" disease or syndrome. In psychiatry, for example, the 1987 *Diagnostic and Statistical Manual* (DSM-III-R; A.P.A., 1987) recognized 292 disorders. It included a novel appendix subtitled "Proposed Diagnostic Categories Needing Further Study"; since then nearly 100 new diagnoses were proposed for the next edition (Pincus et al., 1992). The process of proposing and gaining acceptance of new categories of diagnosis is partly political and often based on cultural assumptions rather than "pure" empirical evidence (Gaines, 1992). Finding new diseases is thus an active process; medicine is consciously oriented to creating disease categories where previously there were none (Freidson, 1970: 252). The case of menopause as a medical syndrome illustrates this process.

Creation of Medical "Problems": The Case of Menopause

Social and economic considerations promote the search for new diseases. For example, menopause, the period of women's lives in which menstruation naturally ceases, is now indexed in the *International Classification of Diseases* (U.S. Department of Heath and Human Services, 1989: 524–525). While menopause is a normal biological process, in the last fifty years, it has come to be seen as a medical problem in the United States and many other Western societies. The Western biomedical literature generally treats menopause as an estrogen deficiency disease or ovarian dysfunction that produces various physical and emotional problems (see Bell, 1990; McCrea, 1983). There is, however, considerable cross-cultural variation in its biophysical, social, and emotional concomitants.

In our culture, symptoms such as hot flashes, headaches, dizziness, fatigue, anxiety, insomnia, irritability, depression, and general emotional problems are typically associated with menopause. Cross-cultural data suggest, however, that women's responses to the cessation of menstruation may be connected to the structure of society and its cultural expectations for women (see Lock, 1993, 1991; Bowles, 1990). For example, in Islamic and many African societies, menopause brings relative freedom from many of the restrictions of women's lives: They are no longer required to be secluded, veiled, and restricted in their male company. These women experience few of the physiological and psychological symptoms attributed to menopause in Western societies (Townsend and Carbone, 1980). Menopause is thus a good example of how social meanings influence individuals' physical experiences and perceptions of their own bodies.

The Western medical construction of menopause, however, ignores these social meanings, reducing the experience to a set of biochemical processes presumed to characterize all female bodies, regardless of cultural or socioeconomic factors. Medical knowledge often becomes detached and independent of the research upon which it is based. Thus, limitations in the original research are not taken into account in the accumulated stock of knowledge. For example, the medical construction of menopause is based in part on clinical studies with small numbers of subjects, typically drawn from patient populations—women whose menopause was surgically induced (e.g., through oophorectomy) or whose problems with menopause had already been medically defined as severe enough to warrant treatment. There are severe methodological limitations to such studies, and cautious researchers know not to generalize too extensively from them to the general populace. Unfortunately, once in the medical literature, these ideas are treated as facts that are presumably generalizable to all women (Kaufert, 1988).

Recent studies of a wider population of middle-aged women have found relatively little evidence of pathology or medical problems. One U.S. study followed the self-reported experiences of 8,050 women over several years before and after menopause; the majority of women did not seek help for menopause-related problems, and those who did experience significant "symptoms" were disproportionately those who reported prior poor health, independent of menopause. The researchers concluded with concern that physicians may be too quickly assuming that these women's problems were due to menopause and, thus, failing to diagnose or treat other, more probable causes such as chronic illnesses, stressful social situations, or preexisting psychological problems like depression (McKinlay et al., 1991). Part of the reason for doctors' acceptance of the methodologically flawed studies is that the medical construction of menopause meshes with physicians' assumptions about bodies and diseases. Thus, to define and treat a normal process as a disease fits the medical model, and the idea that menopause is a disease implies a concrete medical course of action.

In the United States, the definition of menopause as a deficiency disease resulted from the professional efforts of a small, elite segment of the American medical profession during the 1930s and 1940s. A study of the medical literature during this transition shows that this process involved both the "discovery" of a theory of etiology of this "disease" and the development of pharmacologic methods of treatment. Using the paradigms of sex endocrinology, doctors attributed menopause to the deficiency of hormones (in particular, estrogen) regularly produced by the woman's body before cessation of menstruation. The development of an inexpensive synthetic estrogen replacement, DES (diethylstilbestrol), subsequently made the medical management of this "disease" possible (Bell, 1990).

Although these specialists acknowledged that most menopausal women (a common estimate was 85 percent) experienced few or no problems, the efficacy of DES created the possibility of treating *all* menopausal women. Indeed, despite growing criticism and concern over the safety of estrogen replacement therapy (some studies had linked it to cancer and some other serious conditions), by 1975 estrogens had become the fifth most frequently prescribed drug in the United States. A survey done the same year found that an estimated 51 percent of women had taken estrogen for at least three months, with a median use of ten years (see Kaufert and McKinlay, 1985; McCrea, 1983). In 1975 one gynecologist stated:

> I think of the menopause as a deficiency disease like diabetes. Most women develop some symptoms *whether they are aware of them or not*, so I prescribe estrogens for virtually all menopausal women for an indefinite period (quoted in Brody, 1975: 55 [emphasis added]).

In the mid-1970s the scientific literature firmly began to implicate estrogen therapy in iatrogenic diseases, (i.e., those caused by medical treatment). Debates over the curbing of estrogen replacement therapy involved conflicts between the pharmaceutical companies and the Food and Drug Administration, which ruled in 1976 that the industry must prepare a warning on the risks of estrogen for insertion in packages. Subsequently, estrogen use declined dramatically.

The conflict generated a debate within the medical profession itself, highlighting the differences in perspective between biomedical researchers and physicians in clinical practice (Kaufert and McKinlay, 1985). The definition of menopause as a deficiency disease resulted from the efforts of a small elite of specialists, together with the development of a disease etiology that lent itself to medical management and the promotion of a pharmacological agent that could be used in the treatment of the newly created disease.

Denial of Medical "Problems": Tardive Dyskinesia

Despite the general disposition to find new diseases and syndromes, the medical profession sometimes *resists* accepting new disease categories. Social and political factors also account for some constraints against medical "discovery." Tardive dyskinesia is a seriously debilitating, often irreversible disorder of the central nervous system, characterized by a variety of involuntary movements, most notably of the lips, jaw, and tongue. It is a "new" disorder partly because it is a pervasive, iatrogenic side effect of antipsychotic (neuroleptic) drugs, such as chlorpromazine, which came onto the market in the 1950s. In the 1960s and 1970s, the prevalence of tardive dyskinesia increased because neuroleptic drugs were being prescribed more frequently and in higher doses. Even after the syndrome had been identified and named in 1960, many clinicians did not accept or use the diagnostic category (Brown and Funk, 1986: 116–124).

One significant factor in this resistance was that acknowledging the existence and pervasiveness of tardive dyskinesia hurt the economic and political interests of many clinicians. The institutional and professional mandate to control the deviant behaviors of patients often superseded concerns for the drugs' physical risks for patients. The researchers and others who called attention to tardive dyskinesia were generally identified with the National Institute of Mental Health, medical schools, and research institutes, whereas the clinicians who dealt with patients with the syndrome were working in mental hospitals and private psychiatric practice.

Many clinicians simply did not *observe* the disease, even in patients with obvious symptoms. The professional self-interest of these psychiatrists was involved; they relied heavily upon pharmacological methods in their claims for efficacy in the treatment of psychoses, and their claims for recognition and remuneration as medical professionals were linked with their emphasis upon biopsychiatry and psychopharmacology. Since the patients were generally already defined as mentally ill, their complaints could be readily discounted and their overt symptoms attributed to other problems, such as brain disorders (Brown and Funk, 1986). The economic and political interests of these physicians prevented them from recognizing the disease they were creating.

IDEAS AND IDEOLOGIES

Despite the supposed value-neutrality and objectivity of "scientific" medicine, the knowledge produced, held, and used by its practitioners is, with considerable regularity, connected to their personal social location and the larger social situation of medical institutions in that society. In particular, social stratification (by criteria such as social class, age, political power, gender, and race) appears to be closely correlated with ideas about the body, health, illness, and healing. Thus, medical ideas often reflect or serve as ideology.

Ideology is a system of ideas that explains and legitimates the actions and interests of a specific sector (i.e., class) of society. For example, when the coal mining industry was in conflict with coal miners' representatives over black lung disease, the medical ideology of the industry promoted a very narrow definition of the disease, thereby diminishing the industry's legal responsibility toward the victims and its social responsibility for prevention of the syndrome (see Smith, 1987, 1981).

Ideas about health and illness frequently serve as legitimations for the interests of one group over another. A **legitimation** is any form of socially established explanation that is given to justify a course of action (see Berger and Luckmann, 1967: 92–128). In Chapter 6, we examined how ideas of health and illness legitimate the larger social order. Here we shall focus on legitimations for the interests of certain social groups in the stratification system.

In Western industrialized societies, the medical profession has organized itself, as is described further later, specifically to promote its interests. Different professional interests pertain to other health-related occupations, such as nurses, pharmacists, X-ray technicians, midwives, and physical therapists. Incorporated into their ideas about health and healing are legitimations for their occupational statuses and income. Their knowledge about illness simultaneously legitimates their professional domain.

The 1975 "discovery" of Lyme disease, a tick-borne spirochetal infection, illustrates how American rheumatologists successfully claimed the "discovery" and right to define treatment for the disease, superseding the "turf" claims of European dermatologists, who had "discovered" the same (or closely related) condition decades earlier and identified it as ECM (erythema chronicum migrans). By presenting Lyme disease as new and threatening, the mass media enhanced public attention to the disease, and commercial interests fanned public fears to promote a growing range of antitick products for people, pets, and property. Rather than being a discrete, objective entity that was simply medically "discovered," Lyme disease exemplifies the complex process by which a legitimized diagnosis is socially negotiated and developed (Aronowitz, 1991).

Other interests served by medical legitimation include those of the health-related industries: pharmaceutical industries, biotechnological industries, hospitals, nursing homes, and the medical, life, and disability insurance companies. Medical legitimations are especially important for various agencies of social control, such as the courts, mental hospitals, prisons, hospitals, and schools; this role will be discussed further later. Ideas about health and illness are also used to legitimate the interests of such parties as employers, workers, producers, consumers, polluters, environmentalists, and the military.

Ideology influences actions subtly, most often without the actors' awareness. It is incorporated in the language and rituals of everyday interaction, and thus comes to be taken for granted and unnoticed or unexamined (cf. Fisher, 1986; Emerson, 1970). For example, the language used in referring to a patient as "the broken hip in room 305" depersonalizes the ill person, transforming her into a "case" that can be "managed" more readily by a professional team. Even matters of professional dress (such as a uniform, clipboard, and stethoscope) subtly symbolize status differences.

Ideological aspects of thought and practice often go unnoticed because they are often self-confirming. Since ideology shapes people's expectations and what they consider to be evidence, it often produces evidence that confirms those expectations. If, for example, I expect old people to be befuddled, my observations of them are likely to confirm my expectation. Indeed, if an individual protests that he is not befuddled, I may interpret his protestations as further evidence that he is so confused that he cannot see the validity of my judgment. Also, when I treat him as befuddled, he may come to act that way and further confirm my prejudgment. The "evidence" that confirms my expectation is a self-fulfilling prophecy.

Although interest groups tend to be attracted to ideas and practices that mesh with their particular interests, the concept of ideology does not adequately predict any given individual's behavior. We should avoid using this term in any simplistic or deterministic sense. Material interests are not the only motivating force for individuals; for example, spiritual or altruistic motives might lead people to work for conditions that are not in their personal interest. Interest theories, however, suggest that in general people tend to hold ideas and engage in practices that serve or at least do not conflict with their own interests.

Some examples of medical practice in Western industrialized societies show the influence of ideological elements, but there are also ideological aspects to healing practices in other cultures as well. The following examples illustrate some ways that interests influence ideas of health and illness, medical research, and individual diagnosis and treatments in Western bioscientific medicine.

Medicalization

Medicalization is the process of legitimating medical control over an area of life, typically by asserting and establishing the primacy of a medical interpretation of that area (see Conrad and Schneider, 1992; Illich, 1975; Zola, 1983). The process of medicalization is illustrated by the medical treatment of pregnancy and childbirth, as doctors took over a substantial business previously done primarily by midwives.

With the medicalization of childbirth, aspects of women's reproductive lives that are not pathological were brought under the canopy definition of illness. Medical education for the new specialization of obstetrics and gynecology fostered the notion that the events of childbearing—pregnancy, labor and delivery, and puerperium (the period immediately following childbirth)—could best be understood in purely physical and pathological terms (Hahn, 1987). More recently, potency, fertility, and the process of conception have also become medicalized (Becker and Nachtigall, 1992; Tiefer, 1992; Sandelowski, 1991).

The medical profession persuaded the public and the regulators of health care that women needed doctors to manage their pregnancies and childbirth. There is extensive evidence, however, that initial medicalization was linked more with doctors' professional interests than with the patients' well-being. Indeed, when medical control over childbirth was first being consolidated, doctors and hospitals had abysmal records, especially for spreading infection to both mothers and babies (Oakley, 1984; Wertz and Wertz, 1979).

Artificial insemination has similarly been medicalized for reasons unrelated to health per se; the actual process of artificial insemination can be safely and effectively done without advanced technology or medical procedures. Rather, medicalization of this process serves social control functions, for example, by screening applicants (and denying insemination to many), and by treating the process as a response to a husband's fertility ("medical") problems, rather than as a response to a woman's wish to become pregnant. While the determination of the source of a couple's fertility problems is largely a medical process, artificial insemination is not any more a medical concern than is natural insemination. Nevertheless, by medicalizing the process, physicians retain a monopoly over the market and their control is protected by law in several states (Wikler and Wikler, 1991).

The interests of other groups also influence medical ideas and practice. Various industries often exert great pressure and economic influence on medical research. For example, the tobacco industry has spent very large sums of money trying to fight any authoritative medical conclusion that smoking is a health hazard. Manufacturers of products requiring government approval as being safe for sale also have considerable interests vested in the outcomes of research on their products.

Corporate Interests

A good example of how ideology figures into the definition of, diagnosis of, and response to illness can be seen in ideas about occupational health hazards. In recent years manufacturers, unions, workers' rights groups, medical authorities, and several government agencies have been involved in a growing confrontation over issues of the genetic protection of workers and their offspring. One episode occurred in 1979, when the Department of Labor cited and fined American Cyanamid for requiring women to be sterilized to keep their jobs at the company's lead pigments manufacturing operations in West Virginia. Numerous chemicals central to the manufacture of paints, pesticides, herbicides, plastics, and heavy metals have been strongly implicated in reproductive damage. Sterility, miscarriages, and birth defects have been identified with workers' exposure to these chemicals.

In 1984 the UAW (United Automobile Workers union) sued Johnson Controls, the nation's largest producer of batteries, over its exclusionary policies for workers' exposure to lead, the basic raw material of batteries. One worker had undergone sterilization to keep her job; another worker was transferred to a nonexposed job at loss of pay, despite very low probability of becoming pregnant; a male employee's request to transfer to a nonexposed job to avoid reproductive risk was, however, denied. This case eventually resulted in a 1991 landmark decision by the U.S. Supreme Court that personnel practices limiting the employment of fertile women in jobs posing reproductive health hazards constituted sex discrimination and were, thus, illegal under the 1964 Civil Rights Act. This court decision will undoubtedly have long-term policy implications related to several health issues: Are women more at risk than men (who also contribute genetic material to their offspring)? Is the risk to the fetus the most important concern, or should there be concern for male and female workers, as well? Are these reproductive problems only one manifestation of health threats (such as cancer) that might affect all workers? (See Robinson and Giacomini, 1992).

The companies that manufacture such products often sponsor research on these medical issues. In the mid-1960s Dow Chemical Company supported research on cytogenetics, a branch of genetics that focuses on changes in chromosomes. The company's medical director believed that unusual changes in chromosomes, such as breakage and other mutations, might be forewarnings of cancer and birth defects. His studies showed connections between such chromosomal changes and worker exposure to certain toxic chemicals. The medical director and his research associates eventually quit their positions at Dow, asserting that the company was suppressing the damaging research results and refusing to implement policies to inform workers of their existing health conditions or future risks (Severo, 1980). The event of a company's medical director confronting the industry is somewhat uncommon because doctors who are employed or supported by an industry experience inherent constraints against identifying or diagnosing illnesses caused by that industry.

Captive Professionals

The company doctor is a good example of what Daniels (1969) called "**captive professionals**," or those whose presumed professional autonomy is compromised by organizational pressures from the bureaucracies that employ them. Daniels's study noted that psychiatrists practicing in the armed services accommodated their professional judgments to the military's manpower needs and values. Whereas psychiatrists working for mental hospitals tended to diagnose patients as mentally ill (in accordance with the expectations of the employer institutions), psychiatrists working for the military (where sickness reduced active manpower) tended to deny soldiers' claims of illness (Daniels, 1972, 1969; cf. Rosenhan, 1973). The diagnoses made by both of these "captive professionals" served to legitimate administrative decisions of the bureaucracies that employed them (cf. Ingleby, 1982: 136–137).

Similarly, many medical personnel employed by industry are "captive professionals." One Canadian study found that company doctors exhibited a "lack of sympathy with or intolerance of workers' attitudes towards health and safety in the workplace," and often perceived workers' health concerns as "fashions" or unreasonable fears. Rather than press the company to engineer changes in the production process or to initiate expensive monitoring programs, these doctors often emphasized workers' use of protective equipment and the screening and exclusion of supposedly "hyper-susceptible" workers (Walters, 1982). Although the corporate physician is potentially in a position to influence improved occupational health for employees, the professional's employer—not the individual worker—is still the "client," so ethical ambiguity and conflicting pressures are inherent in the structure of the job (Walsh, 1987).

While some professionals' organizational situation makes them clearly vulnerable or "captive" to their employers' interests, all professionals are likely to be influenced by their identification with certain class or status interests. Source of income indirectly affects medical decisions and doctor-patient relationships. For example, there is a tendency for doctors employed by industry not to diagnose occupational diseases, whereas doctors employed by unions or workers' health clinics tend to diagnose such diseases frequently (Lewin, 1987a). Doctors at for-profit hospitals are likewise more likely to urge patients to undergo Caesarian sections, whereas those working at public hospitals are much less likely to decide to perform such operations (Stafford, 1991). And doctors who have mastered a new surgical procedure are less likely to recommend it for patients than doctors who are eager to practice that procedure (Scully, 1980: 195–196).

Whose Interests Are Served?

While ideologies legitimate certain interests over others, they are often accepted by people whose interests are not necessarily served by those ideas. Ideological elements are often subtly diffused in a society through popular culture, educational institutions, mass media, and commercial advertising. For example, whose interests were served by the turn-of-the-century glorification of women's domesticity? Throughout the first half of this century, this ideal was meshed with popular ideas and fears of bacterial contagion to create much more work for housewives, who were taught in school and in women's magazines that they should be occupied with "scientific cleaning" and buying numerous products to protect their families from these dangerous invisible agents (Ehrenreich and English, 1978: 127–164). Interest groups exert power to shape ideology and to have it accepted and disseminated through channels such as the mass media and public education (Berger and Luckmann, 1967: 119–124).

Ideologies are not peculiar to medicine under capitalism and absent under other social and economic arrangements. *All* medical systems embody ideologies, but the nature of these ideologies varies according to the structure of that society. In capitalist societies, the treatment of health and healing as **commodities** to be bought and sold under market conditions produces certain economic benefits for various individual and corporate interests. Medical systems in noncapitalist societies, however, also utilize ideologies to legitimate and promote the interests of certain groups, such as state bureaucracies, dominant ethnic or tribal groups, or patriarchal powers.

Reification: Diseases and Bodies as Objects

Ideas that serve as ideologies often come into use subtly, frequently without explicit intention or awareness that the ideas have ideological uses. One such set of ideas are contemporary medical conceptions of the nature of disease and of the body. The product of this development is the notion that diseases are discrete, identifiable (or potentially identifiable) entities—in short, objects. The body is likewise treated as an object, separate from the person who inhabits it.

This conception illustrates the process of reification and its ideological functions. **Reification** is the "apprehension of human phenomena as if they were things," or something other than human products (Berger and Luckmann, 1967: 89). Reified reality confronts people as something outside themselves, as a nonhuman object. Institutions, social roles, norms, and other social processes are often reified; they come to assume a greater-than-human authority and inevitability. Reification thus entails a certain amount of mystification, as the human roots of phenomena are veiled (see Taussig, 1980).

Reification of disease means conveniently "forgetting" the social processes by which the concept of disease is produced. It means denying the social meanings embodied in symptoms, diagnoses, and therapy, and in the very experience of illness itself. Reification of the body results in an even greater dehumanization because of the close connection between the body and the identity of the individual. For example, an anesthetized body lying on a gurney before surgery on its testicles is medically no more than an object with a pathological entity (disease) in its tissues (things) that must therefore be surgically removed. To the person himself, however, that body and those testicles are an important part of who he is—his very self.

Reification creeps pervasively into the practice of bioscientific medicine because the guise of the scientific process masks the human factors involved in the creation of medical knowledge, as illustrated earlier in this chapter. It also occurs when any individual practitioner fails to acknowledge that a diagnosis or medical disposition is a human creation. The diagnostician constructs a disease identification from an assortment of ambiguous signs and symptoms elicited by human processes, and interpreted in the context of a human evaluation of the patient's social and psychological—as well as physical—condition.

Diagnoses are the product of social interaction, yet rarely does a physician accept authorship of a disease identification. Rather, the disease comes to be seen as a feature or property of the patient (Taussig, 1980). For example, the complex process by which a physician applies the diagnostic label "diabetes" to a patient's condition is forgotten, and the diabetes is treated as an objective thing that the patient "has." The reified disease identification often assumes primacy; if it conflicts with the patient's subjective illness experience, the objectified disease-thing is often treated as more real than the sick person's feelings. To the extent that patients internalize this image of their bodies and diseases, the reified reality shapes even their self-perception and experience.

One of the ideological functions of the reification of disease and the body is an emphasis upon individualistic rather than social or political responses to disease. In the above example of workers' health risks in a chemical factory, the location of disease as a property of individual bodies led to an emphasis on finding which individuals were more likely to be susceptible to work-place toxins. It promoted the idea that those who were identified as being at risk should be counseled to change jobs, rather than reducing the exposure of all workers or eliminating the industrial processes that required the use of toxic substances. Reification transforms occupational disease into a thing that befalls some individuals instead of the result of specific human decisions affecting workers' health.

The emphasis upon disease as an object that occurs within an individual also produces a tendency to locate responsibility for illness in the individual. It is thus one form of **blaming the victim** (Ryan, 1971), a type of legitimation that argues that the victim rather than the agent of a misfortune (e.g., rape, homelessness, or family abuse) was actually responsible for the occurrence. In the case of illness, the sick person is assumed to be responsible for having taken health risks, such as accepting a hazardous job, failing to use seat belts, or moving to an area with polluted water. As described in Chapter 4 the individual is often held accountable for unhealthy lifestyle choices, such as smoking, drinking, poor eating habits, and lack of exercise. The individual's emotional style and characteristic response to stress are also blamed (Crawford, 1977; see also Sontag, 1978).

Such attention to the individual as the locus of disease often results in inattention to the sick person's whole situation. Even extremely caring physicians can lose sight of the sociostructural roots of patients' suffering by focusing upon an utterly individualized image of disease. For example, one study of doctor-patient communication noted the extent to which the patient's larger social predicament (e.g., an extremely stressful work place) was generally ignored or reduced to individualistic treatments, such as recommendation of tranquilizers or a vacation (Waitzkin, 1984).

Instead of examining the work conditions that create stress, attention is focused on how adequately the individual responds to stress. Instead of looking at the marital, family, or work pressures of a compulsive overeater or smoker, emphasis is placed upon the individual's will power to control personal behavior. And when the individual is unable to comply with doctors' orders to get more rest and exercise, the facts that she is a single parent of four young children and works full-time in a stressful, subsistence-level job are considered barely relevant; she is viewed as responsible for her own health. This approach to disease as a condition of the sick individual thus depoliticizes illness causation (McKinlay, 1994). By contrast, adequate social policies for prevention require an awareness of the social causes of illness and the social contexts of the sick person.

THE DEVELOPMENT OF MODERN BIOMEDICINE

We sometimes view the present nature of medical practice as a cultural given. When we think of medical care, our ready mental images include doctors, hospitals, nurses, medical laboratories, operating rooms, X-rays, hypodermic needles, and pills. The institutions, occupations, and technologies that we identify with medical care are, however, the peculiar result of specific political, economic, and social interactions. The history of modern medicine shows that many alternative courses were possible, and that the particular form that medical knowledge and practice have taken in this society made certain medical advances possible but also limited the field by cutting off other potentially fruitful approaches to health and healing.

The paradigm of modern scientific medicine incorporates a number of as-sumptions about the nature of the body and disease that are discussed below. Ideas do not just "happen," however, but rather are produced, accepted, and transmitted in a political and social context. The elevation of this particular paradigm to become *the* medical mode for understanding disease and the body occurred in connection with the political process by which the medical profession gained dominance relative to other social authorities and healers.

Professional Dominance

In the nineteenth century, most medical doctors were barely considered pro-fessionals. Their credentials were relatively easy to achieve (or fake), their body of medical knowledge was skimpy, their tools for diagnosis and therapy were primitive and often dangerous, and their abilities to heal were not particularly impressive. There were several competing kinds of physicians, each with very different ideas about the causes and treatments of sickness. Furthermore, physicians were only a small per-centage of the total number of persons practicing various healing arts, who included, among others, midwives, bone setters, nurses, pharmacists, barbers (who performed minor surgery), herbalists, and folk and religious healers.

Within just a few decades, however, in the early part of the twentieth century medical doctors had achieved virtually total professional dominance. In the process described next, they had successfully eliminated, coopted, or subordinated all com-peting health professionals, and had acquired a state-legitimated monopoly over the health care market in the United States. While medicine enjoys similar professional preeminence in other nations, it lacks the degree of state-legitimated dominance over the entire health care system that characterizes the American situation (cf. Ramsey, 1991; Herzlich and Pierret, 1987; Schepers, 1985; Coburn et al., 1983; Willis, 1983; Berlant, 1975; Freidson, 1970).

A profession is a service occupation characterized by legitimate control over the market for its services and over a body of specialized knowledge or expertise. The **professionalization** of medicine as an occupation is thus a sociopolitical move-ment organized to achieve a "monopoly of opportunities in a market of services or labor and, inseparably, monopoly of status and work privileges" (Larson, 1979: 609). For medicine to achieve professional status, three main developments were necessary: (1) achieving standardization and cohesion within the profession; (2) convincing the state at various levels to grant a monopoly, for example, by requiring medical licenses to engage in healing practices; and (3) gaining public respect and persuading the public to accept the profession's definitions of what problems properly should be brought to it for service.

One definitive characteristic of a developed profession is its autonomy, which is an organizational product of its ability to dominate its area of expertise in the division of labor. In the case of the medical profession, autonomy is evidenced by doctors' legal protection from encroachment by other occupations. A second factor in medical autonomy is the profession's control over the production and application of medical knowledge and skill, especially the training and licensing of physicians. A third indication of medicine's status as a developed profession is its presumed self-regulation with a code of ethics (Freidson, 1970).

In 1847, the American Medical Association (AMA) was established as a professional organization for physicians from the medical belief system dubbed *allopathy*, which was characterized by "heroic" and invasive treatments such as bloodletting, purging, blistering, vomiting, and medicating with powerful drugs (e.g., opium) and poisons (e.g., mercury and arsenic). Allopathic physicians called themselves "regular" or orthodox physicians, but the public was, understandably, attracted to some of the less dangerous forms of medicine practiced by competing approaches such as homeopathy, naturopathy, and hydropathy.

The initial program of the AMA was relatively straightforward: to create internal professional cohesion and standardization by controlling the requirements for medical degrees and by enacting a code of ethics that would exclude "irregular" practitioners from the ranks. These efforts were aimed primarily at reducing the influence of the chief competitors, homeopathic physicians, who had organized the American Institute for Homeopathy in 1844. Between 1850 and 1880, the two camps became increasingly polarized, as the AMA censured members who continued to have dealings with the "enemy." For example, in 1878 the local medical society expelled a Connecticut doctor for having consulted with a homeopathic physician—his wife. "Regular" physicians lost considerable ground in the latter half of the nineteenth century, while homeopathy gained as much public respect and legal considerations as allopathy. "Regular" practitioners accounted for nearly 90 percent of all doctors, but the proportion of "irregular" physicians increased in the mid-1900s. For the latter half of the century, "irregulars" commanded approximately one-fifth of the market (Starr, 1982: 88–99).

The AMA and the "irregular" physicians cooperated, however, in their political efforts to have states enact licensing laws, because they shared a common interest in eliminating competition from persons who had not attended any form of medical school, such as midwives, ministers, pharmacists, and folk healers. The AMA has, from its outset, been especially interested in exposing and prosecuting what it calls "quackery," which is practically defined as all forms of medicating or healing outside the profession's control. A related campaign successfully eliminated much competition from patent medicine manufacturers and eventually subordinated the practice of pharmacy to medical control. Licensing legislation began to specify the quality of the medical education required, and some states set up boards of medical examiners, initially making allowances for various "irregular" forms of professional training alongside the "regular." The courts and legislatures had begun to grant professional prerogatives to thus-approved doctors. Gradually, "regular" medicine coopted and absorbed most "irregular" physicians, but rejected and actively opposed later organized alternatives such as chiropractic and Christian Science (Starr, 1982: 99–112; see also Wolpe, 1990; Baer, 1984).

Scientization of Medicine and Medical Training

The most dramatic change in the medical profession's dominance occurred after the turn of the century. The adoption of "scientific" medicine and the insistence upon standards of rigorous medical education were central strategies in the professionalization process. Science and education did not, however, characterize the actual practice of "regular" medicine at that time. In fact, scientific training was available to only a small elite of physicians, mainly researchers and educators, who had the money to study in Europe (Berliner, 1976).

Control of medical education was critical to a monopoly in the market. In the early 1900s, practicing physicians made relatively poor incomes; one comparison suggests that they earned less than an ordinary mechanic of the day (Berliner, 1976: 584). There appeared to be a growing oversupply of physicians relative to the market of paying clients. Licensing laws had not resulted in fewer physicians but merely more medical schools. While the national population grew between 1870 and 1910 by 138 percent, the number of physicians increased by 153 percent. Many professional leaders objected not only to the numbers of new physicians these medical schools were graduating but also to the fact that they had recruited "undesirable" students: women, blacks, immigrants, and working-class persons. Advocates of reforming medical education believed that medicine could not become a respected profession if its ranks included such lowly elements. Shortly after the turn of the century, the AMA underwent a major internal organization and subsequently made such "reform" its primary focus (Starr, 1982: 112–117).

After a preliminary review of medical colleges, the AMA invited an outside group, the Carnegie Foundation, to conduct a thorough investigation of the approximately 160 medical colleges in the United States and Canada. The resulting report in 1910 was devastating to many medical education programs (Flexner, 1910). The report's foremost objection was to the lack of medical science in the curriculum and training experiences. It recommended that the great majority of medical schools should be closed; that the first-rate schools should be strengthened on the model of Johns Hopkins, which had a singularly science-oriented program; and that a few medium-quality schools should be greatly improved to meet the upper standard. With the support of state legislatures and many universities themselves, the governing body of AMA subsequently became the de facto national accrediting agency for medical schools. The report's recommendations were dramatically supported by funding from numerous philanthropic foundations. By 1934 the nine largest foundations in the U.S. had given over $154 million to implement reforms (Berliner, 1975).[2]

These "reforms" of medical education had exactly the kind of effects the AMA wanted: increased internal cohesion of the profession and increased control of the market. Not only had the supply of licensed physicians been dramatically cut, but the homogeneity of the profession had also been assured by greatly limiting access to medical education for women, blacks, Jews, and all who could not afford the newly required four years of college and four full-time years of medical school. The declining numbers of new physicians adversely affected the poor and rural areas. Flexner had expected that the new highly trained graduates would disperse throughout the country, but in practice they gravitated to the wealthiest regions. The increased cost of their medical education reduced the likelihood that they would accept the modest incomes of practices in small towns and rural areas (Starr, 1982: 123–127). There were likewise fewer doctors for blacks. Due to widespread discrimination and segregation, blacks received treatment mainly from black physicians, but the "reforms" dramatically reduced their numbers (Starr, 1982: 124). Only two of the seven medical schools for blacks survived the "reforms." Since the medical colleges run by "irregular" physicians had been somewhat more open to interracial admissions, their disproportionate demise also reduced opportunities for blacks to become doctors.

In the latter part of the nineteenth century, considerable numbers of women had entered medical practice. In the decade from 1880 to 1890, women doubled their proportional representation of all doctors in the United States (from 2.8 to 5.6 percent); 17 medical colleges for women were founded in that period. After considerable struggle, women began to be admitted to elite medical schools after 1890, and by 1893–94 women constituted 10 percent or more of the student body at 19 of the coeducational schools (Starr, 1982: 117).

Women's acceptance into coeducational settings was far from smooth, however; they experienced considerable harassment from male professors and students (Morantz-Sanchez, 1985). Many physicians believed that women's menstrual cycles made them incapable of professional work. For example, one doctor declared that the " 'periodical infirmity of their sex . . . in every case . . . unfits them for any responsible effort of mind . . . [and that during their menstrual] condition, neither life nor limb submitted to them would be as safe as at other times' " (quoted in Wertz and Wertz, 1979: 57). After the turn of the century, women were increasingly excluded from the profession of medicine. All but three of the 17 women's medical colleges closed, and coeducational medical colleges maintained quotas that, until the 1960s, limited women to about 5 percent of admissions (Starr, 1982: 124).

---

[2]The conspicuous role of the capitalist philanthropies, notably the Rockefeller Foundation (which gave some $66 million to just nine medical schools in the aftermath of Flexner's report), has led some to suggest a direct affinity between capitalist classes and the type of medicine they chose to support (see Brown, 1979; and the critique in Starr, 1982: 228). Even if there were no deliberate collusion, it is true that the outcome was a version of medicine that necessitated extensive expenditures on pharmaceuticals, medical technology, and capital-intensive hospitals, as described further in Chapter 12.

Because they were excluded from mainstream medicine, some women turned to the less prestigious area of public health, such as campaigns for better hygiene, nutrition, and mother-and-child health care. The medical profession often opposed these efforts, which it perceived as threats to its dominance and as competition for health expenditures. For example, female public health advocates campaigned for the Sheppard-Towner Act of 1921, which provided health care for mothers and infants until 1929, when the AMA pressured Congress not to renew funding (Morantz-Sanchez, 1985).

Professional Autonomy and Control

By the 1930s, the medical profession had achieved significant autonomy. It controlled the recruitment and training of new physicians, including the length and content of medical education, as well as the examination and licensing by which new doctors could be admitted to practice. The profession defined (and regularly expanded) the scope of its work, specified its own standards of practice, and maintained the right to enforce them (Freidson, 1970).

The prerogative to define the scope of medical work is connected with the process of *medicalization* by which increasing numbers of areas of life were brought under medicine's purview and control. Childbirth, alcoholism, obesity, infant feeding formulas, and menopause are just a few of the areas that previously were not defined as properly "medical" matters but, through the medical profession's influence, were redefined as issues needing doctors' attention, regardless of whether the medical approach was more effective than nonmedical. Other efforts to expand their markets included the campaign to persuade well persons get an annual checkup.

In defining the scope of its work, the medical profession also eliminated much of its competition. Some professional competitors, such as homeopaths and osteopaths, were coopted; others, such as pharmacists, nurses, anesthetists, and X-ray technicians, were subordinated; whereas still others, such as midwives, clergy, and barber-surgeons, were outrightly driven from legitimate practice (Gritzer, 1981). The AMA also worked to limit public health authorities severely; medical professional interests campaigned (usually successfully) against public dispensaries, the compulsory reporting of tuberculosis, municipal laboratories and vaccination programs, the provision of health services in the public schools, and national public health programs, which were all viewed as competitors in the provision of services and as threats to the profession's autonomous authority over its domain. By controlling licensing, the access to facilities (e.g., hospitals and labs), access to other physicians as backups, and the legitimacy of third-party reimbursement, the medical profession greatly reduced its competition (Dolan, 1980).

The medical profession rapidly consolidated its control over the conditions of its work as the organization of hospitals specifically reflects. In recent years, however, the profession may have lost some of its control in many institutional settings, such as the new for-profit hospital corporations described in Chapter 11. Because of its market monopoly, the medical profession also asserted its control over the terms of its remuneration. American medicine is organized on a fee-for-service basis in which, rather than receiving a set salary, most doctors charge each patient a fee for each service performed. The profession's model of the ideal economic relationship was one of direct payment by the patient-receiver to the health care provider. The rise in importance of third-party payment from the government, insurance companies, labor unions, or fraternal organizations, who paid part or all of some patients' medical fees, represented an intrusion and danger to medical dominance. As Starr (1982: 235) observed, "to be the intermediary in the costs of sickness is a strategic role that confers social and political as well as strictly economic gains." Over the years the medical profession has vehemently asserted its interests in campaigns against national health insurance, Social Security health benefits, Blue Cross and Blue Shield, prepaid health plans, Medicare, and Medicaid. As shown in Chapter 11, the role of third parties has nevertheless increased, resulting in some regulation and limitation of medical practice and payments.

Modernization and Medical Practice

The features of modern medicine are in many ways the products of the broader process of modernization, which has similarly shaped other institutional spheres, such as industry, education, and communications. The specific historical development of the medical profession also contributed to certain structural features of modern medicine.

Several aspects of modernization apply to the development of medicine. One is the trend toward **institutional differentiation**, in which various institutional spheres in society become separated from each other, as each comes to perform specialized functions. Differentiation resulted in the separation of healing functions from the institutions of religion and the family. A second aspect of modernization is **rationalization**, the application of criteria of functional rationality to many aspects of social and economic life. When applied to the division of labor, rationalization promoted bureaucratic forms of organization and an emphasis upon efficiency, standardization, and instrumental criteria for decision making. The structure of the modern hospital reflects this rational principle of organization.

Rational ways of knowing emphasized the use of empirical evidence to explain natural phenomena without reference to nonnatural categories of thought. Weber (1958: 139) observed that this led to the "disenchantment" of the world, meaning that phenomena once held in awe or reverence were stripped of their special qualities and became ordinary. The human body itself has been thus "disenchanted." For example, the modern view of the body contrasts strongly with the medieval notion that the body should not be dissected lest it be unfit for reuniting with the soul in resurrection. Bodies that are considered spiritual temples must be respected; bodies that are disenchanted entities require no special reverence. The key feature of the rationalization process is not so much the particular explanations of phenomena but the belief that all phenomena can be rationally explained. A by-product of this belief is an increased emphasis upon technology and technique by which rational knowledge can presumably be translated into control. Modern societies particularly value rational mastery. For example, we believe that if we can explain what causes a disease, then it is only a matter of time before we can develop a technology or technique for healing or even preventing the disease.

While the process of rationalization occurred in all modernizing medical systems, an additional feature in capitalist societies was **commodification**, or the process by which such qualities as health, beauty, and fitness are transformed into objects that can be bought and sold in the marketplace. Not only material objects such as pharmaceuticals and prosthetic devices but also the entire range of health services become commodities to be bought and sold. Commodification encourages both the sick and the well to become avid consumers of the nebulous product known as health (Featherstone, 1991).

Although these aspects of contemporary Western medical systems are linked with the larger process of modernization, many of the specific characteristics of modern medicine are the products of the historical-political struggle for professional dominance and the assumptions implicit in the biomedical belief system described next. Indeed, it is entirely likely that if different factions and competitors had won those early battles for legitimacy and a share of the medical market, we would today have an entirely different model of medical knowledge, of what constitutes health and health care, and of what it means to be a doctor.

Assumptions of the Biomedical Model

The present system of medical knowledge is based upon a number of assumptions about the body, disease, and ways of knowing. While many of these assumptions have a long history, they do not necessarily produce better medical care. They also deflect attention from nonmedical measures for promoting health, such as nutrition and public health, and as the last part of this chapter illustrates, contribute to serious problems in doctor-patient communication.

Mind-Body Dualism.   The medical model assumes a clear dichotomy between the mind and the body; physical diseases are presumed to be located within the body (Engel, 1977; see also Benoist and Cathebras, 1993; Gordon, 1988; Kirmayer, 1988; Leder, 1984). The medical model also holds that the body can be understood and treated in isolation from other aspects of the person inhabiting it (Hahn and Kleinman, 1983).

The philosophical foundations for this split may go back to Descartes's division of the person into mind and body, or *res cogitans* and *res extensa*. The practical foundations, however, probably lie in medicine's shift to an emphasis upon clinical observation toward the end of the eighteenth century and pathological anatomy beginning in the nineteenth century. Foucault (1973) demonstrated that medicine shifted its ways of viewing the body and developed a "clinical gaze." Previously, physicians "saw" the body indirectly, mainly through patients' descriptions of their experience of a malady. By contrast, the "clinical gaze" emphasized direct clinical observation and physical examinations; technological developments, such as the invention of the stethoscope in 1819, gave physicians access to direct (and presumably more objective) clinical knowledge than previously could be gained only indirectly. Foucault noted that the way the body is viewed has profound political implications. The ascending medical perspective saw the body as docile—something physicians could observe, manipulate, transform, and improve (see also Armstrong, 1983). Increasingly sophisticated pathological anatomy meant that diseases were conceptualized in terms of alterations in tissues that were visible upon opening the body, such as during autopsy. This mode of conceptualizing disease had a profound effect in splitting body from mind in the practice of clinical medicine (Sullivan, 1986: 344–345).

Physical Reductionism.   The medical model not only dichotomizes body and mind, but also assumes that illness can be reduced to disordered bodily (biochemical or neurophysiological) functions. This physical reductionism, however, excludes social, psychological, and behavioral dimensions of illness (Engel, 1977). The result of this reductionism, together with medicine's mind-body dualism, is that disease is localized in the *individual* body. Such conceptions prevent the medical model from conceiving of the *social* body, or how aspects of the individual's social or emotional life might impinge upon physical health. As described in Chapter 3, another result is medicine's general inattention to social conditions that contribute to illness or could aid in healing (Bologh, 1981).

Specific Etiology.   A related assumption of the biomedical model is what Dubos (1959: 130–135) called the "doctrine of specific etiology," or the belief that each disease is caused by a specific, potentially identifiable agent. It developed from the nineteenth-century work of Pasteur and Koch, who demonstrated that the introduction of specific virulent microorganisms (germs) into the body produced specific diseases. One primary focus of scientific medicine became the identification of these specific agents and their causal link to specific diseases. The doctrine of specific etiology was later extended beyond infectious diseases and applied to other diseases, such as deficiency diseases in which the specific etiology was not an intrusive microorganism but the lack of a necessary element, such as vitamin or hormone.

Dubos noted that while the doctrine of specific etiology has led to important theoretical and practical achievements, it has rarely provided a complete account of the causation of disease. He asked why, although infectious agents are nearly ubiquitous, only some people get sick some of the time. Accordingly, an adequate understanding of an illness etiology must include broader factors, such as nutrition, stress, and metabolic states, that affect the individual's susceptibility to infection. As noted in Chapter 2, the search for specific illness-producing agents worked relatively well in dealing with infectious diseases but is too simplistic to explain the causes of complex, chronic illnesses. Also, as Dubos (1959) observed, this approach often results in a quest for a medicinal "magic bullet" to "shoot and kill" the disease, producing an overreliance on pharmaceuticals in the "armamentarium" (stock of weapons) of the modern physician.

The Machine Metaphor.   One of the oldest Western images for understanding the body is a comparison with the functioning of a machine. Accordingly, disease is the malfunctioning of some constituent mechanism (e.g., a "breakdown" of the heart). Other cultures use other metaphors; for example, ancient Egyptian societies used the image of a river, and Chinese tradition refers to the balance of elemental forces (Yin and Yang) of the earth (Osherson and AmaraSingham, 1981). Modern medicine has not only retained the metaphor of the machine but also extended it by developing specializations along the lines of machine parts, emphasizing individual systems or organs to the exclusion of an image of the totality of the body. The machine metaphor further encouraged an instrumentalist approach to the body; the physician could "repair" one part in isolation from the rest (Berliner, 1975).

Regimen and Control.   Partly as a product of the machine metaphor and the quest for mastery, the Western medical model also conceptualizes the body as the proper object of regimen and control, again emphasizing the responsibility of the individual to exercise this control in order to maintain or restore health. Modernizing trends toward rationalization have further encouraged the notion of the standardization of body disciplines, such as diets, exercise programs, etiquette, routines of hygiene, and even sexual activity (Turner, 1984: 157–203).

This brief history shows that the knowledge and practice we know as medicine have their roots in sociopolitical processes. The ideas and assumptions of biomedicine forcefully influence economic and power relationships both within the relationship between practitioner and patient and in institutions (e.g., law) of the larger society. We must remember that these medical realities are socially produced.

SUMMARY

What we know about health, illness, and the body is socially constructed. Both lay and professional medical knowledge are influenced by social, economic, and political factors. The categories and even the very language for describing and understanding diseases are likewise subject to powerful social influences. Diseases and disease syndromes are "discovered" and professionally accepted through concrete social processes; other disease categories are similarly denied, dropped, or disavowed by social processes. Such social influences shape not only ideas but indeed also the experiences of our own and others' bodies and bodily conditions.

The nature of modern medicine is partly determined by the larger process of modernization, especially the extension of rationalization to the body and ways of knowing about and treating the body. In capitalist societies, the additional societal process of the commodification of health and health care has altered the economic meaning of medical services, as health has become an ambiguous product to be bought and consumed.

Medical knowledge sometimes serves ideological purposes, legitimating the interests of certain persons or groups. Ideological aspects of thought and practice are typically very subtle, and often go unnoticed by people who believe and use them. The medicalization of various areas of life and the uses of medicine in service of various institutional goals illustrate some of the ways ideology influences medical ideas and practice. The tendency of bioscientific medicine to treat diseases and bodies as objects masks the social history of ideas of disease and the social processes of finding disease. Reification also leads to a view of disease as a property of the sick person, thus reducing the significance of the social and environmental causes of the disease and the social context of the person's illness.

Many characteristics of the contemporary medical establishment can be traced to political developments in the recent history of the profession. Certain features of modern medicine are the results of the assumptions of the biomedical approach itself, which is characterized by its dichotomization of mind and body, physical reductionism, the doctrine of specific etiology, the machine metaphor for the body, and an emphasis upon bodily regimen and control. These assumptions have concrete implications for the delivery of health care.

RECOMMENDED READINGS

Articles

H. TRISTAM ENGLEHARDT, "The disease of masturbation: Values and the concept of disease," pp. 15–24 in J. W. Leavitt and R. L. Numbers, eds., *Sickness and Health in America*. Madison: University of Wisconsin Press, 1978.

FRANCES MCCREA, "The politics of menopause: The discovery of a deficiency disease," *Social Problems* 13(1), 1983: 111–123.

CATHERINE KOHLER RIESSMAN, "Women and medicalization: A new perspective," pp. 190–220 in P. Brown, ed., *Perspectives in Medical Sociology*. Prospect Heights, Ill.: Waveland Press, 1989.

BRYAN S. TURNER, "The government of the body: Medical regimens and the rationalization of diet," *British Journal of Sociology* 33(2), 1982: 254–269.

VIVIENNE WALTERS, "Company doctors' perceptions of and responses to conflicting pressures from labor and management," *Social Problems* 30(1), 1982: 1–12.

Books

SAMUEL BUTLER, *Erewhon*. New York: New American Library, [1901] 1960. A fictional utopia based on dramatically different definitions of health and illness.

BARBARA EHRENREICH and DEIRDRE ENGLISH, *For Her Own Good: 150 Years of the Experts' Advice to Women*. Garden City, NY: Doubleday, 1978. Locating women's health in the larger context of patriarchal relations, the authors show how women were persuaded by "experts" to accept numerous constraining (and often dangerous) practices in many areas of their lives on the grounds that they were "for their own good."

ELIOT FREIDSON, *Profession of Medicine: A Study of the Sociology of Applied Knowledge*. New York: Dodd, Mead, 1970. This classic study of the structure of medical knowledge and professional autonomy serves as a useful basis for understanding current debates about the status and proper roles of medicine and various other health-related occupations.

PAUL STARR, *The Social Transformation of American Medicine*. New York: Basic, 1982. A sweeping history of the medical profession's rise to professional dominance, Starr's interpretation is nonetheless overly idealistic, attributing the success of medical dominance more to American attitudes and values than to the triumph of the economic interests and political maneuvering that he amply documents.

DAVID SUDNOW, *Passing On: The Social Organization of Dying*. Englewood Cliffs, NJ: Prentice-Hall, 1967. This sensitive ethnography shows how social organization and interaction in hospital settings produce varying definitions of sickness and even death.

CHAPTER TEN

Modern Biomedicine: Knowledge and Practice

Social constructions enter the practice of Western medicine through not only the ideas and professional organization of biomedicine, but also the routine social interactions between medical personnel and their patients. Detailed examination of doctor-patient interactions show how professional dominance is maintained at the interpersonal level. Many of the problems of this relationship are due to social-structural factors in medical training and practice. Other very important factors are embedded assumptions of the medical model of disease and treatment. Some of these medical assumptions also make it difficult for physicians and the society as a whole to respond effectively to the emerging dilemmas in modern health care: the proper ends of medical treatment and the limits of medicine.

When people turn to medical professionals for help, they typically enter the patient role. Unlike the sick role, which is defined by broader social expectations (see Chapter 6), the patient role involves primarily the reciprocal expectations and norms held by the doctor and patient.[1] These expectations are emotionally charged; doctors and patients alike are often deeply dissatisfied with the actual situation.

Although each patient negotiates a different relationship with each particular doctor, a number of general social-structural factors shape the doctor-patient relationship. Two factors in particular are at the root of many of the problems in Western medical practice: (1) professional dominance, and (2) rationalization of the body in the medical model. Professional dominance creates and exacerbates social chasms between doctor and patient, while the medical model's rationalization of the body creates enormous discontinuities between medicine's paradigm of disease and curing on the one hand, and patients' experience and understanding of their illness and their needs on the other.

Although individual doctors could do much to overcome these problems in their own work with patients, these two characteristics are thoroughly embedded in the structure of the profession, medical education, hospital and other medical institutional structures, and the organization of medical practice. Without structural change, they will continue to limit the potential for individual change in the doctor-patient relationship. While the issue of patient (or consumer) dissatisfaction is a genuine concern, a more serious problem is that inadequacies in the doctor-patient relationship may gravely impede the very process of healing. The following discussion suggests some of the ways these social-structural factors may diminish the healing effectiveness of medical practitioners.

PROFESSIONAL DOMINANCE

The professionalization of medicine produced social distance between the practitioner and the sick person. The doctor is assumed to be the relatively knowledgeable "expert"; the patient, the relatively ignorant recipient of the doctor's professional ser-

---

[1]The role of patient is qualitatively different relative to other professional and nonprofessional workers (such as nurses, technicians, or hospital orderlies), and varies dramatically according to institutional context (such as doctor's office, hospital, patient's home, clinic).

vices. Indeed, typically the patient is limited in ability to judge whether the doctor is using adequate medical knowledge, making competent treatment recommendations, and providing good service.

The greater the **social distance** between two people, the less sensitivity either is likely to have toward the other's problems. Doctors who themselves have had extensive experience in the patient role may be more empathetic toward their own patients (cf. Hahn, 1985a). In addition to the social distance inherent in the expert-layperson dichotomy, physicians are often separated from their patients by other factors: gender, ethnicity, and socioeconomic background. Status differences according to gender often supersede status differences between doctor and patient. Thus, for example, male doctors were rarely interrupted by their patients, whereas female doctors were interrupted somewhat more frequently (West, 1984: 150). Social distance also figures into the hierarchy of hospital and other institutional settings, where a greater social distance among the various levels of staff as well as between staff and patients results in insensitivity to each others' problems (Freidson, 1970: 109–136; see also Gubrium, 1975).

The sick person who wants medical help is in an intrinsically weak position. Power differences between doctor and patient have been further widened by medical control in both the larger arena of politics and law, and the narrower situation of the structure of medical practice. Maintaining a position of professional power serves to legitimate physicians' economic rewards and professional autonomy. For example, when patients are in awe of doctors' knowledge and skill, they are more likely to defer to physicians' judgment and to consider high fees to be reasonable.

Professional power also protects physicians from potentially damaging problems such as therapeutic failure. If a diagnosis is incorrect or a treatment does not work, the distance in knowledge between doctor and patient reduces the likelihood that the patient would be able to evaluate whether the failure was due to the doctor's lack of knowledge or skill. One study found that in a hospital setting doctors and other staff limited information given to patients and their families as a protective device in the management of medical mistakes (Millman, 1976). Sometimes keeping patients ignorant of their condition enables the doctor to manage them more effectively by preventing emotional responses that the physician might find disruptive or unpleasant. While individual doctors do not necessarily consciously engage in these protective legitimations, the very structure of the profession promotes them.

Information Control

One of the foremost ways doctors protect their professional power is by controlling the flow of information to the patient. On the one hand, the doctor cannot possibly, even in a long-term relationship, communicate to the patient everything the expert knows relevant to the limited actual circumstances of the patient's condition. On the other hand, patients need information about their condition: What is wrong with me? How serious is it? What is the expected outcome? What are my treatment options?

The more information patients have, the better able they are to understand their situation, evaluate options (including whether they are getting adequate medical care), and participate in treatment decisions. Such evaluation and decision making is, however, often threatening to the physician's control of the case. As a result, some physicians consider the "good" patient to be one who trustingly accepts the doctor's judgment and obediently complies with doctor's orders, full of unquestioning appreciation of the doctor's ministrations.

Although the doctor-patient relationship is based upon reciprocal role expectations, many doctors cast patients in stereotypical roles that serve to justify information control and doctors' dominant position relative to patients. One such expectation is the notion that patients are generally medically ignorant and childlike, and unable to comprehend explanations of the causes, alternative treatments, and expected outcome of their conditions (Segall and Roberts, 1980; see also Millman, 1976). Several studies have found that the majority of physicians consistently and markedly underestimated their patients' level of comprehension (McKinlay, 1975).

Information control involves both information gathering and information giving. The doctor controls the medical interaction, deciding how much and which information to seek, and how much and which information to impart to the patient. The rationale and method for this model of a medical encounter are discussed further later. The medical interview and clinical examination consist of many such information-gathering and -giving decisions. Doctors control the information-gathering aspect by framing questions, cutting off patients' statements, ignoring certain patient input as irrelevant, and actively eliciting other input. The doctor decides whether and how extensively to conduct a physical examination, which tests to have done, and what follow-up study is needed; these aspects of a consultation are highly variable, a matter of the doctor's discretion (Fisher, 1983).

The medical interview is a constrained, prestructured form of talk. West (1983) found that patient-initiated questions are "dispreferred." Her detailed analysis of 21 medical exchanges showed that only 9 percent of the 773 questions were initiated by patients. The doctors' control of the interviews was further evident in that they did not respond to 13 percent of the relatively few questions put to them by their patients; patient assertiveness thus resulted in *less* response from doctors, whose pervasive dislike of patient-initiated questions was linked with the physicians' reluctance to answer "too many" such questions (West, 1984: 156). Patients sensed that their questioning was not the preferred pattern for the interaction; when they did pose questions, nearly half (46 percent) exhibited some anxiety, such as stutters or nervous giggles. By contrast, the patients answered all but 2 percent of the doctors' questions, which tended to be phrased in a way that limited patients' options for answering (e.g., "Do you feel X, or do you feel Y?").

How patients express themselves and certain of their personal characteristics are also important factors influencing the amount and quality of information physicians give them. One study of interaction in a hospital family practice clinic found that doctors gave more information to their patients who appeared to be better educated, younger, or more anxious about their health problems. Patients with communicative styles that were more active and affectively expressive tended to receive more information; patients who were more passive, asked few questions, and exhibited few worries or emotions about their conditions received less information about their conditions and treatments. Since well-educated patients were also disproportionately represented among those with active communicative styles, these findings suggest that some patients are doubly disadvantaged in doctor-patient communication (Street, 1991; see also Street, 1992).

Information-giving and question-asking exchanges between doctor and patient vary significantly according to social class. A British study of general practitioners' consultations found that patients' social class differences accounted for a significant proportion of the variance in both the information doctors gave in answer to questions and in the explanations volunteered by the doctors. Doctors may misinterpret working-class patients' reticence to ask questions as due to their lack of interest, but this study suggested that such patients' diffidence may be due more to the social distance between them and the doctor, and perhaps also to learned patterns of deference to higher social classes (Pendleton and Bochner, 1980).

Another study of 51 general practitioners in southern Wales found a wide range of doctor-patient communication strategies (Comaroff, 1976). Some physicians viewed the interaction as a one-way provision of professional skill in which the patient was passive recipient with nothing of value to contribute. Other doctors had more complex patterns of interaction with patients and were less likely to have a single, simple stereotype of their patients and their input. These data suggest that the differences are not due just to variations in individual doctors' personal need for power, but also to their differing images of their professional role. While related to power, these images are more a matter of ideals and ideologies.

Uncertainty and Control

Information control includes basic communication about diagnosis and treatment. Sometimes, even long after a doctor has a working diagnosis, the patient is not told what the problem may be. Before the enactment of a series of laws in the United States in the 1970s, it was possible for doctors to perform surgery, put patients on medication, and order other treatments without the patients' informed consent.

The issue of informed consent is particularly problematic in medical experimentation and clinical trials of treatments not yet proven safe or effective. One notorious instance of medical science misconduct was the Tuskegee syphilis study, begun in 1932 and continued until 1972, when a Public Health Service worker "blew the whistle" to the press. The U.S. Public Health Service had recruited in Alabama some 400 black men who had syphilis at the time they were enrolled in the project; it also monitored 200 uninfected control subjects. The research was supposed to document the course of untreated syphilis, including autopsy after the subject died. Research subjects were recruited with misleading promises of "special free treatment" (actually spinal taps done without anesthesia—lab tests, not treatments), and they were denied antibiotic therapy in the 1940s when it became the effective treatment for syphilis (Edgar, 1992; King, 1992; Jones, 1981). Outrage over the Tuskegee study led directly to the 1974 National Research Act, which established procedures to guard the rights of human subjects of research.

The central principle of protection for research subjects also applies to medical treatments: informed consent. This principle means that researchers and physicians should give enough information about the procedures, their risks, and benefits so that the subject or patient can decide whether to consent to the treatment. Just what kind and how much information is necessary or desirable is, however, still debated.

Especially in the treatment of potentially fatal or particularly fearsome diseases, such as cancer, many doctors prefer to tell their patients as little as possible. As recently as the 1960s, most physicians routinely withheld from patients diagnosis of feared diseases and prognosis of impending death. One study found that 95 percent of physicians did not disclose a diagnosis of cancer to patients (Oken, 1961; see also Glaser and Strauss, 1968). The same questionnaire, distributed nearly two decades later, found a complete reversal: 90 percent of the physicians claimed they disclosed all information (Novack et al., 1979). But although physicians believe they are giving their patients all relevant information, many patients are dissatisfied with both the amount and the quality of information they receive (McIntosh, 1974). One explanation for this dissatisfaction is that while doctors now usually disclose even unpleasant diagnoses (e.g., cancer, AIDS), their information giving is still selective. For example, a physician may give considerable information about treatment options, while downplaying or withholding information about prognosis (i.e., prospects for recovery or probable course of the disease). Thus, the physician retains considerable control, especially over the patient's willingness to accept the recommended treatment (Miyaji, 1993).

Even for nonfatal illnesses, many doctors do not communicate their full diagnosis or prognosis. Doctors may want to "protect" patients from unpleasant information. This paternalistic approach may simultaneously protect the doctor from dealing with the unpleasant reactions such knowledge might evoke. Giving bad news is very uncomfortable for physicians, as one surgeon explained:

> I really hate this part of the work. I feel terrible . . . always . . . it never seems to get easier. . . . I know it's not my fault . . . I didn't give the patient the disease . . . but I always somehow feel that it is . . . and besides . . . I never really know what to say. They sure never had a course on this part of medicine when I went to school, but let me tell you, I could sure use it now . . . and I usually don't ever get to know these patients who think their lives are in my hands. How am I supposed to deal with it? I hate doing it . . . but I can't avoid it! (quoted in Taylor, 1988).

In response to this stress, physicians adopt complex strategies to routinize the painful task, including telling the truth, professing uncertainty, evading the issue, and dissimulation. One study found that the majority viewed their role as selecting and interpreting information for patients (Taylor, 1988). In deciding where and how much to tell, they consider such factors as the certainty of the diagnosis, whether medical science understands the disease's natural course, whether there are potentially effective therapeutic options, and whether the patient is competent to understand information and make decisions on the basis of that information (Drickamer and Lachs, 1992).

Uncertainty is an inherent difficulty for both doctor and patient. While precision, certainty, and control are goals of bioscientific medicine, clinical practice rarely comes close to meeting such goals. Real patients' problems are often complex, and even highly trained physicians cannot know everything about every possible problem. Diagnoses have, at best, only a certain probability of accuracy; straightforward diagnoses of well-known diseases have only a higher probability of accuracy than those of complex, poorly understood diseases. Pressures for certainty in diagnosis may lead to excessive medical testing (Kassirer, 1989). Control in treatment is likewise often elusive; much therapy is a matter of trial and error. Rather than resolve ambiguity, technological medicine often produces greater expectations at the same time as more arenas for uncertainty. For example, technological capabilities for keeping alive premature infants who would otherwise have died shortly after birth but now may survive with serious debilities increase the range of medical uncertainty for doctors who must decide whether to use these technologies for a particular infant (Beresford, 1991).

Medical training provides some preparation for dealing with clinical uncertainty (Fox, 1957), but routine medical practice often involves judgments whose accuracy and effects are uncertain and, in some cases, unknowable. While practicing physicians do acknowledge a number of areas of uncertainty (Gerrity et al., 1992), they are uncomfortable with uncertainty as an indicator of personal inadequacy, failure, error, or lack of knowledge. One physician, describing his experience with medical mistakes, commented:

> Many situations do not lend themselves to a simple determination of whether a mistake has been made. Seriously ill, hospitalized patients, for instance, require of doctors almost continuous decision-making. Although in most cases no single mistake is obvious, there always seem to be things that could have been done differently or better: administering more of this medication, starting that treatment a little sooner. . . . The fact is that when a patient dies, the physician is left wondering whether the care he provided was inadequate. . . . Medicine is not an exact science; errors are always possible, even in the midst of the humdrum routine of daily care. Was that baby I just sent home with a diagnosis of mild viral fever actually in the early stages of serious meningitis? Will that nine-year-old with stomach cramps whose mother I just lectured about psychosomatic illness end up in the hospital tomorrow with a ruptured appendix? . . . A doctor has to confront the possibility of a mistake with every patient visit (Hilfiker, 1984).

The patient's situation in the face of uncertainty is even more anxiety-producing because the patient lacks medical expertise. Doctors often prolong patients' uncertainty, even after their own uncertainty about the disease or therapy has been reduced or resolved. Waitzkin and Stoeckle (1972) suggested that physicians may use their control over patient uncertainty to preserve their power and keep their options open. For example, the head of one pediatric ward had a policy of aggressively treating children with leukemia up to the moment of death; no child was ever labeled terminal, no matter how unsuccessful the treatment. The mother of a child who was obviously succumbing asked this doctor, "Is my child critical?," to which the doctor replied, "No." Another member of the staff asked him privately, "Why did you tell her the child is not critical, when we know he has only a few weeks to live?" The doctor's answer: "He is not technically critical until he is on some life-support system." To control information about the child's status further, he ordered that the records not be shown or otherwise divulged to the distraught mother. His opinion was that if the mother knew how near to death her child was, she might refuse the course of chemotherapy he had ordered for the boy.

Doctor-patient negotiations over information vary according to the type of illness. In the course of the long-term treatment of chronic illness, the balance of power is often altered, requiring a renegotiation of the doctor-patient relationship. Patients are likely to become increasingly expert about their specific condition and thus more assertive in challenging their doctors (cf. Herzlich and Pierret, 1987: 212; Calnan, 1984).

Doctor-patient communication is especially problematic in the face of the uncertainty related to diseases such as multiple sclerosis (MS), a gradually debilitating, incurable disease of the nervous system. Because many MS victims are in young adulthood, when serious chronic illness is least expected, doctors at first may not consider the diagnosis. MS creates uncertainty for both the doctor and patient partly because its early symptoms are unclear or elusive. Another reason is that the diagnosis is fearsome to both the sufferer and the doctor because MS is incurable and potentially severely debilitating. Physicians thus frequently fail to diagnose MS correctly or postpone telling their patients of the diagnosis until it is inevitable.

One study suggested that this protective strategy for the doctor can create significant problems for the patient, perhaps leading to iatrogenic emotional difficulties (Stewart and Sullivan, 1982). Lacking physician confirmation that their symptoms were indeed related to a "real" illness, many MS patients were viewed by family, friends, and doctors as hypochondriacs or as "imagining things." As a result many sufferers experienced symptoms of stress that were actually more troublesome than the MS-related symptoms themselves. They lost faith in their doctors, shopped around for others, challenged physicians' diagnoses, and self-diagnosed (actions that typically elicited very negative reactions from physicians). Similarly, a study of interactions in a clinic for chronic illness sufferers showed that a major concern of the patients was to convince others—especially doctors—of the reality of their diseases. This was done by elaborating their illness behavior, but the sicker they behaved, the less likely doctors were to believe them. Likewise, their "doctor shopping" to confirm the fact of their illnesses increased the likelihood that doctors would label them as "crocks" (Alexander, 1982).

Especially when medical knowledge about repetitive strain injuries was in the early stages of development, sufferers engaged in a similar search for doctor-patient communication in which their expression of pain would be taken seriously, as a legitimate problem. The medical consultation, thus, became a situation in which patients needed to convince the doctor of the reality of their symptoms, especially pain and disability. They feared being labeled as "neurotic," "crocks," or "malingerers." When physicians must serve as both curers and gatekeepers (e.g., determining whether workers' compensation or disability leaves are legitimate), doctor-patient communication can be even more strained or adversarial (Reid et al., 1991).

One researcher analyzed in detail the transcripts of three such doctor-patient encounters that were marked by tension, ambiguity, and no apparent resolution (Paget, 1983). Without much background about the patient, the reader sees in the transcript an apparently neurotic woman, overly preoccupied with little details of her body's functioning. After these three meetings, her doctor's assessment was that the patient's health was good and that her problem was "nerves." The transcript takes on an entirely different meaning, however, when we realize that the woman had recently had an operation for cancer. Her primary agenda in each of these encounters was clearly to address her fears that her cancer would metastasize or was not fully excised, but those fears *never* once became a topic of discourse. The doctor did not acknowledge that her fears existed or that they might be legitimate; he only heard her seemingly minor complaints about her teeth and her scalp. Indeed, an analysis of the doctor's responses to her input shows that he was not really listening to *any* of her expressions, perhaps because he had already defined them as the product of her "nerves," and therefore medically unreal or unimportant. She too contributed to the ongoing misunderstanding between them by referring only indirectly to the operation in the first encounter and not at all thereafter. She was afraid to express her fears and yet afraid to ignore them. The patient's uncertainty regarding her cancer produced fear, but this unnamed fear led to expressions that the doctor labeled as psychosomatic. His response—disconfirming the reality of her problem—produced further ambiguity, which only exacerbated the woman's fears.

Often such patients come to view physicians as evasive, nonsupportive, insensitive, uncaring, or dishonest. One MS patient said:

> I went to seven or eight doctors in less than two years. I'd tell them about my pins-and-needles feelings, or my numbness, or my weak arms and they'd all do the same thing—nothing. I really got upset with those doctors. They'd usually just say that my problems were normal for a woman my age (25) and things like that. And I'd get really uptight because they would just give me a valium and not try to find out what was really wrong. Some of them thought I was going off my rocker. They thought I was imagining the problems. . . . One of them just threw up his arms and said he didn't know what was wrong with me. Now isn't that some way for a doctor to act. I got so I didn't believe any of them. I knew something was wrong and felt they could find out if they would just try (quoted in Stewart and Sullivan, 1982: 1401).

In such situations the doctors' inability or unwillingness to communicate a diagnosis resulted in the patient's suffering and loss of trust in the doctor-patient relationship.

At the same time, however, total disclosure of all information is neither possible nor helpful for the patient. For instance, too great a barrage of information about a diagnosis and multiple treatment options can overwhelm the patient and, in effect, make patient participation in decision making impossible. Similarly, if a doctor discloses all of the remotely possible diagnoses, it would unnecessarily raise the patient's anxiety. Brody (1992) argues for a new ethic for doctor-patient relationships in which most power is shared with patients, without eschewing the beneficial aspects of the doctor's power as expert. He suggests that:

> . . . physicians most effectively empower patients neither by reflexively disclosing nor by reflexively withholding any particular sort of information. They empower patients by creating an atmosphere that encourages participation and dialogue (Brody, 1992: 136).

The Micropolitics of Professional Dominance

When a patient interacts with a doctor, the relationship is not symmetrical. In addition to the physician's presumed medical expertise, a number of microstructural factors increase the relative power of the doctor in the medical encounter. The professional dominance of doctors is enhanced by their control over minute parts of their interaction with patients.

Language Use.   Doctors control even seemingly medically irrelevant aspects of the doctor-patient interaction, such as humorous exchanges and other sociability (West, 1984: 152; see also Todd, 1983). Several patterns of language use reflect the subtle ways in which dominance is asserted. For example, interrupting is an assertion of whose input to the interaction is more important. Doctors frequently interrupted their patients, whereas they were seldom interrupted *by* their patients.

Doctors' unilateral use of false-familiar terms increases the gap between doctor and patient. For example, many doctors expect to be addressed deferentially by their title ("Dr. Jones"), but regularly address patients—regardless of age or other status—by their first names. Another false-familiar practice is the routine use of the condescending question, "How are we today?" Likewise, the use of diminutives is a subtle assertion of doctors' dominance and condescension. For example, one study of doctor-patient interactions in two gynecological settings (public clinic and private practice) found that doctors frequently used diminutives in talking to patients. For example, a doctor teaching women to perform breast self-examinations said, "Just march your little fingers . . ." (Todd, 1983).

The Dossier.   The doctor typically has far more information about the patient than the patient has about the doctor. Such one-sided familiarity serves to remind the patient which party is dominant (Stimson and Webb, 1975). The medical record functions as a third agent, introducing the patient (and personal details about the patient, such as marital status and age) even before the face-to-face interaction. One researcher observed that doctors often appear to be more oriented to the patient's objectified record or chart than to the patient (West, 1984: 132—133). Records can indeed take on a reality greater than that expressed by patients themselves. Patients' narratives of their illness experiences often bear little resemblance to the case record (see Kleinman, 1988).

Patients typically lack access to or control over these records. They are prevented from seeing their charts, reading their records, or challenging items of information in their files. Particularly in institutional settings such as hospitals, control over medical records is a form of social control over inmates (Goffman, 1961). In ordinary office practice too, patient records often contain information that is discrediting. For example, a doctor in a group practice may read a colleague's comment that a patient is a constant complainer and accordingly decide not to give that person's current problem serious attention.

Social Organization of Space.   The physical setting of most medical encounters is likewise supportive of the physician's dominance. Medical staff have the uniforms and "props" of authority—white coats, stethoscopes, framed certificates, and complicated equipment. Office and hospital consultations are on doctors' "home field," which is organized to their specifications. For example, rarely is the doctor's office arranged so that doctor and patient are seated in equally important positions; much of the interaction may in fact occur in the examining room with the patient undressed and in an awkward posture. Studies of the uses of space, posture, and gesture demonstrate that such differences are related to power and stratification (Henley, 1977).

Social Control of Time.   Significantly, doctors exert considerable control over the time spent with patients. One useful indicator of relative power in a dyad (i.e., a two-person interrelationship, such as teacher-student or executive-underling) is which party is in a position to make the other wait for access to his or her presumably more precious time. Typically, the patient waits to see the doctor rather than the reverse. In private practice, physicians often overbook patients to assure that every block of office consultation time is filled, but they are more sensitive to the need for customer satisfaction than doctors in clinic or institutional settings, where patients are not free to take their business elsewhere.

The allocation of time spent with patients depends partly upon the expectations and rewards for doctors in a particular institutional setting. One study found that prenatal patients in one hospital experienced different waiting times and received very different amounts of doctor time depending upon whether they were being seen in the obstetrics clinic, family practice clinic, or midwife service. Reflecting different organizational—as well as health care—objectives, residents in obstetrics spent an average of five to ten minutes with a prenatal patient, and expected clinic nurses to do the job of communicating information about pregnancy and delivery. By contrast, midwives spent an average of 20 minutes with patients, and family practice residents spent up to 45 minutes with patients. The researcher noted that family practice residents were encouraged and rewarded for the time spent with patients, whereas obstetric residents were discouraged from devoting time to "normal" pregnancies and were informally sanctioned if they failed to process their share of the patient work-load fast enough (Lazarus, 1988).

One study showed that 73 percent of patients' visits to doctors lasted 15 minutes or less (Lawrence and McLemore, 1983). Because doctors' goals include the efficient, task-oriented use of this brief time, the interview and examination are directed to gathering information that they believe is directly relevant to fairly routinized diagnostic decision rules. A British study corroborated the impact of a sense of time constraints on doctor-patient communication. Even when time is actually available for more medical work, doctors narrow the objectives of their routine (and typically uninteresting) practice by thinking not "What can I do for this patient?" but "What can I do for this patient in the next six minutes?" (Horobin and McIntosh, 1983: 328). One physician commented on his tight control of patient interactions:

> The doctor's primary task is to manage his time. If he allows patients to rabbit on about their conditions then the doctor will lose control of time and will spend all his time sitting in a surgery [office consultation] listening to irrelevant rubbish. Effective doctoring is characterized by a "quick, clean job" (quoted in Byrne and Long, 1976: 93).

In much American practice of medicine, the sense of time constraints is further heightened by the more direct linkage of physicians' income with the number of patients seen and the number of specific medical services provided.

Patients are unlikely to know the criteria by which the doctors are judging their input, and often the information about the problem that the patient wants to give is discarded or interrupted by the doctor. One study found that, on average, doctors cut off patients' descriptions of their complaints within the first 18 seconds (Beckman and Frankl, 1984). This practice is particularly problematic because patients only rarely readily reveal the important reasons that triggered their visit (Good and Good, 1982). For example, a patient may start out by presenting a "simple" problem such as a persistent rash, but may have really come to the doctor mainly to obtain reassurance that he does not have heart disease like his brother who recently had a heart attack. If given the time to present all their concerns, patients frequently identify three or four problems, of which the first mentioned is often not the most serious.

Doctors' information-giving time is likewise greatly constricted by the brevity of the ordinary medical encounter. One study found that only about 9 percent of a session was devoted to communicating information about the illness to the patient. If an average session is ten to fifteen minutes, the information-giving part is barely one minute. An analysis of 336 encounters in several outpatient settings showed that doctors spent little time informing their patients, overestimated the time they did spend, and underestimated their patients' interest in obtaining information (Waitzkin, 1985).

THE DOCTOR-PATIENT RELATIONSHIP

Broader structural factors also shape the pattern of miscommunication between doctors and their patients. As described in Chapter 8, patients come to the medical encounter with fundamentally separate (and often irreconcilable) expectations and goals from those of their doctor: What am I doing and why? What are the central facts about my situation? How should we proceed to make sense of this? What is my expected outcome?

Rationalization and the Medical Model

As outlined in Chapter 9, modern biomedicine has developed a conception of disease as separate from the person experiencing it. Rationalized medicine views the body as an object; the body is incidentally inhabited by a person who can potentially help or hinder the task of treating diseases of the body. People cannot, however, simply leave their bodies at the repair shop. While individual doctors may choose to relate to their patients as persons and not just bodies, such an approach is not an essential part of curing in the biomedical model. In many ways, the training and socialization of medical personnel actively discourages them from seeing their patients as whole persons with social, emotional, aesthetic, spiritual, and other health-related facets to their lives.

Medical training emphasizes technical skills in diagnosing and treating pathologies (physiological deviations that constitute or characterize disease). Thus, doctors are trained to approach a medical encounter with a patient with the goal of efficient diagnosis of a pathology and active treatment intervention. By contrast, the patient comes to the doctor with a broader, and more often vague, set of goals. The patient's needs may be related to a range of problems, some of which are unrelated or only indirectly related to an identifiable pathology or bodily condition. The patient may be experiencing illness but lack a clinically detectible pathology. The illness may also be a chronic condition in the face of which the doctor's active intervention is not very effective, although the patient may suffer from certain socioemotional aspects of the illness and its management. With a narrow disease-oriented training, doctors are likely to misunderstand completely what these patients need.

Most persons seeking medical help do not need the kind of medical intervention that physicians have been trained to appreciate. In medical school, internships and residencies, the emphasis is upon the "interesting" cases, which are typically acute and dramatic, and thus challenging—but not impossibly so—for the doctors' diagnostic skills. Cases often are defined as interesting if they offer the chance to practice new surgical techniques; once the doctor has mastered these procedures, such cases become less interesting (Scully, 1980: 166–171). In ordinary office practice, however, such "interesting" cases are proportionately very rare, and doctors are likely to be bored and impatient with the majority of patients' health problems.

One hospital's head midwife, who was involved in training obstetric residents, noted:

> It is a rare medical student who wants to sit with a woman in labor. Residents will even pass on watching normal deliveries. They see people as pathology, as a uterus. I rarely see the art of medicine, the understanding of seeing a patient as a total entity—where she is going, where she has been. I heard a resident say that "If I never do another normal vaginal delivery, it won't be too soon." They train for pathology but go into private

practice with normal patients. There is more money in it, and it is the least amount of time for the most amount of money (quoted in Lazarus, 1988: 39).

In general practice, which includes most of the work done by general practitioners, pediatricians, family practitioners, internists, and obstetrician-gynecologists, only about 15 percent of consultations are for the kind of acute, major, or life-threatening conditions that are likely to be "interesting." By far the largest proportion of office visits are for seemingly minor, self-limiting conditions or for well-person preventive care; chronic illnesses are the second largest category. Physicians whose medical training was oriented toward "interesting" cases find such routine work far less rewarding. One doctor exclaimed:

> Our skills are absolutely wasted . . . frustration and boredom set in. There are days when you go home and think, "Have I got to do this for another twenty years?" You've done a lot of work but you really haven't done anything for anybody. . . . There's no stimulation at all . . . (quoted in Horobin and McIntosh, 1983: 321).

Labeling Patients

Doctors' socialization leads to negative stereotypes of patients. The use of such stereotypes does vary according to the institutional setting; doctors in private practice are less likely than doctors on hospital staff to use pejoratives openly to refer to patients, although they may hold some of the same negative attitudes (cf. Hahn, 1985b). Nevertheless, the values reflected in these attitudes toward patients are encouraged in both the self-selection of doctors and their medical education. Doctors learn that "real" medicine is about pathologies, not patients.

In a U.S. study, 439 family physicians anonymously answered a questionnaire about those patient characteristics to which they responded negatively (Klein et al., 1982). The doctors reacted negatively not only to various social and personal traits of their patients but also to certain medical conditions, especially those for which medical treatment offered little or no likelihood of cure or clear alleviation. The authors suggested that physicians particularly dislike situations, such as emphysema, senility, diabetes, arthritis, psychiatric conditions, and obesity, that challenge their faith in the potency of bioscientific medicine. While they may find a challenging case with a high probability of a dramatic cure "interesting," they dislike conditions, such as back pain, chronic vague pains, headaches, and chronic fatigue, that offer little probability of cure while bringing their competence or diagnostic skills into question. Furthermore, they dislike conditions for which they believe the patient or others are responsible, such as sexual behavior, auto accidents, suicide attempts, and other self-inflicted injuries (Klein et al., 1982; see also Smith and Zimmy, 1988; Hahn, 1985b; Jeffery, 1979; Roth, 1972).

One study found the leading common characteristics of patients that doctors label as "gomers" ("*get outta my* emergency *room*") were illnesses and/or personal characteristics that created management difficulties for the hospital staff (Leiderman and Grisso, 1985). Many patients were identified as "gomers" because their conditions defied solution by modern medical intervention. Their deterioration under treatment was thus a source of frustration and ideological doubts for doctors, especially the beginning doctors who typically staffed hospital emergency rooms and clinics.

Many of the other derogatory terms used for patients reflect similar values. A widespread distinction in doctors' stereotyping of patients is between "sick people" and "trolls." The latter term is applied to patients whom doctors believe lack a "real" disease and to those held culpable for the cause of and/or the failure to control their condition. Other derogatory terms for undesirable patients include "albatross," "turkey," and "crock." Medical education encourages compassion for "sick people" but contempt for "trolls." Such negative stereotypes often supersede even the medical model itself in informing the doctor's understanding of a case, thus leading to failed empathy (Stein, 1986).

Medical students, interns, and residents learn and use extensive slang terms for their patients, patients' conditions and bodies, hospital situations, and working conditions. While use of slang serves other psychosocial functions, such as a safety valve for stressful working conditions and emotionally charged work, it also serves to distance doctors from their patients and confirm negative stereotypes (see Coombs et al., 1993). Even though patients generally do not understand the meanings of insider talk among the medical staff, the terms reflect and produce problems of doctors' empathy. Consider, for example, the effect on interns' attitudes of routinely referring to patients under their care by such terms as: "BW" (beached whale, i.e., obese), "slug" (not motivated to move around out of bed), "dud" (not an interesting case), "supratentorial" (patient's problem is considered to be psychological, not physical), or "HOWDY" (hypertensive, obese, white, diabetic, yahoo). Medical professors' routine use of vulgar or derogatory humor about patients and their conditions to make lectures more entertaining may encourage such stereotyping and failed empathy among medical students (Konner, 1987).

Contempt for "trolls" is particularly encouraged in the United States by the use of student-doctors to staff emergency rooms and clinics that serve a disproportionate number of these "undesirable" patients compared to fee-for-service private practice. The characteristic contempt is illustrated in this quote from a junior resident in an emergency room:

> At least 40–50 percent are gomers. Some weeks there is nothing but alcohol-induced diseases. The other night on call I met only three people with genuine diseases—having nothing to do with anything they ever did to themselves. I spend hours [with them] and check them everyday, but some guy who comes in with alcoholic pancreatitis—I'll tune him up and fire him out the door, and not give two shakes about him (quoted in Mizrahi, 1986: 102).

Hospital staff generally admitted that they often treated undesirable patients less thoroughly. Sometimes the stereotypes led to misdiagnoses and other medical mistakes (Mizrahi, 1986). For example, a homeless person brought unconscious to the emergency room may be treated as a "gomer" under the assumption that the condition was alcohol-induced, whereas a thorough treatment might discover that the symptoms resulted from a serious neurological problem.

Doctors' negative stereotypes of patients are also based upon social and personal characteristics. Doctors tended to consider "undesirable" those patients whose behavior violated the physicians' personal norms, even those with little or no relevance to health. The largest category of social characteristics (33 percent) eliciting negative responses from doctors included such violations as being dirty, smelly, vulgar, chronically unemployed, promiscuous, homosexual, malingering, or on welfare, Medicaid, or workers' compensation. Doctors' expectations of patients are based largely upon white, middle-class values that are accentuated by the self-selection and professional training processes. Social class differences also appear to figure into some negative stereotypes (Klein et al., 1982).

Doctors' often unrecognized value judgments of patients can result in failed empathy and less adequate care, as illustrated by one resident who admitted that he had detested patients who demanded Vistaril (an antianxiety drug often used in pain control) (Stein, 1986). He had viewed them as not legitimately sick but rather as weak, irresponsible, and dependent. Coming from a religious, rural, self-sufficient background, he valued patients who were self-sufficient in their health care and who rarely complained. Until he himself experienced considerable pain from minor surgery (and quickly wrote himself a prescription for Vistaril), he had a strong negative stereotype of patients whose requests for pain medication did not mesh with his personal values.

A study of the medical education process showed how both the structure of medical training and professional ideology work against the development of humanistic doctor-patient relationships.[2] New physicians are taught to avoid interaction with patients, to restrict the time spent with them, and to limit the patient input they listen to in medical interviews (Mizrahi, 1986: 118–119). This study concluded that the very structure of internship and residency teaches doctors to get rid of noninteresting patients. Reflecting both the attitudes of his supervisors and his personal experience with enormous time pressures, one junior resident said, " 'There are different kinds of ideal patients. When you're an intern, the ideal patient is someone you can get out and get out quickly' " (quoted in Mizrahi, 1986: 74–75). Interns and residents, for example, were informally rewarded for quickly and efficiently taking patient histories, and they learned not to bother with inquiring about social aspects of the cases because nobody noticed or appreciated if that were done.

Medical students learned, formally and informally, that what their professors and supervisors really wanted them to do was to narrow their clinical findings efficiently to biophysical data relevant to possible pathology. One senior resident explained:

> I guess I could use the excuse that I don't have the time to do that [deal with patient's social problems]. . . . It would be nice to bullshit with your patients for an hour or so and get a feel for their social situation. . . . It may affect the complaints they present

---

[2]For more detailed and textured description of the medical education process and its impact on treatment of patients, see Cassell, 1991; Davis-Floyd, 1987; Groopman, 1987; Konner, 1987; Light, 1980; Scully, 1980; Bloom, 1979; Coombs, 1978; Becker et al., 1961; Merton et al., 1957.

with. . . . If I was Marcus Welby [a former TV physician] and saw one patient per week, maybe I would be more concerned. I doubt it though, because it's really not appealing to me. If I really wanted to do it, I would have majored in social work or psychiatry. What appeals to me is treatment of sick people by diagnosing their diseases and giving medications. *I like good hard facts and physical findings*—things I can deal with on a tangible basis—not some intangible nebulous feeling of what their social situation is (quoted in Mizrahi, 1986: 95 [emphasis added]).

This attitude reflects the medical model's separation of the disease from the socio-emotional aspects of the patient's illness; doctors are socialized to view the nonbio-physical aspects as "fuzzy," "soft" facts that are ultimately irrelevant to their essential task.

TRANSFORMING THE SICK PERSON INTO A CASE

Just as the medical paradigm views the body as separate from the person, so too does the interaction between doctor and patient often involve isolating salient information about the sick body from the sick person. One of the effects of most medical encounters is to transform the sick person into a medical case. Drawing from their medical training and the biomedical paradigm for interpreting disease and pathology, physicians use the medical encounter for relatively narrow goals: the efficient eliciting and honing of facts relevant to a medical diagnosis, the precise application of a set of decision rules for proceeding, and active therapeutic intervention. Although their understanding of the medical encounter is informed by rational biomedicine, it is also the product of situational factors, cultural biases, and subjective influences that are often subtly embedded in the doctors' practice of medicine itself (Stein, 1986; see also Mishler, 1984).

Social Influences on Medical Judgments

The process of locating and interpreting medical evidence is always socially mediated. Such medical judgments as the factors that the diagnostician considers relevant, the clues that are thought worth seeking and thus are elicited in conversation and testing, and those that should be overlooked or discarded often entail social as well as biological attributes. For example, doctors treating elderly persons sometimes do not carry out routine tests in physical examinations, because they assume patient problems are due to senility or old age (Glassman, 1980).

Both the patient and the doctor often treat the diagnosis as a conclusion rather than a working hypothesis. Even before the diagnosis is reached, the physician's expectations and hunches may limit the clues examined. A study of medical thinking showed that doctors tended to develop hypotheses very early in an intake interview, often basing their hunches on only the patient's general appearance and one or two presenting complaints (Kassirer and Gorry, 1978). The physician's expectations are often subsequently self-confirming; contradictory clues are neither noticed nor sought (Jones, 1982: 156–161).

Medical evidence is typically ambiguous and multifaceted. In both scientific and other medical systems, the process of reaching a diagnosis is one of pattern forming. Despite extensive diagnostic technologies, the art of diagnosis in modern medicine is highly imprecise. A study of diagnostic failures in myocardial infarction (heart attacks) showed that physicians who relied on technological assessment, in place of their own observation and clinical skills, were likely to make a mistaken diagnosis (Zarling et al., 1983). U.S. data on autopsies show that in biomedical terms one out of three diagnoses were erroneous, and that in one out of ten cases the error could have contributed to the patient's death (*The New York Times*, 1987a; see also Altman, 1988b; Sullivan, 1983). To form a pattern, one must actively select pieces of evidence to cluster into an understanding. This process necessarily entails deciding which pieces of information to include and which to exclude (see Locker, 1981).

Similarly, in the interpretation of evidence and treatment decisions nonphysical elements, such as the emotional or social situation of the ill person, become part of the pattern.[3] Often the person creating the pattern is not aware of these elements; instead moral judgments and ideological assumptions enter the process under the guise of objective physical observations. For example, in examining X-rays of workers' lungs for symptoms of asbestosis, company physicians saw very different patterns than did doctors not connected with the industry (Brodeur, 1974: 174).

There is no necessary connection between the many diagnoses and possible treatments. Numerous, sometimes contradictory treatment options exist in any single medical system, and social factors influence which one the doctor recommends. Individual practitioners differ in the *decision rules* that they follow in choosing certain treatments for the same condition. (Decision rules are a form of knowledge that provides a set of minimally acceptable criteria for selecting a mode of treatment, such as surgery or medication.) A British study of ear, nose, and throat specialists revealed that widely varying decision rules determine whether an adenotonsillectomy should be performed. Some relied heavily on a physical examination (and practitioners disagreed over what to look for in the examination); others attached no significance to examination findings and relied instead on the case history. Some recommended surgery only when several signs were present on examination; others considered the existence of only one sign sufficient (Bloor, 1976).

Social judgments also enter into physicians' decision rules. Often the therapy proposed by a doctor varies greatly from patient to patient, even when the same biophysical conditions are present. When recommending hysterectomies (surgical removal of the uterus, resulting in sterility), physicians often included in their decision rules such factors as the woman's age, ethnicity, poverty, marital status, and whether she was on welfare, had had multiple abortions, and had already had children (Fisher, 1986). Thus, a more serious biophysical condition in a 25-year-old white woman with no children might be less likely to be treated with a hysterectomy than a less serious condition in a 35-year-old black woman with four children.

[3]This is not a criticism; effective treatment probably should take the sick person's entire situation into consideration. The issue here is the extent to which uncritical assumptions and ideological biases often enter the process and are treated as part of "objective" reality, without the participants' awareness.

Similarly, studies show that the social attitudes, beliefs, and personal characteristics of physicians influence the treatment options they offer their patients with breast cancer. For instance, although breast-conserving surgery is medically recommended for the majority of women whose cancer is in an early stage, older women (the vast majority of cancer patients) are significantly less likely to be offered this treatment option than younger women (Ganz, 1992).[4]

Judgments of social worth also enter into medical decisions. Studies of treatment decisions and other actions in hospital emergency services show that the young are treated as being more valuable than the old and that welfare cases are treated as being less worthy than those not on welfare. Especially disvalued persons, such as those labeled "drunks" and "PIDs" (women with pelvic inflammatory diseases, often assumed to be due to promiscuity), are given even less prompt and considerate treatment (Roth, 1972; see also Sudnow, 1967).

An appreciation of the social construction of ideas of illness, together with an awareness of the flexible processes by which these ideas are applied in diagnosis and therapy, helps explain how cases are constructed. Medical decision making is powerfully influenced by social assumptions that are often implicit and unacknowledged. The creation of a medical case shows that not only medical knowledge but also medical practice is a social construction.

Depersonalization of the Patient

Patients also bring an understanding—sometimes fragmented and contradictory—of the nature of their illness. They enter the medical encounter with an array of important social, emotional, and situational concerns. Drawing from cultural models, the patients have some interpretation of their own illness. Furthermore, they are likely to be struggling with problems of meaning, at least in the instance of feared, serious illness, including: Why me? Who is responsible? Why this disease? What will this do to my identity and my future?

Serious miscommunication and depersonalization occur when the doctor disconfirms or ignores patient concerns and understandings. Box 10.1 illustrates a gravely flawed exchange between doctor and patient. The doctor, intent only upon his biophysical assessment, has failed to hear the person, ignoring or interrupting her attempts to explain her illness. In conducting the interview and writing this report, the doctor is using the technically correct forms he learned in his training. However, in the medical record he produces, the patient is dehumanized and transformed into a reified, thing-like case, very unlike the person who, as revealed in the transcript, speaks eloquently of her commitments, fears, stresses, economic and social problems.

In transforming Mrs. Flowers into a medical case, the doctor reduces her to her hypertension, her noncompliance with the medical regimen, her early signs of heart

---

[4]A more cynical interpretation of these differences is that the physician's financial gain is a major component in decision rules. Several studies have shown surgery rates to be much higher where physicians are paid on a fee-for-service basis, and surgeons (and hospitals) earn far more for a radical mastectomy than for breast-conserving surgery (Montini and Ruzek, 1989).

failure, and her medications. The doctor, following the technically correct approach to interviewing and treating, has completely missed the person with her complex social, psychological, and economic problems. His control of the interview consistently constrains Mrs. Flowers's presentation of her concerns; she is frequently ignored or interrupted when talking about the very matters that brought her to see the doctor. The doctor permits her to speak about her physical complaints, but disallows her psychological or social problems. The interview elicits only facts about her biophysical diseases and medical treatment. Even though Mrs. Flowers's human suffering is very much a part of her chronic illness, it is relegated to a perfunctory referral to a social worker (Kleinman, 1988: 134–136).

The disease orientation of the medical model and the doctor's professional distance from the patient combine to turn the complex person into a rationalized case with its biophysical parts neatly separated from its social, emotional, spiritual, and economic elements. In this situation, the doctor is also so culturally distant from the patient that he is ignorant of the ideas and social practices that inform her own understanding of her situation. For example, she refers to her "high blood"—a folk illness in lower-class black American subculture. Since "high blood" is believed to

---

BOX 10.1   *THE CREATION OF A MEDICAL CASE*

Background: Mrs. Flowers is returning to the clinic, where she had previously been treated for her hypertension. She is 39 years old, black, the mother of five children. She lives with four of her children, her mother, and two grandchildren in an inner-city ghetto. She works at present as a waitress in a restaurant, but periodically she has been unemployed and on welfare. She has been married twice, but both of her husbands have deserted her. As a result, she is a single head of household. Mrs. Flowers is an active member of the local Baptist church, which has been an important source of support to her and her family for many years. She is also a member of a community action group.

In the household of eight, she is the only wage earner. Her mother, Mildred, is 59 and partially paralyzed owing to a stroke that was the result of long-standing and poorly controlled hypertension. Her oldest daughter, Matty, the unmarried 19-year-old mother of two small children, is at present unemployed and pregnant; in the past, she has had a drug problem. Mrs. Flowers's 15-year-old daughter, Marcia, is also pregnant. Their 18-year-old brother, J. D., is in prison. Teddy, a 12-year-old, has had problems with truancy and minor delinquency. Amelia, 11, the baby of the family, is said by her mother to be an angel.

A year ago, Mrs. Flowers's long-time male companion, Eddie Johnson, was killed in a barroom brawl. Recently, Mrs. Flowers has been increasingly upset by memories of Eddie Johnson, by concern for how prison will affect J. D., and by fears that Teddy will get involved with drugs like his older brother and sister before him. She is also concerned about her mother's worsening disability, which includes what she fears may be early signs of dementia.

Dr. Richards: Hello, Mrs. Flowers.
Mrs. Flowers: I ain't feelin' too well today, Doc Richards.
Dr. Richards: What seems to be wrong?

Mrs. Flowers: Um, I don't know. Maybe it's that pressure of mine. I been gettin' headaches and havin' trouble sleeping.

Dr. Richards: Your hypertension is a bit worse, but not all that bad, considering what it's been in the past. You been taking your medicines as you ought to?

Mrs. Flowers: Sometimes I do. But sometimes when I don't have no pressure, I don't take it.

Dr. Richards: Gee whiz, Mrs. Flowers, I told you if you don't take it regularly you could get real sick like your Mom. You got to take the pills every day. And what about salt? You been eating salt again?

Mrs. Flowers: It's hard to cook for the family without salt. I don't have time to cook just for me. At lunch, I'm in the restaurant and Charlie, he's the chef, he puts lotsa salt in everythin'.

Dr. Richards: Well, now this is a real problem. Salt restriction, I mean a low-salt diet, is essential for your problem.

Mrs. Flowers: I know, I know. I mean to do all these things, but I just plain forget sometimes. I got so much else goin' on and it all seems to affect the pressure. I got two pregnant daughters at home and my mother is doin' much worse. I think she may be senile. And then I worries about J. D., and here comes Teddy with the same problems startin' up. I—

Dr. Richards: Have you any shortness of breath?

Mrs. Flowers: No.

Dr. Richards: Any chest pain?

Mrs. Flowers: No.

Dr. Richards: Swelling in your feet?

Mrs. Flowers: The feet do get a little swollen, but then I'm on them all day long at the restaurant—

Dr. Richards: You said you had headaches?

Mrs Flowers: Sometimes I think my life is one big headache. These here ain't too bad. I've had 'em for a long time, years. But in recent weeks they been badder than before. You see, a year ago last Sunday, Eddie Johnson, my friend, you know. Uh huh, well, he died. And—

Dr. Richards: Are the headaches in the same place as before?

Mrs. Flowers: Yeah, same place, same feelin', on'y more often. But, you see, Eddie Johnson had always told me not to bother about—

Dr. Richards: Have you had any difficulty with your vision?

Mrs. Flowers: No.

Dr. Richards: Any nausea?

Mrs. Flowers: No. Well when I drank the pickle juice, there was some.

Dr. Richards: Pickle juice? You've been drinking pickle juice? That's got a great deal of salt. It's a real danger for you, for your hypertension.

Mrs. Flowers: But I have felt pressure this week and my mother told me maybe I need it because I got high blood and—

Dr. Richards: Oh, no. Not pickle juice. Mrs. Flowers, you can't drink that for any reason. It just isn't good. Don't you understand? It's got lots of salt, and salt is bad for your hypertension.

Mrs. Flowers: Uh huh. OK.

Dr. Richards: Any other problems?

Mrs. Flowers: My sleep ain't been too good, doc. I think it's because—

Dr. Richards: Is it trouble getting to sleep?

Mrs. Flowers: Yeah, and gettin' up real early in the mornin'. I been dreamin' about Eddie Johnson. Doin' a lot of rememberin' and cryin'. I been feelin' real lonely. I don't know—

Dr. Richards: Any other problems? I mean bodily problems?

Mrs. Flowers: No, 'cept for tired feelin', but that's been there for years. Dr. Richards, you think worryin' and missin' somebody can give you headaches?

Dr. Richards: I don't know. If they are tension headaches, it might. But you haven't had other problems like dizziness, weakness, fatigue?

Mrs. Flowers: That's what I'm sayin'! The tired feelin', it's been there some time. And the pressure makes it worse. But I wanted to ask you about worries. I got me a mess o' worries. And I been feelin' all down, as if I just couldn't handle it anymore. The money is a real problem now.

Dr. Richards: Well, I will have to ask Mrs. Ma, the social worker to talk to you about the financial aspect. She might be able to help. Right now why don't we do a physical exam and see how you're doing?

Mrs. Flowers: I ain't doin' well. Even I can tell you that. There's too much pressure and it's makin' *my pressure* bad. And I been feelin' real sad for myself.

Dr. Richards: Well, we'll soon see how things are going.

After completing the physical examination, Dr. Richards wrote the following note in the medical record:

April 14, 1980

39 year old Black female with hypertension on hydrochlorothiazide 100 mgs. daily and aldomet 2 grams daily. Blood pressure now 160/105, has been 170/80–110/120 for several months alternating with 150–/95 when taking meds regularly. Has evidence of mild congestive heart failure. No other problems.

Impression: (1) Hypertension, poorly controlled
              (2) Noncompliance contributing to (1)
              (3) Congestive heart failure—mild
              (1) Change aldomet to apresoline
              (2) Send to dietician to enforce lower salt diet
              (3) Social work consult because of financial questions
              (4) See in 3 days, regularly until blood pressure has come down and stabilized

Signed: Dr. Staunton Richards

Dr. Richards also sent a terse note for a consultation to the dietician, which read: "39 year old Black woman with poorly controlled hypertension who does not comply with low salt diet. Please help plan 2 gram sodium diet, and explain to her again relationship of salt intake to her disease and that she must stop eating high salt foods and cooking with salt."

Source: The Illness Narratives: Suffering, Healing, and the Human Condition, by Arthur Kleinman, M.D. Copyright © 1988 by Basic Books, Inc. Reprinted by permission of Basic Books, Inc., Publishers.

result from blood rising to the head, her consumption of pickle juice makes sense as a folk remedy because it is believed to thin or "cut" the blood. Cultural and social factors, such as the limitations posed by her job, make it unlikely that the sick woman would actually follow the difficult instructions for managing her serious illnesses. Rather than understanding these factors, the doctor views what he labels her "noncompliance" as a moral failing. She is not a "good" patient because she does not do what he tells her to do to control her biophysical condition (Kleinman, 1988: 135–136).

An interesting contrast is the inner-city clinic experience of a young black internist from a middle-class background; her understanding of a patient like Mrs. Flowers is remarkably different:

> The more I see, the more appalled I am at how ignorant I have been, insensitive to the social, economic, and political causes of disease. . . . Today I saw an obese hypertensive mother of six. No husband. No family support. No job. Nothing. A world of brutalizing violence and poverty and drugs and teenage pregnancies and—and just plain mind-numbing crises, one after another after another. What can I do? What good is it to recommend a low salt diet, to admonish her about control of her pressure? She is under such real outer pressure, what does the inner pressure matter? What is killing her is her world, not her body. In fact, her body is the product of her world. She is a hugely overweight, misshapen hulk who is a survivor of circumstances and lack of resources and cruel messages to consume and get ahead impossible for her to hear and not feel rage at the limits of her world. Hey, what she needs is not medicine but a social revolution (quoted in Kleinman, 1988: 216–217).

In learning the medical model and the specific techniques of clinical practice, doctors are trained to transform the patient into a case. A study of case presentations—a standard training method in which interns, residents, and fellows in a teaching hospital present formal case studies to their superiors—found that the standard discourse depersonalized patients, referring to them as objects: their disease, their treatment procedure, or a shorthand term for their health status (Anspach, 1988). For example, a pregnant woman is transformed into a "Gravida III, Para I, AbI, black female at 32 weeks gestation" (Anspach, 1988: 363). Furthermore, by using the passive voice and referring to technological procedures, doctors' case presentations also failed to acknowledge the *human* agency in observing or treating. For example, they state, "He was put on phenobarb," rather than "I decided to put him on phenobarb," or "The arteriogram showed that this AVM was fed . . . ," instead of "I requested an arteriogram and interpreted its findings to mean . . ." (Anspach, 1988: 366–368).

The very language and interviewing techniques of the standard doctor-patient interaction result in losing sight of the patient as person and the patient's concerns. For example, physicians recode the patients' expressions into medical terminology, which becomes a shorthand for their medical condition and glosses over possibly relevant nonphysical aspects of the patients' description of their problems (Waitzkin, 1991; Mishler, 1984). In the preceding example, Mrs. Flowers's expressions are transformed into "hypertension, poorly controlled," "noncompliance," and "mild congestive heart failure." In recoding the language for conceptualizing the problem, the patient's perspective is obscured (Cicourel, 1983: 238).

Likewise, the structure of the medical interview leads to inadequate doctor-patient communication and truncated, distorted understandings of the patient's problem. Doctors are trained to use a set of formulas for conducting interviews with patients. One such formula is a "decision tree," a sequence of small decisions that culminates in a diagnosis and treatment plan. Accordingly, doctors elicit information from patients that enables them to narrow the range of possible medical problems down to smaller and smaller "branches." While they are talking with patients, doctors are simultaneously mentally testing hypotheses. Thus, doctors experience patient input that is not immediately relevant to the part of the decision tree they are then considering as disruptive to their line of thought. Similarly, doctors are trained to proceed in the interview by reviewing each of the bodily systems (respiratory system, circulatory system, and so on), often in a verbal check-list format. This routine device guarantees a certain thoroughness, but doctors often become irritated by the "disruption" of a patient who introduces a question or a point relevant to some area of concern other than the immediate item on the check list (West, 1984; see also Waitzkin, 1989a).

Thus, the typical patterns of doctor-patient communication produce a case, a reified representation of a sickness in which the sick *person* is remote or absent. Often subsequent interaction between the patient and doctor as well as other medical staff is based upon this representation, rather than upon any fresh input from the sick person. Such depersonalization results when the focal object of doctors' work is the medical case.

THE ENDS OF MODERN MEDICINE: MORAL DILEMMAS AND SOCIAL POLICIES

Implicit in the medical model of disease and curing are a number of assumptions about life and death and the proper ends of medical intervention. These assumptions are so deeply embedded that rarely are they acknowledged, much less examined. They have contributed to major contemporary problems for medical personnel and for society as a whole about how to deal with death and dying, life and potential life, and "normal" and "abnormal" life. In short, should the foremost goal of medicine be preserving and extending life for all patients?

The Medical Model and the Conquest of Death

Comaroff (1984) suggested that the biomedical model's interventionist stance against disease, which is defined as the disruption of the body's organic functioning, led to the acceptance of the conquest of death as a major goal of medicine. While acknowledging that ultimately all persons will die, the medical model makes it difficult and sometimes impossible to *decide* that any given person shall be allowed to die (cf. Muller and Koenig, 1988; Kleiman, 1985). The focus on the conquest of death also reduces medicine's attention to other needs, such as ameliorating suffering or making mundane improvements in the sick (or dying) person's quality of life.

Contemporary medical dilemmas are in part the result of biomedicine's very successes. Modern technologies enable doctors to prolong lives, even though often they cannot actually cure the disease. For example, the technology of dialysis allows persons with otherwise fatal kidney failure to live three or more years longer. Technological developments enable neonatal intensive care units to reduce the rate of respiratory distress syndrome among undersized infants who would have surely died soon after birth in earlier decades. Other technologies simulate virtually every organic function, artificially supplying the body with breath, food, water, immune responses, heartbeat, excretion, and blood cleansing. Similarly, the extremely expensive technology of organ transplantation extends some lives, often for many years.

Whereas in the recent past people expected that death was inevitable and would occur at its appointed time, now they expect medicine to intervene to prevent death and to prolong life. Indeed, in promulgating the successes of scientific medicine, the profession itself may have raised people's expectations unrealistically high. The idea that medicine can and should intervene to prolong life is consonant with both the medical model and physicians' professional ideologies. Doctors want to assert their control over sickness and the loss of life; many physicians view the death of a patient as a failure. The expectation that the goal of medicine is to prevent death has many negative consequences, however.

Our culture is profoundly uncomfortable with death and dying. It does little to prepare people for their own and others' deaths (Kearl, 1989; see also Elias, 1985). Ariès (1974) documented the historical development of modern taboos about death. Accordingly, as society failed to provide a consensus about how to die a "good death," it segregated sickness and death from normal social interaction. Medical institutions perform the latent function of segregating the unpleasantness of sickness and dying, while aspiring to the manifest function of curing.

Death and dying have become medicalized partly because of expectations that medicine will be able to intervene in the process, and partly because many people are relieved to have their family members' dying supervised by medical personnel in a hospital setting. Death is perhaps less threatening if it is thus removed, sterilized, and routinized. At the same time, however, the dying process is partly cut off from the very institutions of society most likely to be able to provide meaning in the face of death: religion and the family. Some alternative arrangements for dying, such as the hospice movement, encourage demedicalizing and rehumanizing the process.

Nevertheless, to choose an alternative arrangement for dying requires that alternatives be available, affordable, and legally allowed; that doctors and family members be aware and consciously accept that the patient is dying; and that there be mechanisms for dying persons to consider their options and express their intentions regarding death. Many social structures and attitudes in our society make it difficult for people to die with dignity. The specter of an unavoidable, overmedicalized end is not unrealistic: Medical technology makes possible keeping the body "alive" with respirators, feeding tubes, intravenous hydration and antibiotics, heart resuscitators, and the like, long after the person in the body has lost the ability to consider or express a desire to live or die.

The Technological Imperative

Another cultural value that makes it difficult to decide to let nature take its course and allow death to happen is the **technological imperative**, a prevalent idea in most Western societies (especially the United States) that urges that if we have the technological capability to do something, then we should do it. The technological imperative implies that action in the form of the use of an available technology is always preferable to inaction. Indeed, once a technology becomes available, its use becomes almost inexorably routinized and considered standard. The failure to apply this standard care—no matter how inappropriate for the individual patient—would be reprehensible (Koenig, 1988). The technological imperative is deeply embedded in many institutional responses to health crises. For example, most hospitals have created (and thus need to use) several high-technology wards, such as coronary and neonatal intensive care units, deliberately equipped and staffed to provide maximum multiple technological responses to patients' conditions. Similarly, much health insurance gives priority to high-tech medicine (such as treatment in a coronary care unit) over low-tech or nontechnological responses (such as home care with the help of a visiting health aide and nurse).

In arguing that the proper goal of medicine should not be the unquestioned prolongation of life, the ethicist Callahan (1987: 173) wrote that "the existence of medical technologies capable of extending the lives of the elderly who have lived out a natural life span creates no presumption whatever that the technologies must be used for that purpose." Similar but perhaps more difficult questions need to be posed about the uses of technology for prolonging the lives of persons who have not lived out a natural life span (see Hilfiker, 1983; Crane, 1975). What medical intervention should be used, for example, for an accident victim left in a persistent vegetative state, for a medically unsalvageable patient, such as a person with cancer of the esophagus who subsequently has a heart attack, or for an irreparably damaged newborn, such as an infant with anencephaly (congenital lack of a brain) or myelomeningocele (which in severe cases produces paraplegia, the lack of urinary control, and brain damage)?

There are also serious ethical questions about the use of medical responses that themselves cause pain or other suffering. For example, under what conditions should a patient or a patient's family be allowed to refuse a prescribed treatment, such as chemotherapy or surgery? The technological imperative has considerable legal support in many states; patients and their families must go to court to assert (and sometimes lose) the right to decide to refuse treatment or life supports. Other legal and ethical rights are also uncertain. Does a person have the right to obtain a particular treatment, even if it will not cure or even provide certain benefits for that individual? For example, does every person with kidney failure have the right to a transplant?

Because they underlie legal and social policies, such ethical issues are matters for the entire society as well as individual practitioners, patients, and families to consider. These issues are difficult for the courts, in part because the courts have increasingly deferred to the medical profession itself as the proper authority on matters of defining life and death. As noted in Chapter 6, the medicalization of moral authority has undermined the authority of other institutions, such as religion and the family.

On issues such as these, however, there is no technical (i.e., purely medical) answer. The boundaries of life and death are blurred, and biomedicine is incapable of clearly delineating them for the courts in purely technical terms, as illustrated by the ambiguities of court cases involving the abortion of second trimester fetuses and the passive euthanasia of patients in a persistent vegetative state. As Callahan (1987: 179) observed, "The 'sanctity of life' has to be the sanctity of personhood, not merely the possession of a body." Moral and legal rights adhere to *persons*, but there are no neat biomedical criteria to distinguish when or whether a body is a person. The choice of such criteria must come from outside scientific medicine, although they may include medically measurable determinants, such as brain death.

Policy Implications

Our society must come to terms with these issues in order to develop sensible social policies: How shall we pay for the care needed by the sick and dying? Toward what ends shall we train doctors and other medical personnel? How shall we allocate our society's research funding? What kinds of institutional support are required to fulfill our health care goals; for example, should society's focus be on high-tech hospital care, or is more societal support needed for other institutional settings, such as public health programs, real homes for the aged, or home health aides? Such policy decisions regularly require difficult choices, since no society can possibly meet every need of all citizens and thus must set its priorities.

These policy decisions have been thrust on us by the burgeoning costs of high-tech medicine; by the medicalization of birthing, dying, and other areas of life; and by the increasing numbers and proportions of the population who are old and very old. For example, both the physician and hospital portions of Medicare payments are rising dramatically and threaten to deplete those funds. About 25 to 35 percent of Medicare expenditures each year pay for the medical costs of only 5 to 6 percent of the enrollees—those in their last year of life (Scitovsky and Capron, 1986; Lubitz and Priboda, 1984).

In another example, as recently as 15 years ago babies born very prematurely died shortly after birth. Now many of these babies live, although a substantial proportion suffer physical and mental handicaps and chronic illnesses. The main factors in their survival are the new technologies in neonatal wards and intensive nursing. These are very expensive services; the necessary three or four months of hospitalization may cost $90,000 or more. In many parts of the United States the rates of premature birth are rising (French, 1989). Because of the burgeoning cost of such care, even though it is medically effective for some babies, society must examine whether this expenditure is the best use for its moneys (see Rhodes, 1992; Young and Stevenson, 1990; Guillemin and Holmstom, 1986). Might it not be better to spend health care dollars on public health programs that could prevent premature births, such as prenatal care and nutrition programs for women of childbearing age?

Similar allocation questions also apply to decisions about who shall receive high-priced organ transplants and other expensive surgery. What proportion of the nation's health care resources should go to care for the elderly and the dying? What priorities should be given to heroic interventions (such as by-pass surgery) compared to palliative efforts (such as pain relief) or to simple care and nursing? The United States operates with a de facto system of rationing health care: The wealthy buy whatever they want; the middle classes buy what their insurance allows and have the option to deplete their other resources to buy more; and the poor get whatever the state and Medicaid systems, public hospitals, and Medicare (if they are elderly) offer. This form of rationing results in enormous inequities (Fein, 1986; Gill and Ingman, 1986). The nation needs to confront the ethical issues that have been only implicit in its health care system and must ask: What are our priorities, and is this the kind of nation we really want to be?

SUMMARY

Modern biomedical forms of knowledge and practice are the particular result of social, political, and economic processes. The accomplishment of professional dominance by medical doctors in this century gives them both preeminence in the medical division of labor and control over the definitions of health, illness, and healing practices.

Medical professional dominance also creates problems for the treatment of the sick. The layperson-expert gap and other sources of social distance often result in poor communication and failed empathy. Doctor-patient relationships may reflect other social distance, such as that produced by gender and class stratification. Much interaction between doctor and patient serves to protect the power of the physician, which often directly disempowers the patient. Both the socialization of physicians and the social structure of medical practice promote patterns of doctor-patient interaction that disrupt real communication and lead to unsatisfactory treatment.

Assumptions implicit in the medical model have made it difficult for doctors and laypersons to admit to the limits of modern medicine and to consider setting different goals for its practice. By focusing on the conquest of death, medicine overemphasizes an interventionist approach to treatment and has difficulty coming to terms with death and dying. Not only do doctors and their patients need to reconsider the proper ends of medicine, but society as a whole is also confronted with massive ethical, legal, and policy issues about health care and medical treatment.

RECOMMENDED READINGS

Articles

ERIC J. CASSELL, "The nature of suffering and the goals of medicine," *New England Journal of Medicine* 306, 1982: 639–645.
JEAN COMAROFF, "Medicine, time, and the perception of death," *Listening* 19(2), 1984: 155–169.

BYRON J. GOOD and MARY-JO DELVECCHIO GOOD, " 'Learning medicine': The constructing of medical knowledge at Harvard Medical School," pp. 81–107 in S. Lindenbaum and M. Lock, *Knowledge, Power, and Practice: The Anthropology of Medicine and Everyday Life.* Berkeley: University of California Press, 1993.

Books

DANIEL CALLAHAN, *Setting Limits: Medical Goals in an Aging Society.* New York: Simon and Schuster, 1987. Callahan outlines the ethical problems posed by the medicalization of aging and dying, together with the burgeoning proportion of society in the old and very old age brackets. In the context of alternative ideas about the proper role of the elderly, he proposes carefully considered guidelines for setting limits for health care expenditures on persons who have lived a full life span.

BARBARA EHRENREICH and DEIRDRE ENGLISH, *Witches, Midwives, and Nurses: A History of Women Healers.* Old Westbury, NY: The Feminist Press, 1973. A brief historical treatise on how, in the process of medical professional domination, traditional women healers were driven out or subordinated.

MELVIN KONNER, *Becoming a Doctor: A Journey of Initiation in Medical School.* New York: Penguin, 1987. A reflective ethnographic account of experiences of an anthropologist who entered medical school at the age of 33; while not very critical of the medical model of health and illness, the book gives excellent insight into the problems of medical education, hospital structure, and doctor-patient relationships.

EMILY MARTIN, *The Woman in the Body: A Cultural Analysis of Reproduction.* Boston: Beacon Press, 1987. This book analyzes how medical conceptualizations of women's bodies, particularly menstruation, menopause, pregnancy, and childbirth, embody cultural assumptions about women and their life purpose.

MARCIA MILLMAN, *The Unkindest Cut: Life in the Backrooms of Medicine.* New York: William Morrow, 1976. A highly readable ethnography of hospital surgical units, with special attention to the social management of medical "mistakes."

TERRY MIZRAHI, *Getting Rid of Patients: Contradictions in the Socialization of Physicians.* New Brunswick, NJ: Rutgers University Press, 1986. Mizrahi has studied various stages in the training of physicians with a particular emphasis upon what they learned (formally and informally) about how to deal with patients; the serious contradictions in values imparted have important implications for the care of patients.

CHAPTER ELEVEN

Stratification and Power in Health Care Systems

There is enormous variety in how societies respond to the health needs of their members. Economic and social structural arrangements determine how a society cares for members' sick bodies, frail elderly bodies, disabled bodies, infant bodies—the well-being of all its members. This analysis shows the importance of social power in shaping these economic and social structural arrangements. Each society's political economy creates its health care system's goals and policies for achieving those goals.

A health care system is the "aggregate of commitments or resources which any national society 'invests' in the health concern" (Field, 1973: 763). As a system, all parts mutually influence each other, for better or for worse. Changes in one part of the system result in changes in another part. The U.S. health care system includes, for example, patients and other recipients of care; patients' families; doctors and many other providers of care; hospitals, nursing homes, clinics, and other institutional settings for care; insurers and others who pay for health care goods and services; industries that produce the many goods utilized in health care; and levels of government that are not only a major source of insurance but also a source of regulations, research funding, public health programs, and health-related policies.

U.S. PROBLEMS IN COMPARATIVE PERSPECTIVE

In this society health care has been equated with medical care, and most data in Chapters 11 and 12 refer only to medical care, its organization, and its costs. Our social policies have not conceptualized—much less accommodated—a total health care system. The development and possible effectiveness of social policy are ultimately a political process in which powerful interest groups vie to define the agenda. The present emphasis upon medical care of disease (rather than, for example, preventive medicine or public health) is itself the political product of the relative muscle of various interest groups; any attempt to set a broader agenda for the health of the nation would almost certainly be contested by interest groups benefiting from the status quo.

It is useful to compare the health care systems of nations because they show alternative ways of arranging the parts of the system.[1] For example, the Swedish sys-

[1]The following sources are useful for comparisons among various health care systems with particular reference to industrialized societies: Abel-Smith, 1992; Altman, 1985; Banta and Kemp, 1982; Crichton, 1981; Culyer and Jonsson, 1986; Dahlgren and Diderichsen, 1986; Deppe, 1992; Evans, 1983; Field, 1989; Gill, 1980; Ham, 1982; Heidenheimer and Elvander, 1980; Hessler and Twaddle, 1982; Kaufman, 1987; Klein, 1983; Light and Schuller, 1986; Marmor, 1982; Marmor et al., 1983a; Norbeck and Lock, 1987; Organisation for Economic Co-operation and Development, 1990; Rodwin, 1984; Roemer, 1985; Rosenthal and Frenkel, 1992; Saltman, 1991; Sidel and Sidel, 1983; Twaddle and Hessler, 1986.

While many commentators treat developing nations' health care issues as utterly different from those of industrialized countries, we would argue that many of the problems are the same: attention to broad social causes of illness and disease, appropriate technology, the most desirable training and deployment of health care workers, effective public health and preventive measures, and maximum utilization of all health-related resources toward a genuinely humane treatment of people in need. Some sources that deal specifically with health care systems of developing countries include Banta, 1986; Donahue, 1986, 1989; Elling, 1981; Good, 1987; Green, 1989; Heggenhougen et al., 1987; Horn, 1985; Low, 1985; Morgan, 1989; Roemer, 1985; Rosenthal, 1987, 1988; Rowland, 1991; Sidel and Sidel, 1982; Simonelli, 1987; Stebbins, 1986; Waitzkin, 1983a.

tem involves more extensive regulation and control of doctors and hospitals than the U.S. system. It is also more holistic in its concern for health-related issues like nutrition, child care, environmental pollution, and occupational health and safety. The United States could learn from developing nations as well as industrialized ones because our health care system is having to face the fact that the nation's human and financial resources for dealing with health needs are finite, and we need to find ways to maximize the health-producing results of how we use our resources. For example, China has achieved remarkable health gains at relatively little cost per capita (Kristof, 1991). The Chinese system incorporates indigenous health practices and utilizes nonprofessional providers (like the "barefoot doctors," paraprofessionals deployed to rural districts); China also emphasizes public health measures and nutrition. By contrast, the Kenyan system has devoted huge proportions of national health care expenditures to relatively high-technology medicine in a limited number of urban hospitals, and thus has not achieved adequate health care for the vast majority of its people. From such comparisons we might derive policy directions for our own health care system.

Among industrialized societies, there are four broad types of health care system. The U.S. system, exemplifying the *first type*, is in principle a laissez-faire, commodified arrangement. Lack of central planning or significant state controls results in a diverse and relatively uncoordinated mixture of many different institutional programs for the provisions of health services. Profit is a significant motivating factor for many of the system's health service providers, institutions, insurers, and producers of products and technologies. Health care is *sold* in an economic marketplace. The medical profession enjoys large amounts of autonomy in regulating its affairs, conditions of work, and income. The *second type*, a national health insurance system, is similar, except that *all* citizens are insured by third parties (e.g., a government agency or a labor union) that have a significant degree of regulatory control over practitioners and health-related institutions. The Canadian system exemplifies this model. The British National Health Service (NHS) is a prime example of the *third type*, a health service system, in which most facilities are owned by the nation and most physicians (whether in private practice or on hospital staff) are paid from state moneys. Physicians have relatively large amounts of professional autonomy, although the state has greater control over salaries and institutional arrangements than in laissez-faire or insurance systems. Socialized health systems, such as Russia's, give the state even greater centralized control. In this *fourth type*, the state owns and manages health facilities and employs almost all health personnel (see Field, 1973).

In the United States the power of competing interest groups, together with the ideology of free-market competition, has resulted in an amazingly complex, unwieldy, and expensive health care system that is now in crisis. The ideology of a laissez-faire market has obscured the fact that relatively few parts of the health care system are amenable to real market conditions; thus, the notion of competition in this type of health care system is something of a fiction. Nor has the United States maintained "pure" private enterprise, implied in its rejection of national health plans, like Canada's; indeed, in the United States nearly half of all health care payments are *pub-*

lic moneys, collected by city, state, or federal taxes. The only part of the "ideal type" of this kind of health care system that has not been compromised in the United States is that health care has become highly commodified and the drive for profits is, indeed, a central dynamic.

The contradictions implicit in the U.S. health care system have driven it to the brink of crisis. U.S. health care expenditures have been growing dramatically—much faster than other expenses in the consumer price index. Figure 11.1 shows how greatly the proportion of the total U.S. gross national product (GNP) consumed by health care costs increased between 1940 and 1990. In 1990 these expenditures amounted to more than $2,500 per person (U.S.D.H.H.S., 1992). These figures include only expenditures for formal health care (e.g., doctors, hospitals, pharmaceuticals, and medical supplies); they do not include most costs of informal care (e.g., assistance with daily living for persons with chronic illnesses) or most health maintenance and sickness prevention expenses (e.g., nutrition, pollution control, and accident prevention).

Runaway health care costs have eroded the nation's ability to address other public needs, such as education and scientific research. Because most private health insurance is funded through the work place, the rapid rise of health insurance premiums has become a major concern for businesses, especially those which must compete internationally with companies whose benefits per employee cost far less. Thus,

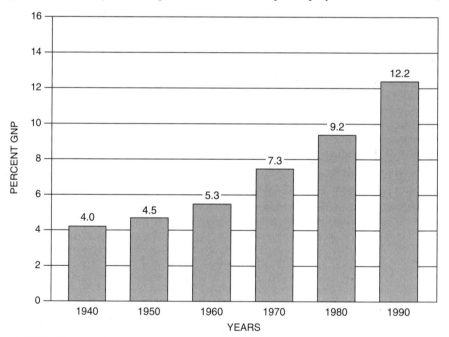

FIGURE 11.1   *U.S. Health Care Expenditures as a Percentage of Gross National Product. Sources: U.S. Department of Health and Human Services, Health, United States, 1991. Hyattsville, MD: National Center for Health Statistics. Note: These data differ from those given in previous editions of this publication, due to Department of Commerce revisions of the gross national product (GNP).*

the rapid rise of U.S. health expenditures diminishes the competitiveness of U.S. products in the international marketplace. Total health expenditures in the United States as a percentage of the gross domestic product[2] (GDP) grew from 7.4 percent in 1970 to 11.8 percent in 1989; by contrast, Canada's expenditures grew from 7.1 percent to only 8.7 percent of its GDP, Germany's from 5.9 to 8.2 percent and the United Kingdom's from 4.5 to 5.8 percent in the same 19 years (Schieber and Poullier, 1991).

The vast majority of Americans are dissatisfied with the health care system in this country. Public opinion polls show that 89 percent of Americans consider the U.S. system to need fundamental change or complete rebuilding. By contrast with two other types of system, only 43 percent of Canadians and 69 percent of the British polled were so dissatisfied. The survey found that under the American system, a much larger proportion of citizens are faced with financial barriers to receiving health care than in Britain or Canada, and that substantial numbers are either not covered by health insurance or severely underinsured (Blendon et al., 1990).

Another study found that approximately half of Americans polled worry about premium and health care costs, as well as whether they will be denied needed care due to inadequate insurance or money for out-of-pocket health expenses (Smith et al., 1992). International comparisons suggest that their fears are well founded. U.S. spending, for every category of health expenditure, is the highest of all nations, but the rate of utilization (e.g., number of doctor visits per person or average number of and length of hospital stays) is well below the average of other industrialized nations (Schieber et al., 1991). These figures suggest that many Americans who experience the kinds of health problems that would be treated by doctors or in hospital in other countries are not utilizing those treatments in the United States; the disproportionately higher costs in the United States may be one important reason why many Americans are not able to utilize needed health care services.

By contrast with the United States, in the two decades since the inception of Canadian national health insurance, substantial gains have been made in making medical services accessible to all Canadians, regardless of ability to pay, and greatly reducing mortality disparities between wealthier and poorer, urban and rural regions (Badgley, 1991). Although some economic barriers still exist, the poor are far less at risk of being denied needed health care, and the middle classes are not in fear of being made poor by health care expenses.

The United States and the Republic of South Africa are the only industrialized nations without some form of comprehensive health care system for *all* citizens (Roemer, 1985). At this writing, the U.S. Congress is considering several proposals for changing the U.S. system, but only some of these proposals would provide for all Americans. In 1993, a presidential commission, headed by Hillary Rodham Clinton, urged a system guaranteeing coverage for all citizens, but not significantly altering the existing status (or financial power) of hospitals, insurers, physicians, manufacturers, and others (see Chapter 12). An alternative set of bills propose a national health insurance program, comparable to Canada's (discussed further in Chapter 12), but

---

[2]The GDP (rather than GNP) is regularly used for international comparisons.

this alternative has not gotten much media attention and is vehemently disfavored by the interest groups that profit from the existing system. Surveys show that the majority of Americans prefer the Canadian arrangement of national health insurance financed by tax money to the present form of public and private health insurance in the United States (*The New York Times*, 1992). Other proposals before Congress do not guarantee universal coverage for citizens but provide mandates or incentives to increase the number of citizens covered by health insurance.

At the same time, however, there is little support in the United States for a national health service like Great Britain's. Indeed, the British are increasingly dissatisfied with their system (as the preceding figures indicate). The British NHS has been seriously underfunded, resulting in shortages, understaffing, and growing waiting lists for nonemergency hospital services (Lohr, 1988). Indeed, in the 1980s, the Thatcher administration encouraged competition from for-profit, private health care providers, with the effect of creating a two-tier system: NHS for the poor, middle, and working classes, and private providers for the as yet small proportion of the upper classes and upper-level employees with private insurance (Whitney, 1991; Clines, 1987).

Although Americans spend much more than citizens of other industrialized nations on health care, they do not enjoy generally better health. In 1990, Americans paid an average of $2,566 per person for health expenses—far more than countries with the next-highest expenditures: Canada, $1,795, and Sweden, $1,421, per capita (U.S.D.H.H.S., 1992: 267). Despite being the industrialized nation with the highest total private and public spending on health care (as a percentage of the GNP or GDP), on several important measures of the health of its people (e.g., life expectancy, infant mortality), the United States ranks far lower than other countries, such as Canada and Sweden, which spend considerably less on health care (Sivard, 1987). The enormous cost disparity is not purchasing Americans generally better health.

High expenditures do not guarantee better health because they are at best only indirectly linked with health-promoting or curing practices. For example, two nations may pay the same amount of money for a program of inoculations, but one nation may obtain far fewer inoculations per capita if the profit margins for the materials or provider services are higher in that health care system. Furthermore, health care expenditures are typically only *medical* care cost; these figures do not account for important differences in other health-promoting expenditures, such as nutrition.

As we examine the allocation of resources for health care, we should not assume that all health care spending necessarily benefits health care recipients; in fact some health care procedures and practices are *detrimental* to people's health. For example, some studies show that due to lack of resources, the poor are less likely to be overmedicated or to undergo unnecessary surgery or lab tests (Gould et al., 1989). The poor are not necessarily worse off for not being able to afford coronary by-pass surgery, Caesarian sections, and lots of tranquilizers. The expensive, high-tech practices that characterize much of modern medicine produce varying results; some are indeed medical wonders, some are merely satisfactory, and still others are negligible relative to the cost, effort, and sometimes pain they involve. Other results are downright iatrogenic, creating illness rather than healing it. In being denied the benefits of medical treatment, the poor have thus been also spared some of the risks.

The U.S. health care system is the product of a long history of considerable political maneuvering, haggling, and contesting (described briefly in this chapter and the next). This system places a particularly heavy emphasis upon *medical* treatment rather than *health* care. As a corollary, its focus is upon institutional and professional forms of care. Furthermore, the U.S. system—even more so than other capitalist systems—emphasizes the commodification of health and health care; making money is one important driving force in the system (cf. Riska, 1985). The interplay of numerous conflicting interests created the existing system, and the same interests would be exerted vigorously in the face of any effort to change the system. Knowledge of the relative power among these interest groups and their use of different power resources is the key to understanding this system.

The following is a greatly simplified sketch of the various economic interests represented in the U.S. health care system. In this chapter we shall consider the social organization and interests of some of the people involved in receiving or providing health care, especially those whose income is derived from providing such care. In Chapter 12 we shall describe the economic interests of large-scale organizations involved in the system, especially hospitals, medical industries, insurance companies, and government agencies. Because these interest groups vary dramatically in their relative power, some historical background of that power is helpful.

The development of economically powerful interest groups as major institutional actors in the U.S. health care policy debates was a nearly inevitable result of the combination of the laissez-faire ideology of the system and the relatively recent expansion of health care profits and markets. The various interest groups, especially the insurance industry whose profits in this sector would be eliminated were the country to adopt a system similar to Canada's, are spending enormous amounts of money on media campaigns, lobbying Congress and other influential politicians, and jockeying for a favorable position relative to other interest groups in the resulting program. It is virtually impossible to predict the political outcome and yet more difficult to anticipate the long-range effects—successes and failures—of some of the proposed changes. In order to think critically about a better future, we need to understand the *structural* sources of the present crises and the *systemic* problems that make the existing health care system so ineffective in providing good, affordable, health care to all citizens.

There now appears to be a general consensus that the U.S. health care system requires significant changes, but there is less consensus on what parts to change and what the long-range objectives should be. If we could build an entirely new system, what might it include? It is useful to imagine alternatives that might better address some of the health needs poorly met by the existing system. We need to consider many criteria—not merely cost—for a better system; for example, our nation could try to provide better access to care for rural and inner-city communities, more preventive measures for all age groups, medical education that discourages overspecialization and encourages better doctor-patient relationships, better decision making about use of surgery, medications, and medical technology, and hospitals that emphasize caring and not merely cost-effective tending of patients.

At root are also some fundamentally moral issues, which we rarely acknowledge or discuss in a public forum. For instance, what kind of nation do we want to be? Do we want to consider health as a commodity that the wealthy can buy in abundance, that the middle classes can afford occasionally in limited measure, and that the poor cannot have at all? Or do we, as a nation, want to consider health, like education, as something we should try to provide for all in order to promote the good of all?

RECIPIENTS

Although the U.S. system is ostensibly an open market of competing providers, health care services and products are not very sensitive to real competition or other market considerations for a number of structural reasons. As a consumer, the recipient-patient is in an inherently weak position, primarily because medicine has become so sophisticated that the patient typically lacks the expertise to evaluate services (e.g., from the doctor or the hospital) and products (e.g., pharmaceuticals or technological devices). Unlike standardized products, medical services are highly variable. To select a pediatrician or to evaluate the advice of a cardiologist, one cannot simply turn to a *Consumer's Report* rating. While there is much an individual can do to become an informed consumer of medical services, the enormous disparity in expertise between professional and patient places the consumer in a relatively weak position.

The market model also assumes that the consumer is the one making the choices in the marketplace, but in medical care the recipient rarely makes such decisions. Although ideologically the U.S. system emphasizes the patient's freedom to choose doctors, the actual choice may be severely constrained by the limited availability of doctors in a region, by insurance that is limited to certain providers, or by the assignment of a patient without private care to a clinic, military, or other institutional doctor. Whereas in 1984, 85 percent of employees' health insurance allowed the open choice of a provider, by 1988 only 28 percent of insured employees had this choice (Califano, 1989). This dramatic change was mainly due to cost-cutting efforts by employers and insurers. Furthermore, only a small proportion of insurance is marketed directly to consumers. Insurance plans are typically marketed to employers, rather than to the health care consumers themselves. Insurers compete only to insure the most profitable pools of employees—those who need the least health care, so market principles do not help reduce prices overall (Bodenheimer, 1990; Altman and Rodwin, 1988).

The recipient's doctor decides in which hospital to place the patient (usually according to where the doctor has privileges to practice). Unlike most other industrialized countries, in the United States the doctor does not relinquish care of (or income from) a patient who is hospitalized. Doctors maintain a relationship with a specific local hospital to which they admit their patients, and they bill their hospitalized patients separately from the hospital bill (Gabel and Redisch, 1979). This arrangement makes the hospital and private practitioner mutually dependent. Patients insured through various forms of "managed care," such as health maintenance organizations (HMOs, discussed further in Chapter 12), are further limited to hospitals participating in their insurance plan. Either way, the patient rarely actually chooses a hospital, and hospitals do not compete for customers in an open market. Like insurance companies, hospitals compete only for the most desirable pools of customers—those with ample insurance and whose care is most likely to result in net income for the hospital.

The doctor is probably the foremost guide of the patient's decisions about health services (Gertman, 1981). The doctor selects the pharmaceuticals and the treatment procedures; the doctor refers the patient to specific other doctors for specialized care and to specific outpatient labs and clinics for diagnostic or therapeutic services. The main decisions left to the patient are whether to accept the professional's decisions (and thus "comply") or to seek the services of another doctor or hospital. Lacking much decision-making power, the patient is hardly a consumer in an open, competitive marketplace.

Another feature of health care decisions that makes them difficult to weigh rationally as in a market situation is the high value our culture places on health and life. When we say our health is "priceless," we imply that we cannot imagine what limit we would pay to preserve that health. The consumer's medical treatment decisions are even more complicated by the fact that they often must be made quickly and under stress. Unlike buying a house, the consumer may have to decide to commit several hundred thousand dollars with no opportunity to "shop around" or even consider other options.

Recipients of medical care are among the least powerful interest groups in the U.S. system. Collectively, some groups of potential patients have wrested benefits from the system, but their successes are related to their political clout (e.g., senior citizens achieving funding of Medicare benefits) and/or their powerful socioeconomic position (e.g., upper-middle-class workers achieving substantial health care benefits from their employers). Less powerful groups of recipients, such as the working poor, have little or no influence against the interests of other parties in the system.

PHYSICIAN-PROVIDERS

The medical "cast of characters," their roles, and their remuneration are the result of numerous historical campaigns, such as medical doctors' achievement of professional dominance (described in Chapter 10). Other occupational groups likewise have asserted their interests in defining their domains, trying to achieve recognition as professions, and attempting to control the conditions of their work and pay. The resulting hierarchy of specialized health care occupations is fluid and changing, but all occupational interest groups utilize whatever resources of power they have to protect their interests. The prestige, power, financial success, and professional autonomy of medical doctors is, however, something of a standard against which other occupational groups measure themselves.

Fee-for-Service Payment

As noted in Chapter 10, medical doctors have achieved a legally recognized monopoly over the provision of most paid health care delivery as well as the training and admission of new personnel. The economic basis of physicians' service is a fee-for-service system in which the doctor typically charges the patient for each service provided at each visit. Technically, this system establishes an economic link between physician-provider and patient-recipient, but few contemporary doctor-patient relationships are so simple, since only about one-fifth of personal health care expenditures are paid directly by patients (Pear, 1993b). Various third parties, such as the government or insurance companies, are the source of the vast majority of payments, as discussed later.

Furthermore, although doctors typically bill on a fee-for-service basis, they are not necessarily paid in this way. For example, a doctor in group practice might receive a percentage of the collective receipts. The idea that the mode of payment forges a direct link between provider and consumer is thus more a myth, harking back to the "good old days" of more personal doctor-patient relationships; it also serves as an ideology to support the interests of physician-providers because the fee-for-service arrangement has allowed them great freedom to set their own terms of remuneration.

In the face of escalating medical costs, many critics are now examining how doctors set their fees. The practice of medicine in the United States is essentially entrepreneurial (i.e., incomes are made in the private business of selling of goods and especially services). What, then, are these services worth? As noted, the market for physicians' services is hardly open and competitive, and few consumers are in a position to barter knowledgeably or with real clout to obtain a "good value." There is considerable evidence that the level of fees is governed primarily by physicians' desired standard of living (Reinhardt, 1987). Overall, the profession is exceptionally well paid—in the top 3 percent of all earners in the United States (Altman and Rosenthal, 1990). If market principles drove the prices of physicians' services, U.S. medical services would cost less than comparable Canadian services because in the United States there are more doctors per capita (i.e., "supply") and because a far larger proportion of U.S. citizens cannot afford needed health care, thus reducing the "demand" for physician services. But physician fees have been relatively impervious to market principles, and U.S. doctors charge 2.4 times what Canadian doctors charge for the same services (Fuchs and Hahn, 1990).

Specialists, particularly surgeons, earn far more than general practitioners and other doctors engaged in the more labor-intensive primary care. Furthermore, during the 1980s, when national spending for physician services nearly doubled, surgeons' and other specialists' incomes grew very rapidly, while primary care doctors' incomes gained by only 5 percent (Pope and Schneider, 1992). By 1992, cardiac surgeons averaged $575,000 annual net income (i.e., earnings after paying costs of offices, insurance, and so on) and neurosurgeons averaged $449,000—several times more than the $119,000 average income of family practitioners, or $124,000 of pediatricians (Eckholm, 1993).

Because the U.S. health care system has no centralized planning or effective controls over the numbers of doctors in the various branches of medicine, there are dramatic and growing imbalances in the supply of specialists (cf. Fryer, 1991). The U.S. Department of Health and Human Services (1980) projected that by the year 2000 there will be an excess of about 150,000 doctors relative to the nation's needs and ability to pay. Despite this overall surplus, there is an expected shortage of family practitioners and other primary care doctors, which will be greatly outweighed by large surpluses of specialists. These imbalances will continue to grow dramatically because since the 1980s there has been a marked and continued drop in the number of medical school graduates who enter residency programs in primary care, such as family practice, rather than specialized programs, such as cardiology (Colwill, 1992).

Interestingly, the oversupply of specialists does not usually lead to competitive pricing. Indeed, rather than competition driving physicians' fees down, the existence of an oversupply of physicians in an area generally increases health care costs because the doctors compensate for the fact that each has fewer patients by raising their fees for each procedure and by recommending more procedures for each patient they treat. There is enormous variation from community to community in the fees charged for the same procedure. For example, an appendectomy would cost as little as $909 in Denver or as much as $1,377 in Los Angeles; a person in New York City would spend $5,123 for a hysterectomy, while the same operation in Dallas would cost $1,996 (Health Insurance Association of America, cited in Morganthau and Murr, 1993).

While variations in the costs of physician training and practice (e.g., office expenses and malpractice insurance) account for a portion of these dramatic differences in fees, they do not adequately explain them (Reinhardt, 1987). In recent years, the U.S. Justice Department has investigated numerous allegations of price fixing by medical professionals, and federal grand juries in several states considered criminal indictments on these charges (Freudenheim, 1988a; Gold, 1988). There is a fine and imprecise line between uniform pricing among doctors in a community and illegal price fixing. Nevertheless, doctors who set fees according to "what the market will bear" rarely undercut the "going" rate; rates are thus seldom particularly competitive within a single community. No matter how honest the fee schedule, the patient typically is not able to evaluate its appropriateness.[3]

Fee setting is in a state of flux because there is considerable struggle between the providers (e.g., doctors, hospitals) and the third-party agencies (e.g., Medicare, insurance companies) that pay the bills (Passell, 1993). For example, in 1988, a study

[3]This analysis focuses primarily on the economic pressures experienced by all physicians, honest and dishonest alike; illegal behavior is one extreme response to the opportunities for gain in medical practice. The intervention of third-party payment processes (e.g., Medicare, Medicaid, and insurance companies) and the bureaucratic management of medical economic transactions increase the opportunities for illegal kickbacks and fraudulent billing. Estimates suggest that between 25 and 40 percent of medical claims involve some form of deliberate overcharging (Roth, 1984). Third-party payers are relatively anonymous and distant from both the provider and recipient of services (e.g., a padded bill might be submitted directly to the third-party payer without scrutiny or verification by the patient).

commissioned by the Department of Health and Human Services recommended a complete overhaul of Medicare payments to doctors (see Smith, 1992, for a thorough analysis of the Physician Payment Review Commission and policy debates). The study found that the existing system of payments overcompensated doctors for invasive procedures such as surgery and for diagnostic tests, characteristic of much specialist care, but did not encourage them to spend time with patients in office visits and other time-consuming medical work, more characteristic of primary care. In 1992 Medicare began to phase in a new fee schedule based on the commission's findings, and commercial insurers may follow suit (Eckholm, 1993).

One analysis of components of physicians' income found that most of the increases between 1980 and 1989 were due to increases in the volume of procedures performed (e.g., surgical procedures and tests) and increased price per service rather than increased time spent with patients and other medical work. The study suggested that because insurance companies and Medicare were more likely to cover costs of surgery than time-consuming office visits, surgeons could command higher fees which were, in turn, less sensitive to market forces (Pope and Schneider, 1992).

Many doctors themselves are dissatisfied with how the fee-for-service arrangement has affected their everyday practice of medicine. One thoughtful physician described his realization of how detrimental these economic considerations had become:

> An aged patient had come in to the office and was talking about her aching feet. She not only had several very real physical problems but she was also very lonely and quite hypochondriacal. . . . As she continued to tell me how tired she was, I realized I wasn't listening. I was angry. What she needed was someone to sympathize with her, gently encourage her, and to make some simple suggestions that might alleviate her suffering. I knew from past experience that that kind of listening and empathetic presence would require at least half an hour, but I would only be able to charge $20 for an intermediate call, Medicare would discount the charge significantly, and my half after overhead, would be, maybe, $8. I also knew that if I just stood up, cut the woman off by giving her a prescription for a pain medicine and scheduled her for next month, I could charge the same $20 and move into the next room where another patient was waiting with a small laceration from which I would earn about $30 in perhaps 10 minutes.
>
> As soon as I recognized what I was angry about, I was ashamed. But the truth of my feelings was nonetheless real. . . . I was looking at my interactions with patients more and more as business transactions (Hilfiker, 1986).

These problems show how unsatisfactory the system of highly commodified health service, in which each aspect of care is delivered as a discrete entity, is for both patient and provider.

Clinical Decisions and Economic Considerations

There is considerable evidence that the present fee-for-service arrangement encourages unnecessary and questionable medical procedures, such as laboratory tests and surgery. Doctors and hospitals can add large markups to charges for lab tests. For example, during an office visit a blood sample may be drawn and sent to a mail-order laboratory for several tests. The physician may then add to the patient's bill not only the actual costs of the lab service but also a sizable profit (Reinhardt, 1987). One study found that doctors who had invested in imaging machines (e.g., radiograph and ultrasound equipment) for their offices ordered 4 to 4.5 times more tests than those who referred their patients to outside facilities in which they had no financial interest. They also charged significantly more per procedure than outside radiologists, resulting in charges that were 4.5 to 7.5 times greater (Hillman et al., 1990a). Provider profit is hardly the only reason for excessive use of testing. Many tests are ordered as part of "defensive" medicine to protect against malpractice suits, whereas others are requested by patients to allay fears of certain illnesses. Some estimates suggest that between 20 and 60 percent of these tests are unnecessary, adding nothing to the patient's diagnosis or treatment (Califano, 1989; Pear, 1987a; Luft, 1983).

Likewise, the fee-for-service system indirectly encourages doctors to resort to surgery rather than less invasive treatments. The decision to operate is based upon a number of discretionary choices, perceptions, evaluations, and decision rules that vary considerably among physicians and medical situations. All surgery involves assessing the probability that the operation will improve function, reduce pain, or increase the quality of life as balanced against the risks of complications from the surgery itself. For example, should a precancerous condition of the uterus be treated with a hysterectomy if the death rate from hysterectomies is greater than that for uterine cancer (Larned, 1977)? Is a carotid endarterectomy (a controversial operation that clears blockages in the major artery leading to the brain) appropriate if the patient is likely to suffer a stroke from the surgery itself (cf. Wilford, 1988)?

The fee-for-service system complicates the medical decision-making process with the added criterion of financial gain for doctor and hospital. For example, if a woman in labor does not give birth quickly, the physician experiences considerable incentive to perform a Caesarian section, a serious abdominal operation for which fee-for-service reimbursement is high and time required is relatively short, rather than work with the mother for a normal vaginal delivery for which the reimbursement is far lower proportionate to the time required. One study of rates of Caesarian sections for women whose previous deliveries had been Caesarians found that financial considerations were a significant predictor of the decision to operate (Stafford, 1991).

Especially for new and unproven procedures, there is considerable potential for physicians to conduct surgery for reasons that are inappropriate relative to the patient's health and needs. For example, a 1987 study found that only 35 percent of carotid endarterectomies were performed for "clearly appropriate indications" (Chassin et al., 1987). Similarly, critics assert that the U.S. rates of coronary by-passes and Caesarean sections are at least double the appropriate level (cf. Rasell, 1993; Califano, 1989; Shabecoff, 1987a). Compared to other industrialized countries, the United States has exceptionally high rates of surgery without concomitant lower rates of mortality. For example, U.S. surgeons perform coronary by-pass operations at six times the rate in England where, under the NHS, surgeons' income is not directly related to the number or type of operations performed, and mastectomies three times more frequently (Payer, 1988). We cannot infer that the difference is due only to unnecessary surgery (see Schwartz, 1984), but the socioeconomic incentive of fee-for-service is certainly one factor promoting high rates of surgery.[4]

In principle, the physician is an advocate for the patient, representing the patient's interests to insurers, hospitals, and other specialists on the case. There is an inherent conflict of interest, however, even for physicians who take their role as advocate seriously, when they are in a position to order for their patients procedures that also happen to be an important source of their own income (Gray, 1991; Luft, 1983). Physicians' judgment may be also subtly influenced by their hospital affiliates' pressures to fill beds. There is wide variation from community to community in the number of operations performed per capita, and studies found that two significant predictors of this difference were the rate of empty hospital beds and the local supply of surgeons (Evans, 1974; Lewis, 1969; see also Barron, 1989; Roth, 1984).

Financial incentives have even more impact on those kinds of physician services that are performed in response to patient demand rather than because of clear-cut medical need. Medical services for fertility or potency problems, sterilizations or abortions, obesity, or chronic pain exemplify these financial interests. A cosmetic surgeon is not likely to counsel a prospective patient that her nose is lovely without surgery.

Another incentive that affects physicians' decisions is their desire to learn the latest surgical procedures. Unlike pharmaceutical innovations, surgical innovations are not required to undergo extensive studies for effectiveness or risks. Nor is demonstrated surgical skill a prerequisite for a physician who does operate; in most states, any licensed medical doctor can legally perform surgery, regardless of expertise (see Barron, 1989; Millman, 1976). For example, in the late 1980s a new surgical procedure was introduced: The doctor removes a diseased gall bladder through a tiny incision, guiding the surgical instruments by watching an image of their movements projected on a screen by a miniature television camera inside the incision. If done correctly, laparoscopic gall bladder surgery can benefit many patients because it requires much less extensive incision than the previous technique. Laparoscopic surgery requires considerably more skill, however, especially because the visual image is a mirror image and because the surgeon's fine control of instruments must be more precise. In the absence of controls over new surgical techniques, many surgeons began practicing the technique on their patients after only a brief introduction, which was rarely taught in a hospital but often sponsored as part of the sales pitch of the companies that sell laparoscopic equipment. After several patient deaths and many serious injuries due to botched surgery, New York State moved to control the use of this new technique (Altman, 1992).

There are, however, no effective nationwide controls to prevent underqualified doctors from practicing this or other newly devised techniques. So long as the U.S. health care system continues to provide economic incentives for inappropriate surgery

---

[4]A possible indicator of the iatrogenic effects of unnecessary medical intervention occurred when, during a 1976 physicians' strike, the Los Angeles mortality rates dropped from an average of 19.8 deaths per 100,000 before the strike to 16.2 during the five-week strike, rising again to 20.4 at the strike's conclusion (*Science News*, 1978).

or other medical procedures, both doctors and hospitals will continue to be subject to the influence of economic considerations in deciding on patient treatment.

Even greater potential for conflict of interest is involved when the physician can receive secondary income from the treatment. When physicians own a "joint venture," such as a freestanding radiation therapy facility, diagnostic imaging facility, nursing home, or psychiatric hospital, they benefit financially by referring their patients, while evading antikickback laws (Mitchell and Scott, 1992). A California study of patients covered by workers' compensation found that physicians who referred patients to physical therapy, psychiatric, or magnetic resonance imaging (MRI) facilities of which they were owners tended to order significantly more services, including a higher proportion of medically inappropriate services, than did a control group of doctors with no financial interest in those facilities (Swedlow et al., 1992).

In 1993 federal regulatory agencies began to investigate some home health care providers, selling such products as drug and nutrition intravenous treatments for patient use at home, with questionable financial relationships with physician-providers. For instance, the investment scheme of T^2 Medical is open only to physician-investors who can refer patients. The company recruits a group of local doctors who make a nominal monetary investment, guarantee startup costs, and receive a significant quantity of shares in the parent company. For a one-time startup fee—quickly recouped from profits—the company helps the doctors set up their local home health products business to which they then refer their patients to obtain home health services and supplies. In addition to their profits on their shares in the parent company, the local doctors can reap thousands of dollars annually depending on how much business they send themselves as investment income, over and above their income for their professional practice (Meier, 1993b).

By 1991, more than 10 percent of U.S. doctors had invested in businesses to which they refer their patients; in some states, such as Florida, more than 40 percent of all doctors have such investments (Pear, 1991a; Pear and Eckholm, 1991). Contrary to claims of proponents of joint ventures, such facilities do not increase access to needed medical services for underserved populations; indeed they appear to have adverse effects on patients' access to care. One study of joint ventures in radiation therapy in Florida found that none of the facilities were located in inner-city neighborhoods or rural areas, compared to 11 percent of nonjoint venture facilities. Joint ventures received 39 percent of their revenues from patients with good insurance coverage, in contrast to 31 percent for nonjoint venture facilities. Furthermore, the principal personnel at joint venture facilities spent 18 percent less time with each patient than those at nonjoint venture facilities. Both the frequency and costs of radiation therapy at freestanding investor-owned facilities were 40 to 60 percent higher in Florida than the rest of the United States, despite the absence of other factors that might explain the difference in use and costs (Mitchell and Sunshine, 1992).

The murky link between physician-investors' conflicts of interest, medically inappropriate treatments, and runaway health care costs is well illustrated by the U.S. program for end-stage renal disease (ESRD), a chronic, debilitating, and often fatal disease of the kidneys. One treatment for ESRD is hemodialysis. When it was first developed, hemodialysis was such an expensive technology that it was systematically rationed. In response to a concerted political campaign by well-organized groups of patients and providers, however, in 1972 the U.S. government passed an amendment to Medicare legislation that provided federal reimbursement for ESRD treatments, regardless of the patient's age.

Even in the first year of the program, the actual costs were many times the projected costs, and since then national expenditures for ESRD treatments have escalated dramatically. By 1991, the ESRD program annual per-patient cost ($29,000) was nine times higher than the average Medicare per-patient cost (Iglehart, 1993). One reason is that the legislation lifted barriers preventing people from being dialyzed and encouraging dialysis for *all* sufferers of ESRD, even though dialysis is not an appropriate or even beneficial treatment for many (Simmons and Marine, 1984). Ironically, the United States, one of the few industrialized nations with no overall policy for the equitable distribution of health care, became the most liberal subsidizer of dialysis for all. In 1989, the U.S. rate of treatment for renal failure was 2.2 times that of Canada and 3.8 times that of all European countries (Iglehart, 1993).

A second reason for the dramatic escalation of ESRD therapy costs was that in the United States, unlike other countries, the dominant mode of treatment was in-center dialysis, rather than the less expensive home dialysis or kidney transplants (Kutner, 1982). After the passage of the ESRD program in 1973, in-center dialysis became a booming business; the number of for-profit dialysis facilities more than tripled in the 1980s alone. To curb runaway costs, in 1983 Medicare reduced the reimbursement rate for outpatient dialysis and subsequently froze the rate altogether. Nevertheless, for-profit dialysis facilities continued to proliferate and earn profits. Physician-owners compensated for reduced reimbursement rates by giving dialysis to more and more patients, including a much larger proportion of patients for whom the treatment is of questionable benefit and those for whom another treatment (e.g., home dialysis or renal transplant) would be more suitable. The for-profit dialysis centers also maintained profits by reducing their operating costs, for example, by substituting less skilled staff for registered nurses and by reusing dialyzers. Such changes raise questions about the quality of their care (Iglehart, 1993; see also Riska, 1985; Miller, 1983). Although many sick people have been helped by the ESRD program, the drive for profits by many participating physicians and dialysis centers have propelled the costs ($6.6 billion in 1991) and influenced professional judgments.

The potential for physician profits on such secondary gains has dramatically increased in recent years with the expansion of high-tech medicine. In 1991, the AMA adopted a policy discouraging physician referral to businesses in which they have an interest, but the policy is only advisory and voluntary, so it carries little weight and no sanctions. The organized American medical profession has been historically very ambivalent about ethical problems tied to financial interests; unlike law, business, and public service, medicine has not seriously addressed financial conflicts of interest as a professional ethical issue until the 1980s. Even though fee splitting, kickbacks, and other questionable commercial practices have been a problem in professional practice since the turn of the century, in the second half of this century, the AMA steadily weakened its stance against abuses to placate its members and reflect their economic interests (Rodwin, 1993, 1992).

Regardless of whether physicians are conscious of their economic interests in clinical decisions, the profit connection in the United States results in very different patterns of patient care than in countries where doctors cannot profit from the treatments they recommend. The ESRD program provides at least one important lesson for U.S. policymakers as they consider how to expand health care access to all citizens: the necessity of restructuring physician payment programs such that conflicts of interest cannot affect physicians' decisions about whether or how to treat their patients.

Malpractice: Economic Burdens and Regulation

The issue of malpractice is related to the socioeconomic basis of provider-recipient relationships. Around the turn of the century, medical societies provided for the mutual defense of members against malpractice suits. Courts deferred to local doctors' judgment as "expert witnesses," which made it virtually impossible for aggrieved patients to get one doctor to testify against another. Furthermore, the medical societies were so successful in protecting their members from suit that they were able to obtain very favorable insurance rates, whereas nonmembers were often unable to obtain insurance at all (Starr, 1982: 111).

In the latter half of the twentieth century, however, the legal and cultural climate changed. Patients became more willing to take doctors to court, partly because of the growing impersonality of economic relationships described previously. Rising expectations of the wonders of medical science may also have both enhanced doctors' prestige and remuneration, while creating unrealistic public beliefs about what doctors could accomplish. Simultaneously, courts allowed the wider use of outside experts and cosmopolitan rather than local standards of care, while legislation—especially since the 1970s—clarified patients' rights, such as the right to informed consent for procedures. The result has been a dramatic increase in malpractice litigation, increasingly large awards to patient-plaintiffs, and soaring malpractice insurance premiums, the cost of which is generally passed on to the consumer.

The expansion of malpractice litigation has created a number of additional powerful interest groups in the health care arena. Malpractice insurance is typically offered as part of a for-profit insurance industry. Lawyers, courts, and layers of legal paper-processing organizations have likewise become major recipients of the health care dollar. An estimated 60 percent of the billions paid annually for malpractice insurance goes not to aggrieved patients but to the insurance and litigation industries (Califano, 1989). At the same time, however, the expense of litigation prevents the vast majority of injured patients from going to court to obtain *any* compensation (cf. Rosenthal, 1988).

Furthermore, the fear of malpractice suits encourages doctors to practice "defensive" medicine in which clinical decisions are made with an eye to protecting themselves from lawsuits. By practicing defensive medicine, hospital staff often construct a patient's chart as a case record designed more to stand up in court than to describe the patient's actual situation. Communication about the patient then takes place informally, off the record, such as by one specialist writing notes to another (Millman, 1976: 145). Defensive medicine also results in unnecessary tests and procedures, costing an estimated $20 billion per year (Califano, 1989). One study estimated that defensive medicine accounts for as much as 15 percent of total physician billings (Freudenheim, 1987a; Reinhardt, 1987). For example, fearing lawsuits if they deliver imperfect babies, obstetricians are more likely to order fetal monitoring during labor and are more likely to perform possibly unnecessary Caesarian sections if the monitor indicates any signs of fetal distress. Another impact of the fear of malpractice suits is that doctors may avoid treating high-risk patients or may shift their practice to a lower-risk specialization; for example, by 1987 more than 12 percent of obstetricians reported that they had left obstetrics and were practicing only gynecology (Tolchin, 1989a).

Physicians' fears of malpractice lawsuits may have indirectly increased the costs of health care, while the vast majority of well-founded cases of malpractice are never brought to court. Most cases that reach the courts are reasonable claims. One study of over 30,000 patients who had been hospitalized found that 3.7 percent had suffered some injury as a result of medical care; of those, 28 percent were injured due to doctor negligence or substandard care. Although 14 percent of the injuries were fatal and nearly 3 percent were permanently disabling, only one out of every 9.6 cases of injury due to negligence resulted in a lawsuit (Brennan et al., 1991). Another study found that most malpractice cases won by patients were, in fact, well-founded cases of substandard care and that the amount of payment awarded closely correlated with the severity of the injury (Taragin and Wilczek, 1992).

While the profit incentive of lawyers and insurers in this system is obvious, theirs is an understandable entrepreneurial response to two unmet needs in the U.S. health care system as it has developed. First, the system has had no adequate method of identifying, controlling, or punishing physicians who were incompetent, negligent, or otherwise detrimental to the health of their patients. One of the prerogatives achieved by medical dominance was the right to peer review: Only doctors could effectively sanction malpractice. Historically, however, doctors were very reticent to judge each other. Once a physician passed the initial screening process and obtained a license to practice, fellow doctors were highly unlikely to constrain that practice, much less to take it away. Indeed, typically doctors in a community supported each other, both legally and more subtly. For example, fellow doctors would cover up for incompetent surgeons by doing "ghost" surgery for them. Similarly, although in principle hospitals could refuse staff privileges to doctors whose practices were medically questionable, most relied on local doctors as the source of patients and thus could not afford to alienate them (Millman, 1976: 120–135).

A second reason for the rise in importance of malpractice suits is that the nation provides few other avenues for a family to obtain recompense for the actual costs created by medical mistakes. Iatrogenic medical practices often create years of additional medical expenses as well as the loss of income due to disability, yet the U.S.

health care system offers little assistance with such costs. Most patients have no safety net of economic help for serious medical problems. Thus, malpractice suits become the last-chance effort to obtain economic relief.

Litigation is, however, a highly unsatisfactory way to provide recompense for medical mistakes because few people with legitimate claims can afford the long and expensive courtroom route. Lawyers typically accept only the cases most likely to win and most likely to obtain a high award, of which the lawyer gets a percentage. In the United States, the vast majority of persons injured by medical mistakes ultimately receive no financial help whatsoever.

By contrast, in Sweden, where equitable access to health care is a citizen's right, these functions are addressed by the public health system. Their Patient Compensation Fund is publicly financed no-fault insurance that compensates both economic and noneconomic aspects of injury, and settles claims rapidly according to a predetermined schedule. The mere fact of injury is sufficient for compensation; claimants do not have to prove that anyone was at fault. Relatively very few claims are arbitrated beyond this point, and patients are generally satisfied that compensation is equitable and objective. A completely separate mechanism, the Medical Responsibility Board—a freestanding national governmental body—deals with malpractice complaints against physicians. It investigates reported incidents and can employ a range of sanctions, from a reprimand to a recommendation that the National Board of Health and Welfare revoke a physician's license to practice. In 1982, the Responsibility Board's rate of disciplinary actions was 3.3 per 1,000 physicians, compared to an average rate of 2.4 per 1,000 by U.S. disciplinary boards (Rosenthal, 1988).

Corporatization of Medical Production

We still have the image of the doctor as a solo practitioner and independent businessperson, but in fact the trend is toward greater corporatization of health care delivery, as medical production converts to corporate forms of ownership and management, such as incorporated group practice, a health maintenance organization (HMO), or a for-profit hospital corporation (Starr, 1982: 420–449). By 1989 about one-half of U.S. doctors were salaried employees (Altman and Rosenthal, 1990). In the 1990s this trend has accelerated as large, for-profit corporations, such as Caremark International, have bought out numerous group practices and clinics nationwide (Freudenheim, 1993b). The projected oversupply of physicians, new patterns of hospital ownership and management, and changes in third-party insurance and government regulation make it likely that yet greater proportions of physicians will be employed in salaried or other somewhat dependent arrangements. Some of these developments are discussed further later.

As a result of these new structural arrangements, health care providers are losing some of the autonomy they gained in their rise to professional dominance (Light and Levine, 1988). Some observers have referred to this as the proletarianization of the medical profession, implying that by being employed in a corporate setting, doctors are being reduced to the status of wage laborers (McKinlay and Stoeckle, 1988;

McKinlay and Archer, 1985). However, while corporatization clearly reduces doctors' independence in some areas of their work, their resulting status is not merely that of the proletariat relative to the industrial bourgeoisie.

The very rise of the technologically advanced, hospital-based medical practices that enhanced the prestige and authority of the medical profession in the first half of the century has in the second half also produced conditions conducive to the profession's corporate dependence. Modern medicine is capital intensive; few solo practitioners can afford to finance even modest practices. Thus, they turn to medical groups, labs, clinics, and hospitals to provide the necessary equipment and support services.

Nevertheless, their relations with their economic sponsors are hardly as disempowering as those faced by the industrial proletariat. Unlike the proletariat, which has only its wage labor to sell, the medical profession retains monopoly control over much needed, complex skill and knowledge (Navarro, 1988). Also, as Derber (1984, 1983) noted, the proletariat is disempowered by the capitalist employers' consolidation of control over the functions of both production capitalization (i.e., supplying costly facilities for making products) and market mediation (i.e., relationships, such as marketing, by which the product is converted into income). By contrast, while increasingly fewer individual practitioners control these two aspects of their medical production, neither are these two functions usually united in a single employer. Typically the production-capitalization functions reside in what Derber (1984: 220) called doctors' "proprietary sponsors" (e.g., hospitals), while the market mediation functions are performed by "market sponsors" (e.g., third-party insurers). While both forms of sponsors place constraints on the conditions of physicians' work, they lack the power enjoyed by capitalist employers over the entire process of production.

Furthermore, the constraints imposed by doctors' sponsors do not reduce all areas of physician control equally. For example, a hospital employer may reduce a physician's control over scheduling and work load, but impose relatively few constraints on the physician's autonomy over technical skills and knowledge (Derber, 1984). The structural situation most threatening to the doctor's professional autonomy is one in which a single agency, such as a for-profit hospital chain, successfully consolidates the production-capitalization functions and the market-mediation functions (e.g., by selling its own prepaid insurance to other employers), while also monopolizing the market in its area (see Gray, 1991).

The trend toward corporatization has also had an impact on patients as well as professional providers. The corporate interests of hospitals and insurers have thrust considerations of cost-effectiveness and profit maximization into the fore. As noted earlier, today proportionately far fewer patients are free to choose their own providers as compared with a decade ago. Who speaks for the interests of the patient-recipient? As we have described, physician-providers often experience conflicting interests in recommending procedures for their patients; nevertheless, their authority used to be a very powerful source of advocacy on behalf of patients (Mechanic, 1986). If a doctor said, "This patient needs to be hospitalized," that decision was once accepted as authoritative by third-party insurers and hospitals. Physicians' sponsors today, however, are more likely to discourage, question, and even override their professional opinions (Rosenthal, 1993a).

NURSE-PROVIDERS AND OTHER HELPING PROFESSIONALS

As noted in Chapter 10, the rise of the medical profession to professional dominance entailed the subordination, cooptation, or elimination of virtually all competing health care professions. For example, in some countries pharmacists are relatively independent and can concoct and dispense most medicines without much control by physicians. When patients are simply able to go to the pharmacist for advice and medicine, however, they have much less need to see the doctor. As early as 1906, the AMA's campaign against patent medicines (i.e., proprietary drugs) produced doctors' legal monopoly over the prescription of powerful medicines. Commercial medicine companies had to market their products to doctors rather than to customers (Starr, 1982: 127–134). As a result the nascent profession of pharmacy was subordinated to the medical profession, although many pharmacists do enjoy relative autonomy in their working conditions.

Nonphysician practitioners in the predominantly male professions of dentistry, podiatry, optometry, pharmacy, and chiropractic have also been able to retain relatively independent practices, even while the medical profession exerts its organizational control. Traditionally female health care professions, such as nursing, have not fared so well; they have been kept subordinate in pay, working conditions, educational programs, and bureaucratic organization. The vicissitudes of nursing as an occupation are almost prototypical of the larger historical process of rationalization of health services delivery, which promoted the ever-increasing specialization of tasks interwoven in complex—usually bureaucratic—organizations. The development of nursing and various allied health professions, such as laboratory technology, physical therapy, and radiological technology, is a result of nearly total gender stratification of medical work.

The Development of Nursing

Early nursing was typically private care by an unpaid member of the family or a paid family helper. It was part of the domestic economy and inextricably linked with women's roles. One of the founders of professional nursing, Florence Nightingale, wrote, "Every woman is a nurse" (1860: 3). She also argued that women should not aspire to be doctors because nursing meshed with their "natural" abilities. Nightingale's hospital reforms envisioned genteel nurses competently running hospitals as domestic managers, completely supportive of and dependent on doctors, who were analogous to the male heads of household (cf. Melosh, 1982; Ehrenreich and English, 1973).

Even today, nursing is a predominantly female occupation; in 1990, 94.8 percent of all registered nurses (RNs) were women, but only 20.1 percent of physicians were women. Table 11.1 shows the distribution of women among several health occupations. The gender segregation of these two jobs means that gender-role expectations figure prominently in the working relationships between doctor and nurse (Brown, 1983). Traditionally, the nurse has been expected to be deferential, nurturing, and submissive, even while taking an active role in the patient's care. In the 1960s, researchers observed a series of strategies by which nurses communicated their recommendations without appearing to make a recommending statement, while physicians asked for nurses' recommendations without appearing to be asking for help (Hughes, 1988; Stein, 1967). While recent studies show nurses to be less deferential and more assertive than in the 1960s, changes in the doctor-nurse interaction occurred more in the behavior of nurses than in the reciprocal roles or expectations of doctors (Porter, 1992; Stein et al., 1990). The historical emphasis upon "womanly" qualities in nursing has been both an ideological hindrance to professional recognition and a basis for nurses to seek a distinctive, caring way of relating to patients in contrast to the impersonality of the bioscientific medical model (Reverby, 1987a).

In the early twentieth century, two major developments in medical care shaped the direction of nursing: the shift to hospital-based care and the growing emphasis upon scientific medicine. The latter, together with many technological developments, created the need for highly trained assistance for doctors; the knowledge and skills required of nurses expanded rapidly. RNs are the single largest group of health care professionals, accounting for about one-fifth of all health workers (Melosh, 1982).

Previously hospitals had been little more than sick wards of the poor-house, staffed by minimally qualified nurses drawn from the lowest social classes. Male attendants worked in men's wards and female attendants in women's wards. Only those who had no family or means of private care were nursed in hospital settings. In response to the technological developments and public relations campaigns described in Chapter 12, however, middle- and upper-class persons began to use hospitals for

TABLE 11.1   Selected Health Occupations by Total Employment (1990)

Occupation	Total Employed (in thousands)	Black (%)	Hispanic (%)	Female (%)
Physicians	575	3.2	4.4	20.1
Dentists	150	1.5	2.7	10.1
Registered nurses	1712	7.1	2.4	94.8
Laboratory technicians and technologists	317	13.4	6.8	75.7
Dental hygienists	84	1.1	3.3	99.8
Licensed practical nurses	445	16.5	4.4	95.0
Nursing aides and orderlies	1506	31.2	6.9	89.2

Source: U.S. Bureau of the Census, *Statistical Abstract of the United States, 1992.*Washington, DC, 1992: 392–394.

sickness, surgery, and childbirth. As medical and nursing education became hospital-centered, hospitals became more prestigious and profitable rather than totally charitable institutions. Their new fee-paying clientele accordingly expected a much higher standard of care (Melosh, 1982: 15–35; Rosenberg, 1987: 212–236).

Hospitals were expanding rapidly and needed the very kind of disciplined, trained workers they found in nurses; however, the profession was further subordinated as it lost control over nursing education. Hospital administrators established nursing schools so that the student nurses would serve the hospital. Student nurses put in 60- and 70-hour workweeks for two or three years of ward service in exchange for their subsistence and a small sum (typically $10 a year) for uniforms and books (Rosenberg, 1987: 220–221). The economic disincentives and the structural subordination of nurses made the occupation increasingly unattractive to men. For women, however, nursing was one of the few "respectable" occupations and was considered an appropriate preparation for marriage as well as a source of income.

Along with the growing emphasis upon scientific training of medical doctors in the early decades of the twentieth century, many voices within nursing urged greater professionalization and standardization of training. By mid-century, there was considerable division between those nurses advocating hospital training and those urging higher education (Melosh, 1982: 67–76). At stake was the relatively greater professional independence of nursing as well as ideas about the proper role of the nurse.

Technological developments in medicine, especially in the second half of the century, further increased specialization in hospital nursing. After World War II, when hospital-based medical care expanded rapidly, nursing was organized according to stratified functions, with routine bedside tasks and lower-skill nursing tasks relegated to LPNs (licensed practical nurses), aides, and orderlies, under the direction of RNs (registered nurses). While this practice resulted in cost savings in hospital payrolls and some organizational prestige for RNs, it also resulted in RNs serving as managers more than as nurses. Greater prestige and pay were incentives for some upper-echelon nurses to specialize for work in the intensive care unit, cardiac unit, or operating room.

Beginning in the 1970s and developing rapidly in the 1980s, hospitals have been reorganizing the nursing labor process in a system called *primary nursing*, in which a single professional nurse (RN) is responsible for completion of all physicians' orders for a set of patients. This reorganization greatly tightens the hospital management's control by unambiguously identifying a single employee responsible for all nursing tasks for each patient (Brannon, 1990). The system has produced greater opportunities for nurses to do patient education and psychosocial caring, but only where hospitals have been willing to pay for enough RNs to cover all the work previously done by the lower-paid strata of nursing staff. Combined with inadequate hospital staffing levels and higher proportions of seriously ill inpatients, however, primary nursing greatly intensifies nurses' workload, increases time pressures, stress, and the likelihood of dangerous errors (Noble, 1993).

The Socioeconomic Status of "Female" Health Professions

The structural subordination of nursing relative to both physicians and hospital bureaucracies has worked severely against the economic interests of nurses. Nurses' wages have historically been low, and between 1971 and 1987 pay raises failed to keep apace of increases in the cost of living. In 1989 the average salary paid by hospitals for nurses at the top of the pay scale was only $32,160 (Tolchin, 1989b), or less than one-third of the average nonspecialist physician's net income.

Patients and their insurance companies are not generally billed separately for nursing services, as they are for the services of, for example, radiologists, anesthesiologists, and physical therapists. Thus employers of nurses try to keep wages low and to maximize the labor they can extract for those wages. Relative to other professions with comparable years of training, hospital nurses experience several other important occupational disadvantages: unfavorable hours and shift work, high stress, and little opportunity for advancement in status or pay. For example, in 1986 RNs received a maximum salary that was 36.4 percent higher than the starting salary; by comparison, accountants received a 192.7 percent increase, engineers received 183.6 percent, and chemists received 231 percent (Tolchin, 1989b).

The hospital nurse shortage of the 1980s was, in part, a by-product of this change in the labor process, although it was also due to the unattractively low salaries identified with nursing and the expanded opportunities for women as health professionals outside hospital nursing (e.g., as doctor or nurse-practitioner). As hospitals reorganized into the primary nursing model, they hired more RNs at the expense of the less well-paid LPNs and other ancillary nursing personnel. Between 1985 and 1989, wages for general-duty RNs increased by 11.0 percent, while wages for LPNs increased only 0.2 percent, and nursing assistants' wages dropped by 3.7 percent (Pope and Menke, 1990). The professionalization of nursing is somewhat akin to "occupational gentrification," (Sacks, 1988) in that as jobs are upgraded, they become increasingly unaffordable to the working classes who previously occupied them (e.g., by requiring four years of college training rather than two-year community college degrees).

In the health care industry, most of the occupations are gender segregated (i.e., one gender accounts for 70 percent or more of those employed). Table 11.1 shows that the health-related occupations of greatest power, prestige, and income are concentrated mainly among white men. Women make up at least 75 percent of all health industry workers, while constituting only about 42 percent of the national work force. Not only are predominantly female occupations generally low paid, but women also earn less than men in the same job categories (Aries and Kennedy, 1986).

Predominantly female health care occupations are also characterized by relatively low amounts of professional autonomy. Nurses, medical technologists, dental hygienists, and other auxiliary workers frequently assume many of the less interesting and more time-consuming tasks of hospitals and doctors' offices. These "physician extenders" are able to do as much as 80 percent of the routine tasks of office medical practice; similarly, dental assistants can assume tasks such as cleaning, patient education, and X-ray work that would otherwise account for most of the dentist's time. The amount the doctor or dentist can charge for these services is roughly the same, regardless of whether they are done by the doctor or dentist or delegated to a relatively low-paid assistant.

The medical profession has used its regulatory and educational controls to prevent serious competition from these auxiliary professions (Brown, 1983, 1978). Their control also enables them to suppress the wages paid to other health care professionals. For example, by using the states' Medical Practice Acts to abolish private X-ray laboratories, radiologists (MDs) were able to control the terms of employment of X-ray technicians and technologists, and to prevent them from competing with radiologists' own labs and those of hospitals.

Similarly, the independent practice of medicine by physicians' assistants was made illegal in all states where the licensing boards are controlled by doctors. Since 1971, however, a majority of states have amended their Medical Practice Acts to allow nurses to diagnose some conditions, prescribe some drugs, and perform other medical duties under certain conditions; similarly, since 1978 federal guidelines have allowed direct reimbursement to nurse-practitioners for Medicare patients. Home health care is one area in which nurse-practitioners have been particularly active; they have also served extensively in locations (such as the inner city and remote rural areas) considered undesirable by many physicians. With the predicted surplus of physicians, it remains to be seen whether these less expensive providers will be allowed to continue to practice (Sorkin, 1986).

The tension between physicians and other health care professionals is best illustrated by the competition posed by a new professional classification, the nurse-midwife. Obstetricians have vehemently opposed allowing them to deliver babies. Where they were not successful in preventing nurse-midwives from practicing, physicians often were able to limit the conditions under which they could practice (Brown, 1978). Nurse-midwives' inability to obtain independent insurance also prevented their practice in many states. The market for infant deliveries is shrinking, and there is a marked oversupply of obstetricians (U.S. Department of Health and Human Services, 1980). As a surgical specialty, obstetrics has responded to this market condition by greatly increasing the number of Caesarian sections. By contrast, nurse-midwives are trained to help the mother to have her baby naturally; they emphasize a more holistic approach to the mother and child, including both prenatal and early infancy care and education. Their market strategy has been to offer comprehensive services at a much lower cost while appealing to consumers looking for a more satisfying birth experience. Thus far, both groups of providers have been somewhat successful; obstetricians have kept their incomes high, despite fewer deliveries, and nurse-midwives have attracted a growing number of customers while enjoying a greater professional autonomy than most nurses (Little, 1982).

For patients, there is no obvious immediate benefit of these conflicts among health care professionals. For example, giving nurses greater professional recognition and pay may create a happier work force, which may or may not result in better patient care. It may actually increase the professional distance between the nurse and patient. Greater emphasis upon nonphysician providers should be more cost-effective, but the patient will not necessarily realize any financial benefits if the savings go to a hospital chain, insurance company, or group medical practice. Although many of the predominantly female health care professions hold ideals of providing greater caring and patient service compared to the medical profession, the trend toward their specialization and professionalization may promote the further disempowerment of the patient.

NONPROFESSIONAL HEALTH CARE WORKERS

The health industry employs a vast number of nonprofessional workers, such as orderlies, clerks, receptionists, kitchen help, and housekeeping staff. Employment in the health industry reflects patterns of stratification in the larger society, especially occupational segregation by gender, class, and race. White men from well-to-do families disproportionately occupy the jobs at the top of the health industry, while health care work at the bottom of the stratification heap is typically done by black women. Black workers are overrepresented in the menial and low-status occupations, such as practical nurse or home health aide (Aries and Kennedy, 1986). Black women are particularly concentrated in the nursing home and home care labor markets, and are far more likely than white women working in such nonhospital services to have earnings below the poverty level (Feldman et al., 1990).

Furthermore, women and blacks are concentrated in occupations with the least opportunity for advancement. Especially in hospital settings, there is almost total lack of job mobility, even though various workers can and do perform tasks appropriate to higher echelon workers. The resulting structural inequality promotes conflict, with the technical and managerial elite (doctors and administrators) separated from and opposing the interests of the lower-status workers. Although some of this conflict is muted by the professional ideals of nurses and others, there is a growing pressure for unionization and other collective expressions of worker dissatisfaction (Sacks, 1988; Ehrenreich and Ehrenreich, 1978).

The interests of nonprofessional health workers, like those of nurses and doctors, do not necessarily coincide with the interests of patients. At the same time, however, the health care system's failure to compensate, regulate, and educate its lower-level care givers adequately, has been seriously detrimental to patients. One study of patient abuse in a nursing home noted that the personnel recruited were socially marginal, poorly educated or trained, and generally uncommitted to their work. Their low-paid, low-prestige custodial care of a powerless population of elderly patients promoted neglect and abuse (Stannard, 1973).

Similarly, the U.S. health care system's recent emphasis upon home care has resulted in a new cadre of underpaid, undervalued aides who help the infirm with cooking, cleaning, bathing, dressing, and moving about their homes. Although some home health aides work for nonprofit agencies, many are employed by commercial agencies contracted by Medicare, state or city agencies, or insurance companies.

By the end of 1987, there were some 50,000 such workers in New York City alone. Most earned less than $7,000 per year (an income at or below the poverty level), and had no job security, no overtime pay, and few or no medical benefits (Iverem, 1988). A 1985 study by the Hunter College School of Social Work (Donovan, 1987) found that 99 percent of these workers were women with a median age of 47; 70 percent were black, 26 percent were Hispanic, and nearly half were immigrants. The typical home health aide was the primary breadwinner for her household, with three to four children to support. Because of their poor remuneration, these women and their families had had no health insurance for 92 percent of their *own* health problems in the previous year (cf. Feldman et al., 1990).

Thus, while federal, state, and private insurers enjoy the cost savings of home care compared with hospitalization, their savings are subsidized by a large number of poor working women. Home health aides are even more disadvantaged than similarly unskilled workers in hospitals because they have none of the social interaction, reassurance, job stability, economic rewards, or prestige associated with working in a medical setting. Further incentives to exploit home health aides exist when the agency employing them operates as a for-profit health industry (Fine, 1988).

SUMMARY

The social organization of health care services in any health system reflects the stratification and power of various interest groups in that society. Because of the commodified, laissez-faire system in the United States, these interests are particularly obvious as they compete for available resources and control. Social stratification and power are important considerations for understanding the quality of health services; these structural factors strongly influence how people behave. Stratification is related to the social distance between patient and providers and between various levels of health service workers; it is also related to imbalances in the socioeconomic power of recipients and providers.

The stratification and power of these interest groups are also linked to structural incentives and disincentives that affect the quality of health services. Many of the problems of the U.S. health care system can be best understood in light of these powerful socioeconomic structural features, which any attempt to solve the problems of quality, access, and cost must address. In Chapter 12 we shall continue our examination of the socioeconomic interests in U.S. health care with a discussion of the large-scale organizations that are increasingly powerful in this system.

RECOMMENDED READINGS

Articles

Nancy Aries and Louanne Kennedy, "The health labor force: The effects of change," pp. 196–207 in P. Conrad and R. Kern, eds., *The Sociology of Health and Illness*. New York: St. Martin's Press, 1986.

Doris R. Fine, "Women caregivers and home health workers: Prejudice and inequity in home health care," *Research in the Sociology of Health Care* 7, 1988: 105–117.

John B. McKinlay, "A case for refocusing upstream: The political economy of illness," pp. 509–523 in P. Conrad and R. Kern, eds., *The Sociology of Health and Illness*. New York: St. Martin's Press, 1994.

Howard D. Schwartz, Peggy L. de Wolf, and James K. Skipper, Jr., "Gender, professional-ization and occupational anomie: The case of nursing," pp. 559–569 in H. D. Schwartz, ed., *Dominant Issues in Medical Sociology*. New York: Random House, 1987.

Books

Susan Reverby, *Ordered to Care: The Dilemma of American Nursing*, 1850–1945. Cambridge: Cambridge University Press, 1987. A thoughtful reexamination of the role of nursing in its economic and organizational setting.

CHAPTER TWELVE

Economic Interests and Power in Health Care

The health care system in the United States is essentially a *medical* care system. As noted in Chapter 11, medical care is not the same as health care. Medical care generally emphasizes acute illness and inadequately addresses other health needs; it emphasizes curative interventions and gives much less attention to prevention, palliation, and basic care. With the development of high-technology and specialized medicine, the medical care system has become hospital based and heavily reliant on large, bureaucratic organizations.

The structure and functions of these medical organizations reflect the structure of the larger society. The medical care system is stratified largely according to the class, gender, ethnic, and other divisions in the whole society. In the United States, the medical care system is a major part of the larger system of economic production and consumption; it is structured to allow various interest groups to make significant profits and to control considerable resources in medical production. Although we tend to think of medical care as a small-scale service offered by individual providers, such as a family doctor or a nurse, in a laissez-faire medical system such as that of the United States, medical care is big business. The powerful economic interests involved in medical businesses—medical groups, hospitals, nursing homes, pharmaceutical companies, insurance companies, medical technology corporations, and so on—often supersede the interests of both sick people and individual health care providers.

As noted in Chapter 11, there is considerable evidence that the American health care system is in crisis. A large proportion of the citizens are not served by the system, and many of those who are served receive insufficient and inferior care. Despite many cost-cutting efforts, the amount spent on health care consumes an enormous proportion of the nation's gross national product, and the costs of most medical treatment continue to spiral upward.

The dramatically increased scale of profits and power commanded by medical businesses has been itself a factor in the crisis of the U.S. health care system. Cost-accelerating profits that in the 1950s seemed like merely deplorable inconsistencies in the system have escalated by the 1990s to an unsustainable burden, depriving many people of their sense of security in matters of health and illness, and threatening to tear apart a minimally integrated health care system. Well-financed interest groups are also pouring resources into influencing any government rethinking of health care policies; each is vying to protect and enhance its power and profits. In this chapter we offer an overview of some of these large-scale medical care organizations. In addition to examining the structural power of health care businesses, we shall hold the U.S. system up to three criteria for evaluation: quality, cost, and access. We shall describe some of the social-structural factors that influence these three aspects.

HEALTH CARE INSTITUTIONS

The provision of health care in large-scale institutions, such as hospitals, is a relatively recent phenomenon. In the early nineteenth century, most sick people were treated and nursed in their homes. Almshouse wards were the main form of hospital, nursing home, and insane asylum, offering a modicum of care and custody to indigent persons without a stable home or family members to provide care. These were hardly desirable places to go to get well. They were run as charitable institutions, with utterly paternalistic organization as well as little real curative function (Rosenberg, 1987; Rosner, 1986).

The Development of the Modern Hospital

By the time of the early twentieth century reformation of the medical profession (described in Chapter 9) hospitals too had changed dramatically. Both hospitals and medicine were becoming more rationalized: science oriented, specialized, and bureaucratized. Many towns established community hospitals, which lacked the stigma of the poorhouse wards. The rapid development of new medical "tools," such as antiseptic conditions for surgery, X-rays, and clinical laboratories, provided an important rationale for centering care in hospitals, which could capitalize these facilities and provide the necessary support staff. Thus, by the 1920s hospitals were capital-intensive institutions. Their prestige and growth hinged on the practice of surgery (Rosenberg, 1987: 337–352).

One reason for the increase of middle- and upper-class hospital patients was the growing faith in the efficacy of medicine; another was the concerted advertising by hospitals, depicting well-appointed private rooms and immaculate conditions. An especially important factor was that many physicians urged that their patients be treated in hospitals. In some cases, this insistence was related to the fact that surgeons themselves owned the hospitals in which they practiced; in many other cases, the doctors' insistence was due to the convenience and growing technological advantages of performing procedures in hospital. Income from private patients made community hospitals economically viable. Hospital-admitting privileges became crucial to physicians' careers; hospitals in turn became dependent upon doctors to bring in private patients (Rosenberg, 1987: 237–261). Nursing too was changed from an untrained domestic task to a hospital-oriented and -trained occupation, bringing discipline and efficiency to the care of paying patients. By the 1920s American hospitals were, therefore, being transformed from charitable enterprises to bureaucratic organizations selling medical commodities in an impersonal marketplace. The very technology and specialization of tasks that made hospitals plausible sites for the centralized practice of medicine have also been major sources of the spiraling costs leading to the present U.S. health care crisis.

Hospital Ownership and Control

One of the biggest changes in the last 40 years has been in how hospitals are owned and controlled. Before the 1970s most hospitals were operated primarily as not-for-profit enterprises. Some not-for-profit hospitals are public institutions, funded mainly from tax revenues of a city, county, state, or national government. Private not-for-profit institutions include community hospitals run by local boards as well as hospitals run by various religious and charitable organizations. Since the early years of private patient hospitalization, there have been private, for-profit hospitals—typically proprietary hospitals set up by several doctors in a community, but small groups of investors could not readily keep pace with the costs of capitalizing modern high-tech hospitals. Since about 1980, increasingly, for-profit hospitals are owned by business corporations with investor-stockholders. There are still many not-for-profit hospitals, but their numbers are dwindling and they are increasingly left caring for a disproportionate number of the sickest and poorest patients, who are turned away from for-profit hospitals due to inability to pay for hospital care (Gray, 1991; 1983).

There is a rapidly growing trend in the United States toward the proprietarization and corporatization of health care facilities, such as hospitals, nursing homes, psychiatric hospitals, and freestanding clinics and outpatient surgery centers. **Proprietarization** is the process by which a greater proportion of health care institutions are operated explicitly for profit. **Corporatization** is the process by which a relatively small number of investor-owned corporations control a greater concentration of proprietary interests. Between 1977 and 1982, while the total number of U.S. hospitals declined by 2 percent, the number of investor-owned chain hospitals increased by 40 percent (Gray, 1983). Furthermore, this ownership was highly concentrated, with only four firms controlling approximately 70 percent of the more than 700 investor-owned hospitals (Berliner and Burlage, 1987).

For example, Columbia Healthcare Corporation bought a number of small, failing hospitals to get a market toehold in cities such as Houston and Miami; then it acquired Galen Health Care, a 73-hospital chain. In 1993 Columbia announced merger with the HCA (Hospital Corporation of America), which would become the world's largest investor-owned hospital group with 190 hospitals in 26 states (Jones, 1993). By 1991, about a quarter of all nonfederal acute-care hospitals were owned by investor-owned corporations (Lindorff, 1992). And the proportion of investor-owned specialty hospitals, such as short-term psychiatric hospitals and nursing homes, was even greater.

For-profit hospitals have been highly profitable for investors. For instance, in 1980 Humana, one of the largest chains, had a 33.6 percent return on equity and a 34.4 percent five-year average earning per share, compared to a median for all industries of 16.1 and 14.3 percent, respectively (Sorkin, 1986: 87). Interestingly, studies have found that for-profit acute-care hospitals are not more cost-efficient than their not-for-profit counterparts, but rather are more expensive to operate. At the same time, however, the study found no evidence that patients admitted to for-profit acute-care hospitals were treated less well than those in not-for-profit hospitals (Sloan, 1988; Institute of Medicine, 1986).

Although initially, after a corporate buyout of a hospital, for-profit hospitals may realize some economies of scale (e.g., better prices on supplies bought through the united purchasing power of the chain), these studies suggest that for-profit hospitals cannot in the long run further reduce costs and maintain the same quality without seriously diminishing their profits. Indeed, if they eventually buy out or drive their nonprofit competitors to bankruptcy, they may be in a position to increase their profits by driving up prices (Jones, 1993). Since profits are their foremost reason for existence, investor-owned hospitals have no incentive to return cost savings to the payers of medical costs. The unprecedented power and potential for market monopoly of for-profit hospitals is a significant and growing problem that any viable U.S. health care policy must address.

Another change in the structure and power of medical businesses is that they are frequently connected within large, integrated nationwide or international corporations. The corporatization of health care has involved both horizontal and vertical integration. **Horizontal integration** is the process by which a corporation acquires large numbers of productive facilities, such as hospitals or nursing homes, across widespread markets (Salmon, 1985; Siegrist, 1983). One brokerage firm predicted that before the end of the century, 80 percent of all U.S. hospitals will be part of chains (cited in Salmon, 1985). These chains are transforming health care into a large-scale, high-stakes industry, described by one editor of the *New England Journal of Medicine* as "the medical-industrial complex" (Relman, 1980).

Vertical integration describes the conglomerate control over several levels of production, such as hospitals, nursing homes, hospital supply companies, pharmaceutical companies, prosthetic supply companies, medical office complexes, and home health care agencies (Salmon, 1985). Vertically integrated industries have increased capacity to control diverse aspects of the market and to shift resources when one part of the business becomes less profitable. One particular form of vertical integration portends great structural change in the health care industry. When hospitals or clinics are owned by the same corporation as insurers or payment managers, considerable market control is concentrated. For example, Humana operated two community hospitals in Chicago, subsequently purchased a chain of freestanding ambulatory care centers to serve as feeders to the hospitals, and then proposed a new teaching hospital to which the community hospitals would funnel patients—all ideally integrated through Humana Care Plus, a comprehensive health insurance program (Berliner and Burlage, 1987). As described in Chapter 11, such concentration greatly reduces the autonomy of professionals working in the system, reducing their ability to serve as advocates for patients. Patients too are severely limited in the affordable options open to them; their weak leverage is further reduced by a very powerful economic system.

Hospital Costs and Financing

Any effort to address the U.S. health system crisis must confront the costs of hospital care. Payments to hospitals account for the largest single category of national health expenditures. Not only have costs of hospital care risen far faster than the cost of living in the United States, they have also consumed an ever greater proportion of total national health expenditures. Whereas in 1929, the costs of hospital care amounted to 18 percent of all U.S. health spending, they were 30 percent by 1950, 37 percent by 1970, and 44 percent in the early 1990s (Gibson, 1980; 1982; Letsch, 1993). Hospital costs have been notoriously difficult to control.

One ironic source of spiraling hospital costs has been competition among hospitals. Hospitals are not marketed directly to patient-consumers, but rather to physicians who admit the patients. In order to be economically successful, hospitals must attract enough of the "right" kind of patient, that is, those with ample resources (usually insurance) to pay their bills. Thus, to appeal to the doctors who will send them the desired patients, hospitals purchase increasingly sophisticated technologies, hire support staff to utilize the new technologies, and renovate physical facilities, often providing economic incentives such as subsidized office space for the participating physicians. Physicians encourage acquisition of new technologies both to improve their skills and abilities to treat patients, and to increase the profitability and prestige of their practices. Patient expectations, too, promote hospital competition for advanced technology by their broad faith in scientific medicine to come up with a "technological fix" for every malady (Rushing, 1984).

Many of these expensive investments are, however, not really needed in the community; many services are duplicated (see Glaser, 1991). For example, all five hospitals in one city may have purchased and staffed an expensive magnetic resonance imaging (MRI) unit, but none of them may have real use for more than one-eighth of the MRI's capacity, so the costs for each use must be high. Then in order to recoup more of the expense of the unit, the hospitals encourage their physicians to order more MRI scans for their patients. State regulatory agencies tried to contain these cost-escalating practices by requiring a certificate of need before purchases of certain equipment, but most such regulations failed to reduce costs substantially (Roth, 1984) and sometimes resulted in bribes and fraud (Lindorff, 1992). One important reason that states cannot adequately limit technology purchases, however, is that the medical profession quickly accepts many technologies as the "standard" for care. If an expensive technology, even if not yet of proven benefit, is considered a basic standard for good medical care, how could a state deny any hospital the right to purchase it?

The proliferation of technologies from the minor (e.g., blood tests) to the massive (e.g., neonatal intensive care units), have driven up hospital costs not only because they are expensive to acquire and house but also because they require costly specialized support workers. Whereas modernizing capital expenditures in industrial production usually decrease labor costs, technological investments in hospital production generally increase labor expenditures.

U.S. hospitals are far more labor intensive than their European counterparts. In 1985, they employed 2.75 hospital personnel per occupied bed, compared to 2.13 in Canada, 1.85 in Sweden, and 1.21 in Germany (Glaser, 1991). U.S. hospitals have higher rates of staffing of skilled medical personnel—an expensive part of hospital budgets. Another difference may be low hospital occupancy rates, since many U.S. communities have an oversupply of hospital beds relative to the population—especially the insured population.

A further explanation is that U.S. hospitals employ far more personnel to administer their fiscal and bureaucratic operations. Lacking universal or standardized health insurance, in the United States every patient must be screened for type and amount of insurance coverage or other method of payment, and the hospital must communicate with payers for review and approval of specific services, as well as conduct elaborate billings and payment collections. Taken together, these labor costs contribute to enormous disparity between U.S. and European hospital costs. In 1987, the United States spent $969 per capita on hospitals, compared with $754 in Canada, $422 in Germany, and $296 in Belgium (Glaser, 1991).

Hospital Reimbursements.   Hospitals obtain their payments in one of four modes of reimbursement. The annual budget mode is characteristic of hospitals operated out of federal, state, or city tax revenues; the budget is set in advance and is unrelated to the units of service actually delivered. A second form is billing based on charges that are set, with no necessary relationship to cost, for each item of service (e.g., use of operating room, each lab test and medication, each day's use of a hospital room). This method of billing was employed since the beginning of private patient use of hospitals, but it has virtually disappeared due to pressure from insurers and government regulatory agencies concerned with controlling costs.

A third, more sophisticated method of billing is retrospective cost reimbursement, by which insurers and hospitals negotiate an agreement about the costs for services provided. This approach forces hospitals to "debundle" charges, making it less likely that they can subsidize an expensive facility by overcharging for other, inexpensive services. It does not, however, prevent a hospital from charging what "the market will bear" for the debundled charges, so it has had limited success in holding down costs. A fourth, more recent and complex approach is prospective reimbursement, by which insurer and/or public agency attempts to predict, on the basis of previous experience and rates of cost increases, the costs for various services in the coming year. The hospital may bill for only that averaged amount, regardless of actual costs. This approach resembles an annual budget arrangement, except that the hospital bills numerous insurance companies, government agencies, and individuals, rather than a single sponsor (McCarthy, 1981). Prospective reimbursement plans were introduced in order to cap costs and simplify hospital billing arrangements, but they have had unintended negative consequences.

The diagnosis-related group (DRG) is the most widely known form of prospective reimbursement. DRGs are the basis of payment for all hospital billing in some highly regulated states, such as New Jersey (see Morone and Dunham, 1984). In 1983, in an effort to contain spiraling hospital costs, the federal government also adopted DRGs as a basis for Medicare reimbursement (Ruggie, 1992; Smith, 1992). In this system, each procedure or service that can be provided to a hospital patient is placed in a diagnosis-related category (for example, in New Jersey there are 467 categories), each with a price fixed by computing what similar hospitals had been charging for like cases. The hospital is not paid more if the actual services cost more; if the actual services cost less, the hospital keeps the difference. This plan eliminates the proliferation of hospital procedures and services previously encouraged when hospitals gained from each additional billable service. On the other hand, it places pressures on doctors not to request services that may be beneficial, and it promotes the early discharge of patients—"quicker and sicker."

At the same time, however, shorter hospital stays leave many hospitals under-utilized. Concomitant with the decline in hospitalization and the reduction of length of stay promoted by DRGs, hospital occupancy rates dropped from 69.7 percent in 1980 to 56.6 percent in 1985, creating economic difficulties for hospitals with limited other means of raising revenue (Smith, 1992; Moss, 1987). One strategy used by hospitals to compensate for lost revenues was the aggressive promotion of outpatient care, which was encouraged by insurers who expected cost savings relative to inpatient care. Because both hospital and freestanding outpatient services have increased their outpatient costs to the point of nearly equaling the expense of inpatient services, private and federal insurers are now trying to set limits for these services as well (Kramon, 1988b). These developments illustrate the economic and political jockeying for position among powerful elements of the health care system: hospitals, insurers, and government regulators.

Hospitals can remain financially stable—and in some cases even highly profitable—if they can control the mixture of *payers* of their patients' bills. Those in a position to accept proportionately few patients with payers (such as Medicare) that severely restrict the hospital's charges (and no patients without insurance or other means of paying) can be economically comfortable. Indeed, there is evidence that for-profit hospitals realize profits not by managing their health care delivery more efficiently but by effectively manipulating the reimbursement system (Pattison and Katz, 1983). Hospital competition for high-paying patients has led to serious problems of access to needed care.

Problems of Access. Most inner-city and rural hospitals, however, do not have the luxury of controlling the mixture of payers, since they are often the only hospital available to a population. Many of them end up in dire financial straits, and their patients experience serious problems of access to needed health care. Many rural hospitals serve a relatively small, widely dispersed population; rural poor or uninsured persons including many farm families who cannot afford private insurance must rely on these hospitals to partially subsidize their care.

Rural hospitals accounted for a disproportionately large number of the more than 500 hospitals that closed between 1980 and 1987 (DeFriese et al., 1992). Some failed hospitals were outmoded and/or substandard, but many were the only ones available to the populace (Reinhold, 1987). Many rural areas have difficulty attracting physicians to practice in their areas, and losing a local hospital to which physicians can admit patients may further disadvantage the community. Closure of rural hospitals also decreases access to emergency medical care. Although the vast majority of the U.S. population lives in urban areas, some 70 percent of trauma fatalities occur in rural areas. There are workable substitutes for small rural community hospitals (e.g., outpatient satellite clinics, helicopter evacuation, and paraprofessional EMS teams), but these require national or statewide policymaking and funding for restoring access to health facilities in rural areas (Rutledge et al., 1992; see also Christianson et al., 1990; Straub, 1990).

Changes in the method of hospital reimbursement have had the unintended consequence of reducing access to hospital services for many areas in the United States.

Before the introduction of DRGs, hospitals typically used cross-subsidization to pay for unprofitable services such as emergency rooms. Because emergency rooms are used disproportionately by uninsured and underinsured patients, they are unlikely to generate enough income to cover costs, and in predominantly poor areas they account for massive losses to hospitals. In New York City, for instance, the emergency room was the avenue to hospital admission for half of all patients (French, 1988). DRGs do not take into account the fact that poor people are more likely to be sicker and suffer multiple conditions and complications compared to those who are well-off. Unable to afford primary care, poor persons appear at emergency rooms when they are extremely sick, requiring extensive medical attention. Furthermore, because many poor people lack the resources and safe conditions to be adequately nursed at home, hospitals must keep them longer. Thus, stays at inner-city hospitals are typically longer than average, but DRG limits are based on average stays (Tolchin, 1988b). Many nonpublic hospitals have responded by eliminating their emergency room services. In Los Angeles, where 27 percent of all nonelderly adults and 30 percent of all children have no health insurance, 15 hospitals closed or downgraded their emergency rooms between 1986 and 1988; the remaining hospitals were posting multimillion dollar annual losses on their emergency services (Reinhold, 1988).

In the inner cities, public hospitals, operated by city or other government bodies, are where most of the urban poor, the underinsured, and the uninsured go for treatment. A 1991 survey of public hospitals found that uninsured patients accounted for 52 percent of outpatient visits and 30 percent of inpatient days in public hospitals. Public hospitals lost an average of $40 million in 1988, due to care that was not reimbursed by Medicare, Medicaid, or private insurance. Although tax revenues subsidized part of that loss, the lack of adequate funding resulted in serious overcrowding, understaffing, and other cuts in services (Hilts, 1991; Stout, 1991).

For-profit hospitals frequently refuse to serve patients who cannot pay or transfer them—often in medically unstable conditions—to public hospitals or those nonprofit hospitals willing to accept indigent patients. This extensive "dumping" of undesirable patients puts an added burden on inner-city hospitals, especially the publicly financed hospitals that become the poor's last resort. In Chicago in 1983, after the governor had placed a ceiling on state payments for hospital services to the poor, transfers of patients from private hospitals to the county public hospital increased from an average of 100 per month to 450 per month. A subsequent study found that of 467 patients transferred to Cook County Hospital from private hospitals, 89 percent were black or Hispanic, 81 percent were unemployed, and nearly a fourth were medically endangered by the transfer (Schiff et al., 1986). In outrage over this and similar instances, Congress outlawed the "dumping" of patients in April 1987. Seven years later, however, a study found that federal agencies were not enforcing the act and had punished only 9 percent of the 268 hospitals cited for the illegal practice (Public Citizen Health Research Group, 1993; see also Himmelstein et al., 1984).

The trend toward proprietarization and corporatization of health care in the United States is closely linked with this underfunding of accessible care for the poor and underinsured (Whiteis and Salmon, 1987), especially when for-profit hospitals displace previously not-for-profit hospitals (see Gray, 1991). For example, in the 1980s, when Medicaid hospital payments did not rise proportionate to payments by commercial insurers or Medicare, for-profit hospitals reduced their share of Medicaid patients (Davis, 1991).

For-profit hospitals (and sometimes, too, not-for-profit hospitals that emulate big businesses) engage in marketing and demarketing strategies to maximize their revenues. *Demarketing* is a euphemism for the practice of actively discouraging "undesirable" patients who seek their services.

For example, economically depressed Brownsville, Texas, is served by two hospitals, both owned by for-profit chains. Despite their very low occupancy rates (40 and 50 percent), they regularly turn away all but the most critical emergency cases if patients cannot pay. In addition to these hospitals' concern for profitability, the plight of poor patients is made more desperate by the fact that Texas has one of the least adequate of all state programs of health services for the poor; only those whose income is below 60 percent of the poverty level are covered by Medicaid insurance. The administrator of one Brownsville hospital said, "We ask all the patients for money. . . . We work with the poor patients and tell them we'd be happy to set up a payment program" (quoted in Tolchin, 1988b). Critics charge that the hospitals aggressively intimidate patients into leaving without health care service (Tolchin, 1988a). One survey of physicians found that those practicing at for-profit hospitals were two to three times as likely to report their hospital discouraged admissions of uninsured, Medicaid, and Medicare patients (Schlesinger et al., 1987). Nonpaying or low-paying patients also may be subjected to long waits and inferior facilities compared to full-paying patients.

A more subtle marketing strategy of profit-oriented hospitals is "cream skimming," or the targeting of a market of highly desirable patients, typically middle- and upper-class persons with good insurance who need treatments that cost the hospital relatively little. Although physicians are still the main source of hospital referrals, more hospitals are engaging in direct advertising and marketing gimmicks to overcome declining occupancy rates. One hospital, for example, advertised refunds to patients who received unsatisfactory service, such as cold meals. Another sent out dollars-off coupons for its clinic (Sorkin, 1986). "Frills" have been added to attract patients, such as cozy birth centers that provide champagne for the new parents. To the extent that some hospitals are successful in attracting the "cream" of patients, others are worse off, especially if DRG payment rates are involved, because their patient mix no longer includes those who are least expensive to treat.

A related form of "cream skimming" is the investment in specialty hospitals. By 1987 more than one-third of the 1,375 for-profit hospitals in the United States were devoted exclusively to specialty care, such as psychiatric care, treatment for substance abuse, and physical rehabilitation. This emphasis was prompted partly by the fact that specialized care is not subject to much federal cost-containment pressure; nearly all patients are privately insured, are younger than Medicare recipients, and tend to stay about three times as long as patients in acute care hospitals. Another feature that yields higher profits is that little expensive technology is required.

Although the long-term profitability of specialty hospitals may be greatly reduced by government or insurer cost-containment measures, the immediate impact has been to siphon desirable patients away from general hospitals (Freudenheim, 1987b).

By contrast, the nursing home industry—75 percent of which is controlled by for-profit companies—has become somewhat less profitable than it once was because it relies very heavily (over 50 percent) upon government subsidies through Medicare and Medicaid. When government reimbursements were liberal, nursing home chains made huge profits and expanded rapidly. In California the average nursing home made a profit of 41 percent on net equity in 1978–79. In those boom years, for-profit chains grew as much as 900 percent in just four years (see Harrington, 1984). When government funding became more restrictive, however, the chains did not fare so well. For example, Beverly Enterprises, which owned 1,003 nursing homes, lost $30.5 million in 1987, despite revenues of over $2 billion (Feder, 1988).

The profit motive in specialty hospitals, especially those such as nursing homes and psychiatric hospitals where patients are relatively isolated and powerless, raises serious questions about the quality of care. For example, in the 1980s, there were numerous reports of patient neglect and abuse in for-profit nursing homes. Such institutions had a very high proportion of unskilled workers, barely earning the minimum wage, with a turnover rate of nearly 80 percent, which led to frequent understaffing (Feder, 1988). Understaffed nursing homes relied heavily on drugs and physical restraints to control patients until 1987 when changed federal regulations reduced the rate of restraint from about 40 percent to less than 20 percent of nursing home patients (Belkin, 1993).

The profit motive has also made specialty hospitals particularly prone to fraud, unethical marketing, and overcharging. For example, in 1991, Psychiatric Institutes of America, the nation's largest and most profitable chain of private psychiatric hospitals with 73 psychiatric hospitals nationwide, were implicated in systematic fraudulent practices. Investigators identified such abuses as inflating bills for medications and services, billing for services never rendered, altering diagnoses and treatments to match insurance coverage, admitting insured patients who did not need hospitalization, keeping patients against their will, and releasing patients—regardless of their condition—as soon as their insurance was exhausted (Kerr, 1991a, 1991b). Similar allegations of fraud and unscrupulous marketing prompted federal investigation of several large, for-profit chains of head-injury rehabilitation centers (Kerr, 1992).

Overcharging and outright fraud contribute to the rapidly rising costs of medical care, both directly as when fraudulent Medicare claims are paid and indirectly as insurance companies pass on inflated costs by increases in premiums. Although many hospitals do not engage in such unscrupulous business practices, the added costs created by those that do are enormous. Federal, state, and local government regulatory agencies must then spend additional moneys trying to detect and control abuses of the system, adding yet more to the actual costs of the health care system. The trends toward proprietarization and corporatization are not inevitable; the government could, for example, decide to redirect funds into public health care programs or public or not-for-profit hospitals for all. These growing hospital corporations, however, wield massive political and economic force that they use to influence government policy-making to keep the hospital industry and their position in it as profitable as possible.

MEDICAL INDUSTRIES

Vast and profitable industries have developed to supply products and processes for medical care. They manufacture, distribute, and market known products, while continuously researching and developing new ones. The most obvious example is the pharmaceutical industry, which markets large numbers of both prescription and over-the-counter drugs. Other industries supply everything from the mundane to the exotic, from the simplest devices to the most complex, including monitors for various organ functions, radiological equipment, laboratory equipment, prosthetic devices, surgical equipment, medical office and hospital supplies and equipment, and intravenous solutions.

Costs

Changing medical technologies involve not only innovations in material objects (e.g., drugs, equipment, and devices), but also the development of new procedures and scientific and technical knowledge bases. Rapidly changing medical technology has been a major source of the increases in hospital and physician-related costs to pay for new technological equipment, to build and adapt spaces to use it, and to hire and supervise the specialized workers to operate it. Estimates from the U.S. Office of Technology Assessment attribute between one-third and three-quarters of increased expenditures for hospital care to the costs of medical technology (Banta et al., 1981).

Expenditures for prescription drugs also contributed a disproportionate amount to the rapid increase in U.S. health care expenditures. In the 1980s, the prices for prescription drugs increased more than 150 percent, or three times the rate of inflation (Novak, 1993). A considerable portion of these price increases went to corporate profits. Between 1988 and 1992, the pharmaceutical industry's pretax profits were five times the profit levels of other U.S. industries. A study done for Congress by the Office of Technology Assessment asserted in 1993 that the pharmaceutical industry had made "excess profits" of more than $2 billion per year (Freudenheim, 1993a). In European countries, where government agencies control drug prices, prescription costs are about 60 percent of the U.S. level (*Dollars and Sense*, 1993).

New drugs are often extremely costly because they involve expensive research and development processes, including the costs of clinical trials required for federal approval, marketing, product liability insurance, as well as corporate profits. The declared costs of research and development of new products is far higher in the drug industry than in many other types of manufacturing. Drug manufacturers estimate that 16.7 percent of their revenues are used for research. The majority of that research is not devoted to finding remarkable cures, however. Much research is in order to find patentable alternatives to drugs made by rival companies or to drugs whose patent is soon to run out. FDA officials estimate that only about 40 percent of new drugs approved in 1993 represented any significant medical advancement (Rosenthal, 1993).

A more important component of the cost of pharmaceuticals in the United States is marketing expenses, which account for about 25 percent of the wholesale price paid by the pharmacist (Roemer, 1986: 17) or an estimated 20 percent of pharmaceutical corporations' entire budgets (Rosenthal, 1993b). Marketing is a particularly important factor in profits on prescription drugs; because doctors—not consumers—decide which drug to order, competitive pricing has little impact. Advertising aimed at the physician-prescriber attempts to achieve brand loyalty, especially when there is little real difference among the competing products. In 1988, drug companies spent more than $5,000 per doctor promoting their products (Wilkes and Shuchman, 1989).

One reason that many medical technologies and drugs are so expensive over the course of a patient's lifetime is that they are not *resolutions* of a problem but merely partial *responses* to it. For example, the iron lung was a response to some needs of polio victims but did not resolve the problem of the disease itself; a resolution came with the development of the polio vaccine. While they may prolong some people's lives, improve some people's functioning, or hold some people's dangerous symptoms in abeyance, even impressive technological developments often do not fully resolve the medical problem for which they were invented. For example, as described in Chapter 11, end-stage renal disease (ESRD) is fatal, but dialysis technology can keep many patients alive, although it is very expensive. In 1991, the cost was about $29,000 per year (Iglehart, 1993). Dialysis cannot cure the diseases that cause kidney failure, nor can it restore patients to full health. While some recipients may live for several years, nationally only about 30 percent survive more than five years. Some patients are able to function nearly normally, but the majority are sufficiently disabled by their illness that they are unable to work outside their home (Plough, 1986: 20, 21). Such medical costs are, thus, not one-time expenses for a single illness episode, but rather continue to mount so long as recipients live.

Modern medicine is struggling to respond to many chronic illnesses that are not so amenable to a "technological fix" as were the acute infectious diseases prominent a few decades ago. For example, in 1993, the five top-selling prescription drugs, together generating annual U.S. sales of about $5.5 billion, included two drugs for high blood pressure, one for ulcers, one for high cholesterol, and one for depression (Freudenheim, 1993a). The most frequently dispensed drugs are predominantly for chronic illnesses or conditions that the drugs are not actually able to cure: ulcers, hypertension, anxiety, heart disease, arthritis, angina, and menopause. Patients must typically take such medications for many years, often for the rest of their lives.

Some new drugs and technologies do, however, save money. For example, new vaccines can prevent outbreaks of serious diseases. New screening devices can detect illnesses earlier when they are more readily cured. New inventions can make surgery safer or simpler. New drugs for conditions such as ulcers can make costly surgery unnecessary; however, whether this substitution saves money depends upon whether the course of drugs is less expensive than the operation.

Another major reason for the increased costs of drugs and medical technologies has been the medicalization of problems not previously treated as medical issues (as described in Chapters 9 and 10). The medicalization of menopause, childbirth, old age, hyperactivity, alcoholism and other substance abuse, emotional troubles, and the like has resulted in the prescription of a number of technological medical responses—drugs, devices, and procedures—that have all contributed to the greatly increased cost of treating these "conditions."

Regulation

Many interest groups are involved in the creation and utilization of new medical technologies. Three obvious parties are the manufacturers who profit from their sales, the physicians and hospitals who may choose to employ them, and the regulatory agencies that have varying degrees of power and responsibility over them. Other groups, including research scientists, political figures, media representatives, consumer groups, insurers, and patients, are also involved, sometimes in complex ways. Because of the rapid pace of technological development in medicine and because of the enormous economic, social, and health stakes involved, ongoing critical analysis of medical products and technologies is important. The complexity and sheer quantity of new developments, however, make it difficult for even well-endowed and powerful nations to monitor them adequately. Developing countries are far less able to evaluate and control the use of new products and technologies, so the regulation of medical products marketed by transnational corporations has become a worldwide problem.

In the United States.   The Food and Drug Administration (FDA) regulates pharmaceuticals, and has the power to allow or ban their sale and control their labeling; the Federal Trade Commission (FTC) has some additional regulatory authority over the content of advertising claims made for health-related products. In 1938 Congress authorized the FDA controls, but a "grandfather" clause exempted preexisting drugs from scrutiny. Drug regulations required evidence of safety and truth in labelling and, since 1962, proof of efficacy (for a fascinating account of the politics of FDA regulation, see Silverman et al., 1992; Silverman and Lee, 1974). Initially, only pharmaceuticals and cosmetics were regulated; in 1976 after tragedies such as the Dalkon Shield deaths, the FDA was given authority to regulate medical devices. To date, however, medical procedures such as new forms of surgery are not regulated or even systematically evaluated.

Many technologies have not been independently evaluated for safety or effectiveness whatsoever, or they were employed widely prior to systematic evaluation, and many continue to be used long after studies resulted in negative assessments. Products and technologies that have been poorly, belatedly, or negatively evaluated include electronic fetal monitors, prenatal ultrasound screening, intrauterine devices, silicon-gel breast implants, oral contraceptives, an artificial heart valve, and coronary care units (Ewigman et al., 1993; Hilts, 1993, 1992; Ratcliff, 1989).

Often the decision to utilize a medical technology is part of a complex web of changes in medical practice in which related changes are not carefully evaluated because of the assumptions implicit in the **technological imperative** (i.e., the belief that if we have the technological capability to do something, then we should do it), as discussed in Chapter 11. Electronic fetal monitor (EFM) technology was introduced in the late 1960s and aggressively marketed in the 1970s (before the United States had any regulatory procedures for new medical technologies). EFM involves placing monitors (usually external) on the woman in labor to provide machine-recorded measures of fetal heart rate and strength of contractions. Many physicians were sold on the prospect of using EFM to detect early signs of "problem" deliveries, and hospitals invested in the technology as a less labor-intensive way to monitor several women in labor simultaneously. There was also widespread faith that technology would provide a more scientific and safe process for labor and delivery (Kunisch, 1989).

Thus, long before adequate research on the effectiveness, accuracy, and side effects of EFM technology had been done, the devices had already been widely sold to hospitals throughout the United States and accepted in medical training as the appropriate standard for care. Doctors learned that "good" obstetrical care meant using the monitors; high-tech deliveries also enhanced their professional prestige and justified hospital childbirth in an era in which both were being challenged. High-tech deliveries meshed with Western cultural values emphasizing technology (such as monitors, anesthesia, and surgery) as mastery over nature; these values further legitimated obstetricians' control over the childbirth process (see Davis-Floyd, 1990; Treichler, 1990). Likewise, hospitals considered themselves up to date if their labor and delivery rooms were equipped with the monitoring machines. The cost of the equipment could be passed on to patients and their insurers, and often hospitals could realize profits through increased use of testing and monitoring technologies.

The decision to buy the monitors led almost inexorably to the decision to use them for all laboring women, not merely the 10 to 15 percent who might be at risk of problem deliveries. Probably the foremost reason that EFM technology became a standard for medical intervention in labor and deliveries is that machine readouts were accepted in courts as evidence against malpractice suits (Kunisch, 1989).[1] The decision to use monitors for all births combined with the fear of malpractice suits led to a rapid increase in the rate of delivery by Caesarian section (i.e., major abdominal surgery on the mother). In the first decade of EFM use, the rate of surgical deliveries more than tripled. Although the rates have leveled off, in 1990 Caesarian sections still accounted for 23.5 percent of all deliveries, compared to 16.5 percent in 1980 before widespread use of EFM (U.S. Department of Health and Human Services, 1992: 232).

Because of machine errors and mistakes in reading the monitor information, much of this surgery is medically unnecessary. Research on the accuracy and effec-

[1] More recently, with the incentive of secondary income, some doctors have invested in home fetal monitoring services used months before the hospital fetal monitoring, for which patients' insurance is billed some $5,000 per pregnancy (Meier, 1993a).

tiveness of EFM technology, as well as the appropriateness of Caesarian sections as medical intervention, came *after* the technologies and standard procedures were already in place. Indeed, the first large-scale trial of EFM came more than 15 years after monitors had first been marketed. By the 1980s, assessments of EFM concluded that the technology provided little benefit in low-risk labors and was costly (especially in escalating costs of unnecessary surgery) and dangerous (see Kunisch, 1989, for a review of these reports). Nevertheless, because employment of EFM technology is motivated by the complex and unexamined factors described earlier, physicians and hospitals are slow to become more discriminating, utilizing it only for high-risk cases.

Medical technologies often have harmful or undesirable side effects. They may even cause illness (iatrogenesis) and death. The evaluation of their safety is difficult, however, partly because it may take years for the bad effects to become evident. For example, in the 1940s and 1950s, unaware of the dangers of radiation, many physicians and dentists used X-rays and other radiological imaging frequently and indiscriminately, thus delivering relatively large doses of radiation to their patients. Since the effects of such radiation are cumulative and may take many years to culminate in disease, which even then may be attributable to multiple causes, the safety of early radioactive technologies was not readily questioned.

Safety is also always relative. The risks of dangerous side effects of a drug or procedure must be weighed against the probabilities and risks of the condition itself as well as of alternative therapies (Banta et al., 1981). For example, oral contraceptives carry the risk of unpleasant, dangerous, and even fatal side effects, but pregnancy and childbirth create serious health risks too. Regulators have not yet resolved issues arising from the fact that safety is also relative to certain characteristics of the patient population. Regulations often restrict drugs that are unsafe for children, for example, but fail to limit those that are unsafe for the elderly (Ray et al., 1990). Risks must also be weighed against the potential health benefits. Dangerous side effects might be more acceptable in a drug for potentially fatal AIDS than in one for baldness, weight loss, or acne.

The importance of the powerful regulation of these new products and technologies is amply illustrated by the tragedies created by several dangerous products. Between 1958 and 1962, some 10,000 children were born with severe birth defects as a result of thalidomide, a sedative prescribed for their mothers to reduce nausea in pregnancy. The drug was not approved in the United States due to the tenacious efforts of a single medical officer with the FDA. The thalidomide disaster spurred the passage of the U.S. Drug Act of 1962 and changed the criteria for testing drug safety (Silverman and Lee, 1974).

A similar tragedy occurred in the United States and elsewhere for children whose mothers took prescribed diethylstilbestrol (DES) during pregnancy. Between 1943 and 1970, DES, a synthetic estrogen, was widely prescribed for women in the United States, despite early and growing evidence of its carcinogenic (cancer-causing) properties and its ineffectiveness for many purposes for which it was prescribed (e.g., preventing miscarriage). Subsequently, researchers found that DES caused iatrogenic disease in the children born to pregnant recipients, and that several million sons and daughters may have been thus affected (Weiss, 1983). Thus far, DES has been responsible for several hundred cases of cancers of the vagina, cervix, or testicles, but researchers are now discovering more insidious side effects, including immune system defects, urological and genital defects, and reproductive problems (Brody, 1993).

The case of DES children illustrates the effects of poor scientific analysis and shoddy clinical trials, lack of regulatory control over doctor experimentation with unapproved drugs, and the readiness of a portion of the medical community to prescribe a potent substance that was not fully understood or proven safe and effective (Dutton et al., 1988; see also Bale, 1990; Bell, 1986; Direcks and Hoen, 1986; Apfel and Fisher, 1984). It also illustrates the difficult problem of how to adequately regulate and control an industry capable of producing tragic iatrogenic effects (see McDonnell, 1986; Braithwaite, 1984).

The tragedies caused by the Dalkon shield, an intrauterine device (IUD) for contraception, illustrate the need for greater regulation of medical devices, as well as pharmaceuticals. In 1968 the shield was introduced and entrepreneurially promoted by a respected gynecologist, who later sold the invention to Robins, a large pharmaceutical company. The government then had no effective regulation for medical devices. No agency checked the doctor's claims of safety and effectiveness, and the manufacturer had no legal accountability for using those inaccurate claims in its advertising. Several million women in the United States and overseas had the device inserted. Despite numerous reports of health- and life-threatening side effects due to the IUDs, massive infections, and dangerous abnormal pregnancies, the company did not issue physicians any warnings about its dangers until after the first documented death (Perry and Dawson, 1985; see also Yanoshik and Norsigian, 1989; Dowie and Johnston, 1987; LaCheen, 1986).

When it became obvious that there were serious medical problems with the device, Robins anticipated a drop in U.S. sales and decided to market the shield internationally. The company offered the U.S.-sponsored development agency, AID, a 48 percent discount on bulk packages of unsterilized shields. Robins continued international sales of the device for two years after lawsuits and deaths forced them to cease U.S. sales; Dalkon shields, previously distributed in developing nations, were still being inserted in new patients through 1980 (Hartmann, 1987). In the face of extensive U.S. lawsuits (by about 200,000 eligible claimants), Robins filed for bankruptcy, limited its liability by paying $2.3 billion to a trust, and simultaneously provided its shareholders the highest rate of appreciation of any security on the New York Stock Exchange. The terms of the trust provided that some injured women would receive some payment with the amount depending, not on degree of injury, but on the number of eventual claims sharing the trust and whether the trust funds were depleted. However, there was virtually no provision for foreign women injured by the product (Sobol, 1991).

While some evidence pertaining to safety (and effectiveness) can be deduced from the chemical properties of substances and devices, and further data can be gained from experiments on animals, medical industries and the FDA need to test innovations on human subjects. Early procedures for drug approval allowed clinical trials done under uncontrolled circumstances to be used as evidence of safety and effectiveness. Any licensed physician was permitted to experiment on patients with drugs before FDA approval, and pharmaceutical companies provided large quantities of free samples for so-called "clinical trials." There are numerous professional incentives for doctors to experiment to find new applications for approved drugs; such results were publishable sources of professional prestige. Only in the 1970s, however, were experimenters required to obtain the informed consent of patients; previously many subjects did not even know that they were taking experimental drugs.[2] Because of the great medical and commercial interest in the many aspects of women's reproductive lives, women—especially poor and Third World women—have been disproportionately used as guinea pigs in medical research (Ford, 1986; Marcelis and Shiva, 1986; Ward, 1986; Oakley, 1984).

In the Third World.   The contrast between the First and Third World in medical device and drug abuses shows the importance of strong regulation in counteracting the market interests of these industries. Whereas in the United States and other First World countries, regulatory agencies and knowledgeable physicians can prevent the misuse or abuse of pharmaceuticals and other medical products, Third World countries lack the money and expertise necessary to control them. In developing countries, medical industries continue to sell unsafe products that were banned or highly controlled in Western markets.

Transnational drug corporations have been attracted to the global marketplace, but have frequently exploited developing countries' lack of expertise and inability to control the sale of pharmaceuticals, infant formulas, contraceptives, and the like. Dangerous drugs are sold over the counter in many countries, while the labeling, package inserts, and desk reference information provided by manufacturers fail to mention many dangers and claim many unproven uses. For example, anabolic steroids can cause birth defects, liver tumors, and irreversible masculinization of females, but are readily sold over the counter in Malaysia, Brazil, and several African nations as an appetite stimulant (often specifically for children) to relieve exhaustion, fatigue, and malnutrition (Muller, 1982).

Although by the beginning of the 1990s, many transnational pharmaceutical companies had voluntarily curbed some of the most flagrant marketing abuses, people in developing nations are still at great risk due to their countries' inability to regulate the industry and enforce drug laws controlling the manufacturing, marketing,

---

[2]The requirement of informed consent has not been totally effective in eliminating abuses, however, since many patients cannot evaluate information they are given and may not understand the risks. While most universities and hospitals have procedures for monitoring consent, clinical experiments done by individual practitioners or in small clinics are not adequately monitored, and serious abuses are still occurring. For example, in 1987 two anesthesiologists administered—without consent—the drug Dilantin to about 250 women in labor as part of an experiment to determine whether the drug (an approved treatment for epilepsy) could reduce fetal stress in Caesarian births (*The New York Times*, June 1, 1988b).

and dispensing of "prescription" drugs (Silverman et al., 1992). In 1968, the World Health Organization established criteria for drug promotion, and in 1988 updated and strengthened its criteria for the ethical advertising, especially of prescription drugs. Despite these efforts, drug advertisements often omit important information about precautions, side effects, and contraindications; they often feature expensive photos with little relevance to the medical value of the products (Herxheimer et al., 1993).

A related exploitation of the global marketplace was the aggressive and often misleading marketing of infant formulas to Third World families, who could not afford to sustain their babies on purchased formula and lacked the sanitary conditions necessary to prepare and store it. Once they had abandoned nursing their infants, however, mothers were trapped into buying formula, which cost an estimated 85 percent of the family's entire income. Babies became malnourished, dehydrated, and died. In 1981 *Newsweek* estimated that some 1 million children were dying each year from malnutrition and infection due to substitution of commercial formulas for breast milk (cited in Bodenheimer, 1984). Few developing nations had the power, knowledge, or resources to prevent the aggressive marketing of formula, however. In 1977, an international grass-roots boycott was organized against Nestlé, which controlled half of the entire Third World infant formula market, and its many subsidiaries; while never achieving enough leverage to attain a victory, the boycott did pressure Nestlé into a compromise. In 1981, the World Health Organization adopted a clear but voluntary code on the marketing of infant formula; the vote was 118 to 1, with the Reagan administration casting the sole dissenting vote (Van Esterik, 1989; Norris, 1982; see also Ledogar, 1975).

Commercial misrepresentation is particularly unfortunate for developing nations, which have small health care budgets but massive health care needs. If pharmaceutical companies persuade poor people or poor nations to spend a large proportion of their budgets on expensive commercial preparations for which there are inexpensive, perhaps even homemade substitutes, they are depriving people of the other benefits that money could have bought. Worse yet is when the expensive commercial preparation is ineffective or dangerous. For example, many pharmaceutical companies actively market profitable drugs for diarrhea in developing countries, where conditions make it a common and dangerous problem. Some, such as clioquinol, are ineffective for most causes of diarrhea and have serious side effects (such as neurological damage and blindness); others, such as Lomotil, can stop the flow of diarrhea but exacerbate the more serious problem of dehydration. The best treatment (oral rehydration therapy) is, however, of no commercial value, since the materials used are inexpensive, readily available sugar and salts. The aggressive marketing of the dangerous but profitable drugs thus diverts funds from therapies that could do vastly more good (Muller, 1982). The story of the more than ten-year international battle to force CIBA-Geigy to cease worldwide marketing of some of its dangerous and medically unnecessary drugs—especially clioquinol—exemplifies the enormous power and outright arrogance of large transnational companies in the face of evidence and opposition from concerned scientists, consumer groups, health organizations, and courts, assessing the company significant damages (Silverman et al., 1992).

Profits and Products

The free enterprise model of technological development and marketing in the United States means that the profit motive is a particularly important influence in shaping the creation and marketing of new drugs and technologies. One critic argued that the proliferation of technological innovation is inevitable, because "expansion is an absolute necessity for capitalist enterprises" (Waitzkin, 1979: 1263). While the profit motive is not the only determining force, it is certainly influential.

On the one hand, the quest for profits has motivated some impressive research; many of the technological advances of bioscientific medicine might not have occurred were it not for the investment of much research time and money. Private enterprise is not the only way a society could organize its research incentive, however; indeed, we gain much—perhaps most—of our medical advances from government-supported research in universities and government research centers. Nevertheless, in the United States many medical changes have come out of the private sector.

On the other hand, the profit orientation has greatly limited the scope of research and development; the medical industries are understandably interested only in new developments that will produce marketable commodities. In recent years, the profit incentive has influenced even university and medical school research centers, which are licensing patents, becoming partners with corporate interests that manufacture and market new devices and procedures, and seeking to develop "technology parks" on their campuses. Thus, academic research centers jeopardize their ability to evaluate new technologies objectively (Wright, 1987).

In the United States, the decision to develop and market a drug depends primarily upon economic considerations; drugs to meet people's actual health needs are often of limited commercial interest (known as "orphan drugs"). The industry is not likely to fund research on a cheap, readily available remedy, even if it may be the best treatment for a condition. For a drug to be profitable, it must be patentable; natural substances and shelf chemicals are not, so they are not researched, even if they may be highly effective. The search for patentable commodities also means that much research is directed to substitute drugs and/or technologies. Many "new" drugs are in fact existing drugs that are only marginally changed to justify a new patent, obtain and hold a market share, or create a new market (e.g., for home use and not just hospital use).

Marketability increasingly depends upon whether the cost of the drug or technology will be reimbursed by third-party payment. For example, if Medicare is not likely to pay for a new treatment for the elderly, then companies are not likely to invest in its development (Pear, 1988a). Drugs for developing nations are likewise of little commercial interest; although large numbers of people need some of these medications, researching and producing them would not be profitable. This general profit orientation does not mean that individual companies always gauge all policies to maximize profits. For example, when a drug developed by Merck for parasitic worms in livestock and dogs turned out to be a safe and effective treatment for a human parasitic infection causing river blindness among more than 18 million people in Africa,

Merck offered to make the drug available without charge through the World Health Organization (*The New York Times*, October 22, 1987). Likewise Searle, a leading producer of heart drugs, offered free supplies of certain drugs to needy patients not covered by private or government insurance programs (Altman, 1988a). In the 1980s there was a greatly increased effort by multinational drug companies, with private philanthropic foundation support, to address the needs of developing countries. Several companies set up research institutes on tropical diseases; others addressed Third World parasitic infection problems, while others improved antimalarial treatments and vaccines (Silverman et al., 1992).

Pharmaceutical companies are not attracted to developing drugs for small markets; government research institutes do most of what research is done. Many known cures for relatively rare conditions would not be commercially produced if it were not for special government incentives (Asbury, 1981).

Interestingly, recent government incentives have themselves led to high drug prices by eliminating possible competition. The 1983 Orphan Drug Act granted seven-year market monopolies to companies developing treatment for relatively rare diseases. For example, Genentech was granted orphan-drug status for its version of the human growth hormone, for which it charged some $10,000 to $20,000 for a year's supply—at a hefty gross margin of 90 to 95 percent—for annual sales in 1987 of $86 million (Pollack, 1988). Some orphan drugs, like Ceredase, which is the only treatment for a rare hereditary disease, are actually discovered and initially tested by non-profit researchers rather than drug companies. Nevertheless, because of their limited market, a monopoly for their production is protected by the Orphan Drug Act, so the producer is allowed to set whatever price it chooses. In the case of Ceredase, the price was $380,000 for the first year of treatment at the recommended dosage (*The New York Times*, 1992).

In the United States, much medical research and new medical technological developments have been directed toward maximizing profits. Sometimes the interests of these corporations coincide with the needs of the sick, but there is no structural reason for this to occur. A market-oriented, profit-maximizing industry does not give first priority to the actual needs of the citizenry.

ECONOMIC INTERESTS AND THIRD-PARTY PAYMENT

The system of payment for health care in the United States is extremely complex; indeed, its very complexity makes it more costly. Ultimately, the American people pay all health care costs, but there are three main patterns by which the health care dollars are directed from the people to the providers: by direct payment by the consumer; from government taxation at various levels; and through private insurance companies, both for-profit and not-for-profit. Several large-scale agencies in government and the insurance industry have become extremely powerful factors in the health care system, and the interests they represent are influential in dealing with the providers as well as the recipients of health care. Their reimbursement policies and regulations become in effect nationally significant health policies. In many instances, these agencies overlap, such as when the government makes private health insurance companies the fiscal intermediaries for public funds; private companies thus profit by charging for administrative overhead. In addition, the foremost purchasers of private insurance are not the health care recipients but their employers, so the interests of business and other employers figure into this complex system.

Despite our national rhetoric regarding private enterprise, public funding is the single largest source of payments for health care, and reliance upon public funding is steadily increasing. In 1966, government payments (federal, state, and local funding) covered only 25.5 percent of all health care expenditures. By 1991, government payments accounted for 44 percent of all health care expenditures, compared to the 37 percent covered by private insurance and the 19 percent coming directly from patients (Letsch, 1993).

The existence of insurance for some citizens encouraged the inflation of costs for all, thus increasing the disparity in the affordability of health care for those with ample coverage and those with insufficient or no coverage. In the health care marketplace, demand is not a function of need. Many people need health care but cannot demand it, because they lack the means to pay.

Insurance functions to create the demand for goods and services among persons not wealthy enough to afford them easily otherwise. If a service or health care product is covered by insurance for enough people to create a sufficient market demand, prices spiral upward. For example, the expansion of Medicare and some private insurance coverage to home health care products and services created a profitable market. Because both private and public insurance provide piecemeal coverage and relatively weak regulation of the many industries involved, there are few incentives for providers and manufacturers to reduce the costs of needed, insurance-covered services or products.

The spiraling costs of U.S. health care, described in Chapters 11 and 12, have greatly contributed to the sense of crisis in the whole system, but they are not the foremost cause. Far more serious is the perception—especially on the part of ordinary citizens and the payers of private health insurance—that the present arrangement of health care insurance does not *secure* the health care of Americans. Americans have become afraid that they will be denied good medical care when they and their loved ones need it, afraid that they will lose their health insurance coverage, afraid that their insurance will not cover important medical needs, afraid that they could be thrown into poverty by uninsured costs of catastrophic illness or long-term nursing care. The following discussion documents the extent to which Americans' fears are, indeed, well founded. Until the health care system in the United States provides the security that all citizens will obtain good quality health care when they need it, the crisis will not have been resolved.

C. Wright Mills (1959) reminds us that we are often trapped in our private "troubles," when we fail to realize that they are the result of public issues. The private struggles for health care and health insurance experienced by families across the

United States are, indeed, the product of government and corporate policies which need to be reevaluated and changed. Boxes 12.1, 12.2, and 12.3 use a composite portrait of one family's private "troubles" to illustrate the larger systemic source of our crisis in health security.

BOX 12.1   *AN INSURANCE NIGHTMARE[5]*

Barbara was 40 when her husband divorced her, changed jobs, and moved out of state, leaving her and her two daughters without health insurance. Although she had been trained as a cosmetologist, workers in that field are often not able to obtain affordable health insurance. With little previous clerical experience, she considered herself lucky to find a job as a clerk-typist at a small university. The job had low pay—only $820 per month when she began in 1989, but at least it had a good benefits package—or so Barbara thought.

As the university struggled with soaring premium costs for employee health care, it made employees pay a greater and greater share. Shortly after Barbara began her job, the university announced that it would pay only a fixed amount per employee annually for all insurance premiums; the employees who wanted to be covered under the plan would have to pay the balance. In the first year of this so-called "flexible benefits" plan, the university paid a total of $110 per month toward Barbara's insurance coverage (life, disability, medical, and dental), but the premiums for family medical insurance alone cost $220 each month. During Barbara's second year on the job, the university's health insurer significantly increased the premiums because two employees had incurred significant medical expenses the preceding year. Although health costs had increased nationally by over 10 percent, the university increased its benefits "contribution" by 4 percent in the same year that the health insurance premiums for Barbara's family of three increased to $300 per month. The cost to Barbara amounted to nearly 30 percent of her after-tax income!

For a look at the larger picture, statistics show:

- At least 5 million women between 40 and 65 have no insurance as a result of divorce, death, or retirement of their spouse (Bodenheimer, 1990).
- Health insurance companies "redline" (i.e., do not offer coverage to) workers in entire industries, such as barber and beauty shops, convenience stores, hotels, restaurants, and construction (Light, 1992).
- Many insurers also engage in "policy churning," a practice that deliberately creates a regular turnover each year. By offering employers attractively low first-year prices, they sign on new group accounts but pay out very little because they build in a 12-month waiting period for most expensive health needs. In the second year, they increase the premiums dramatically for all but the lowest-risk groups, knowing that those companies can and will change to cheaper insurance elsewhere. Small companies are particularly vulnerable because risk cannot be spread over a large number of employees (Light, 1992).

---

[5] This story is a hypothetical composite of two persons' actual problems; identifying features have been changed to protect their anonymity.

Private Insurance

The very idea of and need for health insurance is a relatively recent development. Before the turn of the century, medical services consumed a small proportion of a family's budget. Doctors and other healers charged comparatively modest fees, which often were adjusted according to a person's ability to pay or were payable in kind (e.g., with a chicken or sack of potatoes). Pharmaceuticals were simple and inexpensive. The family itself provided most of the nursing care. Even then, however, lost income due to sickness could be devastating to a family.

With the rapid expansion of technologically sophisticated, hospital-centered medicine beginning in the early part of the twentieth century, costs quickly began to climb. Thus citizens encountered a greatly increased risk that the expenses incurred for treatment would exceed the family's ability to pay. The Depression of the 1930s created another major impetus for insurance, as voluntary hospitals experienced massive reductions in income due to patients' inability to pay. They supported (and financially underwrote) health insurance as a way to stabilize their incomes (Feigenbaum, 1987; Fein, 1986; Starr, 1982). In this climate, the idea of using health insurance to spread the financial risks over time and across a population of insured came to fruition.

In industrialized countries of Europe such as Sweden, Denmark, and Switzerland, national programs of compulsory health insurance were developed as early as 1883. These state-subsidized programs were not instituted mainly for medical costs (which were as yet small proportions of people's expenses) but rather for income maintenance—"sick pay." Nevertheless, their existence later enabled European nations to expand national coverage to include medical costs not just for workers but for all citizens (Starr, 1982: 237–240).

Blue Cross, created in the 1930s, was the foremost early form of health insurance in the United States. Actively encouraged by the American Hospital Association, Blue Cross was a not-for-profit hospital insurance plan based upon noncompeting territorial divisions in which participants paid premiums according to communitywide ratings. Although organized labor favored a national health insurance program instead, it accepted the Blue Cross alternative indirectly by including such insurance in bargaining agendas for labor contracts. When commercial insurers discovered that health insurance was an economically viable enterprise, several began to compete by offering coverage for expenses, such as doctors' fees, not insured by Blue Cross. In response Blue Cross developed its companion plan, Blue Shield, for nonhospital services.

Initially, the AMA opposed Blue Cross and other forms of third-party payment on the ideological grounds that they came between the doctor and patients, and restricted doctors' decisions about treatment. The AMA also committed considerable energies and funds to fighting various legislative attempts to create a national compulsory health insurance. Eventually, the medical profession agreed to accept Blue Shield, because it was given some control over the program and believed that such insurance would defuse the momentum toward a national program. By keeping health insurance out of the public sector, the medical profession gained a large measure of control and greatly increased its income (Starr, 1982: 290–334; see also Law, 1974).

Although Blue Cross had the benefit of preferred corporate status and tax treatment, as well as a much lower ratio of administrative costs to profit than commercial insurers, it began to lose its competitive edge in the 1950s. Blue Cross had been conceived as a plan for an entire community, and premium rates were based upon local experience with participants' hospital utilization and costs; risks were thus widely spread. The initial institutional goal was to stabilize hospital use and income; income from insurance itself was not important. The commercial insurers, however, explicitly sought income from insurance; their competitive strategy was to approach employers of low-risk groups and offer them much lower premiums than possible by the community-rating method of Blue Cross. Eventually, Blue Cross had to abandon its communitywide risk pool in order not to lose all the contracts for coverage of lower-risk employees (Feigenbaum, 1987; Starr, 1982: 327–331). The enduring effect of this development has been that certain groups (such as employees of very large corporations and those in occupations with fewer health problems) obtain insurance coverage at comparatively reasonable rates. Others (such as workers in companies with disproportionately large numbers of older and minority employees) are likely to receive little or no employment-related health insurance because their experience-rated premiums are too expensive for employers to absorb. One growing problem is the lack of regulation of the insurance industry; like the savings and loan industry in the 1980s, some insurance companies in the 1990s are severely undercapitalized, and, when they become insolvent, persons who thought they were insured are left unprotected.

Commercial insurance companies make money primarily in two ways: by paying out less in benefits than they receive in premiums, and by investing premium funds before disbursing them as benefits. Commercial insurers generally pay out a much smaller percent of their income in benefits than do Blue Cross and Blue Shield (McCarthy, 1981). Furthermore, insurance companies' portfolios frequently include investments in other for-profit health care ventures. For example, Connecticut General Insurance (also the holding company for Aetna) merged with the Insurance Company of North America and diversified its holdings; the new corporation, CIGNA, invested in a physician group in California, bought numerous for-profit hospitals in this country and elsewhere, and operates several HMOs. In addition, a subsidiary company acquired substantial investments in several for-profit health care chains, including Humana, HCA, and Beverly Enterprises. Thus, CIGNA became the third-largest diversified financial company, ranked by assets, in the United States (Wohl, 1984).

Control over such large sums for investment is a significant source of economic and political power for major insurance companies (Bodenheimer, 1990). The scale of their financial interests and power is indicated by the fact that insurance lobbyists to state legislatures outnumber lobbyists representing other interests (Bodenheimer, 1990). The insurance industry's contributions to congressional candidates in 1990 was $10.9 million (Makinson, 1992) and as health care reform became an issue in the 1992 national elections, the industry spent $18.6 million in congressional campaign contributions (Pear, 1991b; see also, Kemper and Novak, 1993; Podhorzer et al., 1993; Brightbill, 1991). Clearly, for-profit health insurance has become a big business, often exceeding in power (and sometimes buying out) the hospitals that originated the idea of health insurance.

Forms of Private Insurance.   To make benefit expenditures predictable and thereby assure a desirable profit margin, many commercial insurers offered indemnity plans, in contrast to Blue Shield's earlier service coverage. Indemnity plans specify limits to the costs borne by the insurer by imposing deductibles, copayments, limits on per-service payments, and annual and/or lifetime ceilings on payments for various types of service (Feigenbaum, 1987). Unlike the service plans offered by Blue Cross, Blue Shield, and some commercial insurers, indemnity plans involve no incentive for the insurer to pressure providers to keep costs down, because the excess is borne by the insured. Since individual health care recipients often have little choice among or leverage over hospitals and other providers, many persons covered by limited indemnity plans find themselves underinsured. Indemnity plans account for a decreasing proportion of the group insurance market since the mid-1980s, as employers and insurers shift to some form of *managed care* for cost

---

BOX 12.2   *THE INSURANCE NIGHTMARE CONTINUES*

Barbara began to look for a better job, but she was trapped by her insurance needs. Because her younger daughter had a history of asthma, no insurer would offer affordable private coverage for the family. Some employers offered no health insurance whatsoever, while others had group policies that excluded coverage for preexisting conditions, like Mary Ellen's asthma. So Barbara kept her job at the university and began to work a second job (with no benefits) at night.

Meanwhile, the insurer again steeply increased the premiums, so the university changed insurers. Barbara was temporarily relieved that her new premiums were only $235 per month, although she was concerned that the new arrangement had much higher deductibles and copayments, amounts she would have to pay out of pocket if the family used any medical services. Her relief was short-lived, however, because eight months later the insurance company declared bankruptcy, leaving employees struggling with mountains of paperwork for claims and negotiations with unpaid providers. Although eventually the state covered the employees' insured health expenses for the remainder of their contract, the university again searched for an affordable group insurance plan.

The larger picture shows:

- An estimated 6 percent of Americans have been denied coverage because of conditions such as diabetes, high blood pressure, birth defects or other problems indicating the potential for needing expensive care (Himmelstein et al., 1992).
- With very little federal regulation and uneven regulation by the states, the insurance industry can become precipitously undercapitalized; when health insurance companies and prepaid health care programs declare bankruptcy, the persons they were supposed to cover lose not only the health care for which they have prepaid but also their protection for coverage of preexisting conditions and other excludable health problems.

savings, as well as to shift a greater proportion of cost and risk to the insured and providers.

Managed-care forms of private insurance operate by negotiating with or hiring a limited number of health care providers, negotiating with or directly operating health care facilities (hospitals, offices, laboratories, therapeutic centers, and so on), and intensely screening prospective utilization of insured medical care. Thus, managed care severely limits, either directly or indirectly the choice of physician and hospital. By 1990, various forms of managed care accounted for 25.3 percent of group health insurance premiums, compared to less than 1 percent in 1984 (Hoy et al., 1991).

Preferred Provider Organizations (PPOs) involve an employer or insurance underwriter's contract with a limited number of doctors, hospitals, and other providers to offer services for the insured at a discounted rate. Insured patients who choose other providers must bear the difference in cost and often a higher copayment, as well. Likewise, the point-of-service plan, an adaptation of the PPO concept, typically allows enrollees to use services of off-network providers at a higher cost to the patient. Unlike other PPOs, however, they utilize network primary care physicians as gatekeepers to limit access to all other physicians, such as surgeons and specialists (Sullivan and Rice, 1991).

HMOs are prepaid health plans utilizing preferred providers who are either independently contracted or employed by an HMO group practice. Some HMOs, such as Kaiser in California and HIP in New York, are not-for-profit organizations; most, however, are profit seeking. As the name implies, health maintenance organizations are supposed to be particularly interested in prevention and health maintenance, with the expectation that this emphasis would reduce subsequent costs for acute care and illness treatments. Such long-term savings are difficult to achieve, however, because, as a form of insurance, HMOs are rarely involved in a person's entire illness-causing or preventive experience. An employee may be covered for a few years and then have a different insurer; HMOs also go out of business. Important health maintenance factors such as nutrition are outside the control of the HMO.

Cost and Access.   In the 1970s the federal government hoped that HMOs would contain health care costs better than other forms of insurance. It encouraged recipients of government insurance (e.g., Medicare) to use prepaid, preferred provider plans, but the anticipated efficiency gains and cost containment have not resulted, and premiums have risen rapidly (Freudenheim, 1988c). Indeed, several studies have shown that most HMOs in the 1980s were not more cost-efficient than conventional insurance plans, yet cost more in employee contributions, contributed to overall inflation of premium costs for all types of private insurance, and were sometimes engaged in outright fraudulent practices (Morone, 1990; PROPAC, 1988; see also Altman and Rodwin, 1988). Initially HMOs attempted to reform health care delivery in a group practice model, like the not-for-profit Kaiser plan, but large commercial insurers also created HMOs as a device to vertically integrate their investments in the industry.

By 1990 most HMOs were owned by commercial insurers (Bodenheimer, 1990) for which the HMO structure realized profits by controlling in a single agency patient utilization, provider reimbursement, and hospital costs. Increasing evidence suggests that patient dissatisfaction with HMOs is due largely to the limitations most HMOs impose to increase profitability: long waits to schedule appointments, long hours in the waiting room, followed by too little time with the doctor, severely limited selection of doctors, inconvenient locations and hours, shuttling patients from one doctor to another, and impersonal treatment (Rubin et al., 1993). Many HMOs and other prepaid plans create a conflict of interest for the doctors they employ or contract because they base their remuneration on expectations of low rates of referral to specialists and hospital utilization. With these incentives, doctors can maximize their earnings by decreasing medical services for their patients. This conflict of interest, which is the reverse of the conflict of interest under fee for service, can have perverse effects on the quality of care (Rodwin, 1993).

The financial collapse of several HMOs, including the giant Maxicare, which once covered over 2 million persons, paid substantial dividends to investors, and was touted as the best-managed HMO in the industry, left many enrollees uninsured and providers unpaid, highlighting the inadequate regulation of the industry (Freudenheim, 1989; Holden, 1989). The number of HMO failures per year increased from one in 1984 to 53 in 1988, and HMO mergers increased dramatically in the same period, leading to regulatory legislation in most states. The long-term effectiveness of the regulations for protecting consumers and creditors, as well as their effects on costs and competitiveness in the industry, remain to be seen (Christianson et al., 1991).

One of the biggest problems for persons counting on private health insurance is that as health costs have escalated rapidly, insurance companies and employers have passed on a significant part of that burden to the insured.[6] Between 1985 and 1987, as health care costs soared, the costs borne by employers rose by 35 percent, while those borne by employees increased by 58 percent. Some companies have dramatically raised the deductibles and out-of-pocket expenses to be paid by the employee, while others have dropped family coverage. Yet others have initiated *flexible benefits plans*, a euphemism for contributing a fixed amount toward premiums for *all* employee benefits, regardless of costs, and expecting employees to pay the rest (Kramon, 1988a). Although this form of cost shifting is relatively new, by 1990, 14 percent of all firms had such cafeteria-style benefits plans (Sullivan and Rice, 1991). Between 1980 and 1991, while the premium cost for an employee and family increased by 241 percent, employee out-of-pocket expenses increased by over 500 percent (Rasell, 1993; Short, 1988). Overall, between 1980 and 1989, the share of employees' health premiums paid for by employers declined from 80 to 69 percent, leaving the employee paying the rest (Levit et al., 1989).

---

[6] A growing problem has been that cost-cutting practices by insurers (especially private companies) and providers have made sick people themselves responsible for most of the paperwork for insurance claims. As a result, debilitating illness often results in an inability to collect insurance benefits while bills mount. An entire new business has arisen to process a claimant's paperwork in exchange for a percentage of the resulting benefits, thus further reducing the insured person's actual health care coverage.

BOX 12.3   *AN UNENDING NIGHTMARE?*

Subsequently, Barbara's employer decided to self-insure; that is, the university collected employees' premiums but set aside a portion of its own assets until the premium pool was sufficiently large to cover outlays. Thus, the employer saved some of the expense of commercial insurance, especially marketing costs and profit margin, and simultaneously controlled the assets, while briefly collecting earnings on the insurance pool. Under the new plan, Barbara's premiums were $255 per month. The university paid $130 toward her premium, with nothing left over for her life or disability insurance premiums.

The self-insured plan retained the terms (e.g., deductibles and copayments) of the prior commercial plan, but added a new cost-saving device: It affiliated with a PPO (preferred provider organization). If Barbara's family used doctors and hospitals not on the preferred provider list, she had to pay considerably larger deductibles and copayments each visit. So Barbara had to find completely new doctors, selected from the ones on a negotiated list. After she established relationships with the new doctors, she had to change twice more because the approved list was continually changing. Barbara's family has not used the PPO enough yet to discover that her insurance includes some "gotcha" clauses—elaborate rules for eligibility which, if not followed precisely, will disqualify even their legitimate claims.

Although the self-insured plan is more stable, Barbara's worries are not over. Next year her older daughter starts college. She has a good scholarship offer to an excellent college in another state, but Barbara worries whether her daughter ought to go to a nearby state college in order to be near the preferred provider hospitals and doctors. Barbara also worries whether her employer will decide to retroactively exclude her younger daughter's asthma from coverage. Just this year, the university excluded coverage for AIDS, hospitalization for mental illness and substance abuse, and dependent teenagers' pregnancies. Will they, in the near future, exclude or limit coverage for her family's needs, too?

The larger picture shows:

- Employer self-insurance is an important recent trend; in 1975, only 5 percent of employees were covered by self-insured plans. By 1985, more than 50 percent were in self-insured plans, which now control a market share greater than that of commercial insurers or Blue Cross/Blue Shield plans (Bodenheimer, 1990; Sullivan and Rice, 1991).

- Both commercial insurers and self-insured companies use complex coverage to reduce the number and costs of claims they must pay. See Light (1992) on eligibility rules, claims harassment, exclusion by association, and other tactics to deny coverage.

- Self-insured employers are not restricted by the same regulations as the insurance industry. In the 1990s, a U.S. Supreme Court decision affirmed the employer's power to set limits on coverage, including retroactive changes in the nature and level of coverage, so employees can find themselves seriously underinsured and without recourse.

Exact figures are not available on the number of persons who are *underinsured* due to seriously limited health plans; often employees do not discover how poorly they are insured until they are denied benefits during an actual health crisis. Employer cost-cutting measures are likely to lead to an increase in the proportion of Americans who are under- or uninsured (Farley, 1985). Some policy analysts argue that patients should have to pay a substantial share of the costs of each use of health care services (e.g., higher deductibles) in order to make them more selective and cost-conscious. The Rand Health Experiment of 1974–82 found that while cost sharing did reduce the demands for health services, it did *not* result in good decisions about those demands; in fact, financial barriers reduced the use of health services even when those services were needed and appropriate (Lohr et al., 1986). Greater cost sharing likewise does not lead to more competitive pricing and consumer "shopping" (Marquis, 1984). In the United States, lack of adequate insurance essentially means severely limited access to health care.

The U.S. system of private insurance is structurally inefficient and expensive to administer because it is based upon the exclusion and discrimination of denying coverage to those who need the most health care. In order to maximize profits, insurance companies compete to avoid insuring higher-risk persons—those likely to actually need health care (Light, 1992). They issue complex policies with elaborate exclusions, such as excluding all costs of care for conditions that patients had before becoming covered by that insurance policy, and different terms of coverage for different groups of employees. To screen all claims by insured patients to enforce these exclusions and other restrictive terms, commercial insurance companies spend 33.5 cents for each dollar of benefits provided. These administrative costs are 14 times those of Medicare (2.3 cents per dollar), because all persons covered by Medicare have the same coverage and terms (Brandon et al., 1991).[7]

This estimate of insurers' administrative inefficiency does not include the cost of paperwork on the part of the providers and claimants, which further add to the costliness of the U.S. health care system. The administrative, overhead, and marketing costs of commercial insurance companies have increased faster than the costs of providing health care. Some analysts have suggested that a public program of universal coverage would save enough on these costs that efficiency savings alone would pay for insurance for more than 10 million Americans who are presently without coverage (Brandon et al., 1991).

Public Programs

The number, type, and quality of health care programs financed from tax revenues by various levels of government demonstrate the complexity and inadequacy of the U.S. health care system. The federal government, for example, directly provides care for large numbers of persons in the military and their dependents, veterans' hospitals, and federal prisons. The largest federal health insurance programs

---

[7] Recent proposals for "managed competition" among large networks of insurers would not eliminate most of these administrative costs and may actually increase the costs for advertising, marketing, and commissions (Clancy et al., 1993).

subsidize some care for the poor (Medicaid) and elderly (Medicare). The federal government also finances much health-related research, and has at times supported medical education and other training programs. State, county, and municipal governments also fund health care, by maintaining, for example, public hospitals, nursing homes, community health services, and health programs. State governments are also cosponsors of Medicaid and other health services for the indigent. The quality of and access to medical care provided by these many programs vary widely across the nation, but there is no national organization or central planning to coordinate or regulate even the public efforts, much less to connect public and private programs.

Medicare.   Medicare was enacted in 1965 to finance acute medical care mainly for elderly Americans. Coverage was expanded in 1972 to include people with chronic kidney disease or long-term disabilities. By 1991, Medicare covered 34.9 million Americans. The program has two parts: Part A is hospital insurance, funded by a portion of the Social Security payroll tax. Part B is supplementary medical insurance (SMI) for physicians' services, outpatient care, laboratory fees, and home health care; because it is funded through general federal revenues, its growth as a budget item contributes to the federal deficit and pits health care financing against other expenses, such as defense. Partly in response to the influence of hospitals, doctors, and other interest groups, from the outset Medicare was aimed at the acute medical care of the elderly. Chronic illness and long-term care, which are of limited relevance to acute care hospitals and to many doctors, were not part of the plan, even though they affect the health status and economic well-being of the elderly as much or even more than acute illness. Thus, Medicare does not cover many needed health services and products.

Before Medicare, only about one-third of the elderly had health insurance; private insurance rates were outside the means of most older Americans. The enactment of Medicare immediately increased the average health care utilization rate among the elderly by more than 30 percent (Sorkin, 1986). Although it dramatically increased access to health care, Medicare failed to protect beneficiaries from destitution in the face of health care costs, because its cost-sharing provisions did not limit liabilities in the event of catastrophic illness and did not cover most long-term or nursing home care.

The financing of Medicare has been problematic from the outset. To overcome the objections to the programs by doctors, insurance companies, hospitals, and various other interest groups, Medicare legislation created less of a public health care program and more of an infusion of public money into private channels (Fein, 1986: 69–92). Initially, there were few cost-control regulations in the program. Partly because of the increased utilization of health care services but largely because of rapidly increasing charges by various providers, the expenditures were far more than anticipated. A limited cost-control measure was introduced in 1972, but it was largely ineffective. Between 1979 and 1982, expenditures under Medicare grew much faster than general inflation: hospital care by a rate of 17.2 percent per year, physician services by a 19.2 percent rate (Gibson et al., 1982; Sorkin, 1986). Part of the costliness was due to the fact that high tech medicine and labor-intensive medical care are not as responsive to efficiency and other cost-savings measures as other industries; and part was due simply to overexpansion, greed, and in some case outright fraud on the part of providers, hospitals, and insurance administrators.

While the AMA initially fought against the creation of Medicare, the medical profession has been among its prime beneficiaries, and now generally supports the program and its expansion. To secure the cooperation of physicians, the initial Medicare legislation allowed reimbursement of doctors' "usual and customary fees," so long as those fees were "reasonable." Such vague language, especially in the context of a seldom competitive fee-setting process, led to rapid inflation. Fees increased disproportionate to other rates of inflation; the number of elderly treated increased, and the number of medical services ordered by doctors for their Medicare patients rose markedly. Under Medicare, doctors who had previously treated the needy elderly for a fraction of their normal charges could receive their "customary" full payments. Physicians who had previously been frustrated by their inability to treat their pensioner-patients with the best available methods could, under Medicare, prescribe therapies without prejudice of ability to pay. The influx of Medicare funding provided stability for both physician and hospital income, much as private health insurance had done three decades earlier (Fein, 1986: 80–92). The very complexity of Medicare regulations and reimbursement paperwork, however, adds enormously to the cost of the program. The waste of resources on administrative costs in the United States is particularly highlighted by contrasts with Canada and Great Britain, where insurance company intermediaries are eliminated and providers deal directly with the government rather than struggle with billing and collections (Himmelstein and Woolhandler, 1986; see also Fein, 1986: 157; Lee, 1982).

A major ongoing problem has been that some providers do not accept Medicare rates of reimbursement, so patients must bear the cost of the difference (Fein, 1986: 88–92). Because reimbursement is still based upon fee-for-service rates, there is no incentive for physicians to reduce the number of services or recommend less costly services. New Medicare regulations are regularly being proposed to try to contain costs, to ascertain greater physician cooperation, and to get better care for the moneys spent. The process is essentially a political one in which providers and insurers have disproportionately powerful voices (cf. Marmor et al., 1983b). Whether successful regulations will be enacted or have their desired effect remains to be seen. While Medicare has been an important contribution to the health of covered citizens, it is less and less sufficient for their needs, and less able than ever to cover the increasing proportion of the eligible population. Without major restructuring and massive new sources of funding, Medicare is not a program upon which citizens may rely for the future.

Medicaid.   Medicaid was created at the same time as Medicare, but was organized very differently. Because Medicaid is funded through general revenues rather than a trust fund, and because it is perceived as charity rather than deserved aid, the program is particularly vulnerable to cutbacks at every funding level. Each state operates its own program, with federal contributions varying according to the scope of the state's program, relative level of income, and certain features of providers and recipients. Thus several states that have instituted highly restrictive Medicaid programs do not receive as large a proportion of federal funds as they could with a broader program. The federal program includes health care for persons covered by federal Supplemental Security Income (SSI), which assists blind, disabled, and elderly persons; members of families eligible for Aid to Families with Dependent Children (AFDC); and pregnant women in certain income brackets. Many states have defined the criteria for Medicaid so stringently that they exclude more than half the people who could be covered under federal guidelines (Fein, 1986: 108–112; for a critical history of Medicaid, see Stevens and Stevens, 1974). Only 35 percent of Americans living in poverty have health care coverage through public assistance, mainly Medicaid (Ries, 1991).

Due to deficiencies in Medicare coverage, Medicaid has become a significant source of funding for health care for the elderly. Some states use Medicaid to pay Medicare premiums, deductibles, and copayments that poor elderly persons cannot afford. Medicaid also covers services, such as long-term care, not provided by Medicare (after recipients have exhausted their resources and become poor enough to meet Medicaid guidelines). More than 65 percent of U.S. nursing home residents are supported by Medicaid (Pear, 1993a). In New York, for example, approximately 30 percent of all Medicaid spending went for nursing home care. Children constitute 46 percent of the Medicaid-eligible population, but consume only about 13 percent of Medicaid funds; the elderly used 41 percent of Medicaid dollars, while representing only 13 percent of those eligible (Kolbert, 1991). Thus, Medicaid has not functioned primarily as a source of health care for lower-class persons, especially children, among whom poverty rates are approaching a 30-year high. Rather, its main recipients appear to be those who were made poor by the costs of health care in disability and old age (Fein, 1986: 112).

The House Select Committee on Aging reported that 90 percent of single elderly patients "spend down" to the poverty level after one year in a nursing home by paying nursing home charges that average $22,000 per year; half of the couples with one spouse in a nursing home reach poverty level within six months, and the well spouse is left destitute, often with many years of life ahead. Thus, Medicaid has become the de facto long-term care supplement to Medicare, paying about half of all expenditures for nursing home care (Crickmer, 1988).

The administrative costs of Medicaid are higher than for Medicare. Many states parcel out portions of the program to various local agencies or institutional providers; the several layers multiply administrative costs. Furthermore, unlike Medicare, Medicaid eligibility must be determined by complex formulas and continually reviewed, since agencies have a state-directed imperative to trim rolls and discourage coverage. Medicaid is governed by federal, state, and often local regulations (for patient eligibility, services covered, and the like), the sheer volume and complexity of which create enormous administrative costs. A substantial portion of the funds that Americans believe are used for health care is actually going to the mere administration of public insurance programs (Fein, 1986).

Ironically, the greatest documented abuses of Medicaid funding have been on the part of unscrupulous providers, often abetted by the politically motivated purchasing policies of state and local agencies. For example, in 1971 the California legislature passed the Medical Reform Act, facilitating the assignment of Medicaid recipients to HMOs contracting with the state. The legislature had reasoned that these large health care contractors would be more efficient, reduce utilization (which had become "excessive" under fee-for-service payment plans), and thus be more cost-effective than previous arrangements with independent providers. In fact, however, the welfare HMOs charged more. Compared to other HMOs, which spent about 10 percent of the premium dollar on administration and profits, welfare HMOs used 52 percent of state payments for administration and profits (Lewis, 1976). Subsequent investigations also showed that the utilization of services had been cut by using foreign physicians who spoke limited English, by contracting with proprietary hospitals 30 to 50 miles from the client population, by offering only brief office hours, and by denying emergency services and referrals to specialists (Gabel and Redisch, 1979). Subsequent research found that persons enrolled in Medicaid-paid HMOs suffered considerably worse health outcomes than those whose Medicaid paid for conventional fee-for-service visits (cited in Davis, 1991).

The structure of Medicaid has thus encouraged a two-tiered system of medical care, with the service to those covered by Medicaid being distinctly inferior. Medicaid has, however, increased the access of the poor to *some* medical assistance; after the implementation of the program, poor families used significantly more physician services and hospitalization. Likewise, when government cutbacks reduced Medicaid rolls, the poor with no insurance had significantly less access and utilization than those with Medicaid (Davis, 1991). It has not given the poor access to mainstream medical care, however; for example, poor children are particularly likely to be treated in hospital outpatient services rather than by private physicians. Nor has the program enabled the poor to obtain sufficient medical attention relative to their generally greater health needs (Marmor, 1983).

The two tiers of the American health care delivery system appear to be further and further apart, as cost-cutting measures make even the middle classes vulnerable to restrictions on the freedom of choice of providers, limitations on covered services, and prohibitively high copayment levels. While the poor are the first to be limited, more restricted, and less well served, all but the wealthiest in American society are experiencing severe economic limits in their health care. For example, the state of Oregon and Alameda County in California became the first U.S. government units to plan the explicit rationing of health care for the poor by attempting to give priority to medical procedures that save the most lives and give a better quality of life to more people. For example, prenatal care, children's immunizations and certain other preventive measures, and treatment of acute and chronic illnesses are given high priority; organ transplants, plastic surgery, speech therapy, and dental care receive low priority. While for now explicit rationing applies mainly to Medicaid recipients, it is likely to be adopted by insurers of the middle class as well (Gross, 1989).

The Uninsured and Underinsured

Since most private insurance is linked with the fringe benefits of certain kinds of employment, large numbers of Americans have no health insurance whatsoever; others are insured only occasionally or have extremely limited benefits. Premium costs for adequate amounts of insurance are much lower for large group coverage, such as that purchased by businesses, and they are virtually prohibitively expensive for individual purchasers. Table 12.1 shows the percent of the U.S. population who in 1989 were without any health care coverage (public or private); it also shows the distribution of health care coverage by age, sex, race, income, poverty status, and age.

In 1993, an estimated 38.9 million Americans had *no private or public coverage* for their medical expenses; an estimated 53 million were without health coverage for part of the year. Despite large, steady increases in government health spending for Medicaid and Medicare and other programs, the number of persons uninsured has increased significantly throughout the 1980s. Whereas in 1977, only 13.8 percent of the under-65 population was uninsured, by 1987 an additional 10 million persons— a total of one out of six nonelderly persons—were in the ranks of the uninsured (Rice, 1991). Furthermore, due to loss of employment and cutbacks in employment benefits, the *rate* of increase in numbers of uninsured persons also increased between 1989 and 1992 (Pear, 1993; Steinmetz, 1993).

TABLE 12.1   Percent of the U.S. Population with Health Care Coverage by Poverty Status, Race, and Age, 1989

| | Percent Covered by | | | Percent with |
| | Private | | Public | no |
Poverty Status	Insurance	Medicare	Assistance	Coverage[a]
In poverty	28	12	35	33
under 65	26	2	36	36
65 and over	46	94	28	2
Not in poverty	84	12	2	10
under 65	85	1	2	12
65 and over	82	95	4	1
Race				
White	79	13	4	13
under 65	79	1	4	15
65 and over	81	95	5	1
Black	57	9	17	20
under 65	58	2	17	22
65 and over	44	91	18	3
All persons[b]	76	13	6	14

[a] Includes other sources of coverage (e.g., V.A., military).

[b] Includes other races.

Source: Peter Ries, "Characteristics of persons with and without health care coverage: United States, 1989," *Advance Data* 201, June 18, 1991, p. 2.

Certain segments of the population were particularly hurt. Table 12.1 highlights the plight of the working poor, those people whose jobs provide no health insurance benefits, but who earn somewhat too much to be eligible for Medicaid and yet too little to afford private, non group insurance. Employed persons and their dependents account for approximately 70 to 75 percent of the uninsured population (Rice, 1991). Furthermore, since these estimates are based on those uninsured at the time of the survey, the number of those uninsured at some time in the year is probably far higher because many workers become temporarily laid off or have only seasonal work. Another 50 million Americans are *underinsured*; they have some health insurance but it is inadequate to protect them from financial disaster in case of serious or prolonged illness (Himmelstein et al., 1992.

Blacks and Hispanics are particularly likely to be uninsured because they are disproportionately represented among the working poor, in jobs paying no insurance benefits, and in regions of the United States where labor is less commonly unionized (see Ginzberg, 1991). For example, the percentage of Mexican-Americans under the age of 65 who are uninsured is approximately 3.5 times that of white, non-Hispanics. Among the uninsured Mexican-Americans, more than half were gainfully employed but were living at or below the poverty level (Treviño et al., 1991).

Particularly troubling is the high proportion of children who are without health insurance. In 1989, approximately 12 million U.S. children were uninsured, and much of the recent increase is uninsured middle-class children whose numbers increased by 20 percent between 1987 and 1989. According to the Children's Defense Fund, approximately 40 percent of the nation's children have no health coverage from employer-based insurance. And the proportion is growing; between 1990 and 1991, 284,000 children lost coverage that previously had come through a parent's employer (Whitmire, 1992).

Public assistance becomes the only possible source of health coverage for many children because without employer-based group insurance, families cannot afford private insurance. While there was more than a 30 percent increase in child poverty compared to the preceding decade, in 1987 Medicaid actually served 400,000 fewer children (Johnson, 1989). States vary widely in the income threshold for Medicaid coverage, such that in some states more than half of all children whose families earn less than the poverty level are not covered by Medicaid. For example, while Wisconsin, Rhode Island, and Maine had only about 10 to 11 percent uninsured children among those below the poverty level, New Mexico excluded 44 percent, and Texas excluded 51.4 percent of poor children from Medicaid coverage (Cartland and Yudkowsky, 1993).

Having no health insurance severely limits people's access to health care, often forcing them to postpone care which could prevent a problem from becoming a serious or even life-threatening illness. In the 1960s and 1970s, the gap in access to medical care between the nonpoor and the poor or near-poor had been steadily closing, but in the 1980s the gap widened dramatically (Davis, 1991; Rice, 1991; Freeman et al., 1987). For example, lack of health insurance led to fewer women getting prenatal care, and their newborns were disproportionately likely to have serious health problems (see Braverman et al., 1989). Large numbers of children were not getting minimally necessary inoculations during their preschool years, and more families were using hospital emergency rooms as their only accessible entry to any health care.

Furthermore, public insurance programs rarely cover all needed expenses; for example, in 1986, Medicare covered only about 40 percent of elderly persons' actual health care expenses (Dowd, 1987). Medicaid coverage is worse than that of Medicare, in that Medicaid pays doctors, on average, only 69 percent of what Medicare pays, and an even smaller proportion of what private insurers pay (Pear, 1991). As a result, many doctors refuse to accept Medicaid patients, and many Medicaid-insured patients are shunted into overcrowded and sometimes inferior-quality clinics for what services they do receive (Rosenthal, 1990).

Even seemingly small medical expenditures become financially catastrophic for families with low incomes and poor health insurance. One study found that in 1977 two-thirds of all families spending 20 percent or more of their income on medical care and one-half of those spending 10 percent or more were below the poverty level. The growing numbers of persons living in poverty, together with cutbacks in Medicaid funding, make it likely that many Americans will experience financially catastrophic medical bills (Berki, 1986).

Problems of access to and the underutilization of health care services also appear to have grown during the 1980s. One study found that between 1982 and 1986 Americans' overall rate of hospitalization declined from 9 to 7 percent, while per capita physician visits declined from 4.8 to 4.3 percent. Some of this decline may be due to reductions in *overutilization* in response to cost cutting by providers, insurers, government agencies, and employers. There are indications, however, that the decline is also due to decreased access to physician care for certain segments of the population that are particularly likely to be in poor health: Those who are poor, black, and/or uninsured. Table 12.2 shows indicators of potential underuse of medical care.

TABLE 12.2   Indicators of Potential Underuse of Medical Care, 1986

Problem	U.S.	Low Income	Black	Hispanic	Uninsured
Percent with chronic illness without physician visit in a year	17	18	25	22	20
Among persons with one or more physician visits in year, percent with serious symptoms who did not see or contact a physician	41	42	39	53	67
Percent pregnant women without first trimester prenatal care	15	30	17	27	20
Percent of persons with hypertension without blood pressure check in a year	20	15	30	30	22
Percent without a dentist visit in a year	38	57	50	47	—

Source: Howard E. Freeman, Robert J. Blendon, Linda H. Aiken, Seymour Sudman, Connie F. Mullinix, and Christopher R. Corey, "Americans report on their access to health care," *Health Affairs* 6(1), 1987: 14. Reprinted by permission of Project HOPE, Millwood, Virginia.

It suggests that the lack of insurance, minority status, and low income are all related to the insufficient use of medical services for identifiable chronic and serious illness (e.g., cancer, heart disease, and stroke), for serious symptoms (e.g., loss of consciousness, unexplained bleeding, and chest pain when exercising), and for prenatal care.

National Health Insurance: The Canadian Model

National health insurance is a perennial issue in the United States. As early as 1914 and with increasing fervor in the 1930s and 1940s, some American health reformers were urging social insurance legislation comparable to that in Europe. Insurance companies and the AMA vigorously fought these proposals (Starr, 1982: 240–289). The idea of a national health insurance has been raised in Congress many times since, but America has not yet enacted *any* comprehensive health care program for its citizens.

In light of the large numbers of uninsured and underinsured Americans and the rapidly escalating burden of health care expenditures, many U.S. policymakers are debating the merits of the Canadian national health insurance. Since 1972, a national program has covered all Canadian citizens for hospitalization, physician care, and many ancillary services. Private insurers are legally excluded from the health care arena. Health care providers are mostly in the private sector, but the government controls expenses through its monopoly on payment (for example, with a binding fee schedule). Many incentives for excessive surgery and other costly procedures have been eliminated. Because all citizens are covered by the same level and kind of insurance, administrative costs in Canada are far lower than in the United States; for instance, U.S. hospital administrative costs average 24.8 percent of overall spending—about 2.5 times the rate of Canadian hospitals (Woolhandler et al., 1993).

Canadian doctors have many incentives to work in primary care and to locate their practices in the kinds of communities, such as rural or inner-city areas, that would be seriously underserved in the United States. The Canadian government maintains a smaller proportion of specialists (about one for every four primary care physicians, compared to one to one in the United States). Canadian doctors are paid far less than U.S. doctors, but they remain the best-paid professionals in Canada. Doctors are paid on a fee-for-service basis, according to a fixed, annually negotiated schedule, but there are some caps on the total amounts doctors can earn. There is no evidence that Canadian doctors are sufficiently dissatisfied with their system to leave to practice elsewhere, and Canada has a higher proportion of applicants for medical school than in the United States (Adams, 1993; Rosenthal, 1991; *Consumer Reports*, 1990; Wolfe, 1990).

Patients are free to choose their own doctor, although they must be referred by a primary care physician to use services of specialists. When Canadians consult the doctor or go to the hospital, they simply show their medical card; they are not billed at all. Health care providers may not add on any charges, such as copayments, over those covered by the national insurance program. Canada's program covers most medical services, including many (e.g., long-term home care and nursing-home care) not covered by medical insurance in the United States. The provinces are allowed but not required to cover additional services, such as physiotherapy, eyeglasses, and adult dental care (Kane, 1993; Rosenthal, 1991; Wolfe, 1990).

Control over the hospital sector also keeps costs down. Diagnostic tests are centralized, which provides no profits to physicians or labs. Hospitals are run by each province on an annual budget basis, with no incentives to overbuild or invest in duplicates of expensive technological devices. Authorization for purchase of new technology is more conservative in Canada than in the United States. The policy in Canada is to wait until there is strong evidence of the medical effectiveness, safety, and usefulness of expensive technology, and then to purchase gradually while gauging the actual rate of use of facilities. These controls have enabled the Canadian system to keep its health care expenditures to a much smaller portion of the country's GNP, while providing very high rates of access to health care for all citizens (Wolfe, 1990; Marmor et al., 1983a; Lee, 1982; Marmor, 1982).

The Canadian system does have several drawbacks, however, compared to health care services afforded by upper-class Americans. There are sometimes substantial waits, especially for nonemergency hospital procedures. Provincial facilities for some high-tech procedures and testing may not be located conveniently. The system also has an operative form of rationing, especially of very expensive services such as organ transplants. For example, a person with unfavorable prospects for long-term health benefits from a kidney transplant would be less likely than in the United States to be able to obtain one. Despite these drawbacks, even in years of underfunding, Canadians are highly satisfied with their system (Blendon et al., 1990). In a survey of ten industrialized nations, Canada had the highest proportion (56 percent) of citizens who stated the health care system needed only minor changes (the Netherlands, France, and Germany were the next most satisfied). The United States was at the bottom, with only 10 percent agreeing that only minor changes are needed (L. Harris Associates, cited in *The New York Times,* 1991).

Had the United States enacted a national health program such as Canada's several decades ago, it might have realized similar cost controls and universal health care access. Now, however, vested interests profiting from the laissez-faire American system have become so entrenched, economically centralized, and powerful that it would be extremely difficult to establish any economical national health plan, even one as limited as national health insurance. A few decades ago, U.S. hospitals could have been organized as public facilities, but now many are organized as for-profit businesses with major investments to protect. Expensive high tech medical equipment has already been purchased; excessive hospital rooms have already been built. Likewise, health insurance is big business; without eliminating the profit and paperwork of third-party payments, a national health plan could not realize the kinds of savings of the Canadian system. Stringent government controls could prevent national health insurance from creating yet another inflationary spiral of health costs, but is there sufficient political will to take such a strong stand (Marmor et al., 1983a)?

A national insurance program would probably resolve one major aspect of the current crisis in the U.S. health care system: the access of poor and middle-class people to adequate physician and hospital care. National health insurance also has the potential, if implemented with certain regulatory safeguards, of improving the quality of care received by nonwealthy citizens. Absent major structural changes to eliminate or greatly restrict profit taking, however, a national health insurance program would probably not be able to reduce or even control costs.

The American people could decide that affordable health care for all is a sufficiently important value to warrant such structural changes. The enormous political and economic power of the vested interests of hospital corporations, insurance companies, medical industries, and health care providers would almost certainly be utilized to fight those changes.

Our society needs to consider whether health care is a basic human right that a government should provide for its citizens. Does a country have obligations to provide universal health care, comparable to universal education? To how much and what kind of health care or medical care do people have a right? What priority should health care expenditures have, relative to other national spending in such cases as the military, education, highways, and the environment? Our society's health policy reflects the larger values of the nation: What kind of a people do we want to be? Perhaps the current crisis in the American health system will encourage public discourse on these broader moral and political issues.

SUMMARY

Continuing our sketch of the U.S. medical system, in this chapter we focused on large-scale organizations such as hospitals, insurance companies, health maintenance organizations, and medical industries. As American medicine has become increasingly specialized and reliant on high technology, these organizations have consolidated their power and economic interests. The corporatization of hospitals has changed the economic situation for patients, and affected the autonomy of physicians and other health care professionals. Insurance companies have become powerful agents in the health care system, creating regulations and controlling access to health services. In an array of poorly articulated programs, government agencies are also significant third-party payers and direct providers of health services. Medical industries, especially those researching and developing new pharmaceuticals and technologies, have substantial economic interests in health-related markets. Always a loosely regulated, relatively unplanned, laissez-faire arrangement, the American health system is now powerfully dominated by large, for-profit industries.

This system has resulted in major problems of access and cost. The quality of care available under the system is mixed; much is outstanding, but much is terrible. While the poor receive generally lower-quality medical care, spending lots of money on medical services does not guarantee good quality. Structural incentives, which are related to profitability, are responsible for both the achievements and failures of the American medical system. The problems of the American system clearly illustrate a key theme emphasized throughout this volume: Health and illness are socially produced, especially by structural features of power and stratification.

CONCLUSION

Throughout this book, we have outlined numerous ideas about how society affects the body, health, and illness. These ideas, however, are not mere abstractions, removed from people's actual lives. Real people get sick, experience afflictions, and try to find help; real people also enjoy health, and successfully use their bodies to enrich themselves and to fulfill their goals. Even seemingly abstract social factors, such as social control, economic organization and cultural practices, are—for individuals—very real in their consequences.

The issues we raise in this text suggest the diverse points at which social arrangements might be changed to help reach the goal of a healthier society. We hope we have stimulated readers to consider many ways to promote health in this society and globally. It is necessary to have a genuinely holistic understanding of the connections between the mind, body, and society to envision the far-ranging possibilities for enhancing health. We need to go way beyond narrow medical conceptions of health and to appreciate the entire web of socioenvironmental contexts that promote health. From such a holistic perspective, we might not only imagine changes in obvious problem areas, such as nutrition, water pollution, occupational health, and health care financing, but also consider possible health-promoting alterations in areas such as urban landscapes, automobile design, dependent care programs, media messages, and uses of leisure. A broad, holistic perspective to health transforms our ways of thinking about what is relevant to health and to illness prevention.

Similarly, we have suggested points of influence for improvements in the prevention and treatment of illness. Since power is such a pivotal factor in both illness causation and treatment, when we envision healthier alternative social arrangements, we should give special attention to considering changes in the exercise of power and to social arrangements that encourage the empowerment of individuals. Likewise, we have noted the importance of access to resources to stay healthy or to get well. Alternative scenarios for a healthier society need to pay close attention to social inequalities and the way we choose to distribute the resources necessary to be well or to be alive.

While the social arrangements that influence our health may seem remote and objectlike, they are human products and as such can be humanly changed. It is necessary, however, for us to move beyond the boundaries of our individual lives to effect many measures that potentially have a wide-ranging ability to prevent illness and death. Our purpose in examining the institutional sources of illness and problems in health care is not to blame but rather to suggest some of the points at which social structure and social policy can be changed. Understanding the complex interrelationships of these arrangements prevents naïve notions that an isolated new program, policy change, or medical innovation will alone produce dramatic changes in people's health. While most envisioned changes are matters of policy and social organization, some needed changes are embedded in cultural values and stubbornly change-resistant social structures; while still human products, they often change more slowly. Nevertheless, becoming aware of the human sources of the social arrangements that shape our lives is a first step in making effective efforts to change those forces.

RECOMMENDED READINGS

Articles

Karen Davis, "Inequality and access to health care," *The Milbank Quarterly* 69(2) 1991: 253–273.

Carol McCarthy, "Financing for health care," pp. 272–312 in S. Jonas, ed., *Health Care Delivery in the United States.* New York: Springer, 1981.

J. Warren Salmon, "Profit and health care: Trends in corporatization and proprietization," *International Journal of Health Services* 15(3), 1985: 395–418.

Roberta G. Simmons and Susan Klein Marine, "The regulation of high cost technology medicine: The case of dialysis and transplantation in the U.K.," *Journal of Health and Social Behavior* 25, 1984: 320–334.

Howard Waitzkin, "Health policy in the United States: Problems and alternatives," pp. 475–491 in H. Freeman and S. Levine, eds., *Handbook of Medical Sociology.* Englewood Cliffs, NJ: Prentice-Hall, 1989.

Books

Bradford Gray, *The Profit Motive and Patient Care: The Changing Accountability of Doctors and Hospitals.* Cambridge, MA: Harvard University Press, 1991. This is a useful analysis of various ways the pursuit of profit affects the contemporary health care system.

John B. McKinlay, ed., *Issues in the Political Economy of Health Care.* New York: Tavistock, 1984. This volume contains excellent articles on the social production of health and illness, capital interests and the role of the state, for-profit medical care, the pharmaceutical industry, and political-economic relationships between physicians and their sponsors.

Charles E. Rosenberg, *The Care of Strangers: The Rise of America's Hospital System.* New York: Basic, 1987. This book is a fascinating social history of hospitals and the place of various medical professions within them; it offers an excellent background for understanding contemporary policy issues.

APPENDIX A

Literature in the Sociology of Health and Illness

I. Social science journals in health and illness

Culture, Medicine, and Psychiatry (D. Reidel), quarterly
International Journal of Health Services (Baywood), quarterly
Journal of Health and Social Behavior (American Sociological Association), quarterly
Medical Anthropology Quarterly (American Anthropological Association and Society for Medical Anthropology), quarterly
Social Science & Medicine (Pergamon Press [U.K.]), 24 issues per year
Sociology of Health and Illness: A Journal of Medical Sociology (Basil Blackwell [U.K.]), quarterly
Women and Health (Haworth Press), quarterly

II. Sources on current issues, social policy, and health ethics

Disability Studies Quarterly (Brandeis University, Department of Sociology), quarterly
Hastings Center Reports (The Hastings Center), bimonthly
Health/PAC Bulletin (Health Policy Advisory Committee), bimonthly
Health Affairs (Project HOPE), bimonthly
Journal of Health Politics, Policy, and Law (Duke University, Department of Health Administration), quarterly
Journal of Public Health Policy (National Association for Public Health Policy), quarterly
Milbank Quarterly (Milbank Memorial Fund), quarterly
The Network News (National Women's Health Network), bimonthly

III. Medical and public health journals

American Journal of Public Health (American Public Health Association), monthly
The Lancet (Lancet [U.K.]), weekly
Medical Care (American Public Health Association, Medical Care Section), monthly
New England Journal of Medicine (Massachusetts Medical Society), weekly

IV. Periodicals with good coverage of health and health policy issues

The Economist (U.K.), monthly
The New York Times, daily
The Wall Street Journal, daily

V. Newsletters and magazines

The Disability Rag (Avacado Press), bimonthly
Health Facts (Center for Medical Consumers), monthly
Health Letter (Public Citizen's Health Research Group), monthly
Rehab Brief (U.S. Department of Education, National Institute on Disability and Rehabilitation Research), monthly
The Swedish Information Service, occasional factsheets
University of California, Berkeley Wellness Letter (School of Public Health), monthly

VI. Indexes and abstracts

Abstracts in Anthropology
American Statistics Index
Cumulative Index to Nursing and Allied Health Literature
Hospital Literature Index
Index to International Statistics
Index Medicus
Psychological Abstracts
Public Affairs Information Service
Social Sciences Index (most important source for social science journals)
Sociological Abstracts
Statistical Reference Index
Women's Studies Abstracts

VII. Useful bibliographies and dictionaries

Dorland's Illustrated Medical Dictionary
International Bibliography of Social and Cultural Anthropology
Medical Sociology: An Annotated Bibliography, 1972–1982
The Oxford Companion to Medicine

VIII. Sources of current statistical data

U.S. Department of Health and Human Services, Public Health Service, Centers for Disease Control, National Center for Health Statistics:
   Advance Data, regular reports of data from *Vital and Health Statistics*, with analysis
   Health, United States, annual compendium of data on health and health care
   Monthly Vital Statistics Report
   Morbidity and Mortality Weekly Report (publication of the Center for Disease Control in Atlanta, Ga.)
   Vital Statistics of the United States, annual report
   Vital and Health Statistics, occasional reports

U.S. Dept. of Commerce, Bureau of the Census:

   Statistical Abstract of the United States, annual
   U.S. Census of Population, every ten years
   Current Population Reports, occasional reports between decennial censuses

United Nations Educational, Scientific and Cultural Organization:
  Statistical Yearbook, annual

IX. Unpublished papers

Serious students in the field should attend meetings of professional associations and obtain copies of unpublished papers presented there; these papers are frequently preliminary versions of work that is later published in journals or books, so the unpublished version, while less polished, makes information accessible at least a year earlier. The papers for a conference are often abstracted in a booklet available to registrants. Professional associations have reduced student rates for membership and conference registration. Especially recommended are the meetings of:

American Sociological Association (meets usually in August)
Society for Medical Anthropology (meets as a division of the annual meetings of the American
    Anthropological Association, usually in November or December)
Society for the Study of Social Problems (meets jointly, usually in August, with the American
    Sociological Association)

APPENDIX B

Visual Resources

We have found visual resources, such as films and videos, to be invaluable in teaching the sociology of health and illness. Many of these resources are available in multiple formats (film, VHS, $^3/4''$ video). Listed below are the formats we have used, but distributors or film libraries may offer others.

Asbestos: The Way to Dusty Death. ABC News Production, 1978, 16 mm., 52 minutes, color. Depicts effects of asbestos, environmental and occupational health issues, and the politics of regulation.

Barefoot Doctors of Rural China. Diane Li Productions, 1975, 16 mm., 50 minutes, color. Illustrates the use of paramedical workers for massive public health efforts, family planning, and combination of Western and traditional Chinese medical knowledge.

Bottle Babies. Tricontinental Films, 1976, 16 mm., 30 minutes, color. Documents the effects of bottle feeding on the health of Third World babies and examines the role of multinational corporations' marketing of formula.

The Brain. WNET, 1984, VHS, each episode 60 minutes, color. The fourth episode "Stress and Emotion," describes the physiology of stress and how one's sense of control affects capacity to deal with stresses.

The British Way of Health. London Television, 1976, 16 mm., 28 minutes. Illustrates some aspects of the National Health System, with glimpses of three levels of physicians and their work.

Captives of Care. Australian Film Commission, 1973, 16 mm., 50 minutes, color. Docudrama that dramatizes the struggles for autonomy and independence of residents of an institution for persons with disabilities, many of whom were involved in making the film.

Clockwork. California Newsreel, 1982, VHS, 25 minutes, color. Demonstrates the impact of factory production management techniques, from early Taylorism to contemporary computer-assisted regulation.

Crisis at General Hospital. PBS Video, 1984, VHS, color. Examines the impact of inadequate funding for health care, especially for hospitals serving the urban, underinsured poor populations.

D.E.S.: An Uncertain Legacy. National Film Board of Canada and University of California, 16 mm., $^3/4''$ video and VHS, 58 minutes, color. Examines the development, use, and subsequent iatrogenic problems of the artificial hormone diethylstilbestrol.

The Deadly Deception: The Tuskegee Study of Untreated Syphilis in the Negro Male. WGBH/ Films for the Humanities and Sciences, 1993, VHS, 56 minutes, color. Documentary on a large-scale ethically questionable biomedical research project and its social aftermath.

Deadly Deceptions. INFACT, 1991, VHS, 29 minutes, color. Oscar-winning documentary on the spiral of deceptions surrounding health and environmental hazards in General Electric's operation of nuclear weapons production in the United States.

Doctors and Dollars. PBS, 1993, VHS, 57 minutes, color. Depicts the issues involved in doctors' self-referral and conflicts of interest.

Does Doctor Know Best? Annenberg/CPB, 1989. VHS, 60 minutes, color. Using a case study, panel discusses critical ethical and medical issues in doctor-patient relationships.

Ending Hunger in the Garden State: Recommendations and Reform. New Jersey Commission on Hunger, 1987, VHS, 35 minutes, color. Probes the extent of the problem of hunger and various responses in one of the wealthiest states.

For Export Only: Pesticides (Part I) *and Pills* (Part II). Icarus, 16 mm., $^3/_4''$ video and VHS, 56 minutes each, color. Discusses the pesticides and pharmaceuticals that have been banned or highly restricted in the United States, but are still produced here for export to Third World countries, which have little effective means to control or ban these substances that harm public health and the environment.

Healing and the Mind. PBS/Ambrose Video, 1993, VHS, color. Five-part series. Bill Moyers explores Chinese healing approaches, research on mind-body connections, nonmedical therapies, and U.S. experiences with the importance of the social-emotional factors in health and healing.

Health Care on the Critical List. Public Policy Production, 1985, VHS, 55 minutes (30-minute edition also available), color. Analyzes rising U.S. health care costs and the problems of equity in the health care system; illustrates HMO, PPO, and DRG concepts as approaches to controlling costs, but raises concerns about the long-range quality of health care.

Health Care Rationing. PBS, 1991, VHS, 58 minutes, color. Compares the case of Oregon's efforts to devise a fair system for rationing health care for the poor with the situation of Chicago inner-city poor people whose access to health care is denied by the de facto system of rationing according to who can pay.

Hospice: An Alternative Way to Care for the Dying. Billy Budd Films, 1979, 16 mm., 25 minutes, color. Documents the hospice movement, which emphasizes holistic caring for the dying patient and family, typically in the home.

Hungry for Profit. Robert Richter Productions, 1984, 16 mm., 86 minutes, color. Explores the role of multinational agribusiness in worsening problems of hunger in the Third World by encouraging the use of inappropriate technologies and the growth of export crops in the quest for profits.

Inventing Reality. PBS/Millennium series, # 8, 1992, VHS, 60 minutes, color. Depicts the healing approaches of a Mexican Huichol shaman, in comparison with an innovative Canadian cancer treatment center, underlining differences of underlying assumptions of nonbiomedical healing systems.

The Killing Ground. ABC News Production, 1979, 16 mm., 52 minutes, color. Examines the environmental and public health effects of toxic waste dumping, and critically looks at the politics of regulation and cleanup.

Medicine at the Crossroads. WNET and BBE Productions, 1993, VHS eight-part series, each episode 60 minutes, color. The episodes "The Code of Silence" on doctor-patient communication and "Life Support" on the ethics of death and aging in various countries are very relevant.

The Mind. WNET, 1988, VHS, each episode 60 minutes, color. The episodes "Aging" and "Pain and Healing" are particularly useful.

No Heroic Measures. Carle Medical Communications, 1984, ³/₄″ video or VHS, 23 minutes, color. Explores the ethical, legal, and emotional issues involved in the withdrawal of technological life supports.

The Politics of Food. Yorkshire Television, 1988, VHS, 2 hours, color. Covers political sources of hunger and famine, problems with food aid, politics and agricultural policies, and alternative political approaches.

Prescriptions for Profit. PBS, 1989, VHS, 60 minutes, color. Questions marketing practices of the pharmaceutical industry.

The Reckoning. California Newsreel, 1979, 16 mm., 27 minutes, color. Describes research about the health impacts of unemployment in two British cities; disproportionate footage of researchers looking at computer printouts.

Rich Man's Medicine, Poor Man's Medicine. Icarus, 1976, 16 mm., 45 minutes, color. Compares traditional native healing with high-priced, highly technological medicine in Gabon, Senegal, and Kenya.

Setting Limits. Medical University of South Carolina, 1988, VHS, 47 minutes. Lecture by ethicist Daniel Callahan about the proper ends of medicine and appropriate medical care for the aged and dying.

The Skin Horse. Central Independent Television PIC, 1983, VHS, 1 hour, color. Evocative documentary that deals with sexuality and disability.

Song of the Canary. New Day Films, 1978, 16 mm., 57 minutes, color. Provocatively examines occupational health problems, using case studies of chemical and textile workers.

Strange Sleep. PBS ("Nova" series), 1980, VHS, 45 minutes, color. Docudrama that covers the invention of anesthesia and the social factors surrounding its acceptance.

Taking Our Bodies Back: The Women's Health Movement. Cambridge Documentary Films, 1974, 16 mm., 33 minutes, color. Examines the development and issues of the women's health movement; contains graphic material about self-help techniques and abortion.

To Taste a Hundred Herbs. New Day Films, 1986, 16 mm., 58 minutes, color. Portrays the linkage of traditional Chinese medicine, religion, Chinese village life, and the role of the doctor.

Tibetan Medicine: A Buddhist Approach to Healing. Hartley, 1976, 16 mm., 29 minutes, color. Discusses Tibetan medicine, an interesting contrast to Western biomedicine, that heals both the physical and psychic being.

Titticut Follies. Zipporah Films, 1967, 16 mm., 89 minutes, black and white. Frederick Wiseman's controversial *cinéma verité* documentary (no narration) about a hospital for the criminally insane that illustrates a total institution, with different worlds of staff and inmates.

Who Lives, Who Dies. Public Policy Productions, 1987, VHS, 60 minutes, color. Explores the crisis in the U.S. health care system, and raises issues of health care spending, equity, rationing, and priorities in national spending.

APPENDIX C

Bibliography

Abel, Emily K.
1991   *Who Cares for the Elderly? Public Policy and the Experiences of Adult Daughters.* Philadelphia: Temple University Press.

Abel-Smith, Brian
1992   "Cost containment and new priorities in the European Community," *The Milbank Quarterly* 70(3): 393–415.

Ablon, Joan
1986   "Reactions of Samoan burn patients and families to severe burns," pp. 163–180 in C. Currer and M. Stacey, eds., *Concepts of Health, Illness and Disease.* Leamington SPA: Berg.

Adams, Orvill
1993   "Understanding the health care system that works," pp. 113–141 in A. Bennett and O. Adams, eds., *Looking North for Health: What We Can Learn from Canada's Health Care System.* San Francisco: Jossey-Bass Publishers.

Ader, Robert, David L. Felten, and Nicholas Cohen
1991   *Psychoneuroimmunology,* (second edition). New York: Academic Press, Inc.

Åkerstedt, Torbjörn
1990   "Psychological and psychophysiological effects of shift work," *Scandinavian Journal of Work, Environment and Health* 16 (supplement): 67–73.

Albrecht, Gary L., and Judith A. Levy
1982   "The professionalization of osteopathy: Adaptation in the medical marketplace," *Research in the Sociology of Health Care* 2: 161–202.

Alexander, Jacqui
1988   "The ideological construction of risk: An analysis of corporate health programs in the 1980s," *Social Science and Medicine* 26(5): 559–567.

Alexander, Linda
1982   "Illness maintenance and the new American sick role," pp. 351–367 in N. J. Chrisman and T. W. Maretzki, eds., *Clinically Applied Anthropology.* Dordrecht, Netherlands: D. Reidel.

Alexander, Ralph W., and Joseph Fedoruk
1986   "Epidemic psychogenic illness in a telephone operators' building," *Journal of Occupations and Medicine* 28(1): 42–45.

Altman, Charles F.
1985   *Social Policies in Western Industrialized Societies.* Berkeley: Institute of International Studies, University of California.

Altman, Lawrence K.
1988a   "Maker gives free heart medicine to needy," *The New York Times*, April 6.
1988b   "U.S. moves to improve death certificate," *The New York Times*, October 18.
1992   "Surgical injuries lead to new rule," *The New York Times*, June 14.

Altman, Lawrence, and Elisabeth Rosenthal
1990   "Changes in medicine bring pain to healing profession," *The New York Times*, February 18.

Altman, Stuart H., and Mark A. Rodwin
1988   "Halfway competitive markets and ineffective regulation: The American health care system," *Journal of Health Politics, Policy and Law* 13(2): 323–339.

American Psychiatric Association
1987   *Diagnostic and Statistical Manual of Mental Disorders*, (third edition, revised). Washington, DC: American Psychiatric Association.

Anderson, Robert A.
1978   *Stress Power.* New York: Human Sciences Press.

Anderson, Ronald, Meei-shia Chen, Lu Anne Aday, and Llewellyn Cornelius
1987   "Health status and medical care utilization," *Health Affairs* 6(1): 136–156.

Andrews, Ahmed, and Nick Jewson
1993   "Ethnicity and infant deaths: The implications of recent statistical evidence for materialist explanations," *Sociology of Health and Illness* 15(2): 137–156.

Angel, Ronald
1989   "The health of the Mexican origin population," pp. 82–94 in P. Brown, ed., *Perspectives in Medical Sociology.* Belmont, CA: Wadsworth.

Angel, Ronald, and Peggy Thoits
1987   "The impact of culture on the cognitive structure of illness," *Culture, Medicine, and Psychiatry* 11(4): 465–494.

Angier, Natalie
1991   "Cancer increases among children," *International Herald Tribune*, June 27: 5.

Anspach, Renee
1977   "From stigma to identity politics: Political activism among physically disabled and former mental patients," *Social Science and Medicine* 13A: 765–773.

1988   "Notes on the sociology of medical discourse: The language of case presentation," *Journal of Health and Social Behavior* 29: 357–375.

Antonovsky, Aaron
1979   *Health, Stress and Coping.* San Francisco: Jossey Bass.
1984   "The sense of coherence as a determinant of health," *Advances* 1(3): 37–50.

1987   *Unraveling the Mystery of Health: How People Manage Stress and Stay Well*. San Francisco: Jossey Bass.

1990   "Personality and health: Testing the sense of coherence model," pp. 155–177 in H. S. Friedman, ed., *Personality and Disease*. New York: John Wiley and Sons.

Apfel, Roberta, and Susan M. Fisher
1984   *To Do No Harm: DES and the Dilemmas of Modern Medicine*. New Haven: Yale University Press.

Aries, Nancy, and Louanne Kennedy
1986   "The health labor force: The effects of change," pp. 196–207 in P. Conrad and R. Kern, eds., *The Sociology of Health and Illness*. New York: St. Martin's Press.

Ariès, Philippe
1974   *Western Attitudes Toward Death: From the Middle Ages to the Present*. Baltimore: Johns Hopkins University Press.

Armstrong, David
1983   *Political Anatomy of the Body: Medical Knowledge in Britain in the Twentieth Century*. Cambridge: Cambridge University Press.

Aronowitz, Robert A.
1991   "Lyme disease: The social construction of a new disease and its social consequences," *The Milbank Quarterly* 69(1): 79–112.

Asbury, Carolyn H.
1981   "Medical drugs of limited commercial interest: Profit alone is a bitter pill," *International Journal of Health Services* 11(3): 451–462.

Atkinson, Paul
1978   "From honey to vinegar: Lévi-Strauss in Vermont," pp. 168–188 in P. Morley and R. Wallis, eds., *Culture and Curing*. Pittsburgh: University of Pittsburgh Press.

Atkinson, Thomas, Ramsay Liem, and Joan Liem
1986   "The social costs of unemployment: Implications for social support," *Journal of Health and Social Behavior* 27: 317–331.

Attie, Ilana, and J. Brooks-Gunn
1987   "Weight concerns as chronic stressors in women," pp. 218–254 in R. Barnett, L. Biener, and G. K. Baruch, eds., *Gender and Stress*. New York: The Free Press.

Back, Aaron
1981   *Occupational Stress: The Inside Story*. Oakland, CA: Institute for Labor and Mental Health.

Badgley, Robin F.
1991   "Social and economic disparities under Canadian health care," *International Journal of Health Services* 21(4): 659–671.

Baer, Hans A.
1984   "A comparative view of a heterodox health system: Chiropractic in America and Britain," *Medical Anthropology* 8: 151–168.

Baird, Vanessa
1992   "Difference and defiance," *New Internationalist* 233 (July): 4–7.

Bakal, Donald A.
1979   *Psychology and Medicine.* New York: Springer.

Baker, Dean
1981   "The use and health consequences of shift work," pp. 107–122 in V. Navarro and D. M. Berman, eds., *Health and Work Under Capitalism: An International Perspective.* Farmingdale, NY: Baywood.

Baker, Susan B., Stephen Teret, and Erich M. Daub
1987   "Injuries," pp. 177–206 in S. R. Levine and A. Lilienfeld, eds., *Epidemiology and Health Policy.* New York: Tavistock.

Bale, Anthony
1990   "Women's toxic experience," pp. 411–439 in R. D. Apple, ed., *Women, Health, and Medicine in America: A Historical Handbook.* New York: Garland Publishing.

Banks, Caroline Giles
1992   " 'Culture' in culture-bound syndromes: The case of anorexia nervosa," *Social Science and Medicine* 34(8): 867–884.

Banta, H. David
1986   "Medical technology and developing countries: The case of Brazil," *International Journal of Health Services* 16(3): 363–373.

Banta, H. David, Clyde J. Behney, and Jane Sisk Willems
1981   *Toward Rational Technology in Medicine: Considerations for Health Policy.* New York: Springer.

Banta, H. David, and Kerry Britten Kemp
1982   *The Management of Health Care Technology in Nine Countries.* New York: Springer.

Barchas, Patricia, and Sally P. Mendoza, eds.
1984a   *Social Cohesion: Essays Toward a Sociophysiological Perspective.* Westport, CT: Greenwood.

1984b   *Social Hierarchies: Essays Toward a Sociophysiological Perspective.* Westport, CT: Greenwood.

Barker-Benfield, Ben
1975   "Sexual surgery in late nineteenth-century America," *International Journal of Health Services* 5(2): 279–298.

Barnet, Richard J., and Ronald E. Mueller
1974   *Global Reach.* New York: Simon and Schuster.

Barnett, Rosalind, Lois Biener, and Grace K. Baruch, eds.
1987   *Gender and Stress.* New York: The Free Press.

Barnouw, Erik
1978   *The Sponsor: Notes on a Modern Potentate.* New York: Oxford University Press.

Barraclough, Solon L.
1991   *An End to Hunger? The Social Origins of Food Strategies.* London: Zed Books, Ltd.

Barringer, Felicity
1993   "Pride in a soundless world: Deaf oppose a hearing aid," *The New York Times*, May 16.

Barron, James
  1989   "Unnecessary Surgery," *New York Times Magazine*, April 16, pp. 25–26,
            43–46.

Bartrop, R. W., L. Lazarus, L. Luckhurst, L. Kiloh, and R. Penny
  1977   "Depressed lymphocyte function after bereavement," *Lancet* 1(8,016):
            834–836.

Bates, Maryann
  1987   "Ethnicity and pain: A biocultural model," *Social Science and Medicine*
            24(1): 47–50.

Becerra, José, Carol J. R. Hogue, Hani K. Atrash, and Nilsa Perez
  1991   "Infant mortality among Hispanics: A portrait of heterogeneity," *Journal
            of the American Medical Association* 265(2): 217–221.

Becker, E. Lovell
  1986   *International Dictionary of Medicine and Biology*. New York: Wiley.

Becker, Gay, and Robert D. Nachtigall
  1992   "Eager for medicalisation: The social production of infertility as a dis-
            ease," *Sociology of Health and Illness* 14(4): 456–471.

Becker, Howard
  1963   *Outsiders: Studies in the Sociology of Deviance*. New York: The Free
            Press.

  1967   "History, culture, and subjective experience: An exploration of the social
            bases of drug-induced experiences," *Journal of Health and Social
            Behavior* 8(3): 163–176.

Becker, Howard, Blanche Geer, Everett Hughes, and Anselm Strauss
  1961   *Boys in White*. Chicago: University of Chicago Press.

Beckman, Howard, and R. M. Frankl
  1984   "The effects of physician's behavior on the collection of data," *Annals of
            Internal Medicine* 101(5): 692–696.

Beecher, Henry K.
  1956   "Relationship of the significance of wound to the pain experience," *Journal
            of the American Medical Association* 161: 1604–1613.

  1959   *Measurement of Subjective Responses: Quantitative Effects of Drugs*. New
            York: Oxford University Press.

Belkin, Lisa
  1993   "Nursing homes try life without restraints," *The New York Times*, March
            24.

Bell, Susan
  1986   "A new model of medical technology development: A case study of DES,"
            Research in the Sociology of Health Care 4: 1–32.

  1990   "Changing ideas: The medicalization of menopause," pp. 43–63 in R.
            Formanek, ed., *The Meanings of Menopause: Historical, Medical and
            Clinical Perspectives*. Hillsdale, NJ: The Analytic Press.

Bendelow, Gillian
  1993   "Pain perceptions, emotions and gender," *Sociology of Health and Illness*
            15(3): 273–294.

Bennett, Jon, and Susan George
    1987   *The Hunger Machine: The Politics of Food.* Cambridge: Polity Press.

Benoist, Jean, and Pascal Cathebras
    1993   "The body: From an immateriality to another," *Social Science and Medicine* 36(7): 857–865.

Ben-Sira, Zeev
    1985   "Potency: A stress-buffering link in the coping-stress-disease relationship," *Social Science and Medicine* 21(4): 397–406.

Beresford, Eric B.
    1991   "Uncertainty and the shaping of medical decisions," *Hastings Center Report* (July–August): 6–11.

Berger, Peter
    1967   *The Sacred Canopy: Elements of a Sociological Theory of Religion.* Garden City, NY: Doubleday.

Berger, Peter, and Thomas Luckmann
    1967   *The Social Construction of Reality.* Garden City, NY: Doubleday.

Bergsma, Jurrit
    1982   *Health Care: Its Psychosocial Dimensions.* Pittsburgh: Duquesne University Press.

Berki, Sylvester E.
    1986   "A look at catastrophic medical expenses and the poor," *Health Affairs* 5(4): 138–145.

Berkman, Lisa F., and S. Leonard Syme
    1979   "Social networks, host resistance, and mortality: A nine-year follow-up study of Alameda County residents," *American Journal of Epidemiology* 109: 186–204.

Berlant, Jeffrey L.
    1975   *Profession and Monopoly: A Study of Medicine in Great Britain and the United States.* Berkeley: University of California Press.

Berliner, Howard S.
    1975   "A larger perspective on the Flexner Report," *International Journal of Health Services* 5(4): 573–592.

    1976   "Starr wars," *International Journal of Health Services* 13(4): 671–675.

Berliner, Howard S., and Robb K. Burlage
    1987   "Proprietary hospital chains and academic medical centers," *International Journal of Health Services* 17(1): 27–45.

Berman, Daniel M.
    1978   *Death on the Job: Occupational Health and Safety Struggles in the United States.* New York: Monthly Review Press.

Bieliauskas, Linas
    1982   *Stress and Its Relationship to Health and Illness.* Boulder, CO: Westview.

Bird, Chloe I., and Allen M. Fremont
    1991   "Gender, time use, and health," *Journal of Health and Social Behavior* 32(2): 114–129.

Birke, Lynda
    1986   *Women, Feminism and Biology: The Feminist Challenge*. New York: Methuen.

Black, Douglas
    1980   *Inequalities in Health: Report of a Research Working Group*. London: Department of Health and Social Services.

Blaxter, Mildred
    1983   "The causes of disease: Women talking," *Social Science and Medicine* 17: 59–69.

    1990   *Health and Lifestyles*. New York: Tavistock/Routledge.

Blaxter, Mildred, and Elizabeth Paterson
    1982   *Mothers and Daughters: A Three-Generational Study of Health Attitudes and Behavior*. London: Heinemann.

Blendon, Robert J., Robert Leitman, Ian Morrison, and Karen Donelan
    1990   "Satisfaction with health systems in ten nations," *Health Affairs* 9(2): 185–192.

Bloom, Samuel W.
    1979   "Socialization for the physician's role: A review of some contributions of research to theory," pp. 3–52 in E. C. Shapiro and L. M. Loenstein, eds., *Becoming a Physician: Development of Values and Attitudes in Medicine*. Cambridge, MA: Ballinger.

Bloor, Michael
    1976   "Bishop Berkeley and the adenotonsillectomy enigma: An exploration of variation in the social construction of medical disposals," *Sociology: The Journal of the British Sociological Association* 10(1): 43–61.

    1991   "A minor office: The variable and socially constructed character of death certification in a Scottish city," *Journal of Health and Social Behavior* 32(3): 273–287.

Bloor, Michael, M. Samphier, and L. Prior
    1987   "Artefact explanations of inequalities in health: An assessment of the evidence," *Sociology of Health and Illness* 9(3): 231–263.

Blyton, Paul
    1985   *Changes in Working Time: An International Review*. New York: St. Martin's Press.

Bodenheimer, Thomas S.
    1984   "The transnational pharmaceutical industry and the health of the world's people," pp. 187–216 in J. B. McKinlay, ed., *Issues in the Political Economy of Health Care*. New York: Tavistock.

    1990   "Should we abolish the private health insurance industry?" *International Journal of Health Services* 20(2): 199–220.

Bogin, Meg
    1982   *The Path to Pain Control*. Boston: Houghton Mifflin.

Bohus, B., J. M. Koolhaas, and S. M. Korte
    1991   "Psychosocial stress, anxiety and depression: Physiological and neuroendocrine correlates in animal models," pp. 120–138 in A. R. Genazzani, G.

Nappi, F. Petraglia, and E. Martignoni, eds., *Stress and Related Disorders: From Adaptation to Dysfunction*. Park Ridge, NJ: The Parthenon Publishing Group.

Bologh, Roslyn
    1981   "Grounding the alienation of self and body: A critical, phenomenological analysis of the patient in western medicine," *Sociology of Health and Illness* 3(2): 188–206.

Bolton, Ralph
    1989   "Introduction: The AIDS pandemic, a global emergency," *Medical Anthropology* 10: 93–104.

Bookchin, Murray
    1962   *Our Synthetic Environment*. New York: Harper and Row.

Bordo, Susan
    1989   "The body and the reproduction of femininity: A feminist appropriation of Foucault," pp. 13–33 in A. Jaggar and S. Bordo, eds., *Gender/Body/Knowledge: Feminist Reconstructions of Being and Knowing*. New Brunswick, NJ: Rutgers University Press.
    1990   "Reading the slender body," pp. 83–112 in M. Jacobus, E. F. Keller, and S. Shuttleworth, eds., *Body/Politics: Women and the Discourses of Science*. New York: Routledge.

Boston Women's Health Collective
    1992   *Our Bodies, Our Selves*. Revised edition. New York: Simon and Schuster.

Botkin, Daniel B., and Edward A. Keller
    1982   *Environmental Studies*. Columbus, OH: Charles E. Merrill.

Bowles, Cheryl L.
    1990   "The menopausal experience: Sociocultural influences and theoretical models," pp. 157–175 in R. Formanek, *The Meanings of Menopause: Historical, Medical and Clinical Perspectives*. Hillsdale, NJ: The Analytic Press.

Brandon, Robert M., Michael Podhorzer, and Thomas H. Pollak
    1991   "Premiums without benefits: Waste and inefficiency in the commercial health insurance industry," *International Journal of Health Services* 21(2): 265–283.

Brannon, Robert L.
    1990   "The reorganization of the nursing labor process: From team to primary nursing," *International Journal of Health Services* 20(3): 511–524.

Braudel, Fernand
    1973   *Capitalism and Material Life: 1400–1800*. New York: Harper and Row.

Braverman, Harry
    1974   *Labor and Monopoly Capital*. New York: Monthly Review Press.

Braverman, Paula, Geraldine Oliva, Marie Grisham Miller, Randy Reiter, and Susan Egarton
    1989   "Adverse outcomes and lack of health insurance among newborns in an eight-county area of California, 1982 to 1986," *New England Journal of Medicine* 321(8): 508–513.

Brennan, Troyen A., Lucian L. Leapre, Nan M. Laird, Liesi Hebert, A. Russell Localio, Ann G. Lawthers, Jos. P. Newhouse, Paul C. Wilder, and Howard Libit

1991   "Incidence of adverse events and negligence in hospitalized patients—results of the Harvard Medical Practice Study I," *The New England Journal of Medicine* 324(6): 370–776.

Brenner, M. Harvey
1976   *Estimating the Social Costs of Economic Policy: Implications for Mental and Physical Health, and Criminal Aggression.* Report to the Congressional Research Service of the Library of Congress and Joint Economic Committee of Congress. Washington, DC: Government Printing Office.

1979   "Mortality and the national economy," *Lancet* 2(8,142): 568–573.

Brightbill, Tim
1991   "Political Action Committees: How much influence will $7.7 million buy?" *International Journal of Health Services* 21(2): 285–290.

Brodeur, Paul
1974   *Expendable Americans.* New York: Viking.

Brody, Elaine M.
1990   *Women in the Middle: Their Parent-Care Years.* New York: Springer Publishing Company.

Brody, Howard
1992   *The Healer's Power.* New Haven: Yale University Press.

Brody, Jane E.
1975   "Physicians' views unchanged on use of estrogen therapy," *The New York Times*, December 5.

1983   "Research lifts blame from many of the obese," *The New York Times*, March 24.

1993   "The adult years are bringing new afflictions for 'DES babies,' men as well as women," *The New York Times*, February 10.

Brooke, James
1993   "A hard look at Brazil's surfeits: Food, hunger and inequality," *The New York Times*, June 6.

Brown, Carol A.
1978   "The division of laborers: Allied health professions," pp. 73–82 in S. Wolfe, ed., *Organization of Health Workers and Labor Conflict.* Farmingdale, NY: Baywood.

1983   "Women workers in the health service industry," pp. 105–116 in E. Fee, ed., *Women and Health: The Politics of Sex in Medicine.* Farmingdale, NY: Baywood.

Brown, E. Richard
1979   *Rockefeller Medicine Men: Medicine and Capitalism in America.* Berkeley: University of California Press.

Brown, Leigh Patricia
1988   "Designs take heed of human frailty," *The New York Times*, April 14.

Brown, Lester, William U. Chandler, Christopher Flavin, Jodi Jacobson, Cynthia Pollock, Sandra Postel, Linda Starke, and Edward C. Wolf
1987   *State of the World, 1987.* New York: W. W. Norton.

Brown, Peter J., and Marcia C. Inhorn
    1990   "Disease, ecology and human behavior," pp. 187–214 in T. M. Johnson and C. F. Sargent, eds., *Medical Anthropology: A Handbook of Theory and Method*. New York: Greenwood.

Brown, Phil, and Steven C. Funk
    1986   "Tardive dyskinesia: Barriers to the professional recognition of an iatrogenic disease," *Journal of Health and Social Behavior* 27: 116–132.

Brown, Phil, and Edwin J. Mikkelsen
    1990   *No Safe Place: Toxic Waste, Leukemia and Community Action*. Berkeley: University of California Press.

Bullinger, Monika
    1990   "Environmental stress: Effect of air pollution on mood, neuropsychological function and physical style," pp. 244–250 in S. P. Allegra and A. Oliverio, eds., *Psychobiology of Stress*. Boston: Kluwer Academic Publishers.

Burkholder, John R.
    1974   "The law knows no heresy: Marginal religious movements and the courts," pp. 27–52 in I. Zaretsky and M. Leone, eds., *Religious Movements in Contemporary America*. Princeton: Princeton University Press.

Burkitt, Denis P.
    1973   "Some disease characteristics of modern Western civilisation," *British Medical Journal* 1: 274–278.

Burns, Robert B.
    1979   *The Self Concept*. New York: Longman.

Bury, Michael
    1982   "Chronic illness as biographical disruption," *Sociology of Health and Illness* 4(2): 167–182.

    1988   "Meanings at risk: The experience of arthritis," pp. 89–116 in R. Anderson and M. Bury, eds., *Living with Chronic Illness: The Experience of Patients and Their Families*. London: Unwin Hyman.

    1991   "The sociology of chronic illness: A review of research and prospects," *Sociology of Health and Illness* 13(4): 451–467.

Buss, Terry F., and Stevens F. Redburn
    1983   *Mass Unemployment: Plant Closings and Community Mental Health*. Beverly Hills: Sage.

Butler, Samuel
    [1901] 1960 *Erewhon*. New York: New American Library.

Buytendijk, Jacobus
    1974   *Prolegomena to an Anthropological Physiology*. Pittsburgh: Duquesne University Press.

Byrne, Patrick S., and Barrie E. Long
    1976   *Doctors Talking to Patients*. London: Her Majesty's Stationery Office.

Califano, Joseph A.
    1989   "Billions blown on health," *The New York Times*, April 12.

Callahan, Daniel
    1987   *Setting Limits: Medical Goals in an Aging Society*. New York: Simon and Schuster.

1989   *What Kind of Life: The Limits of Medical Progress*. New York: Simon and Schuster.

Calnan, Michael
1984   "Clinical uncertainty: Is it a problem in the doctor-patient relationship?" *Sociology of Health and Illness* 6(1): 74–85.

1987   *Health and Illness: The Lay Perspective*. New York: Tavistock.

Cameron, H. M., and E. McGoogan
1981   "Prospective study of 1152 hospital autopsies: Inaccuracies in death certification," *Journal of Pathology* 133: 273–283.

Cannon, Walter B.
1929   *Bodily Changes in Pain, Hunger, Fear, and Rage*. New York: Harper and Row.

1942   " 'Voodoo' death," *American Anthropologist* 44: 169–181.

Cant, Sarah L., and Michael Calnan
1991   "On the margins of the medical marketplace? An exploratory study of alternative practitioners' perceptions," *Sociology of Health and Illness* 13(1): 39–57.

Caplan, Gerald, and Marie Killilea
1976   *Support Systems and Mutual Help: Multidisciplinary Explorations*. New York: Grune and Stratton.

Caplan, Robert D.
1972   "Organizational stress and individual strain: A sociopsychological study of risk factors in coronary heart disease among administrators, engineers, and scientists." Unpublished Ph.D. dissertation, The University of Michigan.

Carpenter, Eugenia S.
1980   "Children's health care and the changing role of women," *Medical Care* 18(12): 1208–1218.

Cartland, Jenifer D. C., and Beth K. Yudkowsky
1993   "State estimates of uninsured children," *Health Affairs* 12(1): 144–151.

Cartwright, Anne
1967   *Patients and Their Doctors*. New York: Atherton.

Cartwright, Samuel A.
1851   "Report on the diseases and physical pecularities of the Negro race," *New Orleans Medical and Surgical Journal* 7: 691–715.

Cash, Thomas F., Barbara Winstead, and Louis Janda
1986   "The great American shape-up," *Psychology Today* 20(4): 30–37.

Cassedy, James H.
1977   "Why self-help? Americans alone with their diseases, 1800–1850," pp. 31–48 in G. Risse, R. L. Numbers, and J. W. Leavitt, eds., *Medicine Without Doctors: Home Health Care in American History*. New York: Science History.

Cassell, Eric J.
1976   "Disease as an 'it': Concepts of disease revealed by patients' presentation of symptoms," *Social Science and Medicine* 10: 143–146.

1982   "The nature of suffering and the goals of medicine," *New England Journal of Medicine* 306: 639–645.

1986   "Ideas in conflict: The rise and fall (and rise and fall) of new views of disease," *Daedalus: Journal of the American Academy of Arts and Sciences* 115(2): 19–41.

Cassell, Joan
1991   *Expected Miracles: Surgeons at Work*. Philadelphia: Temple University Press.

Cassidy, Claire M., Hans Baer, and Barbara Becker
1985   "Selected references on professionalized heterodox health systems in English-speaking countries," *Medical Anthropology Quarterly* 17(1): 10–18.

Catalano, Ralph
1991   "The health effects of economic insecurity," *American Journal of Public Health* 81(9): 1148–1152.

Center for Philosophy and Public Policy
1985   "Air pollution: The role and limits of consent," *Report from the Center for Philosophy and Public Policy*, volume 5, number 5. Hyattsville, Md.: University of Maryland.

Center for Study of Responsive Law
1982   *Eating Clean: Food Safety and the Chemical Harvest*. Washington, DC: Center for Study of Responsive Law.

Chapman, Simon, Ron Borland, David Hill, Neville Owen, and Stephen Woodard
1990   "Why the tobacco industry fears the passive smoking issue," *International Journal of Health Services* 20(3): 417–427.

Charles, Nicke, and Marion Kerr
1987   "Food for feminist thought," *Sociological Review* 34(3): 537–572.

Charmaz, Kathy
1983   "Loss of self: A fundamental form of suffering of the chronically ill," *Sociology of Health and Illness* 4: 167–182.

1987   "Struggling for a self: Identity levels of the chronically ill," *Research in the Sociology of Health Care* 6: 283–321.

1991   *Good Days, Bad Days: The Self in Chronic Illness and Time*. New Brunswick, NJ: Rutgers University Press.

Chase, Laurie
1980   "Mass psychogenic illness," *Science for the People* 12(2): 18–19.

Chassin, Mark R., Jacqueline Kosecoff, R. E. Park, Constance Winslow, Katherine Kahn, Nancy Merrick, Joan Keesey, Arlene Fink, David Solomon, and Robert Brook
1987   "Does inappropriate use explain geographic variations in the use of health care services? A study of three procedures," *Journal of the American Medical Association* 258(18): 2533–2537.

Chavkin, Wendy, ed.
1984   *Double Exposure: Women's Health Hazards on the Job and at Home*. New York: Monthly Review Press.

Cherfas, Jeremy, and Roger Lewin, eds.
1980   *Not Work Alone: A Cross-Cultural View of Activities Superfluous to Survival*. Beverly Hills: Sage.

Chernin, Kim
    1981   *The Obsession: Reflections on the Tyranny of Slenderness*. New York: Harper and Row.

Chesney, Margaret A.
    1991   "Women, work-related stress, and smoking," pp. 139–155 in M. Frankenhaeuser, V. Lundberg, and M. Chesney, eds., *Women, Work and Health*. New York: Plenum Press.

Chrisman, Noel J.
    1977   "The health-seeking process: An approach to the natural history of illness," *Culture, Medicine and Psychiatry* 1: 351–377.

Christianson, Jon B., Ira Moscovice, and Anthony Wellever
    1990   "Institutional alternatives to the rural hospital," *Health Care Financing Review* 11(3): 87–90.

Christianson, Jon B., Douglas R. Wholey, and Susan M. Sanchez
    1991   "State responses to HMO failures," *Health Affairs* 10(4): 78–92.

Cicourel, Aaron V.
    1983   "Hearing is not believing: Language and the structure of belief in medical communication," pp. 221–239 in S. Fisher and A. Todd, eds., *The Social Organization of Doctor-Patient Communication*. Norwood, NJ: Ablex.

Clancy, Carolyn M., David U. Himmelstein, and Steffie Woolhandler
    1993   "Questions and answers about managed competition," *International Journal of Health Services* 23(2): 213–218.

Claybrook, Joan, and staff of *Public Citizen*
    1984   *Retreat from Safety*. New York: Pantheon.

Cleary, Paul D.
    1987   "Gender differences in stress-related disorders," pp. 39–72 in R. Barnett, L. Biener, and G. K. Baruch, eds., *Gender and Stress*. New York: The Free Press.

Clines, Francis X.
    1987   "Britain's health service: Is it curing or hurting?" *The New York Times*, June 3.

Cobb, Leonard A., George Thomas, David H. Dillard, K. Alvin Merendino, and Robert A. Bruce
    1959   "An evaluation of internal mammary artery ligation by a double-blind technic," *New England Journal of Medicine* 260: 1115–1118.

Cobb, Sydney, and Stanislav Kasl
    1977   *Termination: The Consequence of Job Loss*. Publication No. 77–224. Cincinnati: National Institute for Occupational Safety and Health.

Coburn, David, and C. Lesley Biggs
    1986   "Limits to medical dominance: The case of chiropractic," *Social Science and Medicine* 22: 1035–1046.

Coburn, David, George M. Torrance, and Joseph M. Kaufert
    1983   "Medical dominance in Canada in historical perspective: The rise and fall of medicine?" *International Journal of Health Services* 13(3): 407–432.

Cockburn, Alexander
    1988   "Live souls," *Zeta Magazine* 1(2): 5–15.

Cockerham, William C.
    1978   *Medical Sociology.* Englewood Cliffs, NJ: Prentice-Hall.

Cohen, Marc J., and Richard J. Hoehn
    1991   *Hunger, 1992.* Washington, DC: Bread for the World Institute on Hunger and Development.

Cohen, Mark Nathan
    1989   *Health and the Rise of Civilization.* New Haven, CT: Yale University Press.

Cohen, Stanley, and Laurie Taylor
    1976   *Escape Attempts: The Theory and Practise of Resistance to Everyday Life.* London: Allen Lane.

Colwill, Jack M.
    1992   "Where have all the primary care applicants gone?" *The New England Journal of Medicine* 326(6): 387–393.

Comaroff, Jean
    1976   "Communicating information about non-fatal illnesses: The strategies of a group of general practitioners," *Sociological Review* 24(2): 269–290.

    1978   "Medicine and culture: Some anthropological perspectives," *Social Science and Medicine* 12B: 247–254.

    1982   "Medicine: Symbol and ideology," pp. 49–68 in P. Wright and A. Treacher, eds., *The Problem of Medical Knowledge: Examining the Social Construction of Medicine.* Edinburgh: Edinburgh University Press.

    1984   "Medicine, time, and the perception of death," *Listening* 19(2): 155–169.

    1985   *Body of Power, Spirit of Resistance: The Culture and History of a South African People.* Chicago: University of Chicago Press.

Comaroff, Jean, and Peter Maguire
    1981   "Ambiguity and the search for meaning: Childhood leukaemia in the modern clinical context," *Social Science and Medicine* 15B(2): 115–123.

Conrad, Peter
    1985   "The meaning of medications: Another look at compliance," *Social Science and Medicine* 20: 29–37.

    1986   "The social meaning of AIDS," *Social Policy* 17(1): 51–56.

    1987   "The experience of illness: Recent and new directions," *Research in the Sociology of Health Care* 6: 1–31.

    1988   "Worksite health promotion: The social context," *Social Science and Medicine* 26(5): 485–489.

Conrad, Peter, and Joseph W. Schneider
    1992   *Deviance and Medicalization: From Badness to Sickness.* Philadelphia: Temple University Press.

Conrad, Peter, and Diana Walsh
    1992   "The new corporate health ethic: Lifestyle and the social control of work," *International Journal of Health Services* 22(1): 89–111.

Consumer Reports
1990   "A look at the Canadian alternative," (September): 614–617.

Coombs, Robert H.
1978   *Mastering Medicine: Professional Socialization in Medical School.* New York: The Free Press.

Coombs, Robert H., Sangeeta Chopra, Debra R. Schenk, and Elaine Yutan
1993   "Medical slang and its functions," *Social Science and Medicine* 36(8): 987–998.

Cooper, Richard S.
1987   "Has the period of rising mortality in the Soviet Union come to an end?" *International Journal of Health Services* 17(3): 515–519.

Cooper, Richard S., and Arthur Schatzkin
1982   "The pattern of mass disease in the U.S.S.R.: A product of socialist or capitalist development," *International Journal of Health Services* 12(3): 459–480.

Corea, Gena
1992   *The Invisible Epidemic.* New York: Harper Collins.

Coulter, Harris L.
1984   "Homoeopathy," pp. 57–79 in J. W. Salmon, ed., *Alternative Medicines: Popular and Policy Perspectives.* New York: Tavistock.

Council on Scientific Affairs
1991   "Hispanic health in the United States," *Journal of the American Medical Association* 265(2): 248–252.

Cousins, Norman
1989   *Headfirst: The Biology of Hope.* New York: E. P. Dutton.

Cowie, Bill
1976   "The cardiac patient's perception of his heart attack," *Social Science and Medicine* 10: 87–96.

Crane, Diana
1975   "Decision to treat critically ill patients: A comparison of social versus medical considerations," pp. 301–333 in J. B. McKinlay, ed., *Health Care Consumers, Professionals, and Organizations.* Milbank Reader, No. 2. Cambridge, MA: MIT Press.

Crawford, Robert
1977   "You are dangerous to your health: The ideology and politics of victim blaming," *International Journal of Health Services* 7(4): 663–680.

1984   "A cultural account of 'health': Control, release, and the social body," pp. 60–103 in J. B. McKinlay, ed., *Issues in the Political Economy of Health Care.* New York: Tavistock.

Crewe, Nancy M., and Irving K. Zola, eds.
1983   *Independent Living in America.* San Francisco: Jossey-Bass.

Crichton, Anne
1981   *Health Policy Making: Fundamental Issues in the U.S.A., Canada, Great Britain, and Australia.* Ann Arbor, MI: Health Administration Press.

Crickmer, Barry T.
1988   "How to handle long-term health care," *The New York Times*, January 18.

Crittenden, Ann
1981   "Bangladesh hunger linked to feudal system," *The New York Times*, December 11.

Csikszentmihalyi, Mihaly
1990   *Flow: The Psychology of Ultimate Experience*. New York: HarperCollins.

Csordas, Thomas
1983   "The rhetoric of transformation in ritual healing," *Culture, Medicine, and Psychiatry* 7(4): 333–375.

Csordas, Thomas, and Steven Cross
1976   "Healing of memories: Psychotherapeutic ritual among Catholic Pentecostals," *Journal of Pastoral Care* 30: 245–257.

Culyer, A. J., and Bengt Jonsson, eds.
1986   *Public and Private Health Services: Complementaries and Conflicts*. Oxford: Basil Blackwell.

Cummings, Judith
1984   "Restrictions on smoking spreading across U.S.," *The New York Times*, February 1.

Cushman, John H.
1993   "U.S. to weigh blacks' complaints about pollution," *The New York Times*, November 19.

Dahlgren, Goeran, and Finn Diderichsen
1986   "Strategies for equity in health: Report from Sweden," *International Journal of Health Services* 16(4): 517–537.

Danaher, Kevin
1985   "How the U.S. and Europe caused Africa's famine," *Utne Reader* 11: 101–103.

Daniels, Arlene K.
1969   "The captive professional: Bureaucratic limitations in the practice of military psychiatry," *Journal of Health and Social Behavior* 10(4): 255–265.
1972   "Military psychiatry: The emergence of a subspecialty," pp. 145–162 in E. Freidson and J. Lorber, eds., *Medical Men and Their Work*. Chicago: Aldine Atherton.

Davis, Joel
1984   *Endorphins: New Waves in Brain Chemistry*. Garden City, NY: Doubleday.

Davis, Karen
1991   "Inequality and access to health care," *The Milbank Quarterly* 69(2): 253–273.

Davis-Floyd, Robbie
1987   "Obstetric training as a rite of passage," *Medical Anthropology Quarterly* 1(3): 288–318.
1990   "The role of obstetrical rituals in the resolution of cultural anomaly," *Social Science and Medicine* 31(2): 175–189.

1992   *Birth as an American Rite of Passage.* Berkeley: University of California
              Press.

DeFriese, Gordon H., Glenn Wilson, Thomas C. Ricketts, and Lynn Whitener
1992   "Consumer choice and the national rural hospital crisis," pp. 206–225 in
              W. M. Gesler and T. C. Ricketts, eds., *Health in Rural North America.*
              New Brunswick, NJ: Rutgers University Press.

Deppe, Hans-Ulrich
1992   "German unification and European integration," *Health/PAC Bulletin*
              (Spring): 22–27.

Derber, Charles
1983   "Sponsorship and the control of physicians," *Theory and Society* 12:
              561–601.

1984   "Physicians and their sponsorship: The new medical relations of produc-
              tion," pp. 217–254 in J. B. McKinlay, ed., *Issues in the Political Economy
              of Health Care.* New York: Tavistock.

Devisch, Renaat
1987   "Interweaving the vital flow and the symbolic function in healing," paper
              presented to American Anthropological Association.

Devisch, Renaat, and Antoine Gailly
1985   "A therapeutic self-help group among Turkish women, Dertleşmek: 'The
              sharing of sorrow,' " *Psichiatria e Psicoterapie Analitica* 4(2): 133–152.

Dew, Mary Amanda, Evelyn J. Bromet, David K. Parkinson, Leslie O. Dunn, and Christopher
M. Ryan
1989   "Effects of solvent exposure and occupational stress on the health of blue-col-
              lar women," pp. 327–345 in K. Ratcliff, M. Ferree, G. Mellow, B. Drygulski
              Wright, G. Price, K. Yanoshik, and M. Freston, eds., *Healing Technology:
              Feminist Perspectives.* Ann Arbor: The University of Michigan Press.

Diamond, Marian Cleeves
1988   *Enriching Heredity: The Impact of the Environment on the Anatomy of the
              Brain.* New York: The Free Press.

DiMatteo, M. Robin, and Howard S. Friedman
1982   *Social Psychology and Medicine.* Cambridge, MA: Oelgeschlager, Gunn,
              and Hain, Publishers.

Dingwall, Robert
1976   *Aspects of Illness.* New York: St. Martin's Press.

Direcks, Anita, and Ellen't Hoen
1986   "DES: The crime continues," pp. 41–49 in K. McDonnell, ed., *Adverse
              Effects: Women and the Pharmaceutical Industry.* Toronto: Women's
              Educational Press.

Doherty, William J., and Thomas L. Campbell
1988   *Families and Health.* Beverly Hills: Sage.

Dohrenwend, Barbara, and Leonard Pearlin
1982   "Report on stress and life events," pp. 55–88 in G. R. Elliott and C.
              Eisdorfer, eds., *Stress and Human Health.* New York: Springer.

Dolan, Andrew K.
   1980   "Antitrust law and physician dominance of other practitioners," *Journal of Health, Politics, and Law* 4: 675–689.

Dollars and Sense
   1993   "Drug price blues," (May): 23.

Donahue, John M.
   1986   *The Nicaraguan Revolution in Health*. South Hadley, MA: Bergin and Garvey.

   1989   "International organizations, health services, and nation building in Nicaragua," *Medical Anthropology Quarterly* 3(3): 258–269.

Donovan, Jenny L., and David R. Blake
   1992   "Patient compliance: Deviance or reasoned decision-making?" *Social Science and Medicine* 34(5): 507–513.

Donovan, Rebecca
   1987   "Poorly paid home health care workers subsidize an industry" [letter to the editor], *The New York Times*, May 16.

Douglas, Mary
   1966   *Purity and Danger: An Analysis of Concepts of Pollution and Taboo*. London: Routledge and Kegan Paul.

   1970   *Natural Symbols: Explorations in Cosmology*. London: Barrie and Jenkins.

Dow, James
   1986   "Universal aspects of symbolic healing: A theoretical synthesis," *American Anthropologist* 88(1): 56–69.

Dowd, Maureen
   1987   "U.S. health care faulted in Senate," *The New York Times*, January 13.

Dowie, Mark, and Tracy Johnston
   1987   "A case of corporate malpractice and the Dalkon Shield," pp. 629–637 in H. D. Schwartz, ed., *Dominant Issues in Medical Sociology*. New York: Random House.

Doyal, Lesley
   1983   "Women, health and the sexual division of labour: A case study of the women's health movement in Britain," *Critical Social Policy* 7: 1–33.

Drickamer, Margaret A., and Mark S. Lachs
   1992   "Should patients with Alzheimer's disease be told their diagnosis?" *New England Journal of Medicine* 326(18): 947–951.

Drinka, George Frederick
   1984   *The Birth of Neurosis: Myth, Malady, and the Victorians*. New York: Simon and Schuster.

Droge, David, Paul Arntson, and Robert Norton
   1986   "The social support function in epilepsy self-help groups," *Small Group Behavior* 17(2): 139–163.

Drummond, Hugh
   1980   *Doctor Drummond's Spirited Guide to Health Care in a Dying Empire*. New York: Grove.

Dubos, René
   1959   *The Mirage of Health.* Garden City, NY: Doubleday.
   1968   *Man, Medicine and Environment.* Baltimore: Penguin.

Dull, Diana, and Candace West
   1991   "Accounting for cosmetic surgery: the accomplishment of gender," *Social Problems* 38(3): 54–70.

Dunnell, Karen, and Ann Cartwright
   1972   *Medicine Takers, Prescribers, and Hoarders.* London: Routledge and Kegan Paul.

Durkheim, Emile
   [1893] 1964 *The Division of Labor in Society.* New York: The Free Press.
   [1897] 1951 *Suicide: A Study in Sociology.* New York: The Free Press.
   [1915] 1965 *The Elementary Forms of the Religious Life.* New York: Collier/Macmillan.

Dutton, Diana
   1986   "Social class, health and illness," pp. 31–62 in L. Aiken and D. Mechanic, eds., *Applications of Social Science to Clinical Medicine and Health Policy.* New Brunswick, NJ: Rutgers University Press.

Dutton, Diana, Thomas A. Preston, and Nancy E. Pfund
   1988   *Worse Than the Disease: Pitfalls of Medical Progress.* New York: Cambridge University Press.

Dye, James W.
   1981   "Man a machine: A philosophical critique," *Journal of Biological Experience: Studies in the Life of the Body* 3(2): 44–60.

Eastwell, Harry D.
   1982   "Voodoo death and the mechanism for dispatch of the dying in East Arnheim, Australia," *American Anthropologist* 84(1): 5–18.

Eckholm, Erik
   1977   *The Picture of Health: Environmental Sources of Disease.* New York: W. W. Norton.
   1989   "River blindness: Conquering an ancient scourge," *The New York Times Magazine*, January 8.
   1990   "What makes the 2 sexes so vulnerable to epidemic?" *The New York Times*, September 16.
   1992   "AIDS, fatally steady in the U.S., accelerates worldwide," *The New York Times*, June 28.
   1993   "Health plan is toughest on doctors making most," *The New York Times*, November 7.

Economist, The
   1985   "The western way to die," 296(7,409): 75–78.

Edgar, Harold
   1992   "Outside the community," *Hastings Center Report* 22(6): 32–35.

Ehrenreich, Barbara, and John Ehrenreich
   1978   "Hospital workers: Class conflicts in the making," pp. 41–49 in S. Wolfe,

ed., *Organization of Health Workers and Labor Conflict*. Farmingdale, NY: Baywood.

Ehrenreich, Barbara, and Deirdre English
1973   *Witches, Midwives, and Nurses: A History of Women Healers*. Old Westbury, NY: The Feminist Press.
1978   *For Her Own Good: 150 Years of the Experts' Advice to Women*. Garden City, NY: Doubleday.

Eisenberg, David M., Thomas L. DelBanco, Catherine S. Berkey, Ted J. Kaptchuk, Bruce Kupelnick, Jackie Kuhl, and Thomas C. Chalmers
1993a   "Cognitive behavioral techniques for hypertension: Are they effective?" *Annals of Internal Medicine* 118: 964–972.

Eisenberg, David M., Ronald C. Kessler, Cindy Foster, Frances E. Norlock, David R. Calkins, and Thomas L. Delbanco
1993b   "Unconventional medicine in the United States," *New England Journal of Medicine* 328(4): 246–252.

Elias, Norbert
1978   *The Civilizing Process*, Vol. 1. New York: Urizen.
1982   *Power and Civility*. New York: Pantheon.
1985   *The Loneliness of Dying*. Oxford: Basil Blackwell.

Elling, Ray H.
1981   "Political economy, cultural hegemony, and mixes of traditional and modern medicine," *Social Science and Medicine* 15A: 89–99.
1986   *The Struggle for Workers' Health: A Study of Six Industrialized Countries*. Farmingdale, NY: Baywood.

Emerson, Joan P.
1970   "Behavior in private places: Sustaining definitions of reality in gynecological examinations," pp. 74–97 in H. P. Dreitzel, ed., *Recent Sociology #2: Patterns of Communicative Behavior*. New York: Macmillan.

Engel, George L.
1971   "Sudden and rapid death during psychological stress: Folklore or folk wisdom?" *Annals of Internal Medicine* 74: 771–782.
1976   "Psychologic factors in instantaneous cardiac death," *New England Journal of Medicine* 294: 664–665.
1977   "The need for a new medical model: A challenge for biomedicine," *Science* 196: 129–136.

Engels, Friedrich
[1845] 1973   *The Conditions of the Working Class in England in 1844*. Moscow: Universal.

Englehardt, H. Tristam
1978   "The disease of masturbation: Values and the concept of disease," pp. 15–24 in J. W. Leavitt and R. L. Numbers, eds., *Sickness and Health in America*. Madison: University of Wisconsin Press.

Engler, Rick
1986   "Political power aids health and safety," *In These Times*, January 15–21: 16–17.

English-Lueck, June Anne
    1990   *Health in the New Age: A Study in California Holistic Practices.* Albuquerque: University of New Mexico.

Epstein, Paul, and Randall Packard
    1987   "Ecology and immunity," *Science for the People* 19(1): 10–20.

Epstein, Samuel S.
    1978   *The Politics of Cancer.* San Francisco: Sierra Club Books.

    1990a   "Losing the war against cancer: Who's to blame and what to do about it," *International Journal of Health Services* 20(1): 53–71.

    1990b   "Corporate crime: Why we cannot trust industry-derived safety studies," *International Journal of Health Services* 20(3): 443–458.

Ettorre, Elizabeth, and Elianne Riska
    1993   "Psychotropics, sociology and women: Are the 'halcyon days' of the 'malestream' over?" *Sociology of Health and Illness* 15(4): 503–524.

Evans, Robert G.
    1974   "Supplier-induced demand: Some empirical evidence and implications," pp. 162–173 in M. Perlman, ed., *The Economics of Health and Medical Care.* London: Macmillan.

    1983   "Health care in Canada: Patterns of funding and regulation," *Journal of Health Politics, Policy, and Law* 8(1): 1–43.

Everett, Melissa
    1984   "Coffee: How it gets to your cup," *Whole Life Times*, January-February: 20–23.

Ewan, Christine, Eva Lowy, and Janice Reid
    1991   " 'Falling out of culture': The effects of repetition strain injury on sufferers' roles and identity," *Sociology of Health and Illness* 13(2): 168–192.

Ewigman, Bernard G., James P. Crane, Fredric D. Figoletto, Michael L. LeFevre, Raymond P. Bain, Donald McNellis, and RADIUS Study Group
    1993   "Effect of prenatal ultrasound screening on perinatal outcome," *New England Journal of Medicine* 329(12): 821–827.

Eyer, Joseph
    1977   "Prosperity as a cause of death," *International Journal of Health Services* 7: 125–150.

    1984   "Capitalism, health and illness," pp. 23–58 in J. B. McKinlay, ed., *Issues in the Political Economy of Health Care.* New York: Tavistock.

Eyer, Joseph, and Peter Sterling
    1977   "Stress-related mortality and social organization," *Review of Radical Political Economics* 9(1): 1–44.

Fagerhaugh, Shizuko, and Anselm Strauss
    1977   *Politics of Pain Management: Staff-Patient Interaction.* Reading, MA: Addison-Wesley.

Fallon, April E., and Paul Rozin
    1985   "Sex differences in perception of desirable body shape," *Journal of Abnormal Psychology* 94(1): 102–105.

Fanon, Franz
    1963   *The Wretched of the Earth*. New York: Grove.

Farb, Peter, and George Armelagos
    1980   *Consuming Passions: The Anthropology of Eating*. Boston: Houghton Mifflin.

Farley, Pamela J.
    1985   "Who are the underinsured?" *Milbank Memorial Fund Quarterly* 63: 476–503.

Fauci, Anthony
    1988   "How far will AIDS spread in the United States," *The Futurist* 22(4): 41–42.

Featherstone, Mike
    1991   "The body in consumer culture," pp. 170–196 in M. Featherstone, M. Hepworth, and B. S. Turner, eds., *The Body: Social Process and Cultural Theory*. London: Sage.

Feder, Barnaby
    1988   "What ails a nursing home empire," *The New York Times*, December 11.

Feigenbaum, Susan
    1987   "Risk bearing in health care finance," pp. 105–144 in C. J. Schramm, ed., *Health Care and Its Costs*. New York: W. W. Norton.

Fein, Rashi
    1986   *Medical Care, Medical Costs: The Search for a Health Insurance Policy*. Cambridge: Harvard University Press.

Feldman, Penny Hollander, with Alice M. Sapienza and Nancy M. Kane
    1990   *Who Cares for Them? Workers in the Home Care Industry*. New York: Greenwood Press.

Feller, Barbara
    1983   "Americans needing help to function at home," *Advance Data*, Report Number 92.

Fenn, Richard
    1978   *Toward a Theory of Secularization*. SSSR Monograph Series, No. 1. Storrs, CT: Society for the Scientific Study of Religion.
    1982   *Liturgies and Trials: The Secularization of Religious Language*. Oxford: Basil Blackwell.

Feshbach, Murray
    1984   "Soviet health problems," *Society* 21(3): 79–89.

Fettner, Ann Guidici
    1987   "Where there's smoke, there's ire," *Village Voice* 32(5): 25.

Feuerstein, Michael, and Eric Skjei
    1979   *Mastering Pain*. New York: Bantam.

Field, Mark G.
    1973   "The concept of the 'health system' at the macrosociological level," *Social Science and Medicine* 7: 763–785.

Field, Mark G., ed.
    1989   *Success and Crisis in National Health Systems: A Comparative Approach*. New York: Routledge.

Fielding, Jonathan E., and Kenneth J. Phenow
  1988   "Health effects of involuntary smoking," *New England Journal of Medicine* 319(22): 1452–1460.

Figlio, Karl
  1982   "How does illness mediate social relations?: Workmen's compensation and medico-legal practices, 1890–1940," pp. 174–217 in P. Wright and A. Treacher, eds., *The Problem of Medical Knowledge: Examining the Social Construction of Medicine.* Edinburgh: Edinburgh University Press.

Findlay, Steven
  1988   "There's no place like home," *U. S. News and World Report*, January 25: 68–70.

Fine, Doris R.
  1988   "Women caregivers and home health workers: Prejudice and inequity in home health care," *Research in the Sociology of Health Care* 7: 105–117.

Fine, Michelle, and Adrienne Asch
  1988   "Disability beyond stigma: Social interaction, discrimination and activism," *Journal of Social Issues* 44(1): 3–21.

Finkler, Kaja
  1989   "The universality of nerves," pp. 171–179 in D. Davis and S. Low, eds., *Gender, Health, and Illness: The Case of Nerves.* New York: Hemisphere Publishing Corporation.

  1994   *Women in Pain: Gender and Morbidity in Mexico.* Philadelphia: University of Pennsylvania Press.

Fischer, Claude
  1983   "The friendship cure-all," *Psychology Today* 17(1): 74–78.

Fisher, Sue
  1983   "Doctor talk/Patient talk: How treatment decisions are negotiated in doctor-patient communication," pp. 135–157 in S. Fisher and A. Todd, eds., *The Social Organization of Doctor-Patient Communication.* Norwood, NJ: Ablex.

  1986   *In the Patient's Best Interest: Women and the Politics of Medical Decisions.* New Brunswick, NJ: Rutgers University Press.

Flexner, Abraham
  1910   *Medical Education in the United States and Canada.* Bulletin, Number 4. New York: Carnegie Foundation for the Advancement of Teaching.

Ford, Anne Rochon
  1986   "Hormones: Getting out of hands," pp. 27–40 in K. McDonnell, ed., *Adverse Effects: Women and the Pharmaceutical Industry.* Toronto: Women's Educational Press.

Foucault, Michel
  1973   *The Birth of the Clinic: An Archaeology of Medical Perception.* New York: Tavistock.

  1978   *The History of Sexuality: An Introduction.* New York: Pantheon.

Fox, Renée C.
  1957   "Training for uncertainty," pp. 207–241 in R. K. Merton, G. C. Reader,

and P. L. Kendall, eds., *The Student Physician*. Cambridge: Harvard University Press.

Frank, Jerome D.
1973   *Persuasion and Healing*. New York: Shocken.

Franke, Richard W.
1987   "The effects of colonialism and neo-colonialism on the gastronomic patterns of the Third World," pp. 455–479 in M. Harris and E. B. Ross, eds., *Food and Evolution: Toward a Theory of Food Habits*. Philadelphia: Temple University Press.

Franke, Richard W., and Barbara H. Chasin
1981   *Seeds of Famine: Ecological Destruction and the Development Dilemma in the West African Sahel*. Montclair, NJ: Allanheld, Osmun.

1992   "Kerala state, India: Radical reform as development," *International Journal of Health Services* 22(1): 139–156.

Frankel, Glenn
1986   "Even the diseases are segregated," *International Herald Tribune*, July 17.

Frankenhaeuser, Marianne
1981   "Coping with stress at work," *International Journal of Health Services* 11(4): 491–510.

1991   "The psychophysiology of sex differences as related to occupational status," pp. 39–61 in M. Frankenhaeuser, U. Lundberg, and M. Chesney, eds., *Women, Work and Health*. New York: Plenum Press.

Frankenhaeuser, Marianne, and Bertil Gardell
1976   "Underload and overload in working life: Outline of a multidisciplinary approach," *Journal of Human Stress* 2(3): 35–46.

Freeman, Howard E., Robert J. Blendon, Linda H. Aiken, Seymour Sudman, Connie F. Mullinix, and Christopher R. Corey
1987   "Americans report on their access to health care," *Health Affairs* 6(1): 6–18.

Freidson, Eliot
1970   *Profession of Medicine: A Study of the Sociology of Applied Knowledge*. New York: Dodd, Mead.

French, Howard
1989   "Tiny miracles become huge public health problems," *The New York Times*, February 19.

Freudenheim, Milt
1987a   "Debate widens over expanding use and growing cost of medical tests," *The New York Times*, May 30.

1987b   "Specialty health care booms," *The New York Times*, November 24.

1988a   "Doctors' concern: Fixing prices and price fixing," *The New York Times*, December 18.

1988b   "Prepaid programs for health care encounter snags," *The New York Times*, January 31.

1989   "Maxicare Health seeks bankruptcy protection," *The New York Times*, March 17.

1993a   "Drug makers propose self-control on prices," *The New York Times*, March 16.

1993b   "Physicians are selling practices to companies as changes loom," *The New York Times*, September 1.

Freund, Peter E. S.
1982   *The Civilized Body: Social Domination, Control and Health*. Philadelphia: Temple University Press.

Freund, Peter E. S., and George Martin
1993   *The Ecology of the Automobile*. Montreal: Black Rose.

Friedl, John
1982   "Explanatory models of black lung: Understanding the health-related behavior of Appalachian coal miners," *Culture, Medicine, and Psychiatry* 6(1): 3–10.

Friedman, Gary D.
1987   *Primer of Epidemiology* (third edition). New York: McGraw Hill.

Friedman, Meyer, and Ray H. Rosenman
1974   *Type A Behavior and Your Heart*. New York: Fawcett Crest.

Friedman, Samuel R.
1993   "A.I.D.S. as a sociohistorical phenomenon," pp. 19–36 in G. L. Albrecht and R. S. Zimmerman, eds., *Advances in Medical Sociology*, Vol. III: The Social and Behavioral Aspects of A.I.D.S. Greenwich, CT: JAI Press.

Friedmann, Georges
1961   *The Anatomy of Work*. Glencoe, IL: The Free Press.

Fries, James F.
1990   "An introduction to the compression of morbidity," pp. 35–41 in P. R. Lee and C. L. Estes, eds., *The Nation's Health*. Boston: Jones and Bartlett Publishers.

Fromm, Eric
1965   *Escape from Freedom*. New York: Avon Books.

Fryer, George E., Jr.
1991   "The United States medical profession: An abnormal form of the division of labor," *Sociology of Health and Illness* 13(2): 213–230.

Fuchs, Victor R., and James S. Hahn
1990   "How does Canada do it?" *The New England Journal of Medicine* 323(13): 884–890.

Funkenstein, Daniel, S. H. King, and M. E. Drolette
1957   *Mastery of Stress*. Cambridge: Harvard University Press.

Gabel, John R., and Michael A. Redisch
1979   "Alternative physician payment methods: Incentives, efficiency, and National Health Insurance," *Milbank Memorial Fund Quarterly* 57(1): 38–59.

Gaines, Atwood D.
1992   "From DSM-I to III-R: Voices of self, mastery and the other: A cultural constructivist reading of U. S. psychiatric classification," *Social Science and Medicine* 35(1): 3–24.

Ganz, Patricia A.
1992   "Treatment options for breast cancer—beyond survival," *New England Journal of Medicine* 326(17): 1147–1149.

Garfield, Jon
1980   "Alienated labor, stress, and coronary disease," *International Journal of Health Services* 10(4): 551–559.

Garrison, Vivian
1977   "Doctor, espiritista, or psychiatrist: Health-seeking behavior in a Puerto Rican neighborhood of New York City," *Medical Anthropology* 1(2): 67–183.

Garson, Barbara
1977   *All the Livelong Day*. New York: Penguin.

1988   *The Electronic Sweatshop*. New York: Simon and Schuster.

Gartner, Alan, and Tom Joe
1987   "Introduction," pp. 1–6 in A. Gartner and T. Joe, eds., *Images of the Disabled, Disabling Images*. New York: Praeger.

Gellhorn, Eric
1969   "The consequences of the suppression of overt movements in emotional stress: A neurophysiological interpretation," *Confinia Neurologica* 32: 289–299.

George, Susan
1982   *How the Other Half Dies*. Montclair, NJ: Allanheld, Osmun.

Gerrity, Martha S., Jo Anne L. Earp, Robert F. DeVellis, and Donald W. Light
1992   "Uncertainty and professional work: Perceptions of physicians in clinical practice," *American Journal of Sociology* 97(4): 1022–1051.

Gertman, Paul M.
1981   "Physicians as guiders of health services use," pp. 258–279 in J. B. McKinlay, ed., *Health Care Consumers, Professionals, and Organizations*. Milbank Reader, No. 2. Cambridge, MA: MIT Press.

Gibson, Robert
1980   "National Health Expenditures, 1979," *Health Care Financing Review* 2 (1): 1–36.

1982   "National Health Expenditures," *Health Care Financing Trends* 2 (5): 1–9.

Gibson, Robert, Daniel Waldo, and Katherine Levit
1982   "National health expenditures, 1982," *Health Care Financing Review* 5(1): 13–15.

Gill, Derek
1980   *The British National Health Service: A Sociologist's Perspective*. Bethesda, MD: U.S. Department of Health and Human Services, Public Health Services, National Institutes of Health.

Gill, Derek, and Stanley R. Ingman
1986   "Geriatric care and distributive justice: Problems and prospects," *Social Science and Medicine* 23(12): 1205–1215.

Gill, Sam D.
1981   *Sacred Words: A Study of Navajo Religion and Prayer*. Westport, CT: Greenwood.

Ginzberg, Eli
 1991 "Access to health care for Hispanics," *Journal of the American Medical Association* 165(2): 238–241.

Glaberson, William
 1987 "Misery on the meatpacking line," *The New York Times*, June 14.

Glaser, Barney, and Anselm Strauss
 1968 *Time for Dying*. Chicago: Aldine.

Glaser, William A.
 1991 "Paying the hospital: American problems and foreign solutions," *International Journal of Health Services* 21(3): 389–399.

Glass, David
 1977 "Stress behavior patterns and coronary disease," *American Scientist* 65: 177–187.

Glassman, Marjorie
 1980 "Misdiagnosis of senile dementia: Denial of care to the elderly," *Social Work* 25(4): 288–292.

Glassner, Barry
 1989 "Fitness and the postmodern self," *Journal of Health and Social Behavior* 30: 180–191.

Glazer, Nona Y.
 1990 "The home as workshop: Women as amateur nurses and medical care providers," *Gender and Society* 4(4): 479–499.

 1993 *Women's Paid and Unpaid Labor: The Work Transfer in Health Care and Retailing*. Philadelphia: Temple University Press.

Glenn, Evelyn Nakano, and Roslyn L. Feldberg
 1977 "Degraded and deskilled: The proletarianization of clerical work," *Social Problems* 25(1): 52–64.

Gliedman, John
 1979 "The wheelchair rebellion," *Psychology Today* 13(3): 59–64, 99–101.

Gliedman, John, and William Roth
 1980 "The unexpected minority: Why society is so mystified by handicap," *New Republic* 182(5): 26–30.

Goffman, Erving
 1959 *The Presentation of Self in Everyday Life*. Garden City, NY: Doubleday.

 1961 *Asylums*. Garden City, NY: Doubleday.

 1963 *Stigma: Notes on the Management of Spoiled Identity*. Englewood Cliffs, NJ: Spectrum/Prentice-Hall.

Gold, Allan R.
 1988 "Competition squeeze seen in leading to more medical antitrust cases," *The New York Times*, December 8.

Goldoftas, Barbara
 1991 "Hands that hurt," *Technology Review* 94(1): 42–50.

Goldsmith, Frank, and Lorin E. Kerr
 1982 *Occupational Safety and Health*. New York: Human Sciences Press.

Goldstein, Michael S.
    1992   *The Health Movement: Promoting Fitness in America.* New York: Twayne
                Publishers.
Goldstein, Michael S., Dennis Jaffe, Carol Sutherland, and Josie Wilson
    1987   "Holistic physicians: Implications for the study of the medical profession,"
                Journal of Health and Social Behavior 28(2): 103–119.
Good, Byron
    1977   "The heart of what's the matter: The semantics of illness in Iran," *Culture,
                Medicine, and Psychiatry* 1: 25–58.
Good, Byron, and Mary-Jo Delvecchio Good
    1981   "The meaning of symptoms: A cultural hermeneutic model for clinical
                practice," pp. 165–196 in A. Kleinman and L. Eisenberg, eds., *The
                Relevance of Social Science for Medicine.* Dordrecht, Netherlands: D.
                Reidel.
    1993   " 'Learning Medicine': The constructing of medical knowledge at Harvard
                Medical School," pp. 81–107 in S. Lindenbaum and M. Lock, eds.,
                Knowledge, Power, and Practice. Berkeley: University of California Press.
Good, Charles M.
    1987   *Ethnomedical Systems in Africa: Patterns of Traditional Medicine in Rural
                and Urban Kenya.* New York: Guilford.
Good, Mary-Jo Delvecchio, and Byron Good
    1982   "Patient requests in primary care clinics," pp. 275–295 in N. J. Chrisman
                and T. W. Maretzki, eds., *Clinically Applied Anthropology.* Dordrecht,
                Netherlands: D. Reidel.
Good, Mary-Jo Delvecchio, Byron J. Good, Arthur Kleinman, and Paul E. Brodwin
    1992   "Epilogue," pp. 198–207 in M. J. Delvecchio Good, B. J. Good, A.
                Kleinman, and P. E. Brodwin, eds., *Pain as Human Experience: An
                Anthropological Perspective.* Berkeley: University of California Press.
Gordon, Deborah
    1988   "Tenacious assumptions in Western medicine," pp. 19–56 in M. Lock and
                D. R. Gordon, eds., *Biomedicine Examined.* Dordrecht, Netherlands:
                Kluwer.
Gore, Susan
    1978   "The effect of social support in moderating the health consequences of un-
                employment," *Journal of Health and Social Behavior* 19: 157–165.
Gould, Jeffrey, Becky Davey, and Randall Stoffard
    1989   "Socioeconomic differences in rates of Cesarean section," *New England
                Journal of Medicine,* 321(4): 233–239.
Gould-Martin, Katherine, and Chorswang Ngin
    1981   "Chinese Americans," pp. 130–171 in A. Harwood, ed., *Ethnicity and
                Medical Care.* Cambridge: Harvard University Press.
Graham, Hilary
    1985   "Providers, negotiators, and mediators: Women as the hidden carers," pp.
                25–52 in E. Lewin and V. Oleson, eds., *Women, Health, and Healing:
                Toward a New Perspective.* New York: Tavistock.

Gray, Alastair McIntosh
    1982   "Inequalities in health, The Black Report: A summary and comment," *International Journal of Health Services* 12(3): 349–380.

Gray, Bradford H.
    1983   *The New Health Care for Profit: Doctors and Hospitals in a Competitive Environment.* Washington, DC: National Academy Press.
    1991   *The Profit Motive and Patient Care: The Changing Accountability of Doctors and Hospitals.* Cambridge, MA: Harvard University Press.

Green, Jeremy
    1983   "Detecting the hypersusceptible worker: Genetics and politics in industrial medicine," *International Journal of Health Services* 13(2): 247–264.

Green, Linda Buckley
    1989   "Consensus and coercion: Primary health care and the Guatemalan state," *Medical Anthropology Quarterly* 3(3): 246–257.

Gritzer, Glenn
    1981   "Occupational specialization in medicine: Knowledge and market explanations," *Research in the Sociology of Health Care* 2: 251–283.

Groopman, Leonard C.
    1987   "Medical internship as moral education: An essay on the system of training physicians," *Culture, Medicine, and Psychiatry* 11: 207–227.

Gross, Jane
    1989   "What medical care the poor can have: Lists are drawn up," *The New York Times*, March 27.

Grossinger, Richard
    1990   *Planet Medicine.* Berkeley: North Atlantic Books.

Gruchow, William
    1979   "Catecholamine activity and infectious disease episodes," *Journal of Human Stress* 5(3): 11–17.

Guarasci, Richard
    1987   "Death by cotton dust," pp. 76–92 in S. L. Hills, ed., *Corporate Violence.* Totowa, NJ: Rowman and Littlefield.

Guarnaccia, Peter, and Pablo Farias
    1988   "The social meaning of *nervios:* A case study of a Central American woman," *Social Science and Medicine* 26(12): 1223–1231.

Guarnaccia, Peter J., Victor DeLaCancela, and Emilio Carrillo
    1989   "The multiple meanings of *ataques de nervios* in the Latino community," *Medical Anthropology* 11: 47–62.

Gubrium, Jabor F.
    1975   *Living and Dying at Murray Manor.* New York: St. Martin's Press.

Guillemin, Jeanne H., and L. L. Holmstrom
    1986   *Mixed Blessings: Intensive Care for Newborns.* New York: Oxford University Press.

Guralnik, James M., and Edward L. Schneider
    1990   "The compression of morbidity: A dream which may come true, some

day!" pp. 42–53 in P. R. Lee and C. L. Estes, eds., *The Nation's Health*. Boston: Jones and Bartlett Publishers.

Gusfield, Joseph R.
1981   *The Culture of Public Problems: Drinking-Driving and the Symbolic Order*. Chicago: University of Chicago Press.
1991   "Risky roads," *Society* 28: 10–16.

Gussow, Joan Dye, ed.
1978   *The Feeding Web: Issues in Nutritional Ecology*. Palo Alto: Bull.

Haber, Suzanne N., and Patricia Barchas
1984   "The regulatory effect of social rank on behavior after amphetamine administration," pp. 119–132 in P. Barchas and S. P. Mendoza, eds., *Social Hierarchies: Essays Toward a Sociophysiological Perspective*. Westport, CT: Greenwood.

Haehn, Klaus-Dieter
1980   "Heilpraktikerbesuche chronisch Kranker: Frequenz und Motivation," *Diagnostik* 13: 145–146.

Hahn, Harlan
1988   "The politics of physical differences: Disability and discrimination," *Journal of Social Issues* 44(1): 39–47.

Hahn, Robert A.
1985a   "Between two worlds: Physicians as patients," *Medical Anthropology Quarterly* 16(4): 87–98.
1985b   "A world of internal medicine: Portrait of an internist," pp. 51–111 in R. A. Hahn and A. D. Gaines, eds., *Physicians of Western Medicine*. Dordrecht, Netherlands: D. Reidel.
1987   "Divisions of labor: Obstetrician, woman, and society in *Williams Obstetrics*, 1903–1985," *Medical Anthropology Quarterly* 1(3): 256–282.

Hahn, Robert A., and Arthur Kleinman
1983   "Biomedical practice and anthropological theory: Frameworks and directions," *American Review of Anthropology* 12: 305–333.

Hall, Bob, and Mary Lee Kess
1991   *Green Index, 1991–1992*. Washington, DC: Island Press.

Ham, Christopher
1982   *Health Policy in Britain*. New York: Macmillan.

Hammond, Phillip E.
1974   "Religion, pluralism, and Durkheim's integration thesis," pp. 115–142 in A. Eister, ed., *Changing Perspectives in the Scientific Study of Religion*. New York: Wiley.

Haraszti, Miklos
1978   *A Worker in a Worker's State*. New York: Universe.

Harburg, Ernest, Edwin H. Blakelock, and Peter J. Roeper
1979   "Resentful and reflective coping with arbitrary authority and blood pressure," *Psychosomatic Medicine* 41(3): 189–202.

Harburg, Ernest, John C. Erfurt, Louise Haunstein, Catherine Chape, William Schull, and M. A. Schork

1973   "Socio-ecological stress, suppressed hostility, skin color, and black-white male blood pressure, Detroit," *Psychosomatic Medicine* 35: 276–296.

Harding, Jim
1981   "The pharmaceutical industry as a public-health hazard and as an institution of social control," pp. 274–291 in D. Coburn, C. D'Arcy, P. Ness, and G. M. Torrance, *Health and Canadian Society: Sociological Perspective.* Pickering, Ont.: Fitzhenry and Whiteside.

1986   "Mood-modifiers and elderly women in Canada: The medicalization of poverty," pp. 51–86 in K. McDonnell, ed., *Adverse Effects: Women and the Pharmaceutical Industry.* Toronto: Women's Educational Press.

Harrington, Charlene
1984   "The nursing home industry," pp. 144–154 in M. Minkler and C. L. Estes, eds., *Readings in the Political Economy of Aging.* Farmingdale, NY: Baywood.

Harris, Marvin
1985   *The Sacred Cow and the Abominable Pig: Riddles of Food and Culture.* New York: Simon and Schuster.

Harrison, James, James Chin, and Thomas Ficarrotto
1992   "Warning, masculinity may be dangerous to your health," pp. 271–285 in M. S. Kimmel and M. A. Mesner, eds., *Men's Lives.* New York: Macmillan.

Hartmann, Betsy
1987   *Reproductive Rights and Wrongs: The Global Politics of Population Control and Contraceptive Choice.* New York: Harper and Row.

Harwood, Alan
1977   *Rx: Spiritist as Needed: A Study of a Puerto Rican Community Mental Health Resource.* New York: Wiley.

1981a   "Mainland Puerto Ricans," pp. 397–481 in A. Harwood, ed., *Ethnicity and Medical Care.* Cambridge: Harvard University Press.

Harwood, Alan, ed.
1981b   *Ethnicity and Medical Care.* Cambridge: Harvard University Press.

Hatfield, Elaine, and Susan Sprecher
1986   *Mirror, Mirror . . . : The Importance of Looks in Everyday Life.* Albany: State University of New York Press.

Hayes, Dennis
1989   *Behind the Silicon Curtain: The Seductions of Work in a Lonely Era.* Boston: South End Press.

Haynes, Suzanne G.
1991   "The effect of job demands, job control and new technologies on the health of employed women," pp. 157–169 in M. Frankenhaeuser, U. Lundberg, and M. Chesney, eds., *Women, Work and Health.* New York: Plenum Press.

Haynes, Suzanne G., M. Feinleib, and W. B. Kannel
1980   "The relationship of psychosocial factors to coronary heart disease in the Framingham Study, III: Eight-year incidence of coronary heart disease," *American Journal of Epidemiology* 3: 37–58.

Health Letter
1987   "Tranquilizing air traffic controllers," 3(12): 11–12.

Heggenhougen, Kris, Patrick Vaughan, Eustace Muhondwa, and J. Rutabanzibwa-Ngaiza
1987   *Community Health Workers: The Tanzanian Experience*. Oxford: Oxford Medical Publications, Oxford University Press.

Heidenheimer, Arnold J., and Nils Elvander, eds.
1980   *The Shaping of the Swedish Health System*. New York: St. Martin's Press.

Helman, Cecil
1978   " 'Feed a cold, starve a fever'—Folk models of infection in an English suburban community and their relation to medical treatment," *Culture, Medicine, and Psychiatry* 2: 107–137.

1985   "Communication in primary care: The role of patient and practitioner explanatory models," *Social Science and Medicine* 20(9): 923–931.

Henley, Nancy M.
1977   *Body Politics*. Englewood Cliffs, NJ: Prentice-Hall.

Herxheimer, Andrew, Cecilia Stalsby Lundborg, and Barbro Westerholm
1993   "Advertisements for medicines in leading medical journals in 18 countries: A 12-month survey of information content and standards," *International Journal of Health Services* 23(1): 161–172.

Herzlich, Claudine
1973   "Health and illness: A social-psychological analysis," *European Monographs in Social Psychology*, vol. 5. London: Academic Press.

Herzlich, Claudine, and Janine Pierret
1987   *Illness and Self in Society*. Baltimore: Johns Hopkins University Press.

Hess, John L.
1987   "Malthus then and now," *Nation*, 244(15): 496–500.

Hessler, Richard M., and Andrew C. Twaddle
1982   "Sweden's crisis in medical care: Political and legal changes," *Journal of Health Politics, Policy, and Law* 7(2): 440–459.

Heurtin-Roberts, Suzanne, and Efrain Reisin
1990   "Folk models of hypertension among black women: Problems in illness management," pp. 222–250 in J. Coreil and J. D. Mull, eds., *Anthropology and Primary Health Care*. Boulder, CO: Westview Press.

Heyward, William L., and James W. Curran
1988   "The epidemiology of A.I.D.S. in the U.S.," *Scientific American* 259(4): 72–81.

Hibbard, Judith H., and Clyde R. Pope
1993   "The equality of social roles as predictors of morbidity and mortality," *Social Science and Medicine* 36(3): 217–225.

Hilbert, Richard A.
1984   "The acultural dimensions of chronic pain: Flawed reality construction and the problem of meaning," *Social Problems* 31(4): 365–378.

Hilfiker, David
1983   "Allowing the debilitated to die: Facing our ethical choices," *New England Journal of Medicine* 308: 718.

1984   "Making medical mistakes," *Harper's Magazine* 268(1606): 59–65.

1986   "A doctor's view of modern medicine," *New York Times Magazine*, February 23.

Hill, Carole E.
1973   "Black healing practices in the rural South," *Journal of Popular Culture* 6(4): 849–853.

Hill, Joanna M.
1989   "Neuropeptides and their receptor as the biochemicals of emotion," pp. 61–74 in D. Palermo, ed., *Coping with Uncertainty: Behavioral and Developmental Perspectives*. Hillsdale, NJ: Laurence Erlbaum Associates.

Hill, Rolla B., and Robert Anderson
1988   *The Autopsy: Medical Practice and Public Policy*. Boston: Butterworth.
1991   "The autopsy crisis reexamined: The case for a national autopsy policy," *The Milbank Quarterly* 69(1): 51–78.

Hillman, B. J., C. A. Joseph, M. R. Mabry, Jonathan Sunshine, S. D. Kennedy, and M. Noether
1990a   "Frequency and costs of diagnostic imaging in office practice: A comparison of self-referring and radiologist-referring physicians," *New England Journal of Medicine* 323: 1604–1608.

Hillman, Mayer, John Adams, and John Whitelegg
1990b   *One False Move—A Study of Children's Independent Mobility*. London: Policy Studies Institute.

Hills, Stuart L., ed.
1987   *Corporate Violence*. Totowa, NJ: Rowman and Littlefield.

Hilts, Philip J.
1991a   "U.S. reports drop in infant deaths," *The New York Times*, April 6.
1991b   "Public hospital wait for bed can be days, U.S. study says," *The New York Times*, January 30.
1992   "U.S. cracks down on health devices made before 1976," *The New York Times*, February 24.
1993   "F.D.A. to toughen testing of devices," *The New York Times*, March 5.

Himmelstein, David, Steffie Woolhandler, Martha Harnly, Michael Bader, Ralph Silber, Howard Backer, and Alice Jones
1984   "Patient transfers: Medical practice as social triage," *American Journal of Public Health* 74: 494–496.

Himmelstein, David, and Steffie Woolhandler
1986   "Cost without benefit: Administrative waste in U.S. health care," *New England Journal of Medicine* 134(7): 441–445.

Himmelstein, David, Steffie Woolhandler, and Sidney M. Wolfe
1992   "The vanishing health care safety net: New data on uninsured Americans," *International Journal of Health Services* 22(3): 381–396.

Hinds, Michael de Courcy
1987   "Consumer Groups' Dishonor Roll of '87," *The New York Times*, December 5.

Hochschild, Arlie
1983   *The Managed Heart: Commercialization of Human Feeling*. Berkeley: University of California Press.

1989   *The Second Shift*. New York: Viking Penguin.

Hoffman, Lily M.
1989   *The Politics of Knowledge: Activist Movements in Medicine and Planning.*
             Ithaca: State University of New York Press.

Hokanson, J. E., and M. Burgess
1962   "The effects of three types of aggression on vascular processes," *Journal
             of Abnormal and Social Psychology* 648: 446–449.

Holden, John M.
1989   "Maxicare posts $17.2 million loss; regulators contest Chapter 11 status,"
             American Medical News, April 21.

Homola, Samuel
1968   *Backache: Home Treatment and Prevention*. West Nyack, NY: Parker.

Horn, James J.
1985   "Brazil: The health care model of the military modernizers and tech-
             nocrats," *International Journal of Health Services* 15(1): 47–68.

Horobin, Gordon, and Jim McIntosh
1983   "Time, risk, and routine in general practice," *Sociology of Health and
             Illness* 5(3): 312–331.

Horton, Elizabeth
1985a   "Unfriendly persuasion," *Science Digest* 93(12): 214.
1985b   "Why don't we buckle up?" *Science Digest* 93(2): 22.

Horwitz, Ralph I., Catherine M. Viscoli, Lisa Berkman, Robert M. Donaldson, Sarah M.
Horwitz, Carolyn J. Murrary, David F. Ransohoff, and Jody Sindelar
1990   "Treatment adherence and risk of death after a myocardial infarction," *The
             Lancet* 136 (September 1): 542–545.

Hotz, Robert Lee
1993   "Experiment to aid growth of short children resumes," *Los Angeles Times*,
             June 29.

Houben, Gerard J.
1991   "Production control and chronic stress in work organizations,"
             International Journal of Health Services 21(2): 309–327.

House, James S.
1974   "Occupational stress and coronary heart disease: A review and theoretical
             integration," *Journal of Health and Social Behavior* 15: 17–27.

1981   *Work Stress and Social Support*. Reading, MA: Addison-Wesley.

House, James S., Karl R. Landis, and Debra Umberson
1988   "Social relationships and health," *Science* 214 (July): 540–545.

House, James S., Ronald C. Kessler, A. Regula Herzog, Richard P. Mero, Ann M. Kinney,
and Martha J. Breslaw
1990   "Age, socioeconomic status and health," *The Milbank Quarterly* 68(3):
             383–411.

House, James S., Anthony J. McMichael, James A. Wells, Berton H. Kaplan, and Lawrence
R. Landerman
1979   "Occupational stress and health among factory workers," *Journal of Health
             and Social Behavior* 20(2): 139–160.

Howard, Robert
    1985   *Brave New Workplace.* New York: Penguin.
Hoy, Elizabeth W., Richard E. Curtis, and Thomas Rice
    1991   "Change and growth in managed care," *Health Affairs* 10(4): 18–36.
Hughes, David
    1988   "When nurse knows best: Some aspects of nurse/doctor interaction in a
                casualty department," *Sociology of Health and Illness* 10(1): 1–22.
Hunger, U.S.A.: A Report by the Citizens' Board of Inquiry into Hunger and Malnutrition in the United States.
    1968   Boston: Beacon.
Hunt, Linda, M., Brigitte Jordan, and Susan Irwin
    1989   "Views of what's wrong: Diagnosis and patients' concepts of illness,"
                Social Science and Medicine 28(9): 945–956.
Hunt, Sonja M.
    1989   "The public health implications of private cars," pp. 100–115 in C. J. Martin
                and D. V. McQueen, eds., *Readings for a New Public Health.* Edinburgh:
                Edinburgh University Press.
Hurowitz, James C.
    1993   "Toward a social policy for health," *New England Journal of Medicine*
                329(2): 130–133.
Iglehart, John K.
    1993   "The American health care system: The End Stage Renal Disease
                Program," *The New England Journal of Medicine* 328(5): 366–371.
Illich, Ivan
    1975   *Medical Nemesis: The Expropriation of Health.* London: Calder and
                Boyars.
Ingleby, David
    1982   "The social construction of mental illness," pp. 123–143 in P. Wright and
                A. Treacher, eds., *The Problem of Medical Knowledge: Examining the
                Social Construction of Medicine.* Edinburgh: Edinburgh University Press.
Institute of Medicine
    1986   *For-Profit Enterprise in Health Care.* Washington, DC: National
                Academy Press.
Irwin, Susan, and Brigitte Jordan
    1987   "Knowledge, practice, and power: Court-ordered Cesarean section,"
                Medical Anthropology Quarterly 1(3): 319–334.
Ivancevich, John M., and Michael T. Matteson
    1988   "Type A behavior and the healthy individual," *British Journal of Medical
                Psychology* 61: 37–56.
Iverem, Esther
    1988   "New York's home health-care system facing a labor crisis," *The New
                York Times*, January 28.
Jackall, Robert
    1977   "The control of public faces in a commercial work situation," *Urban Life*
                6(3): 277–302.

Jackson, Michael
    1983   "Knowledge of the body," *Man* 18: 327–345.

Jacobson, Alan M., and Joan B. Leibovich
    1984   "Psychological issues in diabetes mellitus," *Psychosomatics* 25(1): 7–15.

Jahoda, Marie, Paul Lazarsfeld, and Harry Zeisel
    1971   *Marienthal: The Sociography of an Unemployment Community*. Chicago: Aldine Atherton.

Janes, Craig
    1986   "Migration and hypertension: An ethnography of disease risk in an urban Samoan community," pp. 175–211 in C. Janes, R. Stall, and S. Gifford, eds., *Anthropology and Epidemiology: Interdisciplinary Approaches to the Study of Health and Disease*. Dordrecht, Holland: D. Reidel.

Jeffery, Roger
    1979   "Normal rubbish: Deviant patients in casualty departments," *Sociology of Health and Illness* 1(1): 90–107.

Johnson, Allen
    1978   "In search of the affluent society," *Human Nature* 1: 50–59.

Johnson, Daniel M., J. Sherwood Williams, and David Bromley
    1986   "Religion, health and healing: Findings from a southern city," *Sociological Analysis* 47(1): 66–73.

Johnson, James H., and Irwin G. Sarason
    1978   "Life stress, depression and anxiety: Internal-external control as a moderator variable," *Journal of Psychosomatic Research* 22: 205–208.

Johnson, Julie
    1989   "Children's health seen as declining," *The New York Times*, March 2.

Johnson, Thomas M.
    1987   "Premenstrual syndrome as a Western culture-specific disorder," *Culture, Medicine, and Psychiatry*, 11: 337–356.

Johnson, Thomas M., and Carolyn F. Sargent
    1990   *Medical Anthropology: A Handbook of Theory and Method*. New York: Greenwood Press.

Jones, James H.
    1981   *Bad Blood: The Tuskegee Syphilis Experiment*. New York: Free Press.

Jones, Kathryn
    1993   "A hospital giant comes to town, bringing change," *The New York Times*, November 21.

Jones, R. Kenneth
    1985   "The development of medical sects," pp. 1–22 in R. K. Jones, ed., *Sickness and Sectarianism: Exploratory Studies in Medical and Religious Sectarianism*. London: Gower.

Jones, Russell A.
    1982   "Expectations and illness," pp. 145–167 in H. S. Friedman and M. R. DiMatteo, eds., *Interpersonal Issues in Health Care*. New York: Academic.

Jourard, Sidney M.
    1964   *The Transparent Self.* New York: D. Van Nostrand.

Kahn, Robert L.
    1981   "Work and health: Some psychosocial effects of advanced technology," pp. 17–37 in B. Gardell and C. Johansson, eds., *Working Life.* New York: Wiley.

Kane, Rosalie A.
    1993   "Delivering and financing long term care in Canada's ten provinces," pp. 89–101 in A. Bennett and O. Adams, eds., *Looking North for Health: What We Can Learn from Canada's Health Care System.* San Francisco: Jossey-Bass Publishers.

Kaplan, Howard, Robert Johnson, Carol Bailey, and William Simon
    1987   "The sociological study of AIDS: A critical review of the literature and suggested research agenda," *Journal of Health and Social Behavior* 28: 140–157.

Kaplan, Jay, Stephen Manuck, Thomas Clarkson, Frances Lusso, David Taub, and Eric Miller
    1983   "Social stress and atherosclerosis in normocholesterolemic monkeys," *Science* 220(4,598): 733–735.

Karasek, Robert, and Töres Theorell
    1990   *Healthy Work: Stress, Productivity and the Reconstruction of Working Life.* New York: Basic Books.

Karliner, Joshua N., and Daniel Faber
    1988   "The other revolution: Nicaragua's environmental crisis," *Utne Reader*, January–February: 54–65.

Kasl, Stanislav V.
    1975   "Issues in patient adherence to health care regimens," *Journal of Human Stress* 1(1,975): 5–17.

Kasl, Stanislav V., and Sidney Cobb
    1966   "Health behavior, illness behavior, and sick role behavior," *Archives of Environmental Health* 12: 246–266.

Kassirer, Jerome P.
    1989   "Our stubborn quest for diagnostic certainty: A cause of excessive testing," *New England Journal of Medicine* 320: 1489–1491.

Kassirer, Jerome P., and G. A. Gorry
    1978   "Clinical problem solving: A behavioral analysis," *Annals of Internal Medicine* 89: 245–255.

Kastenbaum, Robert
    1971   "Getting there ahead of time," *Psychology Today* 5: 52–54, 83–84.

Katz, Alfred
    1979   "Self-help groups: Some clarifications," *Social Science and Medicine* 13A: 491–494.

Katz, Alfred, and Eugene I. Bender, eds.
    1976   *The Strength in Us: Self-Help Groups in the Modern World.* New York: New Viewpoints.

Katz, Alfred, and Lowell Levin
    1980   "Self-care is not a solipsistic trap: A reply to critics," *International Journal of Health Services* 10: 329–336.

Kaufert, Patricia
    1988   "Menopause as process or event: The creation of definitions in biomedicine," pp. 331–349 in M. Lock and D. R. Gordon, eds., *Biomedicine Examined*. Dordrecht, Netherlands: Kluwer.

Kaufert, Patricia, and Sonja M. McKinlay
    1985   "Estrogen-replacement therapy: The production of medical knowledge and the emergence of policy," pp. 113–138 in E. Lewin and V. Olesen, eds., *Women, Health, and Healing: Toward a New Perspective*. London: Tavistock.

Kaufman, Caroline
    1987   "Rights and the provision of health care: A comparison of Canada, Great Britain, and the United States," pp. 491–510 in H. D. Schwartz, ed., *Dominant Issues in Medical Care*. New York: Random House.

Kaufman, Martin
    1971   *Homeopathy in America: The Rise and Fall of a Medical Heresy*. Baltimore: Johns Hopkins University Press.

Kaufman, Sharon R.
    1988   "Toward a phenomenology of boundaries in medicine: Chronic illness experience in the case of stroke," *Medical Anthropology Quarterly* 2(4): 338–354.

Kaur, Narinder
    1990   "Impact of consumer culture on health," pp. 131–143 in B. Chaudhuri, ed., *Cultural and Environmental Dimensions on Health*. New Delhi: Inter India Publications.

Kearl, Michael
    1989   *Endings: A Sociology of Death and Dying*. New York: Oxford.

Kemper, Vicki, and Viveca Novak
    1993   "What's blocking health care reform?" *International Journal of Health Services* 23(1): 69–79.

Kerr, Peter
    1991a   "Chain of mental hospitals faces inquiry in 4 states," *The New York Times*, October 22.
    1991b   "Mental hospital chains accused of much cheating on insurance," *The New York Times*, November 24.
    1992   "Centers for head injury accused of earning millions for neglect," *The New York Times*, March 16.

Kessler, Ronald C., James House, and Blake Turner
    1987   "Unemployment and health in a community sample," *Journal of Health and Social Behavior* 28: 51–59.

Kiecolt-Glaser, Janet K., and Ronald Glaser
    1991   "Stress and immune function in humans," pp. 849–867 in R. Ader, D. Felten, and N. Cohen, eds., *Psychoneuroimmunology* (second edition). New York: Academic Press.

Kiev, Ari
    1968   *Curanderismo: Mexican-American Folk Psychiatry*. New York: The Free Press.

King, Patricia A.
1992   "The dangers of difference," *Hastings Center Report* 22(6): 35–38.
Kingsport Study Group
1978   "Smells like money," *Southern Exposure* 6(2): 59–65.
Kinley, David, Arnold Levinson, and Frances Moore-Lappé
1981   "The myth of humanitarian foreign aid," *Nation*, 233(2): 41–43.
Kircher, Tobias, Judith Nelson, and Harold Burdo
1985   "The autopsy as a measure of accuracy of the death certificate," *New England Journal of Medicine* 313: 1263–1269.
Kiritz, Stewart, and Rudolf H. Moos
1974   "Physiological effects of social environments," *Psychosomatic Medicine* 36(2): 96–114.
Kirmayer, Laurence J.
1988   "Mind and body as metaphors: Hidden values in biomedicine," pp. 57–94 in M. Lock and D. R. Gordon, eds., *Biomedicine Examined*. Dordrecht, Netherlands: Kluwer.
Kleiman, Dena
1985   "Changing way of death: Some agonizing choices," *The New York Times*, January 24.
Klein, David, Jackob Najman, Arthur Kohrman, and Clarke Munro
1982   "Patient characteristics that elicit negative responses from family physicians," *Journal of Family Practice* 14(5): 881–888.
Klein, Rudolf
1983   *The Politics of the National Health Service*. London: Longman.
Kleinfield, N. R.
1986   "The ever-fatter business of thinness," *The New York Times*, September 7.
Kleinman, Arthur
1978   "The failure of Western medicine," *Human Nature* 1: 63–68.
1980   *Patients and Healers in the Context of Culture: An Exploration of the Borderland Between Anthropology, Medicine, and Psychiatry*. Berkeley: University of California Press.
1984   "Indigenous systems of healing: Questions for professional, popular, and folk care," pp. 138–164 in J. W. Salmon, ed., *Alternative Medicine: Popular and Policy Perspectives*. New York: Tavistock.
1988   *The Illness Narratives: Suffering, Healing, and the Human Condition*. New York: Basic.
1992   "Pain and resistance: The delegitimation and relegitimation of local worlds," pp. 169–197 in M. Delvecchio Good, P. E. Brodwin, B. J. Good, and A. Kleinman, eds., *Pain as Human Experience: An Anthropological Perspective*. Berkeley: University of California Press.
Kleinman, Arthur, and Joan Kleinman
1991   "Suffering and its professional transformation: Toward an ethnography of interpersonal experience," *Culture, Medicine and Psychiatry* 15(3): 275–301.

Knutsson, Ander S., Bjorn G. Jonsson, Torbjörn Åkerstedt, and Kristina Orth-Gomer
    1986   "Increased risk of ischemic heart disease in shift workers," *The Lancet* 2:
              86–92.

Koenig, Barbara
    1988   "The technological imperative in medical practice: The social creation of
              a 'routine' treatment," pp. 465–496 in M. Lock and D. R. Gordon, eds.,
              Biomedicine Examined. Dordrecht, Netherlands: Kluwer.

Kolata, Gina
    1989   "Ambivalence over pill grows with risk data," *The New York Times*,
              January 8.

Kolbert, Elizabeth
    1991   "Medicaid in New York: Costs surge but care for poor still lags," *The New
              York Times*, April 15.

Konner, Melvin
    1987   *Becoming a Doctor: A Journey of Initiation in Medical School*. New York:
              Viking.

Koos, Earl L.
    1954   *The Health of Regionville*. New York: Columbia University Press.

Kotarba, Joseph A.
    1975   "American acupuncturists: The new entrepreneurs of hope," *Urban Life*
              4(2): 149–177.

    1977   "The chronic pain experience," pp. 257–272 in J. Douglas, ed., *Existential
              Sociology*. Cambridge: Cambridge University Press.

Kotzsch, Ronald
    1985   "How our food choices affect the world," *East West Journal*, June: 15–19.

Kramon, Glenn
    1988a   "Employees paying ever-bigger share of medical costs," *The New York
              Times*, November 22.

    1988b   "Good medicine, better business," *The New York Times*, May 15.

Kristof, Nicholas D.
    1991   "Chinese grow healthier from cradle to grave," *The New York Times*, April
              14.

Krohne, Heinz Walter
    1990   "Personality as a mediator between objective events and their subjective
              representation," *Psychological Inquiry* 1(1): 26–29.

Kuhn, Thomas S.
    1970   *The Structure of Scientific Revolutions*. International Encyclopedia of
              Unified Science, Vol. 2, No. 2. Chicago: University of Chicago Press.

Kunisch, Judith R.
    1989   "Electronic fetal monitors: Marketing forces and the resulting contro-
              versy," pp. 41–60 in K. S. Ratcliff, ed., *Healing Technology: Feminist
              Perspectives*. Ann Arbor: University of Michigan Press.

Kunitz, Stephen, and Jerrold Levy
    1981   "Navajos," pp. 337–396 in A. Harwood, ed., *Ethnicity and Medical Care*.
              Cambridge, MA: Harvard University Press.

Kunzle, David
1981   *Fashion and Fetishism: A Social History of the Corset, Tight-Lacing and Other Forms of Body Sculpture in the West.* London: Rowan and Littlefield.

Kutner, Nancy
1982   "Cost-benefit issues in U.S. national health legislation: The case of the end-stage renal disease program," *Social Problems* 30(1): 51–63.

LaCheen, Cary
1986   "Population control and the pharmaceutical industry," pp. 89–136 in K. McDonnell, ed., *Adverse Effects: Women and the Pharmaceutical Industry.* Toronto: Women's Educational Press.

Lack, Dorothea Z.
1982   "Women and pain: Another feminist issue," *Women and Therapy* 1(1): 55–63.

Laing, Ronald, and Aaron Esterson
1965   *Sanity, Madness and the Family.* New York: Basic.

Lakoff, Robin T., and Raquel L. Scherr
1984   *Face Value: The Politics of Beauty.* Boston: Routledge and Kegan Paul.

Lardy, Nicholas R.
1983   *Agriculture in China's Modern Economic Development.* Cambridge: Cambridge University Press.

Larned, Deborah
1977   "The epidemic of unnecessary hysterectomy," pp. 195–208 in C. Dreifus, ed., *Seizing Our Bodies: The Politics of Women's Health.* New York: Vintage.

LaRocco, James M., and James S. House
1980   "Social support, occupational stress and health," *Journal of Health and Social Behavior* 21: 202–218.

Larson, Magali Sarfatti
1979   "Professionalism: Rise and fall," *International Journal of Health Services* 9(4): 607–627.

Latham, Michael C.
1987   "Strategies for the control of malnutrition and the influence of the nutritional sciences," pp. 330–345 in J. Price, G. Hinger, J. Leslie, and C. Hoisington, eds., *Food Policy: Integrating Supply, Distribution and Consumption.* Baltimore: Johns Hopkins University Press.

Latour, Bruno, and Steve Woolgar
1979   *Laboratory Life: The Social Construction of Scientific Fact.* Beverly Hills: Sage.

Laumann, E. O., J. H. Gagnon, S. Michaels, R. T. Michael, and J. S. Coleman
1989   "Monitoring the AIDS epidemic in the United States: A network approach," *Science* 244: 1186–1189.

La Veist, Thomas A.
1992   "The political empowerment and health status of African Americans: Mapping a new territory," *American Journal of Sociology* 97(4): 1080–1095.

1993   "Segregation, poverty and empowerment: Health consequences for African Americans," *The Milbank Quarterly* 71(1): 41–64.

Law, Sylvia
1974   *Blue Cross—What Went Wrong?* New Haven: Yale University Press.

Lawrence, Linda, and Thomas McLemore
1983   "1981 National Ambulatory Medical Care Survey," *Advance Data*, Report Number 88.

Lawrence, Philip
1958   "Chronic illness and socioeconomic status," pp. 37–49 in E. G. Jaco, ed., *Patients, Physicians and Illness*. New York: The Free Press.

Lazarus, Ellen S.
1988   "Theoretical considerations for the study of the doctor-patient relationship: Implications of a perinatal study," *Medical Anthropology Quarterly* 2(1): 34–58.

Lazarus, Richard, ed.
1966   *Psychological Stress and the Coping Process*. New York: McGraw Hill.

Leavitt, Judith W.
1987   "The growth of medical authority: Technology and morals in turn-of-the-century obstetrics," *Medical Anthropology Quarterly* 1(3): 230–255.

Leder, Drew
1984   "Medicine and paradigms of embodiment," *The Journal of Medicine and Philosophy* 9: 29–43.

Ledogar, Robert J.
1975   *Hungry for Profits: U.S. Food and Drug Multinationals in Latin America*. New York: IDOC/North America.

Lee, Sidney
1982   "Health policy, a social contract: A comparison of the United States and Canada," *Journal of Public Health Policy* 3(3): 293–301.

Lefcourt, Harold M.
1973   "The function of the illusions of control and freedom," *American Psychologist* 28: 417–425.

Leiderman, Deborah, and Jean-Anne Grisso
1985   "The GOMER phenomenon," *Journal of Health and Social Behavior* 26: 222–231.

Lennerlof, Lennart
1988   "Learned helplessness at work," *International Journal of Health Services* 18(2): 207–222.

Lerner, Michael
1992   *Surplus Powerlessness*. Atlantic Highlands, NJ: Humanities Press, Intl.

Leslie, Charles, ed.
1976   *Asian Medical Systems: A Comparative Study*. Berkeley: University of California Press.

Letsch, Suzanne W.
1993   "National health care spending in 1991," *Health Affairs* 12(1): 94–110.

Levi, Lennart
    1978   "Quality of the working environment: Protection and promotion of occupational mental health," *Working Life in Sweden* 8.
    1981   *Preventing Work Stress*. Reading, MA: Addison-Wesley.

Levin, Lowell S., and Ellen L. Idler
    1981   *The Hidden Health Care System: Mediating Structures and Medicine*. Cambridge, MA: Ballinger.

Levin, Lowell S., Alfred H. Katz, and Erik Holst
    1976   *Self-Care: Lay Initiatives in Health*. New York: Prodist.

Levine, Jon D., N. C. Gordon, and H. Fields
    1978   "Mechanism of placebo analgesia," *Lancet* 2(23): 654–657.

Levine, Seymour, and Sandra G. Wiener
    1989   "Coping with uncertainty: A paradox," pp. 1–16 in D. S. Palermo, ed., *Coping with Uncertainty: Behavioral and Developmental Perspectives*. Hillsdale, NJ: Lawrence Erlbaum Associates.

Levine, Sol R., and Abraham Lilienfeld, eds.
    1987   *Epidemiology and Health Policy*. New York: Tavistock.

Levins, Richard, and Richard Lewontin
    1985   *The Dialectical Biologist*. Cambridge: Harvard University Press.

Levit, Katherine R., Mark S. Freeland, and Daniel R. Waldo
    1989   "Health spending and ability to pay: Business, individuals, and government," *Health Care Financing Review* 3: 10–12.

Levy, Sandra M., and Lynda A. Heiden
    1990   "Personality and social factors in cancer outcome," pp. 254–282 in H. S. Friedman, ed., *Personality and Disease*. New York: John Wiley and Sons.

Lewin, Tamar
    1987a   "Company sues its workers' doctors," *The New York Times*, June 9.
    1989   "Ailing parent: Women's burden grows," *The New York Times*, November 24.

Lewis, Charles E.
    1969   "Variance in the incidence of surgery," *New England Journal of Medicine* 281: 880–884.
    1976   "Health maintenance organizations: Guarantors of access to medical care?" pp. 220–240 in C. Lewis, R. Fein, and D. Mechanic, eds., *A Right to Health: The Problem of Access in Primary Care*. New York: Wiley-Interscience.

Lewis, Ioan M.
    1971   *Ecstatic Religion: An Anthropological Study of Spirit Possession and Shamanism*. Harmondsworth, England: Penguin.

Liem, Ramsay
    1981   "Economic change and unemployment: Context of illness," pp. 54–78 in E. Mishler, L. AmaraSingham, S. Hauser, R. Liem, S. Osherson, and N. Waxler, eds., *Social Contexts of Health, Illness, and Patient Care*. Cambridge: Cambridge University Press.

Light, Donald W.
  1980   *Becoming Psychiatrists: The Professional Transformation of Self.* New York: Norton.
  1992   "Excluding more, covering less: The health insurance industry in the U.S.," *Health/PAC Bulletin,* Spring: 7–13.

Light, Donald W., and Sol Levine
  1988   "The changing character of the medical profession: A theoretical overview," *Milbank Quarterly* 66 (supplement 2): 10–32.

Light, Donald W., and Alexander Schuller, eds.
  1986   *Political Values and Health Care: The German Experience.* Cambridge, MA: MIT Press.

Lilienfeld, David E.
  1991   "The silence: The asbestos industry and early occupational cancer research—a case study," *American Journal of Public Health* 81(6): 791–800.

Lin, Nan, Mary W. Woelfel, and Steven C. Light
  1985   "The buffering effect of social support subsequent to an important life event," *Journal of Health and Social Behavior* 26: 247–263.

Lindheim, Roslyn
  1985   "New design parameters for healthy places," *Places* 2(4): 17–27.

Lindorff, Dave
  1992   *Marketplace Medicine: The Rise of the For-Profit Hospital Chain.* New York: Bantam Books.

Lipowski, Zbigniew J.
  1973   "Affluence, information inputs, and health," *Social Science and Medicine* 7: 517–529.

Little, Marilyn
  1982   "Conflict and negotiation in a new role: The family nurse practitioner," *Research in the Sociology of Health Care* 2: 31–59.

Livneh, Hanoch
  1991   "On the origins of negative attitudes toward people with disabilities," pp. 181–196 in R. P. Marinelli and A. E. Dell, eds., *The Psychological and Social Impact of Disability* (third edition). New York: Springer Publishing Co.

Lock, Margaret
  1990   "On being ethnic: The politics of identity breaking and making in Canada, or, Nevra on Sunday," *Culture, Medicine and Psychiatry* 14(2): 237–254.
  1991   "Contested meanings of the menopause," *The Lancet* 337 (May 25): 1270–1272.
  1993   "The politics of mid-life and menopause: Ideologies for the second sex in North America and Japan," pp. 330–363 in S. Lindenbaum and M. Lock, eds., *Knowledge, Power, and Practice.* Berkeley: University of California Press.

Lock, Margaret, and Nancy Scheper-Hughes
  1990   "A critical-interpretive approach in medical anthropology: Rituals and routines of discipline and dissent," pp. 47–72 in T. M. Johnson and C. F. Sargent, *Medical Anthropology: A Handbook of Theory and Method.* New York: Greenwood.

Locke, Steven, Robert Ader, Hugo Besedovsky, Nicolas Hall, George Solomon, and Terry Strom, eds.
    1985   *Foundations of Psychoneuroimmunology*. New York: Aldine.

Locker, David
    1981   *Symptoms and Illness: The Cognitive Organization of Disorder*. New York: Tavistock.

Lohr, Kathleen, R. H. Brook, C. J. Kamberg, G. Goldberg, A. Leibowitz, J. Keesey, D. Reboussin, and J. P. Newhouse
    1986   *Use of Medical Care in the Rand Health Insurance Experiment: Diagnosis and Service-Specific Analysis in a Randomized Control Trial*. Santa Monica, CA: Rand.

Lohr, Steve
    1988   "British health service faces a crisis in funds and delays," *The New York Times*, August 7.

Longmore, Paul K.
    1987   "Screening stereotypes: Images of disabled people in television and motion pictures," pp. 65–78 in A. Gartner and T. Joe, eds., *Images of the Disabled, Disabling Images*. New York: Prager.

Loscocco, Karyn A., and Glenna Spitze
    1990   "Working conditions: Social support and the well-being of female and male factory workers," *Journal of Health and Social Behavior* 31(4): 313–327.

Low, Setha M.
    1985   *Culture, Politics, and Medicine in Costa Rica*. Bedford Hills, NY: Redgrave.

Lowe, Marian, and Ruth Hubbard, eds.
    1983   *Woman's Nature*. New York: Pergamon.

Lubitz, Jim, and Ronald Priboda
    1984   "Uses and costs of Medicare services in the last two years of life," *Health Care Financing Review* 5: 117–131.

Luft, Harold
    1983   "Economic incentives and clinical decisions," pp. 103–123 in B. Gray, ed., *The New Health Care for Profit: Doctors and Hospitals in a Competitive Environment*. Washington, DC: National Academy Press.

Lundberg, Ulf
    1976   "Urban commuting: Crowdedness and catecholamine excretion," *Journal of Human Stress* 2(3): 26–31.

Lurie, Elinore E.
    1981   "Nurse practitioners: Issues in professional socialization," *Journal of Health and Social Behavior* 22: 31–48.

Lynch, James J.
    1979   *The Broken Heart*. New York: Basic.
    1985   *The Language of the Heart*. New York: Basic.

Lynch, James J., and Paul J. F. Rosch
    1990   "The heart of dialogue: Human communication and cardiovascular

health," pp. 31–52 in H. Balner, ed., *A New Medical Model: A Challenge for Biomedicine?* Amsterdam: Swets and Zeitlinger.

Lyon, Margot L.
    1990   "Order and healing: The concept of order and its importance in the conceptualization of healing," *Medical Anthropology* 12(10): 249–268.

Macalister, Malcolm
    1992   "The $225,000 habit," *Observer Magazine* (November 8): 22.

MacDougall, J. M., T. M. Dembroski, J. E. Dimsdale, and T. Hackett
    1985   "Components of Type A, hostility and anger-in: Further relationships to angiographic findings," *Health Psychology* 4: 137–152.

MacLennan, Carol A.
    1988   "From accident to crash: The auto industry and the politics of injury," *Medical Anthropology Quarterly* 2(3): 233–250.

MacMahon, Bryan, and Thomas F. Pugh
    1970   *Epidemiologic Principles and Methods.* Boston: Little, Brown.

Mairs, Nancy
    1987   "Hers," *The New York Times*, July 9.

Makinson, Larry
    1992   "Political contributions from the health and insurance industries," *Health Affairs* 11(4): 120–134.

Maloney, H. Newton
    1987   "Anti-cultism: The ethics of psychologists' reactions to new religions." Paper presented to the American Psychological Association.

Malthus, Thomas Robert
    [1798] 1965 *Essay on the Principle of Population as It Affects the Future Improvements of Society*, reprinted as *First Essay on Population, 1798.* New York: Kelley.

Mansour, Jared
    1987   "Eating culture: Food as junk commodity," *Critique* 25: 14–16.

Marcelis, Carla, and Mira Shiva
    1986   "EP drugs: Unsafe by any name," pp. 11–26 in K. McDonnell, ed., *Adverse Effects: Women and the Pharmaceutical Industry.* Toronto: Women's Educational Press.

Maretzki, Thomas, and Eduard Seidler
    1985   "Biomedicine and naturopathic healing in West Germany: A historical and ethnomedical view of a stormy relationship," *Culture, Medicine, and Psychiatry* 9(4): 383–421.

Marmor, Theodore
    1982   "Canada's path, America's choice: Lessons from the Canadian experience with National Health Insurance," pp. 77–96 in R. L. Numbers, ed., *Compulsory Health Insurance: The Continuing American Debate.* Westport, CT: Greenwood Press.

    1983   "Rethinking national health insurance," pp. 187–206 in T. Marmor, ed., *Political Analysis and American Medical Care.* Cambridge: Cambridge University Press.

Marmor, Theodore, Wayne L. Hoffman, and Thomas C. Heagy
    1983a   "National Health Insurance: Some lessons from the Canadian experience,"

pp. 165–186 in T. Marmor, ed., *Political Analysis and American Medical Care*. Cambridge: Cambridge University Press.

Marmor, Theodore, Donald Wittman, and Thomas C. Heagy
  1983b   "The politics of medical inflation," pp. 61–75 in T. Marmor, ed., *Political Analysis and American Medical Care*. Cambridge: Cambridge University Press.

Marmot, M. G., M. Kogevinas, and M. A. Elston
  1987   "Social/economic status and disease," *Annual Review of Public Health* 8: 111–135.

Marquis, M. Susan
  1984   *Cost-Sharing and the Patient's Choice of Provider*. Santa Monica, CA: Rand.

Martin, Emily
  1987   *The Woman in the Body: A Cultural Analysis of Reproduction*. Boston: Beacon Press.

Mausner, Judith S., and Anita Bahn
  1985   *Epidemiology: An Introductory Text* (second edition). Philadelphia: W. B. Saunders.

May, Clifford
  1985   "Reporter's notebook: Images far from Ethiopia's famine," *The New York Times*, April 7.

McCarthy, Carol
  1981   "Financing for health care," pp. 272–312 in S. Jonas, ed., *Health Care Delivery in the United States*. New York: Springer.

McCarty, Richard, Karin Horwatt, and Maria Konarska
  1988   "Chronic stress and sympathetic-adrenal medullary responsiveness," *Social Science and Medicine* 26(3): 333–341.

McCrea, Frances
  1983   "The politics of menopause: The discovery of a deficiency disease," *Social Problems* 13(1): 111–123.

McElroy, Ann, and Patricia K. Townsend
  1985   *Medical Anthropology in Ecological Perspective*. Boulder, CO: Westview.

McGuire, Meredith B.
  1982   *Pentecostal Catholics: Power, Charisma, and Order in a Religious Movement*. Philadelphia: Temple University Press.

  1983   "Words of power: Personal empowerment and healing," *Culture, Medicine, and Psychiatry* 7: 221–240.

  1985   "Religion and Healing," pp. 268–284 in P. Hammond, ed., *The Sacred in a Secular Age*. Berkeley: University of California Press.

  1988   *Ritual Healing in Suburban America*, with the assistance of Debra Kantor. New Brunswick, NJ: Rutgers University Press.

  1992   *Religion: The Social Context*. Belmont, CA: Wadsworth.

McGuire, Meredith B., and Debra J. Kantor
  1987   "Belief systems and illness experiences: The case of non-medical healing groups," *Research in the Sociology of Health Care* 6: 221–248.

McIntosh, Jim
    1974   "Processes of communication, information-seeking, and control associated with cancer," *Social Science and Medicine* 8A: 157–187.

McKeown, Thomas
    1979   *The Role of Medicine: Dream, Mirage, or Nemesis?* Princeton: Princeton University Press.

McKinlay, John B.
    1972   "The sick role, illness, and pregnancy," *Social Science and Medicine* 6: 561–572.

    1975   "Who is really ignorant—Physician or patient?" *Journal of Health and Social Behavior* 16: 3–11.

    1994   "A case for refocusing upstream: The political economy of illness," pp. 509–523 in P. Conrad and R. Kern, eds., *The Sociology of Health and Illness: Critical Perspectives*, 3rd edition. New York: St. Martin's Press.

McKinlay, John B., and Joan Archer
    1985   "Towards the proletarianization of physicians," *International Journal of Health Services* 15(2): 161–195.

McKinlay, John B., and Sonja M. McKinlay
    1977   "The questionable effect of medical measures on the decline of mortality in the United States in the twentieth century," *Milbank Memorial Fund Quarterly* 55: 405–428.

McKinlay, John B., Sonja McKinlay, and Robert Beagle Role
    1989   "Trends in death and disease and the contribution of medical measures," pp. 14–45 in H. E. Freeman and S. Levine, eds., *Handbook of Medical Sociology* (fourth edition). Englewood Cliffs, NJ: Prentice-Hall.

McKinlay, John B., and John D. Stoeckle
    1988   "Corporatization and the social transformation of doctoring," *International Journal of Health Services* 18(2): 191–205.

McKinlay, Sonja M., D. J. Brambilla, N. E. Avis, and John B. McKinlay
    1991   "Women's experience of the menopause," *Current Obstetrics and Gynaecology* 1: 3–7.

McQueen, David, and Johannes Siegrist
    1982   "Social factors in the etiology of chronic disease: An overview," *Social Science and Medicine* 16: 353–367.

Mechanic, David
    1976   "Illness, illness behavior, and help-seeking," pp. 161–175 in D. Mechanic, ed., *The Growth of Bureaucratic Medicine*. New York: Wiley.

    1978   *Medical Sociology*. New York: The Free Press.

    1986   *From Advocacy to Allocation: The Evolving American Health Care System*. New York: The Free Press.

Medvedev, Z., and R. Medvedev
    1971   *A Question of Madness*. New York: Alfred Knopf.

Meier, Barry
    1993a   "Effective? Maybe. Profitable? Clearly," *The New York Times*, February 14.

    1993b   "Doctors' investments in home care grow, raising fears of ethical swamp," *The New York Times*, March 19.

Melamed, Elissa
    1983   *Mirror, Mirror: The Terror of Not Being Young.* New York: Linden.
Melosh, Barbara
    1982   *The Physician's Hand: Work, Culture, and Conflict in American Nursing.*
                Philadelphia: Temple University Press.
Melzack, Ronald, and Peter Wall
    1983   *The Challenge of Pain.* New York: Basic.
Members of the Working Party
    1975   "Occupational accidents," pp. 65–90 in Members of the Working Party,
                eds., *Research for a Better Work Environment: A Summary of Reports on
                Four Central Research Areas.* Stockholm: LiberFörlag.
Merton, Robert K., George C. Reader, and Patricia L. Kendall, eds.
    1957   *The Student Physician.* Cambridge: Harvard University Press.
Michaels, David
    1988   "Waiting for the body count: Corporate decision-making and bladder can-
                cer in the U.S. dye industry," *Medical Anthropology Quarterly* 2(3):
                215–232.
Milio, Nancy
    1985   "Health policy and the emerging tobacco reality," *Social Science and
                Medicine* 21(6): 603–613.
Miller, Frances H.
    1983   "Secondary income from recommended treatment: Should fiduciary prin-
                ciples constrain physician behavior?" pp. 153–169 in B. Gray, ed., *The
                New Health Care for Profit: Doctors and Hospitals in a Competitive
                Environment.* Washington, DC: National Academy Press.
Millman, Marcia
    1976   *The Unkindest Cut: Life in the Backrooms of Medicine.* New York: William
                Morrow.
    1980   *Such a Pretty Face: Being Fat in America.* New York: W. W. Norton.
Millon, Theodore, Catherine Green, and Robert Meagher, eds.
    1982   *Handbook of Clinical Health Psychology.* New York: Plenum.
Mills, C. Wright
    1956   *White Collar.* New York: Oxford University Press.
    1959   *The Sociological Imagination.* New York, Oxford.
Mintz, Sidney
    1979   "Time, Sugar, and Sweetness," *Marxist Perspectives* 8: 56–73.
Mishler, Elliott
    1984   *The Discourse of Medicine: Dialectics of Medical Interviews.* Norwood,
                NJ: Ablex.
Mitchell, Jean M., and Elton Scott
    1992   "Physician self-referral: Empirical evidence and policy implications,"
                Advances in Health Economics and Health Services Research 13: 27–42.
Mitchell, Jean M., and Jonathan Sunshine
    1992   "Consequences of physicians' ownership of health care facilities—Joint
                ventures in radiation therapy," *New England Journal of Medicine* 327(21):
                1497–1501.

Miyaji, Naoko T.
1993   "The power of compassion: Truth-telling among American doctors in the care of dying patients," *Social Science and Medicine* 36(3): 249–264.

Mizrahi, Terry
1986   *Getting Rid of Patients: Contradictions in the Socialization of Physicians.* New Brunswick, NJ: Rutgers University Press.

Moeller, Dade W.
1992   *Environmental Health.* Cambridge, MA: Harvard University Press.

Moerman, Daniel
1979   "Anthropology of symbolic healing," *Current Anthropology* 20(1): 59–66.

1983   "Physiology and symbols: The anthropological implications of the placebo effect," pp. 156–167 in L. Romanucci-Ross, D. Moerman, L. Tancredi, eds., *The Anthropology of Medicine: From Culture to Method.* South Hadley, MA: Bergin and Garvey.

Montini, Theresa, and Sheryl Ruzek
1989   "Overturning orthodoxy: The emergence of breast cancer treatment policy," *Research in the Sociology of Health Care* 8: 3–32.

Moody, Edward
1974   "Magical therapy: An anthropological investigation of contemporary satanism," pp. 355–382 in I. Zaretsky and M. Leone, eds., *Religious Movements in Contemporary America.* Princeton: Princeton University Press.

Moore, Wilbert E., and Melvin Tumin
1949   "Some social functions of ignorance," *American Sociological Review* 14: 787–795.

Moore-Lappé, Frances, and Joseph Collins
1977   *Food First: Beyond the Myth of Scarcity.* New York: Houghton Mifflin.

1986   *World Hunger, Twelve Myths.* New York: Grove.

Moos, Rudolf H., and Ralph Swindle, Jr.
1990   "Person-environment transactions and the stressor-appraisal-coping process," *Psychological Inquiry* 1(1): 30–32.

Morantz-Sanchez, Regina M.
1985   *Sympathy and Science: Women Physicians in American Medicine.* New York: Oxford.

Morgan, Lynn
1989   " 'Political will' and community participation in Costa Rican primary health care," *Medical Anthropology Quarterly* 3(3): 232–245.

Morgan, Myfanwy, D. Patrick, and J. Charlton
1984   "Social network and psychological support among disabled people," *Social Science and Medicine* 19: 489–497.

Morganthau, Tom, and Andrew Murr
1993   "Inside the world of an HMO," *Newsweek*, April 5: 34–40.

Mormede, Pierre, Robert Dantzer, Bruno Michaud, Keith W. Kelley, and Michelle Le Moal
1988   "Influence of stressor predictability and behavioral control on lymphocyte

reactivity, antibody responses and neuroendocrine activation in rats," *Physiology and Behavior* 43: 577–583.

Morone, James A.
1990   "American political culture and the search for lessons from abroad," *Journal of Health Politics, Policy and Law* 15(1): 129–143.

Morone, James A., and Andrew B. Dunham
1984   "The waning of professional dominance: DRGs and the hospitals," *Health Affairs* 3(1): 73–87.

Moroney, Robert M.
1980   *Families, Social Services, and Social Policy: The Issue of Shared Responsibility*. U.S. Department of Health and Human Services (DHHS Publication No. [ADM] 80-846). Washington, DC: Government Printing Office.

Moss, Abigail
1987   "Recent declines in hospitalization: United States, 1983–86," *Advance Data*, Report No. 140.

Moss, Gordon Ervin
1973   *Illness, Immunity, and Social Interaction*. New York: Wiley.

Moss, Ralph W.
1980   *The Cancer Syndrome*. New York: Grove.

Muller, Jessica H., and Barbara A. Koenig
1988   "On the boundary of life and death: The definition of dying by medical residents," pp. 351–374 in M. Lock and D. R. Gordon, eds., *Biomedicine Examined*. Dordrecht, Netherlands: Kluwer.

Muller, Mike
1982   *The Health of Nations*. London: Faber and Faber.

Mumford, Lewis
1963   *Technics and Civilization*. New York: Harcourt, Brace, and World.

Murphy, Jane M.
1964   "Psychotherapeutic aspects of shamanism on St. Lawrence Island, Alaska," pp. 53–83 in A. Kiev, ed., *Magic, Faith, and Healing*. New York: The Free Press.

Murphy, Robert F.
1987   *The Body Silent*. New York: Henry Holt.

Mutchler, Jan E., and Jeffrey A. Burr
1991   "Racial differences in health and health care service utilization in later life: The effect of socioeconomic status," *Journal of Health and Social Behavior* 32(6): 342–356.

Muwakkil, Salim
1991   "Living fast, dying young in America's inner cities," *In These Times* 15(7): 7.

Najman, Jake M.
1993   "Health and poverty: Past, present and future," *Social Science and Medicine* 36(2): 157–166.

National Institute on Disability and Rehabilitation Research

| 1986 | "Rehabilitation of nonwhite disabled people," *Rehab Brief*, volume IX number 20. |

1987   "Low back pain," *Rehab Brief*, volume IX, number 9.

1993   "Disability statistics," *Rehab Brief* XIV, issue 8.

National Safe Workplace Institute

1990   *Beyond Neglect: The Problem of Occupational Disease in the U.S.* Chicago: National Safe Workplace Institute.

National Safety Council

1986   *Accident Facts:* 1986 Edition. Chicago: National Safety Council.

Navarro, Vicente

1981   "Work, ideology, and science: The case of medicine," pp. 11–38 in V. Navarro and D. M. Berman, eds., *Health and Work Under Capitalism: An International Perspective.* Farmingdale, NY: Baywood.

1988   "Professional dominance or proletarianization?: Neither," *Milbank Quarterly* 66(supplement 2): 57–75.

1989   "Race *or* class, or race *and* class," *International Journal of Health Services* 19(2): 311–314.

1991   "Race *or* class or race *and* class: Growing mortality differentials in the United States," *International Journal of Health Services* 21(2): 229–235.

Navarro, Vicente, and Daniel M. Berman, eds.

1981   *Health and Work Under Capitalism: An International Perspective.* Farmingdale, NY: Baywood.

Neal, Helen

1978   *The Politics of Pain.* New York: McGraw Hill.

Nelkin, Dorothy, and Michael S. Brown

1984   *Workers at Risk: Voices from the Workplace.* Chicago: University of Chicago Press.

Nelkin, Dorothy, David P. Willis, and Scott V. Parris

1991   *A Disease of Society: Cultural and Institutional Responses to A.I.D.S.* New York: Cambridge University Press.

Nelson, Bryce

1983   "Bosses face less risk than the bossed," *The New York Times*, April 3.

New York Times, The

1979   "A.M.A. softens a policy critical of chiropractors," July 25.

1986a   "Census study reports 1 in 5 adults suffers from disability," December 23.

1986b   "Your cigarettes or your job, workers are told," January 25.

1987a   "Alcohol-related deaths seen under-reported; autopsies find diagnostic errors," July 21.

1987b   "Merck offers free distribution of new river blindness drug," October 22.

1988   "Pregnant women received drug, without consent, hospital says," June 1.

1989   "For mothers, elderly present second burden," May 13.

1991   "Global checkup: Views in 10 nations," May 2.

1992   "74% of Democrats and 53% of Republicans favor a national health insurance financed by tax money: The voters' views," November 4: 34.

Newman, Sandra J.
    1976   *Housing Adjustments of Older People*. Ann Arbor: Institute for Social Research, University of Michigan.

Nichter, Mark
    1987   "Kyasanur forest disease: An ethnography of a disease of development," *Medical Anthropology Quarterly* 1(4): 406–423.

Nichter, Mark, and Elizabeth Cartwright
    1991   "Saving the children for the tobacco industry," *Medical Anthropology Quarterly* 5(3): 236–256.

Nightingale, Florence
    1860   *Notes on Nursing: What It Is, and What It Is Not*. New York: Appleton.

Noble, Barbara Presley
    1993   "Pushing nurses to a breaking point," *The New York Times*, January 10.

Noble, Kenneth B.
    1986   "Certain numbers can kill," *The New York Times*, December 28.

Norbeck, Edward, and Margaret Lock, eds.
    1987   *Health, Illness, and Medical Care in Japan*. Honolulu: University of Hawaii Press.

Norris, Ruth, ed.
    1982   *Pills, Pesticides, and Profits: The International Trade in Toxic Substances*. Croton on Hudson, NY: North River Press.

Novack, Dennis, Robin Plumer, Raymond Smith, Herbert Ochitill, Gary R. Morrow, and John M. Bennett
    1979   "Changes in physician attitude toward telling the cancer patient," *Journal of the American Medical Association* 241(9): 897–900.

Novak, Viveca
    1993   "The other drug lords," *International Journal of Health Services* 23(2): 263–273.

Novek, Joel, Annalee Yassi, and Jerry Spiegel
    1990   "Mechanization, the labor process, and injury risks in the Canadian meat packing industry," *International Journal of Health Services* 29(2): 281–296.

Nuckolls, Katherine B., John Cassel, and Berton V. Kaplan
    1972   "Psychosocial assets, life crisis, and the prognosis of pregnancy," *American Journal of Epidemiology* 95: 431–441.

Numbers, Ronald L.
    1977   "Do it yourself the sectarian way," pp. 49–72 in G. Risse, R. L. Numbers, and J. W. Leavitt, eds., *Medicine Without Doctors: Home Health Care in American History*. New York: Science History.

Oakley, Ann
    1984   *The Captured Womb: A History of the Medical Care of Pregnant Women*. Oxford: Basil Blackwell.

O'Donnel, Mary
    1978   "Lesbian health care: Issues and literature," *Science for the People*, May–June: 18–19.

Ohrbach, Susie
1981   *Fat Is a Feminist Issue.* New York: Berkeley.

Oken, Donald
1961   "What to tell cancer patients—A study of medical attitudes," *Journal of the American Medical Association* 175: 1120–1128.

Olesen, Virginia, L. Schatzman, N. Droes, D. Hatton, and N. Chico
1990   "The mundane ailment and the physical self: Analysis of the social psychology of health and illness," *Social Science and Medicine* 30: 449–455.

Omran, Abdel R.
1971   "The epidemiologic transition: A theory of the epidemiology of population change," *Milbank Memorial Fund Quarterly* 49: 509–538.

Organisation for Economic Co-operation and Development
1990   *Health Care Systems in Transition: The Search for Efficiency.* Paris: OECD.

Osherson, Samuel, and Lorna AmaraSingham
1981   "The machine metaphor in medicine," pp. 218–249 in E. Mishler et al., *Social Contexts of Health, Illness, and Patient Care.* Cambridge: Cambridge University Press.

Osterweis, Marian, Arthur Kleinman, and David Mechanic, eds.
1987   *Pain and Disability: Clinical, Behavioral, and Public Policy Perspectives.* Washington, DC: Institute of Medicine, National Academy Press.

Overfield, Theresa
1985   *Biologic Variation in Health and Illness.* Menlo Park, CA: Addison-Wesley.

Paget, Marianne A.
1983   "On the work of talk: Studies in misunderstandings," pp. 55–73 in S. Fisher and A. Todd, eds., *The Social Organization of Doctor-Patient Communication.* Norwood, NJ: Ablex.

Pappas, Gregory, Susan Queen, Wilbur Hadden, and Gail Fisher
1993   "The increasing disparity in mortality between socioeconomic groups in the United States, 1960 and 1986," *New England Journal of Medicine* 329(2): 103–109.

Parker, Richard
1981   "Lappé: take dictators off the dole," *Mother Jones* 6(1) January: 12–13.

Parsons, Talcott
1951   *The Social System.* Glencoe, IL: The Free Press.

1966   *Societies: Evolutionary and Comparative Perspectives.* Englewood Cliffs, NJ: Prentice-Hall.

1972   "Definitions of health and illness in light of American values and social structure," pp. 107–127 in E. G. Jaco, ed., *Patients, Physicians, and Illness.* New York: Macmillan.

Passell, Peter
1993   "The dangers of declaring war on doctors," *The New York Times*, March 21.

Pattison, Robert V., and Hallie M. Katz
1983   "Investor-owned and not-for-profit hospitals: A comparison based on California data," *New England Journal of Medicine* 309: 347–353.

Payer, Lynn
    1988   *Medicine and Culture: Varieties of Treatment in the United States, England, West Germany, and France.* New York: Henry Holt.

Pear, Robert
    1984   "Interpreting the results of the yearly U.S. physical," *The New York Times,* January 22.

    1987   "Medicare expansion imperiled by high costs," *The New York Times,* September 20.

    1988   "Fate of newest treatments is often determined by Medicare," *The New York Times,* January 14.

    1991a   "AMA acts to curb profits from referrals," *The New York Times,* December 12.

    1991b   "Low Medicaid fees seen as depriving the poor of care," *The New York Times,* April 2.

    1993a   "U.S. considers aid on long-term care," *The New York Times,* February 21.

    1993b   "Clinton's health-care plan: It's still big, but it's farther away," *The New York Times,* June 13.

    1993c   "Increase found in those without health coverage," *The New York Times,* December 15.

Pear, Robert, with Erik Eckholm
    1991   "When healers are entrepreneurs: A debate over costs and ethics," *The New York Times,* June 2.

Pearlin, Leonard I.
    1983   "Role strains and personal stress," pp. 3–32 in H. B. Kaplan, ed., *Psychosocial Stress: Trends in Theory and Research.* New York: Academic.

Pearlin, Leonard I., and Carm Schooler
    1978   "The structure of coping," *Journal of Health and Social Behavior* 19: 2–21.

Pellegrino, Edmund D.
    1976   "Prescribing and drug ingestion: Symbols and substances," *Drug Intelligence and Clinical Pharmacy* 10: 624–630.

Pelletier, Kenneth, and Denise L. Herzing
    1988   "Psychoneuroimmunology: Toward a mind-body model," *Advances: Institute for the Advancement of Health* 5(1): 27–56.

Pelletier, Kenneth R.
    1985   *Healthy People in Unhealthy Places: Stress and Fitness of Work.* New York: Dell.

    1992   *Mind as Healer, Mind as Slayer,* 2nd edition. New York: Dell.

Pendleton, David, and Stephen Bochner
    1980   "The communication of medical information in general practice consultations as a function of patients' social class," *Social Science and Medicine* 14A(6): 669–673.

Perry, Susan, and Jim Dawson
    1985   *Nightmare: Women and the Dalkon Shield.* New York: Macmillan.

Peterson, Iver
  1986   "Surge in Indians' diabetes linked to their history," *The New York Times*, February 18.

Pettingale, K. W.
  1985   "Towards a psychobiological model of cancer: Biological considerations," *Social Science and Medicine* 20(8): 779–787.

Pfeffer, Richard M.
  1979   *Working for Capitalism*. New York: Columbia University Press.

Physicians' Task Force on Hunger in America
  1985   *Hunger in America: The Growing Epidemic*. Middletown, CT: Wesleyan University Press.

Pickering, Thomas G., Gary D. James, Peter L. Schnall, Yvette R. Schlussel, Carl F. Pieper, William Gerin, and Robert A. Karasek
  1991   "Occupational stress and blood pressure," pp. 171–186 in M. Frankenhaeuser, U. Lundberg, and M. Chesney, eds., *Women, Work and Health*. New York: Plenum Press.

Pilisuk, Marc, and Susan H. Parks
  1986   *The Healing Web: Social Networks and Human Survival*. Hanover, NH: University Press of New England.

Pincus, Harold A., Allen Francis, Wendy Wakefield Davis, Michael B. First, and Thomas A. Widigen
  1992   "DSM-IV and new diagnostic categories: Holding the line on proliferation," *The American Journal of Psychiatry* 149(1): 112–117.

Pinder, Ruth
  1988   "Striking balances: Living with Parkinson's disease," pp. 67–88 in R. Anderson and M. Bury, eds., *Living with Chronic Illness: The Experience of Patients and Their Families*. London: Unwin Hyman.

Plough, Alonzo L.
  1986   *Borrowed Time: Artificial Organs and the Politics of Extending Lives*. Philadelphia: Temple University Press.

Podhorzer, Michael, Lorraine Driscoll, and Edwin S. Rothschild
  1993   "Unhealthy money: The growth in health PACs' congressional campaign contributions," *International Journal of Health Services* 23(1): 81–93.

Polednak, Anthony P.
  1989   *Racial and Ethnic Differences in Disease*. New York: Oxford University Press.

Polefrone, Joanna M., and Stephen B. Manuck
  1987   "Gender differences in cardiovascular and neuroendocrine responses to stressors" pp. 13–38 in R. Barnett, L. Biener, and G. K. Baruch, eds., *Gender and Stress*. New York: The Free Press.

Pollack, Andrew
  1988   "The troubling cost of drugs that offer hope," *The New York Times*, February 9.

Poloma, Margaret
    1985   "An empirical study of perception of healing among Assemblies of God members," *Pneuma* 7(1): 61–82.

Poole, C. J. M., G. R. Evans, A. Spurgeon, and K. W. Bridges
    1992   "Effects of a change in shift work on health," *Occupational Medicine* 42: 193–199.

Pope, Gregory C., and Terri Menke
    1990   "Hospital labor markets in the 1980s," *Health Affairs* 9(4): 127–137.

Pope, Gregory C., and John E. Schneider
    1992   "Trends in Physician Income," *Health Affairs* 11(1): 181–193.

Population Reference Bureau
    1982   *Population Bulletin* 37(2): 30–31.

Porter, Sam
    1992   "Women in a woman's job: The gendered experience of nurses," *Sociology of Health and Illness* 14(4): 510–527.

Posner, Tina
    1977   "Magical elements in orthodox medicine," pp. 141–158 in R. Dingwall, C. Heath, M. Reid, and M. Stacey, eds., *Health Care and Health Knowledge*. London: Croom Helm.

Post, Stephen G.
    1992   "DSM-III-R and religion," *Social Science and Medicine* 35(1): 81–90.

Pratt, Lois
    1976   *Family Structure and Effective Health Behavior*. Boston: Houghton Mifflin.

PROPAC (Prospective Payment Assessment Commission)
    1988   *Medicare Prospective Payment and the American Health Care System: Report to Congress*. Washington, DC: U.S. Government Printing Office.

Public Citizen Health Research Group
    1993   "Patient dumping continues in hospital emergency rooms," *Health Letter* 9(6): 1–6.

Quick, Allison
    1991   *Unequal Risks: Accidents and Social Policy*. London: Socialist Health Association.

Rahkonen, Ossi, Eero Labelma, Antti Karisto, and Kristina Manderbacka
    1993   "Persisting health inequalities: Social class differentials in illness in the Scandinavian countries," *Journal of Public Health Policy* (Spring): 66–81.

Ramsey, Matthew
    1977   "Medical power and popular medicine: Illegal healers in 19th century France," *Journal of Social History* 10(4): 560–587.

Rasell, Edie
    1993   "A bad bargain: Why U.S. health care costs so much and covers so few," *Dollars and Sense* 186 (May): 6–8, 21.

Ratcliff, Kathryn Strother
    1989   "Health technologies for women: Whose health? Whose technology?" pp. 173–198 in K. S. Ratcliff, ed., *Healing Technology: Feminist Perspectives*. Ann Arbor: University of Michigan Press.

Ratliff-Crain, Jeffrey, and Andrew Baum
1990   "Individual differences and health: Gender, coping and stress," pp. 226–253 in H. S. Friedman, ed., *Personality and Disease*. New York: John Wiley and Sons.

Ray, Wayne A., Marie R. Griffin, and Ronald I. Shorr
1990   "Adverse drug reactions and the elderly," *Health Affairs* 9(3): 114–122.
1990   "Racism and health: The case of black infant mortality," pp. 34–44 in P. Conrad and R. Kern, eds., *The Sociology of Health and Illness*, 3rd edition. New York: St. Martin's Press.

Reid, Janice, Christine Ewan, and Eva Lowy
1991   "Pilgrimage of pain: The illness experiences of women with repetition strain injury and the search for credibility," *Social Science and Medicine* 32(5): 601–612.

Reinhardt, Uwe E.
1987   "Resource allocation in health care: The allocation of life styles to providers," *Milbank Quarterly* 65(2): 153–176.

Reinhold, Robert
1987   "As hospitals close, rural America tries to cope with a void," *The New York Times*, July 6.
1988   "Crisis in emergency rooms: More symptoms than cures," *The New York Times*, December 8.

Relman, Arnold S.
1980   "The new medical-industrial complex," *New England Journal of Medicine* 303: 963–970.

Renner, Michael
1988   "Rethinking the role of the automobile," *Worldwatch Paper*, No. 84. Washington, DC: Worldwatch Institute.

Reverby, Susan
1987a   "A caring dilemma: Womanhood and nursing in historical perspective," *Nursing Research* 36(1): 5–11.
1987b   *Ordered to Care: The Dilemma of American Nursing, 1850–1945.* Cambridge: Cambridge University Press.

Rhodes, Robert P.
1992   *Health Care Politics, Policy, and Distributive Justice: The Ironic Triumph.* Albany: State University of New York Press.

Rice, Dorothy P.
1990   "The medical care system: Past trends and future projections," pp. 72–93 in P. R. Lee and C. L. Estes, eds., *The Nation's Health*. Boston: Jones and Bartlett Publishers.
1991   "Ethics and equity in U.S. health care: The data," *International Journal of Health Services* 21(4): 637–651.

Richardson, James T.
1993   "Religiosity as deviance: Negative religious bias in and misuse of the DSM-III," *Deviant Behavior* 14(1): 1–21.

Richardson, Stephen A., Norman Goodman, Albert Hastdorf, and Stanford Dornbush
1963   "Variant reactions to physical disabilities," *American Sociological Review* 28: 429–435.

Ries, Peter
    1991   "Characteristics of persons with and without health care coverage: United States, 1989," *Advance Data* 201 (June 18): 1–9.

Riessman, Catherine Kohler
    1989   "Women and medicalization: A new perspective," pp. 190–220 in P. Brown, ed., *Perspectives in Medical Sociology*. Prospect Heights, IL: Waveland Press.

Riska, Elianne
    1985   *Power Politics and Health: Forces Shaping American Medicine*. Helsinki: The Finnish Society of Letters.

Risse, Guenter, Ronald L. Numbers, and Judith W. Leavitt, eds.
    1977   *Medicine Without Doctors: Home Health Care in American History*. New York: Science History.

Ritenbaugh, Cheryl
    1982   "Obesity as a culture-bound syndrome," *Culture, Medicine, and Psychiatry* 6(4): 347–361.

Robbins, Thomas, and Dick Anthony
    1982   "Deprogramming, brainwashing, and the medicalization of deviant religious groups," *Social Problems* 29(3): 283–297.

Robinson, A. A.
    1988   "The motor vehicle, stress, and circulatory system," *Stress Medicine* 4: 73–176.

Robinson, James C., and Mita K. Giacomini
    1992   "A reallocation of rights in industries with reproductive health hazards," *The Milbank Quarterly* 70(4): 587–603.

Rodin, Mari
    1992   "The social construction of premenstrual syndrome," *Social Science and Medicine* 35(1): 49–56.

Rodwin, Marc A.
    1992   "The organized American medical profession's response to financial conflicts of interest: 1890–1992," *The Milbank Quarterly* 70(4): 703–741.
    1993   *Medicine, Money and Morals: Physician Conflicts of Interest*. New York: Oxford University Press.

Rodwin, Victor G.
    1984   *The Health Planning Predicament: France, Quebec, England, and the United States*. Berkeley: University of California Press.

Roebuck, Julian, and Robert Bruce Hunter
    1975   "Medical quackery as deviant behavior," pp. 72–82 in F. Scarpitti and P. McFarlane, eds., *Deviance: Action, Reaction, Interaction*. Reading, MA: Addison-Wesley.

Roeder, Beatrice A.
    1988   *Chicano Folk Medicine from Los Angeles, California*. Folklore and Mythology Studies, vol. 34. Berkeley: University of California Publications.

Roemer, Milton I.
    1985   *National Strategies for Health Care Organization: A World Overview*. Ann Arbor: Health Administration Press.
    1986   *An Introduction to the U. S. Health Care System*. New York: Springer.

Roemer, Milton I., and Ruth J. Roemer
    1981   *Health Care Systems and Comparative Manpower Policies.* New York: Marcel Dekker.

Romalis, Shelly
    1985   "Struggle between providers and recipients: The case of birth practices," pp. 174–208 in E. Lewin and V. Oleson, eds., *Women, Health, and Healing.* New York: Tavistock.

Rosenberg, Charles E.
    1987   *The Care of Strangers: The Rise of America's Hospital System.* New York: Basic.

Rosenbloom, Sandra
    1988   "The mobility needs of the elderly," pp. 21–71 in *Transportation in an Aging Society: Improving Mobility and Safety for Older Persons,* Volume 2. Washington, DC: Transportation Research Board, National Research Council, Special Report 218.

Rosenhan, David L.
    1973   "On being sane in insane places," *Science* 179: 250–258.

Rosenman, Ray H., Richard J. Brand, C. David Jenkins, Meyer Friedman, Reuben Strauss, and Moses Wurm
    1975   "Coronary heart disease in the Western Collaborative Group Study: Final follow-up experience of $8\frac{1}{2}$ years," *Journal of the American Medical Association* 233: 872–877.

Rosenthal, Elisabeth
    1990   "Health problems of inner city poor reach crisis point," *The New York Times,* December 24.
    1991   "In Canada, a government system that provides health care to all," *The New York Times,* April 30.
    1993a   "Insurers second-guess doctors, provoking debate over savings," *The New York Times,* January 24.
    1993b   "Drug companies' profits finance more promotion than research," *The New York Times,* February 21.

Rosenthal, Marilynn
    1987   *Health Care in the People's Republic of China: Moving Toward Modernization.* Boulder, CO: Westview.
    1988   *Dealing with Medical Malpractice: The British and Swedish Experience.* Durham, NC: Duke University Press.

Rosenthal, Marilyn M., and Marcel Frenkel, eds.
    1992   *Health Care Systems and Their Patients.* Boulder, CO: Westview Press.

Rosner, David
    1986   *A Once Charitable Enterprise: Hospitals and Health Care in Brooklyn and New York, 1885–1915.* Princeton: Princeton University Press.

Ross, H. Laurence, and Graham Hughes
    1986   "Drunk driving: What not to do," *Nation* 243(20): 663–664.

Roth, Julius
    1972   "Some contingencies of the moral evaluation and control of clientele: The case of the hospital emergency service," *American Journal of Sociology* 77: 839–856.

1976   *Health Purifiers and Their Enemies: A Study of the Natural Health Movement in the United States with a Comparison to Its Counterpart in Germany*. London: Croom Helm.

1984   "The application of 'sociological wisdom' to issues of cost escalation and cost containment," *Research in the Sociology of Health Care* 3: 257–280.

Rothe, J. Peter
1991   *The Trucker's World: Risk, Safety and Mobility*. New Brunswick, NJ: Transaction Publishers.

Rowland, Diane
1991   "Health status in East European countries," *Health Affairs* 10(3): 202–215.

Rubel, Arthur, Carl O'Nell, and Rolando Collado-Ard'on
1984   *Susto: A Folk Illness*. Berkeley: University of California Press.

Rubin, Haya R., Barbara Gandek, William H. Rogers, Mark Kosinski, Colleen A. McHorney, and John E. Ware
1993   "Patients' ratings of outpatient visits in different practice settings," *Journal of the American Medical Association* 270(7): 835–840.

Ruggie, Mary
1992   "The paradox of liberal intervention: Health policy and the American welfare state," *American Journal of Sociology* 97(4): 919–944.

Rushing, William
1984   "Social factors in the rise of hospital costs," *Research in the Sociology of Health Care* 3:27–114.

Rutledge, Robert, Thomas C. Ricketts, and Elizabeth Bell
1992   "Emergency medical services in rural areas," pp. 226–248 in W. M. Gesler and T. C. Ricketts, *Health in Rural North America: The Geography of Health Care Services and Delivery*. New Brunswick, NJ: Rutgers University Press.

Ruzek, Sheryl B.
1979   *The Women's Health Movement*. New York: Praeger.

Ryan, William
1971   *Blaming the Victim*. New York: Vintage.

Sacks, Karen
1988   *Caring by the Hour: Women, Work and Organizing at Duke Medical Center*. Urbana: University of Illinois.

Sacks, Oliver
1984   *A Leg to Stand On*. New York: Summit.

1990   *Seeing Voices*. London: Pan Books.

Sagan, Leonard
1987   *The Health of Nations*. New York: Basic.

Saks, Mike, ed.
1992   *Alternative Medicine in Britain*. Oxford: Clarendon Press.

Salmon, J. Warren
1985   "Profit and health care: Trends in corporatization and proprietization," *International Journal of Health Services* 15(3): 395–418.

Saltman, Richard B.
1991   "Emerging trends in the Swedish health system," *International Journal of Health Services* 21(4): 615–623.

Saltonstall, Robin
1993   "Healthy bodies, social bodies: Men's and women's concepts and practices of health in everyday life," *Social Science and Medicine* 36(1): 7–14.

Sandelowski, Margarete
1991   "Compelled to try: The never-enough quality of conceptive technology," *Medical Anthropology Quarterly* 5(1): 29–47.

Sandler, Dale, Richard B. Everson, and Allen Wilcox
1988   "Passive smoking in adulthood and cancer rise," *American Journal of Epidemiology* 121(1): 37–48.

Sapolsky, Robert M.
1982   "The endocrine stress-response and social status in the wild baboon," *Hormones and Behavior* 16: 279–292.

1989   "Hypercortisolism among socially subordinate wild baboons originates at the CNS level," *Archives of General Psychiatry* 46: 1047–1051.

1990   "Stress in the wild," *Scientific American* 252: 116–123.

Schachter, Stanley
1968   "Obesity and Eating," *Science* 16: 751–756.

Scheder, Jo C.
1988   "A sickly-sweet harvest: Farmworker diabetes and social equality," *Medical Anthropology Quarterly* 2(3): 251–277.

Scheer, Jessica, and Nora Croce
1988   "Impairment as a human constant: Cross-cultural and historical perspectives on variation," *Journal of Social Issues* 44(1): 23–37.

Schensul, Stephen L., and Jean J. Schensul
1982   "Healing resource use in a Puerto Rican community," *Urban Anthropology* 11(1): 59–79.

Scheper-Hughes, Nancy, and Margaret M. Lock
1986   "Speaking 'truth' to illness: Metaphor, reification, and a pedagogy for patients," *Medical Anthropology Quarterly* 17: 137–140.

1991   "The message in the bottle: Illness and the micropolitics of resistance," *The Journal of Psychohistory* 18(4): 409–432.

Schepers, Rita
1985   "The legal and institutional development of the Belgian medical profession in the nineteenth century," *Sociology of Health and Illness* 7(3): 314–341.

Schieber, George, and Jean-Pierre Poullier
1991   "International health spending: Issues and trends," *Health Affairs* 10(1): 106–116.

Schieber, George I., Jean-Pierre Poullier, and Leslie M. Greenwald
1991   "Health care systems in twenty-four countries," *Health Affairs* 10(3): 22–38.

Schiff, Robert L., Daiv Ansell, James Schlosser, Ahamed Idris, Ann Morrison, and Steven Whitman
1986   "Transfers to a public hospital," *New England Journal of Medicine* 314(9): 552–559.

Schiller, Nina Glick
    1992   "What's wrong with this picture? The hegemonic construction of culture in AIDS research in the United States," *Medical Anthropology Quarterly* 6(3): 237–254.

Schlesinger, Mark, Judy Bentkover, David Blumenthal, Robert Musaccico, and Janet Willer.
    1987   "The privatization of health care and physicians' perceptions of access to hospital services," *Milbank Quarterly* 65(1): 25–58.

Schmale, Arthur H.
    1972   "Giving up as a final common pathway to changes in health," pp. 20–40 in Z. Lipowski, ed., *Advances in Psychosomatic Medicine*, Vol. 8. Basel: S. Karger.

Schmeck, Harold M.
    1985   "73% of Americans suffer headaches," *The New York Times*, October 22.

Schnall, Peter L., and Rochelle Kern
    1981   "Hypertension in American society: An introduction to historical materialist epidemiology," pp. 73–89 in P. Conrad and R. Kern, eds., *The Sociology of Health and Illness* (second edition). New York: St. Martin's Press.

Schneider, Joseph W., and Peter Conrad
    1980   "In the closet with illness: Epilepsy, stigma potential, and information control," *Social Problems* 28(1): 32–45.

    1983   *Having Epilepsy: The Experience and Control of Illness*. Philadelphia: Temple University Press.

Schneider, Keith
    1987   "New product on farms in Midwest: Hunger," *The New York Times*, September 29.

Schneider, Michael
    1975   *Neurosis and Civilization: A Marxist-Freudian Synthesis*. New York: Seabury.

Schor, Juliet B.
    1992   *The Overworked American*. New York: Basic Books.

Schott, Thomas, and Bernhard Badura
    1988   "Wives of heart attack patients: The stress of caring," pp. 117–136 in R. Anderson and M. Bury, eds., *Living with Chronic Illness: The Experience of Patients and Their Families*. London: Unwin Hyman.

Schrank, Jeffrey
    1977   *Snap, Crackle, and Popular Taste*. New York: Dell.

Schreiber, Janet M., and John Homiak
    1981   "Mexican Americans," pp. 264–336 in A. Harwood, ed., *Ethnicity and Medical Care*. Cambridge: Harvard University Press.

Schwartz, Barry
    1973   "Waiting, exchange, and power: The distribution of time in social systems," *American Journal of Sociology* 79: 841–870.

Schwartz, Hillel
    1986   *Never Satisfied: A Cultural History of Diets, Fantasies, and Fat*. New York: Macmillan.

Schwartz, Howard D., Peggy L. de Wolf, and James K. Skipper, Jr.
1987   "Gender, professionalization, and occupation anomie: The case of nursing," pp. 559–569 in H. D. Schwartz, ed., *Dominant Issues in Medical Sociology*. New York: Random House.

Schwartz, Miriam
1984   "A sociological reinterpretation of the controversy over 'unnecessary surgery,' " *Research in the Sociology of Health Care* 3: 159–200.

Science News
1978   "Doctors' strike lowered death rate," October 28: 293.

Scitovsky, Anne, and Alexander M. Capron
1986   "Medical care at the end of life: The interaction of economics and ethics," *Annual Review of Public Health* 7: 59–75.

Scotch, Richard K.
1988   "Disability as the basis for a social movement: Advocacy and the politics of definition," *Journal of Social Issues* 44(1): 159–172.

Scott, Clarissa S.
1974   "Health and healing practices among five ethnic groups in Miami, Florida," *Public Health Reports* 89(6): 524–532.

Scully, Diana
1980   *Men Who Control Women's Health: The Miseducation of Obstetrician-Gynecologists*. Boston: Houghton Mifflin.

Segall, Alexander, and Lance W. Roberts
1980   "A comparative analysis of physician estimates and levels of knowledge among patients," *Sociology of Health and Illness* 2(3): 317–334.

Seligman, Martin
1992   *Helplessness: On Depression, Development, and Death*. San Francisco: W. H. Freeman.

Selik, Richard M., Kenneth G. Castro, Marguerite Pappaivanou, and James W. Buehler
1989   "Birthplace and the risk of AIDS among Hispanics in the United States," *American Journal of Public Health* 79(7): 836–839.

Selye, Hans
1956   *The Stress of Life*. New York: McGraw Hill.
1975   *Stress Without Distress*. New York: New American Library.

Sennett, Richard, and Jonathan Cobb
1972   *The Hidden Injuries of Class*. New York: Vintage.

Serrin, William
1989   "Playing down unemployment," *Nation* 248(3): 84–88.

Shabecoff, Philip
1987a   "Panel says caesarians are used too often," *The New York Times*, November 3.
1987b   "Vast changes in environment seen," *The New York Times*, November 4.

Shapiro, Joseph P.
1993   *No Pity: People with Disabilities Forging a New Civil Rights Movement*. New York: Random House.

Sharma, Ursula
    1992   *Complementary Medicine Today: Practitioners and Patients.* London: Tavistock/Routledge.

Shekelle, Richard B., S. B. Hulley, J. Neaton, J. Billings, N. Borhani, T. Gerace, D. Jacobs, N. Lasser, M. Mittlemark, and J. Stamler for the MRFIT Research Group.
    1985   "The MRFIT behavior pattern study, II: Type A behavior pattern and incidence of coronary heart disease," *American Journal of Epidemiology* 122: 559–570.

Shilts, Randy
    1987   *And the Band Played On: Politics, People, and the AIDS Epidemic.* New York: St. Martin's Press.

Short, Pamela F.
    1988   "Trends in employee health benefits," *Health Affairs* 7(3): 186–196.

Shorter, Edward
    1982   *A History of Women's Bodies.* New York: Basic.

Shulman, Lawrence C., and Joanne E. Mantell
    1988   "The AIDS crisis: A United States health care perspective," *Social Science and Medicine* 26(10): 979–988.

Sicherman, Barbara
    1978   "The uses of a diagnosis: Doctors, patients, and neurasthenia," pp. 25–38 in J. Leavitt and R. L. Numbers, eds., *Sickness and Health in America.* Madison: University of Wisconsin Press.

Sidel, Ruth, and Victor Sidel
    1982   *The Health of China: Current Conflicts in Medical and Human Services for 1 Billion People.* Boston: Beacon.

Siegrist, Johannes, and Daniel A. Klein
    1990   "Occupational stress and cardiovascular reactivity in blue-collar workers," *Work and Stress* 4(4): 295–304.

Siegrist, Richard B., Jr.
    1983   "Wall Street and the for-profit hospital management companies," pp. 35–50 in B. Gray, ed., *The New Health Care for Profit: Doctors and Hospitals in a Competitive Environment.* Washington, DC: National Academy Press.

Sigerist, Henry B.
    1960   *On the History of Medicine.* New York: M. D. Publications.

Silverman, Milton, and Philip R. Lee
    1974   *Pills, Profits, and Politics.* Berkeley: University of California Press.

Silverman, Milton, Mia Lydecker, and Philip R. Lee
    1992   *Bad Medicine: The Prescription Drug Industry in the Third World.* Stanford, CA: Stanford University Press.

Silverstein, Bret
    1984   *Fed Up.* Boston: South End.

Simmons, Roberta G., and Susan Klein Marine
    1984   "The regulation of high cost technology medicine: The case of dialysis and transplantation in the U.K.," *Journal of Health and Social Behavior* 25: 320–334.

Simon, Philip J.
    1983   *Reagan in the Workplace: Unraveling the Health and Safety Net.* Washington, DC: Center for Study of Responsive Law.

Simonelli, Jeanne M.
    1987   "Defective modernization and health in Mexico," *Social Science and Medicine* 24(1): 23–36.

Sivard, Ruth
    1987   *World Military and Social Expenditures, 1987–88.* Washington, DC: World Priorities.

Skultans, Vieda
    1974   *Intimacy and Ritual: A Study of Spiritualism, Mediums, and Groups.* London: Routledge and Kegan Paul.

Sloan, Frank A.
    1988   "Property rights in the hospital industry, pp. 103–141 in H. E. Frech and R. Zeckhauser, eds., *Health Care in America: The Political Economy of Hospitals and Health Insurance.* San Francisco: Pacific Research Institute for Public Policy.

Small, Gary W., and Jonathan F. Borus
    1983   "Outbreak of illness in a school chorus," *New England Journal of Medicine* 308(1): 632–635.

Smith, Barbara Ellen
    1981   "Black lung: The social production of disease," *International Journal of Health Services* 11(3): 343–359.

    1987   *Digging Our Own Graves: Coal Miners and the Struggle over Black Lung Disease.* Chicago: University of Chicago Press.

Smith, David G.
    1992   *Paying for Medicare: The Politics of Reform.* New York: Aldine de Gruyter.

Smith, Mark D., Drew E. Altman, Robert Leitman, Thomas W. Moloney, and Humphrey Taylor
    1992   "Taking the public's pulse on health system reform," *Health Affairs* 11(2): 125–133.

Smith, Robert C., and George Zimmy
    1988   "Physicians' emotional reactions to patients," *Psychosomatics* 29(4): 392–397.

Smothers, Ronald
    1991   "Employers becoming targets of suits in the fight to halt drunken driving," *The New York Times*, May 26.

Snell, Bradford
    1982   "American ground transport," pp. 316–338 in J. H. Skolnick and E. Currie, eds., *Crisis in American Institutions.* Boston: Little, Brown.

Snow, John
    [1855] 1936 *On the Mode of Communication of Cholera*, reprinted as *Snow on Cholera.* New York: Hafner.

Snow, Loudell F.
    1974   "Folk medical beliefs and their implications for care of patients," *Annals of Internal Medicine* 81: 82–96.

Snyder, Patricia
    1983   "The use of nonprescribed treatments by hemodialysis patients," *Culture, Medicine, and Psychiatry* 7: 57–76.

Sobol, Richard B.
    1991   *Bending the Law: The Story of the Dalkon Shield Bankruptcy*. Chicago: University of Chicago Press.

Society of Actuaries and Association of Life Insurance Medical Directors of America
    1983   *1979 Build Study*. New York: Metropolitan Life Insurance Company.

Soldo, Beth J.
    1985   "In-home services for the dependent elderly," *Research on Aging* 7: 281–304.

Solomon, George F.
    1985   "The emerging field of psychoneuroimmunology," *Advances: Journal of the Institute for the Advancement of Health* 2(1): 6–19.

Sontag, Susan
    1972   "The double standard of aging," *Saturday Review*, September 23: 29–38.

Sorkin, Alan L.
    1986   *Health Care and the Changing Economic Environment*. Lexington, MA: D. C. Heath.

Spillane, Robert
    1984   "Stress at work: A review of Australian research," *International Journal of Health Services* 14(4): 589–604.

Spruit, Ingeborg P., and Daan Kromhout
    1987   "Medical sociology and epidemiology: Convergences, divergences, and legitimate boundaries," *Social Science and Medicine* 25(6): 579–587.

Stafford, Randall S.
    1991   "The impact of nonclinical factors on repeat caesarean sections," *Journal of the American Medical Association* 265(1): 59–63.

Stalk, Jeffrey
    1992   "At issue in the Netherlands: Is sex for the disabled a right?" *International Herald Tribune*, August 4.

Stannard, Charles
    1973   "Old folks and dirty work: The social conditions for patient abuse in a nursing home," *Social Problems* 20(3): 329–342.

Starr, Paul
    1982   *Social Transformation of American Medicine*. New York: Basic.

Stearns, Carol Zisowitz, and Peter N. Stearns
    1986   *Anger: The Struggle for Emotional Control in America's History*. Chicago: University of Chicago Press.

Stebbins, Kenyon Rainier
    1986   "Curative medicine, preventive medicine, and health status: The influence of politics on health status in a rural Mexican village," *Social Science and Medicine* 23(2): 139–148.

    1991   "Tobacco, politics and economics: Implications for global health," *Social Science and Medicine* 33(12): 1317–1326.

Stein, Howard F.
1986   " 'Sick people' and 'trolls': A contribution to the understanding of the dynamics of physician explanatory models," *Culture, Medicine, and Psychiatry* 10: 221–229.

Stein, Leonard I.
1967   "The doctor-nurse game," *Archives of General Psychiatry* 16: 699–703.

Stein, Leonard I., D. T. Watts, and T. Howell
1990   "The doctor-nurse game revisited," *The New England Journal of Medicine* 322: 546–549.

Steinmetz, Greg
1993   "Number of uninsured stirs much confusion in health-care debate," *The Wall Street Journal*, June 9.

Steinmetz, Suzanne K.
1988   *Duty Bound: Elder Abuse and Family Care*. Newbury Park, CA: Sage Publications.

Stellman, Jeanne
1977   *Women's Work, Women's Health*. New York: Pantheon.

Stellman, Jeanne, and Susan M. Daum
1971   *Work is Dangerous to Your Health*. New York: Pantheon.

Stellman, Jeanne, and Mary Sue Henifin
1983   *Office Work Can Be Dangerous to Your Health*. New York: Random House.

Sterling, Theodor D., Elia Sterling, and Helen D. Ward
1983   "Building illness in the white collar workplace," *International Journal of Health Services* 13(2): 277–287.

Stevens, Robert, and Rosemary Stevens
1974   *Welfare Medicine in America: A Case Study of Medicaid*. New York: The Free Press.

Stevens, William K.
1988   "Diarrhea kills surprising rate of U.S. young," *The New York Times*, December 9.

Stewart, David C., and Thomas J. Sullivan
1982   "Illness behavior and the sick role in chronic disease: The case of MS," *Social Science and Medicine* 16: 1397–1404.

Stimson, Gerry, and Barbara Webb
1974   "Obeying doctor's orders: A view from the other side," *Social Science and Medicine* 8A: 97–104.

1975   *Going to See the Doctor*. London: Routledge and Kegan Paul.

Stine, Gerald J.
1993   *Acquired Immune Deficiency Syndrome*. Englewood Cliffs, NJ: Prentice Hall.

Stone, Deborah A.
1979a   "Diagnosis and the dole: The function of illness in American distributive politics," *Journal of Health Politics, Policy and Law* 4(3): 570–591.

1979b   "Physicians as gatekeepers: Illness certification as a rationing device," *Public Policy* 27(2): 227–254.

Stout, H. R.
1885   *Our Family Physician*. Peoria: Henderson and Smith.

Stout, Hilary
1991   "Public hospitals are overloaded, survey shows," *The Wall Street Journal*,
            January 30.

Straub, LaVonne A.
1990   "Financing rural health and medical services," *The Journal of Rural Care*
            6(4): 467–484.

Straus, Murray A., Richard J. Gelles, and Suzanne K. Steinmetz
1980   *Behind Closed Doors: Violence in the American Family*. New York:
            Doubleday.

Strauss, Anselm
1975   *Chronic Illness and the Quality of Life*. St. Louis: C. V. Mosby.

Street, Richard L., Jr.
1991   "Information-giving in medical consultations: The influence of patients'
            communicative styles and personal characteristics," *Social Science and
            Medicine* 32(5): 541–548.

1992   "Communicative styles and adaptations in physician-parent consulta-
            tions," *Social Science and Medicine* 34(10): 1155–1163.

Struck, Miriam
1981   "Disabled doesn't mean unable," *Science for the People*,
            September–October: 24–28.

Sudnow, David
1967   *Passing On: The Social Organization of Dying*. Englewood Cliffs, NJ:
            Prentice-Hall.

Sullivan, Cynthia B., and Thomas Rice
1991   "The health insurance picture in 1990," *Health Affairs* 10(2): 104–115.

Sullivan, Mark
1986   "In what sense is contemporary medicine dualistic?" *Culture, Medicine
            and Psychiatry* 10: 331–350.

Sullivan, Walter
1983   "Autopsies show 1 in 4 diagnoses were wrong," *The New York Times*,
            April 28.

Suls, Terry, and Glenn S. Sanders
1988   "Type A behavior as a general risk factor for physical disorder," *Journal
            of Behavioral Medicine* 11(3): 201–226.

Susser, Mervyn, William Watson, and Kim Hopper
1985   *Sociology in Medicine* (third edition). New York: Oxford University Press.

Suter, Steve
1986   *Health Psychophysiology: Mind-Body Interactions in Wellness and
            Illness*. Hillsdale, NJ: Lawrence Erlbaum.

Sutherland, Allan T.
1981   *Disabled We Stand*. Bloomington: Indiana University Press.

Sutherland, Prudy
1987   "I want sex—Just like you," *Village Voice* 32(14): 25.

Svarstad, Bonnie L.
1976   "Physician-patient communication and patient conformity with medical advice," pp. 220–238 in D. Mechanic, ed., *The Growth of Bureaucratic Medicine*. New York: Wiley.

Swedlow, Alex, Gregory Johnson, Neil Smithline, and Arnold Milstein
1992   "Increased cost and rates of use in the California workers' compensation system as a result of self-referral by physicians," *The New England Journal of Medicine* 327(21): 1502–1506.

Syme, S. Leonard, and Lisa F. Berkman
1976   "Social class, susceptibility, and sickness," *American Journal of Epidemiology* 104: 1–8.

Syme, S. Leonard, and Jack. M. Guralnik
1987   "Epidemiology and health policy: Coronary heart disease," pp. 85–116 in S. R. Levine and A. Lilienfeld, eds., *Epidemiology and Health Policy*. New York: Tavistock.

Sytkowski, Pamela, William B. Kannel, and Ralph B. D'Agostino
1990   "Changes in risk factors and the decline in mortality from cardiovascular disease," *New England Journal of Medicine* 322(23): 1635–1641.

Szasz, Andrew
1983   "The reversal of federal policy toward worker safety and health," *Science and Society* 1(Spring): 25–51.

Szasz, Thomas S.
1970   *The Manufacture of Madness*. New York: Dell.

Taragin, Mark I., L. R. Willett, A. P. Wilczek, R. Trout, and J. L. Carson
1992   "The Influence of standard of care and severity of injury on the resolution of medical malpractice claims," *Annals of Internal Medicine* 117(9): 780–784.

Taussig, Michael T.
1980   "Reification and the consciousness of the patient," *Social Science and Medicine* 14B: 3–13.

Taylor, Frederick
[1911] 1947 *Principles of Scientific Management*. New York: W. W. Norton.

Taylor, Kathryn M.
1988   " 'Telling bad news': Physicians and the disclosure of undesirable information," *Sociology of Health and Illness* 10(2): 109–132.

Taylor, Rosemary C. P.
1984   "Alternative medicine and the medical encounter in Britain and the United States," pp. 191–228 in J. W. Salmon, ed., *Alternative Medicines: Popular and Policy Perspectives*. New York: Tavistock.

Telles, Joel Leon, and Mark Harris Pollack
1981   "Feeling sick: The experience and legitimation of illness," *Social Science and Medicine* 15A: 243–251.

Temoshok, Lydia
1990   "On attempting to articulate the biopsychosocial model: Psychological-psychophysiological homeostasis," pp. 203–225 in H. S. Friedman, ed., *Personality and Disease*. New York: John Wiley and Sons.

Theorell, Töres
    1991   "On cardiovascular health in women," pp. 187–204 in M. Frankenhaeuser,
                U. Lundberg, and M. Chesney, eds., *Women, Work and Health*. New York:
                Plenum Press.

Thoits, Peggy A.
    1983   "Dimensions of life events that influence psychological distress: An eval-
                uation and synthesis of the literature," pp. 33–103 in H. B. Kaplan, ed.,
                Psychosocial Stress: Trends in Theory and Research. New York:
                Academic.

Thomas, V. J., and F. D. Rose
    1991   "Ethnic differences in the experience of pain," *Social Science and Medicine*
                32(9): 1063–1066.

Thrupp, Lori Ann
    1991   "Sterilization of workers from pesticide exposure: The causes and conse-
                quences of DBCP-induced damage in Costa Rica and beyond,"
                International Journal of Health Services 21(4): 731–757.

Tiefer, Leonore
    1992   "In pursuit of the perfect penis: The medicalization of male sexuality," pp.
                450–465 in M. S. Kimmel and M. A. Messner, eds., *Men's Lives*. New
                York: Macmillan.

Tierney, John
    1988   "Wired for stress," *The New York Times Magazine*, May 15.

Tipton, Steven M.
    1982   *Getting Saved from the Sixties: The Transformation of Moral Meaning in
                American Culture by Alternative Religious Movements*. Berkeley:
                University of California Press.

Todd, Alexandra
    1983   "Discourse in the prescription of contraception," pp. 159–187 in S. Fisher
                and A. Todd, eds., *The Social Organization of Doctor-Patient
                Communication*. Norwood, NJ: Ablex.

Tolchin, Martin
    1988a   "Curbs on tuition for doctors raising fears for care of poor," *The New York
                Times*, July 25.

    1988b   "Shift on Medicare to hurt hospitals in the inner cities," *The New York
                Times*, October 19.

    1989a   "Concern over the costs of malpractice liability," *The New York Times*,
                November 5.

    1989b   "Hospitals give record pay rise to attract nurses," *The New York Times*,
                March 26.

Totman, Richard
    1979   *Social Causes of Illness*. New York: Pantheon.

Townsend, John M., and Cynthia L. Carbone
    1980   "Menopausal syndrome: Illness or social role—A transcultural analysis,"
                Culture, Medicine, and Psychiatry 4: 229–248.

Townsend, Peter
    1990   "Individual or social responsibility for premature death: Current contro-

versies in the British debate about health," *International Journal of Health Services* 29(3): 373–392.

Treichler, Paula A.
1990   "Feminism, medicine, and the meaning of childbirth," pp. 113–138 in M. Jacobus, E. F. Keller, and S. Shuttleworth, eds., *Body/Politics: Women and the Discourses of Science*. New York: Routledge.

Treviño, Fernando, M. Eugene Moyer, R. Burciaga Valdez, and Christine A. Stroup-Benham
1991   "Health insurance coverage and utilization of health services by Mexican Americans, Mainland Puerto Ricans, and Cuban Americans," *Journal of the American Medical Association* 265(2): 233–237.

Trostle, James A.
1988   "Medical compliance as an ideology," *Social Science and Medicine* 27(12): 1299–1308.

Trostle, James A., W. Allen Hauser, and Ida Susser
1983   "The logic of noncompliance: Management of epilepsy from the patient's point of view," *Culture, Medicine, and Psychiatry* 7: 35–56.

Trotter, Robert T., and J. A. Chavira
1981   *Curanderismo: Mexican-American Folk Healing*. Athens: University of Georgia Press.

Tudiver, Sari
1986   "The strength of links: International Women's Health Network in the eighties," pp. 187–214 in K. McDonnell, ed., *Adverse Effects: Women and the Pharmaceutical Industry*. Toronto: Women's Educational Press.

Turner, Bryan S.
1977   "Confession and social structure," *Annual Review of the Social Sciences of Religion* 1: 29–58.

1982   "The government of the body: Medical regimens and the rationalization of diet," *British Journal of Sociology* 33(2): 254–269.

1984   *The Body and Society: Exploration in Social Theory*. Oxford: Basil Blackwell.

Turner, Victor W.
1968   *The Drums of Affliction*. Oxford: Clarendon.

1969   *The Ritual Process*. Chicago: Aldine.

Turshen, Meredith
1989   *The Politics of Public Health*. New Brunswick, NJ: Rutgers University Press.

Twaddle, Andrew C.
1981   *Sickness Behavior and the Sick Role*. Cambridge, MA: Schenkman.

Twaddle, Andrew C., and Richard M. Hessler
1986   "Power and change: The Swedish Commission of Inquiry on Health and Sickness Care," *Journal of Health Politics, Policy, and Law* 11(1): 19–40.

United Nations Development Programme (UNDP)
1993   *Human Development Report, 1993*. New York: Oxford University Press.

United Nations, Food and Agriculture Organizations
1992   *The State of Food and Agriculture*. Rome: United Nations.

U.S. Bureau of the Census
1975   *Historical Statistics of the United States, Colonial Times to 1970.*

Bicentennial edition, part 2. Washington, DC.

1992   *Statistical Abstract of the United States: 1992.* Washington, DC.

U.S. Department of Health and Human Services

1980   *Summary Report of the Graduate Medical Education National Advising Committee.* DHHS Publication No. (HRA) 81–651. Washington, DC: Government Printing Office.

1987   *Health, United States, 1986.* Hyattsville, MD: National Center for Health Statistics.

1989   *International Classification of Diseases.* Public Health Service, Health Care Financing Administration. Washington, DC: Government Printing Office.

1992   *Health, United States, 1991.* Hyattsville, MD: National Center for Health Statistics.

U.S. Department of Labor

1981   "Workers on Late Shifts," *Bureau of Labor Statistics,* September Summary: 81–103.

Vågerö, Denny

1992   "Women, work and health in Sweden," *Current Sweden* 387 (January): 1–8.

Van Esterik, Penny

1989   *Beyond the Breast-Bottle Controversy.* New Brunswick, NJ: Rutgers University Press.

Verbrugge, Lois M.

1985   "Gender and health: An update on hypotheses and evidence," *Journal of Health and Social Behavior* 26(3): 156–182.

1986   "From sneezes to adieux: Stages of health for American men and women," *Social Science and Medicine* 22: 1195–1212.

1990   "Longer life but worsening health?: Trends in health and mortality of middle-aged and older persons," pp. 14–34 in P. R. Lee and C. L. Estes, eds., *The Nation's Health.* Boston: Jones and Bartlett Publishers.

1992   "Pathways of health and death," pp. 41–79 in R. D. Apple, ed., *Women, Health and Medicine in America.* New Brunswick, NJ: Rutgers University Press.

Verbrugge, Lois M., and Frank J. Ascione

1987   "Exploring the iceberg: Common symptoms and how people care for them," *Medical Care* 25(6): 539–569.

Verbrugge, Lois M., and Deborah L. Wingard

1987   "Sex differentials in health and mortality," *Women and Health* 12(2): 103–143.

Vogel, Virgil

1970   *American Indian Medicine.* Norman: University of Oklahoma Press.

Volicer, Beverly

1977   "Cardiovascular changes associated with stress during hospitalization," *Journal of Psychosomatic Research* 22: 159–168.

1978   "Hospital stress and patients' reports of pain and physical status," *Journal of Human Stress* 4: 28–37.

Wagner, Melinda Bollar

1983   *Metaphysics in Midwestern America.* Columbus: Ohio State University Press.

Waid, William M.
1984   *Sociophysiology*. New York: Springer-Verlag.

Waitzkin, Howard B.
1971   "Latent functions of the sick role in various institutional settings," *Social Science and Medicine* 5: 45–75.
1979   "A Marxian interpretation of the growth and development of coronary care technology," *American Journal of Public Health* 69(12): 1260–1268.
1983   "Health policy and social change: A comparative history of Chile and Cuba," *Social Problems* 31(2): 235–248.
1984   "The micropolitics of medicine: A contextual analysis," *International Journal of Health Services* 14: 339–378.
1985   "Information giving in medical care," *Journal of Health and Social Behavior* 26: 81–101.
1989   "A critical theory of medical discourse: Ideology, social control, and the processing of social context in medical encounters," *Journal of Health and Social Behavior* 30(2): 220–239.
1991   *The Politics of Medical Encounters: How Patients and Doctors Deal with Social Problems*. New Haven: Yale University Press.

Waitzkin, Howard B., and John D. Stoeckle
1972   "The communication of information about illness," *Advances in Psychosomatic Medicine* 8: 180–215.

Waldron, Ingrid
1976   "Why do women live longer than men?" *Social Science and Medicine* 10: 349–362.
1991   "Effects of labor force participation on sex differences in mortality and morbidity," pp. 17–38 in M. Frankenhaeuser., U. Lundberg, and M. Chesney, eds., *Women, Work and Health*. New York: Plenum Press.
1994   "What do we know about causes of sex differences in mortality?" pp. 42–55 in P. Conrad and R. Kern, eds., *The Sociology of Health and Illness* (fourth edition). New York: St Martin's Press.

Wallston, Barbara S., S. W. Alagna, B. M. DeVellis, and R. B. DeVellis
1983   "Social support and physical health," *Health Psychology* 2: 367–391.

Walsh, Diana Chapman
1987   *Corporate Physicians: Between Medicine and Management*. New Haven: Yale University Press.

Walters, Vivienne
1982   "Company doctors' perceptions of and responses to conflicting pressures from labor and management," *Social Problems* 30(1): 1–12.

Ward, Martha C.
1986   *Poor Women, Powerful Men: America's Great Experiment in Family Planning*. Boulder, CO: Westview.

Wardwell, Walter I.
1982   "Chiropractors: Challengers of medical domination," *Research in the Sociology of Health Care* 3: 207–250.

Ware, Norma C.
1992   "Suffering and the social construction of illness: The delegitimation of ill-

ness experience in chronic fatigue syndrome," *Medical Anthropology Quarterly* 6(4): 347–361.

Warner, Richard
  1986   "Hard times and schizophrenia," *Psychology Today*, 20(6): 50–52.

Warnock, John W.
  1987   *The Politics of Hunger: The Global Food System*. Toronto: Methuen.

Waxler, Nancy E.
  1980   "The social labeling perspective on illness and medical practice," pp. 283–306 in L. Eisenberg and A. Kleinman, eds., *The Relevance of Social Science for Medicine*. Dordrecht, Netherlands: D. Reidel.

  1981   "Learning to be a leper: A case study in the social construction of illness," pp. 169–194 in E. Mishler, L. AmaraSingham, S. Hauser, R. Liem, S. Osherson, and N. Waxler, *Social Contexts of Health, Illness, and Patient Care*. Cambridge: Cambridge University Press.

Waxler-Morrison, Nancy, T. Gregory Hislap, Bronwen Mears, and Lisa Kan
  1991   "Effects of social relationships on survival for women with breast cancer: A prospective study," *Social Science and Medicine* 33(2): 177–183.

Weber, Max
  [1904] 1958 *The Protestant Ethic and the Spirit of Capitalism*. New York: Charles Scribner's Sons.

  [1922] 1963 *The Sociology of Religion*, trans. E. Fischoff. Boston: Beacon.

Weeks, John R.
  1986   *Population: An Introduction to Concepts and Issues*. Belmont, CA: Wadsworth.

Wegman, David H., and Laurence J. Fine
  1990   "Occupational health in the 1990s," *Annual Review of Public Health* 11: 89–103.

Weider, Joe
  1991   "The invisible woman," *Shape* (May): 16.

Weil, Andrew
  1988   *Health and Healing*, revised edition. Boston: Houghton Mifflin.

Weil, Andrew, and Winifred Rosen
  1993   *From Chocolate to Morphine*. (revised and updated edition) Boston: Houghton Mifflin.

Weiner, Herbert
  1992   *Perturbing the Organism: The Biology of Stressful Experience*. Chicago: University of Chicago Press.

Weinstein, Henry
  1985   "The health threat in the fields," *Nation* 240(18): 558–560.

Weir, David, and Mark Shapiro
  1981   *Circle of Poison*. San Francisco: Institute for Food Development Policy.

Weiss, Jay M.
  1972   "Psychological factors in stress and disease," *Scientific American* 226(6): 104–113.

Weiss, Kay
   1983   "Vaginal cancer: An iatrogenic disease?" pp. 59–75 in E. Fee, ed., *Women and Health: The Politics of Sex in Medicine*. Farmingdale, NY: Baywood.

Wertz, Richard W., and Dorothy C. Wertz
   1979   *Lying-In: A History of Childbirth in America*. New York: Schocken.

West, Candace
   1983   " 'Ask me no questions . . . ': An analysis of queries and replies in physician-patient dialogues," pp. 75–106 in S. Fisher and A. Todd, eds., *The Social Organization of Doctor-Patient Communication*. Norwood, NJ: Ablex.

   1984   *Routine Complications: Troubles with Talk Between Doctors and Patients*. Bloomington: Indiana University Press.

West, Patrick B.
   1979   "Making sense of epilepsy," pp. 162–169 in D. J. Osborne, M. M. Greenberg, and J. R. Eiser, eds., *Research in Psychology and Medicine: Social Aspects, Attitudes, Communication, Care, and Training*, Vol. 2. New York: Academic.

Westley, Frances
   1983   *The Complex Forms of the Religious Life: A Durkheimian View of New Religious Movements*. Chico, CA: Scholars Press.

Wethington, Elaine, and Ronald C. Kessler
   1986   "Perceived support, received support, and adjustment to stressful life events," *Journal of Health and Social Behavior* 27: 78–89.

Whiteis, David, and J. Warren Salmon
   1987   "The proprietarization of health care and underdevelopment of the public sector," *International Journal of Health Services* 17(1): 47–64.

Whitmire, Richard
   1992   "Fewer kids, women get health care," *San Antonio Light*, October 22.

Whitney, Craig R.
   1991   "British Health Service, much beloved but inadequate, is facing change," *The New York Times*, June 9.

Wijkman, Anders, and Lloyd Timberlake
   1988   *Natural Disasters: Acts of God or Acts of Man?* Philadelphia: New Society Publishers.

Wikler, Daniel, and Norma J. Wikler
   1991   "Turkey-baster babies: The demedicalization of artificial insemination," *The Milbank Quarterly* 69(1): 5–40.

Wilford, John Noble
   1988   "Common operation aimed at strokes faces new questions about safety," *The New York Times*, February 11.

Wilkes, Michael S., and Miriam Shuchman
   1989   "Pitching doctors," *New York Times Magazine*, November 5.

Wilkinson, Richard G.
   1986a   "Income and mortality," pp. 88–114 in R. Wilkinson, ed., *Class and Health: Research and Longitudinal Data*. New York: Tavistock.

1986b   "Socio-economic differences in mortality: Interpreting the data on their size and trends," pp. 1–21 in R. Wilkinson, ed., *Class and Health: Research and Longitudinal Data*. New York: Tavistock.

Willen, Richard S.
1983   "Religion and law: The secularization of testimonial procedures," *Sociological Analysis* 44(1): 53–64.

Williams, Rory
1983   "Concepts of health: An analysis of lay logic," *Sociology* 17(2): 185–205.

Willis, Evan
1983   *Medical Dominance: The Division of Labour in Australian Health Care*. Sydney: Allen and Unwin.

Wilson, Sharon
1991   "The unrelenting nightmare: Husbands' experiences during their wives' chemotherapy," pp. 237–313 in J. M. Morse and J. L. Johnson, eds., *The Illness Experience: Dimensions of Suffering*. Newbury Park: Sage.

Wohl, Stanley
1984   *The Medical Industrial Complex*. New York: Harmony.

Wolfe, Samuel
1990   "Importing health care reform?: Issues in transposing Canada's health care system to the United States," *Health/PAC Bulletin*, 20(2): 27–33.

Wolinsky, Frederick, and Sally Wolinsky
1981   "Background, attitudinal, and behavioral patterns of individuals occupying eight discrete health states," *Sociology of Health and Illness* 3: 31–48.

Wolpe, Paul Root
1985   "The maintenance of professional authority: Acupuncture and the American physician," *Social Problems* 32 (June): 409–424.

1990   "The holistic heresy: Strategies of ideological challenge in the medical profession," *Social Science and Medicine* 31(8): 913–923.

Woodrow, K. M., G. D. Friedman, A. B. Siegelaub, and M. F. Collen
1972   "Pain differences according to age, sex, and race," *Psychosomatic Medicine* 34: 548–556.

Woolhandler, Steffie, David U. Himmelstein, and James P. Lewontin
1993   "Administrative costs in U.S. hospitals," *New England Journal of Medicine* 329(6): 400–403.

Woolhandler, Steffie, David U. Himmelstein, and Quentin Young
1993   "High noon for U.S. health care reform," *International Journal of Health Services* 23(2): 193–211.

World Health Organization
1981   "Self-help and health: Report on a W.H.O. consultation," Report Number ICP HED 014, 6484 B, Copenhagen: World Health Organization.

Wright, Barbara Drygulski
1987   "Women, work, and the university-affiliated technology park," pp. 352–370 in B. D. Wright, ed., *Women, Work, and Technology: Transformations*. Ann Arbor: University of Michigan Press.

Yago, Glenn
1985   "U.S. lacks transportation policy," *In These Times* 9(15): 7.

Yanoshik, Kim, and Judy Norsigian
  1989   "Contraception, control, and choice: International perspectives," pp.
            61–92 in K. S. Ratcliff, ed., *Healing Technology: Feminist Perspectives.*
            Ann Arbor: University of Michigan Press.
Yates, Alayne
  1991   *Compulsive   Exercise   and   the   Eating   Disorders.*   New   York:
            Brunner/Mazel.
Yelin, Edward
  1986   "The myth of malingering: Why individuals withdraw from work in the
            presence of illness," *Milbank Quarterly* 64(4): 622–649.
Young, Allan
  1976   "Some implications of medical beliefs and practices for social anthropol-
            ogy," *American Anthropologist* 78(1): 5–24.
  1978   "Mode of production of medical knowledge," *Medical Anthropology* 2:
            97–124.
  1980   "The discourse of stress and the reproduction of conventional knowledge,"
            Social Science and Medicine 14B: 133–146.
Young, Ernie, and David K. Stevenson
  1990   "Limiting treatment for extremely premature, low-birth-weight infants
            (500–750 g.)," *American Journal of Diseases of Children* 144(5): 549–552.
Young, James H.
  1967   *The Medical Messiahs.* Princeton: Princeton University Press.
Zarling, Edwin J., Harold Sexton, and Pervis Milnor, Jr.
  1983   "Failure to diagnose acute myocardial infarction: The clinicopathologic
            experience at a large community hospital," *Journal of the American
            Medical Association* 250(9): 1177–1181.
Zborowski, Mark
  1952   "Cultural components in response to pain," *Journal of Social Issues* 8:
            16–30.
  1969   *People in Pain.* San Francisco: Jossey Bass.
Zola, Irving K.
  1966   "Culture and symptoms," *American Sociological Review* 31: 615–630.
  1982   *Missing Pieces: A Chronicle of Living with a Disability.* Philadelphia:
            Temple University Press.
  1983   *Socio-Medical Inquiries: Recollections, Reflections, and Reconsidera-
            tions.* Philadelphia: Temple University Press.
  1993   "Self, identity and the naming question: Reflections on the language of
            disability," *Social Science and Medicine* 36(2): 167–173.

Author Index

Subject Index